NEW CENTURY BIBLE

General Editors

RONALD E. CLEMENTS

M.A., B.D., PH.D. (Old Testament)

MATTHEW BLACK

D.D., D.LITT., F.B.A. (New Testament)

The Book of Psalms

Volume 2

NEW CENTURY BIBLE

Based on the Revised Standard Version

The Book of Psalms

A. A. ANDERSON

M.A., B.D.

Senior Lecturer in Old Testament Studies in the University of Manchester

VOLUME 2

PSALMS 73–150

OLIPHANTS

OLIPHANTS

MARSHALL, MORGAN & SCOTT
BLUNDELL HOUSE
GOODWOOD ROAD
LONDON SE14 6BL

Volume 1 ISBN 0 551 00267 0
Volume 2 ISBN 0 551 00268 9

Made and printed in Great Britain by
Purnell & Sons Ltd., Paulton, Somerset, England.

CONTENTS

Volume 2

COMMENTARY ON THE BOOK OF PSALMS

Psalms 73–150

BOOK III

Psalm 73 The Nevertheless of Faith

This Psalm is didactic in character, and it is related to Ps. 37 and 49, as well as to the Book of Job. It also includes other elements such as expressions of trust (verses 23–5) and a protestation of innocence (verse 13), and therefore it is more than a mere didactic poem depicting the spiritual struggle of its author. It may well be a cultic song: a Psalm of Trust (so Würthwein), or even a Psalm of Thanksgiving (so Mowinckel).

Its *Sitz im Leben* may be the cult (see verse 28*c*), and it could have been recited before the worshipping community. We need not assume that the speaker in the Psalm is the King (so Würthwein, Ringgren, *et al.*); he could well have been an ordinary member of the congregation. The Psalm arose out of individual experience, but it could also apply to Israel and the nations, before God. It deals not only with theodicy as such, but also with the very survival of faith; and it is intended to lead to a deeper trust in Yahweh, which is the presupposition of the divine deliverance.

Its date is uncertain, but most scholars favour a post-Exilic origin, although some would assign it to the monarchical period.

In verses 1–3 we find an outline of the main theme of the poem. God is gracious to the righteous, yet there seem to be certain exceptions. Verses 4–12 state the problem: the wicked are unpunished, and they go from strength to strength; such a situation cannot but create doubts in the minds of the righteous (verses 13–16). The turning point comes at verse 17, and verses 18–28 present the solution which enables the Psalmist to see things in a different light.

The metre is, with a few exceptions, 3 + 3.

A Psalm of Asaph: see Introduction, pp. 46 and 45f.

THE INTRODUCTION TO THE THEME OF THE PSALM **1–3**

1. Truly: this may point to an existing contradiction which is now rejected.

God is good to the upright: *RSV* and *NEB* follow the common emendation of dividing *l^eyiśrā'ēl* ('to Israel' (=*RSVm*)) into *l^eyāšār 'ēl* (i.e. '. . . God (*'ēl*) is good to the upright, Yahweh [*'^elōhîm* is probably due to the Elohistic editor] (is good) to the pure in heart'). This reading improves both the metre and the parallelism, but there is no support for it in the ancient versions. Occasionally verse 1 is viewed as a proverbial saying, the truth of which has been challenged by the experience of life.
pure in heart are those who are loyal to God both in thought and deed, and as such they are fit to enter God's holy place (24:3f.) and to receive his blessing (24:5).

2. my feet had almost stumbled: yet God in his goodness did not let him fall or lose his faith. In this verse 'feet' and 'steps' denote the Psalmist himself (i.e. as part standing for the whole); cf. 38:16 (M.T. 17), 56:13 (M.T. 14), 66:9, 116:8.

3. For I was envious . . .: the poet had a narrow escape, but he does not blame God. The direct cause of his near-disaster was his own spirit of envy and resentment which suspected God's Covenant loyalty (cf. 37:1; Prov. 3:31, 23:17, 24:19). 'To envy', in this context, is not so much to begrudge the good fortune of the wicked as to question God's government of the world. Consequently there is the danger that one might forsake 'the fear of the LORD' (Prov. 23:17).
the arrogant are those who consider themselves to be self-sufficient and who see no need for God (cf. 5:5 (M.T. 6)); therefore the term is synonymous with 'the wicked' (75:4 (M.T. 5)).
when I saw: Dahood (*PAB*, II, p. 186) may be right in translating: 'begrudged the prosperity of the wicked', because the verb *r-'-h* ('to see') may sometimes mean 'too look with envy' (cf. Ca. 1:6).
the prosperity: or 'good health' (so Snaith), although the former term may include the latter.
the wicked: see on 1:1.

THE PROSPERITY OF THE GODLESS **4–12**

4. they have no pangs: lit. 'for there are no bands in their death' (*AV*). Most exegetes divide *l^emôṭām* ('their death') into *lāmô tām*, taking *lāmô* with verse 4*a*, and *tām* ('sound') with verse 4*b* (as in *RSV*). The *AV* rendering suggests that the wicked pass away peacefully (in old age) after a prosperous life (cf. CD xiii:10),

while *RSV* implies that the godless have no illnesses (or afflictions in general) during their lifetime.
their bodies: the Hebrew *ʾûl* is a *hapax legomenon* in the *OT*, but the suggested rendering may be right (cf. G. R. Driver, *CML*, p. 136, n.5).
sleek: or 'fat'. In the *OT* 'being fat' is usually associated with prosperity, which often tends to lead the person concerned to disobedience to God (Dt. 32:15; Neh. 9:25; Jer. 5:28); see on 17:10, 119:70.

5. 'They do not seem to share in the toil (which is the lot) of ordinary people (cf. Job 5:7), nor are they stricken (with illness) as other men (often are).' For the opposite observation, see Sir. 30:14.

6. 'Therefore arrogance has become their status symbol.' 'Chains' (*RSV* **necklace**) were not only used as ornaments but were also worn by men of importance as a mark of their high rank, so e.g. Joseph (Gen. 41:42) and Daniel (Dan. 5:29).
violence covers them: i.e. it has become as natural to them as their own clothing (cf. 109:18ff.).

7. Their eyes swell out with fatness: it may be better to follow G. R. Driver's suggestion that *y-ṣ-ʾ* in this verse does not mean 'to go out', but that it is to be linked with another verb *y-ṣ-ʾ* ('to shine') (cf. Isa. 51:4; Hos. 6:5*c*), hence: 'Their eyes shine out of (their) fatness' (cf. Job 15:25ff.), i.e. in their prosperity they have become presumptuous, and are eager to do mischief. Other exegetes, following LXX and S, read: 'From fatness comes forth their iniquity' (so Oesterley, Kraus, *et al.*).
their hearts overflow . . .: M.T. could be rendered: 'They know no bounds in the scheming of (their) hearts' (cf. Jer. 5:28). The pronoun 'their' is to be supplied from the parallel phrase (verse 7*a*). The word *maśkiyyôṯ*, which is here rendered by 'scheming', is often used to denote idolatrous symbols (cf. *BDB*, p. 967).

8. speak with malice: or 'speak malice itself'; the function of the preposition *bᵉ* ('with') may be to intensify the word following it (cf. Dahood, *PAB*, I, p. 97).
loftily they threaten oppression: according to M.T. 'oppression' (cf. 62:10 (M.T. 11)) belongs to verse 8*a* (so also *AV*, *RV*) but *RSV* (also LXX and V) provides a better parallelism, and restores the prevailing 3 + 3 metre.

9. They set their mouths . . .: the author may be using metaphors derived from the Canaanite mythology, so that the enemies are described as wild mythological monsters. H. Ringgren

(*VT*, III (1953), pp. 267f.) draws attention to two parallels. In *Baal* I*, ii:1–4 (cf. Driver, *CML*, p. 105a) Mot, the god of the underworld, has '(jaws reaching) to earth, lips to heaven (and) a tongue to the stars'. A similar account is found in *Shachar* and Shalim ii: 27–9 (*CML*, p. 123b). Unless this is a coincidence, the Psalmist must have depicted the godless as being like Death, in seeking to devour their victims, in this case the righteous; cf. Isa. 5:14; Hab. 2:5. *RSV* may suggest that the author thought of the wicked as blaspheming God (so Briggs, Kissane, Nötscher). 'Heaven' may be a surrogate for 'God' (cf. Mt. 21:25).

their tongue struts through the earth: either this continues the mythological metaphor, or it depicts the arrogant as slanderers.

10. This verse is difficult. The literal meaning is probably represented by *RSVm*: 'Therefore his people return hither and abundant waters are drained by them.' It is possible that verse 10 also draws upon certain mythological word-pictures (cf. Ringgren, *FP*, p. 45). G. R. Driver suggests: 'Therefore my people (*ᶜammî*) resort unto them (*lāhem* for M.T. *hᵃlōm*) and find no fault with them (*ûmûm lōᵓ yimṣᵉᵓû lāmô*).' Probably the wicked in their affluence appeared so impressive that even their evil seemed to be attractive.

11. How can God know?: the speakers are the godless, and not the people deluded by them (so Kirkpatrick). They do not deny, primarily, the *ability* of God to know, but rather they affirm that God is not interested in the conduct or welfare of his creatures (cf. 10:4, 11:13, 94:9; Isa. 29:15; Ezek. 8:12). They have come to this false conclusion by making a generalization based on a limited experience and a mistaken interpretation of facts (cf. verses 17ff.).

Is there knowledge in the Most High?: the insolent allusion to the Most High (see on 46:4, 47:2) may indicate the extent of their arrogance. They are convinced that God could not care less for the affairs of human beings, and this in turn casts grave doubts as to God's power and nature; it is not far from a practical atheism, but is far worse.

12. The Psalmist sums up his portrayal of the wicked (see on 1:1): they seem to go on flourishing and amassing wealth. Following G. R. Driver's suggestion, we might render the verse: 'Behold, these are the wicked at ease (*yišlāyû* for M.T. *wᵉšalᵉwê*), the wrongdoers (*ᶜᵃwālīm* for M.T. *ᶜôlām*) who increase (their) wealth'. Cf. also *NEB*.

HONEST DOUBTS **13–16**

13. All in vain: this represents a sharp contrast to verse 1: 'Truly God is good to the upright'. From our point of view, the Psalmist's attitude may seem theologically deficient but, against the background of his times, it means that his primary concern is a search for meaning rather than for reward.

kept my heart clean: a different outlook is expressed by Prov. 20:9: 'Who can say, "I have made my heart clean . . . ?" ' (cf. 1QH f. iv:10: 'who shall be clean in your judgment?'). Our poet holds the same view as that presupposed by the Entrance liturgies (Ps. 15, 24; cf. 24:4); see on 119:9.

washed my hands in innocence: as in 26:6. This was a symbolic action affirming the guiltlessness of the person concerned (cf. Dt. 21:6; Isa. 1:16; Mt. 27:24), and it may have been part of the oath of purification.

14. I have been stricken: the writer does not explain the actual nature of his misfortune; it may have been illness or some other affliction.

chastened every morning: lit. 'my chastisement (was with me) every . . .'. *RSV* follows the usual emendation of *w^e^tôḵaḥtî* into *w^e^hûḵaḥtî*.

15. The Psalmist is tempted to argue in the same vein as the wicked, although for a different reason (cf. Job 2:9).

the generation of thy children: the Israelites were 'the sons of the LORD' (Dt. 14:1), and the reference may be to the cultic community. To be untrue to them would mean placing oneself outside this fellowship and outside the Covenant. Budde *et al.* read *bāḡaḏtā* (for M.T. *bāḡaḏtî*) ('you have dealt treacherously') which, they think, has been altered for theological reasons.

16. In verse 15 the Psalmist realized the seriousness of the temptation to follow the reasoning of the godless, yet, on the other hand, the attempt to reconcile his experience with the accepted doctrine seemed an impossible task.

THE TURNING POINT AND THE SOLUTION **17–20**

What had been impossible to achieve by reasoning is now attained by faith or trust in God.

17. the sanctuary of God: lit. 'the sanctuaries . . .' (cf. Jer. 51:51), but the plural may be understood as a plural of amplification or intensity; hence the reference may be to the Jerusalem

Temple. We are not actually told what the Psalmist experienced in the Temple, but Weiser (*POTL*, p. 511) suggests 'an encounter with his God that was brought about by the theophany . . .', while Würthwein thinks of an oracle which was imparted to the Psalmist. Mowinckel (*PIW*, II, p. 36) is of the opinion that in the Temple the worshipper 'submitted to the prescribed ritual acts and received the promise of Yahweh's "justifying" aid.' As a result, his doubts were dispelled and his temptations overcome, and he was able to give thanks for this promise. It is possible that the Psalmist's certainty was based, at least to some extent, upon the salvation-history of the nation. As a member of the people of God, he had already shared in the truth of the assertion in verse 1.

their end will be the manifestation of the divine purpose which is already operative although not necessarily perceptible to all.

18. in slippery places: i.e. their way of life is like a slippery path on which they are bound to fall (see on 35:6; cf. Jer. 23:12). Dahood (*PAB*, II, p. 187) associates *ḥ^a^lāḳôṯ* ('slippery places') with the Ugaritic *ḫlḳ* ('to perish'), and renders: 'Surely to Perdition will you transplant them' (i.e. in the underworld).

ruin: (*m^e^šô'ôṯ*); M.T. has *maššû'ôṯ* ('deceptive ground'), which seems to be a better parallel to 'slippery places' (verse 18*a*); see on 74:3.

19. The suddenness of the disaster emphasizes the transitory nature of the prosperity of the wicked.

terrors: it is not clear whether 'terrors' are the various misfortunes, or demons. Job 18:14 refers to the 'King of Terrors' who is, apparently, Mot, the god of the netherworld, or, more likely, Death personified (cf. Pope, *JAB*, p. 126; see also Job 18:11, 27:20, 30:15; Isa. 17:14).

20. The text is probably corrupt, but it might be rendered: 'As (one despises) a dream after awakening, (so) you, O Lord, will despise their image when you rouse yourself to activity', reading *b^e^'ûr* for M.T. *bā'îr* ('in the city'). More than once the intervention of Yahweh is described in the *OT* as his awakening from sleep (cf. 35:23, 44:23 (M.T. 24), 59:4f. (M.T. 5f.), 78:65f.). 'Their image' may have a reference to the god or gods of the wicked, in whom they place their trust, or it may denote the wicked themselves (cf. 39:6 (M.T. 7)).

THE PSALMIST'S RELATIONSHIP WITH GOD **21–8**

21. The Psalmist ponders on his recent experiences when he was unable to see God's justice at work. 'Soul' and 'heart' (lit. 'heart' (see on 27:3) and 'kidneys' (see on 7:9) respectively) simply stand for the totality of the man himself (as a part for the whole).

22. I was stupid: see on 92:6.

23. I am continually with thee: in the Temple the author has arrived at the certainty of faith that he belongs to God, apparently by belonging to his people; the one being as real as the other.

hold my right hand: H. Gressmann (*Der Messias* (1929), p. 61) has pointed out that to be grasped by one's right hand is symbolic of being honoured, as a King is raised to dignity by his god (cf. Isa. 45:1). It is possible that the expression was derived from the royal ritual, but in the *OT* the phrase usually means to give help and protection, as in 63:8 (M.T. 9); Isa. 41:10,13, 42:6; Jer. 31:32.

24. afterward thou wilt receive me to glory: this familiar phrase presents considerable difficulties in its interpretation, but there is no need to think that the text is corrupt. The real problem is whether it refers to this life or to the life *after* death; commentators are divided on this point. The Israelite view of after-life is characterized by the shadowy Sheol existence which was largely negative. It was only in the late post-Exilic period that a different idea of life after death was gradually formulated. Had the author of this Psalm believed that the after-life *provided* for a final judgment of God, he would have found little difficulty in explaining the prosperity of the wicked and the misfortune of the righteous. Therefore it seems that he also must have shared in the common Sheol belief. On the other hand, Ps. 73 may represent a tentative venture to go beyond the then current beliefs, although the result would be a glimpse rather than a firm faith (cf. Rowley, *FI*, p. 175, n.2). If this was the case, then it is understandable why the Psalmist remained content that God was his portion for ever (verse 26) without giving a more definite shape to his hope. Von Rad reminds us (*OTT*, I, p. 406f.) that 'the idea of a life after death' was not 'some unheard-of novelty, since as early as the time of Ezekiel the cult of a dying and rising god had forced its way into the

Temple itself (Ezek. 8:14)'. There were also the stories about Enoch and Elijah, and their 'ascension' (whatever was meant by it). In view of all this and in face of the insoluble problems, it is only reasonable that some Israelite theologians should explore this possibility which could set them free from the tension between their faith in God and the facts of experience.

afterward: this brings to mind 'their end' in verse 17. While the wicked will be swept away by the forces of Sheol (verse 19*b*), the righteous will be received (or 'taken') by God. Otherwise we should have to follow some such interpretation as that provided by N. H. Snaith (*The Distinctive Ideas of the Old Testament* (1944), p. 89), who suggests that 'afterward' means 'after these temporary distresses', and not life after death. *RP* has 'and leadest me along the path of (*ʾōraḥ* for M.T. *ʾaḥar* ('afterward')) glory' (cf. *JTS*, XLIV (1943), p. 12). For a possible alternative, see Dahood, *PAB*, II, p. 195.

to glory: Snaith (p. 89, n.2) takes it to mean 'honour and prosperity in the things of this life', and not heavenly bliss. This is, of course, the usual *OT* usage, but, if the Psalmist is stating a new hope, then he may have given a new shade of meaning also to the word 'glory'. It is possible that 'glory' refers to Yahweh's saving manifestation (cf. Exod. 16:7,10, 24:16,17, 33:22).

25. Luther gives a splendid paraphrase: 'as long as I have thee, I wish for nothing else in heaven or on earth' (quoted from Weiser, *POTL*, p. 515). The Psalmist is no longer concerned with the prosperity of the wicked, or even his own troubles, as long as he is near God. Sooner or later this must also mean a change in his fortunes, but he leaves the *when* and *how* to God.

26. My flesh . . . may fail: here 'flesh' and 'heart' may be the sum total of one's vitality.

the strength of my heart: lit. 'the rock of my heart'; but 'heart' (*lᵉḇāḇî*) may be a dittograph, and therefore most commentators read 'my rock' (*ṣûrî*) and omit 'my heart'.

my portion: see on 16:5. Von Rad (*PHOE*, pp. 260ff.) explains: 'The "portion" obviously refers initially to the portion of land which was allotted to the individual in the cultic distribution of territory.' According to the ancient traditions, only the tribe of Levi remained without a tribal inheritance, but *their* portion was Yahweh himself (Dt. 10:9). This probably meant that they derived their livelihood from a share in sacrifices and offerings, but it may also have had a reference to their special relationship with Yahweh. In this verse, it is the spiritual aspect that is emphasized; it is upon Yahweh that the Psalmist's existence depends (cf. also 119:57).

for ever: this does not necessarily suggest eternity or immortality, but in the present context some such idea is not impossible (see on 117:2).

27. The Psalmist sums up the fate of the godless. Since God is the source of all life, it follows that to be far from him means to be near death, or in Sheol itself.

who are false to thee: Snaith (*Hymns of the Temple* (1951), p. 106) interprets this as 'every man who seeks intercourse with other deities instead of with Him'. The verb *z-n-h* is frequently used by Hosea in this sense (cf. 1:2, 2:5 (M.T. 7), 3:3, 4:12–15, 9:1), but in our verse it may have a more general meaning (cf. Isa. 1:21), although it may allude to a previously existing relationship; see on 106:39.

28. Finally the author restates his newly gained experience, and he finishes his song with the same theme as he began (verse 1).

to be near God: Ringgren (*FP*, p. 59) points to a possible alternative, namely, 'to draw near God' (i.e. in the Temple worship).

tell of all thy works: LXX and V add: 'in the gates of the daughter of Zion', which (as well as verse 28*c*) may be borrowed from 9:14 (M.T. 15). 'Thy works' could be the help he had received from God, or the phrase may allude to the redemptive work of Yahweh as a whole, of which his experience is only a small fragment.

Psalm 74 Lament over the Destruction of the Temple

This Psalm is a Lament of the Community, mourning over the desolation of the land and, in particular, over the destruction of the Temple, at the hands of foreign invaders.

The life-setting of the Psalm may be a day of fasting, when the sins of the nation would be confessed and prayers offered to God. One such occasion is described in 1 Sam. 7:5f. (cf. Zech. 7:1–6, 8:18f.), and a similar situation is mentioned in 1 Chr. 20:1–19.

A more difficult problem is to determine the event which gave rise to this Psalm, unless we accept F. Willesen's suggestion that it is completely cultic in its origin, and does not refer to any particular historical event (*VT*, II (1952), pp. 289–306). He regards the Psalm as a ritual lament which was part of the cult drama of the New Year Festival, and which deals with the ritual profanation of the Temple. His thesis may fit certain aspects of the Near Eastern ritual pattern, but it is far from clear that Ps. 74 had this significance for the Israelites, and that this view provides the best explanation for the lament.

There are three main events which may possibly have led to the composition of this lament: the destruction of the Temple in 587 B.C., the hypothetical pollution of the Sanctuary during the reign of Artaxerxes Ochus (359–38 B.C.), and the desecration of the Holy Place by Antiochus Epiphanes in 167 B.C. Of these three possibilities the first seems most likely, although the Psalm could have been adapted to other, later, events of a similar nature.

Verses 1–3 contain a call to God and a cry for help. This is followed by a description of the destruction of the Holy Place (verses 4–8) and a lamentation to God (verses 9–11). In verses 12–17 we find a hymnic confession of trust in the divine king, and the Psalm concludes with a final petition (verses 18–23).

The metre of the Psalm is mainly 4+4.

A Maskil of Asaph: see Introduction, pp. 47 and 45f.

THE PETITION TO GOD **1–3**

1. why: this is a frequent opening of the laments, and it reflects the tension within the worshipper(s). Often the present experience conflicts with the current beliefs, and the result of this partly unresolved inner conflict is the bewildered question 'Why?'. See 10:1,13, 22:1 (M.T. 2), 44:24 (M.T. 25), 79:10, 80:12 (M.T. 13), 115:2; Isa. 63:17; Jl 2:17, etc. (cf. Gunkel, *EP*, p. 127).

for ever: i.e. so unbearably long. The Hebrew *neṣaḥ* ('everlastingness, perpetuity') is a synonym of *ʿôlām* ('long duration', see on 117:2), and in actual usage there was little, if any, difference between the two. Both words come near to what we mean by 'eternity' but it is doubtful whether they ever attained such a connotation in the *OT* (cf. J. Barr, *Biblical Words for Time* (*SBT*, 33, 1962), pp. 85f., 117).

thy anger smoke: this is a description of great anger (cf. 18:8 (M.T. 9), 80:4 (M.T. 5); Lam. 2:3). This may point to a certain destructiveness in the character of Yahweh, yet his anger is never capricious or arbitrary. His punishment is not the result of a fitful whim, but the outcome of his holiness confronting a stubborn rebellion.

the sheep of thy pasture: i.e. the flock of your care. See on 100:3.

2. Remember thy congregation: the verb *z-k-r* has in this context a twofold significance. It points back to the previously existing relationship, and it implores Yahweh to intervene on behalf of his people (see Childs, *MTI*, pp. 34ff.). God is not reminded of the Covenant as if he had forgotten it, but rather the people allude to their election as the reason for their boldness in asking for God's help (cf. 106:4).

'Congregation' (*ᶜēḏāh*) should be, strictly speaking, a gathering of people assembled by appointment, but in many instances this is not the case. In the *OT* *ᶜēḏāh* is often used to denote the nation of Israel, and it is a characteristic expression of the Priestly source in the Pentateuch. Not infrequently a qualifying term is added to *ᶜēḏāh*, e.g. 'the congregation of Israel' (Exod. 12:3,6; Lev. 4:13), 'the congregation of Yahweh' (Num. 27:17, 31:16). In LXX this term is usually translated by *sunagōgē*, and in the Dead Sea Scrolls it is one of the main self-designations of the sect (cf. Leaney, *RQM*, p. 173; Barr, *SBL*, pp. 119–29).

gotten of old: this is probably a reminiscence of Exod. 15:13,16, and of the deliverance from Egypt.

redeemed: cf. Exod. 15:13. For the verb *g-ʾ-l*, see on 119:154.

the tribe of thy heritage: similarly in Jer. 10:16, 51:19 (cf. Isa. 63:17). It probably means 'your very own tribe', i.e. your people (cf. J. Bright, *Jeremiah* (*AB* 21, 1965), p. 78).

Mount Zion: see on 65:1. *AV* has 'this mount Zion', but the pronoun *zeh* ('this') is to be taken as a relative particle (cf. *GK* 138g).

3. Direct thy steps: lit. 'lift up your steps'; this phrase occurs only here in the *OT*, and it may be an appeal to God to intervene. For an alternative rendering, see *NEB*.

the perpetual ruins: the derivation of the Hebrew *maššūʾōṯ* is uncertain. *BDB* (p. 674) suggests 'deceptions' (from *n-š-ʾ*, 'to deceive') but most scholars read *mᵉšōʾōṯ* ('ruins'), as in 73:18. 'Perpetual ruins' would be a hyperbolic description of ruins which had been there for some time, and probably will remain ruins.

in the sanctuary: i.e. in the Jerusalem Temple (cf. 20:2 (M.T. 3), 60:6 (M.T. 8), 150:1); see on 68:17.

THE DESTRUCTION OF THE HOLY PLACE 4–8

4. **have roared:** for the verb *š-ʾ-g*, see on 38:8. LXX and V read: 'have boasted', which is an interpretative rendering. The enemies have behaved blasphemously in the Temple; apart from vocal *worship*, there should be a reverent silence before God. Cf. Hab. 2:20: '. . . the LORD is in his holy temple; let all the earth keep silence before him'.

thy holy place: the Hebrew *môʿēd* comes from the same root as *ʿēḏāh* ('congregation') (see verse 2), and it can denote either an appointed place or time. Thus it can be used of the sacred seasons and appointed feasts (frequent in the Priestly source; cf. Lev. 23:2,4, etc.); it can also designate either the assembly which takes part in the celebration of the festivals (cf. Lam. 1:15) or the place of the festive assembly (Lam. 2:6).

signs for signs: for *ʾôṯ*, see on 71:7. The actual significance of these signs is not clear. Some exegetes see here an allusion to the symbols and rites of the Israelite religion, which had been replaced by idolatrous equivalents (cf. 1 Mac. 1:45–9), while others interpret these signs as military standards (cf. Num. 2:2). This latter suggestion seems more likely if the Psalm refers to the destruction of the Temple in 587 B.C. (see also verse 9). Cf. H. H. Rowley, *The Zadokite Fragments and the Dead Sea Scrolls* (1952), pp. 73f.

5. The text of this verse is obscure, and all the renderings are merely tentative suggestions (cf. G. R. Driver, *JBL*, LXVIII (1949), p. 58). The writer is probably describing the destruction of the woodwork in the Temple; the inside walls were lined with boards of cedar (1 Kg. 6:16), and they were carved with figures of cherubim, palm trees, and flowers (1 Kg. 6:29). See also F. Willesen, *VT*, II (1952), pp. 303ff.

6. **its carved wood:** this is the rendering of the Hebrew *pittûaḥ* which may also suggest objects engraved on metal or stone (cf. M. Noth, *Könige* (*BK* 9_2, 1965), p. 101); Kissane proposes 'sculptures', thinking of the pillars of brass, the brazen sea, and similar objects. It is possible that the author had in mind the removal of all the valuable metal objects as well as the decorative plating (cf. 2 Kg. 18:16).

7. **thy sanctuary:** *miḳdāšeḵā* while some MSS. have the plural

miḵdāšêḵā (see verse 8*b*). The Temple was set on fire, and the reference is, most likely, to the events of 587 B.C., when Nebuzaradan (2 Kg. 25:9) put the Temple and the city to the torch.
to the ground they desecrated: Oesterley (*TP*, p. 348) suggests that the whole 'building has been profaned, from the highest pinnacle to the ground' but the allusion may be to the breaking down of the walls of the sanctuary (cf. *GK* 119gg), or it may suggest that it was *utterly* defiled.
the dwelling place of thy name: (cf. Dt. 12:11), i.e. either the place which is called by Yahweh's name (so Davies), or the place where he has set his name, where his name 'tented' or 'tabernacled' (cf. Clements, *GT*, pp. 116f.). The 'dwelling place' (*miškān*) was originally used of the temporary dwelling of a nomad (cf. de Vaux, *AI*, p. 295), and it was employed by the *OT* writers as a name for the abode of Yahweh, especially his tent-dwelling in the wilderness. At a later time it was used to denote the Temple (cf. 26:8, 46:4 (M.T. 5), 84:1 (M.T. 2)) and, perhaps, other sanctuaries (cf. 87:2). For a similar usage in Canaanite literature, see *ZAW*, LXXV (1963), pp. 91ff.

8. They said to themselves: lit. '. . . in their heart' (see on 27:3).
We will utterly subdue them: reading *nînēm* (from *y-n-h*, 'to oppress'); similarly S: 'let us destroy them'. M.T. has *nînām* ('their offspring'), which is also suggested by LXX, T, and Jerome, although it does not give a satisfactory rendering.
they burned: rather 'let us burn' (*niśrōp̱*), which is suggested by S and one Greek MS. This destructive action was directed against the 'meeting places of God' (*mô*^{ca}*ḏê* *ʾēl*); cf. verse 4. *AV*, *RV* render: 'synagogues of God', but this is unlikely. There may well have been synagogues in Palestine by the Maccabean period, and perhaps even earlier (cf. *DNT*, VII, pp. 798–841), but it is doubtful whether our Psalm refers to them. LXX speaks about the 'feasts of Yahweh (i.e. the LORD)', and similarly T, S, and V; this seems to be a strong testimony against the 'synagogues' in this verse (cf. Rowley, *WAI*, pp. 213–29). Furthermore, in verse 4 *mô*^{c}*ēḏ* was used of the Temple, and it is possible that the plural form employed here is a plural of extension or amplification (cf. *GK* 124b). Those scholars who follow the LXX in rendering 'festivals of God' (as Kissane) would have to change the verb 'burn' into something like 'cease' (e.g. *našbēṯ*, 'let us put an end to . . .').

THE LAMENT TO GOD **9–11**

9. We do not see our signs: see verse 4. The reference may be to the symbols of Jewish religion, such as the sabbaths, festivals, etc. (so Kirkpatrick; cf. Exod. 31:13,17; Ezek. 20:12). The non-observance of them would be regarded as a great calamity (Lam. 2:6). A more likely view is that the signs are the military standards or ensigns (see Yadin, *AWBL*, p. 139). Kraus (*PBK*, p. 517) has suggested that these signs are 'omens' (*Offenbarungszeichen*) or priestly oracles (?); this would fit in well with the rest of the verse. On the other hand, verse 9*a* may be misplaced because it is possible that 'our signs' are intentionally contrasted with 'their own signs' in verse 4*b*.

any prophet: this would seem to favour the Maccabean date, because the cessation of prophecy was characteristic of that period (cf. 1 Mac. 4:46, 9:27, 14:41). Yet we also know of other times when the voice of prophecy was, more or less, silent (cf. 1 Sam. 3:1; Lam. 2:9). There was, apparently, no prophet who could give an answer to the people's perplexed question: 'How long?'. For 'prophet' (*nāḇîʾ*), see on 105:15.

10. scoff: the Hebrew *ḥ-r-p* means 'to say sharp things against another person or group' or 'to taunt'. In this case the reproach may have been expressed not so much in actual words as in deeds. The destroyed places, and in particular the Temple, would be an ever-present reproach, far louder than any words.

revile thy name: (cf. verse 18*b*), i.e. by what they have done and are still doing. Thus they claim to have triumphed over Yahweh, and so they abuse his name or honour (see on 20:1).

11. Why: see verse 1. Verse 11 is a description of the apparent indifference of God to the plight of his people.

hold back thy hand: or, 'Why do you hold your power in check?' For the opposite idea, see Isa. 52:10. This may be another instance where *yāḏ* ('hand') may denote the 'left hand' (cf. Dahood, *PAB*, I, p. 44) which balances 'thy right hand' in verse 11*b*.

in thy bosom: this phrase (verse 11*b*) is in some disorder; M.T. means 'consume thy right hand from the midst of your bosom' which, if correct, is very odd. *RSV* and most exegetes emend the M.T. *kallēh* ('consume') into *tiḵlāʾ* (from *k-l-ʾ*, 'to keep, withhold'), and change the preposition *m*(*in*) ('from') into *bᵉ* ('in').

THE HYMNIC CONFESSION OF TRUST 12–17

12. Yet God my King . . .: or 'Yet (you), O God, are my King . . .'. Perhaps we should add *we'attāh* ('Yet you'), as in verses 13–17. The speaker may be the community personified (so Baethgen) or a representative of the people. For 'king' (*melek*) as a divine title, see on 68:24. LXX and V read 'our king'.
salvation: or 'saving acts' (the noun is in plural form); see on 35:3.
in the midst of the earth: or simply 'in the earth'.

13. There is a difference of opinion whether this and the following verses refer to the traditions of the Creation, or whether they give a figurative description of the Exodus events. The former alternative seems more likely, but it is possible that for the Psalmist the *Heilsgeschichte* included not only the Exodus but also the Creation (cf. 65:6 (M.T. 7)).
Thou didst divide the sea: N. C. Habel (*Yahweh versus Baal* (1964), p. 65) argues that we have here an 'application of the Canaanite "battle for kingship" imagery to the revelation of Yahweh's kingship', and he remarks that 'a dragon myth is not necessarily a creation myth' (*loc. cit.*). Oesterley (*TP*, p. 348), on the other hand, thinks that this Psalm represents the 'old creation-myth, so well known to us from Babylonian and other sources' which was still 'current in Israel even in the Psalmist's days, and men still told the story of how God had *defeated*, frustrated, and rendered ineffective, the mighty powers of Chaos . . .'. The appropriation of foreign myths and their re-interpretation by the Israelites was not a sign of weakness but rather an expression of their theological vitality. The primary purpose of this take-over was polemical, and the re-interpreted myth was not necessarily regarded as a 'doctrinal statement' (cf. O. Kaiser, *Die Mythische Bedeutung des Meeres in Ägypten, Ugarit und Israel* (*BZAW*, 78, 1959), p. 158). Eichrodt (*TOT*, II, p. 115) suggests that the myth of the Chaos conflict was 'of no consequence for Israel's understanding of the world', but that it belonged 'to the treasure-house of poetry, on which poets and prophets liked to draw in order to clothe their thoughts in rich apparel'; roughly speaking this may be right.

In the Ugaritic myths the Sea (*Yām* or *Yamm*) was the opponent of Baal (cf. *ANET*, pp. 130f.; Jirku, *MK*, pp. 54, 79); the battle between the two concerned kingship, and it was not associated with creation. On the other hand, in the Babylonian myth the struggle between Marduk and Tiamat resulted in the creation of the world (see *DOTT*, pp. 5–13). In 74:13–17 it seems that the motif of the fight with the dragon *was* linked with the idea of creation. In 146:6 Yahweh is described as the creator of the sea.

the dragons: O. Eissfeldt (*Kleine Schriften*, III, 1966, p. 259) reads the singular *tannîn* (for M.T. *tannînîm*), and he regards it as one of the names for the Chaos waters; the other names may be Rahab (see on 89:10), Leviathan (see verse 14), the Sea, the fleeing serpent (cf. Job 26:13; Isa. 27:1). The word *tannîn* is of uncertain etymology, but it is found in the Ugaritic texts (cf. Gordon, *UT*, p. 498). In Exod. 7:9,10,12; Dt. 32:33; Ps. 91:13, it simply means a 'serpent' but even in these occurrences W. Zimmerli (*Ezechiel* (*BK* 1314, 1967), p. 707) sees an emphasis on its threatening nature. Of more interest is the use of *tannîn* as a parallel to the sea (Job 7:12) and to Rahab (Isa. 51:9); here it seems to be a synonym for the primeval sea. Ps. 148:7 employs *tannîn* to denote the great creatures of the sea, or the marine animals in general. In its figurative use it can signify the Pharaoh (or Egypt), as in Ezek. 29:3: 'Pharaoh king of Egypt, the great dragon that lies in the midst of his streams . . .' (cf. also Ezek. 32:2). In 74:13 some exegetes retain the plural form (*tanînnîm*), and consider the dragons as the 'helpers of Rahab' (Job 9:13), and as part of her army.

14. the heads of Leviathan: the Hebrew *liwyāṭān* appears in the Ugaritic texts as *ltn* (Lotan?), and Baal is said to have slain or conquered this serpent-like monster with seven heads (cf. *ANET*, pp. 137a, 138b). In these texts *ltn* seems to be another name of the sea. This usage has survived, to some extent, in this verse (and Job 41:1?), where Leviathan is the Chaos monster (see Johnson, *SKAI*, p. 99, n.3). In 104:26 Leviathan has become a mere plaything of Yahweh.

as food: the great monster is cast upon dry land as food for the wild beasts. Some scholars have seen here an allusion to the bodies of the Egyptians which were cast upon the sea shore (Exod. 14:30), but the description may belong to the mythical word-picture (cf. Ezek. 29:5, 32:4). The account is slightly reminiscent of Anath's treatment of Mot, the god of the netherworld, whom she killed and cut to pieces (cf. *ANET*, p. 140b).

for the creatures of the wilderness: lit. 'to the people, to the wild beasts' which may simply mean 'to the wild beasts'; cf.

Prov. 30:25: 'the ants are a people not strong'. Some exegetes re-divide the phrase so as to read *l^e^camle^ṣê yām*, 'to the creatures of the sea' (cf. *TRP*, p. 31). This gives a good sense but the word *^c^amlāṣ* is not found elsewhere in the *OT*. *NEB* has 'to the sharks'.

15. springs and brooks: the Hebrew equivalents are singular in form but they may be used collectively. God made a way for the springs and brooks, and he harnessed the threatening waters to a useful service (cf. 104:6–12).

ever-flowing streams: Kissane (*BP*, p. 335) *et al.* find here a reference to the Red Sea (Exod. 14:21f.) and to the Jordan (Jos. 3–4), but it is more likely that, primarily at least, the allusion is to the mythical rivers (see on 46:4). The *nāhār* ('river') is the Hebrew counterpart of the Ugaritic *nhr*, which was an alternative name of the god *Yām* (or *Yamm*) ('Sea') (cf. Gordon, *UT*, p. 442).

16. Both day and night belong to God, for he made them for his service. Von Rad (*OTT*, I, p. 144) thinks that night is 'a survival of the darkness of chaos, now however kept in bounds by a protective order. But the day is light from that primeval light which was the firstborn of the works of Creation'.

the luminaries: the Hebrew *mā^ɔ^ôr* is either collective in meaning (so *RSV*), or it may refer to the moon (so *NEB*). The latter alternative may be more likely, and this verse would provide an example of a chiastic parallelism.

17. the bounds of the earth: Kirkpatrick interprets it as 'divisions of land and sea' (cf. 104:9), while some other exegetes think of the borders that separate people from people (Davies, Cohen). Perhaps it refers to the divisions of the seasons (cf. Gen. 1:14); this would provide a good parallel with verse 17*b*. In Palestine there were, in a sense, only two seasons: the rainy season or winter and the rainless summer (see on 65:10), or seed-time and harvest.

THE FINAL PETITION **18–23**

18. Remember this: see verse 2. Dahood (*PAB*, II, p. 199) takes *zō^ɔ^ṯ* ('this') as a noun meaning 'insults' (of the enemy); see on 7:3.

the enemy scoffs: the object of the verb is not expressed (cf. verse 10), but the action is directed at Israel and therefore at God.

an impious people: lit. 'foolish people' (*AV*, *RV*). The Hebrew

nāḇāl denotes not so much an excusable lack of knowledge or mere ignorance as guilty foolishness and wickedness (cf. Nötscher, *PEB*, p. 163); see on 14:1. The phrase is also used in Dt. 32:6 (of rebellious Israel), and of foreign peoples (*gôy nāḇāl*) in Dt. 32:21 and in Sir. 50:26 (where it refers to the Samaritans).
reviles thy name: this resumes verse 10*b*. The defiling of the sanctuary and the profaning of God's name are synonymous (cf. Lev. 20:3).

19. the soul of thy dove: this may denote the life of Israel which is symbolized by a dove. LXX and S read '(the life of him) who praises you' (i.e. *tôḏeḵâ* for M.T. *tôreḵā* ('your dove')); similarly *NEB*.
the wild beasts: *ḥayyaṯ* (singular in form) may be an error for the plural *ḥayyôṯ*. Kraus (*PBK*, p. 513) suggests *lammāweṯ* ('to death') for M.T. *ḥayyaṯ*.
do not forget: this is a deliberate act of will, and it amounts to a rejection or casting off. Since God is righteous, this would naturally be understood as a punishment.
for ever: see verse 1.

20. for thy covenant: so LXX; M.T. has 'for the covenant'. On *berîṯ* ('covenant'), see on 55:20. The chastised nation appeals to Yahweh's Covenant promises, and (at the same time) this assumes that the people, on their part, have repented of their sins (both collectively and individually). Briggs (*CECBP*, II, p. 160), following Duhm, reads *labberiyyōṯ* ('to the fat ones', i.e. the enemies; see on 17:10), and he takes the phrase 'for they are full' with verse 20*a*, which is metrically more likely, hence '. . . to the fat ones for they are full' (of the spoil they have gained). There is, however, no support for this emendation in the ancient versions. One could also regard *beriyyōṯ* as 'creatures, people' (as in late Hebrew; cf. Sir. 16:16), and as referring to Israel; perhaps 'have regard for (your) creatures (i.e. people) for they have had their fill (of trouble)', similarly *NEB*.
the dark places of the land: the author may have thought of the hiding-places of the fugitives; there, too, the enemies have perpetrated their violence by slaughtering the helpless refugees (cf. 1 Mac. 2:29–38).
habitations of violence: i.e. the places where violence is done.

21. . . . put to shame: *AV*, *RV* are more literal in their rendering: 'O let not the oppressed return ashamed' (when they pray to God).

the poor and needy: see on 43:2 and 35:10.

22. Arise, O God: see on 7:6.

thy cause: i.e. Israel's cause is also that of Yahweh, and therefore the wicked must not be allowed to be permanently victorious over the people of God. It was believed by many that 'with Israel's misfortunes dishonour falls on God's name, and with her destruction Yahweh's name, too, would be exterminated from the world' (Eichrodt, *TOT*, II, p. 477). Yet the disobedient nation is not punished or oppressed by some independent powers, but the active agent behind it all is God. Being just and merciful, he will not give up his people for ever, when they repent.

the impious: on *nāḇāl*, see verse 18. T renders this 'the mad king', thinking, apparently, of Antiochus Epiphanes, who was sometimes called by his opponents Epimanes, or 'madman'.

23. Do not forget: see verse 19.

which goes up continually in defiance of God.

Psalm 75 Judgment Belongs to God

The classification of this Psalm is problematic, because it consists of heterogeneous elements. It opens with a hymnic praise, or a collective thanksgiving (verse 1), followed by an oracle of Yahweh (verses 2–5) which may have been uttered by a priest or a cultic prophet. Verses 6–8 deal with the impending judgment of the wicked, and the language of these verses has an eschatological colouring. The Psalm concludes with a praise to the God of Jacob (verses 9–10). McCullough (*PIB*, p. 399) regards verse 9 as 'an excerpt from an individual's hymn of praise', but the speaker may well be a representative of the community. Gunkel defines this Psalm as a prophetic liturgy which is indefinite enough to fit this poem; others would describe it as a hymn in the form of a prophetic liturgy (so Leslie), or as a Thanksgiving of the community.

Its life-setting is equally uncertain. It is unlikely that the Psalm was used in the celebration of a particular national deliverance, such as the Assyrian overthrow mentioned in 2 Kg. 19:35 (cf. Kirkpatrick, *BPCB*, p. 449), or that it was purely eschatological in its significance. A cultic interpretation is a more reasonable approach although it is not obvious what cultic events are presupposed by this Psalm. Mowinckel links it with the Enthronement Festival of Yahweh.

There is no indication of the date of the Psalm, but Oesterley (*TP*, p. 350) suggests that it is probably 'a comparatively late adaptation of a pre-Exilic hymn'. Kissane assigns it to the Exilic period.

The metre of the Psalm is irregular but the 3+2 rhythm predominates.

To the choirmaster: see Introduction, p. 48.

Do not Destroy: see Introduction, p. 50.

A Psalm of Asaph: see Introduction, pp. 46 and 45f.

A Song: see Introduction, p. 47.

THE THANKSGIVING TO GOD **1**

1. We give thanks: or, 'We praise you'. The repetition of 'We give thanks' is for the sake of greater emphasis. For the verb *hôḏāh* ('to give thanks, praise'), see on 18:49.

we call on thy name: this follows the reading suggested by LXX, S, and V (*wᵉḳārōʾ ḇišᵉmeḵā*). M.T. has 'and your name is near'. Perhaps we should render: 'and they that call upon your name', reading *wᵉḳōreʾê ḇᵉšimᵉḵā*, because the following phrase in M.T. is '*they* recount your wonderful deeds' (cf. *TRP*, p. 31; S and V have 'we recount'). To 'call on Yahweh's name' (see on 20:1) means to invoke him by pronouncing his name aloud (literally, 'to call *with* the name of Yahweh'; cf. W. Beyerlin, *Origins and History of the Oldest Sinaitic Traditions*, Eng. tr. by S. Rudman (1965), pp. 136f.). Theologically, Yahweh's name 'takes the place which in other cults was occupied by the cultic image' (v. Rad, *OTT*, I, p. 183). The expression came to signify the worship of God in general (cf. 80:18 (M.T. 19), 105:1; Isa. 12:4, 41:25; Jer. 10:25). For *nip̄lāʾôṯ* ('wondrous deeds'), see on 9:1.

THE ORACLE OF GOD **2–5**

2. the set time: on *môʿēḏ*, see on 74:4. Although God may appear inactive for the time being, he has appointed a time for judgment. Neither friend nor foe can make decisions for God; he remains absolutely sovereign in all he does. Gunkel (*PGHAT*, p. 328) thinks of an eschatological judgment, but it is more likely that in the first place the reference is to a divine intervention in the near future (cf. 102:13 (M.T. 14)).

I will judge with equity: M.T. emphasizes 'I', suggesting that none other than God will bring about justice and equity. The Hebrew *mêšārîm* is usually regarded as a plural of amplification (cf. *GK* 124e), and it suggests what is straightforward and upright (cf. Isa. 25:7, 33:15).

3. When the earth totters: the verb *m-w-g* ('to melt away') is used figuratively of agitation and helplessness (cf. 46:6 (M.T. 7)). Even if the whole world and its inhabitants were to melt away in fear, God would still be in control.

its pillars: either the bases of the moral order (so Kirkpatrick, Davies), or the foundations of the earth (see on 104:5; cf. 1 Sam. 2:8; Job 9:6, 38:4,6).

Selah: see Introduction, pp. 48f.

4. the boastful: i.e. whose pride is their own self and not God; therefore they do not render homage to him (see on 34:2, 52:1). For 'the wicked', see on 1:1.

Do not lift up your horn: or 'do not be arrogant'. 'Horn' (*ḳeren*) is a well-known symbol of strength and might, pride and dignity (Job 16:15; Ps. 18:2 (M.T. 3), 89:17,24 (M.T. 18, 25), 92:10 (M.T. 11), 112:9); in Dan. 7:7,8,24 'horns' symbolize 'kings', and so also in Ps. 132:17 (a messianic king?). Cf. G. W. Ahlström, *Psalm 89* (1959), pp. 92–5.

5. on high: Dahood (*PAB*, II, p. 209) takes *lammārôm* ('on high') as a divine name, rendering '(against) the Exalted One'.

speak with insolent neck: cf. Job 15:26. LXX has 'speak not unrighteousness against God', reading *ṣûr* ('rock', a frequent divine name; see on 42:9) for M.T. *ṣawwā'r* ('neck'). The LXX reading is adopted by many commentators (cf. *NEB*), and it lends some support to Dahood's suggestion concerning 'on high' (verse 5*a*).

THE JUDGMENT OF GOD **6–8**

6. This verse may be textually corrupt; but the general idea is that it is in vain to look for human help from whatever quarter, and that the only true hope for the nation is God.

not from the wilderness comes lifting up: the wilderness (see on 55:7) probably refers to the steppe-lands in the south. Kraus (*PBK*, p. 523) suggests that the wicked think that the dwelling of God is in the *far* distance, and that therefore they are safe from his presence. If so, 'the wilderness' might be an allusion to the region around Mount Sinai (see on 68:7f.). M.T. reads: '. . . the wilderness of mountains' (so also LXX, S, and V). According to T, these mountains are those in the north, i.e. Syria. Another possibility is to read: '. . . the wilderness to the

mountains', i.e. from the south to the north (cf. Dahood, *PAB*,
II, p. 209).

7. God who executes judgment: or 'but God is the judge'
(*AV, RV*); cf. Isa. 33:22. For *š-p-ṭ* ('to judge'), see on 72.2.
putting down one . . .: cf. 1 Sam. 2:6,7; Ps. 147:6.

8. cup: this word is used figuratively of divine judgment (see
on 60:3); for a similar usage cf. 11:6; Isa. 51:17; Jer. 25:15,28f.,
49:12, 51:7.
well mixed: lit. 'full of spices' (so Kissane; cf. *KBL*, p. 541b),
or 'full of mixed drink' (cf. Aistleitner, *WUS*, p. 189, no. 1611).
The Hebrew *meseḵ* is a *hapax legomenon* in the *OT*, but it occurs in
Ugaritic; G. R. Driver (*CML*, p. 67b) renders *msk* by 'mead'.
shall drain it: lit. 'they shall drain (the dregs) and they shall
drink (them)'. Either the two verbs are complementary (as in
RSV), or they belong to two parallel lines: 'even its dregs they
shall drain, all the wicked of the earth shall drink (it)' (cf. Kraus,
PBK, p. 520). The essence of this verse is that the wicked shall receive their due punishment to the full (cf. G. R. Driver, *VT*, I
(1951), p. 249).

THE PRAISE TO GOD 9–10

9. But I will rejoice: the speaker is either the community as
a whole, or a representative of the congregation. *RSV* follows the
reading of LXX and V (i.e. *ʾāḡîl* for M.T. *ʾaggîḏ* ('I will declare')).
Another possibility is to read *ʾāḡîḏ* (postulating a verb *g-w-d* ('to
make excellent'); cf. the Arabic *ğāda*, 'to be excellent'; so *TRP*,
p. 31; G. R. Driver, *JTS*, XLIV (1943), p. 14), translating 'I will
magnify the Eternal One', taking the preposition *lᵉ* (*RSV* 'for')
as a *lāmeḏ vocativum*, and *ʿōlām* as a divine name (cf. M. Dahood,
VT, XVI (1966), pp. 299–311).
I will sing praises: see on 66:4. For 'the God of Jacob', see on
20:1.

10. the horns of the wicked: (see verse 5), i.e. the might
and pride of the godless will be brought to nothing.
he will cut off: (*yᵉḡaddēaʿ*). M.T. has 'I will cut off' (*ʾaḡaddēaʿ*);
similarly LXX, S, and V. *RSV* is preferable because the subject
of the verb must be God.
the horns of the righteous: i.e. the righteous (see on 1:5) shall
be made strong and they shall be honoured, while the arrogant
shall be humiliated (cf. Mt. 23:12).

Psalm 76 God Triumphant

The main theme of this Psalm is God's victory over his enemies, and this feature has often led to a historical interpretation. The principal historical events suggested have been the military achievements of David, the Assyrian overthrow (2 Kg. 19; Isa. 37) which is implied by the LXX addition to the psalm title: 'with reference to the Assyrians', and the Maccabean victories. It may well be that the reference is to the salvation-history of the nation, and not to one particular event. The Psalm was probably used in the Jerusalem Temple, perhaps at the Feast of Tabernacles, to celebrate the triumphs of Yahweh and the choice of his Holy City as his dwelling-place. Gunkel, Dahood, *et al.* describe the Psalm as a Song of Zion (cf. *EP*, pp. 42, 81) but essentially it is a hymn. Oesterley (*TP*, p. 352) thinks of it as 'a pre-Exilic hymn', repeatedly adapted to new situations.

The Psalm can be divided into four strophes: verses 1–3 magnify the God whose dwelling is in Zion, while verses 4–6 describe the victory of the God of Jacob; the third strophe depicts the divine judge whose power is both absolute and gracious, and the final strophe (verses 10–12) is concerned with homage to God.

The metre of the Psalm is mainly 3 + 3.

To the choirmaster: see Introduction, p. 48.
stringed instruments: see Introduction, p. 48.
A Psalm of Asaph: see Introduction, pp. 46 and 45f.
A Song: see Introduction, p. 47.

THE GOD OF ZION **1–3**

1. In Judah God is known: he is renowned, acknowledged as great (cf. Prov. 31:23; Isa. 61:9). Mowinckel (*PIW*, I, p. 142) renders: 'God hath "made himself known" in Judah'. The term 'Judah' may denote the southern tribe, or may be used as a synonym of 'Israel'.

his name is great: i.e. he has manifested himself through his mighty acts of salvation. Cf. Isa. 63:12; for 'name', see on 20.1.

2. His abode: lit. 'His covert' (see on 27:5). The Hebrew *sōḵ* can be used of a lion's lair (10:9), and it has been suggested that Yahweh is depicted as the lion of Judah (cf. Isa. 31:4). *NEB* 'his tent'.

Salem, according to Gen. 14:18, was the locality or city of which

Melchizedek was king. It is generally agreed that Salem should be identified with Jerusalem (cf. G. v. Rad, *Genesis*, Eng. tr. by J. H. Marks (*OTL*, 1961), p. 174), and the parallelism of 76:2 is a further support for this equation. 'Salem' may be an abbreviation of 'Jerusalem' (so Davies; cf. also D. R. Ap-Thomas, *AOTS*, p. 282), or 'a poetic and religious appellation' (*IDB*, IV, p. 166a). The use of 'Salem' (*šālēm*) may be intended to bring to mind the word *šālôm* ('peace, salvation'): the God who rules in Salem is the one who creates peace in the world (cf. Heb. 7:1f.).

his dwelling place in Zion: some exegetes (e.g. Oesterley, Johnson) add the first word of verse 3 ('there', *šāmmāh*) to the end of verse 2, reading: 'and as for his dwelling place, he has set it (*śāmāh* for M.T. *šāmmāh*) in Zion'; this restores the dominant 3+3 metre. The 'dwelling' or 'dwelling place' (*m*ᵉᶜ*ônāh*) may denote a lair of wild beasts (Job 38:40; Am. 3:4), but figuratively it may be used of the habitation of Yahweh, i.e. of the Temple (cf. 26:8*a*, 68:5*b* (M.T. 6*b*)), or of God as the refuge of men (Dt. 33:27). For 'Zion', see on 65:1. The establishing of Zion as a dwelling was apparently the first work of God in this *particular* section of the *Heilsgeschichte* (cf. J. Schreiner, *Sion-Jerusalem: Jahwes Königssitz* (1963), p. 233).

3. There he broke . . .: 'There' (*šāmmāh*) probably belongs to the preceding verse (see above), or it can be understood as referring to Salem (or Jerusalem), and as pointing to the ritual drama performed within the city itself (cf. Mowinckel, *PStud.*, II, pp. 57ff., 126ff.).

the flashing arrows: lit. 'the flames of the bow'. The origin of the metaphor may be found in mythology, where the lightnings of the storm-god were regarded as his arrows. In the present context the reference may be either to the swiftness of the arrows' flight, or to the incendiary arrows (see on 7:13). The shield (see on 3:3), sword (see on 44:6), and 'weapons of war' represent *all* types of weapons and armour. 'Weapons of war' (cf. 1QH vi:28) is a translation of *milḥāmāh*, which usually means 'war, battle'. Gunkel, Kissane, *et al.* think that some specific, but not further defined, weapon is meant.

Selah: see Introduction, pp. 48f.

THE DEFEAT OF THE FOES **4–6**

4. Glorious art thou: lit. 'You are lighted up' (or 'enveloped in light' (?); cf. 104:2). Many exegetes follow T and Theod in

reading: 'you are awe-inspiring' (i.e. *nôrā'* for M.T. *nā'ôr*; see on 65:5); *NEB* '. . . terrible'.
everlasting mountains: similarly LXX and V reading *ʿaḏ* (which can mean either 'prey', as in Gen. 49:27, or 'perpetuity', as in Hab. 3:6) for M.T. *ṭerep̱* ('prey'). *AV*, *RV* render: 'the mountains of prey'. The 'everlasting mountains' (a plural of majesty?) may denote Mount Zion, or mountains in general, used as a symbol of all that is lasting and mighty. Cf. Isa. 2:2.

5. stouthearted: Kissane (*BP*, p. 344) renders 'the stubborn of heart', as in Isa. 46:12. These men are the rulers and kings of the earth (see verse 12) and their armies. Weiser (*POTL*, p. 525) finds here an allusion to David's victory over the Philistines (cf. 2 Sam. 5:17–25), the account of which has been coloured by the tradition of the Exodus events. Others see here a reference to the deliverance from the Egyptian bondage (for other views, see O. Eissfeldt, *Kleine Schriften*, III (1966), pp. 448–57).
they sank into sleep: i.e. the sleep of death (see on 13:3).
unable to use their hands: lit. 'they did not find their hands', i.e. they had become powerless, 'paralysed' by death.

6. At thy rebuke: see on 9:5. The Psalmist is thinking of the dynamic word of the God of Jacob (see on 20:1), which has power both to create and to destroy.
rider: reading *rōḵēḇ* (cf. LXX, T, S, and V) for M.T. *reḵeḇ* ('chariot'; see on 68:17). The expression 'rider and horse' is reminiscent of Exod. 15:1.
lay stunned: the verb *r-d-m* means 'to sleep deeply'; occasionally it may suggest the influence or presence of the deity (cf. Dan. 8:18, 10:9). The reference in our Psalm is to the sleep of death (see verse 5) brought about by God.

THE DIVINE JUDGMENT **7–9**

7. But thou: the pronoun 'thou' (*'attāh*) is either repeated for the sake of emphasis, or it is due to a scribal error (dittography?). Kissane reads for the first *'attāh* the adverb *ʿattāh* ('now').
terrible: better, 'awe-inspiring' (see on 65:5).
Who can stand before thee: i.e. who can endure God's judgment (cf. 1:5, 130:3; Nah. 1:6). The rhetorical question serves to emphasize the majesty of God (see Gunkel, *EP*, p. 54; Labuschagne, *IYOT*, p. 97).
when once thy anger is roused: lit. 'from then your anger', which does not give a satisfactory sense. Therefore many com-

mentators read *mēʿōz* ('because of the intensity (or 'might') of (your anger)') for M.T. *mēʾāz* ('from then'); cf. 90:11.

8. From the heavens . . .: this does not contradict verse 2 where Yahweh's habitation is said to be in Zion. In *OT* thought there existed a mysterious link, if not identity, between God's heavenly dwelling and his earthly abode (see Clements, *GT*, p. 68).

judgment: (for *dîn*, see on 72:2). God's sentence on the oppressors means deliverance for the oppressed.

the earth feared: it was full of anxiety. The reference may be to Judah and Jerusalem (so Briggs), in which case 'fear' would be a feeling of awe before God. It is possible, however, that the author had in mind the whole world.

9. . . . arose to establish judgment: according to de Vaux (*AI*, p. 156), the judge was seated during the legal arguments but he stood up to pronounce the sentence (cf. Isa. 3:13).

all the oppressed of the earth: either the people of God, oppressed by the foreign powers, or the afflicted out of all the nations (cf. verse 12; Isa. 11:4; Zeph. 2:3). On 'afflicted' (*ʿānāw*), see on 34:2; cf. H. Birkeland, *ʿĀNI und ʿĀNĀW in den Psalmen* (1933), p. 99.

Selah: see Introduction, pp. 48f.

HOMAGE TO GOD **10–12**

10. the wrath of men shall praise thee: this may suggest that even the hostility of men can be made to serve the purposes of God (cf. Rom. 8:28), or that the enmity of men calls forth the punishment of God, and this in turn becomes the reason for praising God (see on 18:49). Many commentators (as *NEB*) emend *ʾāḏām* (**men,** lit. 'man, mankind') into *ʾeḏōm* ('Edom'), hence: 'the wrathful Edom shall praise you' (so Schmidt, Kraus, *et al.*). This could be further balanced by reading 'and the remnant of Hamath (i.e. *ḥamaṯ* for M.T. *ḥēmōṯ* ('wrath')) shall keep your festival' (following LXX and V which have *teḥoggeḵā* for M.T. *taḥgōr* ('you will gird on')). For other possibilities, see Eissfeldt, op. cit., pp. 449–57.

the residue of wrath . . .: this does not make much sense, and therefore some such change as the one outlined above may well be required. The reference to Edom and Hamath (on the Orontes) may denote the distant south and north respectively, suggesting *pars pro toto* the whole inhabited world. See *NEB*.

11. Make your vows: or 'If you make your vows (then fulfil them)' (cf. *GK* 110f). For 'vow', see on 61:5. The people addressed are the nations (so Weiser), those 'all around him' who turn to him (cf. Isa. 19:21). Kirkpatrick, on the other hand, thinks that the Psalmist is speaking to Israel.

to him who is to be feared: lit. 'to the fear' (*lammôrā'*) or 'to him who is the object of fear', as in Isa. 8:13: 'let him be your fear, let him be your dread'. Some scholars delete *lammôrā'* for metrical reasons, or read for it *lannôrā'* ('to the awe-inspiring one'). *NEB* omits this phrase as a gloss.

12. the spirit of the princes: this may refer either to the pride (or courage) of the hostile rulers (so Gunkel), or to their life (so Davies). The Hebrew *rûaḥ* is found some 378 times in the *OT*, and a third of these occurrences denote 'wind' (48:7 (M.T. 8), 78:39) or 'air in motion, breath' (33:6). Life, or one's vitality, may ebb and flow in a way which is reminiscent of the rising and sinking of the wind, and consequently it too can be designated by *rûaḥ* (cf. 31:5 (M.T. 6), 104:29, 143:7, 146:4), which may also express the varied behaviour of men, as well as their changing moods and characteristics. So one may speak of a patient spirit (Ec. 7:8), or an impatient one (Job 21:4), of a broken spirit (51:17 (M.T. 19)), or one proud in spirit (Ec. 7:8), etc. *Rûaḥ* is often used in the phrase 'the spirit of God' which may bestow special gifts upon men (Jg. 13:25; 1 Sam. 11:6, 16:13; 2 Sam. 23:2; Isa. 11:2), or it may act in creation (104:30; Isa. 32:15), judgment (Isa. 4:4, 30:28), etc. For a detailed discussion on this subject, see Johnson, *VITAI*, pp. 23–37; F. Baumgärtel, *Pneuma*, *DNT*, VI, pp. 359–68.

who is terrible . . .: or 'who inspires awe' (see on 65:5) in the kings of the earth. Thus they learn that the real ruler of the world is Yahweh.

Psalm 77 What God is Great like Our God?

This Psalm consists of two main parts: verses 1–10 form an Individual Lament, while verses 11–20 resemble a Hymn. In view of this, some exegetes have regarded this poem as composed of two different fragments, in which case the division may well have come after verse 15. In verses 16–19 the metre is 3+3+3, in contrast to the prevailing 3+3 rhythm in the rest of the Psalm. Perhaps the best explanation is that the Psalmist drew upon older cultic traditions but that the present composition is a literary unity.

The *Gattung* of the Psalm is not clear; Mowinckel, Leslie, *et al.* regard the poem as a National Lament where the speaker is the King or a representative of the community. J. Gray (*VT*, XI (1961), p. 9) considers it as 'a public thanksgiving after relief from distress', but most commentators define it as an Individual Lamentation. The Psalmist is not troubled by purely personal problems but he feels deeply involved in the national disaster which has overtaken his people. The reference to 'Jacob' and 'Joseph' (verse 15) may suggest a northern Israelite origin (Leslie dates the Psalm between 733 and 721 B.C.), but it is more probable that these terms are employed loosely without implying a northern provenance. The Psalm could have originated in the early part of the Exilic period but any other similar national calamity could be equally well suited.

The hymnic conclusion of the Psalm could be explained as a turning away from the contemplation of the unpleasant present experiences, to the praising of the mighty deeds of God, in the past. This is no sentimental journey but a deliberate attempt to renew one's hope and courage by considering God's greatness and majesty, and his special concern for his people in times past.

To the choirmaster: see Introduction, p. 48.

Jeduthun: see Introduction, p. 46.

A Psalm of Asaph: see Introduction, pp. 46 and 45f.

THE LAMENT OVER PRESENT TROUBLES **1–10**

1. aloud to God: the repetition of this phrase stresses the intensity of the Psalmist's appeal to God.

2. In the day of my trouble: or 'In the time of my distress'. The nature of the trouble is the author's personal involvement in the fortunes of his people. Some great disaster must have befallen the nation, and the Psalmist shares fully in it.

I seek the Lord: for the verb *d-r-š*, see on 24:6. 'The Lord' is a rendering of the Hebrew *ʾᵃḏōnāy* (lit. 'my lords'), which may be an ossified form meaning 'lord'. The long vowel (instead of the short *a*) in the ending *-āy* is probably a Massoretic device to stress the sacredness of the word. The term *ʾāḏôn* ('lord') suggests one who has power over men or things, the emphasis being on the emotional aspect rather than upon the legal one (cf. *TDNT*, III, p. 1060).

my hand is stretched out in prayer (cf. 143:6). For this gesture in prayer, see on 28:2. M.T. could be rendered literally: 'my hand is poured out'; T alters the text, reading 'my eye (*ᶜênî* for M.T. *yāḏî*) was poured out' (cf. Lam. 3:49). This emendation, however, is unnecessary.

without wearying: or 'without growing numb'.

my soul refuses to be comforted: I refuse all consolation, because true comfort can only come from God; for a similar expression, see Gen. 37:35; Jer. 31:15.

3. I think of God: lit. '(when) I remember . . .'; see on 119:52.

and I moan: this may be the consequence of bringing to mind God's mighty deeds in the past (see on 42:5), but at the same time it provides the ground for new hope.

I meditate: this is parallel to 'I remember', and not to 'I moan'. Whenever the Psalmist recalls God's help in bygone days, the present situation makes his spirit faint (see on 76:12; cf. 143:4).

Selah: see Introduction, pp. 48f.

4. my eyelids: lit. 'the guards of my eyes', an expression found only here in the *OT*. A difficulty is created by the verb **Thou dost hold** (*ᵓāḥaztā*); *RSV* implies that God, or the thought of God, keeps the Psalmist awake at night. Winton Thomas (*TRP*, p. 32) reads *ᵓaḥūzōṯ* ('are fast closed') for M.T. *ᵓāḥaztā*, but that is no great improvement. *RSV* may well be right; similarly *PLE*: 'Sleepless that thought holds me'.

that I cannot speak: either 'but I did not speak' (i.e. I did not complain; cf. 39:1f. (M.T. 2f.)), or paraphrasing: 'I am unable to describe fully my distress'.

5. I consider the days of old: I think of the time when God's gracious help was clearly manifested in the life of the nation (cf. 143:5).

I remember: in M.T. this phrase belongs to the following verse: 'I call to remembrance my song . . .' (*AV*, *RV*). *RSV* is supported by LXX, S, and V, as well as by the prevailing 3 + 3 metre.

6. I commune: (*hāḡîṯî*; so also LXX, S, and V); this gives a better sense than M.T. which has *nᵉḡînāṯî* ('my song' or 'my music' (*RSVm*)). For the verb *h-g-h*, see on 1:2. G. R. Driver (*HTR*, XXIX (1936), p. 186) suggests *nôḡantî* ('I am downcast') from *y-g-n** which may well underlie the Hebrew *gaṯ* ('wine-press') (cf. *HAL*, p. 198a).

with my heart: probably 'with myself' (cf. Ec. 1:16). For 'heart', see on 27:3.

in the night: Cohen (*PSon*, p. 247) takes it figuratively as denoting 'the period of the nation's darkness in Exile'. It is more likely that 'night' is to be taken literally although the nation's plight was the main theme of the Psalmist's thoughts.

and search my spirit: so also the ancient versions. M.T. has 'my spirit searches' (*RSVm*) or, perhaps, 'he (i.e. God) searches my spirit'.

7. the Lord: see verse 2.

spurn for ever: see on 44:9. The rhetorical questions amount to formally negative statements: God has not forsaken his people for ever.

8. steadfast love: or 'Covenant loyalty' (see on 26:3).

for ever: *neṣaḥ*, see on 74:1.

Are his promises at an end: lit. 'Has (his) word come to an end.' The Hebrew *ʾōmer* may be a 'word (of promise)' or an 'oracle (of salvation)', see on 119:11; this would be the divine answer to the lamentation.

for all time: lit. 'for a generation and generation'; see on 72:5; cf. 79:13, 85:5 (M.T. 6), 89:1,4 (M.T. 2, 5).

9. Has God forgotten to be gracious?: this is another rhetorical question expecting the answer 'No'. It does not imply that God has a bad memory (or might have), but it suggests that he has deliberately (and no doubt for a good reason) rejected his people for the time being. See on 119:16.

shut up his compassion: i.e. he has withheld his pity (see on 51:1) in his (just) anger (see on 74:1). Since the answer is in the negative, the repentance of the people may yet be accepted (cf. Hab. 3:2).

Selah: see Introduction, pp. 48f.

10. This verse is textually uncertain, and therefore its interpretation is problematic.

It is my grief: or 'This is my piercing', i.e. the cause of my distress is the fact **that the right hand of the Most High has changed,** or it is due to my thinking that the power of Yahweh could ever change (cf. Mal. 3:6). The word *šenôṯ* ('to change') can also mean 'the years of . . .'; *AV*, *RV* read: 'the years of the right hand', i.e. the time when God's power was active in Israel. The *RSV* rendering seems slightly more fitting. For 'Most High', see on 18:13, 46:4.

THE MIGHTY DEEDS OF GOD **11–15**

11. I will call to mind: this follows the reading of Ḳ*erê* and of the ancient versions, while *K*e*ṯîḇ* has 'I will mention (or 'proclaim')' (see *BH*; cf. Isa. 63:7). Cf. also Childs, *MTI*, p. 14. The reading of *K*e*ṯîḇ* seems preferable, because it avoids the repetition of practically the same verbal form in the parallel line.

the deeds of the LORD: i.e. the *Heilsgeschichte*, which may include not only the Exodus but also *all* the marvellous works of God (see verse 12). '*Yāh*' (*RSV* **the LORD**) is the shorter form of the divine name 'Yahweh' (see on 68:4).

thy wonders of old: the Hebrew *pele*ʾ ('wonder') may denote what is beyond comprehension (Lam. 1:9) and marvellous (88:10 (M.T. 11), 119:129), or, more often, it describes the mighty works of God both in judgment and salvation (78:12, 88:10,12 (M.T. 11, 13), 89:5 (M.T. 6)). A synonym of *pele*ʾ is *nip̱lāʾôṯ*; cf. *VT*, XI (1961), p. 332.

12. I will meditate: for the verb *h-g-h*, see on 1:2. The subject of the meditation is the story of God's work of deliverance. Whatever may be the present situation, the *Heilsgeschichte* cannot be undone; nothing can annul the redemption from Egypt and the creation of the people of Israel (cf. 143:5).

13. Thy way, O God, is holy: lit. '(is) in holiness', while *AV*, *RV* (also LXX) read 'is in the sanctuary'. 'Thy way' denotes the manner of God's dealings with his people, and it is characterized by holiness (see on 68:17); therefore his ways are incomparable (cf. Isa. 55:8) just as he himself is without an equal; there is no god like the God of Israel (Exod. 15:11). If we follow the reading of *AV*, *RV*, then the allusion may be to the cultic recital of God's dealings with his people. N. C. Habel (*Yahweh Versus Baal* (1964), p. 68) takes *dereḵ* ('way') in the sense of 'dominion' (see on 10:5).

like our God: so LXX and S. M.T. has 'like God'. Only Yahweh is truly great (cf. Dt. 7:21, 10:17; Ps. 95:3) and no other heavenly being can claim equality with him. This verse does not necessarily suggest a recognition of other gods, because the reference may well be to the angelic creatures that serve God.

14. who workest wonders: i.e. the special works of God in nature and in history. For *pele*ʾ ('wonder'), see verse 11 (cf. Exod. 15:11; Ps. 72:18; Isa. 25:1).

among the peoples: see on 66:8. These nations have witnessed the birth and growth of the people of Israel.

15. with thy arm: by your own power and might (cf. Exod. 6:6; Ps. 136:12). For *zᵉrôaᶜ* ('arm'), see on 37:17.

redeem: *g-ʾ-l*, see on 119:154.

the sons of Jacob and Joseph: this expression occurs only here in the *OT*; Kraus takes it as a designation of the whole nation of Israel. In Ob. 18 'the house of Joseph' and 'the house of Jacob' denote the entire people of God, although 'Joseph' can also be used of northern Israel, as in Am. 5:6,15, 6:6.

THE POWER AND MAJESTY OF GOD 16–20

Some scholars have regarded this section as an independent poem (or a fragment of one), but it is more plausible that the Psalm is a literary unity. It may depict either the Exodus events (i.e. the crossing of the Sea of Reeds), or God's conquest of the primeval waters. Perhaps the Psalmist derives his word-pictures from both themes, because at a later time creation was regarded as an integral part of the salvation-history. G. v. Rad comments on Isa. 51:9f. and Ps. 77:16ff. (M.T. 17ff.) that here creation and redemption 'can almost be looked on as one act of dramatic divine saving action in the picture of the strugle with the dragon of Chaos' (*OTT*, I, pp. 137f.).

16. When the waters saw thee: either those of the Sea of Reeds or, more likely, the waters of the primeval Chaos (so Weiser, J. Jeremias); cf. 114:3; Hab. 3:10.

the deep trembled: for *tᵉhôm* ('deep'), see on 71:20, 104:6. The 'deep' (lit. 'deeps') was agitated because of its desire to revolt against God, as well as because of awe and fear.

17. This and the following verse describe the theophany of Yahweh as a storm-god, accompanied by thunder and lightnings, rain and whirlwind (cf. 18:7–15 (M.T. 8–16), 29:3–9).

thy arrows: the noun *ḥāṣāṣ* is, apparently, a fuller form of *ḥēṣ*, ('arrow') (cf. *GK* 93bb), and it is a poetical term for the flashes of lightning.

18. in the whirlwind: *AV* 'in the heaven'. The Hebrew *galgal* is literally 'what goes round', and therefore it can be used of a 'wheel (of a war-chariot)' (Jer. 47:3); as a wheel, it may denote, *pars pro toto*, the whole chariot. It can also signify a whirlwind (cf. Isa. 17:30) and, perhaps, the circuit of the horizon (cf. Kissane, *BP*, p. 350). If we take *galgal* as 'wheel(s)', then the reference is either to the wheels of the divine chariot (cf. Ezek. 3:13), or to those of the war-chariots, in which case the change of *baggalgal* into *kaggalgal* ('like (the noise of chariot-)wheel(s)') might help the construction (cf. Jl 2:5).

19. Thy way was through the sea: here the reference may be to the deliverance at the Sea of Reeds during the Exodus. Some scholars add the vocative 'Yahweh' for metrical reasons (cf. J. Jeremias, *Theophanie* (*WMANT*, 10, 1965), p. 26).
yet thy footprints were unseen: this may mean that although the Israelites experienced the power of God, they did not *see* God himself; therefore faith and trust are necessary, not only in times of trouble but also in the very events of salvation.

20. Thou didst lead thy people: cf. Exod. 15:13. For the verb *n-ḥ-h*, see on 67:4.
like a flock: see on 78:52, 100:3. This description suggests that, on the one hand, God has a claim to obedience from his people, and on the other hand, it gives a certain confidence to the people that God will help his errant but repentant flock.
by the hand of Moses and Aaron: the immediate guidance was by these two leaders of the nation (cf. Num. 33:1; 1 Sam. 12:6; 1 Kg. 8:35; Ps. 103:7; Mic. 6:4). The Psalm finishes rather abruptly, but it is possible that this is intentional. The writer stresses that no obstacles can hinder the work of God's salvation: if such a God is with his people, then nothing can overcome them.

Psalm 78 Praise to the Lord of History

This Psalm begins like a didactic poem (see verses 1–4), but according to its context it is a Historical Psalm which resembles a Descriptive Psalm of Praise (see Introduction, pp. 32ff.). Mowinckel (*PIW*, II, p. 112) describes it as 'a synopsis of sacred history in the style of a hymn'.

Its *Sitz im Leben* is not clear. It is probable that it was used in worship, although its exact function is not easy to define. Weiser (*POTL*, p. 538) suggests that this Psalm *followed* the recital of the *Heilsgeschichte* which was an integral part of the festival cult. On the other hand, it could well be the recital itself, i.e. as much as would be required at this point in the cultic act (the renewal of the Covenant?); cf. K. Baltzer, *Das Bundesformular* (*WMANT*, 4, 1960), pp. 19–28. For a similar cultic occasion, see 1QS i:16–ii:1.

Some recent exegetes have argued that this Psalm was no part of any liturgy. G. E. Wright ('The Lawsuit of God: A Form-critical Study of Deuteronomy 32', *IPH*, pp. 39ff.) affirms that the Psalm 'is not liturgical but didactic, the present purpose being to justify the hegemony of Judah over Ephraim, of Jerusalem over Shiloh'. The former alternative seems, however, more likely.

The date of the Psalm is uncertain. Eissfeldt suggests 930 B.C. as the latest possible date (similarly also Wright), but a late pre-Exilic origin may be more plausible, perhaps the reign of Josiah. We may note the following points: (i) the Solomonic Temple is still standing (see verse 69); (ii) the Davidic dynasty is still in power, which points to a pre-Exilic date; (iii) there is no indication of the Exile and its lessons; (iv) although there is no clear allusion to the fall of Samaria (722 B.C.), the general outlook suggests that the northern kingdom was no longer in existence; (v) the term 'Holy One of Israel' (verse 41) may suggest (but not necessarily) a post-Isaianic date; (vi) the Psalm also reflects something of the Deuteronomic attitude to Zion and the high places, and therefore both may belong to the same period. In view of all this, it seems that the origin of the Psalm is to be found in the pre-Exilic period, later rather than earlier. Cf. Sabourin, *POM*, ii, p. 303.

The metre of the Psalm is mainly 3 + 3.

A Maskil of Asaph: see Introduction, pp. 47 and 45f.

THE OUTLINE OF THE PSALMIST'S PURPOSE **1–8**

1. Give ear: this is a common opening formula of various ancient poems (cf. Gen. 4:23; Jg. 5:3) and of the instruction of Wisdom teachers (cf. Prov. 7:24; Isa. 28:23; cf. also Ps. 49:1 (M.T. 2)). This formula usually consists of two parts, e.g. 'Give ear . . . incline your ears' (78:1), 'Hear this . . . give ear' (49:1 (M.T. 2)), etc. See also H. W. Wolff, *Hosea* (*BK* 14, 1961), pp. 122f.

my teaching: (so also *NEB*) this is preferable to 'my law' (*AV*, *RV*). For *tôrāh* ('law, instruction'), see on 119:1.

the words of my mouth: i.e. my instruction, teaching (cf. Dt. 32:1; Ps. 19:14 (M.T. 15), 54:2 (M.T. 4), 138:4).

2. I will open my mouth: i.e. in order to teach (cf. Job 33:2; Prov. 24:7, 31:26).

parable: or 'instruction'. The Hebrew *māšāl* is discussed in 49:4.

See also A. R. Johnson's article '*MĀŠĀL*', in *Wisdom in Israel and in the Ancient Near East*, ed. by M. Noth and D. W. Thomas (*SVT*, 3, 1955), pp. 162–9.
dark sayings from of old: the Hebrew *ḥîḏāh* ('riddle', see on 49:4) is not merely a pastime but also a test of wisdom (1 Kg. 10:1ff.). In our verse it is practically 'an expression of the sacred secret which is the property of a community and its watchword' (A. Bentzen, *Introduction to the Old Testament*, I (1948), p. 177); or it can be described as an account of the mysterious workings of God in times past.

3. The glorious deeds of God are, of course, known to the people, but the salvation-history contains also the enigmatic encounter between the grace of God and the sin of man, which is beyond comprehension. It comprises both warning and hope, and it is to this aspect that the Psalmist turns.

4. We will not hide them: LXX and Jerome 'They were not hidden' (reading *niḵḥaḏ* for M.T. *neḵaḥēḏ*), i.e. the mighty works of God.
from their children: some scholars read 'from our children' (*mibbānênû*), but this emendation is not really required.
but tell: the subject of the Hebrew participle *mesapperîm* may be either 'we' or 'they' (i.e. the children who will declare Yahweh's deeds to the coming generation). The former alternative gives a slightly better parallelism, and is preferable.
the glorious deeds of the LORD: or 'the praises of . . .' (*AV*, *RV*); but the *RSV* rendering seems more likely. For *tehillôṯ* ('praises, glorious acts'), see on 65:1.
the wonders: or 'the marvellous deeds'; see on 9:1.

5. a testimony: (*ʿēḏûṯ*), see on 119:2. In this verse 'testimony' is parallel to 'law', and Gunkel (*PGHAT*, p. 342) takes them as a command to instruct their children about Yahweh's works of deliverance (cf. Exod. 10:2, 13:14; Dt. 4:9, 6:7). On the other hand, they may be synonymous with *berîṯ* ('Covenant'; see verse 10), and together they may allude to the Sinai tradition. For the opposite view, see v. Rad, *PHOE*, p. 55; cf. 147:19.
Jacob: see on 20:1; this is parallel to 'Israel', the name of the confederation of the twelve tribes (cf. J. Bright, *HI*, pp. 142–6).

6. The oral transmission of the *Heilsgeschichte* is an important duty of every generation of Israelites (cf. 44:1ff. (M.T. 2ff.)). This task is discharged not only in the Temple or sanctuaries, but also at home.

7. their hope: the Hebrew *kesel* can mean 'loins' (Lev. 3:4, 10:15), 'stupidity' (Ec. 7:25), or 'confidence', 'hope' (Job 4:6, 31:24). The underlying sense is 'to be heavy, thick'. In this verse *kesel* is 'hope, trust'; for the idea, see on 71:5.
forget: this is not a slip of memory, but a deliberate disregard (see on 119:16). 'Not to forget' is to remember, to re-present the works of God so that one fully realizes their relevance. For 'commandments', see on 119:6.

8. a stubborn . . . generation: this expression is a *hapax legomenon* in the *OT*, but it may be derived from Dt. 21:18,20 which speaks of the stubborn and rebellious son who was incorrigible and was heading for punishment (see on 68:6). For a similar thought, see Dt. 32:5.
whose heart was not steadfast: lit. '. . . was not fixed', i.e. it was not faithful and constant (1 Sam. 7:3; Job 11:3). One's heart is the perfect mirror of one's true self. See Johnson, *VITAI*, p. 84.
spirit: see on 76:12; here it is practically equivalent to the personal pronoun 'they'.
to God: (*'el 'ēl*) so some Hebrew MSS.; M.T. has 'with God' (*AV*, *RV*).

THE REBELLION AGAINST THE MOST HIGH **9–31**

9. This verse may be textually corrupt. Some exegetes consider it as a later addition because it interrupts the sequence of thought between verses 8 and 10. Certain Jewish commentators thought that M.T. implies that the Ephraimites left Egypt on their own but suffered defeat at the hands of the men of Gath (see 1 Chr. 7:21; cf. Cohen, *PSon*, p. 250), but this is dubious. Weiser (*POTL*, p. 540) argues that the Psalmist was thinking of the final battle of Saul on the mountains of Gilboa, which could be regarded as the point at which the kingship passed from Saul to David. Ephraim, as the chief tribe, could denote the whole of northern Israel (cf. verse 67; 2 Chr. 25:7), and thus it could be seen as a polemic against the Samaritans.
armed with the bow: lit. 'armed with shooting of the bow'; LXX and V '. . . were bending and shooting (with) the bow'. It is possible that *rômê* ('shooting') is a variant or gloss on *nôšeḳê* ('armed'; so *RSV*, *RP*), or vice versa. For 'bow', see on 44:6.
turned back: i.e. fled.

10. God's covenant: for *berîṯ* ('Covenant'), see on 55:20.

'Covenant' as well as 'law' and 'testimony' (verse 5) may denote the sum total of one's duties and responsibilities towards God. To disregard the Covenant means not only to disobey God's law, but also to show ingratitude for the great saving acts of God; they are an integral part of the Covenant, being its historical prologue (cf. K. A. Kitchen, *Ancient Orient and Old Testament* (1966), pp. 90–102).

11. They forgot: see verse 7.

the miracles: (*niplā'ōṯ*), this refers to the wonderful and extraordinary deeds of Yahweh, wrought in the course of Israel's deliverance from Egypt (see on 9:1, 40:5). The miracles testify to God's active presence rather than to a disruption of the natural order.

12. This verse refers in passing to the 'plagues of Egypt' which are described in more detail in verses 43–51 (cf. Exod. 7:1–13:22).

in the fields of Zoan: this location is not mentioned in the Exodus traditions of the Pentateuch. 'Zoan' (LXX 'Tanis') was a city in the eastern part of the Nile Delta. Once it was the capital of the Hyksos, known as Avaris; a few centuries later, it became the capital and residence of Rameses II and his successors; it is apparently mentioned in Exod. 1:11 as the 'store-city' called Raamses. The name 'Tanis' or 'Zoan' is found in post-Ramesside texts (cf. Bright, *HI*, pp. 54f.; H. H. Rowley, *From Joseph to Joshua* (1952), p. 27). 'Zoan' is also mentioned in Isa. 19:11,13, 30:4; Ezek. 30:14.

13. He divided the sea: i.e. the Reed Sea (cf. 106:7), and not the traditional 'Red Sea' (see Bright, p. 112). This event is described in Exod. 14:16,21f., and it is referred to in Jos. 4:23; Neh. 9:11; Isa. 63:12.

like a heap: the Hebrew *nēḏ* is used of the dammed-up waters of the Reed Sea (Exod. 15:8) and of the waters of the river Jordan (Jos. 3:13,16).

14. Here we find a poetic account of Yahweh's guidance of Israel by means of the pillars of cloud and fire, which were the representations of the divine presence (see Exod. 13:21; cf. Ps. 105:39).

15. He cleft rocks: this is a reference to Exod. 17:6 which tells of the striking of the rock of Horeb (cf. Isa. 48:21). The verb *b-ḳ-*ᶜ ('to cleave, divide') is also used in verse 13, and it probably serves to emphasize the wonder-working power of God. He could cleave the waters of the sea to make an escape for his people; he could also cleave the dry rock to bring forth life-giving water (cf. Kraus, *PBK*, p. 544).

as from the deep: *AV*, *RV*: 'as *out of* the great depths (*tᵉhōmôṯ*)'. For *tᵉhôm*, see on 71:20, 104:6. The mention of the primeval waters, now put to good use, stresses the abundance of the water supply, and thus, by implication, the magnitude of Israel's sin.

16. streams . . . out of the rock: this refers to the other instance of the provision of water for the people of Israel, described in Num. 20:8–11. For 'rock' (*selaᶜ*), see on 42:9; verse 15 has *ṣûr*, which is a synonym of *selaᶜ*.

like rivers: lit. 'like rivers of water', which is parallel to 'as from the deep'. For *nāhār* ('river'), see on 46:4, 72:8.

17. Despite the tangible proofs of divine providence, the Israelites continued to doubt the power and goodness of God, and this was the essence of their sin (see on 119:11), or of their rebellion against the Most High (for *ᶜelyôn*, see on 46:4, 47:2).

18. They tested God: the verb *nissāh* means 'to put to the test, try'. It can be used in a neutral sense of trying to *do* something (Dt. 4:34; Job. 4:2), but more often it describes God testing a man to see whether he is obedient (Gen. 22:1; Ps. 26:2), or it depicts man trying God (Exod. 17:2,7; Num. 14:22). See Gunkel, *Genesis* (1966), p. 236; cf. 1 C. 10:9; Heb. 3:9.

by demanding the food: the Psalmist had in mind the theme of manna and quails (cf. Exod. 13). In Num. 11:4–32 we are told how thc Israelites grew tired of the manna which they had with monotonous regularity, and longed for meat; (did they not have any flocks?). The older Jewish commentators thought that the Israelites were only seeking an occasion to test God.

the food they craved: lit. 'food for their soul' or '. . . for their appetite'; *AV*, *RV*: '. . . for their lust'. For *nep̱eš* ('soul, appetite, etc.'), see on 33:19.

19. This verse describes the unwarranted scepticism of the Wilderness generation, which is a well-known phenomenon at most times. Trust which must be propped up by constant proofs becomes a pernicious drug, or turns doubting into an occasion of rebellion.

can God spread a table: this offers a striking contrast to 23:5, and it shows the difference between scepticism and simple trust.

20. The Psalmist resumes verses 15f. (cf. 105:41).

bread . . . meat: i.e. manna and quails.

for his people: this may suggest a touch of sarcasm which is the sign of unbelief rather than of honest doubt.

21. a fire was kindled: the verb *niśśᵉḳāh* is derived either from *ś-l-ḳ* ('to kindle, burn'; so *BDB*), or from *n-ś-ḳ* ('to burn', cf. *KBL*, p. 638a). This 'fire' is probably the same as 'the fire of the LORD' in Num. 11:1,3, and it is used metaphorically of the destructive or punitive anger of God, which may sound very harsh but is nevertheless more than just.

Jacob: (see on 20:1); this term is a synonym of 'Israel', and denotes the twelve-tribe amphictyony (or league).

22. they had no faith in God: *OT* faith is not (at least primarily) an intellectual assent to certain ideas about God. Rather it is an attitude to him which takes seriously his commands and promises. Something of this is seen in Dt. 9:23: 'you rebelled against the commandments of the LORD your God, and did not believe him or obey his voice'. Similarly the Psalmist can say: 'I believe in thy commandments' (119:66), i.e. I take seriously the Covenant obligations in fulfilling them, and I have confidence in God's Covenant promises (cf. Gen. 15:6). Faith in God is an attitude to him, and it involves one's whole being; von Rad (*OTT*, I, p. 171) defines the meaning of the verb 'to have faith' as 'to make oneself secure in Yahweh'. This ideal becomes a reality when one regards the promises of God as statements of what he is *already* doing, and when one accepts his commands not as a burden to be endured but as a privilege to be enjoyed. See also H. Wildberger, ' "Glauben" Erwägung zu *hʾmyn*', *SVT*, 16 (1967), pp. 372–86.

his saving power: lit. 'his salvation'; the Wilderness generation was unwilling to trust in God that he would deliver them (see Exod. 6:2–8). The verb *b-ṭ-ḥ* ('to trust') is a synonym of 'to have faith' (*heʾᵉmîn*), but the latter denotes in the first place (if we may generalize) a relationship, while the former expresses a state of being secure in someone or something. The rebellious generation refused to enjoy safety in Yahweh's saving power; their 'faith' had to be founded upon manna and quails. See also *DNT*, VI, pp. 191f.

23. Although God was angry (see on 74:1), he gave the people their wish.

the doors of heaven: this phrase is found only here in the *OT*. Gen. 28:17 speaks of the 'gate of heaven', and more often we find references to the 'windows of heaven' (Gen. 7:11; 2 Kg. 7:2,19; Mal. 3:10).

24. he rained down: see Exod. 16:4.
manna: this is usually taken as a natural phenomenon. It is produced in the form of excretions by certain insects which suck large quantities of the sap of the tamarisk. During the cool nights the honeydew excretions form themselves into drops of sticky, yellowish substance, not larger than a pea. Manna is usually collected before the sunrise, for the heat of the sun would melt it. If this identification is right, then manna could not very well have formed the whole diet of the Israelites, but this unusual phenomenon (from their point of view) must have been sufficiently impressive to serve as an example of divine providence as a whole. For further details, see *IDB*, III, pp. 259f.
the grain of heaven is another description of manna, suggested by its grain-like form. In 105:40 it is called 'bread from heaven' (similarly in Exod. 16:4), while in 78:25 it is named 'the bread of angels' (cf. Wis. 16:20).

25. Man ate: *PNT* has 'Mere men', in contrast to the angels, but perhaps the meaning is 'Everyone' (so Wellhausen, Davies).
angels: the Hebrew *ʾabbîr* can denote a 'mighty man' (cf. 1 Sam. 21:7; Job 24:22, 34:20), or a 'strong animal', such as steed (Jg. 5:22), bull (Isa. 10:13). J. Gray (*JJR*, p. 290) regards *ʾabbîr* as derived from the root cognate with the Arabic *ʾabara*, 'to impregnate'. A similar form *ʾāḇîr* ('mighty') is used to designate God, e.g. 'the Mighty One of Israel' (Isa. 1:24), or 'the Mighty One of Jacob' (132:2,5; Isa. 49:26, 60:16). Some scholars have suggested that *ʾāḇîr* is a form artificially differentiated from *ʾabbîr*. See also Eichrodt, *TOT*, II, pp. 194–202.

26. This verse prepares the ground for the account of the giving of the quails (Exod. 16:13; Num. 11:31f.).
east wind . . . south wind: this is usually taken to mean a south-east wind; 'east' and 'south' are mentioned separately for poetical reasons.
in the heavens: better 'from the heavens', taking the preposition *bᵉ* (*RSV* 'in') in the sense of 'from' (as in Ugaritic); see on 18:8.
by his power: Dahood (*PAB*, II, p. 235) regards the Hebrew *ʿōz* as meaning 'fortress, stronghold', a poetic name for 'heaven'; hence 'from his fortress'.

27–8. he rained flesh . . .: verses 27f. give a picturesque description of the incident recorded in Num. 11:31f. The 'flesh' is quails, migratory birds which winter in Arabia and Africa. Their southward flight takes place in September–October, and they return northward in March–April. On this particular occasion, a cloud of migratory quails, travelling with the wind, crossed the path of the Israelites, landing in and about the camp. The Psalmist's description is rather apt: the birds descended like a rain, and they seemed to be countless in numbers like the sand of the sea-shores; cf. Snaith, *LN*, p. 233; *IDB*, III, p. 973a.

29–31. God gave the rebels the object of their desire, and he punished them by answering their own prayers. See Num. 11:33f.

THE STUBBORNNESS OF THE FATHERS **32–9**

The Wilderness generation provides a fair picture of most generations: their existence seems to be characterized by a monotonous succession of sin, punishment, repentance, and pardon. The outstanding lesson of all this is the patience and love of God.

32. In spite of all the wonders (see on 9:1, 78:11) wrought by God, the people still did not believe (see verse 22). They were always wanting fresh proofs, but all they really needed was the will and courage to believe (cf. Num. 14:11).

33. This verse probably alludes to the eventual destruction of the Wilderness generation (Num. 14:22f.).

like a breath: the life of the rebels achieved nothing, and it ended in nothing. The Hebrew *heḇel* means primarily 'breath', 'vapour', hence 'wind' (Isa. 57:13). Figuratively it denotes what may be visible but what is empty of substance, profitless, and transient, e.g. 'vanity' (Ec. 1:2, etc.), 'idols' (31:6 (M.T. 7); Jer. 2:5, etc.). *Heḇel* is one of the watch-words of Ecclesiastes; cf. the phrase 'vanity of vanities'.

in terror: *babbehālāh* is probably a word play on *baheḇel* ('in emptiness'; *RSV* **like a breath**). *PNT* has 'in sudden ruin', apparently caused by some disease (cf. Lev. 26:16).

34. When he slew them: i.e. when he punished some of them, the rest 'sought for him'. For the verb *d-r-š* ('to seek'), see on 24:6.

they repented: lit. 'they returned'. The verb *š-w-b* usually means 'to return'. If the object of the verb is Yahweh, it may suggest repentance, i.e. a turning of one's whole existence to God, which manifests itself in trust and obedience (cf. E. Würthwein, '*Metanoeō*'', *TDNT*, IV, pp. 980–9).

sought God earnestly: in view of verses 36–7 we should perhaps paraphrase: 'they sought God in great haste but with little earnestness' (cf. *RP*). Their motive was not their love for God but the desire to avoid punishment.

35. They remembered: i.e. they acknowledged God once more. For *z-k-r* ('to remember'), see on 119:52.

their rock: see on 28:1, 42:9. G. R. Driver has suggested *ṣawwārām* ('their creator') instead of M.T. *ṣûrām* ('their rock'), which gives a better parallel to 'their redeemer'.

Most High God: for *ʾēl ʿelyôn*, see on 46:4, 47:2.

redeemer: see on 119:154. The *gōʾēl* ('redeemer') is a kinsman who has certain obligations towards another person or persons. In a figurative sense it can be used of God, especially in his role as the protector and liberator, who vindicates the rights of the oppressed.

36. they flattered him: i.e. they tried to deceive God. They made promises which they did not mean to keep; it may have been a form of self-deception 'which spent itself in a superficial lip-service and in the observance of cultic rites' (Weiser, *POTL*, p. 541).

they lied to him: either deliberately, or through their self-deception; but in both cases they were responsible for their actions—for the turning of the means of grace into an expression of their disgrace.

37. Their heart: they not only lacked unwavering allegiance to God but they were also unfaithful (see on 27:3). See Johnson, *VITAI*, p. 84; Eichrodt, *TOT*, II, p. 144.

they were not true: or 'they did not take seriously their Covenant responsibilities'. For 'Covenant', see on 55:20.

38. being compassionate: Yahweh is an *ʾēl raḥûm* ('a compassionate God'); cf. Exod. 34:6; Dt. 4:31. For *r-ḥ-m*, see on 51:1.

forgave: the verb *k-p-r* is discussed at 65:3; cf. 1QH f. ii:13; Eichrodt, *TOT*, II, pp. 477f.

did not destroy them: not all of them, for more than once he held back his anger; therefore they did not bear the full brunt of his wrath which they had deserved.

39. He remembered: he took into account the fact that men are flesh (see on 38:3, 56:4)—that is, they are weak and mortal (cf. 103:14ff.; Isa. 40:6ff.). See also Leaney, *RQM*, p. 255.

REFLECTIONS ON THE DELIVERANCE FROM EGYPT **40–53**

40. How often . . .: in Num. 14:22 it is said that the Israelites put God to the test ten times (i.e. again and again). This attempt to put God to the proof is nothing but a rebellion.
the wilderness: for *miḏbār*, see on 55:7. The parallel term 'desert' (*y^eš̂imôn*) may refer to any desert place (cf. Dt. 32:10), but with the article it may denote the Wilderness of Judah in particular (cf. 1 Sam. 23:19,24, 26:1,3), which is, roughly, the region between the central plateau and the Dead Sea, thus lying in the rain shadow. Here *y^eš̂imôn* is synonymous with *miḏbār*, the steppe-lands which were the home of the Israelite clans before their entry into Canaan.

41. The Israelite lack of faith was manifested in testing God (see verse 18) over and over again (for the construction, see *GK* 120d).
provoked: (so also *NEB*) the verb *t-w-h* is a *hapax legomenon* in the *OT*. Its cognate in Syriac means 'to be sorry, regret'; perhaps we should render the M.T. *hiṯwû* by 'they grieved', which is better than 'limited' (*AV*), which ascribes limitations to God.
the Holy One of Israel might be described as an Isaianic title of God; see on 71:22.

42. . . . did not keep in mind: they deliberately neglected (see on 119:52) the salvation-history as if it did not concern them, even though they may have taken part formally in the recital of this *Heilsgeschichte*. They allowed themselves to forget that God had done these mighty acts for *them* also, and this negligence and its consequences distorted their relationship to God.
redeemed: *p-d-h*, see on 119:134.

43. his signs: this refers to the so-called plagues of Egypt, the visible proofs of God at work; see on 65:8. 'His miracles' (*môp̄^eṯāyw*, see on 71:7) in the following line, is synonymous with 'his signs'.
Zoan: see on verse 12.

44. their rivers: the plural noun *y^eʾōrêhem* may be taken as 'their great river' (cf. Gunkel, *PGHAT*, p. 345), or it may refer to the river Nile and its arms or canals. These streams were turned into blood, i.e. they became tainted (by the unusual amount of soil carried down the river, or by the increase of various micro-organisms?); see Exod. 7:17–20; Ps. 105:29; *IDB*, III, pp. 822ff.

45. swarms of flies . . . frogs: this refers to the fourth and second plagues respectively (cf. Exod. 8:20–32; Ps. 105:30f.). These disasters were natural scourges not unknown in ancient Egypt.

46. caterpillars: *ḥāsîl* is probably used as a synonym of *ʾarbeh* ('locust') which is the most common word for locusts (cf. Jl 1:4). The verb *ḥ-s-l* ('to destroy, consume') is also found in the Ugaritic texts with a similar meaning (cf. Gordon, *UT*, p. 398; Dahood, *UHP*, p. 58). In the Exodus narrative (Exod. 10:1–20) this is the eighth plague (cf. 105:34f.).

47. the hail belongs to the seventh plague (Exod. 9:18–26; Ps. 105:32). It ruined the **vines** and the **sycamores** (*NEB* 'figs'), which probably represented the vegetation as a whole. It is unlikely that the writer understood the destruction as absolute. **frost:** the Hebrew *ḥᵃnāmal* is found only here in the *OT*; *RSV* follows the rendering of most ancient versions. *HAL* (p. 321), *et al.* suggest 'deluge'; *NEB* 'torrents of rain'.

48. the hail may be an error for 'pestilence' (*deḇer*; so two Hebrew MSS., Sym) because the effects of the hail were already described in the previous verse. The change of *bārāḏ* ('hail') into *deḇer* ('pestilence') may be supported by interpreting *rᵉšāp̱îm* (*RSV* **thunderbolts**) as 'plagues' (cf. Hab. 3:5 where *deḇer* and *rešep̱* are parallel). In the Ugaritic texts Rešeph is the god of pestilence (cf. J. Gray, *The Legacy of Canaan* (*SVT*, 5, 1957), pp. 201f.). Thus in our verse the allusion may be to the fifth plague (Exod. 9:1–7).

49–51. Here we find an account of the final plague, the death of Egypt's first-born, the climax of the series of punishments (Exod. 11:1–12:36).

49. indignation, and distress: the last word *ṣārāh* ('distress, trouble') seems to be out of place in this sequence, and therefore some scholars read *ṣiwwāh* (so Gunkel, Leslie, *et al.*), rendering: 'he commanded (wrath and indignation)'.
a company of destroying angels: this probably means that the letting loose of God's anger and wrath, was like 'the sending forth of angels (who bring about) calamities' (cf. Exod. 12:23).

50. He made a path: God gave a free course to his anger. For 'anger' (*ʾap̱*), see on 74:1.
he did not spare them: lit. 'spare their soul' (see on 33:19).

51. the first issue of their strength: (so LXX, T, and S), i.e. the first-born. M.T. has 'the firstlings of male strength' (so Wellhausen); cf. Gen. 49:3; Dt. 21:17.

the tents of Ham is found only here in the *OT*; it simply means 'the land of Ham', i.e. Egypt (cf. 105:23,27, 106:22). According to Gen. 10:6, Ham was the ancestor of Egypt (as well as of Cush, Put, and Canaan). For a similar use of 'tents', see 83:6 (M.T. 7), 120:5.

52. he led forth: i.e. out of Egypt. The verb *n-s-*ᶜ is often used of the Israelite journeyings in the Wilderness (cf. Exod. 14:15, 15:22, 16:1, 17:1, etc.).

like sheep: or 'like a flock of small cattle' (i.e. sheep and goats). This is parallel to *ᶜēḏer* ('flock') which may comprise either sheep and goats, or large cattle. 'Flock' and its synonyms are often employed figuratively to denote Israel.

53. they were not afraid: this contrasts with the terror-stricken Egyptians (Exod. 14:24f.) who were overwhelmed by the sea. The theological implications can be seen against the background of the whole Exodus narrative: when Israel feared the Egyptians and doubted Yahweh's power they were in panic (Exod. 14:10ff.), but when they feared Yahweh (Exod. 14:31) they were no longer frightened of any situation.

ISRAEL IN CANAAN 54–5

54. This and the following verse describes what is traditionally known as the Conquest of Canaan, but the writer's interest centres on Zion and Judah, in particular.

his holy land: lit. 'his holy border'; *AV*, *RV* have 'the border of his sanctuary' but the *RSV* rendering is preferable. The Hebrew *gᵉḇûl* can mean both 'border' and 'territory', i.e. the land which is enclosed by a boundary (cf. 2 Sam. 21:5; 1 Kg. 1:3, etc.).

the mountain is either Mount Zion, or Canaan as the mountainous country (so McCullough). The former alternative seems more likely, although Mount Zion may represent the whole land (cf. Clements, *GT*, pp. 50ff.; Exod. 15:17; Dt. 3:25; Isa. 11:9).

55. he apportioned them: either he gave to the Israelites the nations (cf. Jos. 23:4; so Delitzsch, Cheyne), or he granted to them the land of the nations (so Wellhausen, *RP*); the latter suggestion seems more fitting. R. de Vaux thinks that this allotment of the tribal territory was an expression of Yahweh's ownership of the land, and that probably 'the drawing of lots among the Tribes for the Holy Land is only an imaginative extension to the whole people of what in fact took place at the level of the clan and the family' (*AI*, p. 165). Actually the *tribal* territories may have been won by the right of conquest, or by means of gradual infiltration and absorption of the indigenous population.

ISRAEL'S INFIDELITY **56–66**

56. In spite of the awe-inspiring deeds of Yahweh on behalf of Israel, the latter proved ungrateful and rebelled against God.
the Most High God stands probably for 'Yahweh, the Most High', as in 7:17 (M.T. 18), 47:2 (M.T. 3), 97:9. The use of this divine name may stress the folly of the Israelites: they are not rebelling against some inferior divine being, but against the Most High God.
his testimonies may refer both to the Covenant obligations and to the *Heilsgeschichte* (cf. J. Schreiner, *Sion-Jerusalem: Jahwes Königssitz* (1963), p. 31). God had fulfilled his promise to the fathers, but their children did not have enough sense to keep their part of the Covenant.

57. acted treacherously: for *b-g-d*, see on 25:3.
they twisted: or 'they were turned aside' (*AV*, *RV*), perhaps we should render 'they were perverse (cf. Prov. 17:20) like a slack bow' (cf. G. R. Driver in *Alttestamentliche Studien Friedrich Nötscher zum sechzigsten Geburtstag*, ed. by H. Junker and J. Botterweck (1950), pp. 53ff.); cf. also Hos. 7:16.

58. with their high places: the Hebrew *bāmôṯ* is usually rendered 'high places', but it does not follow that they were always identical with mountain tops. Strictly speaking, a *bāmāh* was an elevation (natural or artificial) or a mound which was used for cultic purposes. It could be 'built' (1 Kg. 11:7) or 'torn down' (2 Kg. 23:8), and it could be used either for the worship of Yahweh (1 Sam. 9:14) or, more often, as a pagan sanctuary. For the Ugaritic equivalent *bmt* ('back'), see Gordon, *UT*, p. 373. The high places mentioned by our Psalmist must have practised either a syncretistic cult, or pure and simple Canaanite worship. For further information on *bāmôṯ*, see de Vaux, *AI*, pp. 284–8, 539.
graven images are probably the representations of Baal and Astarte who in Canaan may have assumed the role of Anat, the female counterpart of Baal in the Ugaritic myths. This is inferred by the relative frequency of the respective names. These graven images provoked Yahweh to jealousy, i.e. he was not envious of the idols but he refused to share his claim to Israel's obedience with nonentities. See on 119:139.

59. When God heard: better 'God reacted', i.e. he heard and took action.

rejected Israel: the writer probably means that Yahweh repudiated his Covenant with the twelve-tribe league as such, and chose Judah (and the house of David) as the new nucleus of his people. 'Israel' can hardly mean 'northern Israel' because the amphictyonic shrine at Shiloh 'belonged' to the whole league.

60. his dwelling at Shiloh: in the following line this 'dwelling' is defined as a 'tent' (see on 61:4) but it does not follow that Yahweh's habitation in Shiloh was actually a tent. It is likely that a more permanent structure, or a temple, situated in Shiloh, continued to be called the 'tent of meeting' (1 Sam. 2:22), and that the traditions of the sacred tent were transferred to the Shiloh sanctuary (cf. Kraus, *WI*, p. 176). The forsaking of Shiloh (cf. Jer. 7:12, 26:6) refers to its destruction by the Philistines *c.* 1050 B.C. (cf. Bright, *HI*, p. 165; Rowley, *WAI*, pp. 63f.). Shiloh itself was an Ephraimite city, some 25 miles N. of Jerusalem, and some 12 miles S. of Shechem.

where he dwelt: *AV*, *RV* have 'which he placed' representing the M.T. *šikkēn*. *RSV* follows the ancient versions, reading *šāḵan*.

among men: the Hebrew *bāʾāḏām* could be taken as a place name 'Adam' (cf. Hos. 6:7), but the traditional rendering may well be right.

61. his power: *ʿuzzô* and *tip̄ʾartô* ('his glory') refer, in all probability, to the Ark (cf. 132:8: 'the ark of thy might') which was captured by the Philistines. The event and its background is described in 1 Sam. 4–5. For further details, see G. Henton Davies, 'The Ark in the Psalms', *Promise and Fulfilment* (1963), pp. 51–61; *ASTI*, v (1966–7), pp. 30–47.

62. to the sword: he punished his people by means of foreign invasions (see 1 Sam. 4:2,10,17).

his inheritance: the people of Israel (see on 28:9).

63. Fire devoured: that is, the fire of war. 'Fire' is often used figuratively for the disasters of war, as in Num. 21:28: 'For fire went forth from Heshbon . . . It devoured Ar of Moab . . .' (cf. also Am. 1:4,7,10,12, etc.).

had no marriage song: lit. 'they were not praised (in songs)'. See Ca. 7:1–9; Jer. 7:34, 16:9, etc.

64. their widows made no lamentation: probably the

disaster had assumed such proportions that there was neither time nor opportunity to make proper lamentations for separate individuals (cf. Job 27:15; Jer. 16:4). For 'widow', see on 146:9.

65. the LORD awoke: see on 35:23.

like a strong man . . .: this vivid word-picture describes the fresh intervention of Yahweh. His action appears so bold and energetic that the Psalmist daringly compares Yahweh with a mighty warrior who is stirred to great deeds by strong wine (i.e. not 'overcome with wine' (so Kissane) but '*stimulated* by wine'). Dahood (*PAB*, I, p. 196) reads: 'like a warrior resting after wine', which might describe the apparently complete inactivity of Yahweh during the Philistine domination.

66. he put his adversaries to rout: lit. 'he smote his adversaries backward' (so *RV*), or '. . . from behind', i.e. he struck them while they were fleeing. *AV* (also *NEB*) takes *ʾāḥôr* ('backwards') as '(in the) hinder parts' (so also Gunkel). The reference seems to be the victories of David (and they may also include the achievements of Samuel and Saul).

THE REJECTION OF EPHRAIM AND THE ELECTION OF ZION AND DAVID **67–72**

67. the tent of Joseph: not 'the tribe of Joseph' (i.e. Ephraim), but the sanctuary at Shiloh. Verses 67 and 68 are arranged chiastically so that verse 67*a* is to be contrasted with 68*b*.

he did not choose: that is, he did not renew the prerogatives and leadership of the house of Joseph; in other words, he rejected them as he had rejected Shiloh.

68. he chose the tribe of Judah as the place where his sanctuary should be located, and as a royal tribe.

Mount Zion: see on 65:1.

69. like the high heavens: lit. 'the heights'. This may imply that the Temple was believed to have been patterned after God's heavenly abode (so Briggs), or that the allusion is to the permanence of the heavens: Zion will not be like Shiloh which perished. Later history shows, however, that this promise was not absolute, but that there were certain implicit conditions.

70. his servant: for this honorific title, see on 27:9, 36:1.

took him from the sheepfolds: this is an allusion to 1 Sam. 16:11. Cf. also 11QPs[a] 151:7.

71. to be the shepherd of Jacob: i.e. of the people of God. This is elaborated in 11QPs[a] 151:1. 'Shepherd' is a well-known

figurative title of the king in the ancient Near East (see on 23:1).
Israel his inheritance: see on 28:9.

72. upright heart: see on 27:3, 64:4; cf. 1 Kg. 9:4.

Psalm 79 Wilt Thou be Angry for Ever?

This Psalm is clearly a National Lament which was used as a prayer on certain days of fasting (cf. Zech. 7:2–7; 8:18f.). The particular national calamity that gave rise to this lamentation is uncertain. The usual view, based on early Jewish traditions (cf. *Sopherim* xviii:3), is that the historical setting was the destruction of Jerusalem and the desecration of the Temple, in 587 B.C. This seems reasonable because the events of that year were a disaster *par excellence*, and there is little doubt that they were commemorated on various occasions. It is possible that our Psalm was later adapted to other situations of a similar nature, and this may account for the somewhat indefinite description of the tragic circumstances.

The Psalm follows the general pattern of Laments (see Introduction, pp. 37ff.), and it has certain affinities with Ps. 44, 74. It consists of three main sections; verses 1–4 contain the lamentation over the ruin wrought by the enemy, while verses 5–12 could be described as a prayer of the afflicted nation; the Psalm concludes with an expression of the people's faith in God (verse 13).

The metre is irregular.

A Psalm of Asaph: see Introduction, pp. 46 and 45f.

THE NATION'S LAMENT **1–4**

1. the heathen: lit. 'the nations' (see on 59:5). In verse 6 they are defined as those that do not know God, i.e. that do not recognize the authority of Yahweh.

thy inheritance: the Hebrew *naḥ^{a}lāh* usually denotes the people of God, but here it refers to the land of Israel or to Jerusalem; see on 28:9, 105:11.

they have defiled thy holy temple: it is not explicitly said that the Temple was destroyed, but this is suggested by the parallelism of verse 1*c*. The verb *ṭ-m-ʾ* ('to defile') is also used of Josiah's treatment of the high places (2 Kg. 23:8) which was, more or less, tantamount to their destruction (cf. Lam. 1:10).

2. The enemy defiled not only the Temple but also the dead bodies of the massacred people of God (cf. 4Q176 1–2,i: lines

3–4). The corpses were, apparently, left unburied because the number of dead may have outnumbered the living (cf. Dt. 28:25f.; Jer. 7:33, 8:2, 9:22, 16:4), and the invaders would not trouble themselves with such a task. According to widespread ancient beliefs, to be left unburied was a grievous misfortune, or a terrible punishment. Whether the Israelites actually believed that the treatment of the mortal remains affected the 'shade' of the departed person is uncertain, but they acted as if it did. This may be, however, a survival of certain ancient customs which had lost their original significance. See also A. Heidel, *The Gilgamesh Epic and Old Testament Parallels* (1963), pp. 155–70.
thy saints: i.e. those loyal to God's Covenant. For *ḥāsîḏ*, see on 30:4. It is unlikely that the reference is to the *ḥ^a^sîḏîm* of the Maccabean period (cf. W. O. E. Oesterley, *A History of Israel*, II (1951), pp. 314–21).

3. Verse 3*a* (and 2*c*) is quoted in 1 Mac. 7:17, with the authority of scripture.
like water: this may suggest that the slaughter of the people was very great, and that life had little value.

4. This verse is practically identical with 44:14 (M.T. 15), q.v.

THE PRAYER OF THE REMNANT **5–12**

5. How long introduces the transition from the lament to the supplication (cf. 6:3 (M.T. 4), 13:1 (M.T. 2), 89:46 (M.T. 47)). This question is an implicit expression of hope.
Wilt thou be angry for ever?: probably we should render 'How long, O Yahweh, will you be exceedingly angry?'. The Hebrew *lāneṣaḥ* (see on 74:1) may have the force of a superlative (see D. Winton Thomas, *JJS*, I (1956), pp. 106ff.).
Will thy jealous wrath burn: or '(How long) will your jealous wrath . . .'. *Ḳinʾāh* ('jealousy'; see on 119:139) can also have the meaning of 'anger, wrath'.

6–7. These verses are practically the same as Jer. 10:25. Either the Psalmist quoted from Jeremiah, or the Jeremiah passage may be a later addition (see J. Bright, *Jeremiah* (*AB* 21, 1965), p. 74).
Pour out thy anger . . .: this means to punish because God's anger is not capricious or arbitrary (see on 74:1). The nations that do not know God are those that do not acknowledge his claims (cf. H. B. Huffmon, *BASOR*, 181 (1966), p. 37).
kingdoms: Jer. 10:25 has 'peoples' (*mišpāḥôṯ*), or 'families' (cf. Jer. 1:15).

that do not call on thy name: see on 75:1; i.e. who do not worship Yahweh. Although he uses foreign nations as his instruments for the punishing of the disobedient (cf. Isa. 10:5f.; Jer. 27:6), these 'divine tools' are not passive instruments; they had their own plans and designs, and they worshipped their own gods, or what they believed to be gods. Therefore, sooner or later, a punishment would fall also upon them.

For they have devoured: reading *ʾāḵᵉlû*, with the ancient versions and Jer. 10:25. M.T. has: 'For he has devoured'.

Jacob: (see on 20:1); this is a synonym for 'Israel' or 'the people of God', i.e. Judah (in this context).

his habitation must be the southern kingdom, or the territory of Judah.

8. Do not remember . . .: or, 'Do not hold the sins of our fathers against us', i.e. forgive us. The verb *z-k-r* means not only 'to remember, call to mind', but also 'to act upon (something)'. For the Hebrew *ʿāwōn* ('iniquity'), see on 32:1.

the iniquities of our forefathers: the word *rīʾšōnîm* could be taken as an adjective, hence 'our former iniquities' (*RP* 'our past sins'). If we follow the *RSV* rendering, the sins which brought about the disaster were those of the previous generations, while their children shared in the consequences of the rebellion. The alternative translation suggests that it is the present generation that is responsible for the destruction of Jerusalem and the nation.

thy compassion: (see on 51:1). The Psalmist pleads with God to meet his people with compassion, to renew the previous relationship, and to forgive (cf. H. J. Stoebe, *VT*, II (1952), p. 247).

we are brought low by the disaster and its sequel. Cf. 116:6, 142:6 (M.T. 7).

9. God of our salvation: i.e. the God who grants us deliverance. For 'salvation', see on 35:3.

the glory of thy name: i.e. for the sake of your own honour, lest the nations go on blaspheming you (see verse 10). Some scholars regard *šᵉmeḵā* ('your name') as a gloss from the parallel line, and they read *kᵉḇôḏeḵā* ('your glory'). M.T. may be right, and it has the support of the versions.

deliver us: see on 59:1.

forgive our sins: the prayer of the people is motivated by an awareness that they share in the sins of the fathers (see verse 8), and that they themselves are in need of divine forgiveness; their own sins (see on 32:1) must be purged away (see on 65:3).

for thy name's sake: or 'for the sake of your own reputation' (see on 20:1). This is an appeal to Yahweh's honour, and not to national pride (see Eichrodt, *TOT*, II, p. 481).

10. Where is their God?: this sarcastic rhetorical question on the lips of Israel's enemies, is an expression of derision: their God is nothing, for he is powerless to do anything (so they think). Cf. 42:2,11 (M.T. 3, 12), 115:2; Jl 2:17; Mic. 7:10.

blood of thy servants: cf. Dt. 32:43; 2 Kg. 9:7; although the ruin of Jerusalem and Judah was a divine punishment (see verse 8), many a righteous person perished together with the rebels.

before our eyes: not that they might enjoy the spectacle of the enemies' overthrow, but that they might know that God is just.

11. the prisoners: this is a rendering of the singular *ʾāsîr*, which is taken collectively, parallel to 'those doomed to die' (lit. 'the sons of death'). The reference may be to the exiles in general, although the description may be more poetical than factual (cf. 102:20 (M.T. 21); Isa. 42:7, 49:9, 61:1), or it may describe the prisoners of war (see de Vaux, *AI*, pp. 80f., 254–7).

preserve: some exegetes (so also *NEB*) follow T and S, reading *hattēr* ('set at liberty', from *n-t-r*, 'to be free') for *hôṯēr* ('preserve'). Cf. 105:20, 146:7.

12. Return sevenfold: i.e. requite fully. See on 119:164; cf. Gen. 4:15,24; Lev. 26:18,21,24.

into the bosom . . .: the allusion is to the fold formed by one's outer garment overhanging the girdle, which served the purpose of a pocket (cf. Exod. 4:6; Prov. 6:27; Isa. 65:6; Jer. 32:18; Lk. 6:38). This expression suggests that the recompense will directly affect the guilty party.

the taunts: see on 119:22. The Psalmist had in mind the insults and the blasphemies of the neighbouring peoples, such as the Ammonites, Edomites, Moabites, who reviled the God of Israel both for his exaggerated claims (so it must have appeared to them) and for his powerlessness. Cf. 89:51 (M.T. 52).

THE EXPRESSION OF CONFIDENCE **13**

13. the flock of thy pasture: i.e. the people of your care; see on 100:3. Yahweh's relationship with his people is depicted by means of the familiar shepherd-flock metaphor which, at the same time, expressed a trust in God. This is justifiable only in the context of obedience; otherwise such a confidence would become a self-deception.

. . . will give thanks: or '. . . will praise' (see on 18:49).

for ever: see on 9:5.

thy praise is the recital of the glorious works of God, especially those on behalf of the nation (see on 65:1).

Psalm 80 Restore Us, O God of Hosts

This Psalm is a National Lament (see Introduction, pp. 37ff.) for a day of prayer and penitence. The people intercede for the restoration of Israel, but the particular circumstances which gave rise to this lamentation are not defined with any clarity.

The mention of Ephraim, Benjamin, and Manasseh (verse 2) and the complete lack of any reference to Judah, may suggest that the Psalm was of northern provenance (so Gunkel, Leslie, Eissfeldt). Some other exegetes ascribe it to the Judaean circles which sympathized with their northern brethren (so König, Schmidt). Their motive need not have been purely altruistic, for the collapse of the northern kingdom would remove the last barrier between Judah and the tidal waves of the Assyrian invasions. LXX adds to the Psalm title: 'concerning the Assyrians'; this may be a later, although a correct, interpretation.

If the Psalm is of northern origin, then it may be dated between 732 and 722 B.C., since the central Palestinian tribes still appear to have some national identity, although they are hard pressed. If, on the other hand, the poem was composed in Judah, the reign of Josiah (640–609 B.C.) could provide a suitable background. During this period there was a mounting interest in the fate of the north, and also an awareness of the unity of the people of God, as well as a desire for the restoration of the whole Israel. This culminated in the temporary unification of the south and the north, and therefore the Psalm may come from the first half of Josiah's reign.

The poem is characterized by a refrain in verses 3, 7, and 19. Verse 14 may be a deliberate variant on the refrain, or a corruption of it. Some exegetes would insert a refrain also after verse 10, but this would interrupt the movement of thought.

The metre is mainly 3 + 3.

To the choirmaster: see Introduction, p. 48.

according to Lilies: see Introduction, p. 50.

A Testimony of Asaph: see Introduction, pp. 50 and 45f.
A Psalm: see Introduction, p. 46.

THE PLEA FOR GOD'S HELP **1–3**

1. Give ear: i.e. attend to our prayers.
Shepherd of Israel: this expression is a *hapax legomenon* in the *OT*, but the idea itself is familiar (see on 23:1). 'Israel' may denote either the northern tribes or, more likely, the people of God in their totality (see on 149:2).
Joseph: this may be a designation of the whole nation, although some scholars (e.g. Briggs, Cohen) suggest the northern kingdom (as perhaps in 78:67).
enthroned upon the cherubim: see on 99:1 (cf. 18:10 (M.T. 11)). These mythological creatures formed the cherubim-throne, which eventually came to be associated with the Ark of the Covenant (see Clements, *GT*, pp. 28–35). Originally the metaphor may have been of Canaanite origin (cf. Kraus, *PBK*, 557). Cf. also 1 Sam. 4:4; 2 Sam. 6:2; Eichrodt, *TOT*, II, p. 193.
shine forth: the Ugaritic cognate of the Hebrew *y-p-ᶜ*, means 'to rise up, challenge' (see F. L. Moriarty, *CBQ*, XIV (1952), p. 62), and similarly our verse speaks of the coming and appearing of Yahweh to take up the challenge of the enemies (cf. J. Jeremias, *Theophanie*, *WMANT*, 10 (1965), p. 147).

2. before Ephraim and Benjamin and Manasseh: these three units may represent *all* the northern tribes, or by this time the Galilean clans may already have been exiled; Weiser (*POTL*, p. 547) thinks that the reference is to the 'truncated state of Ephraim at the time of Hoshea' between 732 and 722 B.C. 'Benjamin' is sometimes reckoned with the southern kingdom (1 Kg. 12:21,23; 2 Chr. 11:1,3,23), and sometimes with the northern state (1 Kg. 11:13,32,36).
Stir up thy might: this is a less conspicuous anthropomorphism (see on 35:23) than the similar expression in 44:23: 'Rouse thyself! Why sleepest thou, O Lord?' The current inactivity of God in the affairs of the nation can be described picturesquely as a slumber or sleep, but in actual fact this 'inaction' is part of the divine punishment upon the disobedient (cf. verse 18).
come to save us: lit. 'come to our salvation'. For the form of *yᵉšûᶜāṯāh* ('salvation'), see *GK* 90g; for the thought, see on 35:3, 119:81.

3. Restore us: T took it to mean 'Bring us back from our exile', but it is far more likely that the prayer was for the restoration of the nation's fortunes in general. This may well require a new Covenant or its renewal, because the present circumstances show that the people must have broken the divine Covenant by disobeying its demands.

O God: originally it may have been 'O God of hosts', as in verses 7 and 14, while in verses 4 and 19 we have 'O LORD God of hosts' which may represent a mixed reading. It is very likely that 'God' (*ʾᵉlōhîm*) was substituted for 'LORD' (*yhwh*), but the familiarity with the usual expression created the present reading which is syntactically difficult (see *GK* 125h); we should expect *ʾᵉlōhê ṣᵉḇāʾôṯ* ('God of hosts', as in 89:8 (M.T. 9)). For 'Yahweh of hosts', see on 24:10, 59:5.

let thy face shine: turn to us with your favour and blessing, and restore the broken relationship. See on 31:16, 67:1. This is reminiscent of the so-called Aaronic blessing in Num. 6:24ff.

that we may be saved: see on 54:1.

THE DIVINE ANGER 4–7

4. LORD God of Hosts: see verse 3.

angry with thy people's prayers: the verb *ʿ-š-n* ('to smoke') would usually require *ʾaḇ* ('anger'), as its subject, and therefore G. R. Driver (*HTR*, XXIX (1936), pp. 186f.) associates the verb *ʿāšantā* ('you are angry') with the Aramaic *ʿᵃšēn* ('to be heavy, strong'), rendering: 'how long wilt thou be obdurate against thy people's prayer?' In this verse Yahweh is depicted as being angry with the supplications of his people (LXX and S 'your servant'). 'Prayers' (see on 65:2) may denote the lamentations offered to God on the special days of self-humiliation. The fact that they have not been answered so far is interpreted as due to God's continued anger, which was, no doubt, regarded as fully deserved, even though the exact reason may not have been as clear as in the case described in Isa. 1:15.

5. This verse describes the desperate situation: trouble has become as much a part of the people's life, as food and drink.

bread of tears occurs only here in the *OT*. The idea is found in 42:4: 'My tears have become my food'. In 1QH v:33 there is a reference to 'bread of sighing'; cf. also Job 3:24; Isa. 30:20; Hos. 9:4.

tears to drink: cf. 102:9 (M.T. 10); 1QH v:34.

in full measure: the Hebrew *šālîš* denotes a measure which is one-third of some larger measure (not further defined). A parallel is our 'quarter' for a 'quarter of a pound'. We could paraphrase verse 5*b*: '. . . tears to drink by the "pint".'

6. the scorn of our neighbours: i.e. the object of their scorn. *RSV* reads *mānôḏ* ('shaking (of the head)'), which is an expression of mockery (see on 44:14). M.T. has *māḏôn* ('strife, contention') as if Israel had become the object of contention to its neighbours. See 1QH v:23.

laugh among themselves: some Hebrew MSS., LXX, S, and Jerome, read *lānû* ('us') for M.T. *lāmô*, which could be rendered '. . . laugh at us'; this seems to give a better sense (cf. 79:4).

7. See verse 3.

ISRAEL'S GLORY AND DEFEAT **8–13**

8. a vine: the vine and vineyard are well-known symbols of Israel, although they may be of Canaanite origin. Since the vine was one of the most prized plants, it provided a fitting metaphor for the people of God, the most privileged nation of the nations (cf. Isa. 5:1–7, 27:2–6; Jer. 2:21, 12:10; Ezek. 15:1–8, 19:10–14; Hos. 10:1; Jn 15:1–6). For the vine symbolism, see C. K. Barrett, *The Gospel According to St John* (1956), pp. 393ff. The vine-emblem was also common on Jewish coins (see *IDB*, III, pp. 434f.). In 128:3 'vine' is used metaphorically of a wife, the mother of many children. In our Psalm, Israel, the vine, is brought from Egypt, and is planted in Canaan. The land is prepared by driving out the nations (cf. Exod. 23:28ff.; Ps. 44:2 (M.T. 3), 78:55); this is, of course, a poetic account of the settlement of the tribes; (for another version, see Jg. 1).

9. Thou didst clear the ground . . .: Yahweh is depicted as a vinedresser (cf. Jn 15:1) who prepares the soil for the planting of the choice vine (cf. Isa. 5:2).

10. The mountains were covered . . .: this account portrays Israel's complete possession of the land.

the mighty cedars: lit. 'cedars of God'. The word 'God' (*ʾēl*) may be used to express the superlative degree (cf. *VT*, III (1953), pp. 210ff.; *VT*, XVIII (1968), pp. 121f.). Even the mighty cedars were overshadowed by the vine: Israel was the absolute master of the whole land. For 'cedars', see on 37:35.

11. to the sea: that is, to the Mediterranean sea, the western boundary of the ideal kingdom; the other border mentioned was the River, i.e. the Euphrates (see on 72:8). In Dt. 11:24 the

Land of Promise is described as 'from the wilderness to Lebanon and from the River, the river Euphrates, to the western sea'. The Psalmist probably had in mind the 'empire' of David at its zenith.

12. This and the following verse offer a striking contrast. The same vineyard that was so carefully prepared and made fruitful is now ravaged even by the wild boar. The Psalmist and his contemporaries are not surprised by the punitive destruction of the vineyard (or what it symbolizes) but they are apprehensive about the *continuing* rejection of Israel, which seemed to imply the end of the Covenant between Yahweh and Israel (cf. R. E. Clements, *Prophecy and Covenant* (*SBT* 43, 1965), pp. 40ff.).
walls: they provided a protection for the vineyard (cf. Num. 22:24; Isa. 5:5). Allegorically, the word-picture suggests the withdrawal of the divine protection.

13. The boar from the forest was an unclean animal (cf. Dt. 14:8), and therefore a suitable symbol for the enemies of Israel (cf. 89:41 (M.T. 42)). The Hebrew *yaʿar* ('forest') is written in M.T. with a suspended *ʿayin* which may suggest a variant reading with an *ʾālep̱* (i.e. *mîʾōr* ('from the Nile')), in which case the allusion would be to Egypt.
ravages it: the verb is a quadriliteral (from *k-s-m*, by dissimilating one of the double letters in the intensive form); it is also a *hapax legomenon* in the *OT*. Cf. Yadin, *SWSLSD*, p. 327; 1QM xiv:7.

THE PRAYER FOR DIVINE FAVOUR **14–19**

14. Turn again . . .: this is either an intentional or an accidental variant on the refrain; see verse 3.
Look down from heaven may suggest that the people were aware of their separation from God (cf. 33:13; Isa. 63:15).
have regard for this vine: lit. 'visit this vine'. The verb *p-ḳ-d* in its connotation 'to visit' may imply an action, either for a gracious purpose (i.e. to visit one 'with salvation', as in 106:4), or for a punitive reason (cf. 59:5*b* (M.T. 6*b*), 89:32 (M.T. 33)).

15. the stock: the Hebrew *kannāh* is found only here in the *OT*. LXX understood it as a verb (in the imperative): 'restore' (from the Hebrew *k-w-n*?), while S (similarly T and Jerome) took it as a noun, *kannāʾ* ('stem, root'). M.T. has at the end of this verse the phrase 'upon the son whom thou hast reared for thyself' (*RSVm*), but this is rightly omitted by *RSV* (also by *RP*, *PNT*, *NEB*) as a variant of verse 17*b*.

16. They have burned it with fire: *RSV* reads *śᵉrāpūhā* for M.T. *śᵉrūpāh* ('it is burned . . .') (so *AV*, *RV*; cf. Isa. 33:12).

the rebuke of thy countenance: i.e. the judgment administered by God himself (cf. 104:7) will destroy the enemies.

17. the man of thy right hand may be an illusion to Benjamin (lit. 'son of the right hand'). It is more likely, however, that the reference is to the King, who can be described as sitting at the right hand of God (cf. 110:1).

the son of man: or simply 'the man' (cf. Dan. 7:13). T understood it in a messianic sense, as suggested by its rendering of the parallel verse 15*b* (M.T. 16*b*): 'upon the royal messiah whom you have established for yourself.' This messianic interpretation is unlikely, however, and the 'son of man' may well be either the king (Josiah?) or Israel.

18. we will never turn back . . .: i.e. we shall no more relapse into idolatry, or become rebellious (cf. Jos. 24:16ff.).

give us life: see on 30:3 (cf. 85:6 (M.T. 7); Hos. 6:2).

call on thy name: see on 75:1.

19. For this refrain, see verse 3.

Psalm 81 A Call to Obedience

This Psalm is usually described as a prophetic liturgy made up of two parts (verses 1–5*b* and 5*c*–16). The first part takes the form of a hymn in which verses 1–3 are the introduction, while verses 4–5*b* contain the main section. The second part is in a prophetic style, and it is often regarded as a prophetic oracle. These two sections may imply that they were originally two independent units, but it seems more likely that the present Psalm is a literary unity.

It is not clear what particular festival provided the cultic background. The term 'our feast day' (*ḥaggēnû*, verse 3) points to one of the three pilgrimage festivals, i.e. Passover, Feast of Weeks, and Tabernacles (cf. Exod. 23:14ff.). The reference to the 'new moon' and the 'full moon' (verse 3), if they mean the first and fifteenth day of the month respectively, may well suggest the Feast of Tabernacles which began on the fifteenth day of the seventh month (i.e. Tishri), and lasted seven days (cf. Lev.

23:33ff.; Num. 29:12ff.). At a later date this feast was preceded by 'a day for blowing the trumpets' (Lev. 23:23ff.; Num. 29:1ff.) on the first day of the seventh month, and it is probable that this day and the Feast of Tabernacles (as well as the Day of Atonement on the tenth day) formed a festal complex, and the *Sitz im Leben* of this Psalm. The poem refers to the giving of the law on Mount Sinai (verse 7*b*), or at least to the Decalogue (verses 9–10), and this would fit the Feast of Tabernacles, which was the appropriate occasion for the seven-yearly reading of the law (cf. Dt. 31:10ff.). Mowinckel (*PIW*, I, p. 157) associates the Psalm with the New Year Festival which formed, apparently, part of the Feast of Tabernacles.

There are no certain allusions which would help to fix the date of the Psalm. If the mention of 'Joseph' (verse 5) could be taken to mean northern Israel, then the date may well be before 722 B.C., but this interpretation of 'Joseph' is hardly necessary. A seventh-century date is a reasonable suggestion (so Oesterley, *TP*, p. 371); Deissler (*PWdB*, II, p. 148) thinks that a post-Exilic date is a possibility.

The prevailing metre of the Psalm is 3 + 3.

To the choirmaster: see Introduction, p. 48.
the Gittith: see Introduction, p. 50.
A Psalm of Asaph: see Introduction, pp. 46 and 45f.

THE FESTIVE SUMMONS **1–5b**

1. Sing aloud: i.e. sing for joy (cf. Job 29:13).
our strength: the Hebrew *ʿûz* could be rendered as 'our refuge' (so *NEB*) (see on 84:5), but the *RSV* rendering is more likely (cf. Exod. 15:2; Isa. 12:2; 49:5).
shout for joy: see on 98:4.
the God of Jacob: see on 20:1.

2. Raise a song: utter a song, probably the Psalm(s) appropriate to the occasion, but cf. *NEB*.
timbrel (*tōp*) was a popular, women's musical instrument, often used in dancing (cf. Exod. 15:20; Jg. 11:34; 1 Sam. 18:6; Ps. 149:3, 150:4). It has been suggested (E. Werner, *IDB*, III, p. 474) that the timbrel was not permitted in the Temple; if so, then either verses 1–3 were a poetical call to rejoice in God, or this jubilation took place outside the sanctuary. In 68:25 (M.T. 26) maidens playing timbrels took part in the procession to the Temple.

the sweet lyre: for *kinnôr* ('lyre'), see on 98:5; 'sweet' probably denotes 'sweet-sounding' (*PNT*) or 'melodious'.
the harp: (*nēḇel*), see on 33:2.

3. Blow the trumpet: the reference is to the sounding of a signal rather than to the making of music. The trumpet here (*šôp̄ār*) is the horn, and not the silver trumpet (Num. 10:2). See on 98:6, 150:3.
the new moon: from Num. 29:1,6 it seems that the new moon was the beginning of the lunar month. Some scholars have argued, however, that in the pre-Exilic period each month began with the full moon (cf. N. H. Snaith, *The Jewish New Year Festival: Its Origins and Development* (1947), pp. 89ff.).
the full moon: the reference is probably to the fifteenth day of the month (unless it refers to the beginning of the month), and the Psalmist may have had in mind the first day of the Feast of Tabernacles (cf. Kraus, *WI*, pp. 61–70; Rowley, *WAI*, pp. 88ff.).
our feast day: the Hebrew *ḥaḡ* (see on 118:27) can denote any one of the three great pilgrimage festivals; here the writer may have intended the Tabernacles.

4. For it is a statute for Israel: this section begins with the hymnic *kî* ('for') (see on 89:2), and it provides the reason for rejoicing. The feast is appointed by God (cf. Exod. 23:14ff.), but ultimately the gladness rests upon the fact that God has been gracious to his people.
the God of Jacob: see on 20:1. Some scholars change this phrase into 'for the tents of Jacob' (cf. Mal. 2:12), i.e. 'for the tribes of Israel'; this involves the emendation of *lēʾlōhê* into *leʾohᵒlê*, but it provides a better parallelism with 'for Israel' in verse 4*a*.

5. He made it a decree: (*RV* 'a testimony'), see 119:5. This emphasis upon the antiquity of the regulations and their divine origin may imply that the Psalm is supporting a cultic innovation or a re-introduction of some ancient but neglected practice (cf. 2 Kg. 23:22; Neh. 8:27; Kraus, *PBK*, p. 565).
in Joseph: some scholars (Schmidt, Weiser, Dahood, *et al.*) see here an allusion to the northern provenance of the Psalm, but it is possible that 'Joseph' is simply a synonym of 'Israel'.
when he went out: the subject of the verb is not explicitly stated but the *RSV* rendering suggests that it was God who went over the land of Egypt punishing it (by means of the plagues?). On the other hand, the preposition *ʿal* (*RSV* 'over') can mean 'from' (cf. Driver, *CML*, p. 141; Winton Thomas, *TRP*, p. 34),

in which case the subject would be Israel, and the event the Exodus; this finds some support in LXX and other versions. *NEB* has 'out of'.

THE PROPHETIC CHALLENGE **5c–16**

Some scholars have argued that these verses are no longer in their original order, but there is no agreement as to what the true sequence might have been.

5c. I hear a voice: this may be a scribal note indicating the appropriate reading from the Pentateuch (with which this Psalm was associated), i.e. it may be a lectionary rubric (cf. Winton Thomas, *TRP*, p. 34). It could also be taken as a description of the writer's inspiration (so Gunkel, Weiser, Kraus, *et al.*), and the voice would be that of Yahweh (cf. Num. 24:4,16; 2 Sam. 23:2; Job 4:12–16; Isa. 5:9). *NEB* omits verse 5*c* as a gloss.

6. your shoulder: M.T. has '. . . his shoulder', but the *RSV* reading is what we would expect. Dahood and *NEB* follow M.T.

of the burden: the reference seems to be the Israelite oppression in Egypt when they were employed as forced labour in building projects (cf. Exod. 1:11; *ANEP*, pl. 115).

your hands: M.T. 'his hands'.

basket: the Hebrew *dûḏ* may mean either a basket or a pot (1 Sam. 2:14; Job 41:20 (M.T. 12)). Here it may be some kind of woven container, such as was used in Jer. 24:1f. (cf. also *HAL*, p. 207a). In Egyptian use such baskets may have carried clay or other building materials (cf. *ANEP*, pll. 115, 122).

7. In distress you called: this need not refer to any particular experience, such as Exod. 14:9f., but rather to the whole series of trials before and during the Exodus events.

I delivered you: see on 116:8; cf. 50:15.

I answered you in the secret place of thunder: God answers the needy by giving them help (cf. 65:5 (M.T. 6), 91:15, 108:6, 118:5). The 'place of thunder' is probably the thunder cloud in which, so to speak, Yahweh hides himself (cf. 18:11 (M.T. 12)), and from which he utters his voice (cf. 18:13 (M.T. 14), 104:7). It is also possible that the allusion is to the theophany on Mount Sinai (cf. Exod. 20:18ff.), or simply to the presence of God (cf. 91:15).

I tested you at the waters of Meribah: in 95:8 the people of Israel are said to have tested God (cf. Exod. 17:1–7; Num.

20:1–13). If the reference is to the same event, then our author sees the testing of God as being essentially a testing of men themselves, or he is drawing upon traditions such as Exod. 15:25; Dt. 33:8.

Selah: see Introduction, pp. 48f.

8. Hear, O my people: this is reminiscent of a similar call to the Covenant people in the Book of Deuteronomy (4:1, 5:1, 6:4, 9:1, etc.; cf. Ps. 50:7).

if you would but listen to me: this is no wishful thinking on the part of God, but an implicit command.

9. no strange god among you: this reminds us of Exod. 20:3; Dt. 5:7, i.e. the first commandment (or the second, according to Jewish tradition) of the so-called ethical Decalogue. A 'strange god', or a 'foreign god', is any god but Yahweh (cf. Dt. 32:12; Mal. 2:11; E. Nielsen, *The Ten Commandments in New Perspective* (*SBT*, 2nd ser. 7, 1968), p. 87).

bow down: i.e. fall prostrate in worship (see on 29:2).

10. I am the LORD your God: this could be described as the formula of self-identification which forms part of the preamble of the Covenant (cf. Exod. 20:2; Dt. 5:6; see on 55:20). It is also found in the descriptions of theophanies (cf. Gen. 15:7, 17:1; Exod. 3:6, etc.).

who brought you up is reminiscent of the so-called historical prologue characteristic of many ancient treaties (see G. E. Mendenhall, 'Covenant', *IDB*, 1, pp. 716ff.), and its purpose here is to summarize the saving works of Yahweh, done for his people (cf. Exod. 20:2; Dt. 5:6; Jos. 24:2–13; Neh. 9:6ff.).

Open your mouth wide: this phrase is probably misplaced; Mowinckel (*PIW*, 1, p. 157) transfers it after verse 7 (so also *NEB*), while Kraus (*PBK*, p. 562) places it after verse 5*c*. The latter suggestion may be preferable; the phrase probably means: 'I will put my words into your mouth' (cf. Jer. 1:9). If verse 10*c* is in its rightful place, then it may be a conditional promise to bless the people loyal to the Covenant.

11. my people: here is a note of sadness and irony: in spite of all that God has done for his people, they are still rebellious (cf. Isa. 1:3).

did not listen . . .: i.e. they were not willing to listen and to obey (cf. Dt. 13:8; Jer. 7:24).

Israel would have none of me: that is, they did not think much of God, and this is clearly manifested by their attitude to

God's commandments which they did not obey (cf. 1 Kg. 20:8; Prov. 1:10; Isa. 1:19).

12. their stubborn hearts: lit. 'the stubbornness of their hearts'; cf. Dt. 29:19; Jer. 3:17, 7:24, 9:14, 11:8, 13:10, etc. It is also a favourite phrase in 1QS and CD.

to follow their own counsels is the essence of being stubborn in heart, or self-willed; its punishment is the fact that God allows it to become a habit.

13. walk in my ways: this means to obey the laws of God (cf. Isa. 42:24).

14. If Israel would submit to the will of God, he would subdue all their enemies. Cf. Isa. 48:17ff.

turn my hand against their foes: cf. Isa. 1:25; Am. 1:8.

15. Those who hate the LORD: since in this section the speaker is actually Yahweh, most scholars read 'those who hate him (*meśanᵉʾāw*)', i.e. the object is Israel. The reading of M.T. seems less likely, although it is supported by the versions. *NEB* '. . . who hate them'.

would cringe toward him: they will offer a reluctant homage (cf. 18:44 (M.T. 45), 66:3).

their fate: lit. 'their time', meaning probably 'the time of their subjection' (cf. Jer. 27:7; Ezek. 22:3), referring to the hostile nations. Briggs (*CECBP*, II, p. 213) takes the phrase (with less justification) as 'their fortune', and he applies it to Israel.

for ever: see on 117:2.

16. *NEB* places this verse after verse 7.

I would feed you: M.T. 'he would feed him' which seems to be textually corrupt, as far as the suffix is concerned; cf. verse 16*b*.

the finest of the wheat: lit. 'the fatness of wheat' (cf. Num. 18:12; Dt. 32:14; Ps. 147:14). This usage is reminiscent of the English expression: 'the cream of . . .'.

honey from the rock: this phrase is similar to that in Dt. 32:13, and it probably denotes wild honey. The expression is a metaphorical description of the divine providence. Cf. Job 29:6: 'and the rock poured out for me streams of oil'.

Psalm 82 The Judgment of Yahweh

This Psalm is a short but perplexing composition, and it is difficult to determine its *Gattung*. McCullough (*PIB*, p. 442) describes it as a didactic Psalm, but this does not take sufficient account of other aspects—e.g. the oracular nature of verses 2–7, which Gunkel (*PGHAT*, p. 361) regards as an imitation of a prophetic speech, although it could well be an utterance of a cultic prophet (cf. *ZThK*, XLIX (1952), pp. 1–16). Leslie (*PAP*, p. 120) defines Ps. 82 as a 'New Year hymn which celebrates the Lord as Judge', yet the poem could be understood as a prayer (or an implicit lament) to God. The essence of the Psalmist's problem is the question why the weak and the defenceless are continually deprived of justice; this is explained as due to the mismanagement of the subordinate divine beings who have been entrusted with jurisdiction over mankind. Such a prayer might have been appropriate to the New Year liturgy; according to the beliefs of some Near Eastern peoples, this was the time when the gods assembled to determine the destiny of the year (cf. Mowinckel, *PIW*, II, p. 132). In Israel it was, perhaps, a time of renewal, and of looking forward to better things. According to a late Jewish tradition found in the Mishnah (*Tamid* vii:4), this Psalm was used by the Levites in the Temple on the third day of the week.

The crux of the Psalm is the identity of 'the gods' (*ᵓᵉlōhîm*) in verses 1*b* and 6*a*. The traditional view, which was already taken by T (and apparently followed by the author of Jn 10:34), regards the *ᵓᵉlōhîm* as the judges of Israel, who show partiality, and are strangers to righteousness. It is doubtful, however, whether the term *ᵓᵉlōhîm* was ever used of the earthly administrators of justice (cf. Delitzsch, *BCP*, ii, pp. 401f.). Be that as it may, *ᵓᵉlōhîm* in verses 1*b* and 6*a* cannot refer to human beings, because in that case verse 7 would hardly make sense or would be a mere tautology. A similar suggestion (and equally unlikely) is that which equates these 'gods' with the wicked rulers of other nations which are holding Israel in subjection (so Duhm, Briggs). In more recent years scholars have tended to identify the *ᵓᵉlōhîm* with the national gods of the various peoples of the world, who have been demoted to the position of Yahweh's servants (see G. E. Wright, *The Old Testament Against Its Environment* (*SBT* 2, 1950), pp. 30–41). It is possible that the stories about the pantheons of the various nations provided the prototype for the heavenly assemblies mentioned in the *OT* (see 1 Kg. 22:19–22; Job 1:6,12, 2:1–6; Ps. 29:1, 58:1 (M.T. 2), 103:20f., 148:2; Dan. 7:9f., 10:13,20f.), but it may well be that the Psalmist simply thought of the divine servants of Yahweh; this would include the patron angels of the nations, who formed his heavenly court whatever may have been the origin of these divine beings. A reasonable parallel is the divine assembly mentioned in Job 1–2.

The Psalm is occasionally regarded as of great antiquity (cf. Kraus, *PBK*, p. 570; Dahood, *PAB*, II, p. 269) but it may well be comparatively late, dating from a time when the idea of heavenly intermediaries was reasonably well known.

The metre is mainly 3+3.

A Psalm of Asaph: see Introduction, pp. 46 and 45f.

THE VISION OF THE HEAVENLY COURT **1**

1. God: we should probably read 'Yahweh' (*yhwh*), which must have been changed into 'God' (*ᵓᵉlōhîm*) by the Elohistic editor.

the divine council: or 'the divine assembly'. In a similar manner Marduk convenes the assembly of the great gods (see 'The Creation Epic', *ANET*, p. 68), and El (or/and Baal) presides over the Canaanite pantheon (cf. Pope, *EUT*, pp. 47ff.; Driver, *CML*, p. 37). The *OT* parallels are mentioned in the introduction to this Psalm (see on 58:1). For more details and references, see Kraus, *PBK*, pp. 569ff.

the gods: the meaning of *ᵓᵉlōhîm* in this phrase is discussed in the introduction above. These 'gods' are probably the divine intermediaries who formed Yahweh's heavenly court, and who had responsibility for the proper functioning of human society (cf. Dt. 32:8–9 (LXX)). Whether these divine beings are regarded as 'angels' (so S) or as the demoted gods of the nations (whatever the difference may be), the uniqueness of Yahweh remains perfectly clear. All the other heavenly beings are dependent upon him for their very existence, and they are responsible to him for their actions. When they disregard their duties, they are sentenced to an 'ungodlike' punishment, namely death. It is possible that the inequality of human life and its possibilities suggested to the Psalmist that powers other than Yahweh must be at work in the world. His faith, however, surmounts the arising problems by envisaging a judgment of all the guilty divine beings (cf. Isa. 24:21) who will be deprived of their delegated authority. In the end Yahweh alone will rule the earth with righteousness.

THE DIVINE JUDGE SPEAKS **2–7**

2. How long . . .?: this introductory question is really an indictment, or an accusation of the 'gods', i.e. those who had misused their authority. Yahweh has been patient with the culprits but now he must act, or he is about to intervene.

judge unjustly: or, 'pass unrighteous judgment'. Strict impartiality is required from those who administer justice. One must neither favour the rich, nor be partial to the poor; the latter alternative would be an uncommon phenomenon although not impossible (see Exod. 23:3; Lev. 19:15).

show partiality to the wicked: lit. 'lift up the face of' (cf. Lev. 19:15; Dt. 10:17; Job 34:19; Mal. 2:9).

Selah: see Introduction, pp. 48f.

3. the weak: for the Hebrew *dal*, see H. Birkeland, *ʿĀnî und ʿĀnāw in den Psalmen* (1933), pp. 21ff. It is a synonym of 'poor', and may denote one who has been made helpless, or who has been reduced in status.

the fatherless: one deprived of either parent or both. The care of the weak and the helpless was not unique to Israel but theoretically it was the duty of the Near Eastern kings and the responsibility of at least some of the deities (for references, see H. Wildberger, *Jesaja* (*BK* 10_1, 1965), p. 48; see on 68:5).

maintain the right: lit. 'do justice' (*AV*, *RV*). From this we see that the verb *hiṣdîḳ* is not so much characterized by formality and legality, as by a determination to render effective help to the helpless. The duty and the privilege of the strong are to succour the weak and oppressed (cf. Isa. 1:17, 10:1f.).

the afflicted and the destitute: see on 34:2; cf. 1QH v:14.

4. Rescue the weak: i.e. they are already 'in the hand', or in the power of the unscrupulous (see Am. 2:6f.; Zech. 7:9f.), and therefore one of the functions of the judges is to deliver the afflicted. For 'needy', see on 35:10.

5. Most scholars take this verse as part of the condemnation of the negligent heavenly beings, but Johnson (*SKAI*, p. 90) regards it as a continuation of the description of the wicked mentioned in the previous verse. In either case, the lack of knowledge and understanding is not a childish ignorance, but a deliberate rejection of true wisdom (cf. Isa. 1:3f.).

they walk about in darkness: i.e. they have forsaken the 'paths of righteousness' (Prov. 2:13) and they live in darkness, or in opposition to God (cf. Job 24:13); McCullough renders 'in moral darkness' (*PIB*, p. 445).

the foundations of the earth: cf. 11:3, 75:3 (M.T. 4), 96:10. The expression is usually interpreted as 'the moral order of the world'.

6. I say: Johnson renders: 'I admit', or, to paraphrase: 'I thought (once that you were divine beings and that you would act as such)'. The verse has a slightly ironical tone.
sons of the Most High: *NEB* 'sons all of you of a high god'. This phrase is a *hapax legomenon* in the *OT* but it need not imply an actual 'physical' kinship with Yahweh, as would be the case in a genuine pantheon; it may denote 'divine beings', i.e. those who belong to the class of gods. Yahweh, however, is not merely one of the *ʾᵉlōhîm*, but he is the absolutely supreme one in this class, and he alone is to be worshipped (cf. S. R. Driver and G. B. Gray, *The Book of Job*, I, pp. 9f.). For *ʿelyôn* ('Most High'), see on 18:13, 46:4, 47:2.

7. you shall die like men: this sentence passed on the heavenly beings stresses their dependence upon Yahweh. They may disobey him for a time, but they cannot deprive him of his power; on the other hand, Yahweh may take away not only their delegated authority, but even their very existence. For some remote parallels, see Isa. 14:12–15; Ezek. 28:2,17.
like any prince: J. Gray (*The Legacy of Canaan* (*SVT*, 5, 1957), pp. 198f.) suggests 'Like one of the bright (stars) . . .', taking *śārîm* ('princes') as a masculine plural participle of *ś-r-h*, a cognate of the Arabic *š-r-y* ('to flash'). It is doubtful, however, whether any real gain is made by adopting this interpretation.

THE APPEAL TO GOD 8

8. . . . judge the earth: this may be understood as a response of the congregation to the prophetic vision in verses 1–7.
for to thee belong all the nations: or 'you shall take possession of (i.e. inherit) all the nations'. G. R. Driver (*HTR*, XXIX (1936), p. 187) proposes: 'for thou dost sift the nations', and associates the verb *n-ḥ-l* with the Assyrian *naḫālu*, 'to sift'. This would provide a good parallel to the preceding line.

Psalm 83 Lament in Times of National Crisis

This Psalm is clearly a National Lament (see Introduction, pp. 37ff.) uttered, in the hour of distress, at some service of intercession. The actual calamity is the apparently imminent threat of a foreign invasion, and verses 6–8 list the ten nations involved in this plotting. In spite of the enumeration of the names of the participants, the identification of the particular historical siutation is difficult (see verse 5). If 'Assyria' in verse 8 is taken to mean the Assyrian Empire, then the Psalm may well be dated between the ninth and seventh centuries B.C. (so Weiser). Some have tried to be more explicit, and have suggested the time of Jehoshaphat (cf. 2 Chr. 20:1–30), or that of Jeroboam II, etc., but these specific suggestions are all doubtful. On the other hand, if 'Assyria' is not taken literally, then the date of the Psalm may be post-Exilic, which would fit in with the language of the Psalm and its reminiscences (cf. Deissler, *PWdB*, II, p. 156). Leslie and others place the Lament between the time of Nehemiah (*c.* 444 B.C.) and that of Alexander the Great (*c.* 331 B.C.). The suggested Maccabean origin of the Psalm seems rather late although one of its earliest supporters was Theodore of Mopsuestia.

The Lament begins with an invocation to God and an appeal to him (verse 1). The actual Lament (verses 2–8) describes the scheming of the enemies, and lists the various foes by name. The third section (verses 9–18) is a petition, which is mostly made up of an 'elaborate description of the disaster imprecated on the enemies' (Mowinckel, *PIW*, II, pp. 51f.); some exegetes see here a connection with the ancient cursing formula.

The metre of the Psalm is mainly 3 + 3.

A Song: see Introduction, p. 47.

A Psalm of Asaph: see Introduction, pp. 46 and 45f.

THE PLEA TO GOD **1**

1. do not keep silence: lit. 'let there be no rest to you' (cf. Isa. 62:6f.), i.e. do not be inactive in the present crisis. For 'God' we should read 'Yahweh'.

do not hold thy peace: i.e. do not give us up to our enemies. For this fairly common expression, see on 28:1.

or be still: that is, do not be a disinterested spectator. For 'God' (*ʾēl*), see on 52:5.

THE LAMENT OVER THE IMMINENT DANGER **2–8**

2. The Psalmist makes it clear that the adversaries of the nation are also Yahweh's enemies, and at the same time he implies that Israel is the people of God.

are in tumult: the nations, gathering for their attack upon Israel, appear to the Psalmist like angry waves (cf. Isa. 17:12f.; Jer. 6:23).

who hate thee: see on 68:1. These enemies of Yahweh have lifted up their heads, or they have become overbearing and defiantly arrogant. When the Midianites were defeated by Israel, it is said of them that 'they lifted up their heads no more' (Jg. 8:28). This expression is not identical with the saying that one's head will be lifted up by God (see on 3:3).

3. They lay crafty plans: lit. 'They make crafty (their) counsel (see on 25:14)'. Their planning is not only cunning, but also wily and sinful (cf. Job. 5:12).

thy protected ones: Sym and Jerome have the singular which may denote the Temple (cf. Ezek. 7:22) as Yahweh's treasure (cf. Boylan, *PSVP*, II, p. 68). M.T. refers to the worshipping community as those who are hidden or protected by Yahweh (cf. 27:5, 31:20 (M.T. 21)).

4. let us wipe them out . . .: i.e. let us annihilate them, let us root them out as a nation (cf. Exod. 23:23; 1 Kg. 13:34; Jer. 48:2).

the name of Israel: for the significance of 'name' (*šēm*), see on 9:5, 41:5. 'Israel' may signify the twelve-tribe league (so Kraus, *PBK*, p. 578), or the southern kingdom as the heir of Israel's election (see on 80:1). When a name is no longer remembered, it means that the reality signified by the name has ceased to exist (cf. Jer. 11:19; Hos. 2:17; Zech. 13:2).

5. with one accord: lit. 'together (with) one mind', i.e. heart (see on 27:3). Some read 'with one heart' (*lēḇ ʾeḥāḏ* for M.T. *lēḇ yaḥdāw*) as in 1 Chr. 12:38.

they make a covenant: i.e. they cut (see on 89:3) a Covenant (see on 55:20), or make a common alliance against Yahweh by being leagued together against his people. The following verses (6–8) enumerate the peoples taking part in this scheming; the coalition comprises ten nations. As far as our present knowledge goes, we do not know of any specific situation in which all the ten national groups were threatening Israel. This fact, among other things, has led some scholars to suggest that the event described is a cultic (and not a historical) situation which depicts the mythological concept of the onslaught of the nations (*Völkersturm*); cf. Kraus, *PBK*, p. 578. It is also possible that we have here a poetical exaggeration which mentions various peoples whose enmity against Israel was typical and/or a present reality (so Nötscher, *PEB*, p. 184; cf. Ringgren, *FP*, pp. 106f., 131, n.14).

6. the tents of Edom: i.e. the people living in the tents of Edom; 'tents of . . .' may serve as a poetical term for a particular nation. Edom was the territory occupied by the descendants of Esau (according to the *OT* tradition), and it stretched from the southern borders of Judah to the Gulf of ʻAqaba (see Baly, *GB*, pp. 239–51).

the Ishmaelites: according to Gen. 25:12–18 their origin was traced back to Ishmael, the son of Abraham by Hagar. G. M. Landes (*IDB*, II, p. 748) regards 'Ishmael' as a gentilic term 'without specific geographical or racial reference', which was applied to various caravan traders, tent-dwellers, and others. In Jg. 8:24 Ishmaelites are synonymous with 'Midianites'.

the Hagrites were a Bedouin tribe living in Transjordan, east of Gilead (1 Chr. 5:10). They, too, may have been regarded as descendants of Abraham through Hagar.

7. Gebal is hardly the Phoenician city of that name (also called Byblos) situated N. of modern Beirut. Most scholars see here a reference to a region S. of the Dead Sea, in the vicinity of Petra, in Edom.

Ammon was traditionally associated with Moab, both being the sons of Lot (Gen. 19:36ff.). From various sources it is known that Ammon was a political state in Transjordan between 1300 and 580 B.C. The post-Exilic references to Ammon may not be to the same ethnic group (cf. *IDB*, I, p. 108). See Baly, op. cit., pp. 232–35.

Amalek was a nomadic tribe wandering in the regions S. of Judah, which, on occasions, may have penetrated the territory of Israel (cf. Jg. 12:15 (a corruption ?); 1 Sam. 30:1f.).

Philistia: see on 56:1.

Tyre was a well-known Phoenician city and port, situated on a rocky isle close to the mainland some 25 miles S. of Sidon and some 35 miles N. of Carmel. Not infrequently Israel was on friendly terms with the rulers of Tyre (e.g. in the time of David, Solomon, Ahab).

8. Assyria: many scholars (e.g. Davies, Schmidt, Weiser, Kraus) identify it with the great empire of Assyria which collapsed in 612 B.C. If this reference is authentic, and the interpretation correct, then the Psalm must be of pre-Exilic origin. On the other hand, Gunkel (*Genesis* (1966), p. 261) suggests that the reference is not to the great Mesopotamian power, but to a small North Arabian tribe. It is, however, unlikely that a comparatively insignificant tribe could have been regarded as the 'strong arm of the children of Lot' (i.e. the Moabites and the

Ammonites). Another possible explanation is that 'Assyria' is simply a loose usage of this particular term to denote the contemporaneous Mesopotamian power; in Ezr. 6:22 it signifies the Persian empire; cf. 1QM i:2, xviii:2, xix:10.
the strong arm: lit. 'the arm of the sons of . . .', an effective help.
Selah: see Introduction, pp. 48f.

THE PETITION IN THE FORM OF AN IMPRECATION **9–18**

9. Midian was a nomadic people, and the vicinity of the Gulf of 'Aqaba in north-western Arabia may have been one of the regions where they could be found from time to time. Occasionally they made incursions into Palestine, and their defeat by Gideon (Jg. 6–8) probably became proverbial for a total defeat (cf. Isa. 9:4, 10:26).
Sisera and Jabin were Canaanite leaders during the time of Barak and Deborah (see Jg. 4–5). Some scholars would place Jabin the king of Hazor, and Sisera, his general (according to Jg. 4:7), into two *different* periods (cf. Gray, *JJR*, p. 267; see also K. A. Kitchen, *Ancient Orient and Old Testament* (1966), pp. 67f.).
the river Kishon: for *naḥal* ('wadi'), see on 36:8. Kishon is a little stream draining the plain of Esdraelon; much of it is dry during the summer months (cf. Baly, *GB*, p. 148).

10. En-dor is not referred to in the account of the war against the Canaanites in Jg. 4–5, but it was situated in the same general area. In Jos. 17:11 En-dor is mentioned together with Taanach and Megiddo, both of which are associated with this battle (cf. Jg. 5:19). Some commentators (e.g. Gunkel, Kraus; so also *NEB*) read 'the spring of Harod' (*ᶜên ḥᵃrōḏ* for M.T. *ᶜên dōʾr*) at the foot of Gilboa, which was one of the locations linked with the Midianite invasion (Jg. 7:1).
dung for the ground: the bodies of the invaders remained unburied, which was both a disgrace and, perhaps, a punishment (cf. 79:3; Jer. 8:2, 9:22; Tob. 1:17).

11. their nobles: the princes of the nations threatening Israel (cf. 107:40).
Oreb and Zeeb were two Midianite leaders, as were also Zebah and Zalmunna. The latter pair are called 'kings' in Jg. 8:5, while Oreb and Zeeb are described as 'princes' (*śārîm*) in Jg. 7:25. G. F. Moore (*Judges* (*ICC*, 1895), pp. 218ff.) suggests that the pronunciation of Zebah and Zalmunna may have been perverted

by 'malicious wit', since they seem to mean 'victim' and 'protection refused' respectively. Kraus *et al.* delete 'Zebah and Zalmunna' as an elaboration from Jg. 8:4ff.; they would read: 'Make . . . like Oreb, and all their princes like Zeeb'. This emendation restores the common 3+3 metre.

12. the pastures of God: LXX has 'the altar (*to thusiastērion*) of God' (similarly also V), while T and Jerome have 'the beauty of God' which probably alludes to the Temple. M.T. seems to suggest that Canaan is Yahweh's land or 'pasture', on which he feeds his flock, Israel. The speakers in verse 12 are the nations who are preparing their onslaught on the people of God.

13. O my God: this prayer may have been uttered by the leader of the community, or by some cultic person speaking in the name of the whole congregation.

like whirling dust: the Hebrew *galgal* is obviously derived from *g-l-l* ('to roll'), and it can denote a 'wheel' (cf. Isa. 5:28; Jer. 47:3). Some commentators suggest that the allusion is to the wheel-shaped calyx of the wild artichoke (*Gundelia tournefortii L.*), which can be driven by the wind, or to the thistledown (so *NEB*, *RP*).

like chaff: for this frequent word-picture, see on 1:4 (cf. Isa. 17:13, 29:5, 40:24, 41:2; Jer. 13:24).

14–15. The community prays for a complete annihilation of the enemies, and the brush fire provides a fitting metaphor for destruction. Verse 14*b* may well refer to a similar conflagration rather than to a volcanic eruption (so Gunkel). Verse 15 continues the colourful and vivid prayer which is reminiscent of an imprecation (58:6–9 and 69:22–28). 'Tempest' and 'hurricane' often accompany the storm-god, but here these phenomena are associated with Yahweh's intervention (cf. Isa. 29:6).

16. Fill their faces with shame: or '. . . with disgrace'; the phrase is a *hapax legomenon* in the *OT*, but for similar thoughts see on 44:15, 69:7.

seek thy name: elsewhere the *OT* writers speak about seeking Yahweh or his face (see on 27:8), but essentially the meaning is the same. For 'name' (*šēm*), see on 20:1. Verse 16*b* is not inconsistent with verse 17*b*, for, although the nations as such might perish, many individuals would survive and might yet serve Yahweh. Their humiliation will lead to homage. Barnes (*PWC*, II, p. 402) thinks that the meaning of verse 16*b* is that the adversaries will seek Yahweh *in vain*, but this seems less likely (see verse 18).

17. let them perish in disgrace: lit. 'and let them be put to shame and let them perish'. The two Hebrew verbs may also be co-ordinated, as in the *RSV* rendering (cf. *GK* 120).

18. Let them know . . .: the Psalmist expects that the calamities of the nations will bring them to their senses and that they will know or recognize the authority of Yahweh (for 'to know' (*y-d-ᶜ*), see on 14:4).

whose name is the Lord: some exegetes (e.g. Gunkel, Kraus, similarly *NEB*) omit 'whose name is' (*šimᵉḵā*) rendering, '. . . that you alone, O Yahweh, are the Most High' (cf. 97:9). Duhm, Oesterley delete the whole phrase (as an explanatory gloss?), reading: '. . . you alone are the Most High', which is metrically desirable; but it seems doubtful whether an emendation for metrical reasons alone can be fully justified.

the Most High: see on 18:13, 46:4, 47:2. The nations thought (as is implied by their attitude) that they and their gods were the masters of the earth (cf. Isa. 10:12ff.), but the subsequent events will show that the real and only Lord is Yahweh, who is in authority above the whole world. He alone is the Most High, without a partner or an equal.

Psalm 84 The Joy of God's House

This Psalm contains several different elements: verses 1, 10, 11f. could well be at home in a Hymn, while verse 2 expresses feelings suited to a Lamentation; verses 8f. are a prayer, and may be an intercession for the King. Most scholars describe Ps. 84 as a Song of Zion, which is at the same time a pilgrim's song similar to Ps. 120–34. Less likely is Schmidt's suggestion (*PHAT*, p. 160) that it is a Gate liturgy, performed by pilgrims and priests.

The most likely setting of the Psalm is the Feast of Tabernacles at which the lordship of Yahweh would be celebrated, and prayers for the Davidic king could be offered (see verse 8). The Psalm may have been sung at the entrance of the Temple, although not necessarily as a liturgy.

The allusion to the King points to a pre-Exilic date, unless verses 8–9 are not original to the song. The Psalm resembles Ps. 42–3, and some exegetes have suggested that all three come from the same author, although written on different occasions. That the Psalmist dwelt among the Gentiles (so Kittel, Weiser, etc.) is not certain (see verse 10). Kissane (*BP*, p. 386) argues that the

Psalm expresses the feelings of the Babylonian exiles who long for their homeland and the Temple. The latter is now in ruins (see verse 3), but God will yet restore it. This interpretation is, however, less satisfactory than the view above, or some variation on it.

The metre of the Psalm is 3 + 2 with occasional variations.

To the choirmaster: see Introduction, p. 48.
The Gittith: see Introduction, p. 50.
Sons of Korah: see Introduction, p. 45.

THE LONGING FOR THE TEMPLE **1–3**

1. How lovely: this expression is reminiscent of Num 24:5: 'How fair are your tents, O Jacob.' The Hebrew *yāḏîḏ* ('beloved', 'lovely') is usually used of persons; thus Benjamin is called 'the beloved of the LORD' (Dt. 33:12); see Ringgren, *FI*, p. 8.
thy dwelling place: the M.T. equivalent (*miškānôṯ*) is plural in form, used probably for the sake of emphasis. See on 43:3, 74:7.
O LORD of hosts: see on 24:10, 59:5.

2. My soul (see on 33:19), **my heart** (see on 27:3), and **flesh** (see on 38:3, 56:4) denote the whole man. In a sense, they are not so much the component parts of the totality called 'man' as three different ways of looking at man.
the courts of the LORD are the object of the pilgrim's longing because it is there that he can fully realize the presence of the 'living God' (see on 42:2), who is the giver and sustainer of all life (cf. *VITAI*, p. 106). For 'courts', see on 96:8. During the visits to the sanctuary the pilgrims 'sojourned' in the courts of Yahweh (see on 65:4), and they 'flourished' there (92:13 (M.T. 14)). Clements (*GT*, p. 74) sees a connection between the pilgrim's 'dwelling' in the Temple and his sojourning in the Holy land, because Mount Zion represents Yahweh's land.

3. sparrow: the Hebrew *ṣippôr* is a generic term for birds (cf. Gen. 7:14; Dt. 4:17; Ezek. 17:23; Dan. 4:12). Sometimes (as in verse 3) the reference may be to some specific bird, in this instance perhaps a sparrow (cf. 102:7 (M.T.8)).
swallow may be the right translation of *d^erôr*. LXX has *trugōn* ('turtle-dove') (so also T, S, and V). Kirkpatrick (*BPCB*, p. 506) points out that the birds which nested in temples were regarded as sacred in the ancient Near East. If so, the purpose of this word-picture is to stress the protection provided by the Temple.
at thy altars: in the Solomonic Temple there seem to have been two altars. The larger of the two was the altar of burnt offerings,

which was situated in front of the Temple (2 Kg. 16:14), while the smaller one was used for incense, and its place was in front of the Holy of Holies (see de Vaux, *AI*, pp. 410f.). King Ahaz may have introduced a third altar (cf. 2 Kg. 16:10–16; J. Gray, *I & II Kings* (*OTL*, 1964), pp. 576ff.). It is very unlikely that the birds built their nests 'in the altars' (so Kissane) or 'at the altars', but rather in their vicinity, i.e. round about the walls of the Temple buildings. Kissane (*BP*, p. 389) thinks that the Psalmist is presenting a picture of desolation, and that *therefore* the birds can build their nests in the altars. This suggestion is doubtful, even for the period immediately after the destruction in 587 B.C. (cf. Jer. 41:4f.).

O Lord . . . my God: this phrase is considered by some commentators (e.g. Kraus, Wanke) as a hymnic addition to the Psalm, which overloads the verse and spoils the metre; it is nevertheless found in all the ancient versions. See on 24:10, 68:24, 91:2.

THE HAPPINESS OF THE PILGRIM 4–7

4. Blessed . . .: see on 1:1.

who dwell in thy house: those who belonged to the Temple staff and who permanently resided in the sanctuary (Neh. 13:4–9); or it may refer to the worshippers who were privileged to enter the Temple (see on 15:1, 23:6) and who, therefore, had the right to dwell in Yahweh's land (see R. E. Clements, 'Temple and Land: A Significant Aspect of Israel's Worship', *TGUOS*, XIX (1961–2), pp. 16–28). It is not improbable that the expression simply means 'those who worship regularly in the Temple' (cf. 23:6, 27:4, 61:4 (M.T. 5)), but hardly 'the inhabitants of Jerusalem' (so Barnes).

ever singing thy praise: i.e. who sing God's praise again and again. For the verb *h-l-l*, see on 119:164.

Selah: see Introduction, pp. 48f.

5. the men: the Hebrew *ʾāḏām* ('man') is used collectively; the plural of *ʾāḏām* does not occur. Its etymological relationship with *ʾaḏāmāh* ('ground') and *ʾāḏōm* ('red') is uncertain (cf. Barr, *SBL*, pp. 144ff.). According to Gen. 2:7, man (*ʾāḏām*) was formed from the ground (*ʾaḏāmāh*), but this may be a play on the two words, and not necessarily an indication of the etymology of *ʾāḏām*. Only rarely is this word used as a proper noun, e.g. at 1 Chr. 1:1.

whose strength is in thee: perhaps 'whose refuge is in you' (so

Kraus; cf. LXX and V). The noun *ʿôz* may be derived from *ʿ-w-z* ('to seek refuge') (so *NEB*) rather than from *ʿ-z-z*, 'to be strong' (cf. *KBL*, p. 693). For the underlying thought, see 27:4f.
the highways to Zion: in M.T. there is no equivalent to 'to Zion', and the Hebrew could be rendered '(those who have) in their heart (i.e. in their mind) the paths of pilgrimage' (*NEB* 'the pilgrim ways'); Johnson (*SKAI*, p. 95) has: 'whose heart is set on pilgrimage'. It is possible that *meṣillôṯ* (*RSV* 'highways') means 'praises' (so G. R. Driver); in 68:4 (M.T. 5) the verb *s-l-l* is used of lifting up (a song), i.e. of praising. This suggestion would provide a good parallel to verse 4*b*. Mowinckel (*PIW*, I, pp. 170f.) thinks that the Psalmist is referring to the processional road leading to the Temple.

6. the valley to Baca: *RV* has 'the valley of Weeping' (reading *beḵeh* ('weeping') for *bāḵāʾ* ('Baca' or 'balsam tree'); cf. Ezr. 10:1), similarly also LXX, T, S, and V. *Bāḵāʾ* may be rendered 'balsam tree', but it is doubtful whether the true balsam (*Commiphora opobalsamum L*) ever grew in Palestine; it is native to South Arabia. Therefore it is not clear from what trees the valley took its name if this were actually the case. No such 'Valley of Baca' is known in the *OT* apart from this present passage (cf. 2 Sam. 5:23), but it seems that the allusion is to some arid (?) valley leading to Jerusalem (*NEB* 'the thirsty valley'). The meaning of the whole verse is ambiguous, but a likely explanation is that, even while the pilgrims are on their way to the Holy City, the autumn rains are turning the parched land into pools of water. This well-nigh miraculous transformation of nature is described in a way reminiscent of Isa. 41:17f. (cf. Ps. 107:33; Isa. 35:6f., 48:21; see also *ET*, XLII (1929–31), pp. 558f.); but both may be derived from a common cultic language or source.
they make it: LXX (followed by some commentators) suggests: 'he (i.e. God) makes it' (reading *yešîṯēhû* for *yešîṯûhû*); this emended reading improves the translation.
the early rain: see on 35:10.
with pools: LXX (similarly V) renders: '(for the lawgiver shall give also) blessings', but *RSV* seems more likely. It is possible that we have here a word play on *berēḵôṯ* ('pools') and *berāḵôṯ* ('blessings'); the former are a sign of the latter.

7. they go . . .: i.e. the pilgrims are encouraged by the divine favour (i.e. rain) as they approach the Holy City, and therefore they go 'from strength to strength'. Some scholars understand

the latter phrase as meaning 'from rampart to rampart' until the pilgrims reach the Temple itself (so Kissane, Ringgren). This increase in strength could also be interpreted as the swelling of the ranks of the pilgrims.
the God of gods . . . Zion: reading *ʾēl* ('God') for *ʾel* ('unto'). M.T. could be rendered 'he (i.e. the pilgrim) appears before God in Zion', but *RSV* is supported by LXX and S. The reading of M.T. is sometimes regarded as the result of an ancient emendation to avoid the bold expression 'they shall *see* the God of gods . . .' (*yirʾû ʾēl ʾelōhîm*), for no man can see God and live (Exod. 33:20). The original phrase (if the above suggestion is right) must have had its starting point in a setting where the worshippers actually saw the image of their god, and so the expression 'to see god' became a stereotyped phrase for the visiting of the sanctuary (see on 42:2). It was taken over by the Israelites in its technical sense, but at some later point it came to be regarded as theologically inappropriate; consequently the scribes usually turned the active verb into a passive one; instead of saying that one sees God, they spoke of appearing before God (cf. M. Noth, *Exodus*, (*OTL*, 1962), pp. 191f.).
Zion: see on 65:1.

A PRAYER FOR THE KING **8–9**

Gunkel and some other commentators (e.g. Duhm, McCullough) treat these verses as a later addition to the Psalm, interrupting the flow of thought. On the other hand, the welfare of the King is also the welfare of the people, because he represents his people and is the channel of their blessings. Furthermore, the Jerusalem Temple was a royal sanctuary, and therefore the King had an important role in its cultus. In view of this, a prayer for the King would be as natural as an intercession for the people.

8. O LORD God of hosts: 'God' is probably a variant of 'LORD' (*yhwh*), and should therefore be omitted in translation (see on 80:3). For 'hosts' (*ṣebāʾôṯ*), see on 24:10, 59:5.
give ear: i.e. attend to my prayer and answer me.
God of Jacob: see on 20:1.
Selah: see Introduction, pp. 48f.

9. our shield: the Hebrew *māgēn* is discussed on 3:3. The word 'shield' may well mean 'suzerain', as also in verse 11 (cf. Dahood, *PAB*, II, pp. 278f.); but at the same time it may describe the King (or Yahweh in verse 11) as the defender of his people.

AV, *RV*, following LXX and V, take 'our shield' as a vocative in apposition to 'God', but the parallel line (verse 9*b*) supports the *RSV* rendering.
thine anointed: for the Hebrew *māšîaḥ*, see on 2:2, 89:20; cf. G. Wanke, *Die Zionstheologie der Korachiten* (*BZAW*, 97, 1966), pp. 19f. The anointed one may also be the high priest (cf. Lev. 4:3, 6:22), but the parallelism with 'our shield', points to the King.

GOD AND HIS TEMPLE AS THE SOURCE OF BLESSING **10–12**

10. in thy courts: i.e. in the Temple precincts (see on 96:8). **than a thousand elsewhere:** the word 'elsewhere' is not in M.T. **I would rather be** (*bāḥartî*) seems to belong to the phrase, and the Hebrew *bāḥartî* must represent a locality, as a contrast to 'in thy courts'. Therefore some emend *bāḥartî* into *beḥeḏrî* ('my (own) room') or *baḥaḏāray* ('my (own) chambers'). Whether the particular emendations are right or not, we expect the meaning to be something like 'my (own) house', hence: '. . . than a thousand in my (own) house'. *NEB* '. . . thousand days at home'.
a doorkeeper: lit. 'the standing at the entrance (of the house of God)'; the Hebrew verbal form *histôpēp* is a *hapax legomenon* in the *OT*, and it is associated with *sap* ('threshold'). The *RSV* rendering is misleading, because what the *OT* writers usually mean by a 'Temple doorkeeper' (cf. 2 Kg. 12:9, 23:4; Jer. 35:4, etc.) is a high official of the ranks of the priests or Levites. The allusion here may be to the worshippers standing at the entrance of the Temple and asking for admission to the house of God (see Introduction to Ps. 15); cf. also LXX. The Psalmist prefers to be a suppliant at the Temple gates rather than a dweller in the 'tents of wickedness'. The latter expression is not clear; it could mean the dwelling of 'the godless Gentiles' (so Weiser) or 'the tents of wealth' (emending *rešaᶜ* into *ᶜōšer* ('riches'); so Schmidt, Wanke). The 'tents of wickedness' are probably the habitations of the godless in Israel.

11. the LORD God: see verse 8.
a sun: only here in the *OT* is it used of Yahweh (cf. Isa. 60:19; Mal. 4:2), and therefore some scholars have suggested that the meaning of *šemeš* (in this verse) is 'buckler' or 'battlement' (so Gunkel, Schmidt, G. R. Driver, *NEB*); this is also suggested by T. LXX and Theod either had a different text, or they paraphrased M.T., rendering: 'For the Lord loves mercy and truth'. The most

likely proposal is that *šemeš* ('sun'), like *māḡēn* ('shield'), was a royal title; its use was usually avoided in *OT* because of the prevalent sun-worship in the Near East. For Near Eastern parallels, see the Tell El-Amarna letters (nos. 137, 147, 234, etc.) where the title 'sun' is applied to the Pharaoh (cf. *DOTT*, p. 43; *ANET*, pp. 483ff.).

shield: see verse 9.

favour and honour: (cf. Jn 1:17) for *ḥēn* ('favour'), see on 6:2, 57:1. K. W. Neubauer (*Der Stamm CHNN im Sprachgebrauch des Alten Testaments* (1964), p. 70) suggests that 'honour' (*kāḇôḏ*, see on 19:1) and '(every) good thing' (verse 11*c*), are the outworking of Yahweh's favour (*ḥēn*) which is manifested to those who live in complete accord with the will of God or 'who walk uprightly' (see on 15:2).

12. LORD of hosts: see on 24:10, 59:5.

blessed: see on 1:1.

the man: the Hebrew *ʾāḏām* is rendered by Johnson as 'mankind', which seems unlikely in the present context. We should probably take it in the sense of 'men', as in verse 5.

trusts: see on 78:22.

Psalm 85 Restore Us Again

This Psalm consists of three main parts: verses 1–3, 4–7, and 8–13. The first section describes a particular deliverance of Israel, probably the Return from the Babylonian exile, although this is by no means certain; this brief account is really an implicit praise of God, and it also provides a reason which might move God to help his people in their present affliction (see Westermann, *PGP*, p. 55). The second main section forms a lamentation in which the people plead with God to deliver them from their distress, which is not further defined. The misfortune must have been very grievous (cf. verse 6) and the nation recognized in the troubles the hand of their God. The third part of the Psalm provides the divine answer, and it is often described as a prophetic oracle uttered by a cultic prophet (or priest), or by the Psalmist himself.

It seems that the most suitable definition of this Psalm is a 'National Lamentation' which may have been used in the course of some festival, or on some special day of supplication. Mowinckel *et al.* would argue that the Psalm belonged to the Harvest Festival, and that it was a New Year prayer for a good and blessed New

Year; as such it would not permit an eschatological interpretation (as expounded by Gunkel, Oesterley, *et al.*), or the view that it arose from a particular historical situation (cf. Mowinckel, *Psalmenstudien*, III (1923), pp. 54f.).

The historical interpretation is very likely, although the cult of the Feast of Tabernacles may have provided the *Sitz im Leben* of the Lament.

The date of the composition must be post-Exilic if it alludes to the Return from the Babylonian captivity; on the other hand, this identification is only tentative. McCullough (*PIB*, p. 460) argues that verse 9 may suggest that 'glory' (i.e. Yahweh's presence) was not as yet in the Temple and therefore 'the date might be somewhere between 587 and 516 B.C.'.

This Lament is often associated with Ps. 126, and its language offers parallels with that of Deutero-Isaiah.

The metre is, mainly, 3+3.

To the choirmaster: see Introduction, p. 48.
A Psalm: see Introduction, p. 46.
Sons of Korah: see Introduction, p. 45.

THE MERCIES OF YAHWEH IN DAYS PAST **1–3**

Gunkel (*PGHAT*, p. 373) thought that this section was an expression of a prophetic certainty of the salvation of God in time to come, but the majority of recent commentators have seen in these verses a reminiscence of a past deliverance. There are no clear historical allusions, and therefore it is difficult to specify the event or events that gave rise to this passage, but the reference may be to the Babylonian exile or, less likely, to the deliverance from Egypt.

1. thy land is also 'our land' (verse 9); that is, Yahweh's land has been given to his people. For a detailed discussion, see v. Rad, 'The Promised Land and Yahweh's Land in the Hexateuch', *PHOE*, pp. 79–93.

thou didst restore the fortunes of . . .: the Hebrew *šûḇ šᵉḇûṯ*, lit. 'turn the turning' (or 'bring about a return') means to reverse the fortunes of a person or group. The Massoretes suggest *šûḇ šᵉḇîṯ* ('turn the captivity'; so also T and S); essentially, however, the meaning of both variants is very similar, although *šᵉḇûṯ* is derived from *š-w-b* ('to turn'), while *šᵉḇîṯ* comes from *š-b-h* ('to take captive') (so *BDB*). The former alternative may be more likely (cf. *ZAW*, LXVI (1954), pp. 315ff.; Dhorme, *CJ*, pp. 649f.) but the return envisaged need not necessarily be to the 'Golden Age' (so Oesterley, *TP*, p. 384). Johnson (*CPAI*, p. 67, n.4) thinks that *šᵉḇûṯ/šᵉḇîṯ* is to be associated with *š-b-t** ('to be firm'), and he renders it by 'well-being'.

Jacob: Briggs (*CECBP*, II, p. 231) describes it as a 'term of endearment for the chosen people of Yahweh'. Here it may denote the restored people of God (i.e. those who returned from the Babylonian exile and the remnant that was spared the experience of the captivity). See also G. Wanke, *Die Zionstheologie der Korachiten* (*BZAW*, 97, 1966), p. 57. 'Jacob' is Deutero-Isaiah's favourite designation of the people of God (cf. Isa. 40:27, 41:14,21, 42:24, etc.).

2. Thou didst forgive: lit. 'you have lifted up (and carried away)'.

iniquity (see on 32:1) is seen as a heavy burden of guilt which must be borne by the sinner (cf. Lev. 5:1,17; Num. 5:31; etc.) even though the strain may be too great (cf. Gen. 4:13). There are, however, certain God-ordained means of atonement, and in some cases one can speak of Yahweh as bearing away the guilt of the offender (cf. R. Knierim, *Die Hauptbegriffe für Sünde im Alten Testament* (1965), pp. 219–22).

thou didst pardon: lit. 'you have covered' (similarly *AV*, *RV*); see on 32:1; cf. Knierim, op. cit., pp. 119ff.

sin: for *ḥaṭṭā'ṯ*, see on 32:1, 51:2.

Selah: see Introduction, pp. 48f.

3. Thou didst withdraw: lit. 'you have gathered in' (cf. 1 Sam. 14:19: 'Withdraw (lit. 'gather in') your hand'; Ps. 104:29).

thy wrath: the Hebrew *ʿeḇrāh* usually denotes 'overflowing rage, fury'; e.g. 'I will pour out my wrath like water' (Hos. 5:10). The subject can be either man (cf. Gen. 49:7; Isa. 14:6; Am. 1:11) or Yahweh (90:9,11; Hos. 13:11). Divine wrath is usually the response of God to human sin, when man tries to provoke God and attempts to thwart his purposes; only rarely may the wrath of Yahweh appear irrational to us (cf. Exod. 4:24; 2 Sam. 6:7).

thy hot anger: see on 38:3 (cf. 69:24 (M.T.25), 78:49; Jer. 30:24; Lam. 1:12, 4:11).

THE LAMENT OF THE NATION **4–7**

4. Restore us again: following LXX, S, and V, and reading *hᵃšîḇēnû*. M.T. could be rendered: 'Turn to us' (so Kissane, *BP*, p. 392), but *RSV* and the versions may well be right (cf. 80:3,7

(M.T. 4, 8)). It seems that, in spite of Yahweh's past intervention and help, the situation of the nation has deteriorated. A number of historical events might fit the general description (cf. McCullough, *PIB*, p. 458), yet the allusion may be to the time shortly after the Return from the Exile, irrespective of the interpretation of *šᵉḇûṯ/šᵉḇîṯ* in verse 1*b* (see 126:1). If we grant this identification, then on the one hand we have the glorious promises of Deutero-Isaiah (40–55) while, on the other, there is the harsh reality of the early part of the post-Exilic period. We find glimpses of hardship, disillusionment, and sin in Isa. 59:9–13; Hag. 1:5–11, 2:15ff.; Zech. 1:12. It is probable that this was the historical setting of our Psalm.

God of our salvation is the God who has repeatedly delivered his people in the past; therefore he is a God of salvation, one who is able to grant deliverance in the present also. Weiser (*POTL*, p. 573) points to the existing tension between the past and present, which calls to mind Mk 9:24: 'I believe; help my unbelief'.

put away: reading *hāsēr* (from *s-w-r*; similarly LXX) for M.T. *hāp̄ēr* ('break', from *p-r-r*). The people feel that their troubles are entirely due to Yahweh's indignation (cf. Dt. 32:19f.; 1 Kg. 15:30; 2 Kg. 23:26).

5. be angry: for the verb *ʾ-n-p*, see on 60:1.

for ever: i.e. unbearably long (cf. 89:1 (M.T. 2)), or, in view of the parallelism, 'from generation to generation'.

Wilt thou prolong . . .: lit. 'Will you draw out . . .'. The verb *m-š-k* can be used (alongside the more literal meaning, as e.g. in Gen. 37:28) to denote also the prolongation of one's kindness (cf. 36:10 (M.T. 11); Jer. 31:3).

to all generations: for 'for ever' (see on 72:5).

6. This verse continues the prayer of the people in the form of a question (as in verse 5). The Hebrew pronoun *ʾattāh* ('you') is emphatic, but it may be a dittograph; it is deleted by Delitzsch *et al.* LXX understood the interrogative particle *h*ᵃ and the adverb *lōʾ* ('not'), as a vocative, 'O God' (*hāʾēl*; so also V); this reading seems inferior to that of M.T., and it may have been influenced (?) by verse 8*a*.

revive us again: lit. 'you will return, you will revive'. Here the verbal ideas are co-ordinated (see *GK* 120g), and the principal idea is expressed by the second verb; the verb 'return' serves as a periphrasis for 'again'. The intensive form of *ḥ-y-h* means 'to revive, restore to life', and it is intelligible only against the wider

OT background, where any sort of misfortune or trouble could be regarded as a form of death. Therefore a reversal of fortunes is equivalent to being restored to life (see on 30:3). The natural consequence of this 'revival' will be rejoicing, as the people express their gratitude to God in thanksgiving (cf. 9:1f. (M.T. 2f.), 13:5 (M.T. 6), 14:7, etc.).

7. Show us . . .: i.e. cause us to see and to experience your Covenant loyalty (see on 26:3).

thy salvation: see on 35:3.

THE PROPHETIC WORD OF COMFORT **8–13**

In this section the worshippers appear to be addressed by a prophetic figure who may have been a *šālôm*-prophet (so Kraus, *PBK*, p. 592), i.e. a 'prophet of peace' or the Psalmist himself (so Gunkel, Kissane). A 'prophet of peace' need not be a false prophet similar to those mentioned in Jer. 6:14, 8:11, because the mere contents of an oracle is no criterion of what is true or what is false. A prophecy is true (irrespective of its nature) when it expresses the will of Yahweh in a given situation. We can only guess as to the process whereby the divine answer was received (for an imaginative suggestion, see *POTL*, p. 573).

8. Let me hear: this can be interpreted as 'claiming divine sanction for the answer' (Eaton, *PTBC*, p. 211), but in itself it does not suggest that the communication is a new revelation (cf. Hab. 2:1). It could have been based on earlier oracles of comfort, such as e.g. Isa. 52:7–10, 57:14–21, or it may rest upon the terms of the Covenant which promise blessings to those who are loyal. Such a prophecy (?) need not come into the same category as the stealing of the word of Yahweh in Jer. 23:30.

for he will speak peace: Kraus (*PBK*, p. 588) takes this as a rhetorical question: 'Will he not speak . . .?', taking *hāʾēl* (*RSV* **God**) as an interrogative (*h*ᵃ*lōʾ*) (see verse 6*a*); this would improve the metre, and would avoid the unusual expression: 'God the Lord'. For 'peace', see on 119:165, 147:14.

his saints is synonymous with 'his people'. For *ḥāsîḏ*, see on 30:4.

who turn to him in their hearts: this rendering is based on an emendation, similar to LXX, representing perhaps *w*ᵉ*ʾel yāšûḇû ʾēlāyw libbām*. M.T. has 'but let them not turn back to folly' (*RSVm*, similarly *AV*, *RV*); many exegetes feel that the warning in this context is out of place, and therefore some of them resort to emendations similar to the one adopted by *RSV*. Dahood

(*UHP*, p. 29) renders M.T.: 'And let them not abandon hope', that is: 'turn away from confidence', taking the preposition *l*ᵉ ('to') in the sense of 'from'.

9. his salvation is at hand: this is reminiscent of Isa. 46:13, 51:5, 56:1; Mt. 3:2. For 'salvation', see on 35:3.
those who fear him: (see on 34:7); that is, those who worship God and submit to his Covenant. The natural counterpart of this is that they turn away from evil; a good example is Job (Job 1:1; cf. Dhorme, *CJ*, p. 2).
glory: Syriac has 'his glory', which is a right interpretation of M.T. 'The glory of Yahweh' is discussed on 26:8, 57:5; cf. Isa. 40:5, 60:2, 62:2. Kissane (*BP*, p. 394) suggests that 'glory' in this verse is equivalent to 'peace' (see verse 8), but it is more likely that the allusion is to the presence of God with his people. See *TDNT*, II, pp. 238–42.

10. Steadfast love (see on 26:3) and **faithfulness** (see on 25:5), as well as **righteousness** (see on 33:5) and **peace** (see on 119:165), are personifications of the divine attributes, and they are portrayed as if they were Yahweh's messengers or servants; it is less probable that they are hypostatized. Kissane (*BP*, p. 395; similarly Cohen) suggests that **faithfulness** refers to Israel's fidelity to God, which is answered by Yahweh's steadfast love. In a similar way, **righteousness** denotes 'Israel's observance of the moral law', while **peace** is the divine reward for the nation's obedience. The former interpretation seems preferable, according to which verses 10–13 would describe the coming time of blessings when the land will enjoy spiritual well-being and material prosperity, the two sides of the same coin.
will kiss each other: this rendering would normally require the reflexive form *niššāḳû*; M.T. has the active form *nāšāḳû* ('they kiss'), with the object unexpressed. Another possible reading is *nāšōḳḳû* ('have rushed together'; see Winton Thomas, *TPR*, p. 35), i.e. they will meet together (parallel to verse 10*a*); *NEB* 'join hands'.

11–12. There is a contrast between **the ground** (or 'earth') and **the sky** (or 'the heavens'), and some scholars (e.g. Davies, Cohen, Kissane) argue that verse 11 states that human faithfulness calls forth divine righteousness, that is, the saving help of God within the Covenant context. It may well be, however, that verses 11–12 are simply a restatement of verse 10, using slightly different word-pictures (cf. Isa. 45:8). The right relationship with

God produces harmony between man and nature (cf. 67:6f. (M.T. 7f.); Hos. 2:18).

what is good: Dahood (*PAB*, II, p. 290) takes *ṭôḇ* ('good') in the sense of 'rain', yet in this particular instance *RSV* may be more likely (cf. *Biblica*, XLV (1964), p. 411).

13. Righteousness . . .: Cheyne (*BPPI*, p. 240) has suggested that the meaning of *ṣeḏeḳ* ('righteousness', see on 33:5) might be 'prosperity (regarded as a righteous gift of the Covenant-God)' (cf. Isa. 41:2, 58:8). It is more fitting, however, to view *ṣeḏeḳ* as a personification (cf. 89:14*b* (M.T. 15*b*)).

and make his footsteps a way: or, 'and it (i.e. righteousness) shall prepare the way of his (that is, Yahweh's) footsteps'. The parallelism may imply that the verb *yśm* is a corruption of some such noun as *šālôm* ('peace') (so *NEB*); if so, we may read 'and peace (shall walk) (in) the way of his steps', i.e. peace will follow Yahweh. Cf. 1QS xi:4: 'the way of my steps', and 1QS xi:13: 'he will establish my steps in the way'.

Psalm 86 THE PRAYER OF A NEEDY MAN

The majority of exegetes class this Psalm as a Lament of the Individual (see Introduction, pp. 37f.). That it was intended specifically for the King is not certain, although not impossible (cf. Eaton, *PTBC*, p. 212). The author of this Psalm draws heavily upon the liturgical language of his times, and this accounts for most of the parallels with other Psalms and elsewhere; yet it does not follow that the Psalmist was an incompetent author. The lament is not merely a string of quotations, or an anthology of odd verses and phrases, for the author has left his imprint upon the arrangement of the thoughts of the Psalm.

As in most laments, it is difficult to establish the exact nature of the misfortune which had befallen the writer. The traditional thought forms and liturgical expressions tend to obliterate the *specific* details of the particular troubles. From the Psalm we gather that the Psalmist was 'poor and needy' (verse 1), and in some sort of affliction (verse 7), so that the situation was extremely grave (verse 13). Much of this distress, if not all, was caused by the enemies (verses 14, 17), although there is also an indirect reference to the author's own sin (?) (cf. verse 5). Some scholars (e.g. Schmidt, Oesterley, Deissler) think that the writer was accused of some crime or sin, and that he was pleading for the divine acquittal.

The date of the Psalm is speculative, but the post-Exilic period (late rather than early) may be a reasonable proposal.

The poem can be divided into four sections: verses 1–7, 8–11, 12–13, and 14–17. The first section is a supplication for help, characterized by a series of reasons why God should help the afflicted man, each one of which is introduced by *kî* ('for'). The second part (verses 8–11) is a hymnic expression of confidence in God, which is followed by the third section (verses 12–13) being a thanksgiving, or a response to a favourable oracle; it could also be a vow to offer thanksgiving when the deliverance will have been granted. The concluding section (verses 14–17) contains a further lamentation and prayer. Some scholars (e.g. Schmidt, Leslie) transpose verses 8–13 after verse 17; this improves the sequence of thought, but need not be the original order. Oesterley (*TP*, p. 387) considers the possibility that two or three Psalms may have been combined to form the present composition, but this and similar views have not found many adherents.

The metre of the Psalm is varied, but the long metre (4+4) prevails.

A Prayer of David: see Introduction, pp. 47 and 43f.

THE PRAYER FOR HELP **1–7**

1. Incline thy ear is a frequent formula in prayers and supplications (cf. 2 Kg. 19:16; Ps. 71:2, 88:2 (M.T. 3), 102:2 (M.T. 3); Isa. 37:17; Dan. 9:18; etc.). The phrase is another way of saying: 'Help me'.

poor and needy: for *ʿānî* and *ʾeḇyôn*, see on 34:2 and 35:10 respectively. It is unlikely that this phrase in the Psalter ever denotes membership of a particular party, or that it is an honorific designation; rather, the expression refers to the Psalmist's actual need. As such he has a claim upon Yahweh, the refuge of the afflicted (cf. Isa. 14:32).

2. Preserve my life: lit. '. . . my soul' (see on 33:19), i.e. protect me from trouble; the same phrase occurs also in 25:20.

I am godly: i.e. I am bound to you by the ties of your Covenant (see on 30:4). The noun *ḥāsîḏ* ('godly one', 'faithful, loyal (servant)') is usually used of man, and only rarely of God (as in 145:17; Jer. 3:12). LXX has *hosios* ('holy'); V renders it by '*sanctus*'. For further information, see Nelson Glueck, *HB*, pp. 66–9.

thy servant is probably a circumlocution for 'me'. *ᶜEḇeḏ* ('servant') is discussed on 27:9, 36:1. Briggs (*CECBP*, II, p. 236) takes the term as denoting Israel, but the individual interpretation is more likely.

trusts in thee: see on 78:22.

3. Thou art my God: according to M.T. this phrase belongs to the preceding verse, and it could be understood as a vocative: 'O you, my God, (save your servant . . .)'. The *RSV* proposal (cf. also *NEB*) seems preferable for metrical reasons; it also improves the construction of verse 2*b*. The expression may be an allusion to the well-known Covenant formula: 'I am the LORD your God' (Exod. 20:2; cf. Deissler, *PWdB*, II, p. 168).

be gracious to me: for this comprehensive 'prayer' for help, see on 6:2.

O Lord: some Hebrew MSS. read *yhwh* ('Yahweh') for *ʾaḏōnāy* (see on 77:2), but the latter variant is more probable, because the Psalmist's appeal to God is based upon the existing servant-Lord relationship.

4. Gladden the soul . . .: i.e. make me rejoice in your saving help (cf. 90:14f.).

O Lord: i.e. *ʾaḏōnāy*, not *yhwh*; see verse 3.

I lift up my soul: as in 25:1 (on which see); similarly also in 143:8. For 'soul', see on 33:19.

5. This verse is reminiscent of Exod. 34:6; Num. 14:18.

forgiving: the adjective *sallāḥ* is a *hapax legomenon* in the *OT*. The verb *s-l-ḥ* is of uncertain etymology, but it is quite frequent in the *OT* (see on 103:3, 130:4), and its subject is always God. See 1QS ii:8: 'may he not forgive by covering (or 'wiping out') your iniquities'; cf. 1QH xiv:24. On the subject of the removal of sin in the *OT*, see Eichrodt, *TOT*, II, pp. 443–83.

abounding in steadfast love: the same phrase is found also in Num. 14:18; Neh. 9:17; Ps. 103:8; Jl. 2:13; Jon. 4:2. For *ḥeseḏ* ('steadfast love' or 'Covenant loyalty'), see on 26:3.

6. The verse is similar to 28:2, 55:1 (M.T. 2), 130:2.

my prayer: see on 65:2.

supplication: the Hebrew *taḥanûnôṯ* denotes a supplication for favour, and it is usually directed to God by the needy but loyal servant of Yahweh. See K. W. Neubauer, *Der Stamm CHNN im Sprachgebrauch des Alten Testaments* (1964), pp. 137–40.

7. the day of my trouble: or 'in time of my distress' (as in 77:2 (M.T. 3); cf. 20:1 (M.T. 2), 50:15). If the Psalmist was unjustly accused (so Schmidt), then the 'day of trouble' might be the particular day on which the decision was expected (cf. Kraus, *PBK*, p. 598).

thou dost answer me: or 'you will answer me' (by giving me help, or a favourable decision).

THE INCOMPARABLE GOD **8–11**

This hymnic praise of God expresses the confidence that God is not only willing to answer the prayers of his servants (see verses 5 and 7), but that he is also *able* to do so.

8. This verse is an echo of Exod. 15:11; cf. also 58:1 (M.T. 2), 71:19, 89:6 (M.T. 7); Isa. 45:21; Jer. 10:6.

among the gods: the *ʾelōhîm* ('gods') may refer either to the gods of the nations (so Davies), or, more likely, to the heavenly beings which serve Yahweh (see on 89:6). Whatever the interpretation of this phrase may be, there is but one who deserves the name 'God', and he is Yahweh: 'thou alone art God' (verse 10*b*). The Psalmist has arrived at this conclusion by considering the works of God; there is nothing in the whole world that can be compared with the deeds of Yahweh—even the very universe itself is his handiwork; therefore the doer of these works must be unequalled and supreme (cf. Dt. 3:24).

9. the nations: (*gôyīm*), see on 59:5. For the thought of verse 9*ab*, cf. Isa. 2:3, 45:23; Am. 9:7. Since Yahweh is the only real God without an equal, the day must come when this statement of faith will become a historical reality.

thou hast made: Gunkel, Kraus, *et al.* transfer this phrase to the end of verse 8; metrically this is an improvement.

bow down: see on 29:2.

glorify thy name: (cf. 22:23 (M.T. 24), 50:15,23) by their obedience, as in Mal. 1:6.

10. This verse contains reminiscences of a number of other *OT* passages; for 10*a*, cf. 72:18, 77:14 (M.T. 15), and, for 10*b*, see 2 Kg. 19:15; Ps. 83:18 (M.T. 19).

11. Teach me thy way: this is a repetition of 27:11*a* (cf. 25:4, 143:8,10). The Psalmist is aware that even his loyalty to Yahweh is largely due to the grace of God (cf. 119:12,26,64, etc.); see 1QS x:12f.: 'I will choose according to what he teaches me, and I will delight in what he decrees for me' (so Leaney, *RQM*, p. 234).

walk in thy truth is similar to 26:3*b*; see on 25:5. Perhaps we should render: 'in faithfulness to you' (cf. Nötscher, *PEB*, p. 191; Dahood, *PAB*, II, p. 291).

unite my heart: some exegetes follow LXX, S, and V in reading *yiḥadd* (from *ḥ-d-h*, 'to rejoice'): 'let (my heart (see on 27:3)) rejoice'. M.T. probably means 'make my heart single' (cf. *NEB*), as opposed to a double heart, or divided loyalty (see on 12:2; cf. 1 Chr. 12:33; Jer. 32:39; Ezek. 11:19f.).

to fear thy name: see on 34:7,9, 85:9. For 'name', see on 20:1.

THE VOW OF THANKSGIVING **12–13**

12. I give thanks . . .: see on 18:49, 30:12.

with my whole heart: with absolute sincerity (cf. Dt. 6:5, 10:12; Ps. 119:2). Verse 12*a* is practically the same as 9:1*a* (M.T. 2*a*).

I will glorify . . .: see verse 9.

for ever: see on 89:1 Dahood (UHP, p. 36) takes the Hebrew *ʿôlām* ('eternity') as a divine name, and the preposition *l*ᵉ ('for') as a *lāmeḏ vocativum* (see on 75:9), rendering 'O Eternal'.

13. great is thy steadfast love: i.e. your Covenant loyalty (see on 26:3) is unlimited; cf. 57:10 (M.T. 11).

. . . delivered my soul: or '. . . rescued me' (see on 33:19).

the depths of Sheol: as in Dt. 32:22 'Sheol' (see on 6:5) in Hebrew thought was the underworld, and the dwelling place of all the dead. The word 'depths' does not point to any divisions in Sheol, such as are described in later apocalyptic literature (see Russell, *MMJA*, pp. 364ff.); the author simply uses the language of the popular belief that Sheol was a place far below the surface and in the very depths of the earth (63:9 (M.T. 10), 71:20). The underworld is the opposite of heaven (Job 11:8; Ps. 139:8; Isa. 7:11; Am. 9:2), being the location furthest removed from heaven; therefore it can denote a practically complete separation from the world of the living and from God (cf. Barth, *ETKD*, p. 83). To be delivered from Sheol, or from its power, means to be restored to a relationship with God; without this deliverance the afflicted would be helplessly lost. It is also possible that our Psalm was part of a royal liturgy, in the course of which the King suffered ritual humiliation and was brought near to the gates of the netherworld. In the end he was delivered from the grasp of death, and was endowed with a new vigour (cf. Johnson, *SKAI*, pp. 116, 121).

THE RENEWED LAMENTATION **14–17**

14. This verse repeats nearly word for word 54:3 (M.T. 5), q.v.

15. See verse 5, and its close parallel in Exod. 34:6.

slow to anger: i.e. God is very forbearing and long-suffering (cf. Num. 14:18; Ps. 103:8, 145:8; Prov. 14:28, etc.; also 1QH i:16, xvi:16, xvii:17). See van Imschoot, *ThOT*, I, p. 64.

16. Turn to me . . .: as in 25:16.

give thy strength: or '. . . your refuge' (so Gunkel; see on 84:5).

the son of thy handmaid: (cf. 116:16), this may be an alternative expression for 'your servant' (see on 36:1). Literally the reference is to a 'slave born in the house' (cf. de Vaux, *AI*, pp. 81ff.), and the point is probably that such a person is a permanent slave, bound to his master for ever. Thus it has nothing to do with the piety of the Psalmist's mother (cf. McCullough, *PIB*, p. 467).

17. a sign of thy favour: for *ʾôṯ* ('sign'), see on 65:8. Mowinckel (*PIW*, II, p. 66) understands it as a 'favourable token'; if obtained, it would be interpreted by an oracle. It is more likely that the sign which the Psalmist expects is actual deliverance; *NEB* 'proof of thy kindness'.

put to shame: the enemies will be confounded (see on 35:4) when they see that Yahweh has intervened on behalf of the afflicted man (cf. Isa. 49:13).

Psalm 87 Zion as the Spiritual Centre of the World

Exegetically this brief Psalm is one of the most problematic in the whole Psalter, but one thing stands out clearly: the poem stresses the significance of Zion, and therefore it could be described as a Hymn of Zion (see Introduction, pp. 33ff.); to this *Gattung* are usually assigned Ps. 46, 48, 76, 84, 122, 137 (cf. Barth, *IP*, p. 20).

As verse 7 implies, the Psalm was probably associated with a dance procession, but dancing need not only have been restricted to one particular festival (e.g. the Feast of Tabernacles). Kraus (*PBK*, p. 601) has argued that this procession may have been part of the representation of the election of Jerusalem, which expressed itself in the capture of the city and in the bringing of the Ark to Zion. It is possible that the Songs of Zion (including our Psalm) may have been sung by pilgrims outside the gates of the Holy City (cf. Kraus, *WI*, p. 210). For a different, but far less likely, interpretation, see Barnes, *PWC*, II, pp. 415ff.

A difficult problem is the mention of the foreign countries in verse 4. One suggestion is that the Psalmist is describing a future vision of Zion as the world-centre of Yahweh's worship, for all peoples symbolized by Egypt (Rahab), the then major Mesopotamian power (Babylon), as well as Philistia, Tyre, and Ethiopia. A variation of this view is to assume that the allusion is to the proselytes from various lands, who had come to Jerusalem for the particular festival (so Weiser). The presence of the comparatively few foreign converts could be taken symbolically of the universal worship of Yahweh, in the time to come (cf. Isa. 19:19–25, 45:22f., 56:6ff.; Zech. 2:11, 8:22f.; Mal. 1:11). Another possibility is the interpretation which sees here a mention of the Jews of the Dispersion; they, too, will be given the same privileges as their compatriots living in Judah. This may well be the most likely view, although the proselytes too should be included among the Jews of the *Diaspora*.

The date of the Psalm is either Exilic (so Oesterley, *TP*, p. 390) or, more likely, post-Exilic. The emphasis upon Zion and its special position in comparison with the 'dwelling places of Jacob' (see verse 2*b*) may allude to some of the questions raised by the Samaritan schism (see Kraus, *PBK*, p. 602).

Many scholars have proposed various re-arrangements of the present order of verses (e.g. Gunkel, Schmidt, Kraus), but it may be wiser to retain the M.T. line order, which is also supported by the versions.

The metre, if any, is irregular; but the text of the Psalm may have become corrupt.

A Psalm of the Sons of Korah: see Introduction, pp. 46 and 45.

A Song: see Introduction, p. 47.

A HYMN IN PRAISE OF ZION **1–3**

1. On the holy mount: lit. 'on the hills of holiness', probably because Jerusalem was situated on several hills (so Gunkel, *PGHAT*, p. 380); cf. 125:2, 133:3. It is possible that the 'hills' should be understood as a plural of amplification, or that the 'holy mountains' may have a mythological significance and refer to the primeval mountains (cf. Kraus, *PBK*, p. 602).

stands the city he founded: this is a paraphrase of M.T. which only has one word: *y^e^sûḏāṯô* ('his foundation'); while LXX reads 'his foundations'. The pronoun 'his' has no antecedent, and is therefore strange. It is possible that the third person masculine pronominal suffix (*RSV* 'his') is a corrupt abbreviation of *yhwh* ('Yahweh'; so Davies). Historically Jerusalem was a pre-Israelite foundation, although the writer may have had in mind the building of the Temple. Traditionally, however, it was said that Yahweh had founded Zion (cf. Isa. 14:32).

2. the gates of Zion: the gates were usually the centres of social and economic life of the town or city (see on 69:12), and as such they could well stand for the *whole* city (cf. 122:2). So in Dt. 12:15 we read: 'within any of your towns', or literally '. . . any of your gates' (cf. Dt. 16:18). For 'Zion', see on 65:1. When the Psalmist says that Yahweh 'loves the gates of Zion', he probably means that God has chosen Jerusalem (cf. 132:13) and protects her (48:3 (M.T. 4)).
the dwelling places of Jacob: the Hebrew *miškānôṯ* may sometimes denote the Jerusalem Temple (see on 74:7), but in this verse it probably signifies other Israelite sanctuaries (so Kraus, Deissler, Eaton). Other exegetes think that the reference is to the Israelite towns and cities (so Kissane, McCullough), or even to the Jewish settlements in the *Diaspora*, or Dispersion. The first suggestion is, however, more likely, for the contrast seems to be between Zion as a religious centre, and other cities (i.e. sanctuaries) of a similar significance. If the Psalm is comparatively late, this may be an allusion to the Samaritan temple on Mount Gerizim, although this seems unlikely. Verse 2 probably offers an explanation as to why Yahweh chose Jerusalem rather than any other Israelite shrine.

3. Glorious things: this may be a reference to the various prophetic promises to Jerusalem, such as in Isa. 2:2ff., 60:15f., to the Songs of Zion, sung by the pilgrims, or to verses 4–6.
are spoken: some scholars (e.g. Duhm, Briggs, Deissler) read *m^e^ḏabbēr* ('he speaks', or 'is about to speak') instead of M.T. *m^e^ḏubbār*; the subject would be Yahweh, and verse 3 could be regarded as an introduction to the oracle-like utterance in verses 4–6. The verb *d-b-r* can be used both of speaking and of singing, as in Jg. 5:12, where Deborah is told to *speak* a song. Weiser (*POTL*, p. 582) and some other commentators transfer verse 6 immediately after verse 3, but see also *NEB*.
city of God: (see on 48:1); the same expression is found in 46:4

(M.T. 5), while in 48:1,8 (M.T. 2, 9) we have 'the city of our God' (in 101:8 and Isa. 60:14 'the city of the LORD'). The reference is clearly to Jerusalem.

Selah: see Introduction, p. 48f.

THE ORACLE CONCERNING THE JEWS OF THE DISPERSION **4–6**

The interpretation of this section is far from clear. Verse 4 is in the form of a direct divine utterance, while verses 5–6 are described as a 'prophetic exposition' (Eaton, *PTBC*, p. 215). The five countries mentioned in verse 4 probably represent *all* the Jews and proselytes (i.e. 'in-comers', so Weiser, *POTL*, p. 583) of the *Diaspora*, or Dispersion, unless the author envisages a world-wide turning to Yahweh at the end-time.

4. Among those who know me: i.e. those who recognize my claims and worship me. Kissane (*BP*, p. 402) thinks that the speaker is the Psalmist himself, in which case we should render 'to my acquaintances'; but *RSV* seems to be right.

Rahab was originally the name of a mythological creature (see on 89:10), but at a later time it was used to denote Egypt (Isa. 30:7). The reason for this extension of usage may have been the belief that in some way Egypt was part of the hostile primeval Chaos; the same idea would be true also of all other powers which threatened Israel.

Babylon: if the Psalm is post-Exilic, as it may well be, then the name must denote the Mesopotamian empire contemporary with the Psalmist. The actual *Babylonian* (or neo-Babylonian) rule began at the end of the seventh century B.C. and collapsed in 539 B.C. (cf. Bright, *HI*, pp. 341ff.).

Philistia was the territory of the ancient Philistines (see on 56:1), and the name has survived in the modern term 'Palestine'.

Tyre: see on 83:7.

Ethiopia: the Hebrew *kûš* can denote either Nubia or Ethiopia (cf. E. A. Speiser, *Genesis* (*AB* 1, 1964), p. 66).

This one was born there: the writer may be thinking of all the Yahweh worshippers who were born in foreign lands, yet Zion (so in verse 5) is to be called 'Mother' (following LXX and adding *ʾēm*, or reading it instead of the first *ʾîš* ('man')) and each man, whatever his place of birth, is also born in Zion, i.e. he is a citizen of Jerusalem. To be 'born' in Zion means to be 'recorded for life in Jerusalem' (Isa. 4:3), and this spiritual citizenship does not depend upon the fact that one happened to be born in

Zion, but rather upon one's obedience to Yahweh. So Ezekiel (13:9) states: 'My hand will be against the prophets . . . they shall not be in the council of my people, nor be enrolled in the register of the house of Israel'. This register or list is apparently the same as the 'book of the living' (69:28 (M.T. 29); cf. Exod. 32:32; Dan. 12:1; Mal. 3:16). For the word-picture of Jerusalem as a mother of many children, see Isa. 49:20f., 50:1, 54:1, 62:4f., 66:7f.

5. the Most High: see on 18:13, 46:4, 47:2. He is the one who has established Zion (see on 48:8). Pope (*EUT*, p. 50) renders verse 5*c*: 'It is Elyon himself who begot her (him?)'.

6. he registers the peoples: i.e. his worshippers from among all the nations of which the five alluded to in verse 4 are but a representative example.

This one was born there: probably 'the one(s) born there' (i.e. in the Dispersion). For this use of *zeh* ('this'), see Dahood, *PAB*, I, p. 152.

THE TEMPLE FESTIVAL 7

7. Singers and dancers: both singing and dancing (see on 30:11) were expressions of religious rejoicing, and had their place in Israelite worship. Dancing is not described in detail by the *OT* writers, but the activity must have been common enough not to require a special mention.

alike say: the verb 'say' is not in M.T., but may rightly represent the meaning of the verse.

All my springs are in you: ultimately the reference is to something which is the source of blessing and joy, but the immediate allusion is not clear. Kirkpatrick (*BPCB*, p. 522) suggests that the Psalmist is speaking metaphorically of 'fountains of salvation' (cf. Isa. 12:3), but this may equally well be a parallel to 36:9: 'For with thee is the fountain of life' (cf. Jer. 2:13). It is possible to think of Zion as the source of the streams of Paradise, as in 46:4 (M.T. 5). Gressmann, Gunkel, Kraus read *kullām ᶜōnê bāḵ* ('they all sing of you', similarly Oesterley, Leslie, *RP*, *NEB*, *et al.*), for *kol maᶜyānay bāḵ* ('all my springs are in you').

Psalm 88 A Godly Man in Perpetual Trouble

This is one of the most tragic songs in the Psalter, and it has been traditionally used as a Psalm suitable for reading on Good Friday.

According to the usual classification, it belongs to the Individual Laments (see Introduction, pp. 37f.), although some of the older scholars (e.g. Wellhausen, Briggs) took it as a National Lamentation. Structurally the Psalm exhibits certain peculiarities: it lacks any explicit expression of trust in Yahweh (see, however, verse 1) and a vow of praise; on the other hand, there is a threefold introductory petition and subsequent lamentation (verses 1–2 and 3–9*a*, 9*bc* and 10–12, 13 and 14–18).

The situation portrayed is a life-long trouble (see verse 15)—perhaps some grave illness, although it would be pointless to speculate as to its exact nature (leprosy, palsy, etc.). Due to this affliction, the Psalmist has been deserted by friends, and, above all, he feels that even God has cast him off. Some commentators (e.g. Olshausen, Wellhausen, Cheyne) have thought that the conclusion (or some other part) of the Psalm has been lost, and that this section may have contained some words of hope; this is, of course, possible, but there is no evidence for this suggestion. As it is, the Psalm creates an impression of unrelieved gloom without a ray of light (but see verse 1). The most striking fact is that the afflicted man prays at all (cf. Rodd, *PEPC*, II, p. 31), and therefore the lament is a fine testimony to the faith of its author and to his need for God. Barnes (*PWC*, II, p. 420) rightly describes this Psalm as 'the story of Job left half-told'; the writer's painful experiences are reminiscent of Job's anguish, but the Psalm lacks the occasional glimpses beyond the present trials and tribulations.

E. Jones (*The Cross in the Psalms* (1963), p. 63) suggests that in 'all probability the Psalm was used in association with penitential rites during the expiatory ceremony', although if this were the case, one might have expected some confession of sin.

The date of the Psalm seems to be post-Exilic, especially in view of its similarities with the Book of Job.

The metre of the Psalm is irregular, but 3 + 3 prevails.

A Song: see Introduction, p. 47.

A Psalm: see Introduction, p. 46.

Sons of Korah: see Introduction, p. 45.

the choirmaster: see Introduction, p. 48.

Mahalath Leannoth: see Introduction, p. 50.

A Maskil: see Introduction, p. 47.

Heman the Ezrahite: in 1 Kg. 4:31 a man called Heman is named among the famous sages of that time, while in 1 Chr. 2:6

Heman is called the son of Zerah, so that 'Ezrahite' might mean 'belonging to the family of Zerah', if the reference were to the same person. 1 Chr. 15:17 mentions a 'Heman the son of Joel', a Levite who was a leader of the Temple music, together with Asaph and Ethan. He is said to have 'prophesied' with musical instruments (1 Chr. 25:1), and he is called the 'king's seer' (1 Chr. 25:5). Dahood (*PAB*, II, p. 302) suggests: 'Heman the native-born'.

THE INVOCATION AND PRAYER **1–2**

1. my God, I call for help: M.T. has 'God of my salvation'. *RSV* follows the usual emendation *ʾelōhay šiwwaʿtî yômām* (for M.T. *ʾelōhê yešûʿāṯî yôm*) which improves the parallelism (cf. 22:2 (M.T. 3)) and the construction of the sentence. On the other hand, the alteration removes the glimmer of hope implicit in 'God of my salvation' (see on 27:1). Kraus (*PBK*, p. 608) sees in this phrase an expression of certainty: Yahweh is the God who has previously delivered the Psalmist, and who is still able to do so. Following M.T., the rest of the verse should be rendered: '. . . by day I cry out, in the night (I am still) before you' (similarly Weiser, Kraus, Deissler).

2. my prayer: see on 65:2.

my cry: the Hebrew *rinnāh* is a ringing cry, either in joy (42:5 (M.T. 6), 47:1 (M.T. 2), 105:43), or in sorrow (17:1, 61:1 (M.T. 2)). Here it is practically identical with 'lamentation'.

THE LAMENTATION OF THE AFFLICTED MAN **3–9a**

3. my soul is a circumlocution for 'I' (see on 33:19).

is full: i.e. 'is sated'. While others are sated with the goodness of God's house (65:4 (M.T. 5)), the forsaken sufferer is conscious of the ebbing away of his life and vitality.

my life draws near to Sheol: that is, the *quality* of the Psalmist's life is becoming more and more like that of the shadowy existence of the dead in Sheol. The etymology of Sheol is uncertain, but some would derive it from *š-ʾ-l* ('to ask, inquire'); so Sheol would denote the place where inquiries could be made of the dead, concerning the future, etc. (cf. 1 Sam. 28:3–19). Another view is that 'Sheol' is to be explained from *š-ʿ-l*, ('to be hollow'), while L. Köhler (*ThZ*, II (1946), pp. 71–4) suggests that 'Sheol' is a formation from *š-ʾ-h*, ('to be desolate'), indicating a place of desolation. Albright (for references, see Johnson, *VITAI*, p. 91, n.1) links 'Sheol' with the Babylonian *shuʾāra*, which was the home of Tammuz (originally the Sumerian deity of vegetation) in the underworld. In spite of the etymology, the nature of Sheol is reasonably clear from the many references to it in the *OT* (see on 6:5). Cf. Tromp, *PCD*, pp. 21ff.

4. I am reckoned: the writer is already regarded as dead (for a similar metaphor, see on 22:18), or as one who goes down to the Pit (for this expression, see on 28:1, 143:7; cf. *ANET*, p. 135a (viii)). **Pit** may denote either Sheol or the grave which, in a sense, forms the entrance into the netherworld, and as such may suggest the whole. E. Jones (*The Cross in the Psalms*, p. 64) thinks that verse 4 implies a 'protestation of innocence', but, if so, God is punishing the Psalmist unjustly (see verses 6–8). The author may simply be stating facts and beliefs without any attempt to reconcile them. He knows that God's hand is heavy upon him (see verses 6ff., 14, 16ff.), but he may also be aware that he has not committed any sin deserving such a prolonged punishment. Nevertheless, he must have been convinced that God is merciful and just (cf. verses 10–12), even though the writer is unable to resolve the existing contradiction and tension.
no strength: (so *KBL*). *RV* renders 'no help' (so LXX, S, *BDB*); similarly *NEB*. The Psalmist is probably thinking of the shades or the dwellers in the underworld (see verse 10), who are often depicted as weak and powerless (cf. Isa. 14:9ff.).

5. like one forsaken among the dead is a very free translation of *bammēṯîm ḥop̄šî*; this may be textually corrupt. *AV* has 'Free among the dead', which is a reasonable literal rendering. The main problem is caused by the word *ḥop̄šî*; its usual meaning is 'free'. Thus the Hebrew slave served six years, and in the seventh he went out *free*. In our verse the word may be used slightly ironically: to be free among the dead means to be liberated, not only from pain and trouble, but also from all that is precious and desirable (cf. Job 3:17ff.; Ec. 9:10). The Ugaritic equivalent of *ḥop̄šî* is *ḫpṯt* which Driver (*CML*, p. 140) renders by 'netherworld', and Aistleitner (*WUS*, p. 116) by 'uncleanness'. In the light of this, we might render verse 5*a*: '(I am) unclean among the dead' (and so separated from the living). J. Gray (*The Legacy of Canaan* (*SVT*, 5, 1957), p. 200) reads *kimᵉṯê maḥpešeṯ* ('as men of corruption'), while *RP* follows the suggestion of Graetz, *kammēṯîm nimšaltî* ('I am become like unto the dead').
like the slain: who had fallen in the battle, and had been buried in a mass grave (cf. Ezek. 32:20–32).

in the grave: the Hebrew *ḳeḇer* ('grave') is a synonym of *bôr* ('pit'), as well as of 'Sheol'. The latter is not simply the sum total of all the graves, although every grave is a manifestation of the netherworld. The *OT* writers do not define the exact relationship between Sheol and the grave (cf. A. Heidel, *The Gilgamesh Epic and Old Testament Parallels* (1963), p. 170), but the above explanation may be a fair summary of the view of the *OT* in general. Literally, the grave or the burial place could be either a trench in the soil or, more often, a cave, hollowed out of a rock, or a natural underground hollow. Ideally one was interred in a family tomb (cf. Gen. 49:29–32; 2 Sam. 21:14), but the poor, the fallen in battle, and others might be buried in a common grave (cf. 2 Kg. 23:6). See Eichrodt, *TOT*, II, p. 212–16; Tromp, *PCD*, pp. 129ff.
remember no more: i.e. one whose life is drawing near Sheol (see verse 3) is separated from God, although theoretically this separation is not as yet absolute. There remains the possibility that God might decide to deliver the unfortunate man who is, for the time being, *like* the dead who can no more expect help from God, or who are cut off from God's hand (verse 5*d*). It may be true to say that Yahweh's power extended also to Sheol (cf. 139:8; Am. 9:2), but for some reason or other he did not wish to interfere with the existence of those in the underworld. This negative attitude may have been emphasized in order to break down the popular cult of the dead and necromancy. Von Rad (*OTT*, I, p. 275) has pointed out that it was believed that the dead were in a state of permanent uncleanness, and as such they were excluded from the worship of Yahweh and cut off from the Covenant institutions and its blessings.

6. the depths of the Pit is another roundabout expression for Sheol (as in Lam. 3:55), and it does not imply any divisions in the underworld (see on 86:13). The phrase may mean 'the netherworld in the depths (of the earth)' (cf. 63:9 (M.T. 10)).
the regions dark and deep: darkness is one of the characteristics of Sheol (cf. 143:3; Lam. 3:6; see also the 'Descent of Ishtar to the Nether World', *ANET*, pp. 107ff.). The Hebrew equivalent of 'deep' is not an adjective but a noun (lit. 'in the deeps' (*AV*, *RV*), i.e. in the depths of the sea (as in Exod. 15:5)). This does not contradict the interpretation of verse 6*a*, because the earth itself was believed to rest upon the waters of the great abyss (see on 72:8), and consequently both metaphors could equally well

denote the netherworld (see Jon. 2:5f. (M.T. 6f.); cf. Barth, *ETKD*, p. 82). LXX and S read 'in the shadow of death' (i.e. *b*^e^*ṣalmāweṯ* for M.T. *bim*^e^*ṣōlôṯ* ('in the depths')), but M.T. seems preferable (cf. however Job 10:21f.).

7. Thy wrath: the afflictions have been brought about by God's anger (see on 85:3), but the Psalmist does not inform us as to what had roused the divine wrath, neither does he assert his innocence, nor does he confess his sins.

all thy waves are probably not simply the waves of tribulation (see verses 16f.) but also the metaphorical waters of the abyss (see on 42:7). LXX reads for verse 7*b*: 'you have brought upon me all your waves'; this suggests the verb ᵓ*innîṯā* for M.T. ᶜ*innîṯā* ('you have afflicted'), which seems quite satisfactory.

Selah: see Introduction, pp. 48f.

8. my companions: that is, my intimate friends, rather than mere acquaintances (as *AV*, *RV*). The Psalmist was forsaken by his former friends, not so much on account of the disease itself, as because he was regarded as a man smitten by God and therefore a potential danger to his associates. Some illnesses (e.g. leprosy and certain skin diseases) would render a man unclean (see Lev. 13:45f.), and consequently he would be excluded from society and worship. It does not follow that our Psalmist must have been a leper, even though he may have been treated like one. For similar descriptions of trouble, see Job 19:13–22, 30:9–15; Ps. 31:11 (M.T. 12).

I am shut in: following the reading of LXX, S, and V (which have *kālūᵓ ᵓ*^a^*nî* for *kālūᵓ*); this may be a correct interpretation of M.T. It is difficult to say what this confinement actually was; it could have been a primitive sort of quarantine (cf. Lev. 13:4,46), or an actual imprisonment (so T, *NEB*; cf. Jer. 32:2); or it might also be a metaphorical account of troubles in general (cf. Lam. 3:7). The author probably felt shut in, or restricted by his misfortunes (cf. 142:7 (M.T. 8); see also the 'Prayer of Lamentation to Ishtar', *ANET*, pp. 384f.).

9a. my eye grows dim: see on 38:10. The allusion is not so much to the gradual loss of sight as to the loss of one's vitality (see on 13:3). The eye was thought of as a mirror of both one's misery and happiness (see Job 17:7; Ps. 6:7 (M.T. 8), 31:9 (M.T. 10)). In the Hebrew there may be a deliberate word play on ᶜ*ênî* ('my eye') and ᶜ*ōnî* ('sorrow' or 'affliction').

THE REASONS WHY GOD SHOULD HELP **9bc–12**

This section is a continuation of the lamentation in verses 3–9*a*, but at the same time it is an implicit praise of God (cf. Deissler, *PWdB*, II, p. 175). The following rhetorical questions are essentially 'veiled' prayers for help (cf. 85:5f. (M.T. 6f.)).

9bc. Every day I call: i.e. I offer my prayers all day long. **I spread out my hands:** the Hebrew phrase occurs only here in the *OT*, but the gesture itself is a common one in prayer (see on 28:2)

10. wonders: see on 77:11. The situation of the Psalmist is so desperate that it would nearly require a miracle to save him. The miracles of Elijah (cf. 1 Kg. 17:17–24) and Elisha (cf. 2 Kg. 4:18–37), as well as the 'translation' of Enoch (Gen. 5:24) and Elijah (2 Kg. 2:11), show that, although normally Yahweh was not concerned with the dead, his *power* was not limited by anyone or anything, but by himself.

the shades: the Hebrew *r^epā'îm* is of uncertain origin. *BDB* (p. 952) links it with *r-p-h* ('to sink, relax'), so that the noun would denote 'the sunken, powerless ones'; while Driver (*CML*, p. 10, n.2) accepts the suggestion that it should be associated with *r-p-'* ('to heal' or 'to be united'); hence the noun could designate the dead 'as a massed community leading a common life in the netherworld'. For other proposals, see Johnson, *VITAI*, pp. 88ff. Yet, irrespective of the etymology, the word *r^epā'îm* clearly suggests the inhabitants of Sheol, who are little more than shadows of their former selves, and therefore the word 'shades' is a reasonable paraphrase. What survives in Sheol is not some immortal soul or spirit, but rather the *whole* man in the form of a shadowy 'replica' which defies any further definition (see Eichrodt, *TOT*, II, p. 214). It is of some interest that the same(?) word is used to signify the prehistoric inhabitants of Canaan (cf. Gen. 14:5, 15:20; Dt. 3:11; Jos. 12:4; etc.). The term is also found in Phoenician inscriptions (cf. G. A. Cooke, *A Textbook of North Semitic Inscriptions* (1903), p. 29), and in the Ugaritic texts (see Driver, *CML*, pp. 10, 155a; Gordon, *UT*, p. 485); but these instances do not, as yet, solve our problems (cf. also J. Gray, pp. 92f., 154). See also Tromp, *PCD*, pp. 176–80.

to praise thee: this is no longer in the power of the shades, for, being ritually unclean, they are separated from the cult and from praising God (cf. v. Rad, *OTT*, I, p. 277f.). Furthermore, since

Yahweh's help and Covenant loyalty are no longer experienced in Sheol, there is no occasion to pay homage to God. The Psalmist, however, is not in the underworld in the full sense of the word, and therefore there is an element of hope.

Selah: see Introduction, pp. 48f.

11. steadfast love, or 'Covenant loyalty', is not manifested in **the grave** (see verse 5), which is here a synonym of Sheol, nor are the deeds of God's faithfulness (see on 36:5) recounted in Abaddon, because his promises are given only to the living. 'Abaddon' is a transliteration of the Hebrew *ʾ*^{a}*ḇaddôn*, which elsewhere is found only in the Wisdom literature (Job 26:6, 28:22, 31:12; Prov. 15:11, 27:20). It is derived from *ʾ-b-d* ('to perish'), and means 'destruction, ruin'; it is employed as a designation of the netherworld. In Rev. 9:11 the word has become the name of the angel of the underworld. Cf. Tromp, *PCD*, p. 80.

12. darkness (see verse 6) and **the land of forgetfulness** are two graphic terms of Sheol. The netherworld is a 'land of forgetfulness' because its inhabitants are soon forgotten (cf. 31:12 (M.T. 13); Ec. 9:5), and they themselves know nothing (Job 14:21; Ec. 9:5). This particular view of the dead may not have been accepted by all Israelites, as is implied by the practice of necromancy (Dt. 18:11; 1 Sam. 28:8–19; Isa. 8:19, etc.). LXX has 'a land forgotten (by you, i.e. God)'.

thy saving help: lit. 'your righteousness' (see on 33:5). The Psalmist simply states the commonly accepted view, and he does not provide any explanation as to *why* the divine help is not extended to those in Sheol.

ANOTHER INTRODUCTORY PRAYER **13**

For the morning as a conventional and opportune time for prayer, see on 44:5.

A FURTHER LAMENTATION **14–18**

14. . . . cast me off: see on 89:38. For a similar view, cf. 74:1.

Why dost thou hide thy face: see on 10:1, 13:1, 27:9.

15. close to death: LXX, S, and Jerome must have read *yāgēa*^{c} ('weary') for M.T. *gōwēa*^{c} (from *g-w-*^{c}, 'to expire, die'). M.T. may be right, and it probably means 'I have been seriously ill (from my youth up)'; similarly *NEB*.

I suffer thy terrors: i.e. I have borne the terrors sent by you (cf. 55:4f. (M.T. 5f.)).

I am helpless: the real meaning of the Hebrew *ʾāp̱ûnāh* is uncertain, because the verb *p-w-n* is not attested elsewhere in the *OT*. A number of scholars emend it to *ʾāp̱ûḡāh* ('I am benumbed'; from *p-w-g*, 'to grow numb').

16. thy wrath: (see on 38:3). The Hebrew equivalent is plural in form which may be a plural of amplification (*GK* 124e): 'your fierce anger'.

thy dread assaults: cf. Job 6:4. The Psalmist sees in all his afflictions the hand of God; it is less likely that the 'dread assaults' are personified as 'angels of the divine wrath' (Eaton, *PTBC*, p. 218).

destroy me: for the unusual Hebrew verbal form, see *GK* 55d.

17. The misfortunes surround the distressed man like the flood waters (see verse 7*b*) and they threaten to overwhelm him, so that the situation is very critical.

18. Verse 18*a* is an echo of verse 8*a*.

my companions are in darkness: or 'the darkness (of Sheol has taken the place of) my familiar friends' (for a parallel, see Job 17:14). Perhaps we should follow G. R. Driver in taking *mḥšk* (*RSV* 'darkness') as a participle *m*^{e}*ḥaśśēḵ* (from *ḥ-ś-k*, 'to withhold, refrain'), continuing the finite verb in verse 18*a* ('you have caused . . . to shun . . .'), and rendering: '(you) have removed (my intimate friends)'; this is also implied by Jerome and S.

Psalm 89 The Promises to David and Present Reality

This Psalm consists of three main sections. Verses 1–18 can be described as a Hymn praising Yahweh's Covenant loyalty, his faithfulness, and power. The second section (verses 19–37) is a review of the Davidic Covenant and its promises in the form of an oracle. Its exact nature is not clear; it could be an expansion of Nathan's prophecy in 2 Sam. 7:4–17, or both may be elaborations of an original dynastic oracle; but these are only two of the possible suggestions (see introduction to verses 19–37). The third section comprises verses 38–51, while verse 52 is a doxology to the third Book of the Psalter. Verses 38–45 contain a lament over the misfortunes of the Davidic king, which may be either historical or liturgical in nature. This is followed by a prayer for Yahweh's intervention and deliverance (verses 46–51).

This brief summary of the Psalm shows that its *Gattung* is not immediately apparent. Some exegetes regard it as a composite work, made up of two or three independent poems. In the view of some scholars, the Psalmist was not so much an author as a compiler. Leslie (*PAP*, pp. 273f.) attributes the hymn (verses 5–18) to a north Israelite source, written before 721 B.C. (cf. Gunkel, *EP*, pp. 416, 419), while verses 19–37 he derives from the 'Temple repertoire' in Jerusalem. All this forms the groundwork for the national lament for the King, composed at the earliest *c.* 701 B.C. Other exegetes link the Psalm with the events following the death of Josiah (2 Kg. 23:29–30) or the exile of Jehoiachin (2 Kg. 24:8–17), yet there is little explicit evidence for this in the Psalm itself. A reasonable suggestion is that of Deissler (*PWdB*, II, p. 182) who thinks that the Psalm may have been composed *c.* 520 B.C. against the background of the hope that the Davidic kingdom might soon be restored (cf. Hag. 2:20–3; Zech. 4:6–14, 6:12f.). It is very likely that the Psalmist drew upon older cultic material, especially for verses 1–37, although he need not have used old poems in their entirety; thus the result seems to be a reasonably intelligible unity (cf. *VT*, XI (1961), pp. 321ff.). Cf. also Sabourin, *POM*, II, pp. 239ff.

Another line of interpretation is to see in the Psalm a pre-Exilic liturgy which involved the ritual humiliation of the King at the annual New Year Festival. This would be reminiscent of a similar ritual act in the corresponding Babylonian festival (see Johnson, *SKAI*, pp. 103f.; cf. Ringgren, *IR*, p. 236), although we should not overlook the dissimilarities; the ritual degradation of the Judean king need not have been associated with the so-called 'dying and rising god' myth. J. M. Ward (*VT*, XI (1961), p. 338) has argued that the lament in verses 38–51 may have been occasioned by the 'division of the Davidic-Solomonic kingdom, and the failure of Judah to realise its grandiose hope of universal dominion'. Therefore it could have been part of the liturgy of the coronations of successive Judean kings, as a lament 'over the frustration of the dynastic promise' (p. 339). Weiser (*POTL*, p. 591) also places the Psalm in the pre-Exilic period, and he links it with the Covenant Festival, 'when the accession to the throne of both the heavenly King and the earthly king were celebrated'.

The metre of the Psalm is predominantly 3 + 3 in verses 16–45, and 4 + 4 in the remainder.

Maskil: see Introduction, p. 47.

Ethan the Ezrahite: a man of this name was a sage in Solomon's time (1 Kg. 4:31); in 1 Chr. 15:17,19 it is the name of a Levitical singer.

THE HYMN IN PRAISE OF YAHWEH **1–18**

1. thy steadfast love, O LORD: reading *ḥᵃsāḏeḵā* for M.T. *ḥasᵉḏê*, following LXX and Theod, while M.T. has 'the acts of devotion of Yahweh'. For *ḥeseḏ* ('steadfast love'), see on 26:3; the plural form, *ḥasᵉḏê*, is used in 107:43 of Yahweh's acts of salvation (also in 17:7, 25:6; Isa. 63:7), and in Isa. 55:3 it alludes to the evidences of Yahweh's Covenant loyalty to David (cf. 101:1).
for ever: the word *ʿôlām* (see on 9:5) is used as an adverbial accusative. It denotes not so much eternity in our sense of the word, as a boundless time referring either to the distant past, or to the time to come. Sometimes the extent of *ʿôlām* may be limited by the context: a man may remain a slave for ever (Dt. 15:17), i.e. as long as he lives; at other times *ʿôlām* indicates a long life, as in 1 Kg. 1:31, where Bathsheba says to David: 'May my lord King David live for ever!' Johnson (*VITAI*, p. 97) takes this expression as a wish that the King may ever 'enjoy good health' and 'unceasing prosperity' (p. 98). For a more detailed discussion of this word, see T. Boman, *Hebrew Thought Compared with Greek* (1960), pp. 151–4; J. Barr, *Biblical Words for Time* (*SBT* 33, 1962), pp. 65–70, 85–90.
I will proclaim: lit. 'I will make known' in my songs of praise. Cf. 71:15, 109:30, 145:21.
thy faithfulness: for *ʾᵉmûnāh*, see on 36:5. The expression is synonymous with 'thy steadfast love', and probably suggests Yahweh's loyalty to his Covenant promises, both to the nation and to the King.
to all generations: better 'through all generations'; this is parallel to 'for ever' (verse 1*a*), meaning in this context 'as long as I live'.

2. For: the Hebrew *kî* introduces the main part of the hymn which provides the explanation and motivation for the praise. This *kî* is also one of the main characteristics of a hymn (cf. Gunkel, *EP*, pp. 42f.). M.T. reads 'For I said', while *RSV* and others transfer *ʾāmartî* ('I said') to verse 3 (changing it into *ʾāmartā* ('you have said'), following LXX, S, and V).
thy steadfast love: the pronoun 'thy' is not expressed in M.T.,

but the parallel line justifies its addition on the principle of the double-duty suffix (see on 3:3).

was established for ever: lit. 'shall be built up' (*AV*, *RV*), i.e. shall be maintained. This expression probably prepares the way for verse 4. 'For ever' has as its counterpart 'the heavens' in the next line, and both indicate the enduring quality of Yahweh's faithfulness and loyalty.

is firm as the heavens: reading *tikkôn* (following LXX, Sym, and V) for M.T. *tāḵīn*, ('(as for the heavens) you shall establish (your faithfulness in them)').

3. Thou hast said is transposed here from verse 2*a* (see above).

I have made a covenant: lit. 'I have cut . . . .'. This is a technical term for the making of a Covenant, and it refers to the ritual in which the sacrificial animal was cut into two in order that the contracting parties might pass through it (see Gen. 15:10; Jer. 34:18). This symbolic action may have contained an implicit curse: 'Let me so die if I do not keep the Covenant'. Therefore Yahweh, too, threatens the Covenant breakers, saying that he will make them 'like the calf which they cut in two and passed between its parts' (Jer. 34:18). The 'Covenant' (see on 55:20) refers to the Davidic covenant and not to the Sinaitic (see D. J. McCarthy, *CBQ*, XXVII (1965), pp. 235–40). It is possible that both these Covenants may have been similar in form to the vassal-treaties (cf. 132:12), although a number of scholars have argued that the Davidic covenant was not dependent upon the fidelity of the ruling Kings (cf. R. E. Clements, *Abraham and David* (*SBT*, 2nd ser., 5, 1967), pp. 47–60; Ringgren, *IR*, pp. 119f.).

my chosen one: the Davidic king stands in a closer relation to Yahweh than any other person, for he has been particularly chosen by the deity (and not by the people). Therefore *bᵉḥîrî* ('my chosen one') may serve as a royal epithet (cf. 2 Sam. 21:6 (*RSVm*); Ps. 106:23; 11QPsᵃ Ps. 151 A, verse 6; *TDNT*, IV, pp. 155–9). In the *OT*, election or divine choosing is for a particular task or service, and therefore it is linked with certain conditions (cf. P. Altmann, *Erwählungstheologie und Universalismus im Alten Testament* (*BZAW*, 92, 1964), pp. 30f.). A repudiation of the responsibilities could imply that the chosen person (or people) has forfeited his election (see H. H. Rowley, *The Biblical Doctrine of Election* (1950), pp. 95–120); see on 105:43.

I have sworn: i.e. I have taken a vow, the terms of which are stated in verse 4. This promise is irrevocable, but it can be repudiated by the recipient for himself (see verses 30ff.).

my servant: the Hebrew *ʿebed* can be used as an honorific title (see on 36:1), but it is by no means an exclusively royal title (cf. Ringgren, *IR*, p. 232). Similarly also in the Ugaritic texts (cf. *DOTT*, p. 120) King Keret is called 'servant of El'. (For further references, see G. W. Ahlström, *Psalm 89* (1959), p. 49.)

4. **your throne** is parallel to 'your descendants', and both refer to the Davidic dynasty; see on 93:2. The emphasis upon the Davidic covenant is a characteristic of this Psalm. Weiser (*POTL*, p. 591) argues that the disastrous events of the writer's time called in question particularly the promise to the house of David, and this accounts for the special stress on this subject.

Selah: see Introduction, pp. 48f.

5. **Let the heavens praise:** a renewed introit to the hymn; the characteristic *kî* ('for') in verse 6 introduces the further motivation. 'The heavens' (see on 19:1) may signify the 'angelic host' (Cohen), or the 'heavenly beings' (so Davies).

thy wonders: for *peleʾ*, see on 77:11. This 'wonder' or 'wondrous work' may be understood as the giving of the Davidic covenant (so Ahlström), while Kissane suggests the settlement in Canaan; Boylan thinks of 'the wondrous deeds which Yahweh performed for Israel and David' (*PSVP*, II, p. 103).

the assembly of the holy ones: i.e. of the heavenly beings, such as are mentioned, e.g., in 82:1. In the Ugaritic texts the 'holy ones' are synonymous with 'gods' (cf. *Baal* III*, B:18f.; *CML*, p. 78f.; *ANET*, p. 130a). 'Assembly' (*ḳāhāl*) is often rendered in LXX by *ekklēsia*, but occasionally by *sunagōgē*. *Ḳāhāl* may denote a gathering of people either for a good or a bad purpose (cf. 26:5). The assembly can be composed of the community in general (149:1), or of a particular class of people, such as the prophets (1 Sam. 19:20) or the evildoers (26:5). In the Psalter *ḳāhāl* often signifies the worshipping community, or the cultic assembly (cf. Barr, *SBL*, pp. 119–29). In this Psalm the *ḳāhāl* consists of the divine beings or the holy ones (cf. 34:9 (M.T. 10); see on 82:1, and M. Noth, 'The Holy Ones of the Most High', *LPOE*, pp. 215–28).

6. This verse emphasizes the incomparability of Yahweh. Nothing and no one in heaven or among the heavenly beings is equal to him, and none of them has a name; therefore they have

no claim to receive worship (see Vriezen, *RAI*, p. 36). Other peoples may worship the sun, the moon, and the stars; but, in fact, they were made by God in order to serve *him* (see verse 11).
the heavenly beings: lit. 'sons of gods' (*RSVm*), i.e. those belonging to the class of gods (*ʾēlîm*); see on 29:1. In 1QS xi:8 there is a reference to 'the sons of the heavens', which may be a periphrasis of our phrase.

7. a God feared: i.e. a God regarded with awe.
the council of the holy ones (cf. 1QH iv:25) is synonymous with 'the assembly of the holy ones' (verse 5*b*) and 'the heavenly beings' (verse 6*b*). All three expressions refer to the angelic beings who act as servants of God. For *sôḏ*, ('council'), see on 25:14.
great: (so also *NEB*.) This is the rendering of the perplexing *rabbāh*, which may be regarded as a verb (third person feminine singular) or as a feminine adjective. Dahood (*PAB*, I, p. 26) takes it as an archaic third person masculine singular verb ('He is great'), while some others emend, reading either *raḇ* ('great', masculine singular; so LXX and S) or *raḇ hûʾ* ('He is great').
terrible: better 'awe-inspiring, awesome'; for *nôrāʾ*, see on 65:5.

8. Lord God of hosts: see on 24:10, 59:5.
who is mighty as thou art, O Lord: or (following LXX and V) 'who is like you? (You are) mighty, O Lord' (similarly *PNT*). The incomparability of Yahweh finds some parallels in the literature of other peoples. It is said of Shamash, the Mesopotamian sun-god: 'no one among the gods is equal with thee' (ANET, p. 387a). (For other references, see Ahlström, pp. 66f.) The Hebrew *ḥᵃsîn* ('mighty') is a *hapax legomenon* in the *OT*, and it is usually regarded as an Aramaism, although it does not necessarily indicate a late date for the composition of the Psalm. 'Lord' is a translation of *yāh*, a shorter form of the divine name 'Yahweh' (*yhwh*); see on 68:4.
with thy faithfulness: lit. 'and your faithfulness (is).' *PNT* offers a good paraphrase: 'and truth is your garment'. For *ʾᵉmûnāh*, see verse 1.

9. Thou dost rule . . .: Yahweh is the ruler of the raging sea because he is its conqueror; so he has taken over the place which in Canaanite thought belonged to Baal (cf. *CML*, p. 87a, *ANET*, p. 137a). For the mythological significance of the sea, cf. 46:2 (M.T. 3), 74:13. The *exact* relationship between Baal's fight against the Sea and Yahweh's conflict with the primeval waters is uncertain.

when its waves rise: the primeval deep had been defeated by Yahweh, and its waters are now controlled by him: he 'set a bound which they should not pass' (104:9). Sometimes they may show their restlessness, but the command of Yahweh remains valid: 'Thus far shall you come, and no further, and here shall your proud waves be stayed' (Job 38:11).

10. Thou didst crush Rahab: it seems that Rahab is either another name for the Chaos waters or one of the marine monsters (cf. Pope, *JAB*, p. 70; O. Kaiser, *Die Mythische Bedeutung des Meeres in Ägypten, Ugarit und Israel* (*BZAW*, 78 (1959), pp. 142–52). The word is a transliteration of the Hebrew *rahaḇ*, which is usually linked with the verb 'to act arrogantly, boisterously' (cf. *BDB*, p. 923a). This mythological dragon was defeated by Yahweh (Job 26:12; Isa. 51:9), in spite of her helpers (Job 9:13); the latter are reminiscent of the helpers of Tiamat, the Babylonian Chaos-monster, who marched at her side when she fought Marduk (see *ANET*, p. 67a). The actual relationship between the story of Rahab and the Babylonian creation myth is not clear; both may originate from a motif common to the peoples of the ancient Near East. 'Rahab' can also be used as a symbol or nickname (?) of Egypt (87:4; Isa. 30:7; cf. Ezek. 29:3, 32:2).

with thy mighty arm: i.e. with your own power. The Hebrew *zᵉrôaᶜ* ('arm') is a common metaphor for 'might' (Exod. 6:6; 1 Sam. 2:31), 'protective strength' (Dt. 33:27). See on 37:17.

11. To Yahweh belong the heavens and the earth, i.e. the whole universe, because he has created it (cf. Gen. 14:19; Exod. 19:5; Ps. 50:12). For 'world' (*tēḇēl*), see on 24:1.

12. The north and the south as the two extremities of the world probably denote the whole universe, i.e. the world from end to end. On the other hand, there may be some mythological associations: 'north' (*ṣāp̄ôn*) was known in the Ugaritic myths as the dwelling place of Baal (or Hadad); see on 48:2. In Jos. 13:27 'Zaphon' is a place on the east bank of Jordan in the territory of Gad, but this location has no bearing on this verse. The word could be used also with a religious significance in the *OT* (cf. 48:2 (M.T. 3); Isa. 14:13), and it may denote the abode of God. Ahlström (op. cit., p. 74) suggests that *ṣāp̄ôn* can also mean 'heavens' (cf. Job 26:7; Isa. 14:13) because the mountain of God, the Temple, and the heavens are all closely associated, since they signify the dwelling place of God. In the *OT*, *ṣāp̄ôn* can serve as a geographical term: 'north'; this usage is easily understandable, because Mount Zaphon was directly N. of Palestine, and therefore 'Zaphon' could indicate the north. The derivation of *ṣāpôn* is not certain; it may be derived either from *ṣ-p-h* ('to look out'), or from *ṣ-p-n* ('to hide').

In view of the possible mythological significance of 'north', one might expect a similar association in connection with the 'south' (*yāmîn*, 'the right', as one faced eastwards); but there is little evidence for it. Schmidt (*PHAT*, p. 167) identifies it with the Amanus (range) (cf. Ca. 4:8; also *Verbum Domini*, XLI (1963), pp. 11–20). More likely is the suggestion that verse 12 is arranged chiastically, and that therefore 'north' is synonymous with Mount Hermon, while 'south' refers to Tabor geographically S. of Hermon. LXX (similarly V) reads *thalassan* ('sea', a translation of *yām*) for 'south' (*yāmîn*) but M.T. offers the more likely version. Dahood (*PAB*, II, p. 308) and *NEB* read 'Amanus' for 'the south'.

Tabor is a mountain some 1,850 feet high, situated at the north-east corner of the plain of Jezreel; it may well have been an Israelite cultic centre (cf. Hos. 5:1). For more details, see Kraus, *WI*, pp. 165–72.

Hermon is one of the highest peaks of the Anti-Lebanon range in ancient Syria (see on 42:6). Theoretically it may have been a place of Yahweh's worship, but here there is nothing to suggest it. In Jg. 3:3 it is called Baal-Hermon, which links it with the Baal cult.

Verse 12 reaffirms that Yahweh is the creator of the world, and that even Tabor and Hermon will praise *him*, and no other god.

13. mighty arm: see verse 10; cf. 1QM xi:4.

thy hand may mean 'your left hand', parallel to 'your right hand' (see on 74:11).

high thy right hand: this is probably symbolic of Yahweh's might, and may be similar in meaning to Exod. 6:6 '(and I will redeem you) with an outstretched arm (and with great acts of judgment)'. Cf. Dt 5:15, 7:19, 26:8.

14. Righteousness (see on 33:5) and **justice** (see on 36:6, 119:7) characterize Yahweh's rule: they form the foundation on which his kingship is established (see on 97:2). Some scholars have pointed to various Near Eastern parallels (cf. Kraus, *PBK*, p. 621) where righteousness and justice appear as divine beings. Ahlström (p. 78) regards them as hypostases which may, perhaps, be identified with the cherubim or seraphim, but this seems less likely; see *VT*, VIII (1958), pp. 426ff.

steadfast love (see on 26:3) and **faithfulness** (see on 25:5) also appear to be personified 'as angels attending God's Presence' (Kirkpatrick, *BPCB*, p. 535). These two words are frequently associated in the Psalter (see on 25:10; cf. 40:10,11 (M.T. 11, 12), 57:3 (M.T. 4), 61:7 (M.T. 8), 115:1, 138:2). That these two hypostases (as well as 'righteousness and justice') were actually represented in the Temple and its ritual, or that they were identified with the four beings envisaged in Ezek. 1:4–25, is doubtful (cf. Ahlström, p. 82).

15. Blessed . . .: see on 1:1. The 'people' (*ᶜam*) is the cultic community (see on 66:8), which is identical with Israel.

who know the festal shout: the Hebrew *teʳûᶜāh* ('festal shout') is the noise of shouting, or the noise created by the musical instruments (see on 27:6 and P. Humbert, *La 'terouᶜa': analyse d'un rite biblique* (1946)). In this context *teʳûᶜāh* is the response of the people; they know not only *what* to shout ('Hallelujahs' (?), so Gunkel, or 'Yahweh is king' (?)) but they have also experienced the *significance* of the acclamation. They praise Yahweh, not simply because it is the right thing to do, but because they are overwhelmed by his goodness and majesty.

who walk . . .: i.e. who enjoy Yahweh's favour and blessings. For the phrase 'the light of thy countenance', see on 4:6 (cf. 44:3 (M.T. 4); Prov. 16:15).

16. who exalt in thy name: the Hebrew *gîl* ('exult, rejoice') may originally have been associated with cultic dancing (cf. Isa. 9:3). In the present context it may mean to utter exclamations of joy, and to make mention of Yahweh's name (see on 20:1; cf. 9:14 (M.T. 15), 13:5, 21:1 (M.T. 2)).

all the day: probably 'always' (cf. 52:1 (M.T. 3); Isa. 65:5).

and extol thy righteousness: M.T. has 'and through your righteousness they are exalted' (similarly LXX and V). Dahood (*PAB*, II, p. 315) takes the verb *r-w-m* to mean both 'to rejoice' and 'to be high'; if so, verse 16*b* could be rendered 'they rejoice in your righteousness' (see on 33:5); cf. L. Kopf, *VT*, IX (1959), p. 249.

17. the glory of their strength: or, '(you are) their glorious strength' (cf. *GK* 128p). For *tip'eret*, ('glory, splendour, beauty'), see on 71:8.

our horn is exalted: i.e. our strength is made mighty. 'Horn' is used as a symbol of strength (see on 75:4). In Canaanite religion

'Bull' can be a divine epithet (see J. Gray, *The Legacy of Canaan* (*SVT*, 5 (1957), p. 117), but it is not certain that this fact has any bearing upon the above idiom (cf. Ahlström, p. 93).

18. our shield belongs to the LORD: better 'our shield is indeed Yahweh', taking the preposition *l*ᵉ ('(belongs) to') as an emphatic *lāmeḏ* (so G. R. Driver, Johnson, *et al.*); the same may be true of *l*ᵉ in verse 18*b*. For the emphatic *lāmeḏ*, see F. Nötscher, *VT*, III (1953), pp. 379f.; M. Dahood, *Biblica*, XXXVII (1956), p. 339. 'Shield' (*māḡēn*) and its possible meaning 'suzerain' (so Dahood) is discussed on 3:3.

our king: better, 'the Holy One of Israel is truly our king' (see above). For the divine title 'Holy One of Israel', see on 71:22. A number of scholars interpret this verse similarly to *RSV* (so Oesterley, Kissane, Cohen, Kraus), in which case the King is the Davidic ruler who is described as the shield or protector of his people. In *NEB* the reference is to Yahweh.

THE COVENANT WITH DAVID **19–37**

This section is often viewed as an expansion or paraphrase of the words of the prophet Nathan to David in 2 Sam. 7:4–17 (cf. v. Rad, *PHOE*, p. 227), yet the exact relationship between the Psalm and the oracle is not clear. The prose passage in 2 Sam. may be dependent upon this section of the Psalm (so R. H. Pfeiffer), or vice versa. Probably both passages go back to a common source, but in their present form they may represent the end products of a process of successive elaboration of the original dynastic oracle. See further Johnson, *SKAI*, p. 101.

19. speak in a vision: i.e. by a prophet. The allusion is most likely to the prophecy of Nathan (cf. 2 Sam. 7:4) unless the writer had in mind the successive repetitions and elaborations of the basic promise to David, by generations of cultic prophets. This finds a slight support in the term **thy faithful one,** for which M.T. has 'your faithful ones' (*RV* 'thy saints') which may be a fitting description of the prophets (*NEB* 'thy faithful servants'; so also Kraus, *PBK*, p. 622). The singular 'faithful one' (*ḥāsîḏ*) (see on 30:4) is usually taken to refer to David (rather than to Nathan), or to the Davidic king.

and say: Dahood (*UHP*, p. 40) regards the conjunction 'and' as a pleonastic or emphatic *wāw* (cf. P. Wernberg-Møller, *JJS*, III (1958), pp. 321–6), and renders: 'Once you spoke in a vision, to your faithful ones indeed you said'.

the crown: reading *nēzer* instead of M.T. *ᶜēzer* ('help') (*AV*, *RV*). It has been suggested by Dahood (*UHP*, p. 68) that *ᶜēzer* in this verse is a cognate of the Ugaritic *ǵzr*, ('boy'), hence: 'I have set a boy above a strong man'. No emendation (such as in *RSV*) seems required: either we may accept the suggestion based on the Ugaritic *ǵzr*, or we may render literally: 'I have set (i.e. granted) help to a fearless man' (for *gibbôr* ('mighty man'), see on 33:16). Most scholars interpret *gibbôr* as referring to the King (cf. 1 Sam. 16:18; Isa. 9:5 (M.T. 4)).

one chosen from the people: (so also LXX and V) the Hebrew *bāḥûr* may also mean 'a young man' (so T; cf. verse 3) and we could translate: 'I have exalted a young man (or 'a youth') above (or 'from among') the people'. Dahood (*PAB*, II, p. 316) thinks that *ᶜam* (*RSV* 'people') means here 'a hero', but this seems unlikely.

20. I have anointed him: by means of Samuel; see on 2:2. From now on the chosen one becomes the anointed one (*māšîaḥ*). According to Mowinckel (*He That Cometh* (1956), p. 78) the anointing and installation of the King are identical with his adoption as Yahweh's son, whose person is henceforth inviolable; he is also equipped to be the ruler over all earthly kings (see verse 27). From 2 Sam. 7:14 and Ps. 89:30ff. (M.T. 31ff.) we see that the promises also contained certain conditions; but, irrespective of the failures of the individual Davidic kings, the Covenant with the Davidic dynasty is an eternal one (see verses 33–7; cf. Lk. 1:32f.; Ac. 13:23; Rom. 1:3. Cf. also L. Schmidt, *Menschlicher Erfolg und Jahwes Initiative* (*WMANT*, 38, 1970), p. 175).

my holy oil is a phrase found only here in the *OT*; for a similar expression cf. Exod. 30:25. See on 104:15; E. Kutsch, *Salbung als Rechtsakt* (*BZAW*, 87, 1963), pp. 1–6.

21. my hand is synonymous with 'my arm', and both are used as symbols of the divine might and power; they represent Yahweh in action (see on 119:173; cf. 37:17). Yahweh will be the King's constant support and strength.

22. shall not outwit him: the derivation of the Hebrew *yaššiᵓ* is not clear. *BDB* (p. 673b) takes it from *n-š-ᵓ* I ('to be a creditor'), rendering '. . . shall not make exactions of him' (similarly LXX), while McCullough, Ahlström, *et al.* derive it from *n-š-ᵓ* II ('to deceive'). *KBL* (p. 951a) links it with *š-w-ᵓ* ('to treat badly'). The general meaning is, however, clear: no enemy shall have the better of him, as suggested by the parallel line. *NEB:* 'shall strike at him'.

23. I will crush: the verb *k-t-t* means 'to crush fine', and it serves as a metaphor for a complete destruction (cf. Dt. 9:21; Isa. 30:14).

strike down: the Hebrew verb *n-g-p* can sometimes be used of an ox goring another ox (Exod. 21:35), or some other animal or person, yet this is not sufficient evidence for assuming a deliberate reference to the so-called bull-symbolism (see verse 17; Ahlström, p. 107). In the *OT* the verb *n-g-p* usually denotes 'to strike, smite' (e.g. in Exod. 12:23; 1 Sam. 25:38; Ps. 91:12).

24. Yahweh's faithfulness (see on 36:5) or trustworthiness, and steadfast love (see on 26:3) or his loyalty to the Covenant promises, will be the King's daily experience (see verse 28).

in my name: or 'through my name' (*NEB*) (see on 20:1).

his horn: or, his strength; see verse 17.

25. his hand: that is, the King's might or dominion. The Hebrew *yāḏ* probably refers to 'his left hand' (see on 74:11), being parallel to 'his right hand'.

the sea . . . the rivers may denote the boundaries of the Davidic kingdom. The 'sea' could well be the Mediterranean, and the 'rivers' might allude to the Euphrates (and its channels?) and the Tigris (so Kissane; cf. 72:8, 80:11 (M.T. 12)), or to the Euphrates and the Nile (so Leslie). On the other hand, the sea (see on 46:2, 74:13) and the rivers (see on 46:4, 72:8) mentioned in this verse may have a mythological significance (cf. Johnson, *SKAI*, p. 24, n.2). Yahweh has established the earth upon the seas and the rivers (ocean currents?), as in 24:2, and he has dominion over the whole universe; consequently, the King, as Yahweh's adopted son or his first-born (see verse 27), has been promised kingship over the whole world (cf. Mowinckel, *He That Cometh* (1956), p. 67). It is unlikely that David is equated with God, or that the former is described as victor over the Chaos waters (cf. Kraus, *PBK*, p. 623; Ringgren, *IR*, p. 226, n.18). The King's world dominion is already experienced in the cult and it will become a universal fact in God's own time.

26. Thou art my Father: i.e. my Father by adoption (2:7). Cf. 'I will be his father, and he shall be my son' (2 Sam. 7:14). Pedersen (*ILC*, III–IV (1953), p. 443) argues that, although the King is inferior to God, 'there is no fixed line between them; they are of the same kin'. There is little doubt that, by the anointing, the King had been lifted above the sphere of ordinary existence; he had been brought into a special relationship with God, but it is less likely that Yahweh and the King were of the *same* kin (see verse 19). The King remained a *man* exalted above his contemporaries by his *office*, and in a sense he was no more than *primus inter pares* (so Johnson, *SKAI*, p. 27), although his relationship to God was closer than that of any other person because of his God-given task.

Rock of my salvation: cf. 18:2 (M.T. 3), 95:1; the same phrase is found in Dt. 32:15. Ahlström (p. 115) thinks that the Semitic tendency to associate deities with mountains, rocks, and stones provides not only a metaphor for strength and permanence, but also indicates that the origin of this concept is the mountain of God, or some divine symbol of stone (cf. G. A. Danell, *Studies in the Name Israel in the Old Testament* (1946), p. 39).

27. the first-born: in Exod. 4:22 it is the people of Israel that is called Yahweh's 'first-born son', while in Jer. 31:9 the expression is used of Ephraim. Obviously it does not denote a physical relationship, such as may have been believed to exist between the Moabites and their god (i.e. from the Moabite point of view; cf. S. R. Driver, *The Book of Exodus* (*Camb.B.*, 1911), p. 32), but it describes the privileged position of the King and the people of Israel. The first-born son enjoyed certain privileges: he received a double share of the inheritance (Dt. 21:17), and eventually he became the head of the family. Of more importance here is the fact that the first-born *belonged* to God (cf. Exod. 13:2, 12f.; Num. 3:13) and was holy (in the *OT* sense of the word). In the Babylonian Creation Epic it is Marduk who is called the first-born of gods (*ANET*, p. 66a (iv:20)).

the highest of the kings: the Davidic king is represented as the *ᶜelyôn* of kings. Although *ᶜelyôn* is frequently used as a divine title (see on 18:13, 46:4, 47:2), its application to the anointed one of God, does not suggest that he is divine. As Yahweh is the Most High above all beings (including the host of heaven), so his adopted son, the King, is the highest of all earthly kings.

28. My steadfast love: (see verse 24) cf. Isa. 55:3. This verse emphasizes the permanence of the God-established Covenant (see on 55:20), or the relationship between Yahweh and the King (see also verses 4, 21, 24, 29, 33–37).

29. his line: lit. 'his seed' or 'his descendants'. The parallelism with **his throne** (see on 93:2) suggests that the actual meaning is 'his dynasty'. Dahood (*UHP*, p. 67) renders verse 29*a*: 'And I shall set his offspring upon his seat', taking *ʿaḏ* (*RSV* **ever**) as 'throne, seat'.

the days of the heavens: this phrase is a *hapax legomenon* in the *OT*, but, for a similar idea, see Dt. 11:21; Ps. 72:5, 89:36f. (M.T. 37f.). The 'days of our years' is a short period of time (90:10) but the **days of the heavens** denotes time that is practically endless (see verse 37). This is not to say that the heavens were thought to be eternal (cf. Isa. 65:17, 66:22), but that they were symbolic of all that was lasting. Their durability ultimately depended upon the will of God, and not upon some inherent indestructibility (cf. Isa. 34:4, 51:6; Mt. 24:35; Mk 13:31; Lk. 21:33).

30–1. These verses state the conditions which are implicit in the election of the Davidic dynasty. Each King must keep Yahweh's law (see on 119:1) and walk in his ordinances (for *mišpāṭ*, see on 119:7). In this context these two parallel terms are synonymous with the **statutes** (*ḥuḳḳôṯ*, see on 119:5,) and **commandments** (*miṣwōṯ*, see on 119:6). All these terms seem to refer to the Covenant obligations.

32. their transgression: or 'their rebellion' (see on 32:1).

the rod: for *šēḇeṭ* see on 23:4, 45:6. Occasionally deities were depicted by the ancients as possessing a short rod or mace (see G. E. Wright, *Biblical Archaeology* (1962), p. 109, fig. 65).

their iniquity, like **their transgression,** is singular in M.T., while the versions (LXX, S, and V) have the plural form in each case. In M.T. the reference is not to some minor sin or failure but to the breach of the Covenant. Consequently the guilty King will be punished, but the Covenant with the Davidic house stands unchanged because God is faithful to his promises (see verses 33f.). By implication this means that God's relationship with the people also remains unaltered, although the evildoers receive their due reward. Yahweh chastises the Covenant breakers, but he refuses to break the established Covenant (see on verse 3); this is stressed again in verses 33f.

34. the word that went forth: cf. Num. 30:12; Dt. 8:3, 23:23; Patton, *CPBP*, p. 22. Ahlström (p. 127) sees in the promise of Yahweh his creative word. As the promise is uttered, the Covenant with the Davidic house is established or created. This may be so, because the divine word is a creative word.

35–7. These verses emphasize still further the *promises* to the Davidic dynasty.

35. Once for all: or 'One thing'.
by my holiness: Yahweh as the highest authority in the universe swears by his own holiness (cf. Am. 4:2) or by himself (Gen. 22:16; Exod. 32:13; Isa. 45:23; Am. 6:8). In Jer. 44:26 he utters an oath by his 'great name', and in Isa. 62:8 by 'his right hand and by his mighty arm'. Essentially, all these expressions are synonymous, and they suggest that the divine promises are guaranteed by God's own character.
I will not lie: i.e. Yahweh's promises are no empty words, or expressions of falsehood (cf. 132:11).

36. his throne: see on 93:2. His dynastic line will be practically timeless, like the sun and the moon and the very skies.

37. it shall stand firm . . .: reading *bᵉᶜôḏ haššaḥaḳ* ('while the heavens') for *wᵉᶜēḏ baššaḥaḳ* ('and a witness in the skies'); *RSV* also supplies the verb. M.T. could be rendered 'and (as) a faithful witness in heaven' (*AV*; similarly LXX, S, and V). This 'witness' may refer to the moon (so G. W. Anderson), while Ahlström takes it as the rainbow (cf. Gen. 9:12–17) symbolizing the unbreakable bond between Yahweh and his chosen King.
Selah: see Introduction, pp. 48f.

THE LAMENT OVER THE SERVANT OF YAHWEH **38–45**

38. But now thou hast cast off: or 'Yet you have spurned' (see on 44:9). *RSV* reads *wᵉᶜattāh* ('But now') for M.T. *wᵉʾattāh* ('Yet you' (emphatic)), which seems preferable (so *NEB*). The verb *z-n-ḥ* is often found in laments (cf. 43:2, 44:23 (M.T. 24), 60:1 (M.T. 3), 74:1, 77:7 (M.T. 8), 88:14 (M.T. 15)), and it suggests a separation from God, if not a broken Covenant relationship. The object of the verb is usually the people of Israel; only here is it used of the King.

39. Thou hast renounced: Hebrew *n-ʾ-r* is found only twice in the *OT*, here and in Lam. 2:7. *BDB* (p. 611) gives it the connotation: 'to abhor, spurn'; Ahlström suggests 'to break' (p.131). Although the exact meaning of the verb is not certain, the general sense is clear: God has repudiated or broken his Covenant with his servant, the King (see on 36:1).
his crown: the verb *n-z-r* means 'to dedicate, consecrate' and the noun *nēzer* may denote 'consecration' as well as a 'crown' (i.e. the sign of one's consecration; cf. Snaith, *LN*, p. 204). *Nēzer* is usually used of the royal and priestly crowns (cf. 132:18), and it signifies not only the wearer's authority but also the sanctity of

his office. Yet Yahweh has dishonoured the crown, or office, of the Davidic king, because the latter has obviously dishonoured his divine sovereign; therefore the misfortunes are the direct result of God's wrath (verses 38 and 46). In Jer. 13:18f. the defiling of the crown is associated with the Exile (cf. Lam. 5:16; Ezek. 21:26f.). This verse is not a contradiction of the previous promises of Yahweh; rather it is an illustration of the punishment threatened in verses 30ff. The Covenant may be broken or repudiated by a particular King, but the promises of Yahweh are still valid for the Davidic *house*; otherwise there would be little point in appealing to the oath given to David (verse 49).

40. all his walls: Ahlström (p. 133) sees here an allusion to the walls of the vineyards (cf. Jer. 49:3), while Oesterley thinks of the walls of the sheepfold which protect the flock, i.e. the nation of Israel. Probably the reference is simply to the defences of the land, which are paralleled by the 'strongholds' in verse 40*b*. So the whole verse depicts the overthrow of the country.

41. despoil him: since the destiny of the nation and that of its king are inseparably linked together for better or worse, the King can symbolize the whole land. On the other hand, it is possible that this and the following verses do not speak about historical events but rather of the ritual humiliation of the King (so Johnson, Ahlström).

the scorn of his neighbours: the noun *ḥerpāh* is often found in the Psalter, with different shades of meaning, but it denotes essentially 'scorn', 'reproach' (see on 119:22). 'Neighbours' (*šᵉḵēnîm*) may refer either to the 'next-door dwellers', or to those in adjacent countries (e.g. in Edom, Moab, Ammon; so Deissler). If the Psalm describes a past event, the reference is probably to foreign neighbours (cf. 44:14 (M.T. 15), 79:4, 80:6 (M.T. 7); Lam. 2:15); but if the Psalm is understood as part of the ritual drama, then the 'neighbours' might be Israelites (symbolizing foreigners?).

42. the right hand of his foes: Yahweh has exalted 'the right hand' (see on 20:6), or the might, of the enemies, and he has made them victorious (cf. Lam. 2:17). Consequently the adversaries rejoice (verse 42*b*), as in Lam. 2:17 (cf. Ps. 35:26).

43. the edge of his sword: lit. 'the rock of his sword' (so Hengstenberg). Eerdmans (*The Hebrew Book of Psalms* (*OTS*, 4, 1947), p. 425) is probably right in connecting the origin of this expression with the time when knives of flint were widely used (cf.

G. E. Wright, p. 121, fig. 73). The rock or flint would form the cutting edge, and at a later time the expression could have been used of the edge of any sword. G. R. Driver (*JTS*, XLV (1944), pp. 13f.) associates the Hebrew *ṣūr* ('rock') with the Akkadian *ṣarāru*, *ṣirru*, 'to gleam, flash'; hence we could render: 'his flashing sword'. Kraus (*PBK*, p. 615) follows Duhm in reading *miṣṣar* (for *ṣûr*), 'from the oppressor'. The expression 'to turn back one's sword' means to make ineffective one's military strength, and the same idea is expressed by the next line (verse 43*b*): the King and his armies have been rendered unable to stand their ground in the battlefield (or in the mimed battle of the ritual drama?).

44. **Thou hast removed the sceptre from his hand:** reading *maṭṭeh miyyāḏô* (so Baethgen) for *miṭṭᵉhārô* ('his brightness', so *AVm*); *AV*, following M.T., renders: 'Thou hast made his glory to cease'. Cf. Isa. 14:5. In Ugaritic we find the noun *ṭhr*, meaning 'jewel, gem' (cf. Gordon, *UT*, p. 406a). M.T. is metrically too short, and its present reading may be due to a textual corruption (haplography?). *RP*, amongst others, has: 'his royal sceptre' (i.e. *maṭṭēh hōḏô* for *miṭṭᵉhārô*). A possible parallel is found in the Epilogue of the Code of Hammurabi (see *ANET*, p. 179a (xxvi:50); cf. Ahlström, p. 147).

his throne to the ground: for *kissēʾ* ('throne'), see on 93:2. This expression is synonymous with the defiling of the royal crown (verse 39) and probably suggests that the royal office has ceased to exist (cf. Deissler, *PWdB*, II, p. 184), or that the King has suffered a military reversal (cf. 132:18; *VT*, XI (1961), p. 337).

45. **the days of his youth** may mean that the King has become prematurely old (which may well have been the experience of Jehoiachin; cf. 2 Kg. 24:8–15), or that he has lost his very life (in actual fact (so Olshausen), or symbolically in the cultic drama).

covered him with shame: so *NEB*. *RP* 'brought him early to gray hairs' (reading *śêḇāh* ('gray hairs') for *bûšāh*, ('shame')); similarly Gunkel, Oesterley, *et al.* (cf. Hos. 7:9). Yet M.T. gives a satisfactory sense. Dahood (*PNWSP*, p. 7) renders: 'You covered him with dryness' (lack of sexual vigour?), linking *bûšāh* with the root *y-b-š* ('to be dry').

Selah: see Introduction, pp. 48f.

THE PRAYER FOR DELIVERANCE **46–51**

46. How long: this introduces the transition from the lamentation to the prayer for deliverance. It is sometimes described as the stereotyped sigh of the Psalmists (see on 6:3).

hide thyself: by refusing to help your servant.

How long will thy wrath burn . . .: this second 'how long' is not in M.T., but it is supplied from the context. For a parallel, see 79:5.

47. Remember . . .: for *z-k-r* ('to remember'), see on 79:8. The vocative 'O Lord' (*ʾᵃḏōnāy*) is an emendation of *ʾᵃnî* ('I', see verse 50). Perhaps we should read (following one MS.) 'Remember, how transitory I am' (i.e. *meh ḥāḏēl ʾānî* for M.T. *ʾᵃnî meh ḥālēḏ*), as in 39:4*c* (M.T. 5*c*). Johnson (*SKAI*, p. 103) suggests: 'I am not everlasting', reading *ʾᵃnî meh ḥālēḏ ʿôlām*, and taking *meh* as a negative, and *ḥālēḏ* as 'lasting', following the Arabic usage of the corresponding terms. See also *SVT*, 4 (1956), pp. 12ff.

for what vanity: or 'Is it for nought that . . .' (i.e. *hᵃšāw*, adding *ʿal me(h)* ('for what') to the end of the previous line, and reading it as *ʿôlām*; see above). M.T. may, however, be retained.

all the sons of men: i.e. mankind. Ahlström (p. 158) suggests that it refers to all the previous kings of Judah.

48. What man . . .: *geḇer* ('man') is sometimes taken to allude to the King (cf. Jer. 22:30; Zech. 13:7). For semantic considerations, see Jacob, *TOTe*, pp. 156f.; Barr, *SBL*, pp. 144ff.

and never see death: this expression occurs only here in the *OT* but it is synonymous with 'and never see the Pit' (44:9 (M.T. 10)), i.e. no man can escape death or Sheol-existence (see on 6:5 (M.T. 6), 30:9 (M.T. 10), 40:2 (M.T. 3)).

Who can deliver his soul . . .: that is, his life or himself. Cf. 1 Sam. 19:11; Ps. 116:4; Jer. 48:6. For 'soul', see on 33:19.

Selah: see Introduction, pp. 48f.

49. See verses 2f.

50. how thy servant is scorned: (cf. verse 41) lit. 'the reproach of your servants'. Many MSS. and S read the singular 'your servant', which may refer to the King, while the plural is read by M.T., LXX, and Jerome (cf. verse 19*a*), which may allude to the people (so Cohen; cf. Lam. 3:45f.; Jl 2:17), or it may be a plural of excellence, denoting the King (so Dahood, *PAB*, II, p. 320).

the insults of the peoples: reading *kᵉlimmaṯ* ('insult') for M.T.

kol rabbîm ('all the many'). M.T. may be retained, in which case the word 'reproach' (*ḥerpāh*) should be mentally supplied from the preceding line, as in *AV*, *RV*.

51. they mock the footsteps of thy anointed: the phrase probably means that Yahweh's chosen one is scorned at every step (so Johnson, *SKAI*, p. 104). Kissane (*BP*, p. 414) suggests: '. . . the lot of thy anointed', while Deissler (*PWdB*, II, p. 184) interprets the expression as referring to the historical record of the Davidic dynasty. A similar usage of 'footsteps' is found in 77:19*c* (M.T. 20*c*). The Targum relates verse 51*b* to the delay of the coming of the Messiah, but this is clearly a late interpretation.

THE DOXOLOGY 52

This doxology was intended to mark the end of the third Book of the Psalter, and it was probably not part of the original Psalm.
Blessed be the LORD: see on 28:6, 41:13*a*.
Amen and Amen: see on 41:13.

BOOK IV

Psalm 90 The Eternal God and Mortal Man

This Psalm is generally regarded as a Communal Lament (see Introduction, pp. 37ff.), but some scholars (e.g. Gunkel, Mowinckel) describe it as belonging to a mixed type. Verses 1–2 (some would also add verse 4) form a hymnic introduction, extolling the pre-existent and everlasting God. Verses 3–12 deal with the theme of man's transience which is further aggravated by sin and its consequences. In a way, verses 3–12 take the place of the actual lament, and they are influenced by Wisdom literature. The final part, verses 13–17, expresses a petition and prayer to God.

Some exegetes have made out a reasonable case for the view that Ps. 90 is composed of two independent poems consisting of verses 1–12 and 13–17 respectively. On the other hand, it is not impossible that the Psalm is a unity, although the writer may have used some older material.

As a Lamentation the Psalm was probably used at the service of penitence and intercession (one such occasion is well depicted in Jdt. 4:9–12). The Lament is set against the background of human mortality and sin, but the immediate reason for this prayer is not clear. All we can say is that the community was obviously in some sort of need (see verse 13) and that the unspecified affliction had lasted for quite a while (verse 15).

The Psalm is attributed to Moses, and as such it is unique in the Psalter. Few (e.g. Maclaren) would accept the Mosaic authorship of this lament; most scholars agree that the composition is of a post-Exilic date, late rather than early. The ascription of the Psalm to Moses may be (at least partly) an appreciation of the poem by later generations.

The prevailing metre of the Psalm is 3 + 3.

Prayer: see Introduction, p. 47.

the man of God: see Dt. 31:1; Jos. 14:6. This same expression is not infrequently used of certain prophets, e.g. of Elijah (1 Kg.

17:18,24; 2 Kg. 1:10) and of Elisha (2 Kg. 4: 7, 9, 21, etc.) as well as of David (2 Chr. 8:14; Neh. 12:24,36) and of the angel of Yahweh (Jg. 13:6,8).

CONFIDENCE IN THE EVERLASTING GOD **1–2**

1. Lord: for *ʾaḏōnāy*, see on 77:2. The divine name 'Yahweh' (*yhwh*) (*RSV* 'LORD') occurs only in verse 13. The choice of *ʾaḏōnāy* may be a deliberate one, intended to stress the majesty of Yahweh whose is the earth and all that is in it (cf. 24:1). **dwelling place:** (cf. Dt. 33:27) some MSS. read 'refuge' (*māʿôz*, see on 27:1), which is supported by LXX *kataphugē* ('refuge', so also V); cf. 71:3, 91:9. For *māʿôn* ('dwelling place'), see on 76:2. God has been, and still is, the refuge of his people 'in all generations', i.e. to each successive generation. Kissane (*BP*, p. 422) understands *beḏōr wāḏōr* (*RSV* 'in all generations') as 'in ages past', because verses 7ff. show that Israel had lost Yahweh's favour. If so, verse 1 would not contradict verses 7ff. (see Gunkel, *PGHAT*, p. 399).

2. The Psalmist applies the birth-metaphor to the origin of the mountains (cf. Job 38:8; Prov. 8:25), and consequently the subject of verse 2*b* may be the earth, and not Yahweh, rendering: 'before the earth and the world were in travail (bringing forth the hills)'. The Hebrew verb *ḥ-w-l* is often used of child-birth (cf. 51:5 (M.T. 7); Isa. 26:17, 45:10, 51:2), and it may have a similar meaning in our verse. In Dt. 32:18 Yahweh is described as the one who gave birth to, or brought forth Israel, and it is not impossible that a similar word-picture could be applied to the creation of the world. It is more likely, however, that, although ultimately Yahweh is behind this process of the bringing forth of the mountains (cf. Gen. 1:11, 20), the immediate 'agent' is the earth; see Eichrodt, *TOT*, II, p. 115, n.1; Jacob, *TOTe*, p. 142.

In view of the birth-metaphor, it is doubtful whether the mountains were regarded as 'the most ancient parts of the earth' (Kirkpatrick, *BPCB*, p. 549).

The most important point of verse 2 is not the account of the creation of the universe but the eternal God who, as the creator, precedes the created world, and whose majesty can hardly be grasped by his creatures. For the 'eternity of El', the chief god of the Canaanite pantheon, see Patton, *CPBP*, p. 16. In a sense Yahweh is like El in his 'eternity', but he does not share in the latter's senility (cf. Pope, *EUT*, p. 34).

THE FRAILTY AND SINFULNESS OF MAN 3–12

3. man: *ʾenôš* in this particular context may suggest man in his frailty (see on 8:4), who is both utterly dependent upon God and mortal (cf. 103:15).

to the dust: this is better than 'to destruction' (*AV*, *RV*). Man is a dweller in a 'house of clay' (Job 4:19; cf. Wis. 9:15; 2 C. 5:1), who has been taken from the ground and who must return to it (Gen. 3:19; 1QH x:4, xii:26).

Turn back: there are several possible interpretations of this phrase. The least likely is Rashi's suggestion, adopted by some commentators, that the expression denotes man's return to God (in repentance). More likely is the view that the Psalmist is speaking of a return to life, i.e. of the rise of the new generations (so Luther, Kissane, Westermann); for a remote parallel, see Isa. 41:4. Thus verse 3*a* and *b* would form an antithetic parallelism. The most likely proposal is to take verse 3*a* and *b* as synonymous lines, speaking of man's inevitable return to the dust.

4. a thousand years: i.e. even a thousand years (cf. the longevity of the ancestral fathers in Gen. 5) is a mere nothing in God's sight, so how much more insignificant was 'threescore and ten' years (verse 10). A millennium to God is no more than a **watch in the night** to a man (cf. 2 Pet. 3:8; Sir. 18:10). A night watch was four hours, and to a sleeping man it was as nothing; no allusion to a guard or watchman was intended.

5. Most scholars agree that there is some textual corruption in verses 5f. but the suggested solutions differ considerably.

. . . sweep men away: lit. 'You sweep them away in a downpour' (or 'as by a flood'). Duhm, Kittel, *et al.* read *zeraʿtām* ('you sow them'; Moffatt 'Year by year thou sowest men').

they are like a dream: lit. 'sleep are they'. Some scholars read *šānāh šānāh* ('year by year') for M.T. *šēnāh* ('sleep'), assuming a haplography and a wrong vocalization); if so, the verb *yihyû* ('they are' or 'they become') should be taken with what follows: 'they become like grass (that) passes away' (omitting 'in the morning' (*babbōḵer*) as a dittograph (or gloss) from verse 6).

6. it flourishes and is renewed: the parallelism of verse 6*b* suggests that both verbs in verse 6*a* are most likely synonymous. Therefore 'is renewed' (*ḥālap̄*) cannot very well suggest a change to decay, a passing away (so Ewald, Deissler), but perhaps it could be paraphrased: 'and is soon past its best'. When the evening comes, it fades and withers. For similar descriptions of human existence, see Job 14:1f.; Ps. 103:15f.; Isa. 40:6f.

7. we are consumed by thy anger: or, 'we waste away because of your anger'. The pronoun 'we' refers to the worshipping community and the tragedy is that life is not only very brief but also full of trouble. The background of the divine-human contrast serves to emphasize the gravity of the situation. Unless God pities his erring servants, their span of life is bound to be an unrelieved sequence of toil and trouble (verse 10).

we are overwhelmed: the verb *nibhal* is often used to describe the experience of fear and terror, inspired by an impending misfortune (cf. Jg. 20:41), or divine judgment (Exod. 15:15; Ps. 6:3 (M.T. 4), 83:17 (M.T. 18); Isa. 13:8, 21:3, etc.).

8. our iniquities: for *ᶜāwōn*, see on 32:1; cf. R. Knierim, *Die Hauptbegriffe für Sünde im Alten Testament* (1965), pp. 237–56. Most scholars tend to think that implicit in *ᶜāwōn* is an awareness of the culpability of the action. This may be true in many cases, but not in all instances (cf. 1 Sam. 20:1,8; 2 Sam. 14:32).

our secret sins: i.e. those hidden from our fellow-men, and perhaps even from ourselves (cf. Ringgren, *IR*, p. 140), but known to God, who 'knows the secrets of the heart' (44:21) and from whom no wrong can be hidden (69:5). Mowinckel (PIW, II, p. 12) thinks that the 'secret sins' may include also unwitting violations of taboo. Briggs (following T) suggests 'our youth', but this possibility does not fit the context; a more reasonable proposal is 'the sins of our youth' (cf. Dahood, *PAB*, II, p. 321).

in the light of thy countenance: that is, the secret sins are not concealed from God but they are, so to speak, before his very eyes. Cf. F. Nötscher, *Zur Theologischen Terminologie der Qumran-Texte* (1956), pp. 100f.

9. pass away: lit. 'turn' or 'decline' (cf. Jer. 6:4). Although their day of life is declining towards the darkness of Sheol, there is no relief from trouble, because they live under the shadow of the divine wrath (see on 85:3) and punishment.

come to an end: lit. 'we complete our years', or 'we spend . . .' (so *AV*, *RV*).

like a sigh: our whole life is one long sigh or moan. The Targum has: 'like the breath of mouth', while *AV*, *RV* render: 'a tale (that is told)', which is a less likely rendition.

10. The years of our life: lit. 'The days of our years, in them there are . . .'. Budde *et al.* delete *yᵉmê šᵉnôṯênû* ('the days of our years', a gloss from the previous verse?) and read *śoḇʿām* ('their fill', i.e. their highest limit) for M.T. *ḇāhem* ('in them'). Whether we assume a textual corruption in verse 10 or not, the point seems to be that 'seventy years' could hardly be taken as the normal *average* age (cf. L. Köhler, *Hebrew Man* (1956), pp. 42–6); rather it could be regarded as the normal *limit* of human life, and only a few individuals would live to see their seventieth birthday. In certain exceptional cases man might reach the age of eighty (or even more). When it is said of man: 'his days shall be a hundred and twenty years' (Gen. 6:3), the writer must have had in mind the utmost limit of human life-span. The author of Jubilees 23:15 seems to voice the right interpretation of this verse when he writes that man has done well if he reaches the age of seventy, but he must be a strong (and healthy) man to attain the limit of eighty years (cf. Sir. 18:9).

their span: following the reading of LXX, T, S, and V (i.e. *roḥbām* for M.T. *rohbām* ('pride')). The word is found only here in the *OT*, and it may suggest that even the best years of our life (if they are lived under the wrath of God) are characterized by toil (see on 55:10) and trouble (see on 36:4). The emendation assumed by *RSV* is not imperative.

they are soon gone: the subject must be 'years of our life', and not the trouble and toil (cf. Ec. 6:12).

we fly away: this has nothing to do with the Egyptian idea that the human 'soul' is like a bird (cf. Leslie, *PAP*, p. 252; H. Frankfort, *Ancient Egyptian Religion* (1961), pp. 96ff.). The above metaphor simply describes the swift passing of human life (cf. Job 20:8).

11. The reason why human existence is full of misery is sinfulness; this is not so much a theological statement as a simple observation of humanity. The rhetorical question (cf. Ec. 2:19, 3:21) in verse 11 apparently suggests that no one really pays any attention to the power or triumph (see on 21:1) of God's anger. Weiser (*POTL*, p. 600) points out that 'men hardly ever realize the ultimate relationship between mortality and sin', and therefore they are not deterred from wrong-doing. Leslie (*PAP*, p. 252) renders verse 11*a*: 'Who knows how to meet . . .'.

according to the fear of thee: Gunkel, *RP*, *et al.* read *ûmî rōʾeh ṯōḵ* for M.T. *ûkᵉyirʾāṯᵉḵā*, which could be translated: 'and who regards the effect (of your wrath)?' Another possibility is the emendation *ûmî yārēʾ ṯōḵ* ('and who fears the stroke (or 'effect, fierceness') of . . .?'—so Wellhausen, Nötscher). *RSV* could be understood as '(who considers) according to his reverence for God, the (reasons for the divine) wrath?'; and the answer is 'No one', although this may be taken as a poetical exaggeration. See also *NEB*.

12. to number our days: Delitzsch (*BCP*, III, pp. 57f.) takes this to mean a contemplation of 'the fleeting character and brevity of our life'. Perhaps we should read: 'to apportion our days so as to . . .' (cf. Isa. 65:12); *PNT* paraphrases verse 11*a*: 'make us know the shortness of our life', i.e. make us realize (by counting, by being mindful) how few our days are.
that we may get . . .: lit. 'that we may bring in a heart of wisdom' (for the use of the verb, cf. 2 Sam. 9:10; Hag. 1:6); the expression probably means: 'that we may acquire a good sense (which begins with the fear of Yahweh)' (cf. Dt. 32:29). Some scholars (Kautzsch, Bertholet, Gunkel, *et al.*) read: 'that we might bring wisdom into (our) heart' (i.e. *ballēḇ* for M.T. *lᵉḇaḇ* ('heart of')).

THE PRAYER FOR HELP **13–17**

13. Return, O Lord: that is, cease punishing us (cf. Exod. 32:12) and return to us by helping us (cf. Dt. 32:26). See on 6:4.
How long?: see on 6:3.
Have pity: for the verb *n-ḥ-m*, see on 71:21; its object is the servants of Yahweh, i.e. his Covenant people. *AV*, *RV* render 'and let it repent thee concerning . . .' (cf. van Imschoot, *ThOT*, II, p. 80).

14. Satisfy us . . .: see on 65:4 (cf. 17:15, 63:5 (M.T. 6)). The intervention of God on behalf of his servants is expected 'in the morning', which some exegetes (e.g. Davies, Cohen, Kissane) interpret as 'quickly, soon'. It is more likely, however, that the expression should be taken more literally; see on 46:5.
thy steadfast love: see on 26:3. God's Covenant loyalty brings with it rejoicing and gladness to those who strive to be loyal themselves. This shouting for joy and rejoicing would be heard in particular on occasions of giving thanks in the sanctuary (cf. Rowley, *WAI*, pp. 260f.).

15. Since toil and trouble (see verses 7–10) have been the people's portion for a long time, their prayer is that God may grant them a lasting blessing. Unless they had been oppressed unjustly by some foreign powers, there could be no question of 'compensation' (as suggested by Kissane).

16. thy work: that is, God's work of salvation, his providential intervention (cf. 92:5 (M.T. 6), 95:9; Isa. 52:10) in the life of the nation or of his servants (see on 36:1).

thy glorious power is parallel to 'thy work' in verse 16*a*. The Hebrew *hāḏār* often signifies the majesty that is characteristic of royal power (see on 96:6; cf. 104:1, 111:3). LXX (followed by V) must have misread M.T., rendering: 'guide (their children)'.

17. the favour of the Lord: or 'the graciousness of . . .' which is preferable to 'the beauty of . . .' (*AV*, *RV*). See on 27:4. For 'Lord', see verse 1.

yea, the work of our hands . . .: this is probably a variant (omitted by *NEB*) on the preceding line (or vice versa), or a mere dittograph. The repetition could, however, be part of the technique of the Psalmist. The phrase may refer to the daily work of the people, and is reminiscent of similar Deuteronomic expressions (cf. Dt. 2:7, 14:29, 16:15, etc.).

Psalm 91 If God is on Our Side, Who is Against Us?

This Psalm has two main parts: verses 1–13, which are reminiscent of a Wisdom poem; and verses 14–16, which could be described as a divine promise in the form of an oracle. Oesterley (*TP*, p. 407) regarded the composition as a 'polemic in devotional form, against the means employed to counteract the assaults of demons', while Mowinckel (*PStud.*, III, pp. 102f.) took the Psalm as a part of a larger liturgy, which gave the divine answer to the lamentation and petition of the afflicted man. Perhaps we should follow Schmidt's suggestion (*PHAT*, pp. 171f.) that this Psalm could be associated with the Entrance Liturgies (cf. Ps. 15, 24). It may have been addressed to those admitted into the Temple, and it may have served the purpose both of instruction and of blessing or promise. The pilgrim(s) in need of divine help was advised to trust in Yahweh (verse 2).

The Psalm has no title, but LXX supplies the heading: 'Praise (in the form) of a song, by David', which may be a later addition based on older psalm titles. Most scholars place the composition of this poem in the post-Exilic period. See also *RB*, LXXII (1965), pp. 210–17.

The prevailing metre is 3+3.

THE DIVINE PROTECTION **1–13**

1. He who dwells: less likely, '. . . who sits enthroned' (Eaton, *PTBC*, p. 224). The Hebrew participle *yōšēḇ* may be read as *yēšēḇ* ('he shall dwell', i.e. the one who says to Yahweh: 'My refuge . . .').
the shelter: (see on 119:114), this may allude to the asylum afforded by the sanctuary (cf. 27:5, 31:20 (M.T. 21), 61:4 (M.T. 5)) and to the divine protection in general.
Most High: see on 18:3, 46:4, 47:2.
who abides: lit. 'he shall abide'.
the shadow of the Almighty: this refers to the 'shadow of thy wings' (as in 17:8, 36:7 (M.T. 8), 57:1 (M.T. 2), 63:7 (M.T. 8)); see verse 4*a*. The expression has nothing to do with the 'shadow thrown by the Temple-crowned Mount Zion' (Barnes, *PWC*, II, p. 442), but it may be purely a figure of speech denoting the protection of Yahweh (see on 17:8, 36:7). 'The Almighty' (*šadday*) is an ancient divine title, and it occurs elsewhere in the Psalter only at 68:14 (M.T. 15), q.v. Vriezen (*RAI*, p. 111) argues that 'El Shaddai' possesses not only a protective character but also a fearsome aspect.

2. will say: so *RSV* following LXX, S, and Jerome, in reading *ʾōmēr* for M.T. *ʾōmar* ('I will say').
My refuge: see on 61:3.
my fortress: see on 18:2.
my God: Yahweh is not a god who belongs to the worshipper (as if he existed only for the sake of the devotee), but rather he is the God who is the Lord, not only of the worshipper, but of the whole world.

3. For he: the pronoun is emphatic, suggesting that the deliverance can only come from Yahweh; he alone is the effective helper.
the snare of the fowler: similarly 124:7, 141:9; Hos. 9:8. This expression may imply a man-made threat or evil rather than a natural disaster. For *paḥ* ('snare'), see on 119:110.
from the deadly pestilence: since 'pestilence' is mentioned in verse 6, most exegetes follow LXX, Sym, and S in rendering: 'from the destructive word', which involves an alteration of *middeḇer* ('from the pestilence of') into *midᵉḇar* ('from the word of'; cf. 38:12 (M.T. 13)). The proposed reading could suggest a treacherous plot, slander, or even false accusation. Weiser

(*POTL*, p. 603), following Duhm, emends *middeḇer* into *mibbôr* ('from the pit of').

4. **with his pinions:** this description is obviously a metaphor, and it is doubtful whether any one actually envisaged Yahweh as a being with wings (but cf. Oesterley, *TP*, p. 208). One could, however, *liken* him to an eagle that protects its young (Dt. 32:11; cf. Isa. 31:5; Mt. 23:37; Lk. 13:34). The wings of the cherubim may have been a symbol of protection (so Kraus, *PBK*, p. 637), but the present word-picture may owe its origin to the proverbial care of the mother bird for her chicks.

under his wings: this is a synonym of 'his pinions' (verse 4). See on 17:8, 36:7.

his faithfulness: (see on 25:5). Yahweh's fidelity to his Covenant promises is like the protection given by a shield (see on 35:2) and a buckler. The latter term, *soḥ^erāh*, is a *hapax legomenon* in the *OT*; its cognate in Syriac (*sāḥartā*) means 'a walled enclosure', while T understood the M.T. *soḥ^erāh* as a 'round shield' (*ᶜ^agîlāʾ*), and this may be right. Some scholars (e.g. Dahood) have suggested *ʾammāṯô* ('his arm') for M.T. *ʾ^amittô* ('his faithfulness'; for references, see *TRP*, p. 38); this would provide a better parallel to 'pinions' and 'wings'. *NEB* transposes verse 4c after verse 7.

5. **the terror of the night:** those who trust Yahweh for protection have no need to fear the attacks of human enemies (cf. Ca. 3:8) or demonic powers (be they real or imagined). The latter were believed to exist and to have great power for evil, but Yahweh can set a man free from all terrifying superstitions, and guard him from every threatening reality. It is possible that the particular allusion is to the night-demon, Lilith (see E. Langton, *Essentials of Demonology* (1949), p. 47); but see also *NEB*.

the arrow that flies by day: (sun's rays?). The reference may be to certain sinister forces that cause such illnesses as sunstroke. Both midnight and midday were thought to be potentially dangerous hours, when destructive influences and powers were at work.

6. **the pestilence** may refer to some plague, or to a demon; Oesterley (*TP*, p. 410) suggests the Babylonian pest-demon, Namtar (cf. *ANET*, pp. 108, 109; see also Exod. 12:29; 2 Kg. 19:35). Nötscher (*PEB*, p. 202) thinks that 'pestilence' and 'destruction' are poetical personifications, and do not refer to demons.

the destruction: the Hebrew *ḳeṭeḇ* may refer to a pestilential epidemic (from *ḳ-ṭ-b*, 'to cut off').

that wastes at noonday: rather 'that works (its) ruin . . .' (similarly *NEB*). The verb is probably derived from *š-d-d* ('to despoil, ruin'); LXX must have taken the verb (*yāšûḏ*) as a noun, *wᵉšēḏ* ('and a demon'). M.T. is more likely, but LXX bears a witness to the interpretation of the Psalm at a later time.

7–8. This hyperbolic word-picture reaffirms the current belief in the rewards and punishments in *this* life. It is less likely that the setting of this metaphor is the battlefield, although it may re-echo some aspects of the Exodus traditions (cf. Exod. 12:23, 14:30); or it may have been borrowed from the martial language appropriate to the Royal Psalms (cf. 3:6f. (M.T. 7f.)). The Psalmist stresses that, irrespective of the numerical strength of the adversaries, the godfearing man will be delivered while the wicked will be punished (cf. Prov. 12:21) by means of some plague or misfortune (see verse 10).

but it will not come near you: this is occasionally regarded as a later addition (so Gunkel, Kraus) or as an intrusion from another verse.

You will only look . . .: or, 'You will certainly behold. . .', i.e. it will surely come to pass (cf. 54:7 (M.T. 9)).

and see the recompense . . .: the Psalmist is not inspired by a malicious joy, but by the certainty that God will manifest his justice and righteousness.

9. you have made the LORD your refuge: M.T. has 'you, O LORD, are my refuge'. *TRP* (p. 38) has *ʾāmartā* ('you have said ("Yahweh is my refuge")') for M.T. *ʾattāh* ('you').

the Most High: see on 18:3, 46:4, 47:2.

your habitation: LXX and V may have read *māᶜuzzᵉḵā* ('your stronghold') for M.T. *mᵉᶜônᵉḵā*. The parallelism may favour the former variant.

10. scourge: for the *negāᶜ*, see on 38:11. Here it is probably used of affliction in general, as a parallel to 'evil' in verse 10*a*.

your tent: i.e. your dwelling; this may also include a man's household possessions (see on 61:4).

11. angels: the word *malʾāḵ* ('messenger, angel') is derived from *l-ʾ-k* ('to send'); the verb itself is not found in the *OT*, but it is used in Arabic, Ugaritic, etc. (cf. Eichrodt, *TOT*, II, p. 23; Gordon, *UT*, p. 426). *Malʾāḵ* is employed in the *OT* of both human and heavenly messengers, and the most important figure among the latter is the *mal'ak yhwh* ('the angel of Yahweh') who often appears as a manifestation of Yahweh himself (see v. Rad, *OTT*, I, pp. 285ff.). In this Psalm the angels are depicted as the guardians of the faithful (cf. Mt. 4:6; Heb. 1:14); what in Exod. 23:20 is said of the people as a whole, is here applied to the individual worshipper of Yahweh.

in all your ways: the writer takes it for granted that all these ways are in accord with the divine will and purpose.

12. they will bear you up: for this metaphor of special care, see Exod. 19:4; Isa. 63:9; Mt. 4:6; Lk. 4:10f.

lest you dash your foot . . .: this is an allusion to possible misfortune and trouble (cf. 35:15, 37:31, 38:16 (M.T. 17); Prov. 3:23).

13. the lion: LXX has *aspida* ('asp'), but M.T. is supported by the parallelism. For a different suggestion, see Winton Thomas (*TRP*, pp. 38f.), who renders *šaḥal* (*RSV* 'lion') and *kᵉpîr* (*RSV* 'young lion') as 'asp' and 'viper' respectively (similarly *NEB*). The lions and serpents in verse 13 may be a symbolic representation of *all* actual and potential enemies and dangers.

THE DIVINE PROMISE **14–16**

14. This verse has a chiastic arrangement (see Introduction, p. 41).

he cleaves to me in love: the verb *ḥ-š-ḳ* may be a Deuteronomic term, and it is used of one's love for another person (Gen. 34:8; Dt. 21:11), of Yahweh's love for Israel (Dt. 7:7, 10:15), and of one's devotion to God (as in this verse). The 'loving of God' is synonymous with 'knowing his name' (cf. 9:10 (M.T. 11), 20:1 (M.T. 2)), and both expressions point to the worshipper's intimate relationship with God, based upon loyalty and obedience to him.

15. One result of this communion with God is the certainty that he will answer the prayers of the needy man, and that his presence is with his servant even in times of trouble.

honour him: or 'bring him to honour' (cf. Jer. 30:19).

16. long life was the desire of all Israelites, and it was commonly regarded as the outward sign of divine favour (cf. Dt. 30:20; Ps. 21:4 (M.T. 5); Prov. 3:2), and as the consequence of one's obedience to the divine Covenant (Exod. 20:12, 23:26).

. . . show him my salvation: the verb *r-'-h* in this context is probably a by-form of *r-w-h* ('to drink deeply, be sated') (for references, see Winton Thomas, *TRP*, p. 23); if so, M.T. *'ar'ēhû* =

ʾarwēhû ('I shall give him to the full (of my salvation)'). For 'salvation', see on 35:3 'To show' in this verse may mean 'to experience' or 'to witness' (cf. Ch. Rabin, *The Zadokite Documents* (1954), p. 43).

Psalm 92 Praise to the Most High

This Psalm has two parts: verses 1–3 form a hymnic introduction to the main part, comprising verses 4–15. The main section of the Psalm explains why it is fitting to praise God. The worshipper may indeed find many reasons for thanking Yahweh, but the Psalmist emphasizes in particular the righteous rule of God.

This poem could be classed as a Hymn or Descriptive Praise (see Introduction, pp. 32f.) with a didactic tone. At the same time it is an Individual Thanksgiving (see verses 10f.), and it seems that the individual deliverance is set in the wider context of God's dealings with men in general. Since God has no favourites, the same principles are operative, not only in the life of one particular individual, but also in the lives of all men everywhere. The nature of the Psalmist's troubles can only be conjectured; he depicts some sort of adversity, but in the end all his doubts were dispelled and all his enemies received their due recompense. There is no indication that the author was thinking of some illness (so Schmidt, Leslie), or that he was grieved by slanderous aspersions. There is, however, the possibility that the poem was a Royal Psalm (so Dahood *et al.*), but the former interpretation seems more likely (a hymnic thanksgiving?).

According to its title, the Psalm was used on the Sabbath. This suggests that at a later time the individual Hymn of Thanksgiving was adapted for congregational use. Mishna (*Tamid* vii:4) states that it was sung by the Levites in the Temple (probably at the morning sacrifice) and that it was given an eschatological significance.

The date may well be post-Exilic, and the metre of the poem is 3+3, except for verse 9 which is a *tricolon* (or a three-line unit) in a 3+3+3 metre; verse 8 should be taken with verse 7*c*.

A Psalm: see Introduction, p. 46.

A Song: see Introduction, p. 47.

for the Sabbath: see the introduction to this Psalm.

A REFLECTION ON GIVING THANKS **1–3**

1. It is good: (cf. 147:1); the precise meaning of the Hebrew *ṭôḇ* is not certain. When God looked at his works of creation, he saw that they were good (*ṭôḇ*), i.e. they corresponded to his design and purpose (cf. Gen. 1:4,10,12, etc.). Similarly the Psalmist may have come to the conclusion that the praise of God (see on 18:49) fits in with the plans of the Most High. *Ṭôḇ* may also have ethical implications, denoting what is right, and what is the proper attitude to God, for 'praise befits the upright' (33:1). Ringgren (*FP*, p. 82) suggests: 'it feels good to praise the Lord'.
to the Lord: Dahood (*PAB*, II, p. 335) renders it: 'O Yahweh', regarding the preposition *lᵉ* ('to') as a *lāmeḏ vocativum*. This would give a better balance to the vocative in verse 1*b*.
to sing praises: the verb *z-m-r* (see on 66:4) is from the same root as *mizmôr*, which is the common word for a psalm or song, usually accompanied by stringed instruments.
thy name: see on 20:1. The reference is to the name 'Yahweh', and not to *ʿelyôn* (see on 18:13, 46:4, 47:2), as is suggested by Briggs (*CECBP*, II, p. 284).

2. Yahweh's **steadfast love** (see on 26:3) and **faithfulness** (see on 36:5) are the main themes of the thanksgiving presented both in the morning and at night. The reference may be to the sacrifices and praises offered by the Temple personnel at the customary hours (cf. Exod. 29:38–41; Ps. 5:3 (M.T. 4), 55:17 (M.T. 18), 134:1). It is equally possible that the writer had in mind the annual festivals which lasted for a whole week (cf. Exod. 23:15; Dt. 16:13). A sharp contrast to verses 2–3 is provided by Isa. 5:11f.
by night: lit. 'by nights'. Briggs (*CECBP*, II, p. 286) took the Hebrew *lêlôṯ* as an intensive plural, 'dark nights', while *AV*, *RV* render it by 'every night' (so also *NEB*).

3. to the music: this is an interpretative addition; it is not in M.T.
the lute: lit. 'a ten(-stringed instrument)'. LXX has in verse 3*a* only one instrument, 'a psaltery of ten strings' (which may represent *nēḇel ʿāśôr*). For **harp** (*nēḇel*), see on 33:2.
the melody: the Hebrew *higgāyôn* is associated with *h-g-h* ('to speak, muse') (see on 1:2), and it can also mean 'meditation' (19:14 (M.T. 15)). In our verse it probably refers to the sounds or melody produced by the lyre (see on 98:5).

THE BOUNDLESS WISDOM AND POWER OF GOD **4–9**

4. For: this introduces the main section (verses 4–15), which gives the grounds for praising Yahweh. The Psalmist is inspired by what God has done, rather than by the contemplation of abstract divine qualities. For this use of *kî* ('for'), see on 89:2.
thy work may be the help granted to the Psalmist, and it is a synonym of 'the works of thy hands'. It is doubtful whether the two expressions allude to two *different* deeds of God (so Barnes). 'The works of thy hands' may describe God's creative activities (cf. 19:1 (M.T. 2), 102:25 (M.T. 26)), but this is not the only usage of this particular phrase (cf. 28:5; Isa. 5:12). The author may also be looking beyond his own salvation to the *Heilsgeschichte* of the whole nation, or he may be alluding specifically to the righteous government of Yahweh (described in verses 7–11) which brought about the Psalmist's deliverance.
sing for joy: for the verb *r-n-n*, see on 33:1.

5. How great are thy works: this is probably an elaboration of the theme stated in verse 4. For similar expressions, see 77:11f. (M.T. 12f.), 106:2, 111:2. In Dt. 11:7; Jg. 2:7 the great 'work of Yahweh' is the deliverance from Egypt.
Thy thoughts suggest the incomprehensible designs and ways of God. In the past the Psalmist may well have doubted the divine providence and justice, but now he realizes that, although the plans of God cannot be fully grasped by human understanding (cf. Isa. 55:8), there can be no question that God *is* loyal and utterly reliable.

6. The dull and stupid man finds it difficult to believe that the world is ultimately governed by divine justice and righteousness. The term **dull man** (*ʾîš baʿar*) occurs only here in the *OT*. Elsewhere *baʿar* is used by itself (49:10 (M.T. 11), 73:22; Prov. 12:1, 30:2), and it is derived from the same root as *beʿîr* ('beasts, cattle'), used in a collective sense. *AV*, *RV* render *baʿar* as 'brutish man'. The Psalmist is not thinking of men who have a low I.Q., but of people who deliberately reject true wisdom, the beginning of which is the fear of Yahweh (Prov. 1:7). In this Psalm, they refuse to believe that evil is doomed, and they do not even realize that in the end wickedness does not pay (see verse 7).

7. the wicked: see on 1:1, 28:3. Although the guilty men flourish like the grass after the rainy season, they are without real permanency, and are destined to perish for ever (verse 7*c*). The wicked (*rāšā*ᶜ) says: 'There is no God' (10:4), and he thinks: 'I shall not be moved' (10:6); thereby he indeed becomes foolish, because he does not discern the ways of God.

evildoers: see on 28:3.

8. on high: lit. 'height', used as an accusative of place. LXX reads: '(but you are) most high'. The vindication of right and the punishment of wrong are guaranteed by the eternal sovereignty of Yahweh, who is not only 'on high', but also the Most High.

9. It is thought that this verse reflects a similar *tricolon* in the Ugaritic texts (III AB. A.8f.): 'Behold, your enemies, O Baal, behold, your enemies you shall smite, Behold, you shall destroy your opponents' (cf. *DOTT*, p. 129; *ANET*, p. 131a). The Psalmist may have been familiar with this Canaanite liturgy (cf. Kraus, *PBK*, p. 643) but the imitation or borrowing (if such it was) need not have been direct. It is by no means certain that the author was thinking of the powers of Chaos; primarily he may have had in mind the same evildoers as were mentioned in verse 7.

THE DOWNFALL OF THE ENEMIES OF THE PSALMIST **10–11**

10. my horn: see on 75:4.

the wild ox: the Hebrew *reʾēm* is sometimes translated as 'buffalo' (cf. Gordon, *UT*, p. 481). LXX has *monokerōs* ('unicorn', so also *AV*) which is unlikely (cf. Dt. 33:17 where the *reʾēm* has more than one horn). The horn or horns of the wild ox are used as a simile of strength; hence Yahweh has endowed the Psalmist with new vigour and vitality (see on 75:4).

thou hast poured over me . . .: lit. 'I am anointed . . .' (so *NEB*); *RSV* adopts the emendation of *ballōṯî* into *ballōṯanî* (so T and S). Perhaps we should render: 'you have made me fat with fresh oil', i.e. you have strengthened me (cf. E. Kutsch, *Salbung als Rechtsakt* (*BZAW*, 87, 1963), pp. 10f.). It is less likely that the author is referring to an actual anointing in public worship (see Weiser, *POTL*, p. 616); Eaton (*PTBC*, p. 226) thinks that the anointing is that of 'the ruler of God's choice'. For 'oil' (*šemen*), see on 104:15.

11. My eyes have seen: cf. 55:7 (M.T. 8), 112:8. This is not so much a malicious joy at the punishment of the enemies as gladness that Yahweh's justice has been clearly manifested. *NEB* renders: 'I gloat over . . .'.

the downfall of my enemies: the word 'downfall' is supplied by the translators, but is not in M.T. The Hebrew *bešûrāy* is a dubious word which Cohen (*PSon*, p. 306) renders: 'them that lie in wait for me' (i.e. from *š-w-r*, 'to behold, watch'). A number of commentators read *b^e^šôr^e^rāy* ('my enemies'; so also most of the ancient versions).

the doom of my evil assailants: some scholars delete *m^e^rē^c^îm* ('evildoers') as a gloss on 'my assailants' (lit. 'those who rise up against me').

THE BLESSEDNESS OF THE RIGHTEOUS **12–15**

12. The righteous: see on 1:5. The flourishing palm tree is used as a simile of the prosperity of the righteous; for a similar idea, see 1:3; Jer. 17:8.

cedar: see on 37:35. For 'Lebanon', see on 29:5. 'Cedar' is often used as a symbol of strength and splendour (cf. Isa. 2:13; Zech. 11:2).

13. The righteous are pictured as trees planted in Yahweh's house, and thriving in the Temple precincts. It is very likely that there existed a link between the Temple and Yahweh's land (see Clements, *GT*, p. 75). The blessing received in the house of God was thought to bring with it material blessings in all spheres of one's life (cf. Isa. 40:31). It is difficult to say whether or not the word-picture was derived from the sight of trees growing in the courts of the Temple (see on 96:8); Kraus (*PBK*, p. 644) cites an Egyptian ritual during which trees were planted before the deity. It is unlikely, however, that this practice had any bearing upon the Psalmist and his ideas.

14. The Israelite ideal was a long and happy life, and the best example is the Deuteronomist's picture of Moses, who is said to have died 'a hundred and twenty years old', and 'his eye was not dim, nor his natural force abated' (Dt. 34:7). In a similar manner the Chronicler describes the death of David, saying that 'he died in a good old age, full of days, riches, and honour' (2 Chr. 29:28). Not dissimilar is the Psalmist's portrayal of the life of the godly man; he will know strength and vigour even in his old age.

bring forth fruit: Dahood (*PNWSP*, p. 20) reads for verse 14*a*: 'They will still be full of juice in old age', deriving the Hebrew *yānûḇûn* (*RSV* 'they . . . bring forth fruit'), not from *n-w-b*, 'to bear fruit', but from *n-w-b* ('to flow').

15. This final verse is an echo of Dt. 32:4.

the LORD is upright: i.e. he is perfect in his relationships with his creatures. The word *yāšār* describes a person as straight in his dealings with others, and it may also suggest the idea of loyalty. Sometimes *yāšār* is used of a straight or level road, either literally (107:7) or in a metaphorical sense (Isa. 26:7). The plural *y^e^šārîm* may be taken as a designation of the worshipping community (cf. 111:1, 140:13 (M.T. 14)).

my rock: for this title of Yahweh, see on 28:1, 42:9, 62:2. T has 'my protector' (*tḳpy*), while LXX reads *ho theos mou* ('my God'); M.T. may have preserved the right reading. *NEBm* has '(my) creator'.

unrighteousness: see on 119:3. The author has pointed out that, although the wicked might prosper for a time (verse 7) and the righteous might be temporarily afflicted (verse 11), there is no unrighteousness in Yahweh. This justification of God or theodicy is based not on intellectual arguments, but upon the writer's personal experience.

Psalm 93 Yahweh's Throne is from of Old

This Psalm is a Hymn or a Descriptive Psalm of Praise (see Introduction, pp. 32f.), but more often it is defined as an Enthronement Psalm (see Introduction, pp. 33ff.).

Its life-setting may have been the Feast of Tabernacles (see Introduction, pp. 52f.), or the so-called Enthronement Festival (a part of the Feast) during which Yahweh was hailed as the king of all and given due homage. Gunkel described the Enthronement Psalms as 'eschatological songs of Yahweh's enthronement' (*EP*, pp. 329, 345), and in a sense this is true, because the cult deals not only with the past and present, but also with the future when the cultic reality will become a historical fact. The Mishnah (*Tamid* vii:4) suggests that Ps. 93 was sung on the sixth day of the week, in anticipation of the time 'that shall be all Sabbath and rest in the life everlasting.' This particular eschatological emphasis seems to be a later interpretation of the Psalm, and it is unlikely that this feature had the same significance for the original author.

Ps. 93 has no title in M.T., but in LXX it is introduced with the following words: 'For the day before the Sabbath when the land (or 'the earth') was resettled. A praise, a song to David'. It is hardly likely that this title is original; rather it is a testimony to the usage and interpretation of the Psalm. It may suggest that this hymn may have been used at a later period to commemorate the return from the Babylonian exile, but this historical event need not be regarded as the *reason* for the composition of this poem, unless it is later than Deutero-Isaiah, and dependent upon him.

The theme of the Psalm is the everlasting kingship of Yahweh, and there is no power in the whole world that can be compared with his majesty and might. Therefore Yahweh's word is trustworthy and reliable.

The hymn begins with a 4+4 metre, which changes into 3+3 +3 at the end of the first verse.

1. The Lord reigns: or 'Yahweh has become king' (so Mowinckel). Both renderings are possible, and the choice depends largely upon the interpretation of the whole Psalm. The older commentators used to argue that the Hebrew perfect in this phrase (i.e. *mālaḵ*) expressed 'not merely a fact . . . but an act' (Kirkpatrick, *BPCB*, p. 564), and they thought of a particular historical happening which could be interpreted as Yahweh's assumption of his royal rule. Some other exegetes regarded the verb as a prophetic perfect (cf. *GK* 106n) referring to the end-time, when Yahweh's kingdom would be established over the whole world. At the present time much of the scholarly discussion on this point is concerned with the question whether the verb *mālaḵ* should be taken in a durative sense ('is king') or in an ingressive sense ('he has become king'; cf. *VT*, III (1953), pp. 188f.; IV (1954), pp. 87ff.; VI (1956), pp. 40ff.; E. Lipiński, 'Les psaumes de la royauté de Yahwé dans l'exégèse moderne', *LPOBL*, pp. 133–272). The former alternative could be understood as asserting Yahweh's eternal kingship, while the latter could refer to a particular act in the ritual, at which point Yahweh was regarded as enthroned at the annual ceremony. Perhaps there is no real contradiction; Yahweh's kingship could be thought of as 'from of old' when he became king by his primeval victory (or by his creative acts?), and this statement of faith could be celebrated in the cult by reliving Yahweh's victory, and by offering homage to the king of kings.

The phrase 'the Lord reigns' is similar in form to such expressions as 'Absalom reigns' (2 Sam. 15:10) and 'Jehu reigns' (2 Kg. 9:13), and they may all amount to a declaration of allegiance, requiring one to take sides. The fact that in the expression *yhwh mālaḵ* the subject is first may indicate that it is Yahweh (and no other deity) who is (or 'has become') king (cf. W. H. Schmidt, *Königtum Gottes in Ugarit und Israel* (*BZAW*, 80, 1966), p. 76). For a parallel, see *ANET*, p. 66a; there the gods acclaim Marduk as the first among gods: 'Joyfully they did homage, "Marduk is king" '.

robed in majesty: the ancient kings were often distinguished by their magnificent robes, sometimes fragrant with perfume (cf. 45:8 (M.T. 9)); but Yahweh is clothed in majesty and might. We need not assume that at this point in the ritual Yahweh was symbolically represented 'as seating himself on his throne' (cf. Taylor, *PIB*, p. 504), because the description of Yahweh's robes is really a metaphorical account of his nature. He has shown himself to be majestic and powerful by his victory over the waters of Chaos and by his creation of the world (if this is the right interpretation of verse 1*c*). It is possible that the word-picture was derived from the investiture of the earthly King at his enthronement (cf. J. Schreiner, *Sion-Jerusalem: Jahwes Königssitz* (1963), p. 204).

the LORD is robed: probably 'in majesty', as in verse 1*a*; there is no need to delete the repeated phrase (cf. verse 3 for a similar stylistic feature).

he is girded with strength: this may well be derived from a military expression: cf. 18:39: 'For thou didst gird me with strength for the battle' (=2 Sam. 22:40).

the world is established: LXX and other versions suggest *tikkēn* ('he has prepared, ordered (the world)'; cf. *tikkantî* ('I have kept steady') in verse 75:3 (M.T. 4)). M.T. derives the verb from *k-w-n* ('to be firm, established') (cf. 96:10). This expression may refer to the creation of the world (cf. 104:5). For 'world' (*tēḇēl*), see on 24:1.

2. throne was the ceremonial seat of a king, and it came to symbolize kingship as a whole. The ancient thrones were of different types; Solomon's (cf. 1 Kg. 10:18ff.) was apparently a well-decorated, high-backed chair. Some scholars have argued that the Ark of the Covenant may also have been, among other things, 'a portable throne for the invisible presence of Yahweh' (G. Henton Davies, *IDB*, I, p. 223), although it is possible that the Ark was associated with Yahweh's throne only when it came to be linked with the cherubim (see on 68:1).

is established: this may be a word play on the same phrase in verse 1 (in Hebrew *nāḵôn* and *tikkôn* respectively).

from of old: it is unlikely that the Psalmist intended a deliberate contrast between Yahweh himself who is **from everlasting,** i.e. from the time which is hidden from our perception, and his throne which was established 'from of old', or 'from that time' when he gained the primeval victory (and/or when he created the world). The author may simply have wished to stress that the 'timelessness' of God guarantees the continuation of his dominion.

3. The floods: lit. 'rivers' (see on 46:4, 72:8). The Psalmist is probably indebted to the Canaanite religious literature for this imagery, especially to the 'battle for kingship' motif. In the Ugaritic myths it is Baal who has a tremendous struggle with *Yam* ('Sea', or the god of the sea) who is also called 'Judge *Nahar*' (i.e. 'Judge River'; see N. C. Habel, *Yahweh Versus Baal* (1964), pp. 52–71; W. H. Schmidt, pp. 10–14). It is very likely that the Israelites were equally familiar with the Babylonian creation story, in which there was the account of Marduk's victory over Tiamat, the primeval deep, and of how he made from her body the heaven and the earth (cf. *ANET*, pp. 60f.). The Psalmist may have had in mind a similar conflict between Yahweh and the unruly waters ('rivers'), or the primeval sea, although the *OT* description is stripped of most mythological elements, and the rest may have been considerably reinterpreted. The use of the Canaanite motifs may serve to emphasize Yahweh's kingship, and it may be an implicit polemic against Baal or any other gods. N. C. Habel (p. 66) argues that there is no actual evidence that Yahweh had fought the 'sea for supremacy on earth', and that this and similar word-pictures are 'a culturally relevant way of saying that Yahweh, not Baal, is king over all cosmic forces.' The latter part of Habel's argument seems true, but the former is doubtful (cf. 74:13, 89:9f. (M.T. 10f.)).

the floods lift up their roaring: the change of tense (i.e. from the perfects in verse 3*ab* to the imperfect in verse 3*c*) may be a poetic device (like the threefold repetition of 'the floods') without any change in the meaning, or it may suggest that the primeval rebellion of the waters will find its counterpart in the end-time, although the latter revolt will be equally futile (cf. Weiser, *POTL*, p. 620). The Hebrew imperfect may be used in its ordinary sense, and it may imply that the floods (symbolizing the elements hostile to the present world-order) would still like to return and cover the earth, but this they are unable to accomplish because Yahweh reigns, and has set a limit which they cannot pass (104:9). It is not unreasonable to suppose that the 'floods' have a double meaning, referring both to the primeval deep and to the hostile nations which 'roar like the roaring of mighty waters' (Isa. 17:12; cf. Isa. 51:9f.).

4. There are several possible translations of this verse, with or without a textual emendation. The following rendering (see also *NEB*) requires no changes: 'Above the thunderous noise of the great waters, (above the thunderous noise of) the majestic surgings of the sea, majestic on high is Yahweh' (cf. G. W. Anderson, *PCB*, 378d). The 'waters' probably refer back to the floods in verse 3, whose limited might is still seen in the stormy sea. If the latter can inspire a certain amount of awe, how much more glorious and majestic is Yahweh, who is in absolute control of the great waters! See on 89:9.

on high suggests the transcendence of Yahweh, although, being what he is, he still remains concerned with the world he has created (cf. 144:7).

5. Thy decrees: or 'Thy testimonies' is understood by Weiser (*POTL*, p. 620) as 'the tradition of the *Heilsgeschichte* which was recited in the Covenant cult', but it may equally well refer to the Covenant as a whole (cf. 119:2) which includes, not only the mighty deeds of Yahweh, but also his promises and commands (cf. 25:10, 132:12). J. D. Schenkel (*Biblica* XLVI (1965), pp. 407ff.) argues that the Hebrew *ᶜēḏōṯêḵā* (*RSV* 'Thy decrees') is to be linked with *ᶜd* ('throne') (cf. also Dahood, *PAB*, II, p. 342), and that verse 5*a* could be rendered: 'Your throne has been firmly established' (cf. verse 2).

are very sure: i.e. very dependable, trustworthy.

holiness befits thy house: the Hebrew *bayiṯ* may denote an ordinary house as well as a temple or palace. The Temple is holy because Yahweh or his name dwells there (cf. Dt. 12:5,11, 14:23f., 26:2; 1 Kg. 11:36, 14:21, etc.), and that holiness demands that all who enter there should be holy (cf. 15:1ff., 24:3ff.). Schenkel (pp. 410ff.) reads: 'in your temple the holy ones shall glorify (you, Yahweh, for a length of days)', taking *naʾᵃwāh* (*RSV* 'befits') in the sense of 'to praise, glorify' (cf. Exod. 15:2), and *ḳōḏeš* ('holiness') as a collective noun: 'saints, holy ones' (cf. *HTR*, LVII (1964), p. 242); the preposition *lᵉ* is given the meaning 'in', for which he cites a parallel in 51:10a (M.T. 12a).

for evermore: *RSV* takes it with the previous phrase, but it is possible that the Psalmist is describing Yahweh as the one who is 'for evermore' (lit. 'for a length of days').

Psalm 94 The Judge of All the Earth

This Psalm is often divided into two main sections: verses 1–15 and 16–23. The first resembles a National Lament (see Introduction, p. 39), while the second is not unlike an Individual Lament (see Introduction, pp. 37ff.). In view of this, some scholars (Gunkel, Leslie, *et al.*) regard this Psalm as a composite work, consisting of two originally independent compositions. Another less likely possibility is to split the Psalm into verses 1–11 and 12–23 (so Schmidt). On the other hand, it is by no means imperative to assume that the Psalm is of a composite nature. It could have been used by some representative of the community, and this might account for the mixture of collective and individual traits in it.

The enemies are not foreign oppressors, but rather men of power within the community itself. In Mowinckel's view (*PIW*, I, p. 227) the representative of the community is, most likely, the King, and therefore the enemies would be foreign peoples; but the former suggestion seems more feasible. The Psalmist's own troubles provide only one concrete example of the widespread breakdown of a just social order (cf. Ps. 14). The social conditions (verses 5ff.) depicted in the Psalm could be applicable to more than one period; some have argued for the time of Isaiah and Micah (e.g. Calès), while others have suggested the late post-Exilic period (so Kraus); the late Persian period may be a reasonable guess.

According to Mishnah (*Tamid* 7:4) the Psalm was sung on the fourth day of the week (i.e. on Wednesday), but clearly this is a late liturgical usage. The Psalm has no heading in M.T., but in LXX and V it is attributed to David, and designated for use on the fourth day of the week.

In its present position, our Psalm is found among the so-called Enthronement Psalms, but it does not follow that it must have been part of the same festival liturgy.

The metre is 3 + 3, with some variations in verses 9–12, 17, 23.

AN APPEAL TO THE RIGHTEOUS JUDGE **1–2**

1. God of vengeance: lit. 'God (*'ēl*) of vengeances' (a plural of amplification?) perhaps, '. . . of complete vengeance' (cf. *GK* 124e). The Hebrew *n^eḳāmāh* is not so much a vengeful vindictiveness as vindication (so also Dahood). To the oppressed it brings deliverance, but to the oppressors punishment (cf. Dt. 32:35f.; Isa. 35:4; Ezek. 25:15ff.).

shine forth: see on 80:1.

2. Rise up: (*hinnāśē*ʾ) in 7:6 (M.T. 7) this expression is synonymous with 'arise' (*ḳûmāh*) and 'awake' (*ʿûrāh*); in both passages the context is Yahweh's judgment. God is the 'judge of the earth' (cf. Gen. 18:25), and he is asked to stand up to pronounce his judgment on the wicked (cf. 76:9 (M.T. 10); Isa. 3:13; de Vaux, *AI*, p. 156). For the idea, see 58:11 (M.T. 12), 76:8f. (M.T. 9f.), 82:8.

the proud: the Hebrew *gēʾeh* ('proud') is associated with *g-ʾ-h* ('to rise up'), and it describes men who have lifted themselves up against God (cf. Job 40:11,12; Ps. 123:4; Isa. 2:12; Jer. 48:29). Their sin consists not of empty boasting, but of a refusal to recognize God as God. Consequently their relationships with other people are also distorted, and are intended to further only their own plans regardless of anything else.

their deserts: for this expression, see on 28:4; cf. Jl 3:4.

THE LAMENT OF THE PEOPLE OF GOD 3–7

3. In this verse of some interest is the stairlike parallelism (see Introduction, p. 42).

how long: see on 6:3.

the wicked: for *rᵉšāʿîm*, see on 1:1, 28:3, 92:7. In the following verses these men are also described as 'evildoers' (*pōʿᵃlê ʾāwen*, see on 28:3) whose violence knows no limits.

exult: the verb *ʿ-l-z* can be used both of one's triumph over foes (2 Sam. 1:20; Jer. 11:15, 50:11), or of exultation in Yahweh and because of him (28:7, 68:4 (M.T. 5), 149:5). The wicked proudly triumph over the weak and unprotected members of the community, but the situation will be quite different when the judge of all the earth arises to establish *his* justice.

4. They pour out: lit. 'They pour forth, they speak insolently', i.e. they pour forth like a flood their insolent speech (cf. 1 Sam. 2:3; Ps. 31:18 (M.T. 19), 75:5 (M.T. 6)). For the co-ordination of the Hebrew verbs, see on 85:6.

5. They crush: the Hebrew *d-k-*ʾ is often used figuratively. So Job is crushed by the words of his friends (Job 19:2), and the afflicted man is crushed at the gate by perverted justice (Prov. 22:22); similarly in this verse the people of God are oppressed

by the miscarriage of justice (cf. 143:3), on the part of their own leaders.
thy heritage: this refers to the Covenant people (see on 28:9).

6. The protection of the weak was the privilege and duty of the strong and of those in a judicial office, etc. The widow, the resident alien (see on 82:3), and the orphan were the objects of the special care of Yahweh, and consequently their ill-treatment was doubly obnoxious to him. Such a state of affairs was not, however, confined to one particular period of Israelite history, as is clear from Isa. 1:15ff.; Jer. 7:5f.; Ezek. 22:7; Mic. 3:1–4; Mal. 3:5; and elsewhere. The 'slaying' of the underprivileged may suggest that they were deprived even of those things which were necessary to their livelihood, or the allusion might be to their legal murder (see verse 21), or both. Oesterley (*TP*, p. 417) regards the verbs of verse 6 as 'an overstatement'—perhaps rightly so, because the language may be figurative (cf. Isa. 1:15ff.), although this need not always be the case (cf. Jer. 7:6,9).

7. The Psalmist cites the very words of the wicked; they think that God is simply not concerned with the rights and wrongs of their society (cf. Job 22:13f.; Ps. 10:11, 73:11). This argument must be the result of their limited experience and faithlessness; they thought that because they had not been punished so far, it must mean that God would *never* seek them out for recompense.
the Lord: the word used is *yāh* (not *yhwh*); see on 68:4. For the term 'God of Jacob', see on 20:1.

THE WARNING TO THE OPPRESSORS **8–11**

This section, with its rhetorical questions, reflects the Wisdom style, and its purpose is to call the wicked to their senses. It might be said that the Psalmist is not so much interested in the punishment of the evildoers as in their 'conversion'.

8. O dullest of the people: or, paraphrasing, 'you have behaved like animals among your own people'. *Bōᶜarîm* (*RSV* 'dullest') is a participle of *b-ᶜ-r* ('to be brutish'); see on 92:6. It seems that those addressed are the Israelites, although 'the people' (*hāᶜām*) need not always be limited to Israel.
Fools: for *kᵉsîl*, see on 49:10, 92:6.
when will you be wise: i.e. when will you learn the fear of the Lord, which is the foundation of all true wisdom (cf. 19:9 (M.T. 10), 25:12).

9. The essence of the argument is that the creator is far superior to his creatures. To the Psalmist it is unthinkable that he who has given so many faculties to human beings does not possess them himself (cf. Prov. 20:12).

10. He who chastens . . .: so *RSV*, following the versions and reading *hayyōsēr* for M.T. *hᵃyōsēr* ('is he not the one who chastens . . .'). The Hebrew *y-s-r* can also mean 'to instruct', which may be more likely in the present context. The thought that Yahweh teaches other nations (see on 59:5) is rather unusual, and it may be linked with the concept of Wisdom in Prov. 8 (cf. Rom. 1:20, 2:14). Some commentators would emend *hᵃyōsēr* to *hayyōṣēr* ('who created (or 'formed') (the nations)'); but M.T. seems satisfactory.

He who teaches men knowledge: M.T. appears to be defective, and a word may have fallen out. One suggestion is to read *hᵃlōʾ yēḏāᶜ* ('does he not know?'; cf. *TRP*, p. 39) instead of M.T. *dāᶜaṯ* ('knowledge'). Another possibility is to assume that the letter *mêm* has dropped out by haplography, and that we should read *middāᶜaṯ* ('without knowledge'), *NEB* '. . . has he no knowledge?'

11. This verse provides the answer to the questions in verses 9f. Yahweh knows not only the deeds of men but even their very thoughts and motives.

that they are but a breath: the allusion may be to 'the thoughts of man' (so Davies, Oesterley, Kraus; cf. 1 C. 3:20), or to men in general. A problem is created by *hēmmāh* ('they'), which is a masculine plural pronoun; its possible antecedent is either 'thoughts' (*maḥšᵉḇôṯ*; a feminine plural) or 'man' (*ʾāḏām*; a masculine singular, used collectively (?)).

breath: *heḇel* can also mean 'vanity, vapour', and it often denotes what is unsubstantial and profitless. This same term occurs also in the Preacher's slogan: 'Vanity of vanities'; see on 78:33.

THE BLESSINGS OF THE RIGHTEOUS **12–15**

12. Blessed . . .: see on 1:1.

the man whom thou dost chasten: this is an echo of Job 5:17 (cf. Prov. 3:12). It may be better to render *y-s-r* by 'to instruct' (so *NEB*), and the parallel line (verse 12*b*) supports this shade of meaning. It is possible, however, that the temporary affliction is regarded as *part* of the divine instruction.

LORD: for *yāh*, see on 68:4.

out of thy law: *tôrāh* ('law') is dealt with on 1:2, 119:1. Although all men are taught wisdom by Yahweh (see verse 10), the law is the special blessing to Israel (as long as it is obeyed). *Tôrāh* may denote religious truths in general (cf. Cohen, *PSon*, p. 310) but it is more likely that the reference is to some form of written law. Leslie (*PAP*, p. 255) thinks that this must point to a time 'after the introduction of the priestly law by Ezra (*c.* 397 B.C.)', but there may be other possibilities.

13. days of trouble: i.e. the time when the wicked seem to have an almost complete power over the righteous. Some read 'in days . . .' (*bîmê*) for 'from days . . .' (*mîmê*) (so Kissane). The man who knows the law of God will not be afraid of tribulation, because he sees a meaning in it; and he also knows that God is faithful to his promises to the Covenant people.

pit: for *šaḥaṯ*, see on 49:9. It may well be a synonym of *bôr*, and both may denote not only pits used for the catching of animals but also the underworld. In this verse *šaḥaṯ* is used figuratively of just retribution or destruction. This is, in a way, the outworking of the principle stated in Prov. 26:27; Ec. 10:8.

14. Here the Psalmist takes up the theme of verse 5, and explains that, even though temporarily life may be difficult, Yahweh will not be disloyal to his people, nor will he abandon permanently his heritage. He 'will not cast away his people, for his great name's sake' (1 Sam. 12:22).

15. justice: for *mišpāṭ*, see on 36:6, 119:7. Here it may suggest a just administration of the laws.

to the righteous: *RSV* follows the reading suggested by Sym and S (i.e. *ṣaddîḵ* for M.T. *ṣeḏeḵ* ('righteousness'), so *AV*, *RV*; cf. 85:10f. (M.T. 11f.)). If the suggested emendation is right, it means that the righteous will once more experience a just treatment.

the upright in heart: for the phrase, see 7:10 (M.T. 11), 119:7. In popular language, such men could be described as 'on the level' in all their dealings (either with God or with men).

will follow it: this is a paraphrase (similarly *NEB*); M.T. has *wᵉaḥᵃrāyw* ('and after it') which some exegetes (e.g. Kittel, Kissane, Kraus) alter into *wᵉʾaḥᵃrîṯ lᵉ* ('and a reward (shall come) to . . .'). *ʾAḥᵃrîṯ* may denote both a 'happy lot or future' (cf. Prov. 23:18, 24:14; Jer. 29:11) as well as a 'final end' (73:17). If the emendation is justifiable, the former must be the meaning here; it would give a good sense although M.T. is not impossible.

CONFIDENCE IN YAHWEH **16–23**

16–17. The rhetorical questions in verse 16 are not an expression of doubt and fear, but rather a stylistic method to emphasize the fact that, when everything seemed hopeless, Yahweh came to the help of the oppressed. The writer also draws attention to verse 17, which depicts the timely intervention of Yahweh (cf. 124:1).

my soul: i.e. I myself (see on 33:19).

the land of silence: lit. 'in silence'; *NEB* 'the silent grave'. In 115:17 'silence' is clearly a synonym of Sheol or the grave, and it has the same meaning in this verse. See also Barth, *ETKD*, p. 72; cf. 4Q184, l. 7: 'the tents of the underworld' (i.e. of silence).

18. When I thought: lit. 'When I said'.

the steadfast love: for this Covenant term, see on 26:3, 51:1. It was Yahweh's loyalty that supported the afflicted man during his tribulations. Cf. 18:35 (M.T. 36), 20:3 (M.T. 4), 41:3 (M.T. 4), 119:117.

19. the cares of my heart: lit. 'my thoughts within me' (*AV*, *RV*). The Hebrew *śarᶜappîm* occurs elsewhere only in 139:23, while another form of it (*śeᶜippîm*) is found in Job 4:13, 20:2 (cf. Dhorme, *CJ*, pp. 49f.). In the present context the meaning of *śarᶜappîm* is 'disquieting thoughts'; *RVm* has 'doubts'.

thy consolations: the Hebrew *tanḥûmîm* (an intensive plural) may denote the comfort given by God (cf. Job 15:11), or the consolation provided by men and women (Job 21:2; Isa. 66:11; Jer. 16:7; cf. 4Q176 1–2, i:4).

my soul is a circumlocution for 'me' (see on 33:19).

20. wicked rulers: lit. 'a throne of destructions' (LXX has *thronos anomias* ('throne of iniquity')). For 'throne' (*kissē*ᵓ), see on 93:2; here it may refer by synecdoche (i.e. the mention of a part when the whole is to be understood) to the person who occupies the throne, or to the seat of power. The reference need not be to the King but, more likely, to the judges who have abused their office and sacred duty and who have spread ruin and destruction (cf. Isa. 10:1f.). Such men can have no fellowship with God.

who frame mischief by statute: they make laws to suit their own plans; they wrong their fellow men under the cover of supposedly divine law (cf. Dt. 1:17). This phrase is, however, ambiguous in M.T., and it could also be rendered: '(Can those who) frame mischief against (your) statute (have fellowship with you?)'; similarly Wellhausen, Oesterley, Kraus, *et al.*

21. They band together: the Hebrew *yāḡôddû* seems to be derived from *g-d-d* ('to cut', or 'to attack'), while T suggests *yāḡûrû*, adopted by *RSV*, although *g-d-d* may have a similar meaning because it is associated with *g^e^ḏûḏ* ('band, troop').

against the life: lit. 'against the soul' (see on 33:19).

the innocent: M.T. has 'the innocent blood' (so *AV*, *RV*); *RSV* may be right either in its paraphrase, or in assuming a change to *ʾāḏām* ('man') for M.T. *dām* ('blood'). In either case the sense of the verse is the same: the wicked condemn the innocent man to death in order to derive some gain from so doing, as in 1 Kg. 21:8–16.

22. . . . my stronghold: see on 59:1. Yahweh is the refuge of the oppressed (cf. 18:2 (M.T. 3)); the verb 'has become' is occasionally taken as a perfect of certainty: 'will surely be' (so Cohen, *PSon*, p. 311).

the rock: for *ṣûr*, see on 28:1, 42:9, 62:2. 'Refuge' (*maḥseh*) is dealt with in 61:3.

23. He will bring back: reading perhaps *w^e^yāšēḇ* for M.T. *wayyāšeḇ* ('he has brought back'), unless the latter is yet another perfect of certainty.

their iniquity: for *ʾāwen*, see on 36:4.

wipe them out: the repetition of this phrase may be a stylistic device to stress the certainty of the divine retribution (cf. 7:16 (M.T. 17)). LXX omits the repeated verb, but this reading may be based on the assumption that M.T. contains a dittography.

Psalm 95 No Worship without Obedience

This Psalm is often described as a Prophetic Liturgy, and it consists of two main parts: verses 1—7*c*, which form a 'double' Hymn, and verses 7*d*—11, which are a prophetic warning. Consequently some scholars have thought that the Psalm was composed of two fragments of originally separate poems (so Cheyne, Wellhausen). It is more likely, however, that the Psalm is a literary unity; a parallel is found in the structure of Ps. 81.

There is some disagreement among commentators as to whether this song should be reckoned as an Enthronement Psalm. The setting of Ps. 95 may well be the Feast of Tabernacles, of which the so-called Enthronement Festival was, apparently, one aspect.

The Mishnah links this Psalm with the New Year Festival (cf. Weiser, *POTL*, p. 625), and this later usage may reflect its original cultic setting. The *Sitz im Leben* of the Psalm seems to be the entry of the worshippers into the Temple courts (cf. verses 2 and 6) during the festival. Whether the different parts of the Psalm were sung by different choirs, groups, or solo singer(s) is a matter of conjecture, although some such procedure seems likely (cf. Sir. 50:16ff.).

The main themes of the Psalm are the kingship of Yahweh, his ownership of the world because he had created it, his care for the Covenant people, and the responsibilities of those who are in a Covenant relationship with him.

LXX assigns this Psalm to David, but this seems to be a late editorial note, although the Psalm may be of pre-Exilic origin; Nötscher, Deissler, *et al.* think that the Psalm is of a post-Exilic date.

The metre is mainly 3 + 3.

PRAISE THE CREATOR **1–5**

Verses 1–2 are a summons to worship Yahweh, while verses 3–5 supply the reason for this call.

1. let us sing: or, 'let us shout for joy'.

let us make a joyful noise: perhaps, 'let us pay homage' (cf. 98:4) since the same verb is used of the cries of allegiance of the people at Saul's coronation (1 Sam. 10:24; cf. Ps. 47:1 (M.T. 2); Zeph. 3:14; Zech. 9:9).

the rock of our salvation: the word 'rock' (*ṣûr*) is a well-known divine epithet (cf. 18:2,31,46 (M.T. 3,32,47), 19:14 (M.T. 15), 28:1, 78:35, 89:26 (M.T. 27); Isa. 44:8; Hab. 1:12), and it may point to the reliability and stability of the divine. The phrase means: 'the rock that is (or 'brings about') our salvation' (cf. 19:14: 'O LORD, my rock and redeemer').

2. Let us come into his presence: perhaps, 'let us greet him' (cf. E. König, *Die Psalmen* (1927), p. 107; Dt. 23:5; Isa. 21:14), or 'let us approach his presence' (i.e. enter the Temple).

with thanksgiving: cf. 100:1; Mic. 6:6.

let us make a joyful noise: better, with Johnson (*SKAI*, p. 59): 'While we acclaim Him with songs' (cf. verse 1*b*); the reference may be to Psalms such as 93, 96–9.

3. the LORD is a great God: i.e. Yahweh is not only a 'great one' but *the* great one. Cf. 77:13: 'What God is great like our God?'

a great King: some commentators (e.g. Gunkel, Kraus) omit 'great', because the same adjective has already been used in verse 3*a*, and overloads verse 3*b*.
above all gods: this phrase presupposes a polytheistic background, and could hardly be of Israelite origin. In the present context the gods of the other peoples are regarded as nonentities, and their mention simply underlines the absolute supremacy of Yahweh (cf. Exod. 15:11).

4. In his hand: lit. 'in whose hand', but the relative particle (*ʾašer*) is usually deleted for metrical reasons.
the depths of the earth: LXX, followed by some exegetes (e.g. Baethgen, Gunkel, Oesterley), reads: 'the distant parts (*merḥakkê*) of the earth'. The *RSV* rendering provides, however, a better parallel to 'the heights of the mountains' (verse 4*b*).
the heights: *NEB* 'the folds'; the etymology of *tôʿāpôṯ* is uncertain (cf. S. R. Driver and G. B. Gray, *The Book of Job*, II, p. 157) but *RSV* is supported by LXX, S, and V. The general thought of this verse is that both the depths of the earth (underworld?) and the summits of the mountains (i.e. the abodes of gods according to the beliefs of many peoples; cf. 68:15ff. (M.T. 16ff.)) are Yahweh's; they are not outside his jurisdiction and rule (cf. 88:10ff. (M.T. 11ff.), Am. 9:2), in spite of other popular beliefs (cf. Isa. 38:18).

5. The sea is his: lit. 'whose is the sea'. *RSV* omits the relative particle (as in verse 4*a*). It is possible that here we find an implicit allusion to the sea as the primeval opponent of God (see on 46:2, 74:13), which is now fully under the divine control (cf. 93:3ff.).
for he made it: i.e. Yahweh's dominion over nature rests upon the fact that he created it, and that he is its undisputed Lord.
for his hands formed the dry land: cf. Gen. 1:9ff.; Ps. 24:1, 89:11 (M.T. 12).

THE PRAISE OF THE COVENANT GOD **6–7c**

This is the second part of the hymn of praise (and not a second *hymn*); it stresses the relationship between Yahweh and his people.

6. O come: this can mean: 'come in' (so *PNT*) or 'let us go in' (cf. Mowinckel, *PIW*, I, p. 156), and it may be an invitation to enter the gates of the Temple.
let us worship and bow down, let us kneel: all three verbs are probably synonymous and emphasize the respect and homage due to God.

the LORD, our Maker: God is, of course, the creator of all beings, but the stress in this verse seems to be upon the making of Israel into the people of God (cf. 100:3).

7. For he is our God: this verse is a variation of the Covenant formula: 'I will be their God, and they shall be my people' (Jer. 31:33; cf. Exod. 19:5f.; 2 Sam. 7:24; Ezek. 11:20, 14:11, 34:31).
the people of his pasture: many commentators (Gunkel, Kraus, *et al.*) assume a textual disorder in the rest of the verse. Kraus reads with S: 'we are his people, the sheep of his pasture' (*PBK*, p. 659). This would correspond with the formula in Jer. 31:33, and with Ps. 100:3. On the other hand, M.T. gives a reasonable meaning, and is attested by LXX and V, and, in any case, the basic meaning remains unaltered. Boylan (*PSVP*, II, p. 139) suggests that 'pasture' is Canaan.
the sheep of his hand: i.e. the flock under his care and protection (cf. Gen. 30:35; Jn 10:11–14).

THE WARNING AGAINST DISOBEDIENCE **7d–11**

It is only right that the people of God should rejoice in their king and in his care, but this ought not to obscure their Covenant responsibilities.

7d. O that today . . .: Gunkel (*PGHAT*, p. 420) takes 'his hand' (verse *7c*) with verse *7d*, and adds 'know' (*d^e^cû*), reading: 'Know his power today' (for similar summons, see Dt. 9:3, 11:2). 'Today' is reminiscent of Dt. 4:40, 5:3, 6:6, 7:11, 9:3, 11:2, etc., and it points to a cultic setting. Mowinckel sees here an allusion to the renewal of the Covenant, and to the proclamation of the commandments.
hearken to his voice: this may refer to verses 8–11, or Ps. 95 may have been preceded by the singing of a song such as Ps. 15.

8. In this and the following verses the speaker is Yahweh, and the oracle was probably proclaimed by a cultic prophet, or priest.
Harden not your hearts: i.e. be not disobedient. In Prov. 28:14 such a stubbornness is contrasted with fearing the Lord.
as at Meribah: (*AV* 'as in the provocation'), this is to be taken with 'when your fathers tested me'. 'Meribah' means 'contention' or 'place of contention', and according to Exod. 17:1ff. it was a name given by Moses to the place where the people of Israel had angered Yahweh (cf. 106:32) by doubting his presence (Exod. 17:7). From Exod. 17:7 one could argue that 'Meribah and Massah' was a double name of this particular place, but it is more

likely that originally they were two different locations (cf. M. Noth, *Exodus* (*OTL*, 1962), pp. 139f.). Meribah, at least, seems to have been situated in the Kadesh (-Barnea) area, in the wilderness of Zin (cf. Num. 27:14; Dt. 32:51; Ezek. 47:19, 48:28).

at Massah: the noun is derived from *n-s-h* ('to test, prove'), and it probably means 'trial' (so Johnson, *SKAI*, p. 60). LXX suggests 'temptation' (cf. Dt. 6:16, 9:22). See above, on 'Meribah'.

the wilderness: (see on 55:7). This may be 'a sandy desert' as well as 'a pasture land'. In the Exodus context the reference would be to areas suitable for grazing.

9. your fathers: i.e. your ancestors.

tested me: see Exod. 17:1ff.; Num. 20:1ff. They had put God on trial because they doubted whether he was in their midst, and whether he was able to provide for them. The later generations, at least, saw in this event a type of rebellion (cf. 78:18,41,56). Verses 7*d*–11 are quoted in Heb. 3:7–11 as an example of disobedience.

though they had seen my work: Boylan (*PSVP*, II, p. 140) argues that the 'work' here was the gift of water, but it is more plausible that it includes all the mighty deeds of God in saving and sustaining Israel (cf. Ps. 78). LXX uses the plural form, *ta erga mou* ('my works').

10. I loathed: i.e. God made them know his displeasure (cf. Num. 14:34).

that generation: M.T. has 'with a generation', while *RSV* follows LXX, S, and Jerome in reading *baddôr hahûʾ*.

who err in heart: i.e. whose will no longer corresponds with that of God, and thus it is parallel with 'they do not regard my ways' (verse 10*c*). For the verb *t-ʿ-h* ('to err'), see on 107:4.

11. I swore in my anger: cf. Num. 14:21ff. Although God pardoned his people as a whole, the rebels had to pay the price for their disobedience.

that they should not enter my rest: i.e. the Promised land (cf. Dt. 12:9); Johnson (*SKAI*, p. 60) renders it by 'my homeland' (cf. Ru. 1:9; Ps. 132:8,14). The Promised land was Yahweh's land, and only those who observed the Covenant had the right to dwell in Yahweh's inheritance and the privilege to enjoy 'his rest'.

Psalm 96 YAHWEH IS KING AND JUDGE

This is another of the so-called Enthronement Psalms which form a subdivision of the Hymns (see Introduction, pp. 33f.); a more non-committal description of them might be 'Psalms Celebrating the Kingship of Yahweh'. Their setting was the Feast of Tabernacles which was probably the Israelite New Year Festival. LXX provides a title for this Psalm: 'When the house was built after the captivity. A Song of David'; this means probably that the translator regarded the Psalm as Davidic, and that it may have been used during the post-Exilic period in the hope and expectation that the new (i.e. rebuilt) Temple would become, sooner or later, the house of prayer for all peoples. This Psalm was also used by the Chronicler (1 Chr. 16) in a composite hymn which was supposed to have been sung by the choirs at the removal of the Ark of the Covenant to Jerusalem. Most commentators agree that the Chronicler's version is dependent upon Ps. 96, although it is unlikely that the hymn is of Davidic origin. The Chronicler's setting may be right in as far as it shows that the composite Psalm in 1 Chr. 16 was used on a cultic occasion commemorating the bringing of the Ark to the Holy City.

It is not impossible that this Psalm is of a post-Exilic date (so Deissler, *PWdB*, III, p. 31), although some of its material may be of more ancient origin. It has many points of contact with other Psalms (e.g. Ps. 9, 29, 93, 98), and it reflects many characteristic themes of Isa. 40–66: e.g., the nothingness of idols (Isa. 40:18ff., 41:23f., 44:6ff.), the appeal to creation as evidence of Yahweh's greatness (Isa. 40:22, 42:5, 44:24, 45:12, etc.), the invitation to nature to praise Yahweh (Isa. 44:23, 49:13, 55:12), and the conviction that all nations will worship Yahweh (Isa. 45:5f., 49:7, 56:3ff., 60:9ff., 66:18). In view of all this, it is possible that Ps. 96 is later than Isa. 40–66 (cf. Kraus, *PBK*, p. 666), but one could also argue that the author(s) of Isa. 40–66 is dependent upon the cultic language of the pre-Exilic period.

The style and thoughts of Ps. 96–9 are similar, and it has been suggested that they were written by the same person (cf. Rhodes, *LBCP*, p. 134); but it is equally possible that, since certain songs belong to the same psalm-type, there are bound to be many similarities.

The hymn itself contains two introductions (verses 1–3 and 7–9) and two main sections (verses 4–6 and 10–13), but this does not mean that the Psalm is composed of two or three separate hymns (e.g. verses 1–6, 7–9, and 10–13; cf. Taylor, *PIB*, p. 517).

The Psalm is essentially an invitation to the whole universe to praise Yahweh because he is its creator and king, as well as its judge. As such, he is superior to all other gods who are in fact mere idols or nonentities.

The metre is irregular.

SING TO THE LORD **1-3**

1. In verses 1–2 we find the stairlike parallelism where the first three lines include the same phrase 'sing to the LORD' (see Introduction, p. 42).

a new song: perhaps, 'the ever-new song'. Just as God's care is never ceasing and new every morning (cf. Lam. 3:22f.), so also the song of his praise must be ever new. It is obvious that, at some point in time, our Psalm was 'new', i.e. newly composed, yet in its liturgical use the newness must be sought in the fact that God's praise is inexhaustible (see on 33:3; cf. 40:3 (M.T. 4), 98:1, 149:1; Isa. 42:10).

all the earth may well indicate all the inhabitants of the world, but the people who are addressed in particular are the people of God (cf. verses 3 and 10).

2. bless his name: i.e. his name (or Yahweh himself) is worthy of adoration and thankful praise (see on 20:1, 48:9, 54:1).

tell: lit. 'proclaim the good tidings', and the content of the good news is 'his salvation'. The exact meaning of 'salvation' depends upon the interpretation of the Psalm; it has been taken to mean some recent deliverance of Israel (such as the Return from Babylon) or Yahweh's victory at the end-time; but it is more likely that it refers to Yahweh's triumph in the creation of the world (cf. verse 5) and to his unbroken rule.

from day to day: i.e. God's praise should be continual.

3. Declare: the Israelites are called upon to share their experience of Yahweh's mighty works, with all the peoples of the world (cf. Isa. 66:18).

his glory: see on 19:1. This is parallel to 'His marvellous works' (see on 9:1), and both may refer to Yahweh's acts of creation (cf. 136:4ff.) and of salvation (verse 2). See on 66:2.

THE LORD ALONE IS WORTHY OF PRAISE **4-6**

These verses form the first main section of the hymn.

4. For great is the LORD . . .: the same phrase is also found in 48:1 (M.T. 2) and 145:3. His greatness is obvious when one considers his mighty deeds, and therefore praise is one aspect of the right attitude towards Yahweh.

he is to be feared: or 'he is awe-inspiring'. In his enemies he inspires terror and fear, but in those who serve him a worshipful awe and a spirit of praise (cf. 99:3).

above all gods: this may imply that the Psalmist believed in the existence of other gods also; yet it is clear that to him these deities were nonentities (cf. verse 5). The idea that the creator god is superior to the other deities may be derived from non-Israelite sources (cf. Kraus, *PBK*, p. 667), and so the polytheistic background may well be part of the metaphor and not an expression of the Psalmist's own beliefs.

5. **the gods of the peoples are idols:** LXX and V call them 'demons', but the Hebrew ʾ^{e}*lîlîm* (whatever its etymology) is probably a term of contempt, at least in this context (cf. *HAL*, p. 54a): they are not ʾ^{e}*lōhîm* ('gods') but ʾ^{e}*lîlîm* ('nobodies'); cf. Isa. 2:8,18,20; 10:10,11; etc.

but the LORD made the heavens: here we have a contrast between Yahweh and the idols. The latter are impotent man-made things, while Yahweh is the creator of everything—including the heavens, the creation of which may have been regarded as a particularly mighty act (cf. 8:3 (M.T. 4)). This appeal to creation as a proof of Yahweh's power may reflect the myth of the combat of the gods (see on 93:3).

6. **Honour and majesty** is the usual pair of words used to describe royal dignity (21:5 (M.T. 6), 45:3 (M.T. 4), 104:1, 111:3). Many exegetes suggest that these two attributes of God are personified and are regarded as his personal attendants, just as the earthly kings are waited upon by their servants. Whether this is so or not, the phrase means that true honour and majesty belong to God (see on 104:1). Weiser (*POTL*, p. 629) regards verse 6 as a description of the theophany (i.e. a cultic theophany) in the sanctuary.

strength and beauty: in 78:61 these terms are used to describe the Ark (or could it refer to the people of Israel?). If we have a personification of divine attributes in verse 6*a*, then the same may be true of verse 6*b*. The whole verse may refer to the cultic representation of Yahweh's theophany, or to the fact of his presence in the Temple; cf. 47:8 (M.T. 9), 68:1 (M.T. 2).

his sanctuary is either God's heavenly dwelling or the restored Temple (so Kirkpatrick, *BPCB*, p. 577). The reference may simply be to the Temple in general.

THE UNIVERSAL CALL TO WORSHIP **7–9**

This section is a renewed introduction, and it exhorts all peoples to praise Yahweh; it is reminiscent of 29:1f. Leslie (*PAP*, p. 78) thinks that the scene depicted in verses 7–9 is the open space before the Temple gates, and he follows Oesterley's suggestion that these verses give us an outline of the order of service at the ceremony of Yahweh's enthronement. This is, however, dubious.

7. Ascribe: acknowledge and proclaim the wonderful deeds of God (cf. Jos. 7:19).

families of the peoples: in 29:1 this exhortation is addressed to the 'heavenly beings', but here it refers to all the nations. The summons to worship Yahweh is directed to the pilgrims also, who were present at this particular festival.

glory and strength: see on 29:1; cf. 1 Chr. 16:28.

8. the glory due his name: i.e. the glorious praise for his marvellous works (cf. 66:2). For 'name', see on 20:1, 48:9, 54:1.

offering: (*minḥāh*) the reference may be to the gifts (i.e. tribute) brought by the subjects to their Lord (cf. Isa. 60:5ff.). See on 40:6.

into his courts: the Jerusalem Temple had several courts, and we know that the Herodian Temple area included the Court of the Gentiles, the Women's Court, the Court of Israel, and the Priests' Court. Only the first of these courts was accessible to Gentiles, and it is possible that the Psalmist now invites the Gentiles to take their place alongside the Israelites (cf. Davies, *Cent. BP*, II, p. 150). G. R. Driver (*JTS*, XL (1939), p. 393, n.3) derives the Hebrew word from the Arabic *ḥaḍara*, and translates 'his presence' (for *RSV* 'his courts'); this finds some support in 1 Chr. 16:29: 'bring an offering, and come before him'. Cf. also the Ugaritic *ḥẓr* ('court'); see Driver, *CML*, p. 138a; Aistleitner, *WUS*, p. 106.

9. Worship the LORD: or, 'bow down in worship of the LORD' (cf. 22:29 (M.T. 30)); see on 29:2.

in holy array: this is usually taken to mean 'garments that are ritually clean' (cf. Lev. 11:24–8), but in recent years attention has been drawn to a Ugaritic parallel in *Keret* I, iii:51 (cf. Driver, *CML*, p. 33) where *hdrt* is parallel to *ḥlm* ('dream'). The Ugaritic *hdrt* may suggest 'theophany', 'revelation', and the same may be true of its Hebrew equivalent (*hadraṯ*). If so, we could render verse 9*a*: 'Bow down to the Lord during (his) holy theophany' or '. . . during the theophany of the Holy One', taking *ḳōḏeš* as a

divine title (cf. *Keret* II, i:10f.); see also Kraus, *PBK*, p. 664; Ps. 29:2; I Chr. 16:29. 'His theophany' (or 'appearance') would provide a good parallel to 'before him' in verse 9*b*.
tremble: Briggs (*CECBP*, II, p. 304) translates 'whirl (before him)' in the sacred pilgrim dance, but it is more likely that the meaning is: 'tremble in fear' before Yahweh (cf. Dt. 2:25; Jer. 5:22, 51:29; Jl 2:6; Zech. 9:5).

YAHWEH IS KING AND JUDGE OF ALL **10–13**
This is the second main section of this Psalm, and in it all nature is invited to rejoice at the good news that Yahweh reigns.

10. Say among the nations: this re-echoes the command given in verse 3, but it is more specific in its contents. The gist of what is to be said is expressed by 'The LORD reigns' (see on 93:1). The Old Latin version contains the famous reading *Dominus regnavit a ligno* ('the Lord has reigned from the tree'). The addition *a ligno* ('from the tree') is obviously a Christian gloss, and the verse was used by many Latin Fathers as a prophecy of Christ's triumph through the Cross. This reading has also inspired the well-known sixth-century hymn: '*Vexilla regis prodeunt*', better known in J. M. Neale's translation: 'The royal banners forward go'.

We are not told how this 'missionary' task was to be accomplished; possibly it was fulfilled through the cultic celebration of Yahweh's kingship. Verse 10*b* may be derived from 93:1, although the writer may have drawn upon cultic phraseology as such. Verse 10*c* is similar to 9:8*b* (M.T. 9*b*) (cf. 7:8 (M.T. 9)), but it is omitted in I Chr. 16:31.
he will judge: this is not necessarily an eschatological event which will take place sometime in the future; it is, at least partly, a present reality in the cultic experience (cf. Eichrodt, *TOT*, I, p. 487). See on 72:2.
with equity: or, 'in fairness'. See on 75:2; cf. 9:8 (M.T. 9), 17:2, 58:1 (M.T. 2), 98:9, 99:4.

11. heavens . . . earth . . . sea constitute the universe of the peoples of antiquity. The whole world, and all that is in it, are invited to glorify their creator, sustainer, and vindicator. Such an appeal is characteristic of Deutero-Isaiah (42:10f., 44:23, 49:13, 55:12ff.).
all that fills it: the reference may be to the waves of the sea (so Kraus, *PBK*, p. 668; cf. 93:3), but it is more likely that the

writer had in mind the creatures that inhabit the sea (cf. 24:1, 98:7; Isa. 42:10).

12. the field: i.e. the open country (as in Jer. 40:7; Mic. 4:10), the home of wild beasts.

Then: so also *NEB*. Most scholars emend *ʾāz* ('then') into *ʾap̱* ('yea'), rendering: 'Also let all the trees . . .'.

13. This verse is similar to 98:9, q.v. (cf. 9:8 (M.T. 9)).

for he comes: this phrase is found twice in this verse but only once in 98:9 and in 1 Chr. 16:33, yet 96:13 may be the better reading, at least for metrical reasons.

The Hebrew *bāʾ* may be either a participle (so most translators, including *RSV*), or a perfect, 'for he has come' (so Weiser, *POTL*, p. 628) which could be an expression of cultic experience. On the other hand, some scholars (cf. Kraus, *PBK*, p. 668) take it in an eschatological sense (cf. Isa. 40:10, 59:19, 62:11).

to judge: i.e. both to punish and to vindicate, to judge and to rule (see on 72:2).

with righteousness: God's judgment is not vindictive, but it is characterized by righteousness or absolute fairness, by giving everyone his due (see also on 33:5).

with his truth: with self-consistency and without arbitrariness (cf. Rowley, *FI*, p. 66ff.).

Psalm 97 The Universal King and His Subjects

The acclamation of Yahweh in verse 1 and the main themes of the Psalm imply that it belongs to the Psalms Celebrating the Kingship of Yahweh, or the so-called Enthronement Psalms (see Introduction, pp. 33f.).

In LXX it has a heading: '(A Psalm of) David; when his land was restored'. It may well be that the translator believed that the Psalm was an ancient song, and that it was used to commemorate the Restoration from the Babylonian exile. Most scholars regard the Psalm as post-Exilic (cf. Kraus, *PBK*, p. 671); but the author may have made use of older material.

This hymn consists of two main parts: verses 1–6 describe the might and majesty of Yahweh, while verses 7–12 deal with the significance and effects of Yahweh's rule over Israel and all the peoples. Many phrases of this poem are found in other Psalms and in prophetic literature, or they are echoes of such expressions. The author of Ps. 97 has been described as 'a masterly hymn-writer', although not an original poet (Kirkpatrick, *BPCB*, p. 579); this seems a fair comment.

The metre of the hymn is mainly 3 + 3.

THE KINGSHIP AND MIGHT OF YAHWEH **1–6**

1. The LORD reigns: for this acclamation of the divine king, see on 93:1.

let the earth rejoice: this summons is addressed, apparently, to the whole universe (cf. Isa. 42:10, 51:5) and/or to its inhabitants.

coastlands: or, 'isles' (see on 72:10). This term may denote the coastlands and islands of the Mediterranean Sea, but in this verse it refers probably to the remotest parts of the earth.

2. The verse begins with a description of Yahweh's theophany, using various word-pictures of older traditions, some of which may go back even to pre-Israelite times (cf. Ps. 29).

Clouds and thick darkness are reminiscent of Yahweh's theophany on Mount Sinai (cf. Dt. 4:11, 5:22), or of the coming Day of Yahweh (cf. Ezek. 34:12; Jl 2:2; Zeph. 1:15). This description points to the awe and mystery which surround God, who is said, metaphorically, to dwell in thick darkness (1 Kg. 8:12; 2 Chr. 6:1; Job 22:13).

righteousness and justice are the basis of all kingship, both divine and human. It helps the weak, and restrains the strong; thus the harmony of the society is fully maintained; cf. 82:3. Verse 2*b* occurs also in 89:14*a* (M.T. 15*a*); cf. 11QPs[a] Creat., verse 3; H. Brunner, 'Gerechtigkeit als Fundament des Thrones', *VT*, VIII (1958), pp. 426ff.

the foundation of his throne: this may refer either to the platform on which the throne is built (cf. Briggs, *CECBP*, II, p. 257), or to its supports and pillars (in various shapes and forms) (cf. Corswant, *DLBT*, p. 280). Perhaps the reference is to the legs of the throne (cf. Gunkel, *PGHAT*, p. 389); on an ivory relief from Megiddo the throne or its arms are supported by sphinxes (*ANEP*, pl. 332). The 'throne of God' may signify the rule or dominion of God (cf. 2 Sam. 3:10), which is characterized by righteousness and justice.

3. Fire is an important element in the descriptions of the theophanies of God (cf. Exod. 19:18, 24:17; Dt. 5:4, 9:10,15, 18:16; Ps. 50:3, etc.); this metaphor may have been suggested by a volcanic activity or, more likely, by a thunderstorm. Thus

God appears 'in fire' (Exod. 19:18), or he may be 'a devouring fire' (Dt. 4:24), and before him is a 'devouring fire' (50:3).
burns up his adversaries: (cf. 68:2 (M.T. 3), 106:18). Some scholars emend *ṣārāyw* ('his adversaries') into *ṣeᶜāḏāyw* ('his steps'), rendering 'and (fire) blazes about his steps' (so Wellhausen, Duhm, *et al.*). This change may improve the parallelism, but it is hardly necessary.

4. His lightnings: for the ancient people at least, a thunderstorm was an awe-inspiring phenomenon, and it is possible that every thunderstorm was regarded as a kind of theophany. The thunder was Yahweh's voice (cf. 29:3ff., 104:7), and the lightnings his arrows and spear (144:6; Hab. 3:11). Yahweh's lightnings also lighten the world (cf. 77:18*b* (M.T. 19*b*)), and suggest that God is near.
the earth sees and trembles: (cf. 77:16 (M.T. 17)). The Hebrew verbs in verses 4–6 are perfects, and consequently many translators prefer the past tense ('saw . . . trembled . . .'). If we have here a cultic presentation of a theophany, then the perfects may refer to the ritual which has just taken place; on the other hand, if we understand the Psalm eschatologically, then the verbs could be regarded as perfects of certainty, picturing future events (cf. Kraus, *PBK*, p. 673).

5. The mountains melt like wax: the mountains, which are a symbol of stability (cf. 30:7 (M.T. 8)), melt before the presence of the Lord (cf. 68:2 (M.T. 3); Mic. 1:4; Nah. 1:5).
before the Lord: i.e. before Yahweh. This is probably a variant on the similar phrase in verse 5*b*, which has *ʾaḏôn* ('the Lord of . . .'). See on 10:12, 140:7.
the Lord of all the earth: cf. Jos. 3:11,13; Mic. 4:13; Zech. 4:14, 6:5. This phrase depicts Yahweh as the ruler and master of the whole universe.

6. The messengers of the divine king are the heavens (cf. Isa. 52:7; see on 19:1), and their message is addressed to the whole world and all its inhabitants.
his righteousness (see on 33:5) is, apparently, parallel with 'his glory' (see on 19:1), and both may refer to Yahweh's work of salvation (cf. 50:6).
all the peoples: see on 66:8. Yahweh's victory will be made manifest not only to the people of Israel, but also to the whole world.

THE MEANING OF YAHWEH'S KINGSHIP 7–12

7. worshippers of images are probably the worshippers of other gods, as contrasted with Israel (cf. Isa. 42:17, 45:16f.; Jer. 10:14ff.). 'Image' (*pesel*) can signify either a molten or a carved image of any suitable material.

are put to shame: i.e. they fail to receive help from their helpless gods (cf. 25:3, 37:18f.; Isa. 1:29, 20:5ff.; Jer. 12:13, 48:13; Mic. 3:7).

who make their boast: i.e. who pride and glory themselves in what is worthless, and so their boast is empty (cf. 1 Kg. 20:11; Prov. 25:14, 27:1).

worthless idols: see on 96:5. This reflects the irony of the idol-worshipper's situation: the object of his praise and worship turns out to be something less than the worshipper himself.

all gods: this may be a synonym of the 'worthless idols' (verse 7*b*), or it may refer to the members of Yahweh's heavenly court (cf. 29:1, 82:1ff.). LXX has: 'his angels', so also V (cf. Heb. 1:6).

bow down before him: LXX, S, *NEB*, *et al.* take the verb as an imperative, but the *RSV* rendering is more natural.

Some scholars see in verse 7 an allusion to Yahweh's victory over other gods (cf. Weiser, *POTL*, p. 634), or an attempt to explain his relationship to the gods of other nations (cf. Johnson, *SKAI*, p. 86). In any case, this verse is a statement of faith, because, on many occasions during Israel's history, the Israelites had witnessed the victories of the nations worshipping such idols.

8. Zion: see on 65:1. Here it is used as a synonym for the inhabitants of Jerusalem.

the daughters of Judah (cf. 48:11 (M.T. 12)) are the 'cities of Judah'. For the expression, see Jos. 15:45: 'Ekron, with its towns (lit. 'and her daughters') and its villages'.

because of thy judgments: i.e. the judgments in overthrowing the forces of the enemy (cf. Johnson, *SKAI*, p. 80).

9. O Lord: this is deleted by some scholars for metrical reasons (so Gunkel, Kraus).

For thou . . . art most high: so also *NEB*; Oesterley *et al.* render: 'For thou art the Most High' (*TP*, p. 425). The Hebrew *ʿelyôn* can be either an adjective 'high, most high', or a divine title 'the Most High' (see on 47:2, 57:2). The former alternative seems more likely, and it provides a better parallelism with 'thou art exalted'.

above all gods: see verse 7*c*.

10. The LORD loves those who hate evil: this rendering presupposes a slight emendation (i.e. *ʾōhēḇ* for M.T. *ʾōhaḇê*, and *śōneʾê* (so S) for M.T. *śineʾû*); M.T. could be rendered: 'You who love the Lord, hate (imperative) evil'. *RSV* provides a better agreement with the following two lines, where the *Lord* is the subject of the verbs, and which describe his relationship with his people (cf. Prov. 8:13; Am. 5:15; for the opposite type of man, see Mic. 3:2).
he preserves the lives of his saints: or 'he protects the lives (i.e. souls) of his loyal servants'. For 'saint' (*ḥāsîḏ*), see on 30:4, 86:2.
from the hand of: or 'from the power of'.
the wicked: see on 1:1, 28:3, 92:7.

11. Light dawns: this reading is suggested by LXX, T, *et al.*, while M.T. has 'light is sown (*zārūaᶜ*)', for which there are some classical parallels (cf. Kirkpatrick, *BPCB*, p. 582) but no *OT* parallel. 'Light' is often a symbol of 'salvation' (cf. 27:1; Isa. 9:2) or of 'blessing' (cf. 118:27; Isa. 58:8,10, 60:1). *NEB* has 'A harvest of light is sown'.
the righteous: i.e. the man who honours his Covenant relationship with God and man (see on 1:5).
joy is the result of Yahweh's intervention on behalf of those who act and think in accordance with the will of God.
the upright in heart is a frequent term in the Psalter (see on 7:10; cf. 11:2, 32:11, 36:10 (M.T. 11), 64:10 (M.T. 11), 94:15); it is a synonym of 'the righteous'.

12. The Psalm ends as it began, with an invitation to rejoice. For verse 12*a*, cf. 32:11*a*.
his holy name: (=*NEB*) lit. 'his holy memorial'. In this context, 'memorial' is obviously an equivalent of 'name', as in Exod. 3:15. See on 135:13.

Psalm 98 God Comes to Rule

In a number of ways Ps. 98 resembles Ps. 96, so much so that both Psalms have been attributed to the same author. It is more likely, however, that the common phrases are due to the common cultic situation and liturgical phraseology. For the life-setting of the Psalm, see introduction to Ps. 96. Essentially this Psalm is a Hymn of Praise for the deliverance which Yahweh has wrought for his people, and which is also relevant to the whole creation.

This salvation may have been the deliverance from the Exile (so Kissane *et al.*), an anticipation of Yahweh's final advent envisaged in a 'prophetic style' as having already come to pass (cf. Oesterley, *TP*, p. 426), or a cultic representation of Yahweh's past and future saving acts (cf. Weiser, *POTL*, p. 637). The whole creation is summoned to rejoice and to acclaim Yahweh as king.

Ps. 98 is sometimes called an 'orphan Psalm' since its title consists only of 'A Psalm' (*mizmôr*, see Introduction, p. 46) without any further qualification. LXX has 'A Psalm of David', while S describes it as dealing with the deliverance from Egypt.

Because there are many points of contact with Deutero-Isaiah, this poem is thought to have been inspired by the coming of Cyrus (cf. McCullough, *PIB*, p. 525), but this similarity could be explained in many other ways.

PRAISE GOD FOR HIS VICTORY **1–3**

1. O sing to the LORD: i.e. celebrate in song the saving acts of God. This is identical with 96:1*a*.

a new song: see on 96:1. If indeed the Psalm had its origin in the last few years of the Babylonian exile, the 'new song' might have been intended to express Yahweh's triumph at the *new* Exodus, just as the people of Israel magnified God at the first Exodus (cf. Exod. 15:1ff.).

for he has done marvellous things: this is at least one of the reasons why Yahweh should be praised. The 'marvellous things' (see on 9:1, 78:11) are defined in verses 2–3 as the victory of Yahweh, manifested in the salvation of his Covenant people.

His right hand and **his holy arm** emphasize that Yahweh has triumphed by reason of his *own* strength without any essential help (cf. 44:3 (M.T. 4); Isa. 59:16, 63:5).

have gotten him victory: lit. 'have wrought salvation for him'.

2. The LORD has made known by having brought about the deliverance, so that it was not only known but also experienced.

he has revealed his vindication: this is parallel to the previous phrase, and consequently 'victory' (lit. 'salvation', see on 35:3) is synonymous with 'vindication' (lit. 'righteousness', see on 33:5), as is often the case in Is. 40–55 (cf. Isa. 46:13, 47:12, 51:5,6,8). The nations learn of Yahweh's victory not simply by hearsay, but they themselves are involved in this event (cf. Isa. 40:5, 52:10).

3. He has remembered: he has actively implemented his Covenant loyalty. See Childs, *MTI*, pp. 41ff.

his steadfast love: see on 26:3, 51:1. After this phrase LXX adds 'to Jacob', which provides a good parallel to 'and his faithfulness to the house of Israel'.
faithfulness (*'ᵉmûnāh*) refers to Yahweh's Covenant with Israel, and this relationship is characterized by a lasting loyalty (see on 36:5; cf. 89:1ff. (M.T. 2ff.)).
the house of Israel is the name of the Covenant people (cf. 115:12, 135:19).
All the ends of the earth: i.e. all the world (cf. 2:8, 22:27 (M.T. 28), 59:13 (M.T. 14), 67:7 (M.T. 8), 72:8; Isa. 45:22, 52:10). It seems that the redemption of Israel will provide the opportunity for the nations to turn to Yahweh (cf. Isa. 45:22ff.).
have seen: Kissane (*BP*, p. 451) suggests 'behold . . .', but there is no need to emend M.T. as we have a good external parallelism in verses 1*b* and 3*a*, 2 and 3*b*.
the victory of our God: i.e. his salvation (see on 35:3).

LET THE WORLD SALUTE THE KING **4–9**

4. Make a joyful noise: or 'Utter your cry of homage . . .'. In 1 Sam. 10:24 this cry consisted of: 'Long live the king', and the above phrase may refer to a similar situation here (cf. 47:1f. (M.T. 2f.); Zeph. 3:14; Zech. 9:9). Such a cry is not simply a wish, but also a recognition of the royal authority and a submission to it.
all the earth: i.e. the whole world and all that is in it (cf. 66:1, 100:1).
break forth into joyous song: lit. 'break forth, and shout in joy' (cf. Isa. 52:9).
sing praises: or 'make melody' (see on 66:4).

5. the lyre (*NEB* 'the harp') was a stringed instrument with a varying number of strings; the minimum may have been three, the maximum, as far as we know, twelve (cf. E. Werner, *IDB*, III, p. 474). It could be used both on religious and secular occasions (cf. Isa. 23:16; see on 43:4).
the sound of melody: i.e. a song. Cf. Isa. 51:3.

6. trumpets (*ḥᵃṣōṣᵉrôṯ*) were straight metal tubes, and those described in Num. 10:2 were made of silver. They were used, primarily, on religious occasions; trumpets were blown during the accession ceremony of Joash (2 Kg. 11:14).
horn (*šôpār*) is one of the best known musical instruments in the *OT*, and it is mentioned some 70 times. Usually it was made of ram's horn, but later also the horns of the ibex and the antelope

were used. The horn was also associated with the enthronement ceremonies (cf. 1 Kg. 1:39).

before the King: i.e. in his presence.

the Lord: some scholars regard this word (*yhwh*) as a gloss on 'the King', since it overloads the line, making it 3 + 4 instead of the usual 3 + 3.

7. Let the sea roar: (=96:11*b*). It is possible that the thundering sea and the 'floods' (verse 8) were intended to remind the hearers of the primeval enemies of Yahweh. Once they roared their defiance of him (93:3), but now they pay homage.

all that fills it: see 96:11.

the world (*tēḇēl*) is probably the dry land in contrast to the sea.

those who dwell in it: see on 24:1*b*.

8. Let the floods clap their hands: the 'floods' are probably the rivers of the earth, although at the same time they may be reminiscent of the primeval Chaos waters (cf. verse 7). The clapping of hands formed a part of the acclamation of the King (cf. 2 Kg. 11:12) and it was an expression of joy (cf. 47:1 (M.T. 2); Isa. 55:12). The same gesture may also signify a malicious joy, as in Ezek. 25:6; Nah. 3:19.

let the hills sing: the floods and the hills form a poetic description for the *whole* created world, just as the sea and the world did in verse 7.

9. This verse is practically identical with 96:13.

for he comes: this is found twice in 96:13, and some would repeat it also here (so LXX (Codex Alexandrinus)).

He will judge: i.e. he will both save and punish. For Israel at least, the emphasis was upon the former aspect, and therefore God's judgment was awaited with joy; because it was characterized by righteousness and equity, it excluded all *false* hopes (cf. 67:4 (M.T. 5)).

with equity: in 96:13 we have 'with his truth', but cf. 96:10.

Psalm 99 Holy Yet Forgiving

This is the last of the so-called Enthronement Psalms (see Introduction, pp. 33f.), and it opens with the characteristic cry: 'The Lord reigns'. Its cultic setting was the Feast of Tabernacles, and the allusions to the Covenant (cf. verses 4ff. and 7ff.) may point to the renewal of the Covenant, which may have formed an important part of the great Autumnal Festival.

The structure of the Psalm is problematic; *RSV* divides it into two strophes, while some other scholars prefer a threefold division: verses 1–3, 4–5, and 6–9, which is partly suggested by the phrase 'Holy is he' (verses 3 and 5) and its more expanded form in verse 9 (cf. the Trisagion in Isa. 6:3). On the other hand, it is possible that there is some sort of refrain in verses 5 and 9.

It is a peculiarity of this Psalm that there is little, if any, dependence upon Deutero-Isaiah, and there is nothing in the Psalm itself which would militate against a pre-Exilic origin.

The metre of the Psalm is irregular.

YAHWEH'S UNIVERSAL KINGSHIP 1–5

Yahweh rules from Zion as the Great king, the ruler of the whole world. He is the Mighty king, but his strength is primarily manifested in righteousness.

1. The Lord reigns: see on 93:1.

let the peoples tremble: the reference is not simply to the peoples of Canaan (so R. H. Kennett, *Old Testament Essays* (1928), p. 197), but also to the inhabitants of the whole world.

He sits enthroned: this is parallel to 'The Lord reigns'. The preposition in 'upon the cherubim' is lacking in M.T.; *AV* suggests 'between', while Leslie (*PAP*, p. 83) has 'above'; *NEB* 'on'. Cf. 80:1.

The biblical cherubim have little in common with the popular concept of cherubs and their innocent baby faces; they were mysterious celestial beings, such as those guarding the garden of Eden (Gen. 3:24), and sometimes they were regarded as personifications of winds or storm-clouds (cf. 18:10 (M.T. 11) = 2 Sam. 22:11). Occasionally they are depicted as winged creatures with an animal body, and with a human and/or animal face or faces (cf. Ezek. 41:18ff.). These mysterious creatures may have formed the cherub-throne of Yahweh, which in time came to be associated with the Ark of the Covenant (see Clements, *GT*, pp. 28–35).

let the earth quake: i.e. the whole world and all that is in it.

2. The Lord is great in Zion: Yahweh is the only true world king (cf. 48:2 (M.T. 3)) whose kingdom is the whole universe, and the earthly centre of his reign is Zion (see on 65:1). Some exegetes are not certain whether the reference is to the heavenly Zion (cf. Oesterley, *TP*, p. 429), or to Jerusalem where was his Temple and the Ark (cf. v. Rad, *OTT*, I, p. 237). The latter alternative is more likely in view of the contents of the

Psalm; see also N. W. Porteous, 'Jerusalem-Zion: the Growth of a Symbol', *Living the Mystery* (1967), pp. 93–111.

he is exalted over all the peoples: this is an affirmation of faith, especially when the apparent might of the nations is contrasted with the continual plight of the people of God.

3. Let them praise: this is a call to all the peoples to give glory to God's name, and to accept the hidden fact that Yahweh does reign; cf. also v. Rad, *OTT*, I, pp. 356ff.

thy great and terrible name: some scholars either omit the pronoun 'thy' (so Briggs), or change it into 'his' (so Wellhausen, Gunkel, Kissane, *NEB*, *et al.*); but there is no real need for this alteration. 'Terrible' might be rendered as 'awesome' or 'awe-inspiring' (see on 65:5).

Holy is he: this may refer either to Yahweh or to his name (so *AV*). The parallel expressions in verses 5 and 9 favour the former alternative. 'Holy' describes not only God's awe-inspiring might, but also his moral majesty (cf. 1 Sam. 6:20; Isa. 6:3ff.); see on 71:22.

4. Mighty King: lit. 'and the king's strength' (*RSVm*). M.T. of verse 4*a* is difficult; the best solution may be to take 'and the strength of' (*weᶜōz*) with verse 3, reading: 'Holy is he and mighty' (similarly *NEB*) (i.e. *weᶜāz*), or 'It is holy and mighty' (cf. Johnson, *SKAI*, p. 62). Verse 4*a* could be rendered: '(You are) a king who loves justice', or if we retain M.T. as it is: 'and a strong one is king . . .' (revocalizing *ᶜōz* as *ᶜaz*).

lover of justice: verses 3*b* and 4*a* could be translated: 'Holy is he and mighty, (yet) a King who loves justice' (cf. *RP*). God's power is not used despotically, but it serves the functioning of true justice and righteousness. Cf. 33:5, 37:28.

thou hast established equity: God's reign is distinguished by absolute justice and equity or fairness; the same thought is repeated in the second part of the verse.

thou hast executed justice and righteousness: i.e. God has brought about and has sustained a just social order through his Covenant law. The same characteristics ought also to mark the rule of his regent, the King of Judah (cf. 2 Sam. 8:15; 1 Kg. 10:9; Isa. 16:5, etc.).

in Jacob: i.e. among the people of God; cf. Isa. 2:6: '. . . thy people, the house of Jacob'. See on 20:1, 85:1; cf. Isa. 40:27, 41:8,14, 43:1,22.

5. Extol: Yahweh is the high and lofty one (Isa. 57:15), anp

therefore it is fitting to extol him and to recognize him as the supreme Lord of all.
our God may be an allusion to the Covenant relationship (cf. Kraus, *PBK*, p. 684; Exod. 20:2; Jos. 24:17,18,24; Neh. 9:32, 10:32ff.). See on 113:5.
worship: i.e. fall prostrate (see on 29:2) in humility before the divine king. This act of homage may have taken place before the Ark of the Covenant (cf. Weiser, *POTL*, p. 642) or in its direction.
at his footstool: the reference may be to the Temple (Isa. 60:13), the Ark (1 Chr. 28:2), Jerusalem (Lam. 2:1), or even the whole earth (Isa. 66:1; Mt. 5:35). In this verse the 'footstool' is probably the Ark (cf. Mowinckel, *PIW*, 1, p. 117), as also in 132:7, or Zion which would correspond to 'his holy mountain' in verse 9. These terms, however, need not be mutually exclusive. The ancient kings are often pictured sitting on their thrones, with their feet on a footstool, probably due to the height of the throne (see *ANEP*, pll. 460, 463).

YAHWEH AND HIS PEOPLE **6–9**

This section outlines Yahweh's relationships with Israel, and this salvation-history, or *Heilsgeschichte*, provides the pattern for the future.

6. This verse is exegetically difficult. Verses 6–8 could be regarded as a historical retrospect of Israel's relationships with God, or they could refer to the present (i.e. there are still in the community a Moses, an Aaron, and a Samuel); some think that the three heroes of the past are depicted as interceding in heaven, as Onias and Jeremiah in 2 Mac. 15:12ff., but this is not likely. The first suggestion seems to be the most plausible one.
Moses and Aaron . . .: the representatives of the priests, while Samuel was a type of the prophets. Johnson (*SKAI*, p. 62) takes 'his priests' and 'those who called on his name' as plurals of excellence, preceded by *bêṯ essentiae*, and renders:

> 'Moses, and Aaron as His priest,
> And Samuel as one who calls on His Name
> Would cry to Yahweh, and He would answer them'.

We may regard Moses as the original Covenant mediator, and Aaron and Samuel as prototypes of priests and prophets respectively.
They cried to the Lord: there are a number of instances where Moses, Aaron, and Samuel are portrayed as exercising inter-

cessory functions (Moses in Exod. 14:15, 17:11ff., 32:11ff., 30ff.; Num. 12:13, 14:13ff.; Aaron in Num. 16:44–8; Samuel in 1 Sam. 7:8ff., 12:16ff.). This verse may have been in the mind of the prophet in Jer. 15:1 where the situation was so serious that even the great intercessors, Moses and Samuel, could not have turned away the impending doom.

and he answered them: i.e. he granted them their request.

7. He spoke to them: most exegetes take this to refer to Moses, Aaron, and Samuel, although some (e.g. Delitzsch) think that the object is 'the whole people' (*BCP*, III, p. 102).

the pillar of cloud was a symbol of the divine presence (cf. Exod. 13:21ff., 14:19ff.; Num. 12:5, 14:14; Dt. 31:15). God is depicted as speaking to Moses, in a pillar of cloud, in Exod. 33:9, and to Aaron in Num. 12:5; there is no such account concerning Samuel, unless 1 Sam. 3:3ff. comes into this category.

they kept his testimonies: see on 119:2. The task of the prophets and priests was not only to hear the voice of God but also to preserve and transmit the terms of the Covenant (i.e. testimonies).

the statutes: (see on 119:5), in this context they are synonymous with 'testimonies', and belong to the Covenant terminology.

8. O LORD our God: see verse 5.

thou didst answer them: the object still seems to be Moses, Aaron, and Samuel, although it is probable that the reference is to the experience of the people of God.

thou wast a forgiving God to them: i.e. to the people. It is less likely that the offenders were Moses, Aaron, and Samuel, even though some of their 'sins' are mentioned in the *OT* (e.g. Num. 20:12 records the unbelief of Moses; Exod. 32:1ff. deals with Aaron's part in the Golden Calf episode; 1 Sam. 8:1ff. describes the failure of Samuel to discpline his own sons).

an avenger of their wrongdoings: i.e. when the people persisted in breaking and neglecting the terms of the Covenant, God punished them (cf. Exod. 37:6f.). The Covenant is not a one-sided affair; it brings blessings upon those who keep it, and curses upon those who set it at nought.

9. See verse 5.

his holy mountain is probably Zion (as in 2:6; Dan. 9:16; cf. Ps. 3:5 (M.T. 6), 15:1, 43:3, 48:2 (M.T. 3)). The holiness of the mountain is a derived quality; only the holiness of God is original.

Psalm 100 Serve The Lord with Gladness

This Psalm is occasionally classed with the Enthronement Psalms (cf. Ringgren, *FP*, p. 18), but there is no explicit reference to Yahweh's kingship, and the song itself is of a very general nature; it would fit most Israelite festivals. The Psalm is obviously a Hymn (see Introduction, pp. 32f.) or a Hymn of Procession (cf. G. Quell, *Das Kultische Problem der Psalmen* (1926), p. 71).

Verses 1–3 may have been sung by the pilgrims approaching the gates of the Temple, while verses 4–5 could have been chanted by a choir within the Temple courts. The purpose of this festal entry was to offer thanks to Yahweh.

This hymn is in some ways an echo of 95:1–7, and it consists of two sections, similar in structure. Verses 1–2 and 4 are introductions, while verses 3 and 5 are the main sections of the hymn, in miniature, stating the grounds for praising God.

The metre is fairly regular 3+3+3.

A Psalm: see Introduction, p. 46.

thank offering: (*tôḏāh*) or 'thanksgiving' (as in verse 4). Originally the reference must have been to a congregational act rather than to a private thank-offering or thanksgiving.

THE GRACIOUS MAJESTY OF YAHWEH 1–3

1. Make a joyful noise: i.e. shout aloud in praise. Cf. 98:4*a*, where the words may have a more specific meaning, such as a cry of homage to the divine king.

all the lands: all the earth rather than 'all the land' (so Gunkel), meaning the people of Israel. Since Yahweh is the Lord of all, it is fitting that *all* peoples should praise him. It is possible that the chosen people of God *represented* all the peoples of the world.

2. Serve the Lord: this may suggest either the wider relationship between the people and their God (as in Jos. 24:14ff.), or worship in particular (cf. Exod. 3:12; 2 Sam. 15:2; Isa. 19:21). The second half of verse 2 seems to support the latter interpretation.

with gladness: this is not an optional extra, but the right mood that befits the blessings which God bestows upon his people (cf. Dt. 28:47).

Come into his presence: i.e. into his Temple (cf. 95:6, 96:8; Isa. 1:12).

with singing: the theme of their songs would be the acts of God in saving and sustaining his people (cf. 107:22).

3. Know: this is more than merely an intellectual exercise; in this context it implies the acknowledgement that Yahweh is God, and a self-involvement in all the demands and responsibilities which the Lordship of Yahweh implies (cf. Dt. 4:39; Isa. 43:10; Jer. 3:13, 14:20).

the LORD is God: this was probably a well-known cultic phrase used to renounce all other gods, and to declare allegiance to Yahweh alone, as the Covenant God (cf. Dt. 4:35ff.; Jos. 24:18; 1 Kg. 18:39). Whether this is an affirmation of monotheism depends upon the definition of the latter, as well as upon the particular setting (cf. J. Barr, 'The Problem of Israelite Monotheism', *TGUOS*, XVII (1959), pp. 52ff.; H. H. Rowley, 'Moses and Monotheism', *From Moses to Qumran* (1963), pp. 35–63).

It is he that made us: the reference is not to the creation of man, but to the formation of the people of God (cf. Isa. 29:23, 43:1,21, 44:2, 60:21).

and we are his: the Hebrew tradition has preserved two alternative readings. *RSV*, *NEB* follow the *Ḳ^e^rê* variant (*w^e^lô*) supported by Aquila, Jerome, and T, while *K^e^ṯîḇ* has *w^e^lōʾ* ('and not (ourselves)'), so also LXX, Sym, S, etc. The former alternative is better since it provides a progression of thought, and is more fitting in the context (cf. Isa. 43:1,21).

we are his people: i.e. we are his possession.

the sheep of his pasture: cf. 74:1, 79:13, 95:7; Isa. 40:11; Ezek. 34:31. This phrase is a synonym of 'his people' (cf. Jer. 23:1f.). The figure of God as shepherd is quite frequent in the *OT* (see on 23:1) as well as in the *NT* (cf. Lk. 15:3–6; Jn 10:1–18).

PRAISE THE ENDURING GOODNESS OF YAHWEH **4–5**

4. Enter his gates: i.e. the gates of the Temple courts (see on 96:8).

with thanksgiving: see on 69:30.

his courts: the crowds would be gathered in the various courts (see on 96:8), and not in the Temple itself.

Give thanks to him: thanksgiving is never a private affair, but an act of the whole worshipping community. They have been blessed as God's people, and as such they offer their thanks.

bless his name: i.e. praise God for his blessings (cf. 34:1 (M.T. 2)); see on 16:7, 104:1.

5. For the LORD is good: here the Psalmist gives the reasons why God is worthy of praise and thanks. The expression of this motivation is in general terms, well established in cultic usage (cf. 106:1, 107:1, 118:1, 136:1). The purpose was not so much to enumerate the various events as to interpret them. See on 106:1.
his steadfast love: or 'his Covenant loyalty' (see on 26:3, 51:1).
his faithfulness: or 'his dependability' (see on 36:5).
to all generations: it is unending.

Psalm 101 The Ideal King and his Rule

Psalm 101 is generally regarded as a Royal Psalm intended for the Davidic king (verse 8); it can be taken as a vow which the King makes at his coronation outlining his future policy and professing his loyalty to the divine Covenant, or it can be viewed as 'an affirmation of the rule which he is wont to exercise' (Johnson, *SKAI*, p. 106). The setting of the Psalm would be the annual festival, in the course of which the King suffered a symbolic ritual humiliation reminiscent of that of the Babylonian kings in their New Year Festival (cf. *ANET*, p. 334a).

The former alternative seems slightly more likely, and the vow could have been uttered, not only at the enthronement of the Davidic prince, but also at the yearly royal festival. The Psalm may be the King's response to the ritual acts whereby he was proclaimed the regent of Yahweh, or whereby he was confirmed in his office. Kraus (*PBK*, p. 689; cf. von Rad, *PHOE*, pp. 221–31) sees in our Psalm a possible influence of the Egyptian royal protocol.

Mowinckel (*PIW*, I, pp. 67f.) describes the poem as a 'Psalm of promise' in which the King pays his homage to Yahweh for the election of the Davidic house and other blessings, and in which he promises to rule the people of God with righteousness and according to the Covenant.

The date of the Psalm is the monarchical period and Deissler (*PWdB*, III, p. 46) suggests a date *c.* 620 B.C.

The metre is, on the whole, 3 + 2.

A Psalm of David: see Introduction, pp. 46 and 43ff.

THE MORAL AND RELIGIOUS STANDARDS OF THE KING 1–4

1. I will sing: in its form this phrase calls to mind the hymnic introductions (cf. Gunkel, *EP*, p. 38). The versions and 11QPs[a] follow M.T.; emendations are not justified.

Verse 1*a* suggests that the theme of the praise is Yahweh's **loyalty** (*ḥeseḏ*: see on 26:3) and **justice** (*mišpāṭ*; see on 36:6, 119:7) although some exegetes (e.g. Davies, Kissane, Weiser, Eaton) see here, at least primarily, an allusion to the King's own Covenant loyalty and obedience. It is more likely that *ḥeseḏ* refers to the proofs of Yahweh's Covenant faithfulness to the Davidic house (cf. 89:1 (M.T. 2)). 'Justice' may be the divine gift to the King enabling him to judge rightly (see on 72:1; cf. Dt. 17:18ff.). For the expression 'loyalty and justice', see Hos. 12:6 (M.T. 5); Mic. 6:8; Mt. 23:23.

2. I will give heed: the exact meaning of the Hebrew *hiśkîl* is uncertain; it can denote such meanings as 'to consider' (Isa. 41:20), 'to teach' (32:8), 'to act wisely' (2:10), 'to prosper' (Isa. 52:13), 'to grasp the inner meaning of something' (106:7), etc.; it can also suggest the composition, or use of a *maśkîl* (see Introduction, p. 47) which is a certain type of poem.

the way that is blameless: this is taken by Johnson (*SKAI*, p. 105) as the theme and title of the Psalm: 'A Faultless Way'. *Dereḵ tāmîm* is a conduct which is characterized by integrity, and those whose life is such can be described as *tᵉmîmê ḏereḵ*, 'whose way is blameless' (see on 119:1).

when wilt thou come to me?: some commentators (e.g. Gunkel, Kraus, Deissler) render, with slight variations: 'Truth will come to me', reading *ʾemeṯ* for *māṯay* ('when'), or 'May truth come before me' (so Leslie, *PAP*, p. 98). For other suggestions, see Kissane, *BP*, p. 459. M.T. may be regarded as a brief prayer by the King in the midst of his ritual humiliation, or as a later addition (so Wellhausen, *PBP*, p. 105). *NEB* has 'whatever may befall me'.

integrity of heart: since the heart was thought to be the centre of the intellect and will (see on 27:3) we might render 'integrity of mind' (cf. 78:72 (M.T. 73)), hence 'I act with integrity' (cf. 1 Kg. 9:4).

my house is either the King's family or the court.

3. anything that is base: lit. 'a word (or 'thing') of Belial'. 'Belial' is a transliteration of the Hebrew *bᵉliyyaᶜal*, a compound noun made up of the negative particle *bᵉlî* ('without') and *yaᶜal*, which seems to mean 'what is profitable' or 'what is of worth'. Therefore *bᵉliyyaᶜal* is either a 'worthless man' or a 'thing of worthlessness' (cf. Dhorme, *CJ*, p. 517; see on 18:4). 'Belial' appears in a dissimilated form as 'Beliar' in the literature of the intertestamental period (see Russell, *MMJA*, pp. 278f.).

I hate . . . who fall away: *NEB* 'I will hate disloyalty'; for 'I hate', see on 68:1. The Hebrew is difficult; *BDB* (p. 962a) gives a possible literal rendering: '. . . to do deeds that swerve'. LXX (T, S) suggests *ᶜōśê* ('those who practise . . .') for *ᶜaśōh* ('to do . . .' (?)), while *RSV* reads 'work of . . .' (*maᶜaśēh*). The word *sēṭîm* (*RSV* 'those who fall away') is a *hapax legomenon* in the *OT*, but many exegetes associate it with *śûṭ* ('to fall away'); LXX translates it by *parabaseis* ('transgressions'), which may be a likely indication of the meaning of *sēṭîm*. Dahood (*PAB*, I, p. 31) suggests: 'I hate the making of images', and he thinks that 'I hate' is a technical term 'in the formula of repudiation of false gods'.

it shall not cleave to me: or 'he shall not remain close to me'. For the verb *d-b-ḳ*, see on 63:8. Johnson (*SKAI*, p. 106) proposes: 'He is no adherent of mine'.

4. Perverseness of heart: or 'A perverse mind' (cf. Prov. 11:20, 17:20).

shall be far from me: lit. 'shall depart . . .'.

I will know nothing . . .: i.e. I will not participate in evil. The verb *y-d-ᶜ* ('to know') describes an experience which involves, not only the mind, but the whole man; it may be both a total response and a total obedience. So the King will have nothing to do with anything that is evil. Cf. also *ANET*, p. 34.

THE KING'S JUST RULE 5–8

5. who slanders: for the form of the Hebrew participle, see *GK* 90m. Slandering one's neighbour involves not only a defamation of his character; it may also lead to a false testimony in a capital charge (cf. Lev. 19:16). Therefore we can understand the severity of the reaction of the King: '(Him . . .) I will destroy' (or '. . . I will silence'; cf. *KBL*, p. 808).

man of haughty looks: lit. '(one) lofty of eyes'; the Hebrew phrase *geḇah ᶜênayim* occurs only here in the *OT*, but it is similar to 'the haughty eyes' in 18:27 (M.T. 28), q.v.; cf. 131:1; Prov. 21:4.

arrogant heart: lit. 'broad of heart'. The allusion is not to a broadminded man but, apparently, to a greedy, covetous individual (cf. Prov. 28:25; 1QS iv:9); *NEB* 'pompous'.

I will not endure: LXX and S (similarly *NEB*) suggest: 'with him I will not eat' (*ʾittô lōʾ ʾōḵēl*, for M.T. *ʾōṯô lōʾ ʾûḵāl*). M.T. finds a parallel in Isa. 1:13, and it is probably a pregnant construction for 'I cannot bear' (cf. Jer. 44:22).

6. This verse provides an antithesis to verse 5.
I will look with favour on . . .: lit. 'My eyes (are) on . . .'. The phrase may suggest 'to look after', 'to care for' (cf. Gen. 44:21; Ps. 33:18, 34:15 (M.T. 16); Jer. 39:12, 40:4).
the faithful in the land: i.e. those loyal to Yahweh (cf. the similar expression in 35:20). They are the ones who shall dwell on Yahweh's holy hill (15:1) and in his land.
dwell with me: they shall be his associates (cf. Cohen, *PSon*, p. 327), and shall receive his favour.
the way that is blameless: as in verse 2.
shall minister to me: the verb *š-r-t* ('to minister') can be used of serving both men in authority and God; its subject may be not only men, but also angels (103:21, 104:4). The Hebrew verb often describes the activities of the Levites (cf. Num. 3:6; Dt. 10:8, 17:12).
7. who practises deceit: see on 52:2.
in my house: cf. verse 2. The expression may refer not only to the royal family and the court, but also to the whole land, as suggested by verse 8.
who utters lies: for *šeḳer* ('lie'), see on 52:3, 119:29.
shall continue: lit. 'shall be established'. No liar shall have a permanent place in the King's favour (cf. Prov. 29:12; Zeph. 1:9).
8. Morning by morning: judgment was usually administered in the morning (see 2 Sam. 15:2; Jer. 21:12; cf. Ps. 46:5 (M.T. 6)), and the King would normally deal with the more difficult legal cases (cf. 1 Kg. 3:16–28). The destruction of *all* the wicked in the land is an ideal rather than a fact; cf. *ANET*, p. 178, where Hammurabi makes similar claims. Dahood (*PAB*, I, p. 300) reads *liḇᵉḳārîm* ('like cattle'), for M.T. *labbᵉḳārîm* ('morning by morning'), but *RSV* seems preferable. J. Schreiner (*Sion-Jerusalem: Jahwes Königssitz* (1963), p. 134) argues that M.T. means 'early in the morning', and not 'every morning', emphasizing the zeal of the King.
I will destroy: see verse 5.
the wicked: see on 1:1, 28:3, 92:7. 'The wicked of the earth' is found also in 75:8 (M.T. 9).
evildoers: for *pōᶜᵃlê ʾāwen*, see on 28:3.
the city of the Lord is Jerusalem which is parallel to 'the land'. The meaning seems to be that what is done in Jerusalem affects the whole land. In 46:4 (M.T. 5) Jerusalem is called 'the

city of God' (or 'the city of our God' in 48:1 (M.T. 2); cf. G. Wanke, *Die Zionstheologie der Korachiten* (*BZAW*, 97, 1966, pp. 100–6)).

Psalm 102 PRAYER TO THE EVERLASTING GOD

This is the fifth of the seven Penitential Psalms of the early Church (the others are Ps. 6, 32, 38, 51, 130, 147), although there is no explicit expression of penitence. It is very likely, however, that the very description of the calamity or illness may serve as an implicit confession of one's sin (cf. verse 10); if God is just, and if he has caused the distress, then it must be ultimately due to one's sin, or the result of the collective responsibility (cf. Jos. 7:1; 2 Sam. 21:1–7).

Some scholars (e.g. Duhm, Schmidt) see the Psalm as composed of two different parts, consisting of verses 1–11, 23–8 and 12–22; or 1–11, 23–4 and 12–22 and 25–8. Verses 1–11 could be described as an individual Lament, while verses 12–22 are clearly hymnic in character, and are sometimes taken as a 'prayer for Zion and its people' (Eaton, *PTBC*, p. 244); they are also reminiscent of prophetic speech. Kraus (*PBK*, p. 695) argues that during Exile the *Heilsgeschichte* of the nation had become obscured by the judgment upon the people of God, and therefore the lament was set in the context of prophetic hope. Verses 23–4 return once more to lamentation, and the final verses (25–8) resume the praise of God, and include prophetic elements.

The more likely explanation is to assume that Ps. 102 is an Individual Lament in which the troubles of the afflicted man are related to, and set against the background of, the destruction of Jerusalem and its hoped-for restoration. Mowinckel (*He That Cometh* (1956), p. 84, n.4) suggests that the Psalm belongs 'to the cultic prayers at the harvest and New Year festival' and that the 'I' of this Psalm refers either to the King or to the cultic representative of the congregation; so the calamity of Zion is also his suffering and 'sickness'.

The Psalm belongs to the Exilic or early post-Exilic age, while Mowinckel (op. cit., p. 85, n.4) thinks that the date of the poem may be between 598 and 587 B.C.

The dominant metre is 3+3.

The title of the Psalm designates it as a prayer (see on 65:2) of 'one afflicted' (for *ʿānî*, see on 34:2) in time of trouble. According to the Mishnah (*Taanith* ii:3), Ps. 102 was one of the Psalms used on days of fasting.

THE INVOCATION OF YAHWEH **1–2**

This introduction to the lament uses the traditional language of liturgy, and therefore it resembles a mosaic of phrases from different Psalms.

1. my prayer: see on 65:2. For the phrase cf. 39:2 (M.T. 3). **my cry:** (see on 18:6) or, 'my cry for help'; this expression is used as a synonym of 'my prayer' (cf. 1QH v:12). N. Snaith (*The Seven Psalms* (1964), p. 70) points out that the Psalmist does not imply that God has been unmindful of him, but that some of the theological difficulties have been caused by the survival of an old-fashioned phraseology (cf. Lam. 3:44: 'thou hast wrapped thyself with a cloud so that no prayer can pass through'). Snaith may be right; but it is difficult to be certain whether expressions of this sort were taken in a 'literal' sense or not. A contrast to the thought of our verse is provided by Isa. 65:24: 'Before they call I will answer, while they are yet speaking I will hear.'

2. Do not hide thy face . . .: see on 13:1, 27:9, 69:17. **in the day of my distress:** as in 59:16. Kraus (*PBK*, p. 696) thinks that the Psalmist is speaking of the day on which the oppressed man and his enemies appear before Yahweh in order to wait for his judgment (cf. 59:16 (M.T. 17)); the suppliant is hoping for an oracle of salvation.

Incline thy ear: so also in 31:2 (M.T. 3), 71:2; for similar expressions, see 17:6, 86:1, 88:2 (M.T. 3); Dan. 9:18.

answer me speedily: see 69:17 (M.T. 18).

in the day when I call: this occurs also in 56:9 (M.T. 10).

THE DESCRIPTION OF THE AFFLICTION **3–11**

3. like smoke: so also *NEB*, following some Hebrew MSS, LXX, T, and Jerome in reading *keʿāšān*; M.T. has 'in smoke'. See on 37:20; cf. 68:2 (M.T. 3); Hos. 13:3.

my bones burn like a furnace: the problem is caused by the Hebrew *môḳēḏ*, which is found elsewhere in Isa. 33:14 and in Lev. 6:9 (the feminine form of the noun). It may denote a 'furnace', 'hearth', or a 'burning mass' (see Snaith, *The Seven Psalms*, p. 73; *AV*, *RV* have 'firebrand'), and probably also a 'fiery heat', 'fire', which may be its meaning here. The Psalmist is depicting in picturesque language the effects of fever, and 'my bones' may refer to one's bodily frame (so Cohen, *PSon*, p. 328;

cf. 6:2 (M.T. 3)), or to one's whole being (35:10). For *ʿeṣem* ('bone'), see Johnson, *VITAI*, pp. 67ff. Because the author is using stereotyped expressions, it is not easy to say whether he was actually suffering from fever (or a similar illness), or whether the word-pictures were simply used to describe the feeling of God-forsakenness which had arisen on account of the affliction.

4. My heart: this is either a circumlocution of 'I' (so *NEB*), or an allusion to the centre of one's strength and vitality (so Cohen, *PSon*, p. 328).

is smitten like grass: my vigour is like the green grass that wilts in the scorching heat of the sun (cf. Isa. 49:10; also Ps. 121:6; Hos. 9:16).

withered: this verb is deleted by some scholars (e.g. Briggs, Gunkel, Oesterley) as an explanatory gloss. LXX renders verse 4*a*: 'I am smitten like grass and my heart is dried up.'

I forget: his troubles are so great that he has lost all his appetite (cf. 1 Sam. 1:7,8; Job 33:20). Some exegetes associate *š-k-ḥ*, not with 'to forget', but with the Ugaritic *ṯkḥ* ('to wilt') (cf. Driver, *CML*, p. 151b; Dahood, *PNWSP*, pp. 11f.), rendering: 'I am wasting away not eating my food'. The same idea is obtained by assuming a transposition of letters, that is, *kāḥaštî* ('I grow lean') instead of *šāḵaḥtî* (cf. 109:24; Snaith, op. cit., p. 74).

my bread: the Hebrew *leḥem* usually means 'bread', but it can also denote 'food' in general (136:25; 147:9); so also in Ugaritic (cf. Gordon, *UT*, p. 427).

5. Because of . . .: there is no verb in verse 5*a*, and therefore many commentators (e.g. Baethgen, Gunkel, Kraus) supply *yāgaʿtî* ('I am weary') (for similar expressions, see 6:6 (M.T. 7), 69:3 (M.T. 4)) at the beginning of the verse. For another possibility, see *NEB*.

my bones cleave to my flesh: *AV* '. . . to my skin' which is the more likely rendering. For a brief discussion on *bāśār* ('flesh'), see on 38:3, 56:4. *AV* follows the meaning of the Arabic cognate of *bāśār* (cf. Gordon, *UT*, p. 377). The Psalmist describes himself as being nothing but skin and bones.

6. a vulture: the meaning of *ḳāʾāṯ* is uncertain. LXX (V) has 'pelican', which is regarded as unclean (cf. Lev. 11:13–18); but, since it is a gregarious water bird, it is hardly fitting in the present context. G. R. Driver (cf. *PEQ*, LXXXVI (1955), p. 16) suggests: 'a desert owl' (so also *NEB*); its name (*ḳāʾāṯ*) may be onomatopoeic, derived from the cries of the bird.

owl: the Hebrew *kôs* may be a general term for owls, which were unclean birds (Lev. 11:17; Dt. 14:16). The word-picture in verse 6 implies that the sufferer was regarded as unclean, and that his situation was made worse by his loneliness. Both ideas would fit a man who was near to death (cf. 88:5 (M.T. 6)). Gunkel (*PGHAT*, p. 438) thinks that the point of comparison is the wailing cries of the birds and those of the stricken man (cf. Job 30:29f.).

the waste places: or 'ruins' (*NEB*).

7. I lie awake: lit. 'I watch'.

I am: some exegetes emend the verb *wāʾehyeh* into *wāʾenheh* ('and I wail') or *wāʾehᵉmāyāh* ('and I groan'). M.T. may, however, be right: 'I am like a restless bird, lonely on a housetop' (cf. 1 Sam. 9:25); similarly Kissane (*BP*, p. 464).

bird: *ṣippôr*, see on 84:3.

8. . . . taunt me: i.e. the adversaries regard the Psalmist's illness (or his troubles in general) as deserved, and the man himself as forsaken by God (cf. 22:7f. (M.T. 8f.), 42:10 (M.T. 11), 44:13 (M.T. 14)).

those who deride me: *BDB* 'those mad against me'. LXX and S suggest *mᵉhalᵉlay* ('those who (previously) praised me'), but the M.T. reading gives a better parallel to 'my enemies' (verse 8*a*).

use my name for a curse: or 'they curse by me'. This may have involved the use of some such formula as that found in Gen. 48:20: 'God make you as Ephraim and as Manasseh', except that the enemies would use this or a similar expression for the purposes of cursing, and not in blessing. In other words, the afflicted man's distress has become proverbial.

9. For a similar thought, see 42:3 (M.T. 4), 80:5 (M.T. 6); 1QH v:33f.

ashes: the Hebrew *ʾēper* is often used as a symbol of mourning and grief (Est. 4:1; Job 2:8; Lam. 3:16), humiliation and penitence (Job 42:6; Dan. 9:3). It is less likely that the sufferer actually ate ashes; rather grief and suffering had metaphorically become his food and drink. Such a man would sit in ashes, as did Job (Job 2:8; cf. Jer. 6:26; Ezek. 27:30; Jon. 3:6), or would put ashes on his head, like Tamar (2 Sam. 13:19). See also Pedersen, *ILC*, I–II (1946), pp. 494f.

10. The singer of the Psalm is fully aware that his misfortune is the result of a just divine punishment (for *zaʿam* ('indignation'), see on 38:3). God, like a hurricane (cf. Job 27:21, 30:22), has taken him up and flung him away from all help and healing (cf. Jer. 23:29). Eaton (*PTBC*, p. 245) sees here a possible ironical allusion to the election of the people of Israel or their King.

11. like an evening shadow: lit. 'like a stretched-out shadow, which is about to be swallowed up by complete darkness (cf. Job 8:9, 14:2; Ps. 109:23, 144:4; Jer. 6:4).

like grass: see on verse 4; cf. Jas 1:11.

THE PRAISE OF YAHWEH'S POWER AND MERCY **12–22**

12. But thou is emphatic and expresses a striking contrast to what precedes. The ephemeral nature of man appears even more fleeting by the implicit comparison with the majesty of God. At the same time the dominion of God is a source of hope to those who trust in him.

O LORD: this is occasionally regarded as a gloss (cf. *BH*); but the parallel in Lam. 5:19 supports M.T.

enthroned for ever: see on 9:7, 29:10. The writer, apparently, re-echoes ancient cultic traditions, such as those mentioned in the so-called Enthronement Psalms.

thy name: (*NEB* 'thy fame') lit. 'thy remembrance' (*AV*), or 'thy memorial' (*RV*); some MSS. and Lam. 5:19 have: 'thy throne'. The cultic pronunciation of the divine name is God's memorial (cf. Childs, *MTI*, p. 71) and successive generations will call upon it (cf. Exod. 3:15).

13. Thou wilt arise: i.e. 'you will take action to maintain the cause of your people' (cf. 7:6 (M.T. 7)).

have pity on Zion: *r-ḥ-m* ('to have pity') is probably a denominative verb (for *raḥ*ᵃ*mîm* ('compassion'), see on 40:11, 51:1), and this prophecy (?) will be fulfilled when Zion (see on 65:1) is rebuilt (cf. verse 16).

it is the time to favour her: this is possibly a variant on 'the appointed time has come', or vice versa (so Briggs, Kraus). For the thought, see Isa. 30:18, 40:1, 49:13; Jer. 30:18; Zech. 1:12,16.

14. thy servants: for *ᶜeḇeḏ* ('servant'), see on 36:1. These are the worshippers of Yahweh, and not foreign rulers such as Cyrus or Artaxerxes (as suggested by Barnes, *PWC*, II, p. 479).

her stones: i.e. though the Holy City is in ruins, even the pitiful remains of her former glory are dear to the people of God (cf. Neh. 4:2). The love for Jerusalem, so characteristic of the Songs of Zion (see Introduction, p. 35), has not ceased with the destruction of the city.

15. The nations will fear . . .: similarly in Isa. 59:19 (cf. Isa. 41:5). The verb *y-r-ʾ* can denote not only 'to fear, be afraid', but also 'to reverence, honour', and the object can be one's parents (Lev. 19:3), the leaders of the people (Jos. 4:14), and very often God (15:4, 22:25 (M.T. 26), 31:19 (M.T. 20)), or his name (61:5 (M.T. 6), 86:11, etc.); see note on 34:7. In 105:15 the peoples shall revere Yahweh because of his self-manifestation in the restoration of Jerusalem (verse 16), which will mark a new era for all nations. Delitzsch, Kirkpatrick, *et al.* see here the beginning of the conversion of the world.

the name: see on 20:1.

thy glory may refer to Yahweh's intervention in the history of his people (cf. Isa. 40:5); see on 26:8, 57:5 (M.T. 6); cf. C. R. North, *The Second Isaiah* (1964), pp. 76f.

16. The verbs in this and the following verse may be prophetic perfects (cf. *GK* 106n) referring to events which are about to come to pass.

. . . will build up Zion: this points to the end of the Exilic or the early part of the post-Exilic period: for similar thoughts, see 51:18 (M.T. 20), 147:2; Isa. 60:10; Mic. 7:11.

he will appear in his glory: see verse 15.

17. the prayer: see on 65:2. 11QPs[a] (p. 20) has *twlʿt* ('worm') for M.T. *tᵉpillaṯ* ('prayer'), and it could be rendered: '(he will regard graciously) the worm of (the destitute)' (cf. Isa. 66:24; see also Job 25:6; Ps. 21:6 (M.T. 7); Isa. 41:14). The 'destitute man' may be a description either of the afflicted man in verses 1–11, or of the nation in Exile (so Cohen, Kissane, *et al.*) The parallelism of verse 17*b* favours the latter alternative.

their supplication is a translation of the same Hebrew noun (*tᵉpillāh*) as in verse 17*a*; LXX suggests *tᵉḥinnāṯām* ('their supplication'), but it is not certain that the translator did not have before him the same word as in M.T.

18. Let this be recorded: the account of how Yahweh had mercy upon his people. This deliverance and restoration is still to come, but when they have taken place, they will be written down as a testimony for future generations. Some exegetes think that 'this' (*zōʾṯ*) refers to the prophecy in verses 13–17 (so Gunkel), which will be set down in writing so that the re-created people of God could offer their praises to Yahweh in the knowledge that it is he who had wrought the new salvation (cf. Isa. 8:1–4, 30:8; Jer. 30:2f.).

a people yet unborn: lit. 'a people created', or 'which shall be created' (cf. Isa. 43:15). The allusion seems to be to the re-creation of Israel from the Babylonian exile. The verb *b-r-ʾ* ('to create') is discussed on 51:10.
the LORD: *yāh*; see on 68:4.

19. that: the Hebrew equivalent is the hymnic *kî* (see on 89:2), which could be rendered: 'for'.
from his holy height: i.e. from heavens, rather than from 'the height of his sanctuary' (*AV, RV*): cf. 14:2, 33:13; Isa. 57:15, 63:15. *Mārôm* ('height', see on 68:18) is parallel to 'heaven' in verse 19*b*.
the LORD: some commentators (e.g. Kraus, Deissler) omit *yhwh* (*RSV* 'the LORD'), while others (e.g. Nötscher, *NEB*) transfer it to the preceding line; it overloads verse 19*b*, but M.T. is supported by 11QPs[a] (p. 20).

20. the prisoners: lit. 'the prisoner'; the Hebrew *ʾāsîr* (see on 68:6) may be used collectively, and it does not necessarily imply the exiles. For **the groans of the prisoners,** see on 79:11, where we find the phrase: 'those doomed to die' (lit. 'the sons of death'). The word *t*[e]*mûṭāh* ('death') is found only here and in 79:11.

21. the name of the LORD: see verse 15*a*.
Jerusalem is the pre-Israelite name of the Holy City, and it is already attested in the Egyptian Execration texts of the nineteenth century B.C. The name probably means 'the foundation of (the god) Salem (Prosperer)' (see *AOTS*, p. 277). The name 'Salem' (*šālēm*) in Gen. 14:18; Ps. 76:2 (M.T. 3), may be an abbreviation of 'Jerusalem' (so *BDB*).
his praise: for *t*[e]*hillāh*, see on 65:1, 119:171.

22. When Zion is restored, all peoples shall gather there to pay homage to Yahweh. This will be the fulfilment of many ancient prophecies and hopes (cf. 47:9 (M.T. 10); Isa. 2:2ff., 60:3–7; Mic. 7:12; Zech. 14:16).
to worship: lit. 'to serve' (for *ʿ-b-d*, see on 106:36).

THE CONTINUATION OF THE LAMENT **23–4**

23. He has broken my strength . . .: so *Ḳ*[e]*rê*, T, and S; *K*[e]*ṯîḇ*, LXX, and V have 'his strength' (*kōḥô* for M.T. *kōḥî*), probably suggesting that God has afflicted the desolate man '(with) his strength'. Since the subject of the verb is not defined, some exegetes read the passive *ʿunnāh* (for M.T. *ʿinnāh*): '(my strength) is broken . . .' (so Kraus, *NEB*).
in mid-course: lit. 'in the way', i.e. in the midst of my life

(cf. Isa. 38:10), before I have come to the end of my journey.
he has shortened my days: he has brought me near to premature death.

24. "O my God," I say: *RP* omits 'I say'. Verse 25, in its present form, seems metrically too long, while verse 24 is too short.
take me not hence: although the same verb is used in 2 Kg. 2:1 of Yahweh being about to take Elijah up to heaven, in our verse the allusion is simply to the Psalmist's untimely death.
in the midst of my days: see verse 23.
thou whose years endure . . .: cf. verse 12. The Psalmist is contrasting his own transitoriness with the timelessness of Yahweh.

THE PRAISE OF THE CREATOR AND HELPER **25–8**

Verses 25f. are quoted in Heb. 1:10ff., and are associated with the manifestation of Jesus Christ.

25. thou didst lay the foundation of the earth: 11QPs[a] (p. 20) has: 'the earth was founded' (*nwsdh* for *yāsaḏtā*), but M.T. seems to be preferable. Yahweh is praised as the creator of the world (i.e. of 'the earth' and 'the heavens').
the work of thy hands: for a similar expression, see 8:3 (M.T. 4); cf. Isa. 44:24, 48:13.

26. The heavens and earth are often considered as symbolic of all that is permanent and enduring (cf. 78:69, 104:5, 119:90, 148:6; Ec. 1:4), but, in comparison with Yahweh, they are like a garment which is worn out sooner or later (a similar idea is found in Isa. 34:4, 51:6). For a remote Ugaritic parallel, cf. Patton, *CPBP*, p. 27; Driver, *CML*, p. 103b.
wear out: the verb *b-l-h* means 'to become old and worn out', and it can be used of garments (Dt. 8:4, 29:5), or figuratively of the earth (Isa. 51:6), bones (32:3), man (Job 13:28), etc.

27. but thou: presents an emphatic contrast to the preceding thought (lit. 'but you are he'). The Hebrew *hû'* ('he') is used to emphasize the uniqueness of Yahweh (cf. Dt. 32:39; Isa. 41:4, 43:10,13, 46:4, 48:12; C. R. North, op. cit., p. 94). See also Dahood, *PAB*, II, pp. 36f.

28. thy servants: see on 36:1. Cf. 69:36 (M.T. 37), which offers a close parallel to our verse.
shall dwell secure: lit. 'shall dwell' (in the rebuilt Jerusalem); cf. Jer. 33:16.
before thee: or 'in your (protective) presence' (cf. 16:11), i.e. in Yahweh's land and in his care.

Psalm 103 The Lord Pities Those Who Fear Him

The Psalm can be described as an Individual Thanksgiving in the form of a Hymn (see Introduction, pp. 35f. and 32f.). It consists of an introduction (verses 1–2), two main sections (verses 3–5 and 6–18), and a conclusion (verses 19–22). The first main section expresses the gratitude of one who has been forgiven and healed from a severe illness (see, however, on 102:3), as well as abundantly blessed by God. The second main section is a praise of Yahweh who has dealt wonderfully with his Covenant people. At the same time the Psalm serves as a warning that the only foundation of true happiness is the fear of Yahweh (see verses 11, 13, 17). The poem was probably recited at the individual's thanksgiving which took place before the congregation (see on 22:22f.).

The Psalm is post-Exilic in origin, late rather than early (so Kraus). This is implied by the allusions to various passages in Isa. 40–66, as well as by the unusual pronominal suffixes in verses 3–5 (cf. *GK* 58g).

The number of verses is 22, but there is no real reason to assume that this was meant to correspond to the number of letters in the Hebrew alphabet.

The prevailing metre is 3+3.

A Psalm of David: see Introduction, pp. 46 and 43ff.

A HYMNIC CALL TO BLESS YAHWEH **1–2**

1. Bless the Lord, O my soul: this is a self-exhortation to praise Yahweh (see on 104:1), and it may be an emphatic way of saying that the Psalmist will most certainly give thanks to God.
all that is within me: lit. 'all my inward parts', i.e. my whole being. It is quite customary in the *OT* for any part of the body to express or denote the activity of the whole man. This linguistic usage is known as synecdoche (see on 94:20), cf. the expression 'All my bones shall say . . .' (35:10).
his holy name: (for *šēm* ('name'), see on 20:1), lit. 'the name of his holiness' (cf. 68:17 (M.T. 18)), as in 33:21, 105:3, 106:47, 145:21.

2. The repetition of verse 1*a* is for the sake of emphasis.
forget not all his benefits: these are the gracious deeds of Yahweh recounted in verses 3–5. 'To forget' is not so much a slip of memory, as a deliberate act of ignoring the goodness of God

(see on 119:16). Similar warnings are frequent in Deuteronomy (4:9,23, 6:12, 8:11, 32:18).

THE FORGIVING AND REDEEMING GOD 3–5

3. who forgives: the verb *s-l-ḥ* (see on 86:5) could be regarded as the only explicit term for forgiveness (cf. Kraus, *PBK*, p. 702), although the idea itself may be expressed by different metaphors (cf. *TDNT*, I, p. 510; *IDB*, II, pp. 315ff.; Eichrodt, *TOT*, II, pp. 443–83). The parallel line (verse 3*b*) shows that the outward sign of forgiveness is healing, just as disease or calamity could be taken as the result of sin (cf. 107:17–20, 130:4). For the hymnic participles, see Introduction, p. 33. See also F. Crüsemann, *Studien zur Formgeschichte von Hymnus und Danklied in Israel*, *WMANT*, 32, 1969, pp. 81–154.

all your iniquity: for *ʿāwōn* ('iniquity'), see on 32:1, 51:2, 90:8. The pronoun 'your' (see *GK* 58g, 91l) refers to 'my soul' (verses 1 and 2), i.e. to the Psalmist himself (see *NEB*).

who heals: the Hebrew *r-p-ʾ* is the regular verb for 'to heal' and it can also be used in a figurative sense (147:3; Isa. 53:5; Jer. 51:8,9). Occasionally it denotes the restoration of fertility (cf. Gen. 20:17; 2 Kg. 2:21; J. Gray, *The Legacy of Canaan* (*SVT*, 5, 1957), p. 154).

all your diseases: cf. Dt. 29:22; 2 Chr. 21:19; Jer. 14:18, 16:4. The word *taḥᵃlūʾîm* (always in the plural) may suggest illness as well as suffering in general (cf. Dt. 29:22).

4. who redeems: for *g-ʾ-l*, see on 119:154 (also 78:35).

your life: i.e. you. For *ḥayyîm* ('life'), see on 21:4.

from the Pit: Targum has 'from Gehenna', LXX reads *ek phthoras* ('from destruction'). The Hebrew *šaḥaṯ* is discussed on 7:15, 49:9. The Psalmist's illness has brought him close to death, so that his healing can be described as a deliverance from the Pit or Sheol (see on 40:2); the reference is not to resurrection.

who crowns you: i.e. who makes you feel like a King on the day of his enthronement (8:5 (M.T. 6), 21:3 (M.T. 4), or like a bridegroom at his wedding (Ca. 3:11). *NEB* 'surrounds me'.

steadfast love and mercy: for *ḥeseḏ*, see on 26:3; and for *raḥᵃmîm*, see on 40:11, 51:1, 119:77, 156.

5. as long as you live: the literal meaning of *ʿeḏyēḵ* is probably 'your ornament' which may be a picturesque term for 'soul' (so Boylan, Deissler). The versions were equally uncertain as to the exact connotation; LXX has 'your desire', T 'the days of your old age', while S has 'your body'. These and similar renderings seem to be interpretative translations, if not guesses. The best solution is to read *ʿōḏēḵî* ('your life'), lit. 'your continuance'. *AV*, *RV* have 'thy mouth' which is an unlikely rendering; *NEB* has 'in the prime of life'.

your youth is renewed . . .: the metaphor may be derived from Isa. 40:31, and the reference is to strength and vitality, suggested by the swiftness of the eagle's movements (Dt. 28:49; 2 Sam. 1:23; Jer. 4:13, etc.). The word-picture has nothing to do with the bird's moulting, because this process is in no sense an exclusive characteristic of eagles or vultures. The Hebrew *nešer* is an eagle, but possibly the term also included vultures (especially the griffon-vultures).

YAHWEH'S COVENANT LOYALTY **6–18**

6. vindication: lit. 'righteousness' (see on 33:5). *Ṣeḏāḳôṯ* ('acts of righteousness') may refer not only to the salvation-history, but also to the present expressions of God's faithfulness (cf. Jg. 5:11). 'Righteousness' is no static attribute of Yahweh, but it manifests itself in such acts as help, deliverance, healing, forgiveness, etc.

justice: *mišpāṭîm*, see on 36:6, 119:7.

7. his ways: or 'his modes of action' (Davies, *Cent. BP*, II, p. 171), or 'his general intention'. In a figurative sense *dereḵ* may denote 'commandments' (cf. 18:21 (M.T. 22), 25:4,9, 37:34, etc.) or 'manner' (Gen. 19:31), 'moral action' or 'character' (39:1 (M.T. 2), 50:23, etc.). The parallelism of verse 7*b* implies that 'ways' is synonymous with 'his acts'. Kraus (*PBK*, p. 703) thinks that the allusion is to the divine plans which are made known to Moses (cf. Am. 3:7); see on 105:26.

8. This verse is reminiscent of Exod. 34:6.

merciful and gracious: as in Exod. 34:6; Ps. 86:15. In 111:4, (112:4), 145:8 we have 'gracious and merciful'. *Raḥûm* ('compassionate, merciful') is always used of God, but see 112:4 (cf. also Dt. 4:31; 2 Chr. 30:9; Neh. 9:17; Jl 2:13; Jon. 4:2).

slow to anger: lit. 'long (with respect to) anger' (see on 86:15).

steadfast love: see on 86:5.

9. He will not always chide: (cf. Isa. 57:16) the verb *r-y-b* means 'to dispute, contend, quarrel, go to law', and it is often used in a legal setting. For the so-called controversy (*rîḇ*) pattern, see H. B. Huffmon, *JBL*, LXXVIII (1959), pp. 285–95; J. Harvey,

Biblica, XLIII (1962), pp. 172–96; M. Delcor, *VT*, XVI (1966), pp. 8–25.

nor will he keep his anger . . .: the Hebrew *n-ṭ-r* can mean both 'to keep, guard' (Ca. 1:6, 8:11) and 'to maintain one's anger' (Jer. 3:5,12; Nah. 1:2; 1QS x:20; CD vii:2, viii:5, ix:2,4,5, xiii:18; cf. the cognate Akkadian *nadāru* ('to be angry') (G. R. Driver, *JTS*, XXXII (1931), pp. 361f.)).

10. sins: for *ḥēṭ*ʾ, see on 32:1, 51:2. Although sins are punished, the primary motivation is the desire to restore the sinner rather than to destroy him. In other words, God's retribution is tempered with his mercy. For a slightly different view, see Isa. 40:1: 'she has received from the LORD's hand double for all her sins' (cf. Job. 34:11).

iniquities: see on 32:1, 51:2, 90:8.

11. as the heavens: for a similar expression, cf. Isa. 55:9 (Ps. 36:5 (M.T. 6), 57:10 (M.T. 11)). Just as the distance between the heavens and earth seemed immeasurable, so also Yahweh's Covenant loyalty (see on 26:3) appeared infinite.

so great is: M.T. has '(so) strong is' (similarly *NEB*; cf. 117:2) although some exegetes emend M.T. *gāḇar* into *gāḇah* ('(so) high is'; so Leslie, Kraus).

who fear him: see on 34:7,9, 85:9, 102:15.

12. our transgressions: Hebrew *pešaᶜ*; see on 32:1, 51:1. This verse describes the removal of the effects of the rebellion and God's complete forgiveness. For a parallel thought cf. Mic. 7:19.

13. The concept of God as father is an ancient one, and it is found not only in Israel, but also among other Near Eastern peoples. In Ugarit, El was the father of the gods as well as the father of mankind (cf. Pope, *EUT*, p. 47). In the *OT*, and often elsewhere, the fatherhood of the deity emphasizes, not the physical, but the social relationship (cf. Gray, op. cit., p. 118). In our Psalm the father-son relationship is dependent not so much upon one's nationality, as upon obedience. The children of God are those who fear him (see verse 11). For the fatherhood of God in the *OT*, cf. Exod. 4:22; Dt. 14:1, 32:6; Isa. 1:2, 45:11, 63:16, 64:8; Jer. 3:4,19, 31:9; Hos. 11:1; Mal. 1:6, 2:10, 3:17; Eichrodt, *TOT*, II, p. 177; Ringgren, *IR*, p. 86; H. W. Wolff, *Hosea* (*BK* 14), pp. 254ff.

14. our frame: i.e. our creatureliness. The noun *yēṣer* ('form, frame, forming') is derived from *y-ṣ-r* ('to form, fashion'), which is used in Gen. 2:7 of the making of man of dust from the ground.

The frailty and weakness of man is one of the reasons why God could be expected to show pity (cf. Job 10:8f; v. Rad, *OTT*, I, p. 459, n.12).

dust: see on 119:23. For the general idea, see Gen. 2:7, 3:19; Job 4:19, 10:9, 34:15; Ec. 3:20, 12:7; 1QS xi:21; 1QH iii:21, x:4,5,12, xii:24,26, xiii:15, xviii:31, etc.

15. As for man: see note on 8:4. Kirkpatrick (*BPCB*, p. 603) renders *ʾenôš* by 'mortal man', while Davies (*Cent. BP*, II, p. 172) suggests 'man at his best'; the former seems more likely.

his days are like grass: this word-picture stresses the transitory nature of human existence. For similar expressions, see Job 14:2; Ps. 90:5f.; Isa. 40:6ff., 51:12.

like a flower which soon fades away. The Hebrew *ṣîṣ* is literally 'a shining or sparkling thing'; and it usually denotes the wild flowers or those in the field, which in the springtime transform even the bleakest landscape into a colourful scenery.

16. The author depicts the withering of the flowers in the dry wind from the desert, and this serves as a suitable metaphor for the short-lived life of man.

17. steadfast love: for *ḥesed*, see on 26:3. In Isa. 40:6ff. it is the abiding word of God that is contrasted with the mutability of man, while in our Psalm the latter is set against the enduring Covenant loyalty of Yahweh.

is from everlasting . . . who fear him: cf. Lk. 1:50. Since the verse is metrically too long, some exegetes suggest *ʿaḏ ʿôlām* ('(is) for ever') for M.T. *mēʿôlām weʿaḏ ʿôlām ʿal yereʾāyw*. Perhaps it might be better to regard *mēʿôlām weʿaḏ ʿôlām* ('from everlasting to everlasting') as a gloss, in which case 'those who fear him' would be parallel to '(their) children's children'.

his righteousness: see on 33:5, 119:40.

18. The Psalmist further defines the characteristics of those who serve (or 'fear') Yahweh (cf. Exod. 20:6; Dt. 7:9); they are the ones who abide by the terms of the Covenant (see on 55:20), and who act obediently (lit. 'remember') towards the commandments (see on 119:4) of God (cf. Num. 15:39).

ALL THE WORKS OF GOD PRAISE HIM **19–22**

For a similar hymn of praise, see 148:1–4.

19. his throne: see on 47:8, 93:2; cf. 11:4; Isa. 66:1.

his kingdom: i.e. his dominion extends over the whole world. Yahweh is the heavenly king who rules over his creation.

20. Bless the Lord: see on 104:1.
his angels: for *mal'āḵ*, see on 91:11. The various angelic beings apparently surround the heavenly throne and wait upon Yahweh to do his bidding.
mighty ones: lit. 'warriors of strength'; this phrase is a *hapax legomenon* in the *OT*, but it occurs in 1QH viii:11, x:34 as a synonym of 'angels'; a similar term is found in 1QH iii:35, which mentions 'the mighty ones of heavens' (*gibbôrê šāmayim*). *NEB* has 'creatures of might'.

21. all his hosts: see on 24:10. These are the hosts of heaven who minister (see on 101:6) unto Yahweh and do his will (lit. 'pleasure'). The reference may be to the stars (cf. 148:2f.), or to the heavenly beings, or both. The Hebrew *ṣᵉḇā'āyw* ('his hosts') is rather unusual, because the plural of the noun usually takes the feminine form.

22. all his works: i.e. all his creation.
Bless the Lord, O my soul: the Psalm ends with the same phrase as that with which it began. This is occasionally described as a cyclic composition in which the author returns to the same point (or phrase) whence he began (cf. Dahood, *PAB*, I, p. 5).

Psalm 104 A Hymn to the Creator of the World

This Psalm is usually defined as 'a Hymn in which the central theme is the works of God in creation'; thus it is often called a Nature Psalm, and its author 'the Wordsworth of the ancients'. It is a Descriptive Psalm of Praise meant either for the individual or the community; the latter alternative is more likely, and the Psalm may belong to the liturgy of the great Autumnal Festival. The theme of Creation would be appropriate to this feast, and so the poem might form a part of the liturgy of the New Year Festival.

Some scholars (e.g. Gunkel, Kirkpatrick, Schmidt) have argued that Ps. 103, 104 are by the same author; both Psalms have the same beginning and the same conclusion; and there are also other stylistic similarities. Much of this can be explained as due to the traditional style, but the identity of authorship is not impossible. Another interesting point is the similarity between Ps. 104, on the one hand, and Gen. 1 and the rather unique Hymn to Aten, on the other; few scholars, however, would suggest a literary dependence. The Priestly account of creation in

Genesis 1 is hardly a *creatio ex nihilo*, and therefore the similarities between Ps. 104 and Gen. 1 may have been derived from a common tradition and worship. On the relationship between our Psalm and the Hymn to Aten, we may quote R. J. Williams (*DOTT*, p. 149): '. . . many of the ideas contained in the Aten Hymn, itself dependent on earlier models . . ., found expression in later religious works. From sources such as these the Psalmist may well have obtained his inspiration.' But, in stressing the similarity between the two, we must not neglect the striking differences.

The metre, with a few exceptions, is 3 + 3. The Psalm opens with a self-exhortation to bless Yahweh, and proceeds to address God in the second person, acknowledging his majesty (verses 1–4). In verses 5–9 the Psalmist describes the founding of the earth and the subjection of the Chaos waters which now serve Yahweh by serving his creatures who are sustained by him (verses 10-18); even the sun and the moon are part of God's world, and he alone is its lord and determines the functions of all things created (verses 19–23). His dominion also includes the sea and all that is in it (verses 24–6), and even the mysteries of life and death are in his hands (verses 27–30). The Psalm concludes with a praise of Yahweh (verses 31–5).

THE MAJESTY OF GOD 1–4

1. Bless the Lord: the meaning is well expressed in Tob. 12:6: 'Praise God, and give thanks to him; and exalt him and give thanks to him in the presence of all the living for what he has done for you'. Similarly, in verse 1, to bless God is not to increase his power by the words of blessing, but it means to praise him and to give him glory for all his works of creation, as the following verses clearly show (cf. Ps. 66:8, 103:1,22, 145:1).
my soul: i.e. 'myself'. So 'Let me bless . . .', or 'I will bless . . .' (cf. 33:19).
O Lord my God: or 'My God', omitting 'O Lord' as a dittograph, thus restoring the dominant 3 + 3 metre.
honour and majesty are the insignia of kings. See on 93:1, 96:6; cf. Job 37:22, 40:10; 11QPs[a] Creat., verse 2.

2. who coverest thyself with light: cf. 1 Tim. 6:16. Oesterley (*TP*, p. 440) sees here an allusion to the Iranian conception of the deity being clothed in light, but the thought may well be more ancient (cf. *ANET*, p. 62, ll. 102f.).

the heavens are likened to a tent stretched out over the whole earth (cf. Isa. 40:22, 42:2, 44:24, 45:12, 51:13; Jer. 10:12, 51:15; 11QPsᵃ Creat., verse 8). The metaphor implies, in its own way, the effortlessness with which God created the world. Perhaps we should render verse 2*b* as: '(You are) the one (reading *hannôṭeh* for M.T. *nôṭeh*) who stretched out . . .'.

3. . . . thy chambers: or '(who laid the beams of) *his* (so M.T.) chambers'. Briggs (*CECBP*, II, p. 337) regards the chambers as 'the successive heights or layers of heaven' (cf. Am. 9:6). In *OT* *ᶜaliyyāh* is often used to denote either a room in the upper storey of a large house, or a room on the flat roof of a house (cf. 1 Kg. 17:19; 2 Kg. 1:2, 4:10). In this verse it probably refers to the royal palace of Yahweh, which is founded on the waters above the firmament (Gen. 1:7). Here, in his heavenly dwelling, Yahweh sits 'enthroned over the flood' (29:10).

the clouds thy chariot: lit. '. . . his chariot'. See on 18:10 (cf. Isa. 19:1; Dan. 7:13; Mt. 24:30). A similar description, 'he who mounts the clouds', was one of Baal's stock epithets (cf. A. S. Kapelrud, *The Ras Shamra Discoveries and the Old Testament* (1965), p. 37).

who ridest: or 'who walketh' (*AV*, *RV*).

the wings of the wind: cf. 18:10*b* (M.T. 11*b*). Some (e.g. Gunkel, Weiser) suggest that the wind is Yahweh's 'winged horse', but, whatever is the exact meaning of this phrase, the underlying purpose is to stress that all nature exists to serve Yahweh (cf. 148:8). In the Mesopotamian story of Adapa (*ANET*, p. 101) we find a mention of the 'wing of the south wind'.

4. the winds thy messengers: lit. '. . . his messengers' (cf. Heb. 1:7). LXX renders: 'who makes his angels winds' (similarly T), which may imply that God makes his angelic messengers assume the form of various natural phenomena, such as wind and lightning. The *RSV* rendition seems to be more likely.

fire and flame: Hebrew *ʾēš wālahaṭ*. An alternative is 'a flaming fire' (so *AV*, *RV*), which is the literal translation of M.T.; but we should expect the participle *lōhēṭ* to have the feminine form.

YAHWEH IS THE LORD OF THE WATERS OF CHAOS **5–9**

Some recent scholars see in these verses an allusion to God's 'struggle' with the powers of Chaos (cf. Ringgren, *FP*, p. 94; v. Rad, *OTT*, I, p. 360) which is a contrast to the creation story in Gen. 1 with its emphasis upon the creative word. On the other hand, the difference may be primarily in the choice of metaphors (derived from Babylonian or Canaanite mythology, or other sources) rather than in the underlying thought itself.

5. **its foundations:** i.e. the earth is conceived as resting upon its foundations, which are sunk into the cosmic sea (cf. Johnson, *SKAI*, p. 52; Stadelmann, *HCW*, pp. 126ff.). It is possible that the 'bronze sea' in Solomon's Temple (1 Kg. 7:23–6; 2 Kg. 25:13) was a symbolic representation of this cosmic sea, and that it played an important role in the Temple ritual (cf. G. E. Wright, *Biblical Archaeology* (1962), p. 141). Probably the marvel of it all is that, however great may have been the hostile forces, Yahweh's might has been far superior, and he has been able to harness these frightening powers to his service.

6. **Thou didst cover it . . .:** or 'The deep covered it (i.e. the earth) as a garment' (reading *kissattāẖ* for M.T. *kissîṯô*). In the beginning, **the deep** (*tᵉhôm*) covered the whole earth (cf. Gen. 1:2) which may have been thought of as already in its present form, with all its mountains and valleys, although submerged by the floods, so that 'the waters stood above the mountains' (verse 6*b*). 'The deep' is usually equated, at least etymologically, with Tiamat of the Babylonian Creation epic (cf. *DOTT*, p. 14); but in the *OT* it is largely 'demythologized' (cf. 71:20); we also find the plural *tᵉhômôṯ* (135:6).

7. **At thy rebuke they fled:** see on 9:5; cf. Isa. 50:2; Nah. 1:4. This verse may be a more picturesque description of Gen. 1:9: 'And God said . . . And it was so!' The waters are viewed as semi-personal, but they are not divine, as Tiamat.

thy thunder is Yahweh's voice (see on 18:13). Similarly it is said of Baal that 'he will utter his voice in the clouds, his flashings (and) lightnings on the earth' (*Baal* II, v:8–9; Driver, *CML*, p. 97b).

8. **The mountains rose . . .:** it seems that the subject should be 'the waters' (see verse 9) (so Gunkel, Kraus, *NEB*, *et al.*). In that case we should render: 'They go up the mountains (i.e. the waters of the Chaos appear as mountain springs), they go down to the valleys (in the form of streams), (and then they go) to the place which you have appointed for them' (cf. E. F. Sutcliffe, *VT*, II (1952), pp. 177–9).

9. The waters of the primeval Chaos are 'gathered together into one place' (Gen. 1:9), and they are set limits which they are

powerless to transgress (cf. Job 26:10, 38:10; Prov. 8:29; Jer. 5:22; see also *ANET*, p. 67, ll. 139–40, where Marduk posts guards lest the waters of Tiamat should escape). Instead of dominating the earth, these waters are now made to serve the creatures of God.

YAHWEH IS THE SUSTAINER OF THE WORLD **10–18**

10. Thou makest springs: or, '(You are) the one who sends forth springs'. In Israelite thought, springs had their origin in the waters of the great abyss, so that the destructive Chaos was utilized for the furthering of life.

11. the wild asses are here representative of all the wild animals. *RP* renders the Hebrew *pᵉrāʾîm* by 'zebras', but the former alternative is more likely (cf. P. Humbert, *ZAW*, LXII (1949–50), pp. 202–6).

12. By them: this refers, not to the wild asses (so Baethgen, Ehrlich), but to the springs and brooks.

they sing among the branches: LXX reads 'from among the rocks' which is less likely.

13. From thy lofty abode: lit. 'From his . . .'. On 'lofty abode' (*ᶜᵃliyyôṯ*), see on verse 3.

thou waterest the mountains by sending rain through the windows of the heavens (Gen. 7:11, 8:2; Mal. 3:10). When the Psalmist speaks here of 'the mountains', he may have in mind, primarily, such things as the upland corn fields and the vineyards on the slopes. In the Ugaritic texts it is Baal who gives 'abundance of rain, abundance of moisture with snow' (*Baal* II, v:6–7; Driver, *CML*, p. 97b). See *DOTT*, p. 147, ll. 70–3, where Aten waters the fields.

the fruit of thy work: is taken by Kirkpatrick (*BPCB*, p. 609) as 'fruit produced by God's manifold operations', while others interpret it as meaning 'rain' which could be regarded as the product of God's work (so Davies, Briggs).

14. Thou dost cause . . .: or '(You are the) one who causes . . .'.

plants for man to cultivate: or 'fodder for the animals that serve man' (*RSVm*); or better 'plants for the sustenance of man' (so Dahood, *PNWSP*, p. 26), which would balance verse 14*a*. 'Plants' (*ᶜēśeḇ*) could be both fodder for animals (Dt. 11:15) and food for men (Gen. 1:29), and could include corn and vegetable products.

that he may bring forth . . .: this describes in more detail the contents of verse 14*b*. Corn, wine, and oil were the three staple products of Canaan (Dt. 12:17).

15. wine to gladden the heart of man: or 'with wine he gladdens . . .'; cf. Jg. 9:13; Ec. 10:19; Sir. 40:20. Taken in excess, however, the same wine would rob a man of his senses, as in the case of Noah (Gen. 9:21, 19:33,35).

oil was used for various purposes. It could be applied for the protection of one's skin (cf. Dt. 28:40; Ps. 92:10; Lk. 7:46), or for healing purposes (Isa. 1:6); it could also be used in sacrifices (Lev. 2:4), in anointing (89:20 (M.T. 21)), or as a sign of gladness (23:5, 45:7 (M.T. 8); Prov. 27:9; Isa. 61:3), as fuel for lamps (Mt. 25:3–8), and for cooking (cf. Num. 11:8).

bread to strengthen man's heart: or 'with bread he sustains the heart of man' (so Dahood, *PAB*, I, pp. 115f.).

16. The trees of the LORD: perhaps 'the mighty trees' (*RP*), or 'the trees of the primeval forests' (Kissane). LXX reads 'the trees of the plain'.

cedars of Lebanon: in biblical times the mountains of Lebanon were the main source of cedars, hence 'the cedars of Lebanon'. See on 37:35.

17. the stork has her home in the fir trees: some scholars (following LXX) read: '. . . her home on top of them (*b^erō^ʾšām*)', i.e. on top of the trees mentioned in verse 16 (similarly *NEB*). The 'fir tree' is thought to be a species of juniper growing in Lebanon (cf. *IDB*, II, p. 293), or the cypress which was native to Canaan.

18. The high mountains: perhaps, the most inaccessible places which would normally be useless but God has made them the homes for wild goats, possibly the Nubian ibex (cf. *IDB*, II, p. 251). This animal may rarely be seen by man but it is not beyond God's providential care.

the badgers are, most likely, the Syrian conies (and not rabbits as might be suggested by the connotation of the English 'conies' (*AV*, *RV*)). In spite of their small size, they are related to elephants.

SUN AND MOON RECEIVE THEIR ORDERS FROM GOD **19–23**

19. Thou hast made: lit. 'He has made'. Perhaps we should read the participle *ʿōśeh* (as in verse 4). The sun and moon are not thought to be divine powers, as among other peoples, but they are creatures of Yahweh serving his purposes. For a different view of the sun, see the Egyptian Hymn to Aten (i.e. the sun disc), in *DOTT*, p. 145, ll. 1–2, 54:

'Thou dost appear beautiful on the horizon of heaven,
O living Aten, Thou who wast the first to live . . .
Thou didst create the earth according to Thy will, being alone'.

seasons may refer to the sacred seasons or to the great festivals (cf. Sir. 43:7: 'From the moon comes the sign for the feast days'). The moon is mentioned before the sun because, in the lunar calendar, it is of greater importance than the sun. Oesterley *et al.* attributes the precedence of the moon to the belief that at one time it was the chief deity of the nomadic Semites.

20. darkness was originally related to the primeval Chaos (Gen. 1:2). In Hebrew thought it was not simply the absence of light, but it had its own independent existence. Both light and darkness have their separate dwellings (Job 38:19), and according to Gen. 1:4, light was good, although darkness was not described as evil. Yet, whatever its origin, it too can serve the total plan of God.

21. seeking their food from God: the **young lions** represent *all* wild animals (as *pars pro toto*) which are equally dependent upon God for their sustenance (cf. Hymn to Aten, l. 17).

22. they get them away: or 'they gather themselves (to their lairs)'.

23. Man's work is part of the God-ordained pattern for human existence. It is unlikely that 'work' and 'labour' refer to two different types of occupation.

THE CREATURES AND THEIR CREATOR **24–30**

24. how manifold are thy works: cf. Hymn to Aten, ll. 52–5 (*DOTT*, p. 147): 'How manifold is that which thou hast made, hidden from view! . . . Thou didst create the earth . . . Mankind, cattle, all flocks . . .'.

wisdom is one of the attributes of God, and it is especially seen in the works of creation (cf. 136:5; Prov. 3:19; Jer. 10:12).

the earth is full of thy creatures: rather than '. . . of thy riches' (*AV*, *RV*, *PNT*).

25–6. The sea appeared to the Israelites even more mysterious and awe-inspiring than the earth. It is perhaps no accident that, when the author of the book of Revelation contemplates the new heaven and the new earth, he comments: 'and the sea was no more' (21:1). Cf. Stadelmann, *HCW*, pp. 154–64.

the ships are thought to be out of place among the various creatures of the sea, which look to God for their food (verse 27); and therefore some scholars (e.g. Gunkel) have read *ʾêmôṯ* ('dreadful things, monsters') for M.T. *ʾoniyyôṯ* ('ships'). On the other hand, it may be said that the Hymn to Aten also, which has a number of similarities with our Psalm, refers to the ships that 'sail upstream and downstream' (line 37).

Leviathan may well be the primeval dragon, also known as Rahab (Job 26:12; Ps. 89:10 (M.T. 11); Isa. 51:9) or dragon ('sea monster') (Job 7:12; Ps. 74:13; Isa. 51:9). In the Ugaritic literature, Leviathan (or Lotan) was the enemy of Baal who smote this tyrant with the seven heads (*Baal* I,*i: 1–3). See the discussion on this subject in Pope, *JAB*, pp. 276ff. In the present verse, unless the reference is to some large fish, the once mighty Leviathan appears as a grotesque figure—a plaything of Yahweh.

27–8. These all refers back to the different types of creatures mentioned previously. They are all dependent upon Yahweh for their very existence (cf. 145:15f., 147:9).

29. thou hidest thy face means to withdraw one's favour or providential care.

when thou takest away their breath: lit. '. . . their spirit', i.e. 'the breath of life' (Gen. 2:7), which comes from God and which, in the end, returns to him (Ec. 12:7). When the body is no longer animated by the breath of life, it reverts to the dust from which it was taken in the first place (Gen. 3:19; cf. Job 34:14f.; Ps. 146:4).

30. they are created: this alludes to the continual process of re-creation, which cannot be understood apart from God. Throughout the successive generations, life and death alike are in the hands of God.

THE PROMISE OF YAHWEH 31–5

These five verses form a hymnic conclusion to this magnificent nature hymn.

31. the glory of the LORD is often used in the descriptions of Yahweh's theophany (e.g. Exod. 16:7,10, 24:16,17, 40:34,35), and it may denote the manifestation of his presence. In the present context the reference is probably to the creative majesty of Yahweh, which calls forth the homage of his creatures. See 19:1 (M.T. 2), where 'the glory of God' is parallel to 'his handiwork'.

may the LORD rejoice in his works: this calls to mind Gen.

1:31 (cf. Prov. 8:31). It may imply a wish that the creatures should continue to be what Yahweh meant them to be.

32. Once more we find a description of Yahweh's power and his absolute supremacy over the created world. One look from him, and the earth trembles (as by an earthquake); one touch, and the immovable mountains smoke (a volcanic eruption?; cf. 144:5). The language is reminiscent of the accounts of Yahweh's theophanies.

33. This verse is practically identical with 146:2. The creature's response to the Creator must be praise in word and deed, so that the word is the beginning of the deed, and the deed the fulfilment of the word.

as long as I live: this may have as its background the current belief of its times, that the 'dead do not praise the LORD, nor do any that go down into silence' (115:17; cf. 6:5 (M.T. 6)). Therefore the Psalmist wishes to use his life upon this earth to praise God.

34. my meditation is, perhaps, this Psalm. See 19:14 (M.T. 15), where we find a similar thought: 'Let the words of my mouth and the meditation of my heart be acceptable in thy sight'. Both expressions (i.e. verse 34 and 19:14 (M.T. 15)) may be described as a dedicatory formula (cf. Lev. 1:3ff.).

35. Let sinners be consumed: this petition for the destruction of the godless may have been derived from the ritual associated with the Covenant renewal, in which the pronouncement of blessings and curses played an important role (cf. v. Rad, *Deuteronomy* (*OTL*, 1966), pp. 167ff.). It may not be far wrong to suggest that the primary function of these curses was to protect the Covenant rather than to destroy the sinner. Similarly the Psalmist may not have been motivated by a hatred of the wicked, but by his desire to see that the Creator is acknowledged as such.

Bless the LORD: see on verse 1.

Praise the LORD: *halᵉlûyāh*, or 'hallelujah'. This phrase includes the shorter form of the divine name *yāh*; see on 68:18.

Psalm 105 THE GOD WHO KEEPS HIS WORD

It has been customary to define Ps. 105 as a Hymn (see Introduction, pp. 32f.) praising the Covenant-God for his faithfulness to his promises. On account of its contents, it could also be described as a History-Psalm (*Geschichtspsalm*) in the style of a hymn. It recites the salvation-history of Israel, beginning with Abraham, Isaac, and Jacob, and concluding with the Settlement in Canaan. The writer briefly alludes to the Sojourn in Egypt, the subsequent oppression, the choice of Moses and Aaron, the plagues and Exodus, but, for some reason, the Sinai events are omitted; it is possible that this episode was dealt with in another part of the liturgy.

Although the Psalm has a didactic character (so Mowinckel), it is primarily a cultic hymn (but cf. Ringgren, *FP*, pp. 98f.); this is reasonably clear from verses 1–6. W. I. Wolverton (*CJT*, x (1964), p. 169) suggests that Ps. 78, 105, 106, in their present form, may be poetical adaptations of older prosaic recitals of the sacral history, in the amphictyonic worship of pre-Davidic times.

Ps. 105:1–15 has been used by the Chronicler in 1 Chr. 16:8–22, alongside Ps. 96 and 106:1, 47f., in association with the celebrations that followed the installation of the Ark in Jerusalem. Ps. 105 is very apposite to this situation, because the fulfilment of the promises spoken of in the hymn could be regarded as finally completed in the triumphant entry of the Ark into Jerusalem. On the other hand, it is unlikely that our Psalm dates from the Davidic period; its composition may well be placed between the early part of the post-Exilic period and the date of the Chronicler (*c.* 300 B.C.). The Chronicler, in quoting the composite poem (1 Chr. 16), is probably reflecting its cultic setting and usage of his own time (cf. Mowinckel, *PIW*, II, p. 200). Originally the *Sitz im Leben* of the hymn may have been the ceremony of the renewal of the Covenant (cf. 1QS i:16–ii:1).

Wolverton (p. 170) has argued that Ps. 106:1–3 actually belongs to Ps. 105, and he may well be right.

The metre of the Psalm is, with a few exceptions, 3+3.

THE CALL TO PRAISE **1–6**

1. This verse seems to be taken from Isa. 12:4. In LXX and V our Psalm is introduced by: 'Praise the Lord'.

give thanks: see on 18:49, 30:12.

call on his name: see on 75:1. It is possible that this expression may have had differing connotations in varying contexts. In the Laments, the afflicted man calls upon the name of Yahweh (116:4), while in Hymns one could rejoice aloud in the divine name with shouts such as 'Praise the LORD' (cf. 104:35: Nötscher,

PEB, p. 228). Luther rendered the phrase 'calls on his name' by 'preach his name'.

his deeds: (cf. 9:11 (M.T. 12)), i.e. the dealings of Yahweh with his people, as they are recounted in the following verses.

2. Sing to him: for *š-y-r*, see on 68:4.

sing praises: the verb used is *z-m-r*, for which see on 66:4. The repetition of the same ideas by means of several synonyms emphasizes the importance of these cultic acts. The praise of God is not simply an enjoyable exercise, but is essential for the maintaining of the right attitude and relationship with him.

his wonderful works: the word *niplā'ôṯ* is discussed on 9:1, 78:11. The Psalmist has in mind the mighty deeds of Yahweh in the Drama of salvation.

3-4. Glory in his holy name: for the verb *h-l-l*, see on 34:3; the phrase occurs elsewhere only in 1 Chr. 16:10. 'His holy name' is a synonym for 'Yahweh'; Davies (*Cent. BP*, II, p. 185) suggests: 'His holy character'.

those who seek: for *b-ḳ-š*, see on 27:8, 40:16; it is also employed in verse 4*b*, and it may be a technical term for making a pilgrimage to Yahweh's sanctuary (cf. W. Beyerlin, *Origins and History of the Oldest Sinaitic Traditions* (1965), p. 123). The verb in verse 4*a* is *d-r-š* (see on 24:6), which means: 'to seek Yahweh in worship and prayer'.

the Lord and his strength: perhaps: 'the mighty Yahweh' (cf. such Ugaritic double names as *kṯr-w-ḫss*; Jirku, *MK*, pp. 61f.). Some scholars read *weʿūzû* ('and seek refuge (in him)') (similarly *RP*), or *weʿuzzû* ('and be strong (in him)') (so also LXX, S, and V). It is possible that 'strength' is simply a synonym of 'presence' (in verse 4*b*).

5. Remember: i.e. call to mind the *Heilsgeschichte* of Israel, or Yahweh's wonderful works (see verse 2*b*), and be thankful.

miracles: for *môp̄ēṯ*, see on 71:7.

the judgments . . .: lit. 'the judgments of his mouth', not the laws given by Yahweh, but the sentence passed by him on the Pharaoh and his people (cf. Exod. 6:6, 7:4, 12:12; Ps. 105:14f.).

6. offspring of Abraham: cf. Isa. 41:8; 1 Chr. 16:13 has 'seed of Israel' (which in *RSV* is altered, following our Psalm); the former reading seems more likely (cf. verse 9). 'Abraham' is rarely mentioned in the Psalter, apart from verses 9 and 42, the only other occurrence is in 47:9 (M.T. 10).

his servant: see on 27:9, 36:1. This can refer either to Abraham or the 'offspring' (so LXX, T, and V, which read: 'his servants').

his chosen ones: the Hebrew *beḥîrāyw* should perhaps be altered into *beḥîrô* ('his chosen one'; see on 89:3), referring to Jacob (see on 20:1, 85:1); so Gunkel, Kraus, *RP*.

YAHWEH'S COVENANT WITH THE FATHERS 7–15

7. The main section of the hymn begins with an affirmation that Yahweh is the Covenant-God. Cf. the self-identification of the giver of the Covenant in Exod. 20:2: 'I am the LORD your God' (also in Dt. 5:6) (see K. A. Kitchen, *Ancient Orient and Old Testament* (1966), pp. 90–102).

his judgments are in all the earth: the allusion is probably to verse 5. Yahweh is no mere national God, but his rule extends over the whole world (cf. Gen. 18:25).

8. He is mindful: the verb is *z-k-r* ('to remember') (see on 8:4, 74:2, 79:8), which in this context is synonymous with 'to be loyal to . . .', i.e. God keeps his Covenant pledge, and he expects the Israelites to do their part in maintaining the Covenant (for *berîṯ*, see on 55:20). 1 Chr. 16:15 has the imperative plural: 'Remember . . .' (referring to the Israelites); but M.T. of Ps. 105 is preferable.

for ever: see on 89:1.

the word that he commanded: denotes the Covenant promises, especially the promise of the land (see verse 11). In a sense 'the word' (*dāḇār*) is parallel to 'his Covenant' (cf. 111:9).

for a thousand generations: for ever, for an unlimited period (cf. Dt. 7:9).

9. the covenant which he made . . .: the verb *kāraṯ*, 'he cut (a Covenant)' is discussed on 89:3. For further details, see Noth, *LPOE*, pp. 108–17. For the Covenant with Abraham, see Gen. 15:18, 17:2ff., 24:7; Lk. 1:72; R. E. Clements, *Abraham and David* (*SBT*, 2nd ser., 5, 1967), pp. 15–34.

his sworn promise: lit. 'his oath' (so *NEB*). Gen. 22:16 mentions such an oath to Abraham, which was later confirmed to Isaac (Gen. 26:3ff.). Its essence was the promise of the land and many descendants.

10. as a statute: the Hebrew *ḥōḳ* (see on 119:5) is synonymous with *berîṯ ʿôlam* ('an everlasting Covenant'; cf. v. Rad, *PHOE*, p. 228), and both point to the promises (see verse 11) inherent in the Covenant. The promises had to be reaffirmed because the specific blessings were not extended to all the descendants of

Abraham, but only to the line through Jacob (cf. Gen. 28:13f., 35:12).

everlasting covenant: cf. Gen. 9:16; Isa. 24:5, 55:3, 61:8, etc. The expression is also found in 1QS iv:22, v:5; 1QSb ii:28.

11. saying: this is lacking in some Hebrew MSS., and may be a gloss emphasizing the actual promise.

the land of Canaan: i.e. the Promised land. 'Canaan' is probably the West Semitic form of the Akkadian *kinaḫna*, which was the Mesopotamian designation of Phoenicia (cf. J. Gray, *I & II Kings* (*OTL*, 1964) p. 229); the name may describe Phoenicia as the 'land of purple', or as the 'land of reeds' (cf. *IDB*, I, p. 494a). Later the term was applied not only to the Phoenician coast but also to the whole of Palestine.

as your portion: lit. 'the lot of your inheritance' (so *AV*, *RV*); cf. 78:55; Dt. 32:9. *Ḥeḇel* may also mean 'share (of the land)' (cf. v. Rad, *PHOE*, p. 82). The pronoun 'your' is plural, while 'you' (in verse 11*a*) is singular; consequently Kirkpatrick (*BPCB*, p. 617) suggests that the 'promise was made to the patriarchs individually . . . but in them to their descendants also'.

inheritance: *naḥ*ᵃ*lāh* is a hereditary possession or a family property, usually the land apportioned to the tribe, or to the individual, by lot. The people of Israel are often described as Yahweh's inheritance (see on 28:9).

12–13. few in number: lit. 'men of number' (as in Gen. 34:30; Dt. 4:27, (33:6); Jer. 44:28; etc.), that is, they are numerable, and therefore comparatively few. The opposite would be 'without number' (e.g. 40:12 (M.T. 13)).

of little account: *AV*, *RV* 'yea, very few', a more literal rendering. Probably we could paraphrase: '(When they were) but a handful (of men)' (cf. *GK* 118x).

sojourners: for *gēr*, see on 39:12. The Patriarchs were semi-nomads, and wandered from place to place (cf. Gen. 12:1–6,10, 20:1, 26:1, 28:2, etc.).

14. he rebuked kings: the allusion is to the Pharaoh (Gen. 12:17) and to Abimelech, king of Gerar (Gen. 20:2f.); the incidents refer to the deliverance of the ancestress of Israel, i.e. Sarah.

15. my anointed ones: for *māšîaḥ*, see on 2:2, 89:20. It is unlikely that the Patriarchs were actually anointed with oil; rather the term *māšîaḥ* is used in a secondary sense to denote one who is called by God and equipped by him for a particular task (cf. Isa. 45:1; E. Kutsch, *Salbung als Rechtsakt* (*BZAW*, 87, 1963), p. 61). The main point of this term is to emphasize the sacrosanctity of the Patriarchs.

my prophets: of all the Patriarchs, only Abraham is called a prophet in the *OT* (Gen. 20:7). J. Lindblom (*Prophecy in Ancient Israel* (1962), p. 96) thinks that *nāḇîʾ* ('prophet') is used in a loose sense, 'referring to a supernormal endowment'. The word *nāḇîʾ* is of uncertain etymology; it may be associated with the Akkadian *nabû* ('to call, name, announce') (cf. also Arabic *nabaʾa* ('to announce, utter a sound')). Hence *nāḇîʾ* may be a 'spokesman (of God)' or 'one who is called (by God)' (if the noun is to be taken in a passive sense). For further details, see Johnson, *CPAI*, pp. 24ff.

THE FORTUNES OF JOSEPH **16–23**

16. he summoned a famine: the famine mentioned is that described in Gen. 41:54, which affected not only Egypt but also Canaan (Gen. 42:5). The Psalmist makes it clear that Yahweh is the sovereign lord both of nature and of history. For the idiom, see 2 Kg. 8:1 (also Am. 5:8, 9:6).

every staff of bread: some scholars (e.g. Kraus, Eaton) think that the 'staff' is the wooden pole used for the storing of the ring-shaped loaves (cf. *KBL*, p. 516a). It is more likely, however, that the expression simply denotes: 'he cut off all food supply' (cf. Snaith, *LN*, p. 171); see also Lev. 26:26; Ezek. 4:16, 5:16, 14:13. This view is supported by Isa. 3:1 which speaks of the 'stay (or 'staff') of bread' and of 'stay of water'. *NEB* '. . . cut short their daily bread'.

17. This verse is an example of the statement of faith that 'in everything God works for good with those who love him' (Rom. 8:28); even Joseph's enforced slavery was made to further the purposes of God (Gen. 45:5,7) and the welfare of his people.

18. hurt with fetters: this is probably a poetic description of Joseph's imprisonment (Gen. 39:20).

his neck was put in a collar of iron: lit. 'his soul entered (into) iron' (similarly *NEB*). The Hebrew *nep̄eš* ('soul') may sometimes denote 'neck' (see on 33:19), or it may be used here as a circumlocution for the personal pronoun, i.e. *he* was put into irons (similarly Wellhausen, Cohen).

19. what he had said may refer to Joseph's prophetic dreams in Gen. 37:5–11, or to his interpretation of the dreams of his fellow-prisoners (Gen. 40:5–23, 41:12f.).

the word of the LORD tested him: Yahweh put Joseph to the test. For *ʾimrāh* ('word'), see on 119:11. Some exegetes (e.g. Gunkel, Kraus) read *niṣrāpāh* ('(the word of Yahweh) was tested (and proved true)') for M.T. *ṣerāpaṯehû* ('it tested him'); but M.T. may be right.

20. The king sent . . .: or 'He (i.e. Yahweh) sent the king' (so Kraus, Deissler). *RSV* is supported by Gen. 41:14: 'Then Pharaoh sent and called Joseph'.

the ruler of the peoples: the Hebrew *mōšēl ʿammîm* occurs only here in the *OT*, and it describes the Pharaoh as the ruler of many lands. At times the Egyptian dominion also included Syria and Palestine.

21. lord of his house: i.e. Joseph was made grand vizier, or the representative of the Pharaoh (cf. Gen. 41:40). Such an office existed in Israel also (cf. 1 Kg. 16:9, 18:3; 2 Kg. 15:5, 18:18,37; etc.), and the official concerned was described as 'the one over the house' or 'master of the palace' (see de Vaux, *AI*, pp. 129ff.).

22. to instruct: (cf. Gen. 41:33) *RSV* rightly follows LXX, S, and V in reading *leyassēr*; M.T. has *leʾsōr* ('to bind') which does not provide a suitable parallel to verse 22*b* ('to teach . . .'). M.T. may be read as *leʾassēr* which may be a byform of *leyassēr* (cf. G. R. Driver, *JTS*, XLIV (1943), p. 20).

his princes: see on 119:23.

at his pleasure: lit. 'in his soul' (for *nepeš*, see on 33:19). LXX, T, and V suggest: 'according to his soul' (*kenapšô*), probably: 'as he wishes'.

ISRAEL IN EGYPT **23–36**

23. In this verse the author briefly describes the descent of Jacob and his family into Egypt (see Gen. 46:1–7).

the land of Ham (see on 78:51) is a poetical synonym of 'Egypt'. The word *miṣrayim* ('Egypt') is of uncertain origin (cf. *KBL*, p. 558) but it occurs already in the Ugaritic texts (see Aistleitner, *WUS*, p. 192) and in the Amarna Letters. Since *miṣrayim* appears to be a dual form, it is often suggested that the allusion is to Upper and Lower Egypt; yet this is far from certain. For further details, see *NBD*, pp. 337ff.

24–5. In these two verses the author has summarized the lengthy sojourn in Egypt (cf. Exod. 1:7ff., 12:40). This and similar summaries were not intended as substitutes for the more detailed accounts, but rather they brought to mind the events of the *Heilsgeschichte*.

He turned their hearts: i.e. Yahweh made the Egyptians hate the Israelites. Here, as in the whole Psalm, the writer is at pains to stress the absolute sovereignty of Yahweh, and therefore the Egyptian hostility is rightly or wrongly attributed to him. Targum took the verb *hāp̄ak̲* in an intransitive sense (as in 78:9): 'Their heart turned to hate . . .' (so also Davies, Leslie). This reading is grammatically possible, but in view of the Exodus story as a whole it seems less likely (cf. Exod. 7:3, 9:12).

to deal craftily: in order to weaken the strength of Israel and to reduce them to permanent slavery; see Exod. 1:10ff., 15f.

26. Moses is mentioned only in five Psalms (77:20 (M.T. 21), 103:7, 106:16,23,32, and in the heading of Ps. 90 (verse 1 in M.T.)). For more detailed information on the name and person of Moses, see *IDB*, III, pp. 440–50; *TDNT*, IV, pp. 848–73.

his servant: see on 27:9, 36:1.

Aaron: the elder brother of Moses (Exod. 6:20, 7:7). See *IDB*, I, pp. 1f.

whom he had chosen as the spokesman of Moses (Exod. 4:14ff.).

27. They wrought: LXX, S, V, *et al.* read *śām* for M.T. *śāmû*, and some scholars suggest *śām bid̲ᵉb̲ārām* ('he wrought (his signs) by their word').

his signs: lit. 'the words of his signs' (for *ʾôṯ* ('sign'), see on 65:8). This may refer either to the predictions concerning the plagues or to the calamities themselves (see Exod. 10:1f.).

among them: i.e. among the Egyptians. Some commentators (e.g. Kraus) read *bᵉmiṣrayim* ('in Egypt') for M.T. *bām* ('among them'), which may have been an abbreviation (?) for the suggested reading.

miracles: for *môp̄ēṯ*, see on 71:7.

the land of Ham: see verse 23.

28. In his account of the plagues, the Psalmist departs from the traditional order in Exod. 7–12, and he omits any reference to the fifth and sixth plagues. The author may have been familiar with the completed P narrative (cf. *IDB*, III, pp. 822ff.), but not necessarily so.

darkness: in the Exodus account this is the ninth plague (Exod. 10:21ff.); Kirkpatrick (*BPCB*, p. 621) has suggested that this calamity was intended to convince the worshippers of the sun-god of Yahweh's unlimited power.

they rebelled against his words: (cf. Num. 20:24) omitting the negative (*lōʾ*) with LXX and S. M.T. has 'and they (Moses and Aaron?) did not rebel . . .', or the negative *lōʾ* could be regarded as an interrogative particle to give the rendering: 'and did they not rebel . . .?'. Another suggestion is to read *welōʾ šāmerû* (and 'they (i.e. the people of Egypt) did not heed (his words)'), for M.T. *welōʾ mārû* (so Weiser, Kraus; similarly *NEB*).

29–30. The tainting of the waters of Egypt is the so-called first plague (Exod. 7:14–24; see on 78:44), while the frogs belong to the second plague (Exod. 8:1–15; see on 78:45).

in the chambers of their kings: the term 'kings' (if correct) may refer to the nobles of Egypt; but we might read *meleḵ hēm* ('they (came even in the chambers of) the king'), or *meleḵ ḥām* ('the king of Ham'), for M.T. *malekêhem* ('their kings').

31. swarms of flies are part of the fourth plague (Exod. 8:20–32; Ps. 78:45).

gnats: (cf. Exod. 8:16f.) *AV*, *RV* render 'lice'. McCullough (*PIB*, p. 562) suggests 'mosquitoes'; *NEB* has 'maggots'.

32–3. hail refers to the seventh plague (Exod. 9:13–35; see on 78:47). The **lightning** was part of the hailstorm (Exod. 9:23f.) which damaged the vegetation of which **vines** and **fig trees** were the representatives.

34–5. the locusts: this belongs to the eighth plague (Exod. 10:12–15); see on 78:46. They destroyed what was left after the hail.

36. The final plague (Exod. 11:4ff., 12:29; see on 78:49ff.) involved the death of the **first-born.**

the first issue . . .: lit. 'the first-fruits of . . .'; *PNT* paraphrases: 'the finest flower of their sons'. For a similar expression, see Gen. 49:3; Dt. 21:17; Ps. 78:51.

THE EXODUS **37–42**

37. Then he led forth Israel is a correct interpretation of M.T. '. . . led them forth'.

with silver and gold: the Israelites are thought to have departed from Egypt laden with valuables (cf. Exod. 3:21, 11:2, 12:35f.), as if with spoil. According to Wis. 10:17 the silver and gold were the people's reward for their slavery in Egypt. Silver (*kesep̱*) and gold (*zāhāḇ*) were the two main precious metals of antiquity. Both were used for the making of ornaments, jewelry, and other objects, as well as in business transactions, etc. At an early period silver was more precious than gold, and therefore silver may have been mentioned first. By the Neo-Babylonian period, gold was generally regarded as the more valuable metal. The silver-gold ratio varied from place to place, and from time to time; of great importance also was the purity of the metal (cf. G. Contenau, *Everyday Life in Babylon and Assyria* (1959), pp. 89f.).

none . . . who stumbled: cf. Isa. 5:27. This emphasizes the effectiveness of Yahweh's guidance (cf. Dt. 8:4).

38. The Egyptians were afraid that even worse disasters might befall them and their land, and therefore they were glad to see the back of their former subjects (cf. Exod. 12:33).

39. a cloud for a covering: (cf. Wis. 10:17) or for protection from the Egyptians (cf. Exod. 13:21). Kirkpatrick (*BPCB*, p. 623) thinks that the purpose of the cloud was to shelter the people from 'the burning rays of the sun in the desert'. In Exod. 13:21 and Ps. 78:14 the cloud served as a guide to the Israelites.

fire to give light: thus leading the people by night (Exod. 13:21f.). The metaphor of the pillars of cloud and of fire may have been derived from the observation of an active volcano, but it is far from certain that such a volcano actually provided the guidance for the people of Israel.

40. For **quails** and **bread from heaven,** see on 78:24, 27f. It is noteworthy that in verses 40f. the author emphasizes only what Yahweh has done, without mentioning the murmuring of the people.

41. the rock alludes to the incident at Rephidim (Exod. 17:1–6, cf. 78:15).

like a river: for *nāhār*, see on 46:4, 72:8; see also 78:16 (cf. Isa. 48:21). This is obviously a poetical exaggeration, but it stresses the miraculous nature of Yahweh's help, and ultimately his limitless majesty.

42. he remembered: i.e. he acted on account of his promise. For the verb *z-k-r*, see on 8:4, 74:2, 79:8. The 'holy promise' (i.e. the divine word) is identical with the Covenant made with Abraham (see verse 9), and the Exodus events are part of the fulfilment (cf. Exod. 2:24; Dt. 7:8).

his servant: see on 27:9, 36:1.

THE BLESSINGS AND RESPONSIBILITY 43–5

43. 'With joy' and 'with singing' (or 'with shouts of triumph', see on 88:2) are reminiscent of Exod. 15, as well as of Isa. 35:10,

51:11, 55:12. It is possible that the Psalm is post-Deutero-Isaiah.

his chosen ones: see on 89:3. The Israelites were a chosen nation because their ancestors were chosen men (see verse 6).

44. the lands of the nations: i.e. Canaan (see on 78:55; cf. Dt. 6:10f.).

the fruit of the peoples' toil: lit. 'the labour of the peoples', i.e. the results of their work, such as fields, plantations, houses, etc.

45. One of the main purposes of the divine acts of salvation was to inspire the people's obedience. The law (see on 1:2, 119:1) was to be kept, not from a fear of punishment, but out of gratitude for what God had already done (cf. 78:7; see also Dt. 4:40, 26:17f.). It is possible that in the cultic setting Ps. 105 was followed by a recitation of the divine law.

Psalm 106 Israel's Ingratitude

This composition, like Ps. 78 and 105, deals with the sacral history of Israel, but the emphasis is upon the tension between the disobedience of the nation and the incredible mercy of Yahweh. Gunkel and a number of other exegetes have regarded Ps. 106 as a Lament of the People (see Introduction, p. 39), but W. I. Wolverton (*CJT*, x (1964), p. 174) may well be right in pointing out that our Psalm 'would have *induced* lament by the people; but it is not itself such a lament'. Cf. Sabourin, *POM*, II, pp. 177f. Perhaps the most likely understanding of the Psalm is gained by assuming that its *Sitz im Leben* is similar to the yearly renewal of the Covenant, depicted in 1QS i:16–ii:18. In this ceremony (according to 1QS) the priests recounted the righteous acts of God (1QS i:21), while the Levites recited the iniquities of the children of Israel (1QS i:23); after this there followed a confession (cf. Leaney, *RQM*, pp. 104–7). Consequently Ps. 106 may have been a similar recital (or 'a liturgical sermon'—so Wolverton, p. 176) of the acts of rebellion of Israel. The cumulative effect of this series of 'historical snapshots' would be to prepare the people for a humble confession of their own sins. The cultic setting could have been the Feast of Tabernacles, although in the Qumran community the renewal of the Covenant was linked with the Feast of Weeks or Pentecost (cf. Leaney, *RQM*, p. 104).

The introductory verses of the Psalm are occasionally taken as the conclusion of Ps. 105 (see below), while verses 4–5 are thought to be a later addition to adapt the poem for a personal devotional use (so Wolverton, p. 175). On the other hand, it is not impossible that verses 1–5 serve as a preparation for the story of Israel's disgrace and Yahweh's grace; without the latter the history of Israel might have been very short.

Although the Chronicler (1 Chr. 16:34ff.) associates our Psalm (i.e. the beginning and the end of it) with David, it must belong to the early post-Exilic period. Verses 27 and 47 seem to presuppose the Exile, and the Psalm as a whole may come from a time after the completion of the Pentateuch, but before the date of the Books of the Chronicles.

The dominant metre of the Psalm is 3 + 3.

HYMNIC CALL TO PRAISE **1–3**

Wolverton (p. 170) suggests that verses 1–3 really belong to the end of Ps. 105 because they do not suit the mood of the present Psalm. This proposal is possible, although changes in the tone of Psalms are not unknown.

1. Praise the Lord: see on 104:35. This phrase is a form of doxology which is frequently used in the fifth book of the Psalter, as well as in the Books of the Chronicler. J. Hempel (*IDB*, II, p. 514b) thinks that the verb *h-l-l*, of which the intensive form denotes 'to praise', may have had a profane use before the Exile, thus being unworthy of the God of Israel. This would account for its comparatively late usage, but, be that as it may, 'Hallelujah' (i.e. 'Praise the Lord') became a very frequent cultic exclamation.

. . . give thanks: see on 18:49, 30:12. This liturgical formula 'O give thanks . . . for his steadfast love endures for ever' is also found in 1 Chr. 16:34; Ps. 100:5, 107:1, 118:1, 136:1; cf. Ezr. 3:11; Jer. 33:11.

for he is good: i.e. benevolent (cf. Imschoot, *ThOT*, I, p. 65). J. Hempel (*IDB*, II, p. 440b) points out that the Hebrew *ṭôḇ* ('good') suggests that 'a person or a thing is in accordance with the acknowledged practical, moral or religious standards'. See on 100:5. *NEB* has 'It is good to give thanks . . .', which is a possible rendering.

his steadfast love: or 'his Covenant loyalty' is endless (for *ʿôlām*, see on 9:5, 89:1). See also on 107:1.

2. Who can utter . . .: the rhetorical question amounts to saying that none is able to express adequately the praise of Yahweh. The verb used is the Aramaic *m-l-l*, which is also found in Gen. 21:7, Job 8:2, 33:3.
the mighty doings: the Hebrew *gᵉḇûrāh* signifies the might or strength of God (21:13 (M.T. 14), 54:1 (M.T. 3), 65:6 (M.T. 7), etc.), or of men (Prov. 8:14) and animals (Job 39:19; Ps. 147:10). The plural form of the noun can also be used of the mighty deeds of Yahweh, especially of those in history (20:6 (M.T. 7), 71:16, 145:4,12, 150:2).
show forth: or 'recount' (lit. 'cause to hear').
his praise: LXX, S, and Jerome have 'his praises' (*tᵉhillōṯāyw*) which provides a better parallel to 'the mighty doings . . .' in verse 2*a*.

3. Blessed are they: for *ʾašᵉrê*, see on 1:1. This verse is a 'congratulation' of the righteous man but essentially it is an exhortation to strive for righteousness.
justice: see on 36:6, 119:7. 'To observe justice' is, in a sense, an imitation of God (cf. 15:2).
who do: (*ʿōśê*) so some Hebrew MSS. and the versions; M.T. has *ʿōśēh* ('who does').
righteousness: *ṣᵉḏāḳāh* is discussed on 33:5, 119:40.

THE PERSONAL PRAYER 4–5

4. Remember me: i.e. grant me your favour for the sake of your Covenant loyalty; see on 8:4, 74:2. LXX and other Greek versions suggest 'Remember us' (i.e. *zoḵᵉrēnû* for M.T. *zoḵᵉrēnî*).
when thou showest favour . . .: lit. 'in the favour of your people'. *Rāṣôn* may mean 'favour, goodwill, acceptance' and in most cases it refers to a divine action expressing God's favour and grace (see *TDNT*, II, p. 743). In our verse *rāṣôn* is parallel to 'salvation' (*yᵉšûʿāh*), see on 35:3.
help me: lit. 'visit me (with your salvation)'. For the verb *p-ḳ-d*, see on 80:14. The Greek versions read 'visit us . . .' (*poḳᵉḏēnû* for M.T. *poḳᵉḏēnî*).

5. that I may see . . .: i.e. that I may share in the blessings of God's people (cf. Jer. 29:32). The Greek versions take the verbs as first person plurals; they do not presuppose a different reading, because this verse is dependent for its interpretation upon the preceding verse. The Psalmist emphasizes an important truth: the happiness of the individual can truly be found only in the well being of the whole nation. This thought provides a corrective to the 'I'm-all-right-Jack' philosophy.

thy chosen ones: see on 89:3.

thy nation: the noun used is *gôy* (see on 59:5); cf. 33:12; Zeph. 2:9. Oesterley (*TP*, p. 451) argues that when *gôy* is used of Israel or Judah, the intention is to describe them as a sinful nation (cf. Dt. 32:28; Jg. 2:20; Isa. 1:4, 10:6), but obviously this is not an absolute rule; see Exod. 19:6: 'a holy nation (*gôy*)' (cf. Exod. 33:12; Jos. 3:17, 4:1; etc.).

thy heritage: i.e. your people (see on 28:9).

THE CONFESSION OF SIN **6**

Although the Psalmist is conscious of his solidarity with the preceding generations, he may also be confessing his own sin as well as that of his generation.

6. have sinned: lit. 'We have sinned together with our fathers' which is a more likely rendering than 'We have sinned like our fathers' (*RP*). For *ḥāṭā*ʾ, see on 119:11.

we have committed iniquity: for the verb *ᶜ-w-h*, see on 51:2.

we have done wickedly: the verb *hiršîaᶜ* is an internal causative form (*GK* 53d), and it is usually found in late writings. It often means: 'to condemn as guilty' (cf. Job 9:20, 10:2, 15:16; Ps. 37:33; etc.); the noun *rāšāᶜ* denotes a man who has been found guilty. Yet neither the verb nor the noun are merely legal terms; they can also point to the corrupt nature of the man concerned. All the three verbs mentioned in our verse are also found in 1 Kg. 8:47 (cf. Dan. 9:5); perhaps they form part of a formula of confession.

THE EXODUS STORY **7–12**

7. when they were in Egypt: the verb is lacking in Hebrew, and the line seems rather short. For 'Egypt', see on 105:23.

thy wonderful works: (see on 9:1, 78:11) the author has in mind the miracles wrought by Yahweh in Egypt, through the instrumentality of Moses and Aaron. In spite of the deliverance from Egypt, the people failed to grasp (i.e. they did not consider; see on 101:2) the significance of the marvellous deeds of Yahweh. They also neglected to remember (see on 119:52) the manifestations of Yahweh's loyalty—or, in other words, they were callous and ungrateful to God for his faithfulness (cf. Exod. 4:8, 14:10ff.).

thy steadfast love: since the Hebrew *ḥeseḏ* (see on 26:3) is here

plural in form, we should render: 'your acts of devotion' (see on 89:1). LXX, T, and Jerome have the singular.
rebelled: *m-r-h* is usually used of men defying the divine authority (Num. 20:10; Isa. 1:20, 50:5, 63:10, etc.).
against the Most High at the Red Sea: so most commentators, reading *ᶜelyôn* ('Most High'; see on 18:13, 46:4, 47:2), for *ᶜal yām* ('at the sea') which seems to be a scribal error; LXX has *anabainontes* ('as they went up' which represents the Hebrew *ᶜōlîm*), so also Barnes, Kissane. 'The Red Sea' is a traditional but inferior rendering of *yam sûp̱*, which may well mean 'the Sea of Reeds'. There are no reeds in either the Gulf of 'Aqaba or the Gulf of Suez, and therefore the reference must be to some inland lake or marshy area N. of the Gulf of Suez. The Hebrew *sûp̱* may be an Egyptian loan word (i.e. *twf* (*y*) ('papyrus'); see *NBD*, p. 1078a). N. H. Snaith (*VT*, xv (1965), pp. 395–8) has argued that *yam sûp̱* was the 'sea at the end of the land', 'the deep sea away to the south with its tides and great depths, all of it very different from the Mediterranean which was close at hand and the only sea they really knew' (p. 398).

8. He saved them: although they deserved to have their wish to serve the Egyptians once more (Exod. 14:12). For the verb *y-š-ᶜ*, see on 54:1.
for his name's sake: i.e. as befits his character, or for the sake of his reputation (cf. 25:11, 31:3 (M.T. 4); Isa. 48:9; Jer. 14:7; etc.). For *šēm* ('name'), see on 20:1. In Exod. 14:18 God saves his people in order that the Egyptians may know that he is Yahweh.
his mighty power: see verse 6.

9. He rebuked . . .: see on 9:5 (119:21). Kraus (*PBK*, p. 729) suggests that the motif is derived from the myth of Yahweh's fight with Chaos (cf. 104:7; Isa. 50:2; Nah. 1:4; Eichrodt, *TOT*, II, p. 114; v. Rad, *OTT*, I, p. 178).
the Red Sea: see verse 7.
it became dry so that the deeps (see on 104:6) became like a desert (see on 55:7), or a dry ground (Exod. 14:21). *RVm* has 'pasture-land' for 'desert'; such a rendering would imply that God led his people, as a shepherd leads his flock, across the sea-bed. Cf. Isa. 63:13, where the prophet asks: 'who led them through the depths? Like a horse in the desert, they did not stumble.'

10. from the hand of the foe: or, 'from the power of him who hated (them)' (similarly LXX); cf. Lk. 1:71.

delivered them: the verb is *g-ʾ-l* (see on 119:154), while in verse 10*a* we have *y-š-ᶜ* (see on 54:1). The verb *g-ʾ-l* is commonly used of a close relative in cases such as blood-revenge, the redemption of property, etc. When it is applied to Yahweh, the basic idea is not so much a ransom by means of a payment as the protection given to the needy.

11–12. These verses describe the destruction of the enemies (see Exod. 14:28, 15:5), which is followed by the praise of the redeemed people (Exod. 15:1–18).

Then they believed: (for *heʾᵉmîn*, see on 78:22) C. H. Spurgeon (*The Treasury of David*, v (1878), p. 76) suggests that this is mentioned 'not to their credit, but to their shame . . . Who would not believe when the fact stares him in the face?'.

they sang his praise: better with some MSS., LXX, S, Jerome, and V: 'and they sang . . .' (*wayyāšîrû* for M.T. *yāšîrû*). For 'praise' (*tᵉhillāh*), see on 65:1, 119:171. Spurgeon (p. 76) aptly remarks that between 'Israel singing and Israel sinning there was scarce a step'.

GOD IS PUT TO THE TEST **13–15**

13. they soon forgot: lit. 'they made haste, they forgot' (so also LXX). For the construction, see on 85:6. 'His works' refer to Yahweh's mighty deeds in Egypt and at the Sea of Reeds. The possibility that the people might forget Yahweh's saving works was a constant worry of the Deuteronomist (Dt. 4:9,23, 6:12, 9:7; cf. also Hos. 2:13 (M.T. 15)).

they did not wait: i.e. they allowed mistrust and impatience to blind them, so that they no longer waited obediently for Yahweh and his plan (see on 33:20). For the murmurings in the wilderness, see Exod. 15:22–5, 16, 17:2f.; Num. 11; Ps. 78:17ff.

14. they had a wanton craving: (cf. *GK*, 117p) similarly in Num. 11:4. The verb *ʾ-w-h* ('to incline, desire') does not necessarily imply a sinful wish or desire (cf. Dt. 12:20, 14:26; 2 Sam. 23:15; Lk. 22:15). The hunger and thirst may have been real enough, but the disbelief in Yahweh's providence was not justifiable, and it led to unreasonable doubting and even to rebellion.

wilderness: see on 29:8, 55:7.

put God to the test: (see on 78:18) rather than 'tempted God' (so *AV*, *RV*). They wanted to dictate to Yahweh rather than to trust him, or receive instructions.

in the desert: *y^e^šîmôn* (see on 78:40) is here a synonym of 'wilderness'.

15. The Israelites received what they had asked for; yet the answer to their prayer was not a favour but a punishment.

a wasting disease: (cf. Num. 11:34) is a translation of M.T. *rāzôn*, which occurs elsewhere in Isa. 10:16; Mic. 6:10. LXX has *plēsmonēn* ('fulness' or 'plenty'); similarly S, V, and Kissane (who reads *rāwôn* ('abundance') for *rāzôn*). Briggs (*CECBP*, II, p. 356) suggests *māzôn* ('food') which could refer to the quails and manna.

among them: lit. 'in their soul' or, perhaps, 'in their throat' (for this use of *nep̱eš*, see on 33:19).

DATHAN AND ABIRAM **16–18**

16. When men in the camp . . .: lit. 'they were envious . . . in the camp' (so *RP*). This incident is described in Num. 16, which depicts, apparently, a double mutiny: that of Korah and certain other Levites, and that of Dathan and Abiram who were of the tribe of Reuben. The Psalmist alludes, however, only to Dathan and Abiram (so also Dt. 11:6), omitting any reference to Korah; he may have been afraid to compromise the well-known Korahite family which formed a guild of Temple singers (cf. Rowley, *WAI*, pp. 173f.). For 'Moses' and 'Aaron', see on 105:26.

the holy one of the Lord is Aaron. According to Lev. 21:6 the sons of Aaron are 'holy to their God'; similarly the high priest's crown bears the inscription: 'Holy to the Lord' (Exod. 39:30). In 2 Chr. 35:3 the Levites are described as: 'holy to the Lord', and in 2 Kg. 4:9 Elisha is called a 'holy man of God'. The Nazirites, too, are said to be 'holy to the Lord'. The characteristic of all these people was, ideally, their separation from what was unclean, and their dedication to Yahweh (see on 34:39).

17. the earth opened: the Hebrew *ʾereṣ* is probably a synonym of 'Sheol' (see on 61:2) or the netherworld (cf. also Num. 16:30–33). The two parallel lines of verse 17 are complementary to one another. The verb *tip̱taḥ* may be a *ḳal* passive (*tup̱taḥ*), so Dahood, *PNWSP*, p. 8, n.4.

18. Fire also broke out . . .: originally this event may have referred to Korah and his company (cf. Num. 16:17, 35; Snaith, *LN*, pp. 254ff.).

the wicked: (Num. 16:26), see on 1:1, 28:3, 92:7.

THE GOLDEN CALF **19–23**

19. a calf: M. Noth (*Exodus* (*OTL*, 1962), p. 247) argues that, as 'the ancient Near East (in contrast to Egypt) knows no theriomorphic deities . . ., the "golden calves" of the royal sanctuaries of Jeroboam are also surely meant as pedestals for the God who is imagined to be standing invisibly upon them' (similarly also v. Rad, *Deuteronomy* (*OTL*, 1966), p. 78). On the other hand, the Ugaritic texts show that not only El, but also Baal could be described as 'Bull' (for references see Pope, *EUT*, pp. 35ff.; J. Gray, *The Legacy of Canaan* (*SVT*, 5, 1957), p. 117; W. H. Schmidt, *Königtum Gottes in Ugarit und Israel* (*BZAW*, 80, 1966), pp. 6f., 21). It is not impossible, however, that these descriptions should be taken metaphorically. The word 'calf' may be a derogatory substitute for 'bull' (*šûr*), which may have been deliberately misrepresented as an idol, although originally it was but a bull-pedestal of Yahweh (see J. Gray, *I & II Kings* (*OTL*), p. 290; *ANEP*, pll. 470–4, 500–1). Vriezen (*RAI*, p. 187) thinks that the bull-figure was a symbol of Yahweh, but not a Yahweh-image, because he was envisaged anthropomorphically. Some scholars (e.g. Barnes) are of the opinion that the bull-image was probably derived from Egypt.

Horeb is the usual designation of Sinai in the Book of Deuteronomy (except Dt. 33:2). Kirkpatrick (*BPCB*, p. 628) suggests that the choice of the term may be an indication that the author had in mind the Deuteronomist's version of the so-called 'apostasy of the golden calf' (Dt. 9:8–21).

worshipped: see on 29:2.

molten image was made by pouring the molten metal into a prepared mold, as against an image carved of stone or wood. Probably the molten images were first made of some common metal, and were later overlaid with gold or silver (cf. Isa. 40:19).

20. the glory of God: (similarly T) lit. 'their glory' (which is Yahweh; similarly *NEB*; cf. Dt. 10:21; Ps. 3:3 (M.T. 4); Hos. 4:7). In Jer. 2:11 we read: 'But my people have changed their glory for that which does not profit'. According to an ancient tradition M.T. *k*ᵉ*ḇôḏām* ('their glory') is a scribal correction for either *k*ᵉ*ḇôḏî* ('my glory') or *k*ᵉ*ḇôḏô* ('his glory'). For the phrase 'glory of God', see on 19:1, 26:8, 57:5; cf. 1QM iv:6,8.

21. They forgot God: see verse 13, cf. 119:16.

their Saviour who delivered them from Egypt. *Môšîa*ᶜ ('saviour') is often used by Deutero-Isaiah as a designation of Yahweh (Isa. 43:3,11, 45:15,21, 49:26). J. Sawyer (*VT*, xv (1965) pp. 475–86) has argued that *môšîaᶜ* has in most cases forensic overtones.

great things: God's acts of salvation and judgment (cf. Dt. 10:21; Job 5:9; Ps. 71:19).

22. Wondrous works (for *niplāʾôt*, see on 9:1, 78:11) are synonymous with **terrible things**, or 'deeds which inspire awe' (for *nôrāʾ*, see on 65:5), and both refer to the plagues in the land of Ham (see on 105:23), i.e. in Egypt, and to the deliverance at the Red Sea (or 'the Sea of Reeds'; see verse 7).

23. Therefore he said: Yahweh resolved to destroy the Israelites (Dt. 9:25) because of their rebellion, but the intercession of Moses (Exod. 32:11ff.) averted the divine wrath (see on 6:1, 74:1).

his chosen one: for *bāḥîr*, see on 89:3.

stood in the breach is a metaphor derived from a military context. Moses is depicted as a fearless warrior standing in the breach of the city wall (cf. Ezek. 22:30) and facing the enemy.

THE RENEWED REBELLION FOLLOWING THE REPORT OF THE SPIES 24–7

These four verses seem to cover the period from the Wilderness generation down to the Exile. The dispersion in the sixth century B.C. is regarded, at least partly, as a punishment for the disobedience of the Israelites in the Wilderness at the time of the Exodus.

24. the pleasant land is Canaan, the Promised Land (as in Jer. 3:19; Zech. 7:14). The exaggerated report of the spies (Num. 13:25–9) disheartened the people, who were more ready to trust the opinions of men than to believe in God (see on 78:22). They even planned to return to Egypt (Num. 14:4).

25. They murmured . . .: as in Dt. 1:27.

did not obey . . .: lit. 'they did not listen to the voice of . . .' (see on 54:2). The particular divine command is summarized in Dt. 1:21: 'Behold, the LORD your God has set the land before you; go up, take possession . . .'.

26. Therefore he raised his hand and swore to them: lit. 'He lifted his hand to them' which is a common gesture in the swearing of an oath (cf. Num. 14:30; Ezek. 20:23; see also Gen. 14:22). In Dan. 12:7 both hands are lifted up toward heaven, while in Rev. 10:5f. it is the right hand that is raised in an oath.

Similarly in 144:8: 'whose right hand is a right hand of falsehood', i.e. who swear falsely.

in the wilderness: see on 55:7. The allusion is to Num. 14:28ff.

27. This verse is nearly the same as Ezek. 20:23.

disperse: (*l^e^hāp̱îṣ*); so *RSV*, *NEB* after T and S (cf. Ezek. 20:23), for M.T. 'would make them fall' (*ûl^e^happîl*), which is a repetition of the same verbal form as in verse 26*b*.

nations: *gôyīm* (see on verse 5 and on 59:5) refers to the dispersion of the people of God among the foreign nations. This punishment is not threatened in Num. 14, but it is mentioned in Lev. 26:33; Dt. 4:27.

FURTHER ACTS OF DISOBEDIENCE **28–33**

28. they attached themselves to . . .: lit. 'they yoked themselves to . . .' (cf. Snaith, *LN*, p. 302) as in Num. 25:3. LXX suggests 'they were initiated' (*etelesthēsan*).

Baal of Peor: the Hebrew *p^eᶜôr* was a name of a mountain in Moab (Num. 23:28) but its location is uncertain; for various suggestions, see H. W. Wolff, *Hosea* (*BK* 14, 1961), pp. 213f. The 'Baal of Peor' was the god of Mount Peor, probably a localization of the well-known Canaanite Baal. Kissane (*BP*, p. 492) argues that 'Baal Peor' was the Moabite god Chemosh worshipped at Peor (cf. S. R. Driver, *Deuteronomy* (*ICC*, 1896), pp. 63f.).

sacrifices offered to the dead: the Hebrew *zeḇaḥ* (see on 40:6) was in the nature of a fellowship meal which either established or helped to maintain a mutual bond of communion between the deity and the worshippers. 'The dead' may refer to the foreign god(s) (cf. Lev. 26:30; Ps. 115:4–8; Wis. 13:10), or the allusion is to certain mortuary cults (cf. Dt. 26:14; (A:II, 132f.; Driver, *CML*, p. 49)).

29. the LORD is a correct interpretative addition. Some MSS. and most of the versions suggest 'they provoked him' (*wayyaḵᶜîsûhû*). Those who forsook the living God (Jer. 10:10) for lifeless idols were struck down by a plague or pestilence (cf. Num. 25:8f.). In Num. 25:5 it is Moses who ordered the judges of Israel to slay the men who had attached themselves to the Baal of Peor.

30. Phinehas was the son of Eleazar the son of Aaron (Num. 25:7) who slew an Israelite and his Midianite wife(?). Some scholars (e.g. Snaith, *LN*, p. 303) regard this incident as unconnected with the previous apostasy. The name 'Phinehas' is apparently of Egyptian origin, meaning 'negro'.

and interposed: *RP* 'and prayed' (so T and S); LXX '. . . made atonement' (*exilasato*; cf. Num. 25:13).

the plague was stayed: as in Num. 25:8 (cf. Num. 16:50 (M.T. 17:13)).

31. . . . reckoned to him as righteousness: for the expression cf. Gen. 15:6, where Abram put his trust in Yahweh, and this was counted to him as righteousness. Cf. Rom. 4:3; Gal. 3:6; v. Rad, *OTT*, I, pp. 171, 379. Gunkel (*PGHAT*, p. 467) takes 'righteousness' (see on 33:5) in the sense of 'reward' which was 'the Covenant of a perpetual priesthood' (Num. 25:13; cf. Sir. 45:23f.).

from generation to generation: see on 72:5.

for ever: see on 9:5, 89:1.

32. They angered him: so with some MSS., LXX, and S. M.T. has no object (*NEB* adds 'the LORD'), but the reference seems to be to Yahweh, and not to Moses. For the incident, see Num. 20:2–13.

the waters of Meribah: see on 81:7, 95:8.

it went ill with Moses: there is no clear information about the details of the happenings during which Moses incurred Yahweh's displeasure. For various explanations, see Snaith, *LN*, p. 276.

THE DESECRATION OF YAHWEH'S LAND 34–46

Nötscher (*PEB*, p. 236) points out that the Psalmist must have had in mind the religious syncretism which bedevilled the Israelites for centuries, and which was largely due to the Canaanites.

34. They did not destroy the peoples: the so-called conquest of Canaan was envisaged as a Holy War, in which the enemy and the booty were to be handed over to Yahweh (cf. Jos. 7:1; 1 Sam. 15:3). (For more details, see G. v. Rad, *Studies in Deuteronomy* (*SBT* 9, 1953), pp. 45–59.) It may well be that the Israelite inability to subdue the whole of Canaan and to destroy its inhabitants was later interpreted (or misinterpreted?) as a disobedience on the part of the nation.

as the LORD commanded: some of the relevant passages are found in Exod. 34:11–16; Num. 33:50–56; Dt. 7:1–5,16, 20:10–8.

35. they mingled with the nations both by intermarriage and by settling among the foreign peoples (cf. Jg. 3:5f.; Ezr. 9:1f.).

. . . learned to do as they did: they adopted Canaanite ways of life and many features of their religion. This is elaborated in verses 36–9.

36. They served: the verb *ᶜ-b-d* may simply mean 'to labour, work' (Exod. 20:9, 34:21), 'to do a particular task' (Gen. 2:5, 3:23), or 'to serve as a slave for one's master' (Exod. 21:2,6; Dt. 15:12,18; etc.). This service can be offered not only to an owner or king, but also to Yahweh (Exod. 3:12; Ps. 22:30 (M.T. 31)) or to other gods (Jg. 2:19; Ps. 97:7) by means of various ritual acts and a particular way of life. A. S. Herbert (*Worship in Ancient Israel* (*Ecumenical Studies in Worship* 5, 1959), p. 11) points out that 'the emphasis is not so much on the worshipper's servile status as on his function to carry out the will of his lord'.

their idols: the noun *ᶜāṣāḇ* ('idol') is always used in the plural (for the form, see *GK* 93ee), and it signifies 'graven images'. It is possible that sometimes there may be an intentional word play between *ᶜāṣāḇ* ('idol') and *ᶜeṣeḇ* ('pain', or some other form of the same root). If correct, the implication may be that those who serve idols bring trouble upon themselves. Such idols would be made of (cf. Dan. 3:1, or at least they might be overlaid with) silver and gold (115:4; 135:15).

which became . . .: Cohen (*PSon*, p. 356) thinks that the reference is to the inhabitants of Canaan, but the writer may have had in mind the idols (as in Jg. 2:3). For 'snare' (*môḳēš*), see on 64:5.

37. One of the adopted evils was human sacrifice (cf. Lev. 18:21; Dt. 12:31; 2 Kg. 16:3, 21:6, 23:10; Jer. 7:31, etc.). See R. de Vaux, *Studies in Old Testament Sacrifice*, pp. 63–90.

demons: the Hebrew *šēḏîm* is found elsewhere only in Dt. 32:17, and its exact meaning is uncertain; in post-biblical usage it is a fairly frequent term for 'demons'. *Šēḏîm* are often connected with the Akkadian *šêdu*, which is the name of certain subordinate spirits invested with power for good or evil, usually represented as winged bulls.

38–9. Most recent commentators (e.g. Weiser, Kraus, Deissler) regard verse 38*bc* as a gloss which may be more appropriate to the preceding verse.

38. innocent blood: the reference is probably to legal murders and the like (cf. 2 Kg. 21:16; Isa. 1:15ff.; Jer. 22:3).

the land was polluted . . .: every breach of God's Covenant desecrates the Holy land (Isa. 24:5), and the transgressors themselves are defiled by their own deeds.

39. played the harlot: the Hebrew verb *z-n-h* ('to be a prostitute') is used only of women, either in common or ritual prostitution. Both kinds of practice were well known in the life and cults of Semitic peoples (cf. *DNT*, VI, 1959, pp. 584–7). 'Prostitution' is used in the *OT* as a metaphor of Israel's perverted relationship to Yahweh. Although common prostitution as such was tolerated in Israel (cf. Gen. 38:14ff.; Jos. 2:2ff.; 1 Kg. 3:16; Am. 7:17; see, however, Lev. 19:29), it was not permissible for a married woman to have extra-marital relationships; any such faithlessness was regarded as a gross indecency and sin. The relationship between Israel and God could be depicted as a marriage-bond (cf. Isa. 1:21, 50:1, 57:7–13; Hos. 2–3), yet Israel preferred to become like an adulterous wife.

40. the anger of the LORD: similar expressions are frequent in the *OT* (e.g. Exod. 4:14; Num. 12:9; Jos. 17:1; Jg. 2:14); see on 38:3.

his heritage: i.e. the people of Israel (see on 28:9). Yahweh abhorred (or 'regarded as an abomination'; *PNT* 'he was filled with horror . . .') his inheritance or his special possession, Israel.

41. into the hand of the nations: i.e. into the power of foreign oppressors (cf. Jg. 2:14, 13:1), such as the Canaanites, Moabites, Midianites, Philistines, Ammonites, etc. The Psalmist is thinking primarily of the period of the Judges, but it is possible that he also intends to recall the rest of the varied history of his people, down to the time of the Exile.

43. Many times he delivered them: the Israelite history seems to be an unending sequence of rebellion and punishment, repentance and deliverance.

in their purposes: G. R. Driver (*JTS*, XLIV (1943), p. 20) renders 'by their disobedience'; *NEB* 'and rebellious still'.

45. He remembered: see on 8:4, 74:2, 79:8; cf. Lev. 26:42; Ps. 98:3. Perhaps we could paraphrase: 'He implemented his Covenant promises for the sake of his wayward people'. For 'Covenant' (*b^e^rîṯ*), see on 55:20, 89:3.

relented: (see on 71:21) or 'pitied' (*AV*, *RV* 'repented'; cf. 2 Sam. 24:16; Jon. 3:9,10).

his steadfast love: or 'his Covenant promises' (see on 26:3).

46. to be pitied: 1 Kg. 8:50 (cf. Neh. 1:11) suggests the meaning: 'And he gave them over to mercy (which they should find) in the sight of all their captors'.

THE CONCLUDING PRAYER **47**
This is probably the congregational response to the recital of Israel's sins and God's mercy.

47. Save us: see on 54:1.
O Lord our God: 1 Chr. 16:35 has 'O God of our salvation', but M.T. of our Psalm is more likely.
gather us: referring either to the Babylonian exiles in particular or to the Jews of the dispersion in general (cf. Dt. 30:3).
give thanks: see on 18:49, 30:12.
thy holy name: for similar expressions see 33:21, 103:1, 105:3, 145:21. The phrase may be a circumlocution for 'you' (i.e. Yahweh).
thy praise: see 65:1, 119:171.

THE DOXOLOGY **48**

48. This verse may not be an integral part of the Psalm, but it may form the conclusion to the fourth book of the Psalter (cf. Kirkpatrick, *BPCB*, p. 634). For the interpretation, see the doxology at the end of Ps. 41 (verse 13). Nötscher (*PEB*, p. 237) thinks that 1 Chr. 16:35f. indicates that by the time of the Chronicler the poem was already the final Psalm of a collection or division.
Praise the Lord: see on verse 1 and 104:35.

BOOK V

Psalm 107 Thanks to the Saving God

This Psalm consists of two main parts: a Thanksgiving (verses 1–32), and a Praise to Yahweh, or Wisdom Hymn (verses 33–42). The first part opens with an introductory call to give thanks to Yahweh (verses 1–3), which is followed by the expression of gratitude by four different groups of people: travellers (verses 4–9), released prisoners (verses 10–16), those recently healed from their illnesses (verses 17–22), and seafarers (verses 23–33). The thanksgiving of each group follows the same pattern: a description of the distress, a prayer to Yahweh, details of the subsequent deliverance, and finally an expression of thankfulness. There is also a double refrain in verses 6 and 8, 13 and 15, 19 and 21, 28 and 31. The Psalm may have been used at a communal thank-offering (cf. Mowinckel, *PIW*, II, p. 42) at which various groups of people offered their thanksgiving sacrifice and their grateful praise.

The concluding Hymn (verses 33–43) has no refrain, and its main theme is the providence of God who is the lord both of nature and of men. Some scholars (e.g. Duhm, Oesterley, Leslie, Kraus) argue that the hymn is a later addition. This suggestion is possible but not absolutely necessary; the evidence is inconclusive either way.

The Psalm may be of post-Exilic origin; Oesterley (*TP*, p. 453) dates it *c.* 300 B.C., but it may be a pre-Exilic composition adapted to the needs of the restored community of the Persian period.

The Psalm has no title; but in LXX and V it begins with 'Hallelujah'.

The metre of the poem is mainly 3 + 3; one of the variations is provided by the refrain in verses 6, 13, 19, and 28, which are in 4 + 3 metre.

THE CALL TO OFFER THANKSGIVING **1–3**

1. This verse is a common liturgical formula which expresses the gratitude of those bringing their thank-offerings to Yahweh

(Jer. 33:11). The phrase 'for his steadfast love . . .' may be the response of the congregation, and should perhaps be rendered: 'Indeed! His steadfast love . . .'. The Hebrew *kî* (*RSV* 'for') is more likely an emphatic particle (cf. Dahood, *PAB*, I, p. 241), meaning 'surely, indeed'. Cf. also 118:1–4, 136:1ff. For further exegesis, see on 106:1.

2. the redeemed of the LORD: the same phrase is found in Isa. 62:12 (cf. Isa. 35:9, 51:10) and many commentators regard the Psalm as post Deutero-Isaiah (so Kirkpatrick, Davies, Barnes, Cohen). In Isa. 62:12 the 'redeemed' are the Babylonian exiles, while in 107:2 they may refer to the four groups of people described in verses 4–32. Kraus (*PBK*, p. 738) suggests that verses 2–3 may be a later addition which adapts the Psalm for the use of the restored deportees.

he has redeemed: for *g-ʾ-l*, see on 106:10, 119:154.

from trouble: or 'from the hand of the enemy' (*AV*). The Hebrew *ṣar* can be derived either from *ṣ-r-r* I ('to be restricted') or from *ṣ-r-r* II ('to display hostility'); in the former case the meaning of *ṣar* would be 'trouble', while in the latter instance 'enemy'. The second alternative seems more likely (so also LXX, *NEB*), while in verses 6, 13, 19, and 28 *ṣar* means 'trouble'.

3. from the lands: cf. 106:47; Jer. 32:37; Ac. 2:8–11.

from the east . . .: i.e. from the four corners of the earth.

and from the south: M.T. has 'and from the sea', i.e. from the west. Most exegetes emend M.T. *ûmiyyām* into *ûmiyyāmîn*, which is presupposed by the *RSV* rendering (similarly *NEB*). The Targum speaks about the 'southern sea', which may allude to that part of the Mediterranean Sea of which Egypt forms the coastline, or it may suggest the Red Sea. The proposed emendation seems a reasonable solution, but cf. Isa. 49:12 ('from the north and from the sea').

GOD DELIVERS THE LOST TRAVELLERS 4–9

4–5. Some wandered: this represents the Hebrew *tōʿê*; M.T. has *tāʿû* ('they wandered'). Since the subject of the verb is not explicitly expressed, some assume that it is to be found in verses 2–3. If these two verses are secondary, then *tāʿû* may be a deliberate alteration to *tōʿê* (similar participles are also found in verses 10 and 23). Originally the word-picture may have referred to lost travellers, while after the Exile the allusion may have been understood as a description of the home-coming of the exiles (cf.

Isa. 43:14–21, 49:10). The account may bring to mind also the experiences of the nation during the first Exodus. The verb *t-ᶜ-h* means 'to wander about aimlessly' or 'to be lost' (Exod. 23:4; Isa. 53:6). It can be applied also to the realm of ethics and religion (cf. 58:3 (M.T. 4), 95:10, 119:110).

in desert wastes: *RSV*, *NEB* (LXX, S) add the word 'way' (*derek̲*) to the next line; M.T. reads 'in the wilderness, in a desert way' (*RV*). For *mid̲bār* ('wilderness'), see on 55:7, and for *yᵉšîmôn* ('desert'), see on 78:40.

a city to dwell in: or, 'an inhabited city'. The travellers were probably not looking for a city in which to settle down, but for a place where they could find food and drink, and guidance.

their soul fainted: i.e. they were utterly exhausted (cf. 1QH viii:29). Their 'soul' (for *nep̄eš*, see 33:19), or their 'vitality', had faded away like the life of a fatally wounded man (Lam. 2:12).

6. Then they cried . . .: this forms the beginning of one of the refrains. Verses 13 and 19 use a slightly different but synonymous verb (*z-ᶜ-q* for *ṣ-ᶜ-q*).

in their trouble: for *ṣar*, see verse 2.

he delivered them: i.e. he snatched them out of their distress. The verb used is the causative form of *n-ṣ-l*, which can denote deliverance from all sorts of trouble (cf. Barth, *ETKD*, p. 125). LXX usually renders it by *ruomai*.

7. a straight way: for *yāšār* ('straight'), see on 92:15; cf. Jer. 31:9. In our verse the reference is to the shortest way to the place of shelter, i.e. the inhabited city (see verse 4).

8. Let them thank: see on 18:49, 30:12. The people addressed may be either the travellers who have been brought to safety or the people in general; the individual experiences of some may represent the saving help of Yahweh to one and all.

for his wonderful works: for *nip̄lāʾôt*, see on 9:1, 78:11.

the sons of men: either the people who have experienced a similar deliverance or the whole nation, the members of which have been the recipients of God's grace both individually and collectively. For *bᵉnê ʾād̲ām*, see on 49:2.

9. The language of this Psalm is reminiscent of Jer. 31:25 (cf. Isa. 29:8; Lk. 1:53). Yahweh is the one who can supply the needs of his people.

THE PRISONERS ARE SET FREE **10–16**
The Targum applies these verses to Zedekiah and the nobles of Israel (i.e. of Judah) in the Babylonian exile, while some later exegetes interpret this passage as describing the misfortunes and the eventual redemption of the Babylonian exiles (so Barnes). Another possibility is to suppose that originally the description was understood literally, but that later it was applied to the Exile. It is very likely that certain kinds of offender were imprisoned (i.e. they were usually thrown into some empty cistern or pit, like Jeremiah (Jer. 38:6)) until the divine decision was given in the particular case (Lev. 24:12; Num. 15:34). Those who were set free had ample cause to praise God.

10. Some sat in darkness . . .: a similar expression is used in Isa. 42:7, of the exiles. J. Muilenburg (see C. R. North, *The Second Isaiah* (1964), p. 113) interprets the Isaiah passage in a spiritual sense 'as a liberation of all the peoples from bondage'. Cf. 143:3.

in gloom: for *ṣalmāweṯ*, see on 23:4.

in affliction: the Hebrew *ᶜᵒnî* means 'affliction, poverty'. Winton Thomas (*TRP*, p. 45) draws attention to the Arabic cognate *ᶜanā*, *ᶜanwa* ('imprisonment'). For 'prisoners', see on 68:6.

in irons: lit. '(prisoners of affliction) and of iron'. In this context 'iron' probably means 'iron fetters'. The Hebrew *barzel* ('iron') is probably a Hittite loan-word. It seems that this metal was a Hittite monopoly for a few centuries (cf. O. R. Gurney, *The Hittites* (1952), pp. 82ff.) because they had discovered the art of smelting and working iron. During the period of the Judges the monopoly on iron in Canaan belonged, apparently, to the Philistines (cf. Bright, *HI*, pp. 164f.).

11. for they had rebelled: the trouble depicted in verse 10 is interpreted as a punishment for sin (cf. verses 17 and 34). This was true of the Babylonian captivity (Isa. 40:2), but obviously the Exile was not the only instance of divine retribution. Any prisoner would quite naturally be regarded as a sinner according to the beliefs of that time (cf. Job 36:8ff.).

the words of God: i.e. 'God's law' (Kissane, *BP*, p. 498). There may be a word play on *himrû* ('they rebelled') and *ʾimᵉrê* ('the words of').

the Most High: see on 18:13, 47:2.

12. Their hearts . . .: i.e. they themselves (cf. Johnson,

VITAI, p. 81). *RSV* and *NEB* follow LXX and V in reading *wayyikkānaᶜ* for M.T. *wayyaḵnaᶜ* ('he humbled (their hearts with . . .)'). For *lēḇ* ('heart'), see on 27:3.

they fell down: lit. 'they stumbled' (cf. 105:37). For a parallel, see Isa. 3:8.

with none to help: similar expressions are found in 2 Kg. 14:26; Ps. 22:11 (M.T. 12), 72:12; Isa. 63:5; Lam. 1:7; Dan. 11:45.

13. For this refrain, see verse 6.

14. he brought them out . . .: i.e. he delivered them. See also verse 10.

broke their bonds . . .: or 'he tore apart their bonds'. This is a figurative description of the liberation of prisoners.

15. This is the second part of the double refrain (see verse 8).

16. This verse may be regarded as an adaptation of Isa. 45:2, or both may be dependent upon a common cultic language. Kirkpatrick (*BPCB*, p. 641) takes verse 16 as a fulfilment of Isa. 45:2, since it can hardly refer to ordinary prisoners.

doors of bronze: according to Herodotus (i. 179) there were one hundred gates in the walls of Babylon, all made of bronze.

THE SICK ARE HEALED **17–22**

17. Some were sick . . .: M.T. 'Fools because of the way of their rebellion and . . .' (similarly *AV*, *RV*, *NEB*). This verse emphasizes the connection between illness and sin; the sinner is a foolish man who despises divine instruction (Prov. 1:7). It is no accident that such a man acts foolishly (see on 14:1); he is skilled in doing evil (Jer. 4:22). Some commentators emend *ʾᵉwîlîm* ('fools') into *ḥôlîm* ('those who were sick', so *RSV*, Kissane, *PNT*, etc.).

their sinful ways: lit. 'the way of their rebellion'. For *pešaᶜ* ('rebellion'), see on 32:1, 51:1.

iniquities: see on 32:1, 51:2, 90:8.

suffered affliction: or 'brought trouble upon themselves'.

18. they loathed . . .: lit. 'their soul loathed . . .' (see on 33:19). Gunkel (*PGHAT*, p. 472) takes *nepeš* ('soul') in the sense of 'throat' (so also Kraus, Deissler), while Leslie prefers the meaning 'appetite'. The parallelism favours *RSV*; for a similar thought cf. Job 6:7, 33:19f.

the gates of death: this metaphor depicts Sheol as if it were either a house or a city (cf. Barth, *ETKD*, p. 78) awaiting the afflicted (cf. 1QH vi:24f.). They are already in the sphere of death, a state characterized by weakness, pain, and loss of vitality (see on 9:13). Cf. Tromp, *PCD*, pp. 152ff.

19. See verse 6.

20. he sent forth his word: i.e. the divine word is seen as an angel or messenger of Yahweh (147:15,18) able to accomplish the task for which it was sent (Isa. 55:11). The idea of 'sending the word' may suggest, among other things, that the stricken man was unable to participate in the cult, and that he cried to God 'from afar' (cf. Kraus, *PBK*, p. 739). The word sent was the oracle of salvation (i.e. of healing), for the word of God heals all things (Wis. 16:12). For a different interpretation of this verse, see Dahood, *PNWSP*, p. 28, n.2; he renders it: 'He sent his pestilence, but He healed them, and delivered them from their boils', reading *dab̲rô* ('his pestilence') for *d^e^b̲ārô* ('his word') and deriving *š^e^ḥîṯôṯ* from *š-ḥ-y*, a cognate of *š-ḥ-n*, 'to be inflamed'.
he healed them: see on 30:2.
and delivered them from destruction: lit. 'that he might deliver from their pits' (cf. Lam. 4:20). *RSV* follows LXX, S, and V. An old but often accepted emendation is to read *way^e^mallēṭ miššaḥaṯ ḥayyāṯām* ('and he delivered their life from destruction') (similarly Gunkel, Deissler, *RP*, *et al.*). For *šaḥaṯ* ('destruction'), see on 7:15, 49:9.

21. See verse 8.

22. sacrifices of thanksgiving were communion sacrifices (for *zeb̲aḥ*, see on 40:6, 106:28), and their main purpose was to express gratitude for the divine help received and to bear testimony to the saving work of God (cf. Eichrodt, *TOT*, I, p. 147; R. de Vaux, *Studies in Old Testament Sacrifice*, p. 33).
songs of joy: (see on 88:2) it does not follow that 'sacrifices of thanksgiving' should be taken in a spiritual sense as 'praises'; rather the account of God's graciousness was part of the sacrificial meal, i.e. the sacrifices of thanksgiving (cf. 22:22,26 (M.T. 23, 27)).

THE SEAFARERS ARE SAVED IN TIMES OF TROUBLE **23–32**
Some scholars (e.g. Kissane) regard this passage also as a metaphorical account of the return from the Exile (cf. Isa. 54:11). It is not certain, however, that this was the original meaning.

23. Some went down to the sea: cf. Isa. 42:10; Sir. 43:24. The Psalmist describes the experiences of those who trade on the great waters, i.e. men whose business takes them across the seas (cf. 1QH iii:14ff.). The Hebrews in general were not a seafaring people, and therefore sea voyages were regarded as particularly dangerous. There were no natural harbours on the Canaanite sea-coast S. of Carmel and, furthermore, most of the coastal towns were dominated for centuries by the Philistines or Canaanites; therefore sailing was not an occupation familiar to the Hebrews in general.

the great waters: cf. 77:19 (M.T. 20). *Mayim rabbîm* may also denote: 'many waters' (cf. *JBL*, LXXIV (1955), pp. 9–21).

24. the deeds of the Lord: i.e. his awe-inspiring power to hurl great winds upon the seas (Jon. 1:4), or to still the raging waves; the main emphasis is upon Yahweh's works of deliverance. It is possible that the description was also intended to call to mind Yahweh's primeval victory over the waters of Chaos (cf. 93:3).

the deep: i.e. the deep sea (cf. 88:6).

25. For he commanded: this is lacking in S.

and raised the stormy wind: LXX and Jerome may have read *wayyaᶜᵃmōḏ* ('and (the storm) arose'; cf. *NEB* and 105:31,34) for M.T. *wayyaᶜᵃmēḏ* ('and he raised . . .').

the stormy wind: lit. 'the wind of tempest', as in 148:8. The same phrase is used in Ezek. 1:4 in connection with theophany (cf. G. A. Cooke, *The Book of Ezekiel* (*ICC*, 1951), p. 9).

the waves of the sea: *RSV* gives a correct interpretation of the M.T. *gallāyw* ('its waves'); so S.

26. They mounted up to heaven: the seafarers, and not the waves; this is made clear by verse 26*b*.

the depths: for *tᵉhômôṯ*, see on 71:20, 104:6.

their courage: lit. 'their soul' (for *nep̱eš*, see on 33:19). The sailors are terrified (cf. 46:6 (M.T. 7), 75:3 (M.T. 4)) and panic-stricken by the frightening storm.

27. like drunken men: (cf. Isa. 19:14; Jer. 23:9) they were apparently sea-sick.

at their wits' end: lit. 'and all their wisdom was swallowed up'. 'Wisdom' (*ḥoḵmāh*) in this context probably refers to the navigational skill of the sailors.

28. See verse 6.

29. he made the storm be still: lit. 'he made the storm into a calm (or 'silence')'; *BDB* (p. 199a): 'he settleth storm into whisper'. Cf. 89:9 (M.T. 10); Mt. 8:26.

the waves of the sea: (so S, suggesting *gallê hayyām*) M.T. has *gallêhem* ('their waves').

30. because they had quiet: the subject is not explicitly stated: the reference may be either to the waves (so Davies, Cohen), or rather to the seafarers (*BDB*, Oesterley, *et al.*).
their desired haven: lit. 'the city of their desire'. *Māḥôz* ('city') is an Akkadian loan-word (*maḫāzu*, 'city'), and it occurs only here in the *OT*, denoting a maritime city.

31. See verse 8.

32. the congregation of the people: i.e. the worshipping community. For *ḳāhāl*, see on 89:5.
praise him: see on 119:164.
the assembly of the elders: Kraus (*PBK*, p. 740) regards this as composed of the cultic representatives of the tribes and clans. The Hebrew *zāḳēn* may denote both an old man or an elder. The term 'elders' may include all adult men (i.e. those who have a beard (*zāḳān*)) or, more likely, the heads of the families (see de Vaux, *AI*, p. 69). Cf. Jg. 20:2; Jer. 26:17.

A HYMN TO GOD **33–43**

Verses 33–8 describe Yahweh's unlimited control of nature, while verses 39–43 show that this special care extends to the poor and needy. The language of this hymn reflects many other *OT* passages.

33. He turns rivers into a desert: *nāhār* ('river') is usually a perennial stream (see on 46:4), but even such a supply of water is ultimately dependent upon God (cf. Isa. 50:2). Cohen (*PSon*, p. 362) suggests that the allusion is to 'land which is abundantly watered by streams', but the literal interpretation is more likely.

34. a salty waste: or 'salt flat'; the expression is probably used metaphorically of an arid, useless land (cf. Dhorme, *CJ*, p. 600), which is the opposite of fruitful soil (cf. Job 39:6; Jer. 17:6; 1QH viii:24).
the wickedness of its inhabitants is the cause of all the troubles. The verse is reminiscent of the punishment meted out to the cities of Sodom and Gomorrah (cf. Gen. 19; Dt. 29:23ff.; Isa. 1:9).

35. Yahweh not only punishes the offenders, but he also blesses the needy. As he is able to reduce a fruitful land to a desert, so also it is in his power to transform a dry waste into pools of water (as in Isa. 41:18; cf. Isa. 35:7, 43:19f., 44:3). He is the God who does even what seems impossible.

36–8. The hungry are settled in a fertile land, and there they establish their city (LXX 'their cities'), a sign of prosperity. Their fields and vineyards yield a good harvest, and this divine blessing will multiply those who were once hungry (cf. Ezek. 36:30, 33–7; also Isa. 49:19f., 54:1).

39–40. Kissane, Kraus, *et al.* transpose verses 39 and 40, but it is possible that verse 39 should be taken as a kind of protasis to verse 40 which may be a quotation from Job 12:21*a*, 24*b* (or vice versa?). These two verses probably suggest that whenever the righteous are oppressed (verse 39), God will punish the offenders (verse 40). Thus Yahweh shows himself to be in control both of the realm of nature and of human society.

princes: or 'nobles' (*n*ᵉ*ḏîḇîm*) (see on 113:8) may refer either to the princes (or 'men of rank') of Israel or to foreign rulers (cf. 83:11 (M.T. 12); Prov. 8:16), probably the former. The Psalmist may have had in mind the experience of the last two Kings of Judah—namely, Jehoiachin and Zedekiah.

trackless wastes: the Hebrew *tōhû* is used, e.g. in Gen. 1:2; Jer. 4:23 of the primeval Chaos (in the phrase *tōhû wāḇōhû*), while in Dt. 32:10; Job 6:18, 12:24 it denotes a wilderness or desert.

41. he raises up: i.e. he protects the needy from continued affliction by setting him on high, above all trouble (see on 59:1). The verb *ś-g-b* means 'to be (inaccessibly) high', and in the intensive form it often has the meaning 'to protect' (cf. 20:1 (M.T. 2), 69:29 (M.T. 30)). For *ʾeḇyôn* ('needy'), see on 35:10, 86:1.

like flocks: their descendants will be numerous (cf. Job 21:11; Ezek. 36:37f.).

42. The upright: (for *y*ᵉ*šārîm*, see on 92:15). Verse 42*a* is similar to Job 22:19, which has *ṣaddîḳîm* ('the righteous') for *y*ᵉ*šārîm* ('the upright').

all wickedness . . .: i.e. all the wicked. The same expression, with slight variations, is also found in Job 5:16. For *ʿawlāh* ('wickedness'), see on 119:3.

43. wise: (cf. Jer. 9:12; Hos. 14:9) the Hebrew *ḥāḵām* has a wide range of meanings, and it can suggest such connotations as 'skilful (in a particular work)', 'shrewd', 'intelligent', and 'wise (ethically and religiously)'. In our setting *ḥāḵām* must describe a man for whom the fear (i.e. reverence) of Yahweh is the basic principle of life.

let him give heed: let him apply the lesson taught by the course of events.

the steadfast love . . .: lit. 'Yahweh's acts of loyalty' (for the plural form of *ḥasᵉḏê*, see on 89:1).

Psalm 108 A Liturgy of Thanksgiving and Prayer

This Psalm is a combination of 57:7–11 (=108:1–5) and 60:5–12 (=108:6–13). For the exegesis, see the relevant passages.

Psalm 109 Be Not Silent, O God

This Psalm could best be described as a Lament of the Individual (see Introduction, pp. 38ff.), although some scholars regard it as a national Psalm of Lamentation (so Mowinckel, Buttenwieser, Eaton). Both suggestions are possible, but it seems more likely that it is a prayer of a private individual, perhaps that of an accused man (so Schmidt, Weiser, Rodd, *et al.*). The Psalm begins with an appeal to God for help and a lamentation (verses 1–5), followed by an extensive imprecation (verses 6–20). Verses 21–9 resume the prayer and complaint at the beginning of the poem, while verses 30–1 form the conclusion as a vow to thank God.

The main problem is the interpretation of the malediction in verses 6–20. There seem to be two main possibilities: either the malediction is a quotation of the curses uttered by the enemies of the Psalmist, or it consists of the words of the Psalmist himself, directed against his accusers or against the chief of them. Kraus (*PBK*, p. 747) has well argued for the former alternative, stressing the following points: (i) at the beginning and at the end of the Psalm the enemies are spoken of in the plural, while in the imprecation itself only one person is addressed (but cf. verses 13 and 15); (ii) verse 28 explicitly states that the foes resorted to curses; (iii) the phrase 'But thou, O God . . .' (verse 21) may suggest that what was said previously (in verses 6–20) refers to the utterance of the adversaries; (iv) the Psalmist's own 'curses' are expressed in verse 29.

This argument is impressive, except for two main details: (i) verse 16*b* may actually refer to the Psalmist (cf. verse 22); (ii) in view of the current belief in the inherent power of the spoken word, it is questionable whether one would venture to repeat such curses originally directed against oneself (cf. Rodd, *PEPC*, II, p. 71). Consequently it may well be that the malediction was spoken by the Psalmist concerning his chief enemy (unless the adversaries are thought of collectively). For other possible interpretations, see *PIB*, pp. 582f.

It is unlikely that the Psalm was used in what might be called ordinary worship; its setting may have been some ritual connected with the obtaining of the divine decision in a serious but complex legal case.

The modern reader may find the vindictiveness of this Psalm rather appalling, but one may recall the words of C. S. Lewis (*Reflections on the Psalms* (1961), p. 31) that the bitterness of some of the Psalmists can be understood 'at least in part because they took right and wrong more seriously'. They also believed that they knew the difference between the two.

The date of the Psalm is uncertain; Oesterley suggests the post-Exilic period (so also Briggs, Davies, Gunkel, Deissler, *et al.*), while Kraus finds nothing in the Psalm that would definitely contradict a pre-Exilic date. The first view is more likely, because the malediction is reminiscent of Jer. 18:19–23 (so Deissler, *PWdB*, III, p. 88).

The metre of the Psalm is irregular.

To the choirmaster: see Introduction, p. 48.

A Psalm of David: see Introduction, pp. 46 and 43ff.

A PRAYER OF LAMENTATION **1–5**

1. Be not silent: or 'Be not deaf (to me)'; see on 28:1. The Psalmist appeals to God to remain inactive no longer.

God of my praise: i.e. the God whom I have praised in the past (cf. Dt. 10:21; Ps. 22:3 (M.T. 4); Jer. 17:14). At the same time, the phrase expresses the writer's confidence that God will help him again, and that he will be his praise once again.

2. wicked . . . mouths: lit. 'the mouth of the wicked and the mouth of deceit'; *RSV* assumes *reša*ᶜ ('wickedness') for M.T. *rāšā*ᶜ ('the wicked') thus providing a better parallel to *mirmāh* (see on 52:4), 'deceit' (so Gunkel, Kissane, Kraus, *et al.*). Some scholars (e.g. Gunkel, Oesterley, Kraus) would delete *ûp̄î mirmāh* ('and the mouth of deceit') which seems to overload the line.

are opened against me: the enemies speak deceitfully against the Psalmist.

against me: lit. 'with me' (*ʾittî*), which may imply that some of the enemies pretend to be on friendly terms (so Briggs, *CECBP*, II, p. 366). Perhaps *ʾittî* could be taken to mean '(even) in my presence' (cf. *NEB*, also Klopfenstein, *LAT*, p. 50 and n.211).

with lying tongues: i.e. the adversaries utter lies. See on 52:4; cf. 10:7, 50:19; 1QH v:27.

3. They beset me: or 'They surround me' (cf. 3:6 (M.T. 7), 69:4 (M.T. 5)).

words of hate: probably 'accusations inspired by hate'; this phrase occurs only here in the *OT*. The Targum suggests *wᵉḏōḇᵉrê* (for M.T. *wᵉḏiḇᵉrê*), 'those who speak (hatred)'; M. T. is, however, to be preferred.

. . . attack me: or, 'they fight me (for no reason whatsoever)'.

4. In return for my love: this phrase is sometimes omitted (so also *NEB*) because it is also found in verse 5. 'Love' (*ʾahᵃḇāh*) in this expression means 'deep friendship' (cf. *TDNT*, i, p. 24).

they accuse me: the verb is *ś-ṭ-n*, from which is derived *śāṭān* ('accuser'; *AV* 'Satan'); see on 71:13; Eichrodt, *TOT*, II, p. 206.

even as I make prayer for them: M.T. (if correct) has 'but I—prayer', probably meaning: 'although I (am all) prayer'. A similar construction is found in 120:7: 'I—peace'. Some commentators (e.g. Nötscher, Kraus) follow S in reading *waʾᵃnî tᵉpillāṯî lāhem* ('and as for me, my prayer was for them'). The reference, however, may be not so much to private prayer, as to the cultic intercessions for those ill and excluded from public worship, and such-like.

5. they reward me . . .: lit. 'they have put (evil) upon me . . .'; S reads 'they have repaid (similarly *NEB*) (me) . . .', *wayyāšîḇû* (for M.T. *wayyāśîmû*).

evil for good: cf. 38:20 (M.T. 21); Prov. 17:13: 'if a man returns evil for good, evil will not depart from his house'; for a concrete example, see 1 Sam. 25:21.

hatred for my love: see verse 4*a* (cf. 35:12, 38:20 (M.T. 21)).

THE IMPRECATION **6–20**

For a general interpretation of these curses, see the introduction to this Psalm, and 58:6–9, 69:22–8.

6. Appoint a wicked man . . .: verse 6*a* is rather ambiguous; a wicked man (i.e. an unscrupulous judge) might not necessarily pronounce a just judgment upon another evildoer; and therefore a common emendation is to read *maršîaᶜ* ('one who declares (him) guilty'). This reading, however, anticipates verse 7*a*. Another suggestion is to revocalize *rāšāᶜ* into *rešaᶜ* ('wickedness'), i.e. 'visit upon him (his) wickedness'.

an accuser: LXX has *diabolos*; *AV* renders the Hebrew *śāṭān* by 'Satan' which is wrong in this context. See on verse 4.
bring him to trial: lit. 'let the accuser stand at his right hand'. This was, apparently, the customary position for the accuser during the 'court session'; cf. Zech. 3:1. The place at one's right hand could also be taken by the helper (see verse 5; 110:5).

7. When he is tried: or 'When he is judged'. All legal pronouncements are ultimately divine decisions (Exod. 18:13–27; Dt. 1:17), and the more difficult cases in particular were largely dependent upon the divine judgment obtained by some means or other (cf. Exod. 28:15; Prov. 18:18; de Vaux, *AI*, pp. 157f.).
guilty: for *rāšāᶜ*, see on 1:1, 28:3, 92:7.
his prayer . . .: i.e. his lamentation and protestation of innocence will turn out to be a mockery of God, or an expression of guilt (*for ḥᵃṭāʾāh*, see on 32:1) because he is actually guilty. Kissane (*BP*, p. 506) takes 'sin' (*ḥᵃṭāʾāh*) in its original sense as 'failure, miss', hence: 'his prayer shall be without avail'. *RP* has 'let sentence be passed upon him for guilt', involving a change of M.T. *ûṯᵉpillāṯô* ('his prayer') into *ûpᵉlîliyyāṯô* ('and his sentence'); cf. Isa. 28:7. This is a reasonable suggestion, but the gain may not justify the emendation.

8. May his days be few: i.e. let him die prematurely (cf. 37:35f., 55:23 (M.T. 24)).
may another seize his goods: or '. . . take his office' (*RV*). Verse 8*b* is quoted in Ac. 1:20, where it is applied to Judas. The Hebrew *pᵉḳuddāh* can denote both 'possessions' (*NEB* 'hoarded wealth') and 'offlce'; most recent exegetes (e.g. Kraus, Deissler, Eaton) prefer the latter alternative, since the former is referred to in verse 11. It is possible that the office in question could have been inherited by his sons.

9. May his children be fatherless: i.e. may they be without protection, and destitute. For *yāṯôm* ('fatherlesss') see on 82:3. This type of collective responsibility is not acceptable to our society, but equally undesirable is its modern counterpart, individual irresponsibility; cf. Eichrodt, *TOT*, II, p. 429.
his wife a widow: widowhood often involved great hardship, and so in a way the punishment was extended to the wife also (and to the children). See de Vaux, *AI*, p. 40; *IDB*, IV, p. 842.

10. . . . and beg: begging must have been a fairly common feature of life in the ancient Near East. The real tragedy was found, primarily, in the sudden change of fortunes. For a similar curse, see Jer. 18:21.

may they be driven out . . .: *AV* 'let them seek *their bread* also out of . . .'. The Hebrew verb *wᵉḏārᵉšû* ('and let them seek') has no object, and it may be an error for *wᵉgōrᵉšû* ('and let them be driven out'; as suggested by LXX and V); cf. Exod. 12:39; Job 30:5. *NEB* 'driven (from their homes)'.

the ruins they inhabit: lit. 'their desolate places', i.e. their dwellings which have been reduced to ruins.

11. the creditor had a considerable power, as seen from 2 Kg. 4:1: 'the creditor has come to take my two children to be his slaves' (cf. Neh. 5:1–5).

seize: the verb used is *n-ḳ-š* ('to knock, strike'), which is not very fitting in the present context. Perhaps it should be linked with the Arabic *naḳaša*, 'to exact money from a person' (cf. Delitzsch, *BCP*, III, p. 179). This would involve the slight change of *š* into *ś*.

strangers: for *zārîm*, see on 54:3.

12. . . . to extend kindness to him: (cf. Jer. 31:3) since the man himself would be dead (verse 12*b*), kindness (see on 26:3) would normally be shown to his family in which his name and memory were believed to continue to exist. Thus, in a way, the dead man goes on existing in his descendants.

nor any to pity: those who were thought to be punished by God were usually avoided, but it must have been difficult to decide when the weak and needy should be helped (as in 82:3; cf. 10:18, 72:4), and when they should be regarded as afflicted for their sins, or those of their fathers, and so be beyond the pale; the *OT* writers generally advocate the former course of action.

13. May his posterity be cut off: for the construction, see *GK* 114k. The extinction of one's family was a great calamity; see verse 12; Job 18:19f.; Ps. 37:28,38.

his name: (*šᵉmô*), i.e. the name (see on 20:1) of the wicked man himself; so some MSS., LXX, Jerome, and V, while M.T. has *šᵉmām* ('their name'), referring to the children (so also *NEB*). For the blotting out of one's name, see on 9:5, 41:5.

in the second generation: LXX and V have 'in one generation' suggesting *ʾeḥāḏ* for M.T. *ʾaḥēr*. The name of the offender will become extinct with the death of his children.

14. the iniquity of his fathers: some scholars emend *ʾaḇōṯāyw* ('his fathers') into *ʾāḇîw* ('his father'), which would correspond to *ʾimmô* ('his mother') in verse 14*b*; yet the versions support M.T. In view of the solidarity of the family, the unrequited sins of the parents may be visited upon their children (Exod. 20:5; Dt. 5:9). This was thought to be primarily the duty of God himself and not so much the responsibility of the 'civil' courts (cf. Dt. 24:16; 2 Sam. 21:1–6). For 'iniquity' (*ʿāwōn*), see on 32:1, 51:2, 90:8.

before the LORD: some scholars (e.g. Gunkel, Kraus, Deissler, also *NEB*) omit this phrase (following S), as a gloss.

. . . be blotted out: see on 51:1. For *ḥaṭṭāʾṯ* ('sin'), see on 51:2.

15. Let them be before the LORD: i.e. the unatoned sins will not be forgotten by God, and the delayed punishment will be brought upon the family of the offenders, cf. 90:8; Lam. 1:22.

his memory: i.e. the memory of him. This follows some MSS. of LXX, in reading *zikrô*; M.T. has 'their memory' which is understood as the remembrance of the forefathers and their descendants (so Kirkpatrick, Cohen). For the expression, see on 34:16. To cut off one's memory is equivalent to blotting out one's name (see verse 13*a*; Childs, *MTI*, pp. 70–3).

16. For . . .: this introduces the reasons for the uttering of the imprecation.

. . . to show kindness: i.e. he deliberately forgot to honour his obligations towards other members of the community; see Glueck, *HB*, p. 69. In other words, he disregarded the basic principles of the life of the Covenant people summed up in the words: 'to do justice, and to love kindness, and to walk humbly' with God (Mic. 6:8).

In view of verse 22*a*, it is possible that **the poor and needy** (see on 34:2 and 35:10 respectively) is a roundabout expression for 'me' (i.e. the Psalmist), although it may also include all those who belong to this category and who may have been afflicted by the heartless enemy.

the brokenhearted is probably one of the objects of the verb 'pursued' (verse 16*b*). The expression 'to (their) death' (*lammāweṯ*) is an emendation (suggested by S) for *lemôṯēṯ* ('in order to slay'). Kissane (*BP*, p. 507) takes the Hebrew *wenikʾēh* ('and the brokenhearted') as a perfect *wenikʾāh* ('so shall he be grieved (in heart even unto death (*lammāweṯ*))'); the *RSV* and *NEB* renderings seem preferable.

17. He loved to curse: actions normally have a retroactive effect upon the doer for better or for worse, and the Psalmist hopes that God will accelerate this process. For cursing in general, see 58:6–9, 69:22–8.

let curses come on him: reading *ûtᵉḇô'ēhû* (with LXX and Jerome) for M.T. *wattᵉḇô'ēhû* ('and it came unto him') (*RV*); *RSV* 'curses' is an interpretative addition.

He did not like blessing: i.e. it went against the grain for him to bless anyone; but it is doubtful whether he had any scruples about receiving blessings.

may it be far from him: this presupposes *wᵉṯirḥaḳ* (so LXX and Jerome) for M.T. *wattirḥaḳ* ('and it was far from him' (*RV*)).

18–19. He clothed himself with cursing: the use of maledictions had become his second nature, and he must have been motivated more by his personal likes and dislikes than by any honest desire to dissociate himself from those who actually despise the law of God by uttering curses.

may it soak into his body: reading *wᵉṯāḇô'* with LXX and Jerome. M.T. has 'and it came into his inward parts like water' (*RV*). This is reminiscent of the ordeal by 'the water of bitterness that brings the curse' (Num. 5:16–28). Probably the opponent of the Psalmist will feel the effects of the curse like a guilty woman who has drunk the 'waters of proof' (cf. Snaith, *LN*, p. 202).

like oil into his bones: the real significance of this expression is uncertain. It is possible that oil was also used in certain rituals (apart from the well-known acts of anointing), or that 'oil' served as a metaphor to depict the pervasiveness of the curse; this same thought seems to have been developed by the description in verse 19.

20. May this be the reward: this is a summary of verses 6–19 (cf. also Isa. 17:14): this is to be the punishment of the godless. Those who take the malediction as a quotation from the words of the enemies sometimes render *pᵉ'ullāh* (*RSV* 'reward') as 'work' (cf. Kraus, *PBK*, p. 747), i.e. the preceding curses are the 'work' of the accusers (see on 71:13). Thus the Psalmist expresses the wish that Yahweh would redirect the curses so that they might come upon the head of their own authors, because there was no justification for the malediction.

against my life: lit. 'against my soul' (see on 33:19), or simply 'against me'.

FURTHER PRAYER AND LAMENTATION **21–9**

21. But thou . . .: this introduces a new theme (cf. 22:19 (M.T. 20), 41:10 (M.T. 11), 86:15).

O GOD my Lord: lit. 'O Yahweh my Lord'. The same combination of divine names is also found in 68:20 (M.T. 21), 140:7 (M.T. 8), 141:8.
deal on my behalf: lit. 'work with me' or '. . . at my side' (cf. *KBL*, p. 100a). *PNT* paraphrases '. . . act in my defence'.
for thy name's sake: see on 106:8.
is good: many commentators read *k^e^ṭûḇ* ('according to the goodness of (your Covenant loyalty . . .)') (cf. T, S) for *kî ṭôḇ* ('because good is . . .').
deliver me: see on 59:1, 107:6.

22. I am poor and needy: see verse 16*b* (cf. 40:17 (M.T. 18)).
my heart is stricken: lit. 'my heart is pierced' by the enmity of the adversaries. Some commentators follow LXX, S, Jerome, and V in reading *ḥōlal* ('troubled') from *ḥ-w-l* ('to writhe') for M.T. *ḥālal* ('is pierced'), which (in this form) occurs only here in the *OT*. For a similar thought, see verse 16 and 55:4 (M.T. 5).

23. I am gone: i.e. I have been made to ebb away, to decline like an evening shadow (see on 102:11).
I am shaken off: so also *NEB*. That is, they are about to get rid of me as if I were a locust (for *ʾarbeh*, see on 78:46). Kissane (*BP*, p. 508) suggests 'I am made bare as by locusts', which is not an impossible rendering; *RSV* and *NEB* provide, however, a slightly better parallelism to verse 23*a*.

24. . . . are weak: lit. 'totter'.
through fasting: Barnes (*PWC*, II, p. 532) thinks that the allusion is to an involuntary fasting caused by the sick man's lack of appetite. On the other hand, it may be a willing abstention from food in preparation for the hoped-for divine decision; (for a similar occasion, see 69:10f. (M.T. 11f.)).
my body: lit. 'my flesh' (for *bāśār*, see on 38:3, 56:4).
has become gaunt: perhaps 'has grown lean for the lack of fat'. *RP* renders '. . . lean for lack of nourishment'; this is a reasonable translation because oil (i.e. olive-oil) may have formed an important part of the staple diet of the Israelites.

25. . . . to my accusers: this is a correct interpretation of M.T. 'to them'. The enemies regard the Psalmist's self-humiliation as an expression of hypocrisy, and therefore they pour their scorn upon him (cf. 69:10f. (M.T. 11f.), also 31:11 (M.T. 12), 79:4, 89:41 (M.T. 42)).
they wag their heads in contempt and supposed holy indignation (cf. 22:7 (M.T. 8); Mt. 27:39).

26. Help me: as in 119:86 (cf. Jos. 10:6).
save me: this is a frequent cry for help in Psalms of Lamentation. Cf. 3:7 (M.T. 8), 6:4 (M.T. 5), 7:1 (M.T. 2), 22:21 (M.T. 22), 31:16 (M.T. 17), 54:1 (M.T. 3), etc.
according to thy steadfast love: for *ḥeseḏ*, see on 26:3. The Psalmist does not appeal to his own righteousness but to the loyalty of the Covenant God.

27. that this is thy hand: i.e. the deliverance of the afflicted man is entirely due to God, it is the work of his hand (cf. 86:17). It is probable that the allusion is to the distress of the author, and is meant to indicate that this trouble had been sent by Yahweh to try the Psalmist (so Barnes, *PWC*, II, p. 533), or as a punishment.
thou, O LORD, hast done it: 11QPs[a] omits 'O LORD', unless 'thou' and 'O LORD' have been transposed, in which case the latter word might have stood in the lacuna.

28. Let them curse: the Psalmist is not afraid of the curses of the enemy if the *blessing* of Yahweh is with him (cf. Jer. 20:11). The word of God is far more powerful than all the curses of men put together. See on 66:20 (cf. Jg. 17:2; 2 Sam. 21:3).
Let my assailants be put to shame: this follows the reading suggested by LXX and V (i.e. *wᵉḳāmay yēḇōšû* for M.T. *ḳāmû wayyēḇōšû* ('they arose and they were ashamed'); cf. *RSVm*).
thy servant: for the use of this term, see on 27:9, 36:1. The Hebrew *ᶜeḇeḏ* ('servant') does not necessarily suggest a royal personage (cf. Eaton, *PTBC*, p. 259).

29. my accusers: see verse 6.
clothed with dishonour: i.e. greatly disgraced (cf. 35:26).
. . . wrapped in their own shame: (cf. 71:13) i.e. their ignominy will be both complete and public.

THE VOW **30–1**

30. With my mouth . . .: that is, I myself shall give thanks (see on 18:49) to God.
I will praise him: see on 119:164.
in the midst of the throng: i.e. in the midst of the congregation, or the worshipping community (as in 22:22 (M.T. 23)).

31. he stands: M.T. has *yaᶜᵃmōḏ*, while 11QPs[a] reads *ᶜmd* ('he stood'; so also LXX, S, and V).
at the right hand . . .: instead of the accuser (see verse 6) it is Yahweh who will stand at the right hand of the needy (see on 35:10, 86:1) to deliver him (see on 54:1). Cf. 16:8, 121:5.

those who condemn him to death: lit. 'those who judge his soul' (for *nepeš*, see on 33:19). This is an unusual expression of which the *RSV* rendering may be a correct interpretation. LXX has 'who pursue my soul (i.e. me)' (*rōḏᵉpîm napšî*). Weiser, Nötscher, *et al.* read *miššōp̄ᵉṭāyw* ('(to save him) from his judges').

Psalm 110 The Enthronement of the King

Exegetically this is one of the most difficult Psalms, and the problems are partly due to the textual corruption. It may well be one of the oldest poems in the Psalter, and this may explain, to some extent, the condition of the text. It is also possible that in the course of transmission it was re-interpreted more than once, and that some verses may have been omitted; this would account for the lack of smoothness which has led some scholars (e.g. König) to doubt its unity.

This Psalm could be classed as a Royal Psalm which was later understood messianically. Its original *Sitz im Leben* may have been the enthronement of the King, or it may have formed part of the annual ritual of the great Autumnal Festival. H. H. Rowley ('Melchizedek and Zadok', *Festschrift für Alfred Bertholet* (1950), pp. 467f.) has suggested that the Psalm was composed for a specific occasion, 'when David was recognized as master of Jerusalem' (p. 469), and written for the purpose of celebrating the enthronement of David and of confirming Zadok's priesthood (see verse 4). This is plausible, but at a later time it may have been used at the accession of successive Davidic kings. According to Rowley's view, the speaker in verses 1–3 and 5–7 is Zadok the priest, while verse 4 is addressed to Zadok by the King, who recognizes the priesthood of the former, just as Abram acknowledged the priestly office of Melchizedek, the king of Salem (Jerusalem (?), cf. Gen. 14:17ff.). The majority of exegetes would regard the speaker in the Psalm as a cultic prophet, or a priest addressing the King. It is likely that the recital of the Psalm was accompanied by various ritual acts, but it would be unwise to reconstruct the enthronement ritual on the basis of this poem, as done by L. Dürr, *Psalm 110 im Lichte der neueren altorientalischen Forschungen* (1929). Cf. also M. Rehm, *Der Königliche Messias* (1968), pp. 320ff.

In the early Christian Church the Psalm was interpreted christologically, although verses 1 and 4 only are quoted or echoed in the *NT*. For verse 1, see Mt. 24:22, 26:64; Mk 12:36,

14:62, 16:19; Lk. 20:42ff., 22:66; Ac. 2:34f.; 1 C. 15:25; Heb. 1:13, 10:13; for verse 4, see Heb. 5:6, 7:17,21.

The metre of the Psalm is irregular.

A Psalm of David: see Introduction, pp. 46 and 43ff.

1. The LORD says to my lord: the Psalm opens with an oracle introduced by the well-known formula *neʾum yhwh*, which might be rendered 'Oracle (or 'Utterance') of Yahweh'. More often than not this phrase is used to conclude a prophetic pronouncement; in the Psalter this formula is found only here (cf. 36:1 (M.T. 2)). For a detailed discussion on its use, see R. Rendtorff, 'Zum Gebrauch der Formel nĕʾum Jahwe im Jeremiahbuch', *ZAW*, LXVI (1954), pp. 27ff. 'My lord' (*ʾadōnî*) is the King, and the term may point to the servant-lord relationship existing between the King and his subjects (cf. 1 Sam. 26:18); perhaps it is a generalization to think that the Israelite king was merely the first among equals.

Sit at my right hand: i.e. Yahweh bids the Davidic king (or David?) take the place of honour (cf. 1 Kg. 2:19; Ps. 45:9 (M.T. 10)), but it is not clear by what ritual action this was symbolized or made effective. It may be associated with the King's standing by the pillar in the Temple (cf. Weiser, *POTL*, p. 694), as depicted in 2 Kg. 11:14, 23:3; 2 Chr. 23:13, 34:31. Another guess is that since the presence of God is closely linked with the Ark, the King's throne may have been placed beside the Ark of the Covenant (in the Holy of Holies?) (cf. Kraus, *PBK*, p. 757). Thus the King could be said to sit, symbolically, at the right hand of Yahweh. The phrase may also suggest that in a way the King shares Yahweh's throne, as may be implied by 1 Chr. 28:5, 29:23; 2 Chr. 9:8; cf. Ps. 45:6 (M.T. 7).

your footstool: see on 99:5. The metaphor may be derived from the sphere of warfare: sometimes the victorious king and his captains would place their feet upon the neck of the defeated enemy (as in Jos. 10:24; Isa. 51:23); similarly Marduk also is said to have stood on the carcass of Tiamat (*ANET*, p. 67). The vassals of a king not infrequently refer to themselves as the overlord's footstool (for references, see Kraus, *PBK*, p. 758; cf. *ANEP*, pll. 460, 463).

2. In this verse the speaker is probably the cultic official in charge of the ceremony, and it is addressed to the King.

your mighty sceptre: see on 2:9; cf. Jer. 48:17; *ANET*, p. 141b, l. 29. The sceptre was the symbol of the might and authority of the King, and verse 2*a* is often taken to mean that Yahweh will wield the sceptre of the King, or extend his dominion. Gunkel *et al.* read *šᵉlaḥ* ('stretch forth' (imperative)), and so parallel with 'rule' in verse 2*b*. In such a case the word 'Yahweh' would have to be changed into 'God' (*ʾᵉlōhîm*), and taken as referring to the King (i.e. 'O God' (so Oesterley)). Yet M.T. may be right, and it is possible that at this point in the ritual the King was invested with the sceptre. G. R. Driver ('Psalm CX: Its Form, Meaning and Purpose', *Studies in the Bible*, ed. by J. M. Grintz and J. Liver (1964), p. 18) suggests: 'he will stretch out (i.e. offer, give) a staff of authority to thee' (that is, the pronominal suffix is given a datival force); cf. *NEB*.

Rule in the midst of your foes: cf. 2:1ff., 83:3ff. (M.T. 4ff.). The King, having received honour and authority, is commanded to exercise his rule as God's vicegerent over all the peoples (cf. 72:8). This word of command is at the same time an implicit promise that he will be triumphant.

3. The interpretation of this verse is difficult.

Your people will offer themselves freely: cf. Jg. 5:2. Weiser (*POTL*, p. 695) sees here a further promise, namely, that 'the people will readily serve the king in times of war'. Kraus (*PBK*, p. 758) regards this verse as a description of the cultic situation: 'Round about you (stand) the nobles (*nᵉḏîḇōṯ*) . . .', and he takes 'your people' (*ʿammᵉḵā*) as a preposition (*ʿimmᵉḵā*), following LXX. M.T. could be translated literally: 'Your people are willingness (itself)', which Johnson (*SKAI*, p. 121) turns into: 'Thou hast the homage of thy people' by vocalizing the consonantal text so as to read *nāḏaḇtā* ('Thou hast made (thy people) willing').

on the day you lead your host: lit. 'on the day of your power' (*RV*), while Johnson (*SKAI*, p. 121) reads 'of thy birth' (i.e. *ḥîlᵉḵā*). 'The day of power' is, apparently, the day of the enthronement of the King; hence it could be described as the day of his birth (cf. 2:7). The *RSV* rendering seems less suitable, because the occasion of the Psalm is the coronation of the monarch. For a different rendering, see *NEB*.

upon thy holy mountains: M.T. has 'in the sacred splendour' which may allude to the festive garments of the people surrounding the King (cf. 29:2, 96:9). The *RSV* reading is supported by some Hebrew MSS., Sym, and Jerome; the same phrase is found in 87:1 where it refers to the hills of Jerusalem. In 133:3 there is a mention of the 'mountains of Zion'. M.T. may well be right.

From the womb of the morning: Johnson (*SKAI*, p. 121) sees here an allusion to the rebirth of the King at dawn, which is also his deliverance from the underworld, and forms part of the ritual drama enacted on this occasion. It is possible that the language of this verse (as also elsewhere) may have a mythological colouring. Some scholars find in 'the morning' (*mišḥār* or *šaḥar*, if *m* is a dittograph) a reference to the goddess mentioned in the Ugaritic texts (see '*Shahar and Shalim*', in Driver, *CML*, pp. 121ff.; Jirku, *MK*, pp. 58f.) and in Isa. 14:12, where the king of Babylon is described as the 'son of Dawn' (*ben šaḥar*). If indeed this verse contains a reminiscence of the liturgy of the Canaanite fertility cult, it does not follow that the use of these well-known metaphors must mean that the Psalmist accepted the mythology itself. For further references; see Rowley, *Festschrift für Alfred Bertholet*, pp. 469f.

like dew your youth will come to you: M.T. has 'you have the dew of your youth', but perhaps we should read *kᵉṭal yᵉliḏtîḵā* ('like dew I have begotten you'); the verb is also suggested by LXX and S, and the expression itself would form a parallel to 2:7. The mythological metaphors of this verse serve to emphasize the special relationship between God and the King. 'Like dew' may have a reference to the invisible working of God; dew was believed to fall from the clouds or heaven (cf. 2 Sam. 17:12; Prov. 3:20; Zech. 8:12), but its descent was imperceptible. It may also have an allusion to the vitality of the King. In 72:6 the Psalmist expresses the wish that the King might be like 'rain that falls on the mown grass, like showers that water the earth'.

4. It is usually understood that verse 4*b* contains another oracle from Yahweh to the King, but an interesting variation has been suggested by Rowley (pp. 461ff.) who argues that in verses 1–3 the King (i.e. David) is addressed by Zadok, while in verse 4 the latter is spoken to by the King, who confirms Zadok in the priesthood. In Rowley's view Zadok was a priest of the Jebusite cultus in the pre-Davidic Jerusalem; thus in Ps. 110 we find 'the priest pledging the submission of the city to the conqueror and the king confirming the priest to his office . . .' (p. 472). Although the majority of commentators follow the traditional interpretation, Rowley's suggestion is worth serious consideration. The general view is that verse 4 is a divine oracle installing the King in the priestly office, which probably differed from that of Abiathar and Zadok (cf. 2 Sam. 8:17).

The LORD has sworn: i.e. the word of Yahweh is unalterable. Cf. 89:35 (M.T. 36); Isa. 14:28; Jer. 22:5; Am. 4:2, 6:8.

priest for ever: the office is conferred once for all.

after the order of Melchizedek: the latter may well have been the Canaanite king of Jerusalem (?), during the time of Abram (cf. Gen. 14:18), who was also the priest of God Most High (*ʾēl ʿelyôn*). The name 'Melchizedek' may mean either 'My (or 'The') king is righteous', or 'Zedek is my king'; both component parts are attested as divine appellatives, if not proper names (cf. Johnson, *SKAI*, pp. 32–42). When David captured Jerusalem, it is thought that he took over the Jebusite kingship, and thus the Psalm may allude to this conferment of the twin offices (i.e. kingship and priesthood) upon David. The Judean kings played an important role in the cult (cf. 2 Sam. 6:13–18; 1 Kg. 8:14, 55f.) but, on the other hand, Rowley (p. 471) points out that what 'is required is not evidence that the King played a priestly part in certain festival rites, but that he ordinarily exercised the functions of the priest, and was as truly the priest *de facto* as he was the King'. Weiser (*POTL*, p. 695) is of the opinion that this oracle is 'directed against the aspirations towards autonomy of a priesthood which was prompted by hierarchical desires and striving for the separation of ecclesiastical power from the secular one'. Cf. also *CBQ*, xxv (1963), p. 308; *VT*, xvii (1967), pp. 36ff.

5. The *RSV* rendering of this verse makes Yahweh the subject of all the verbs in verses 5–7, while the person addressed is the King. Kissane *et al.* suggest: 'My Lord (i.e. the king), because of Thy right hand (i.e. God's), shall smite . . .'; thus the King is made the subject of the verbs while the utterance itself is directed towards God. *RSV* seems more likely but we should assume a change of subject in verse 7.

The LORD is at your right hand: cf. 16:8, 109:31, 121:5. In *ANET*, p. 450a, we find: 'The god Sin at your right hand, the god Shamash at your left.' The Psalmist means to say that, in all that the King does, Yahweh is at his side as his helper; in verse 5 the emphasis is upon military operations. In a metaphorical way, Yahweh *is* the King's right hand that will crush the enemies. Cf. the similar expression in verse 1, where it denotes honour; verse 5 refers to divine protection.

he will shatter: lit. '. . . has shattered' (similarly *NEB*). *RSV* takes the Hebrew tense as a perfect of certainty, or a prophetic perfect (so Kirkpatrick); although the action is as yet in the future, the victory already belongs to Yahweh.

on the day of his wrath: i.e. the day when he will judge the peoples (cf. 2:5,12, 21:9 (M.T. 10); Isa. 13:9,13; Zeph. 2:3). This concept was probably part of the traditions associated with the Autumnal Festival, and it may have been the prototype of the Day of Yahweh.

6. filling them with corpses: *RSV* supplies 'them' (i.e. the nations), while other scholars add 'valleys' (*gē'āyôt*) which may have fallen out due to haplography; Aquila and Jerome read 'valleys' instead of 'corpses'. Some scholars suggest 'full of majesty' (*m^elē' gē'ûṯ*), which would be a description of the King (cf. G. R. Driver, p. 25); cf. *NEB*.

he will shatter chiefs: lit: '. . . head'. The latter might be taken collectively as 'chiefs' or 'head(s) (of the enemies)' (cf. Num. 24:17; Jg. 5:26; Ps. 68:21 (M.T. 22)).

7. Some scholars (e.g. Johnson) see Yahweh as the subject of this verse also, but it seems more likely that the reference is to the King who, during the royal ritual, drinks from the brook (the spring of Gihon?); as a result of this symbolic action he is endowed with power (cf. Kraus, *PBK*, p. 672). Water had a rich symbolic meaning, and this may account for the ritual (cf. G. R. Driver, p. 29). It is less likely that the Psalmist portrays the King as refreshing himself at the brook during a pause in his pursuit after the enemies. R. de Vaux (*AI*, p. 102) suggests concerning Gihon that it 'is much more likely that Solomon was consecrated at Gihon because the sanctuary of the Ark was there' (cf. 1 Kg. 1:38ff.). Cf. also C. Schedl, *ZAW*, LXXIII (1961), pp. 290–7; Sabourin, *POM*, II, p. 250.

he will lift up his head: this is usually taken to mean that he will be triumphant (cf. 3:3 (M.T. 4), 27:6, 140:9).

Psalm 111 His Praise Endures for Ever

This Psalm is a Hymn (see Introduction, pp. 32f.) in praise of the works and goodness of Yahweh, and in form it is similar to a Psalm of Thanksgiving (see Introduction, pp. 35f.). It probably had also a didactic purpose implied by its acrostic structure (see introduction to Ps. 9). The Psalm consists of twenty-two short lines (or half-verses?) which, in M.T., begin with the successive letters of the Hebrew alphabet. The parallelism, if any, is merely formal (see Introduction, p. 42). The alphabetic scheme imposes certain limitations upon the author, and therefore there is little development of thought.

The hymn was sung by an individual (verse 1) during the worship at one of the annual festivals, not necessarily the Feast of the Passover. Weiser (*POTL*, p. 699) regards the poem as the congregation's response (expressed by an individual) to the preceding cultic acts whereby Yahweh's redemptive works have been declared to the worshipping community.

The date of the Psalm may be post-Exilic, as suggested, but not necessarily demanded, by the acrostic arrangement, the lack of genuine parallelism, the didactic character of the conclusion of the Psalm, and the sentiments well attested for the post-Exilic period. Psalm 111 is similar to Ps. 112, and both may come from the same author.

The prevailing metre of the Psalm is 3+3.

1. Praise the Lord: see on 104:35, 106:1. The phrase is either a title to the hymn or a liturgical addition, outside the acrostic scheme.

I will give thanks: see on 18:49, 30:12.

with my whole heart: i.e. unreservedly (see on 119:2).

in the company of the upright: that is, in the cultic community (cf. 22:22 (M.T. 23)) which is not an *ecclesiola in ecclesia* as suggested by Baethgen, Duhm, *et al.* (cf. Gunkel, *PGHAT*, p. 488). For 'company' (*sôḏ*), see on 25:14, 55:14. The term *yāšār* ('upright'), is discussed on 92:15.

in the congregation: for *ʿēḏāh*, see on 74:2; cf. 1:5; 1QH vi:5.

2. the works of the Lord: this refers to his mighty deeds in history and, apparently, does not include the works of creation (cf. v. Rad, *OTT*, 1, p. 449).

studied by all . . .: (see on 24:6) Wellhausen (*PBP*, p. 122) renders: 'worthy of examination . . .'. In later Hebrew the verb *d-r-š* was used of the interpreting of scriptures, from which is derived also the well-known term *midrash*, or exposition.

who have pleasure in them: that is, who have a special, personal interest in the *Heilsgeschichte*, the story of Yahweh's works of salvation. *NEB* has 'all men study them for their delight'.

3. Full of honour and majesty: these two attributes often describe the royal power of Yahweh, and they are also clearly manifested in all his works (see on 90:16, 96:6, 104:1).

his righteousness endures for ever: cf. 112:3,9. He is always faithful to his Covenant promises: to the afflicted this means deliverance, to the oppressor it brings punishment; see on 31:1, 33:5, 119:40. 'For ever' (*lāʿaḏ*) appears in 9:5, q.v.

4. He has caused . . . to be remembered: or, 'He has appointed (lit. 'made') an occasion for the proclamation of his wonderful works.' For this use of *zēḵer*, see Childs, *MTI*, p. 72. Yahweh has not only wrought great salvation, but he has also instituted the transmission of the salvation-history in order that later generations might share in the great events of redemption (cf. Exod. 12:14, 13:8f.). Some scholars (e.g. Luther, Hupfeld, Nötscher, *et al.*) have thought that the allusion is to the Passover, but the Drama of Salvation was not exclusive to the spring festival; Weiser points to the autumn Covenant Festival. For *nip̄lāʾōṯ* ('wonderful works'), see on 9:1 (78:11).
gracious: the adjective *ḥannûn* is used only of God (for a possible exception see on 112:4), and it denotes a lasting characteristic of Yahweh. See K. W. Neubauer, *Der Stamm CHNN im Sprachgebrauch des Alten Testaments* (1964), pp. 127f.
merciful: see on 103:8. The expression **gracious and merciful** may have been part of an older cultic formula.

5. He provides food . . .: *ṭerep̄* ('food', cf. Prov. 31:15) usually means 'prey', and the reason for the choice of this term may have been the acrostic arrangement which required here a line beginning with the letter *ṭ*. The allusion is, most likely, to the giving of the quails and manna in the wilderness (cf. Exod. 16; Num. 11) rather than to the 'spoils of Canaan' (so Barnes).
those who fear him: i.e. those who are faithful to him (see verse 10; also 34:7,9 (M.T. 8,10), 85:9 (M.T. 10); cf. 112:1.
he is mindful: lit. 'he remembers' (see on 79:8). For 'Covenant', see on 55:20, but here *beriṯ* probably means 'Covenant promises'. Cohen (*PSon*, p. 375) thinks of the Covenant with the Patriarchs (so also Kirkpatrick) but it is more likely that the reference is to the Sinaitic covenant (so Briggs, Weiser).

6. the power of his works: or 'his mightiest works', i.e. the dispossession of the peoples of Canaan.
the heritage of the nations: i.e. the land of Canaan which was the possession of the nations (for *gôyīm*, see on 106:5).

7. faithful and just: lit. 'truth and judgment' (*RV*). Yahweh manifests his faithfulness (see on 25:5) to Israel by being true to his promises and his judgment (see on 36:6, 119:7) of the nations by driving them out of their land, due to their sin (Dt. 9:4f.).

The same characteristics are seen in all his dealings; he is never actuated by capriciousness or other inferior motives.

his precepts (for *piḳḳûḏ*, see on 119:4) are trustworthy or reliable. God's demands and laws are essentially a gift to his people (cf. 19:7–10 (M.T. 8–11)) and not a burden. Barnes (*PWC*, II, p. 540) suggests that 'precepts' denote God's 'providences' rather than divine law; but the former alternative seems more likely.

8. they are established: the law, or precepts, of God.

to be performed: or 'they are done' (*RV*, similarly *AV*, *RP*, *PNT*), i.e. they are enacted. The latter alternative seems more likely, balancing verse 8*a*.

for ever and ever: perhaps 'from eternity to eternity', taking the preposition *l*ᵉ in *lāᶜaḏ* to mean 'from', as in Ugaritic (cf. Dahood, *UHP*, p. 30).

uprightness: reading *yōšer* (with LXX, T, S, and Jerome) for M.T. *yāšār* ('upright'); see on 92:15.

9. redemption: the Hebrew *pᵉḏûṯ* can denote 'ransom' (*BDB*, p. 804a), but in connection with Yahweh it can only mean 'redemption', because God did not pay any ransom to the Egyptians (see on 119:134). The Psalmist may have had in mind, not only the Exodus events, but also the successive deliverances of God's people.

he has commanded his covenant: see on 105:8. The usual expression for the making of a covenant is 'to cut a Covenant' (see on 89:3). Our phrase may indicate that the divine Covenant (see on 55:20) was not unlike a treaty between the suzerain and his vassal, which was given by the superior to the inferior party as a sign of favour, the neglect of which would amount to an ungrateful rebellion.

for ever: (*lᵉᶜôlām*), see on 9:5, 89:1.

his name: see on 20:1. Yahweh in his self-revelation is both **holy** (see on 34:9) or, to paraphrase, 'unique in his all-round excellence' and **terrible,** or 'awe-inspiring' (see on 65:5).

10. The fear of the Lord: see on 19:9, 25:12. A humble dependence upon, and obedience to, Yahweh is the foundation of wisdom; it is the awareness of the reality of God. For the same maxim, see Prov. 1:7, 9:10; cf. Eichrodt, *TOT*, II, pp. 268–77.

wisdom: (*ḥoḵmāh*) may have several shades of meaning, but in this particular context it refers primarily to the practical knowledge of the divine laws governing the relationships in life. 'Behold, the

fear of the LORD, that is wisdom; and to depart from evil is understanding' (Job 28:28).
a good understanding: or, 'a good sense', which is better than *AVm* 'good success' (cf. Prov. 3:4*a*).
who practise it: (following LXX, S, and Jerome in reading *ʿōśêhā* for *ʿōśêhem*) i.e. the fear of Yahweh or the 'wisdom'. M.T. has 'who practise them' (i.e. the precepts (?)).
his praise (see on 65:1, 119:171) is endless because the attributes of God are unchanging; their effectiveness and excellence do not decrease.

Psalm 112 The Reward of the Godly Man

In some ways this poem is related to Ps. 111; a number of commentators suggest that both compositions are the work of one and the same author, or that they belong to the same school of thought. Psalm 111 is a Hymn, while Ps. 112 is more like a Wisdom poem, but both possess exactly the same acrostic scheme (see the introduction to Ps. 111), and certain terms and expressions are common to both; e.g.: 'his righteousness endures for ever' (111:1 and 112:2), 'established' (*s*ᵉ*mûḵîm*; 111:8), and 'is steady' (*sāmûḵ*; 112:8).

Ps. 112 could be regarded as the counterpart to Ps. 111; the latter praises the works of Yahweh, while the former magnifies the blessings of the godly man, and could be described as a *midrash*, or exposition, of 111:10. The purpose of Ps. 112 seems to be didactic but a cultic usage cannot be excluded.

The date of the composition is usually thought to be late post-Exilic.

The metre is mainly 3 + 3.

1. Praise the LORD: this phrase is not included in the alphabetic structure of the Psalm. See on 111:1.
Blessed is the man: for this formula of congratulation, see on 1:1. The Psalm is meant to offer not only an encouragement but also a testimony to the blessedness of the righteous man.
who fears the LORD: this is a variation on 'those who fear him' (111:5*a*, q.v.). A **man who fears** (i.e. who shows reverential obedience to) Yahweh has nothing else to fear.
who greatly delights: cf. 1:2. The doer of the law finds in the divine commandments (see on 119:6) both enjoyment and help. For a contrast, see Jer. 6:10.
2. mighty in the land: the Hebrew *gibbôr* ('mighty man')

probably denotes 'a man of substance' (see on 33:16, cf. 37:11) rather than 'a man valiant in war'. There is no need to change *gibbôr* into *g^e^bîr* ('lord', so Oesterley, Kraus).
the generation of the upright: probably 'the family of'; for this use of *dôr* (*RSV* 'generation'), see Dahood, *PAB*, I, p. 82; *JNES*, IX (1950), p. 216. For *y^e^šārîm* ('the upright'), see on 92:15; cf. 111:1.
will be blessed: by God; see on 67:1; cf. 66:20.

3. Wealth and riches are signs of divine blessing (cf. 1 Kg. 3:13; Prov. 3:9f.,16, 13:18); 'the reward for humility and fear of the LORD is riches and honour and life' (Prov. 22:4). 'Wealth' (*hôn*) and 'riches' (*ᶜōšer*) are synonymous; the former may sometimes stress 'sufficiency', the latter 'abundance'. LXX has *doxa* ('glory'), i.e. *hôḏ* for M.T. *hôn*.
his righteousness endures for ever: this phrase occurs also in 111:3 (q.v.) where it is applied to Yahweh, but it seems that in our Psalm it must describe the upright man (see verse 9*b*). This choice of the same expression may be deliberate: in 111:3 'righteousness' denotes Yahweh's constant loyalty to his Covenant relationships, while in 112:3 (and verse 9) the emphasis may be upon the blessings (or 'reward') which the faithful man receives from God who is consistently righteous. Cohen (*PSon*, p. 376) renders *ṣ^e^ḏāḵāh* by 'merit', while McCullough (*PIB*, p. 597) suggests 'righteous deeds'; cf. *TDNT*, II, p. 196.

4. The interpretation of this verse is ambiguous because it is not clear what is actually the subject of the verb 'rises' (verse 4*a*), and to whom the adjectives in verse 4*b* refer.
Light rises in the darkness . . .: i.e. there is happiness in store for the upright (see on 92:15), even in time of affliction. 'Light' (*ᵓôr*) is a frequent symbol of blessedness and life (see on 56:13), or of Yahweh himself (see on 27:1; cf. Jacob, *TOTe*, p. 178). On the other hand, a number of commentators (e.g. Kirkpatrick, Weiser, Deissler, Eaton) argue that the subject of the verb *zāraḥ* is the godfearing man who brings happiness to other upright men. The *RSV* interpretation seems preferable, because this godly man is himself included among the 'upright ones' (see verses 2*b* and 4*a*). Perhaps we should render: 'The light of the upright rises (even) in darkness'; in Isa. 10:17 Yahweh is described as 'the light of Israel' (cf. also Isa. 58:8,10). If the allusion is to Yahweh, then the adjectives in verse 4*b* refer to him, and *RSV* is justified in adding 'the LORD' (*yhwh*; following LXX^A^ and V).

and righteous: Kraus (*PBK*, p. 770) deletes the conjunction *w*[e] ('and'), thus obtaining a nominal clause 'the Righteous one is gracious and merciful', similar to 111:4*b*. If, on the contrary, the adjectives in 112:4*b* are understood as describing the upright man, then these attributes could be regarded as a reflection of the characteristics of Yahweh; the godly man is but a mirror of his God.

5. It is well with the man: or, 'A good man deals graciously' (similarly *AV*, *PNT*, Kissane), because the word order may be due to the acrostic arrangement which requires a word beginning with *ṭ* at the head of the line.

and lends in order to help the needy; he is not governed by the hope of gaining a profit (cf. 15:5). For a similar thought, see on 37:26 (Prov. 14:21).

his affairs: lit. 'his words'. He conducts his business in accordance with justice (for *mišpāṭ*, see on 36:6, 119:7) or integrity. *RV* renders: 'He shall maintain his cause in judgment', but there is no reason why the good man should be dragged to a court. Some exegetes (cf. *TRP*, p. 47) read *d*[e]*rāḵāyw* ('his ways') for M.T. *d*[e]*ḇārāyw* ('his words'; cf. Sir. 49:9), but the improvement is not great.

6. the righteous: see on 1:5.

will never be moved: for the expression cf. 10:6, 15:5, 16:8. 'Never' (*l*[e c]*ôlām*) is discussed on 9:5.

he will be remembered: lit. '(the righteous) will be for an eternal memorial'. After his death his memory will be kept alive by his own family and by those whom he has helped. Just as the works of Yahweh are remembered (see on 111:4) so also the deeds of the godly man will not be forgotten (cf. Prov. 10:7).

7. evil tidings: or 'disastrous news' (as in Jer. 49:23). The righteous man is not exempt from all the human problems and trials, but the difference is that he is not terrified by them. He has, of course, a clear conscience, but above all he trusts in Yahweh (see on 78:22), and his heart is steadfast (see on 57:7). For a contrast, cf. Prov. 10:24.

8. His heart is steady: the verb is *s-m-k* ('to rest, support') (not *k-w-n*, 'to be firm', as in verse 7*b*). The passive participle *sāmûḵ* may suggest that the Psalmist's heart (i.e. his courage; see on 27:3) is sustained by Yahweh (cf. 51:12 (M.T. 14); Isa. 26:3) and therefore he will not be afraid of any possible tribulation. This is a re-statement of verse 7.

until he sees his desire: perhaps, 'until he feasts his eyes on his adversaries' (cf. 54:7 (M.T. 9), 91:8, 118:7; and the Moabite Stone l. 4 (in *DOTT*, pp. 196, 197)), i.e. until he triumphs over his enemies. The emphasis is not upon the Psalmist's gloating (if this were the case) but upon the change of fortunes.

9. He has distributed freely . . .: lit. 'He has scattered, he has given to the poor' or 'He has given generously to . . .' (for the construction, see *GK* 120g). This verse is also quoted in 2 C. 9:9 as a description of the 'cheerful giver' (2 C. 9:7). For 'poor' (*ʾeḇyôn*), see on 35:10, 86:1.

his righteousness . . .: see verse 3*b*.

his horn is exalted: the 'horn' (*ḳeren*) is a symbol of strength and pride. To lift up one's own horn usually means to be proud and boastful (see on 75:4) but in our verse it is God who exalts the righteous man. For 'honour' (*kāḇôḏ*), see on 19:1.

10. The wicked man sees it: i.e. the exaltation of the godly. The verb 'sees' may be used in order to bring out the contrast with verse 8*b*. The upright *sees* the frustration of the schemes of the wicked (see on 1:1, 28:3), while the wicked *sees* the triumph of the righteous.

is angry: i.e. he is vexed at the effect of divine justice.

he gnashes his teeth: this description is a word-picture of powerless rage (cf. 35:16, 37:12). His vexation is so great that he 'melts away', i.e. he has made himself ill with envy and anger (cf. 1:6); *NEB* 'in despair'.

the desire . . .: (cf. 38:9 (M.T. 10)), i.e. the plans, and the things coveted by the wicked come to nothing (Prov. 10:24,28, 11:7). It is not necessary to change M.T. *taʾᵃwaṯ* ('the desire of . . .') into *tiḳwaṯ* ('the hope of . . .'), as is done by Hupfeld, Gunkel, Davies, *et al.*; *NEB* has 'the hopes of . . .'.

Psalm 113 Who is Like the Lord?

This Psalm is one of the so-called 'Hallel Psalms', and it belongs to the 'Egyptian Hallel' (i.e. Ps. 113–18) which is distinguished from the 'Great Hallel' (Ps. 120–36, or 135–36, or sometimes Ps. 136 alone; the ancient Jewish authorities were not agreed as to the extent of the 'Great Hallel'). Another Hallel collection is found in Ps. 146–50 (cf. I. Elbogen, *Der jüdische Gottesdienst* (1924), pp. 494ff.).

Traditionally these Psalms were used at the great annual festivals which included the Passover. On the latter occasion

Ps. 113–14 were sung before the Passover meal, Ps. 115–18 after it (cf. Mt. 26:30; Mk 14:26).

Ps. 113 is a Hymn repeated by the congregation (see verse 1) in praise of the incomparable majesty of Yahweh and of his gracious care for the poor in particular. The Psalm consists of a hymnic introduction (verses 1–3) with a call to praise and to bless Yahweh. The main part of this Hymn (verses 4–9) gives the reasons why God is worthy of praise and homage; the poem concludes with the same words as it began: 'Praise the LORD'. Leslie's reconstruction of its actual performance in the cult is hypothetical (cf. *PAP*, p. 193); he thinks that verse 1 was spoken by the officiating priest, while verses 2–4 and 5–9 were sung by two different Levitical choirs.

The date of the Psalm is uncertain, possibly post-Exilic (so Kirkpatrick, Gunkel, Kraus, Deissler).

The metre is irregular.

THE CALL TO GIVE PRAISE **1–3**

1. Praise the LORD: for the exegesis of this liturgical formula, see on 104:35, 106:1. Note also the threefold repetition of the imperative (second person plural) in the opening verse, for the sake of emphasis: 'Praise!'

servants of the LORD are probably the worshippers of Yahweh in general, although it could refer to the priests and Levites in particular (cf. 134:1, 135:1f.). For *ʿeḇeḏ* ('servant'), see on 36:1; in this context the term has a twofold significance: it emphasizes the privileges of the worshippers as well as their duties and responsibilities.

the name of the LORD occurs three times in verses 1–3, and it comprises primarily the whole self-revelation of Yahweh to his people; the phrase may be a circumlocution for 'Yahweh'. For *šēm* ('name'), see on 20:1; cf. Imschoot, *ThOT*, 1, pp. 195–9.

2. Blessed be the name . . .: see on 104:1. This is an expression synonymous with 'Praise the LORD'.

from this time . . . for evermore: i.e. for ever, without ceasing; so also in 115:18, 121:8, 125:2, 131:3.

3. The name of Yahweh (see verse 1) should be praised throughout the whole world (cf. 66:1), i.e. from the east to the west (cf. 50:1; Mal. 1:11) and at all times (verse 2).

THE SOVEREIGN GOD IS GREAT IN MERCY **4–9**

4. The LORD is high: Yahweh transcends all created things and beings, and all the nations together 'are as nothing before him' (Isa. 40:17); cf. Ps. 46:10 (M.T. 11), 99:2.

nations: for *gôyīm*, see on 59:5, 106:5.

his glory: (see on 26:8, 57:5) or Yahweh himself, is exalted above the heavens (8:1 (M.T. 2); cf. 1 Kg. 8:27) which declare the majesty of God (19:1 (M.T. 2)).

5. Who is like the LORD . . .: this rhetorical question expects the answer: 'No one' (cf. Exod. 15:11; Dt. 3:24; Ps. 35:10; Isa. 40:18,25, 46:5). There is no being in heaven or on earth comparable to God.

our God: this may be an allusion to the Covenant formula: 'And you shall be my people, and I will be your God' (Jer. 30:22; cf. Jer. 24:7, 31:1).

who is seated on high: lit. 'who makes (it) high to sit' (for the Hebrew construction, see *GK* 114n); the principal idea is expressed by the infinitive. In M.T. this phrase begins with a participle which is a characteristic of the main section of the Hymns (see Introduction, p. 33); the same participial expression is also found in verses 6, 7, and 9. A better rendering of verse 5*b* might be: 'who is enthroned on high' (similarly Cohen, Nötscher, Kraus, *et al.*); cf. 29:10, 103:19; *NEB* has 'who sets his throne so high'.

6. who looks far down: lit. 'who makes (it) low to see' (*GK* 114n) or, to paraphrase: 'who condescends to care for (his creatures)'.

upon the heavens and the earth: some commentators (e.g. Gunkel, Oesterley, Nötscher, Kraus, *NEB*) transfer verse 6*b* after verse 5*a*; this makes reasonable sense, but it does not necessarily represent the original order (cf. 33:13f., 138:6).

7, 8a. A quotation from 1 Sam. 2:8, which is part of the Song of Hannah (cf. also Lk. 1:52).

7. He raises the poor: i.e. Yahweh is able to restore to a worthwhile existence those who are reduced to poverty and misery by various misfortunes of life. For 'poor' (*dal*), see on 82:3, and for 'needy' (*'eḇyôn*), see on 35:10, 86:1.

the ash heap was, roughly, the ancient counterpart of the workhouse, and of the more recent geriatric ward. It was the rubbish heap outside the village or town, which had become the pitiful shelter of the poor, the outcasts, and the diseased (cf. Lam. 4:5; also Job 2:8). There they begged, ransacked the refuse dump to find some scraps of food, and slept.

8. to make them sit with princes: M.T. has 'that he may set me with . . .', but most exegetes follow LXX, S, Jerome, and V (as *NEB*) in reading: 'that he may set him . . .' (i.e. the poor and the needy) (*l^ehôšîḇô* for M.T. *l^ehôšîḇî*). This expression is a metaphor for elevation to honour and dignity (cf. Job 36:7); it is not so much exaltation as a restoration of self-respect by giving the person concerned a rightful place in his community.
princes: *n^eḏîḇîm* are men of rank, or nobles, and as such they are rich and powerful (cf. 118:9, 146:3; Prov. 19:6); they have a place of honour in the community, and their words are taken seriously. A good description of such an important man is found in Job 29:1–25. The term may also denote foreign princes, as possibly in 118:9.

9. He gives the barren woman a home: lit. 'He gives a dwelling to the barren one of the household', i.e. he grants her security. The lot of a childless wife must have been hard (cf. 1 Sam. 1:6), for barrenness was often regarded as a disgrace and a curse from God (cf. Gen. 16:2, 20:18; 1 Sam. 1:5; Lk. 1:25; de Vaux, *AI*, p. 41). The Psalmist must have had in mind Hannah who became the mother of Samuel, for he quotes from her prayer.
making her the joyous mother of children: or '(as) a joyful mother of . . .' (similarly Kraus, Deissler). The Psalmist depicts Yahweh as the God who accomplishes the humanly impossible, and he may have intended to point also to the restoration of Zion (cf. Isa. 54:1ff.). This was the interpretation of the Targum, which in its paraphrastic translation makes this verse refer to 'the congregation of Israel'.
Praise the LORD: this resumes the call at the beginning of the Psalm (see verse 1). LXX, Jerome, and V place it at the head of Ps. 114.

Psalm 114 THE AWE-INSPIRING PRESENCE OF GOD

In LXX, S, V, and other versions, Ps. 114, 115 form a single composition, but from the contents alone it seems fairly clear that the two Psalms are independent literary units.

Ps. 114 is the second of the 'Egyptian Hallel' songs (see Introduction to Ps. 113), and it is usually classed as a Hymn although it does not follow what might be described as the conventional hymnic style. In essence it is a praise of God who has delivered his people from Egypt and has brought them into the Promised land.

The date of the Psalm is uncertain but it may be of pre-Exilic origin; Weiser (*POTL*, p. 709) places it before 721 B.C., but a later date may be more likely. Kraus (*PBK*, pp. 780f.) has argued that Ps. 114 may have been based on the cultic traditions of the Gilgal sanctuary (cf. Jos. 3–5), which were at a later time transferred to Jerusalem.

According to a Jewish tradition, Ps. 114 was sung on the eighth day of the Passover festival, while Weiser (*POTL*, p. 709) suggests that originally the Psalm belonged to 'the Covenant Festival of Yahweh'; Schmidt, Mowinckel (cf. *PIW*, I, pp. 114f.) would associate it with the Enthronement Festival, but the evidence is rather slender.

Many commentators see in our Psalm four strophes of two verses each, but this may be an artificial division.

The metre of the Psalm is mainly 3+3.

1. When Israel went forth . . .: the Psalm begins with the Exodus, the birth of the nation. The term 'Israel' (see on 80:1) denotes the so-called 'Greater Israel', or the twelve-tribe league.
Egypt: see on 105:23.
the house of Jacob is a synonym of 'Israel'. It refers to the family of Jacob (Gen. 46:27) which God had multiplied and made into a nation.
a people of strange language: lit. 'a people talking unintelligibly' (cf. Gen. 42:23); the phrase is a *hapax legomenon* in the *OT*, and the verb *l-ᶜ-z* is found only here. Some exegetes render: 'a barbarous people' (LXX *laou barbarou*), but this may be misleading; a people speaking a foreign language usually suggest a hostile nation (cf. Isa. 28:11; Jer. 5:15).

2. Judah became his sanctuary: Westermann (*PGP*, p. 96, n.47) points out that the pronoun 'his' can only refer to Yahweh, and that therefore the Psalm must originally have begun with a verse in which the subject was Yahweh himself. LXX begins our Psalm with 'Praise the LORD', transferred here from the end of Ps. 113. The interpretation of the whole verse is rather complicated and, as yet, no final solution has been found. **Judah** is parallel with **Israel,** and both may refer to the constituent parts of the 'Greater Israel', but, if this is the case, 'Israel' in verse

2 has a more limited meaning than the same term in verse 1. Probably 'Judah' denotes the 'Greater Israel' or 'the people of God' as *pars pro toto* (i.e. 'Judah' as a part of the league can represent the whole) and is synonymous with 'Israel' in verse 2*b*.

Equally problematical is the connotation of 'his sanctuary' (*ḳoḏšô*), lit. 'his sacredness' or 'his holy place' (cf. 20:2 (M.T. 3), 24:3). This may allude to the Jerusalem Temple, or it may imply that Judah (i.e. the whole nation) has become the people of God, or holy to Yahweh (cf. Jer. 2:3). Dahood (*PAB*, I, p. 139) suggests 'his holy throne', while Mowinckel (*PIW*, I, p. 155) 'his sacred dominion'; of the two the latter seems more likely.
his dominion: reading with LXX, S, Jerome, and V *memšaltô* for M.T. *mamšᵉlôṯāyw* (a plural of *local extension* (?); cf. *GK* 124b), 'his kingdom' (*PNT*, Dahood).

3. The sea looked: lit. '. . . saw', but the object of the verb is not expressed. It may, however, be inferred from verse 7; it was Yahweh who at his appearing put the sea to flight (cf. 48:5 (M.T. 6)). The allusion is to the crossing of the sea during the Exodus (cf. Exod. 14:10–31) but, at the same time, the sea (*yām*) both suggests and symbolizes the powers of Chaos (cf. v. Rad, *OTT*, I, p. 178). In the Psalmist's presentation, Yahweh had no need to fight the sea, because his mere appearance was sufficient to overcome any opponent (cf. 77:16 (M.T. 17); Hab. 3:10). For a contrast, see the conflict between Baal and Yam (the 'Sea') in the Ugaritic texts (*ANET*, pp. 130f.). This is not to say that the *OT* writers never used the theme of Yahweh's fight with the unruly waters, or that they never resorted to the poetic personification of the sea as a monster (see on 74:13, 89:9f.; cf. Isa. 51:9f.).
Jordan turned back: this is a laconic but picturesque summary of Jos. 3, which describes the crossing of the river Jordan. The events at the Red Sea (or 'Sea of Reeds') and those at Jordan were already associated in Jos. 4:23.

4. The mountains skipped: this probably refers to the Sinai episode (cf. Exod. 19:18; Jg. 5:5; Ps. 68:8 (M.T. 9)). The verb *r-ḳ-d* may denote 'to dance' or 'to skip about gaily' (Ec. 3:4*b*), but in our word-picture the skipping of the mountains is due to fear, and not to joy (as suggested by Barnes, Deissler); cf. verse 7 and 29:6.

5–6. The rhetorical questions may be tinged with 'gentle irony' (McCullough, *PIB*, p. 604) and the Psalmist's participation in the past events may be explained as due to the cultic representation of the *Heilsgeschichte*, or Drama of Salvation. By this means the past becomes the present; this view rests on the belief that 'God and his action are always present, while man in his inevitable temporality cannot grasp this present-ness except by "re-presenting" the action of God over and over again in his worship' (M. Noth, 'The "Re-Presentation" of the Old Testament in Proclamation', *Essays in Old Testament Interpretation*, ed. by C. Westermann (1963), p. 85).

7. Tremble . . .: or 'Dance . . .' (so *NEB*). Kraus (*PBK*, p. 778) suggests *ʾadôn kol hāʾāreṣ* ('(at the presence of) the Lord of all the earth', as in Jos. 3:11,13; Ps. 97:5; Mic. 4:13; Zech. 4:14) for M.T. *ʾādôn ḥûlî ʾāreṣ*; the resultant meaning is that the sea and Jordan flee, and the mountains skip, at the presence of Yahweh. This seems a reasonable proposal, although it is not supported by the versions.

the God of Jacob: see on 20:1; our Psalmist uses the archaic (?) *ʾelôah* (cf. *BDB*, p. 43a; *HAL*, p. 51a) for *ʾelōhê*.

8. The Psalmist, using poetic licence, describes the events at Kadesh (for details, see M. Noth, *Exodus* (*OTL*, 1962), pp. 139f.); cf. Exod. 17:5ff.; Num. 20:8–11; Dt. 8:15; Ps. 78:15f.,20.

rock into a pool of water: (for *ṣûr* ('rock'), see on 42:9) this description may have been influenced by Isa. 41:18 (or, perhaps, vice versa) with its allusion to the second Exodus, or the End-time (cf. Deissler, *PWdB*, III, p. 106). The Hebrew *ʾagam mayim* ('pool of water') is rendered by C. R. North (*Second Isaiah* (1964), p. 102) 'reedy pools' (cf. Num. 20:11; *HAL*, p. 10b).

the flint into a spring of water: (cf. Dt. 8:15) i.e. out of the flinty rock Yahweh made to spring forth a flowing fountain. The miracle at Kadesh is heightened to emphasize both the majesty of Yahweh and his care for Israel. This 'rock' was famous in Jewish tradition, and we find a variant in 1 C. 10:4.

Psalm 115 The Lord will Bless Us

Some versions (e.g. LXX and V) join Ps. 114 to Ps. 115, but there is little doubt that they are independent compositions. The *Gattung* of Ps. 115 is difficult to define, because it exhibits the characteristics of several psalm-types; verses 1–2 are reminiscent of a National Lament, while verses 3–8 are very much like a Hymn. Consequently the Psalm is usually described as a cultic liturgy which was sung antiphonally (cf. verses 1, 3, 12, 18 with verses 9ff.). Essentially the poem appears to be a liturgical prayer with a strong note of assurance, rather than 'a liturgical hymn of praise' (so Rhodes, *LBCP*, p. 158). When it became a part of the 'Egyptian Hallel' (see introduction to Ps. 113) emphasis may have shifted to the aspect of praise. Originally the Psalm probably arose out of a situation in which the people of Yahweh were oppressed by foreign nations (cf. verses 2, 9ff., 17), and were in need of encouragement. Ps. 115 seems to have supplied this lack: in the Temple the worshipping community was assured of the mercy and constancy of Yahweh.

The Psalm opens with an appeal to God (verses 1–2), which is followed by a hymnic reply (verses 3–8) to the sarcastic question: 'Where is their God?' (verse 2). The answer, however, serves the purpose of a self-encouragement by means of an attempt to understand the current problems of faith and life. Verses 9–11 contain an exhortation to trust Yahweh, and in verses 12–15 there is an expression of assurance and a prayerful wish for blessing. The Psalm concludes with a praise of Yahweh (verses 16–18).

The metre is irregular.

THE PRAYER OF THE COMMUNITY **1–2**

1. Not to us: this is not a 'note of triumph' (so Barnes, *PWC*, II, p. 548), but an emphatic protestation (note the repetition of 'Not to us'). The community is still in trouble, and they pray for deliverance which will glorify the name of Yahweh. For a similar petition, see Dan. 9:18f.

to thy name: or 'to yourself' (i.e. to Yahweh); see on 20:1.

give glory: (cf. 29:1; Jer. 13:16) i.e. act on our behalf in order to magnify your own name or reputation. This thought is similar to that expressed in Ezek. 36:22f. where Yahweh promises to intervene for the sake of his holy name.

steadfast love: if Yahweh were to remain aloof, it would seem that his 'steadfast love' (see on 26:3), or 'Covenant loyalty', had ceased to exist, and that his 'faithfulness' (see on 25:5) had turned into indifference.

2. This verse is practically identical with 79:10*a* (q.v.).

the nations: see on 59:5, 106:5. *Gôyīm* refers to the foreign peoples who may be responsible for the affliction suffered by the people of God. The words 'Where is their God?' suggest that the situation of the nation must have been serious to provoke such a scornful question.

THE OMNIPOTENCE OF GOD AND IMPOTENCE OF THE IDOLS **3–8**

3. Our God is in the heavens: or, 'But our God . . .'. The conjunction *w*ᵉ ('and, but') may be an emphatic *wāw* (see Dahood, *PAB*, I, p. 24) with the force of: 'Truly (it is *our* God who is in the heavens)'. The expression 'our God' brings with it the implicit counter-question: 'But where are *their* gods or idols?'. It may also allude to the Covenant relationship between Yahweh and his people (see on 113:5*a*). 'In the heavens' can imply a contrast between the God of Israel, dwelling in the inaccessible heavens, and the man-made idols of the nations, who are on this earth and of it.

he does whatever he pleases: this ability to act and to accomplish his plans distinguishes Yahweh from the gods of the other peoples (cf. 135:6), at least from the Israelite point of view. Yahweh is the God who made man in his own image, while the idols are gods made in the image of man (or beast).

4. The description of the idols (verses 4–8) is a slight variation on 135:15–18 (cf. Isa. 44:9–20; 46:6f.; Jer. 10:1–9; Hab. 2:18f.). It is possible that the similarity of thought and language which exists between the passages cited is largely due to the common cultic tradition associated with the renunciation of foreign gods (cf. Jos. 24:14f.,23).

Their idols: LXX, S, Jerome, and V have 'idols of the heathen' which is an interpretative rendering.

silver and gold: (see on 105:37) these precious metals probably served as a plating for the idols made of wood or other cheaper material; for a description of the process, see Isa. 40:18ff., 44:9–17; cf. C. R. North, *The Second Isaiah* (1964), p. 86.

the work of men's hands: the Psalmist, apparently, identifies the idols with the gods of the nations, and he does not make any allowance for the view that these images might be thought of as *representations* of the gods. What is condemned by the Psalmist is, strictly speaking, a crude idolatry, but the poetical exaggeration makes plain the futility of idol-worship, especially from a monotheistic viewpoint; cf. Mowinckel, *PIW*, I, p. 98.

5–7. Although the idols have a close likeness to the human form, their mouths, eyes, noses, hands, and feet simply do not function. Therefore these images are far inferior to the men who made them (cf. Wis. 15:17), not to mention the God who is the creator of all things. In a way the satire on the idols is an indirect praise of God; the impotence of these images emphasizes, by contrast, the power and majesty of Yahweh.

8. Those who make them are like them: not so much in appearance as in effectiveness. Those who trust in idols, which are nothing, are bound to become as nothing themselves (cf. 2 Kg. 17:15; Jer. 2:5; Rom. 1:21ff.). A god who is less than a man can only degrade his worshipper. LXX, V, and some commentators regard this verse as a wish (cf. 135:18).

THE EXHORTATION TO TRUST YAHWEH **9–11**

These verses resemble the hymnic introductions which call on the worshippers to praise and to exalt God. Those who take part in the cultic act forming the *Sitz im Leben* of this Psalm are divided into three groups: 'Israel' (or 'the house of Israel', as in verse 12*b*), 'the house of Aaron', and those 'who fear the LORD'; but the actual definition of each group is ambiguous (see on 118:2ff., 135:19f.). Most scholars suggest that the reference is to the laity, priests, and proselytes respectively, but it is quite probable that 'those who fear the LORD' is used as a comprehensive term for both the laity and the priestly class (cf. 22:23 (M.T. 24)). It is unlikely that this expression denotes the Temple servants (cf. *PIB*, p. 608), or an inner circle of the godly (cf. Deissler, *PWdB*, III, p. 109; Johnson, *SKAI*, pp. 114f.).

9. . . . trust in the LORD: see on 78:22.

He is their help: the change from the second person to the third person plural is slightly harsh, but it may be due to the fact that the Psalm may have been performed antiphonally. For 'help and . . . shield', see on 33:20; the phrase may point back, by contrast, to the powerlessness of the idols (verses 4–8), even though it is a stereotyped cultic affirmation.

10. house of Aaron: or 'sons of Aaron' (*PNT*).

11. who fear the LORD: see on 34:7,9, 85:9. If this term refers to the proselytes (cf. Ac. 13:16,26, 18:7), it need not necessarily imply a very late date (cf. 1 Kg. 8:41; Isa. 56:6). Verse 13 suggests that our phrase may be a term inclusive of both the laity and the priests.

THE CERTAINTY OF FAITH **12–15**

12. . . . has been mindful of us: lit. '. . . has remembered us' (see on 79:8). This may be a response to the divine oracle of promise, or a priestly word of comfort (based on divine authority), ending with a blessing (verses 14–15). Weiser (*POTL*, p. 717) thinks that the expression presupposes a cultic act, such as a theophany.

he will bless us: (see on 67:1) i.e. we shall experience his saving presence which bestows upon us those things and conditions which work for our good (cf. *TDNT*, II, pp. 756–9). Another way of saying that God will bless us is 'God will be with us' (as in Gen. 39:2–5). *RSV* rendering follows LXX, S, and V in reading *yᵉḇārᵉḵēnû* for M.T. *yᵉḇārēḵ* ('he will bless us').

13. both small and great: (cf. Jer. 6:13, 16:6, 31:34) the blessing of God extends to all who truly worship him, without any regard for their rank or social importance. It can also mean 'everyone', i.e. the *whole* community.

14. give you increase: lit. 'add upon you'. For the Israelites, one of the greatest blessings was many descendants (Dt. 1:11; Ps. 127:3ff.). The increase of the nation was also the fervent hope of the Exilic and post-Exilic community (cf. Isa. 54:1ff.; Zech. 10:8ff.).

15. who made heaven and earth: i.e. who created the whole world. This seems to have been a common description of God in the *OT* (cf. 121:2, 124:8, 134:3, 146:6). Since Yahweh is the creator of all, he is able to fulfil his promises.

THE PRAISE OF THE COMMUNITY **16–18**

16. The heavens are the LORD's heavens: most versions read: 'The heavens of heavens are (or 'belong to') the Lord's' (i.e. *šᵉmê* for *haššāmayim*), but M.T. may well be right. The above phrase probably has a polemical undertone: the heavens are the dwelling place of God (verse 3, 2:4), and not the stage for the activities of various imaginary gods.

the earth he has given to the sons of men: i.e. the earth and its produce are the gifts of God to mankind (cf. Gen. 1:28); consequently they should give thanks and praise to none other than Yahweh.

17. The dead do not praise: i.e. not only do they lead a shadowy existence, but they are also ritually unclean; thus, excluded from cultic activities, they are separated from Yahweh (or *Yāh*; for this shorter form of 'Yahweh', see on 68:4). For a more detailed discussion, see on 6:5, 30:9, 88:10.

silence is a synonym of Sheol or the underworld (cf. Tromp, *PCD*, pp. 76f.), and it means '(the land of) silence' (see on 94:17). LXX renders it by 'Hades'. Verses 16f. give the *OT* view of the world: it consists of the heavens, earth, and Sheol or the netherworld (cf. v. Rad, *OTT*, I, p. 152).

18. But we . . .: this is an emphatic statement. Although the circumstances are such that death is a likely possibility, the worshippers of Yahweh are convinced that they will not perish; they are confident that they will be delivered and that therefore they will praise God (for this sense of 'to bless', see on 104:1). To praise God means to be alive, and the implication is that a life without the praise of God is a death-like existence (cf. Westermann, *PGP*, p. 159). LXX adds after 'But we' the explanatory gloss, *hoi zōntes* ('the living'; similarly also V).

from this time forth . . .: (cf. 113:2) i.e. as long as we live.

Praise the Lord: see on 104:35, 106:1. LXX and V transfer this cultic exclamation to the beginning of Ps. 116.

Psalm 116 'What Shall I Render to the Lord?'

This Psalm is an Individual Thanksgiving (see Introduction, pp. 35f.) although it contains various elements characteristic of other psalm-types, such as complaint (verse 11), petition (verse 4), and expression of confidence (verse 15). I. Engnell (*Studies in Divine Kingship in the Ancient Near East* (1967), p. 210) describes the poem as a 'royal passion psalm', the conclusion of which is formed by Ps. 117; this seems, however, unlikely. The Psalmist depicts himself as a man who has come to the Temple in Jerusalem (verse 19) to offer a sacrifice of thanksgiving (verse 17) for his deliverance from some very grave danger. We are not told what this misfortune was, and the two most frequent guesses are illness and false accusation. The Psalm was meant to be recited as a thanksgiving and as a testimony before the worshippers in the Temple, while the restored man paid his vows to God (verses 14 and 18). It is of special interest that in the *OT* individual experience and public worship are frequently fused into one whole, to the advantage of the entire congregation.

LXX and V divide Ps. 116 into two independent poems, consisting of verses 1–9 and 10–19, yet there is little justification for this division.

The date of the Psalm may well be late post-Exilic (so Oesterley, Kraus, Deissler, *et al.*), and the Aramaisms in verses 7, 12, and 16 support this view.

The metre of the Psalm is irregular.

GOD HAS ANSWERED THE PRAYERS OF HIS SERVANT **1–2**

1. LXX transfers the phrase 'Praise the LORD' from the end of Ps. 115 to the beginning of Ps. 116.

I love the LORD: so also *NEB*. In M.T. there is no object, and it simply reads: 'I love (because . . .)'; this structure is unusual, but not impossible. It is clear from the context that the Psalmist refers to Yahweh; in the cultic setting of the Psalm this must have been even more obvious. *RSV*, following the older versions, transposes 'the LORD' (*yhwh*) from the end of verse 1*a* and makes it into the object of the verb. In essence this verse anticipates 1 Jn 4:19: 'We love, because he first loved us'. For the verb *ʾ-h-b* ('to love'), see on 26:8, 119:47.

because he has heard: i.e. he has both heard and answered (see on 54:2). Instead of the imperfect *yišmaʿ* ('he will hear'), we should read the perfect *šāmaʿ* (so *RSV* and most translations); the *y* may be a dittograph.

my voice and my supplications: this may well be a 'construct chain with an interposed possessive suffix' (see Dahood, *PAB*, 1, p. 110) so that the rendering should be 'my supplications' (Dahood 'my plea for mercy', loc. cit.), or 'my loud supplications for favour' (similarly LXX, S; see on 86:6).

2. he inclined his ear to me: i.e. he attended to my prayer and helped me (see on 86:1).

therefore I will call on him . . .: lit. 'in my days I shall call', i.e. when in the days of my misfortune I used to cry out to him. The *RSV* can be taken to mean 'I shall *worship* him as long as I live' (cf. 18:3 (M.T. 4)). Oesterley, Kraus, *PNT* suggest 'in the day I cried (to him)' (changing *ûḇᵉyāmay* ('and in my days') into *bᵉyôm* ('in the day'; so also S). Winton Thomas (*TRP*, p. 48) *et al.* read *bᵉšēm yhwh* ('in the name of Yahweh'; see verse 4) for *ûḇᵉyāmay*. *NEB* has 'whenever I have cried to him'.

THE DISTRESS **3–4**

3. The snares of death . . .: i.e. the fingers of death grabbed hold of me. This is a metaphor of grave danger, although the nature of the peril is not defined, probably deliberately so. For details, see on 18:4f., 119:61.

the pangs of Sheol: lit. 'the straits of . . .', but the Hebrew *mᵉṣārê* ('the pangs of . . .') may mean 'the bonds of . . .' (parallel to 'the snares (or 'cords')' in verse 3*a*); this meaning is supported by the related word *ṣ^e^rôr* ('bundle'; so G. R. Driver). The suggested emendation *m^e^ṣōḏê* ('snares of . . .'; cf. *BH*) may not be necessary. Verse 3*b* provides a synonymous parallelism to verse 3*a*, and both depict the Psalmist as already in the shadow of death. For 'Sheol', see on 6:5, 88:3.

I suffered . . .: lit. 'I found . . .', i.e. I found in life nothing but 'distress and anguish'.

4. Then I called . . .: or 'But I kept on calling . . .'. For the expression, see verse 13, cf. 75:1 (M.T. 2); van Imschoot, *ThOT*, I, pp. 196f.

save my life: lit. '. . . my soul' (see on 33:19), i.e. deliver me.

THE GRACIOUS DELIVERANCE **5–11**

5. gracious is the LORD: see on 111:4.

righteous: see on 119:137. He is true to his self-imposed Covenant promises.

our God is merciful: the Covenant God (see on 113:5) manifests himself in loving acts. The verb *r-ḥ-m* usually denotes certain tangible expressions of love, rather than a mere show of emotions (see on 18:1; cf. *TDNT*, II, pp. 480f.).

6. the simple: (*NEB* 'the simple-hearted') see on 19:7, 119:130. The term *p^e^ṯā᾽îm* often suggests persons who are naïve, gullible, or wilfully foolish (so especially in the book of Proverbs); here it probably denotes those who are inexperienced and helpless; over such Yahweh keeps his watchful eye. LXX has *ta nēpia* ('babes').

when I was brought low by illness or some other serious trouble (cf. 79:8, 142:6 (M.T. 7)). The verb *d-l-l* ('to be low') may be used of oppression by an enemy (as in Jg. 6:6), but this is not always the case.

he saved me: or 'he helped me'. For the verb *y-š-*ᶜ, see on 54:1.

7. Return, O my soul: be at rest because God has helped you (cf. 132:8). For a similar form of self-exhortation, see on 42:5 (M.T. 6), 103:1f.

your rest: the Hebrew *mānôaḥ* is used in the plural, and may signify a complete, true rest. For the Aramaic pronominal suffix, see *GK* 91l.

. . . has dealt bountifully: i.e. in his graciousness he has dealt fully with all my adversities (cf. 13:6, 119:17, 142:7 (M.T. 8)). 'With you' refers to 'my soul' in verse 7*a*.

8. Verses 8 and 9 are similar to 56:13 (M.T. 14).

delivered my soul: i.e. saved me (for 'soul', see on 33:19). It

is not clear what kind of troubles had caused the suffering and what had brought the Psalmist near to death. The verb *ḥ-l-ṣ* means 'to rescue, deliver', but the actual affliction or misfortune must be inferred from the context (cf. 6:4 (M.T. 5), 18:19 (M.T. 20), 34:7 (M.T. 8), 50:15, 81:7 (M.T. 8), 91:15, 119:153, 140:1 (M.T. 2); Barth, *ETKD*, p. 129; *TDNT*, VI, p. 1001).
my eyes from tears: this phrase is not found in 56:13 (M.T. 14), and is omitted by *NEB*; it does not fit the preceding verb 'thou hast delivered'. The meaning is, however, clear: God will save his servant from all those things which cause sorrow (cf. Isa. 25:8; Rev. 7:17).
my feet from stumbling: i.e. Yahweh has rescued the Psalmist from imminent ruin or downfall (cf. Prov. 26:28).

9. I walk before the Lord: or 'I will walk . . .', i.e. I will live obediently before Yahweh, I will conduct myself in accordance with his will (cf. Gen. 17:1, 24:40, 48:15).
in the land of the living: see on 56:13. This points back to the poet's deliverance from the land of doom and darkness (Job 10:21).

10. I kept my faith, even when I said: (cf. 2 C. 4:13) *AV* (following LXX) renders 'I believed, therefore have I spoken'. G. R. Driver (*JTS*, XLIV (1943), p. 21) has suggested: 'I thought that I should be carried off (sc. by death)' (similarly *NEB*); this assumes that M.T. *ʾdbr* represents *ʾeṯdabbēr* ('I would be carried off'; cf. *KBL*, p. 199b); a slight variation might be 'I felt sure that . . .'. Klopfenstein (*LAT*, p. 198) translates: 'I have kept (my) faith, therefore I now acknowledge'.
I am greatly afflicted: or 'I was . . .' (so *AV*, *RV*), i.e. 'I was completely helpless in my adversity'.

11. . . . in my consternation: the same expression is found in 31:22 (M.T. 23). *AV*, *RV* have 'in my haste' which is possible but less likely. The verb *ḥ-p-z* usually suggests 'to be in alarm, panic stricken' (cf. 2 Sam. 4:4; 2 Kg. 7:15; Ps. 104:7; 1QM xv:8).
Men are all a vain hope: lit. 'All men are liars'. Schmidt, Kraus, *et al.* find here an allusion to false accusations brought against the Psalmist, but it is more likely that the author was thinking of his fellow-men as deceptive or disappointing in their pretence, or inability to help (cf. Klopfenstein, *LAT*, pp. 199f.); the only real help is Yahweh (verses 6f.). See also 60:11 (M.T. 13), 146:3.

THE THANKSGIVING OF A GRATEFUL MAN **12–19**

12. What shall I render . . .: or 'How can I repay Yahweh?' (similarly *PNT*, *NEB*, Deissler), i.e. How can I thank adequately? **for all his bounty:** the Hebrew *tagmûl* ('benefit, bounty') occurs only here in the *OT*, but synonymous expressions (of the same root) are not uncommon (cf. 103:2; Prov. 12:14). The pronominal suffix used is the Aramaic *-ôhî* ('his'; cf. *GK* 91l) for the usual Hebrew equivalent *-ô*.

13. the cup of salvation: lit. 'the cup of salvations'; it can mean several things: (i) a drink offering (of wine) which was part of the thank-offering (cf. Num. 28:7); (ii) a metaphor of deliverance, and the opposite of the cup of Yahweh's wrath (cf. Isa. 51:17; Jer. 25:15); (iii) a cup connected with some particular ordeal (cf. Num. 5:16–28); (iv) a cup of wine used at the thanksgiving meal (cf. 23:5). The first suggestion seems the most plausible, because 'the cup' must represent something rendered to Yahweh, as an expression of the Psalmist's gratitude (similar to the vows (verse 14) and the sacrifice of thanksgiving (verse 17)).

call on the name of the Lord: the same phrase is used in verse 4, where it describes a call for help of which an important part was the invocation of the divine name. In verse 13 it is more or less tantamount to the proclaiming of Yahweh's name in thanksgiving. For 'name' (*šēm*), see on 20:1.

14. This verse is repeated as verse 18, and it may be an accidental insertion. It is missing in some Hebrew and Greek MSS., and it is deleted by many commentators, probably rightly so.

I will pay my vows: the Hebrew *nēḏer* may mean both 'vow' and 'votive sacrifice'. Here the reference is to the vows (cf. 50:14, 56:12 (M.T. 13)) which are discharged by the offering of the thanksgiving sacrifice.

in the presence of all his people: i.e. before the worshipping community. Thus the performance of the vow has a twofold purpose: it conveys one's gratitude to God and serves as a testimony to God's grace.

15. the death: the Hebrew *māwᵉṯāh* is a feminine form of *māweṯ* ('death') and a *hapax legomenon*; some scholars read *tᵉmûṯāh* ('death') which is attested in 79:11, 102:20 (M.T. 21). The untimely death of the saints (see on 30:4, 86:2), or of Yahweh's loyal dependants, is not a matter of indifference to him; therefore he delivers them from their troubles. For the thought, see on 16:10, 72:14.

16. O Lord, I am thy servant: lit. 'O Lord, for I am . . .' but the Hebrew *kî* ('for') may be taken emphatically '. . . I am indeed . . .' (cf. J. Muilenburg, *HUCA*, xxxii (1961), p. 143). For 'servant' (*ᶜeḇeḏ*), see on 36:1. Some exegetes delete 'for I am thy servant' as a dittograph (cf. *TRP*, p. 48); *NEB* transposes it to the end of verse 4.

the son of thy handmaid: (for this expression, see on 86:16; cf. Exod. 23:12), it is synonymous with 'thy servant', and serves as a humble self-designation: 'the lowest of the servants of God'. It also points to the Psalmist's relationship with God.

Thou hast loosed my bonds: this is, most likely, a figurative description of the deliverance from the bonds of Sheol, i.e. untimely death (see verse 3). Schmidt (*PHAT*, p. 210), on the other hand, takes the phrase literally, but the word *môsēr* ('bond') is usually used metaphorically (cf. Klopfenstein, *LAT*, p. 421, n.866). The preposition *lᵉ* in *lᵉmôsērāy* ('my bonds') may be an Aramaism (cf. *GK* 117n).

17. . . . the sacrifice of thanksgiving: see on 107:22.

call on the name . . .: see verse 13.

18. For exegesis, see verse 14.

19. the courts of the house of the Lord: the Temple courts are referred to in the note on 96:8. In Herod's Temple, the altar of burnt offering was situated in the court of priests (cf. *IDB*, iv, pp. 556f.).

Praise the Lord: see on 104:35, 106:1. LXX adds this expression to the beginning of Ps. 117.

Psalm 117 'Extol Him, All Peoples'

This is the shortest Psalm in the whole Psalter, and one of the songs of praise in the 'Egyptian Hallel' (see Introduction to Ps. 113). Its *Gattung* can be defined as a Hymn (see Introduction, pp. 32f.); it consists of an introductory call to praise Yahweh (verse 1) and the main part of the Hymn, giving the reasons why God should be extolled (verse 2*ab*). It concludes with a renewed call for praise (verse 2*c*).

Because of its brevity, the Psalm is sometimes added either to the end of Ps. 116 or to the beginning of Ps. 118, but neither alternative is satisfactory. The hymn may well be a unit on its own (not a fragment of a longer composition) which served its purpose in the ritual of some of the festivals. Weiser (*POTL*, p. 721) is perhaps, far too positive when he states that Ps. 117 is 'a liturgical formula to introduce the festival hymn which follows the theophany . . .'.

The Psalm may be of post-Exilic origin, and its metre is 3 + 3.

1. This verse is quoted in Rom. 15:11 as one of the proof-texts that the inclusion of the Gentiles was not a divine after-thought.

Praise the Lord: this differs from the concluding formula in verse 2*c*, by its use of the fuller form of the divine name Yahweh instead of the shorter form *yāh* (see on 68:4). For the whole expression cf. 104:35, 106:1.

all the nations: (for *gôyīm*, see on 59:5) Kraus (*PBK*, p. 798) points out that the universalism of this Psalm rests upon the old cultic traditions which exalt Yahweh as the 'High God' who is the king and the lord of the whole world. R. Martin-Achard (*A Light to the Nations* (1962), p. 58) has remarked that the nations (and the whole created world) are often summoned to praise Yahweh, but it is 'by reason of their belonging to the realm of creation and not because they are called to share Israel's faith, that the heathen must glorify God'. This may be largely true, but it is equally clear that at some point in Israel's history there arose the conviction that the other nations also would join one day in the worship of Yahweh.

Extol him: for the verb *š-b-ḥ*, see on 63:3.

peoples: the masculine plural *ʾummîm* occurs only here in the *OT* but there is no need to change it into the more common *leʾummîm* ('peoples').

2. For great is his steadfast love . . .: lit. 'For his Covenant loyalty (see on 26:3) has prevailed (or 'has been mighty') over us (or 'on our behalf')' (cf. 103:11).

faithfulness: lit. 'truth'; see on 25:5.

for ever: see on 9:5. H. Sasse (*TDNT*, I, p. 199) describes *ʿôlām* ('eternity') as the 'hidden or distant time belonging to the remote and inscrutable past or future from the standpoint of the present'.

Praise the Lord: see verse 1. LXX adds this phrase to the beginning of Ps. 118.

Psalm 118 A Liturgy of Thanksgiving

This Psalm concludes the 'Egyptian Hallel' (see introduction to Ps. 113) and according to the Mishnah (*Sukkah* iv:5) it belonged to the Feast of Tabernacles. There is no real reason to doubt that this cultic setting of the Psalm reflects its original usage; therefore the poem refers not to any *particular* historical victory but to an annual cultic experience (cf. Mowinckel, *PIW*, II, p. 28). See F. Crusemann, *Studien zur Formgeschichte von Hymnus und Danklied in Israel* (*WMANT*, 32 1969), pp. 217–25.

The structure of the Psalm is rather complex. Verses 1–4 are a hymnic thanksgiving of the people, while the next section (verses 5–21) is an individual thanksgiving. The speaker seems to be the King or a representative of the nation, and consequently the whole Psalm concerns essentially the fortunes of the entire community. This accounts for the mixture of individual and congregational experiences and acts of worship. The concluding section (verses 22–9) contains various elements: a proverbial expression (verse 22), a praise of Yahweh (verses 23–4), a prayer (verse 25), a priestly blessing and direction (verses 26–7), and the response of the King (verse 28); the final verse repeats verse 1, and this may be a stylistic device in which the writer returns to the initial thought with which the composition began.

The Psalm was performed at the Temple gates (verses 19f.), and therefore it is closely related to the Entrance liturgies (cf. Ps. 15, 24). In a way our Psalm is not properly a thanksgiving (this is suggested by verse 19), but its account of Yahweh's goodness and help is an implicit claim by the speaker that he is righteous and therefore fit to enter the gates of righteousness (cf. S. B. Frost, '*Asseveration by Thanksgiving*', *VT*, VIII (1958), pp. 380f.). Yahweh himself has shown by his saving works that the claim is fully justified, and that further blessings are in store for the King and his people because the righteousness of the ruler is inseparably linked with the righteousness of the people (cf. Johnson, *SKAI*, pp. 6ff.).

The Psalm dates, most likely, from the pre-Exilic times.

The metre is mainly 3+3.

LET THE PEOPLE THANK GOD **1–4**

1. This verse may be a traditional liturgical formula, and it occurs several times in the Psalter (see on 106:1). The Psalm seems to be a liturgy, but it is not exactly clear how it was performed. **give thanks to the LORD:** i.e. recount the wonderful works of Yahweh as a testimony to his goodness and fidelity.

2–4. Let Israel say: LXX (similarly *NEB*) has 'Let the house of Israel', and a number of commentators follow this suggestion; cf. 115:9. LXX repeats the phrase **for he is good** (verse 1*a*) also after verses 2*a*, 3*a*, and 4*a*, but this addition is not justified metrically. The Psalmist refers to three groups of people: Israel, the house of Aaron, and those who fear the LORD; but their identity is not clear. For a brief discussion on this point, see on 115:9–11. Johnson (*SKAI*, p. 114) is of the opinion that 'Israel' denotes the whole nation while 'those who fear the LORD' refers to the general body of worshippers.

THANKSGIVING TO GOD **5–21**

Johnson and many other scholars think that the speaker of these verses is the King. This is more likely than the suggestion that the subject of these verses is the personified Israel, or some ordinary worshipper. If the Psalm is of post-Exilic origin, the reference may be to the representative of the community.

5. Out of my distress: it is quite customary for one giving thanks to God to recall the past misfortunes out of which he has been delivered. The account of the affliction is in general terms, and therefore very indefinite; but from verses 7 and 10ff. we learn that the singer had been surrounded by enemies who nearly brought about his death (verses 17f.). The Hebrew *mēṣar* ('distress') occurs elsewhere in 116:3 ('the pangs of (Sheol)') and Lam. 1:3 ('distress'), and it depicts the adversity as a condition of being hemmed in by trouble. Some commentators (e.g. Johnson, Eaton) interpret the 'distress' as the King's ritual humiliation, unless the language of the Royal Psalms has been 'democratized'. Schmidt (*PHAT*, p. 212) argues that the allusion is to the imprisonment of the Psalmist, but this is far less likely. **I called on the LORD:** or '. . . on Yah' (see on 68:4). The shorter form of the divine name is also used in verses 5*b*, 14*a*, 18*a*, and 19*b*.

the LORD answered me . . .: lit. 'Yah answered me with a broad place', i.e. he set me free from the choking restrictions of my afflictions; see on 18:19.

6. With the LORD on my side: lit. '(With) Yahweh for me'; cf. Rom. 8:31: 'If God is for us, who is against us?' LXX, T, S (and Heb. 13:6) have: 'The Lord is my helper', as in verse 7, but M.T. is preferable for metrical and stylistic reasons (cf. 56:9 (M.T. 10)).

I do not fear: perhaps, 'I shall cease to be afraid'. Kraus (*PBK*, p. 805) sees here a possible allusion to an oracle of salvation, of which an important part is the expression: 'Do not fear' (Lam. 3:57; cf. Isa. 41:10,13). With the increase of the fear of the Lord, the fear of man decreases, and therefore the singer can exclaim: 'What can man do to me?' (as in 56:11 (M.T. 12)).

7. to help me: lit. 'as my helper' (cf. *GK* 119i; *HS* 106g; 54:4 (M.T. 6)). *AV*, wrongly, 'The LORD taketh my part with them that help me' (similarly *RV*).

I shall look in triumph on . . .: lit. 'I shall see on . . .'; cf. 112:8.

those who hate me: this may be a brief description of 'all nations' in verse 10. For the expression, see on 68:1.

8. This and the following verse form an external, repetitive parallelism (see Introduction, pp. 41f.).

to take refuge in the LORD: (see on 7:1, 16:1); many commentators point to a similar experience of Nehemiah, whose escort did not prevent the hostilities of his enemies (Neh. 2:9f., 4:7 (M.T. 4:2)). The attempt to identify the speaker of the Psalm with Nehemiah or with any other known leader of the people, is, however, a mere speculation. 11QPs^{a} reads *lbṭwḥ* ('to trust') for M.T. *laḥ^{a}sôṯ* ('to take refuge').

to put confidence in man: it is unwise to set one's reliance exclusively upon man for although God can use men and women to fulfil his purposes, they themselves must depend upon God. Therefore, with God on our side, we have more than enough; without him, we may not have even enough. For the verb *b-ṭ-ḥ* ('to trust'), see on 78:22.

9. in princes: see on 113:8.

10–12. All nations surrounded me: here we have to consider several possibilities: (i) the reference may be to the foreign enemies in a particular situation (e.g. the neighbours of the Judaean community during the time of Nehemiah); (ii) the description may be part of the ritual humiliation of the King; (iii) the Psalmist may have borrowed the metaphors, proper to Royal Psalms, and have applied them to his own situation (cf. Kraus, *PBK*, p. 805). The second possibility seems the most likely one.

in the name of the LORD: (for *šēm* ('name') see on 20:1), i.e. through Yahweh's self-manifestation as an effective help (see verse 7). Perhaps we should render: 'armed with the name . . .' (cf. 1 Sam. 17:45; Sheldon H. Blank, 'Some Observations concerning Biblical Prayer', *HUCA*, XXXII (1961), p. 76).

I cut them off: probably 'I shall certainly cut them off'. The Hebrew *kî* ('for'; not represented in *RSV*) may be the emphatic *kî* (see J. Muilenburg, 'Usages of Particle *KY* in the Old Testament', *HUCA*, XXXII (1961), p. 143). The verb *m-w-l* means 'to circumcise', and some scholars (e.g. Hengstenberg, Briggs) take it more or less literally. Most of the recent commentators derive the verb from *m-w-l* II ('to ward off') (see *KBL*, p. 502b, *TRP*, p. 48); a similar meaning is also suggested by LXX, T, S, and V.

The repetition of verse 10 in verses 11f. and their antithetic form serves to emphasize the thought that Yahweh's help is more than adequate for all eventualities.

like bees: (cf. Dt. 1:44) i.e. they were both numerous and fierce. LXX suggests 'as bees (surround) wax' which requires the addition of *dōnāḡ* ('wax'). Metrically this is preferable (cf. *NEB*).

they blazed like a fire of thorns: so *RSV* following LXX and V, reading *bāᶜᵃrû* ('they blazed') for M.T. *dōᶜᵃḵû* ('they were quenched'); *RSV et al.* point to the fierceness of the attack, while M.T. stresses the fact that the hostilities of the foes were checked in no time.

13. I was pushed hard: (i.e. by the enemy) so also LXX, S, and V, which suggest *niḏḥêṯî* ('I was pushed') for M.T. *ḏᵉḥîṯanî* ('you pushed me'). In both cases the cause of the trouble must be the enemies, who may be personified by one individual (so Kirkpatrick, Barnes; cf. Johnson, p. 115, n.5). The M.T. reading could refer to Yahweh (cf. verse 18), but one expects a more or less direct allusion to the adversaries.

so that I was falling: or 'that I might fall'.

the LORD helped me: see verse 7.

14. This verse may be a quotation from Exod. 15:2 which belongs to the so-called 'Reed Sea Hymn' (Noth, *Exodus*, p. 123; cf. Isa. 12:2), or the 'victory song of Moses'.

The LORD is my strength: i.e. the source of my strength (see on 78:26). 'The LORD' translates the Hebrew *yāh*; see verse 5.
my song: that is, Yahweh is the subject of my song of praise and thanks. For *zimrāṯ* ('song') we should probably read *zimrāṯî* ('my song'); the last letter (*î*) may have fallen out through haplography. *KBL* (p. 260) *et al.* link the Hebrew word with *zimrāh* ('strength, protection'); similarly Winton Thomas (*TRP*, p. 48) who suggests 'my defence', and *NEB*.
he has become my salvation: i.e. he has become to me the giver of my deliverance (for 'salvation', see on 35:3).

15. Hark, glad songs of victory: lit. 'The voice of rejoicing and salvation' (*AV*, *RV*). For *rinnāh* ('rejoicing'), see on 88:2.
the tents: or 'the dwellings', because most of the Israelites would live in more permanent habitations; the word 'tent' is probably used in a secondary sense (see on 61:4; cf. 91:10), unless the reference is to the tents in which the people may have lived during the festive week.
the righteous: (see on 1:5) are the Covenant people whose life matches their profession. *NEB* renders *ṣaddîḳîm* by 'the victors'.
the right hand stands for Yahweh's *own power* (see on 20:6; cf. 1QM iv:7).
does valiantly: (see on 60:12) i.e. it performs mighty deeds (cf. 1QM xii:10).

16. is exalted: LXX, S, and V have '. . . exalts me' but this reading seems less likely. Kraus (*PBK*, p. 806) thinks that the lifting up of the right hand may be an ancient symbolic gesture on the part of the victor.
does valiantly: 11QPs[a] has *ʿsth gbwrh* ('performs (deeds of) strength'), which is a variation on verse 15*c*. *NEB* omits verse 16*b*.

17. I shall not die: the reference is to a particular situation (either cultic or historical) in which the singer has been delivered from the threat of imminent death, and not to personal immortality or resurrection.
I shall live: the essence of living is to declare the saving deeds of Yahweh. Thus the life of the Psalmist was an impressive testimony to the goodness of Yahweh.

18. The LORD has chastened me: i.e. the misfortune and the humiliation was, primarily, part of the divine discipline. At one time this would have been regarded as a just punishment for sins; now the Psalmist looks at his tribulations as a helpful discipline (cf. v. Rad, *OTT*, I, p. 402; Prov. 3:11f.; Jer. 10:24).

The disciplinary aspect of suffering may, however, include or presuppose the penal aspect also (cf. Am. 4:10).

19. the gates of righteousness: (*NEB* '. . . of victory') i.e. the gates through which only the righteous may enter (verse 20). Kirkpatrick (*BPCB*, p. 697) is of the opinion that the 'gates of righteousness' derived their name from the fact that the Temple was the abode of the God of righteousness (Jer. 31:23), but this seems less likely than the previous explanation. Cf. J. Morgenstern, 'The Gates of Righteousness', *HUCA*, VI (1929), pp. 1–37. The would-be worshippers were asked, at least formally, for a declaration of their faithfulness to the Covenant (see Ps. 15, 24). Those who had been loyal to Yahweh's commands, were accepted as righteous and were admitted to the Temple precincts (cf. Isa. 26:2; for a Babylonian parallel, see Kraus, *PBK*, p. 807). Mowinckel (*PIW*, I, p. 181, n.191) points out that also in Babylonia the different temple gates had symbolic names, such as 'the gate of salvation', 'the gate of life'.

give thanks to the LORD: see on 18:49, 30:12.

20. This is the gate of the LORD . . .: this verse probably comprises the reply of the priestly gate-keepers (cf. 2 Kg. 25:18; Neh. 13:5). The 'gate of the LORD' may be a synonym of the 'gate(s) of righteousness', except that the emphasis may be on the fact that this gate leads to the presence of Yahweh who abides in the sanctuary.

the righteous: or 'Only the righteous' (cf. S. B. Frost, 'Asseveration by Thanksgiving', *VT*, VIII (1958), p. 381).

21. I thank thee: see on 18:49, 30:12. The reason for this thanksgiving is that God has answered the suppliant by granting him salvation (see on 35:3), or help in need (cf. Exod. 15:2). If the Psalm is pre-Exilic, then the allusion may be to the cultic victory of the King (and so also of the nation as a whole); if the Psalm is later, the reference may be to some historical triumph, although the difference between the two is not as great as it may appear to us.

THE PRAISE AND PRAYER OF THE COMMUNITY **22–5**

22. The stone which the builders rejected: this is in all probability a proverbial saying, that what appeared to be worthless has now taken the place of honour. This was also the experience of the singer in verses 5–21: at one point he was hard pressed and near death; now he is delivered by Yahweh and recognized as righteous or victorious.

the chief cornerstone: lit. 'the head of the corner'. It was not necessarily the *only* stone of such a nature, but *one* of the most important parts of the building. The metaphor alludes either to one of the large cornerstones which bind together two rows of stones (especially in the foundations), or to the keystone which completes an arch or structure. In any case its actual function is less important than the surprising change in the significance of the stone in question. Verse 22 is applied to Jesus Christ in Mt. 21:42; Mk 12:10; Lk. 20:17; Ac. 4:11; Eph. 2:20; 1 Pet. 2:7; cf. Leaney, *RQM*, pp. 218f.

23. The community realizes that the deliverance of the King (this seems to be the most likely view) was entirely the work of Yahweh, and that any human contribution was as nothing in comparison with the marvellous works of God.

24. This is the day which the LORD has made: Johnson (*SKAI*, p. 118) renders '. . . on which Yahweh hath acted'. In either case the significance of the day is due to the event(s) celebrated on it.

let us rejoice: for the verb *g-y-l*, see on 89:16.

25. Save us: the Hebrew *hôšîᶜāhnnāᵓ* appears in transliteration as 'Hosanna' which, strictly speaking, represents the shorter form *hôšaᶜnnaᵓ* (cf. V. Taylor, *The Gospel According to St. Mark* (1952), pp. 456f.). In the *OT* this and similar expressions are usually used as a cry for help, but in the *NT* it has become more like a greeting or acclamation. Some scholars (e.g. J. J. Petuchowski, '*Hoshiᶜah na* in Psalm 118:25: a Prayer for Rain', *VT*, v (1955), pp. 266–71) have argued that this phrase was used in prayers for rain, especially at the Feast of Tabernacles.

give us success: cf. Neh. 1:11. *NEB* has 'send us prosperity'.

THE BLESSING **26–7**

26. Blessed be he who enters: the verse may be a liturgical element closely associated with the so-called Gate-liturgies (see Ps. 15, 24). All who enter the Temple precincts receive the priestly blessing (cf. Num. 6:23–7). The phrase **in the name of the LORD** enlarges upon 'Blessed be' (see Sheldon H. Blank, pp. 75–9), i.e. it is Yahweh himself who is ultimately the source of all blessing (see on 67:1); otherwise 'in the name of. . .' might suggest 'with the authority of. . .', as perhaps in Mk 11:9; Jn 12:13. 'He who enters', or 'He that cometh' (*RV*), eventually became a messianic title in later Jewry (cf. Mt. 11:3; Lk. 19:38).

We bless you . . .: the 'we' denotes the priests; nevertheless, it is Yahweh who adds effectiveness to this blessing (as in Num. 6:27). It is probable that the two lines of verse 26 are parallel, in which case the blessing in both phrases is pronounced over the whole procession. Weiser (*POTL*, p. 729) thinks that the first part was addressed to the King, the second to the congregation, while Kissane (*BP*, p. 542) suggests that those 'who are present bless those who are absent'; but these interpretations are less likely than the first proposal.

27. This verse may be a continuation of the priestly blessing in verse 26 (so Weiser, Deissler), but it can equally well be an affirmation by the worshippers.

The LORD is God: or 'Yahweh is El', i.e. he is the highest God (cf. the name 'Elijah'); Kraus (*PBK*, p. 808) finds the origin of this expression in the ancient festival of the Covenant Renewal (cf. Jos. 24:17ff.).

he has given us light: this may be an allusion to the Aaronic blessing in Num. 6:24ff. Rightly or wrongly, it also reminds us of Am. 5:18, which states that the day of Yahweh was expected to be a day of light. Perhaps the meaning of the phrase is 'he has given us victory' (cf. Est. 8:16).

Bind the festal procession with branches: *AV*, *RV*, *RP* render 'Bind the sacrifice with cords', but this translation seems less likely, because there is no evidence that the sacrificial victim was tied with ropes to the altar (cf. Ezek. 40:38–43). The difficulty is partly created by the word *ḥaḡ*, which usually means a 'pilgrimage festival'; whether it denoted 'sacrifice' is doubtful (but cf. Exod. 23:18; Schmidt, *PHAT*, p. 212). In recent years it has been customary to translate *ḥaḡ* by 'procession' (see on 26:6), or 'festal dance', and to interpret the whole verse in the light of Mishnah (*Sukkah* iv:5f.), which describes how on the Feast of Tabernacles the procession of worshippers used to go round the altar. They also carried the *lulab*, a bundle of branches made up from myrtles, willows, and palms (it also included a citron; cf. *Sukkah* iii:4; see also Lev. 23:40). During the procession the altar was covered with the branches, and the expression 'up to the horns of the altar' may not be inappropriate, even in this instance. It is not impossible that our Psalmist envisaged a similar procession. The verb 'bind' (*'isᵉrû*) could be taken to mean 'begin (the festal procession)' (cf. *BDB*, p. 64a), or 'Join (in the dance)' (so Johnson, *SKAI*, p. 118).

horns of the altar were the projections at the four corners, and they were regarded as the most sacred parts of the altar. Their original significance is, however, uncertain (see de Vaux, *AI*, p. 414). In the early period, to grasp the horns of the altar was tantamount to a claim for divine protection (1 Kg. 2:28); unless the person concerned was actually guilty (or the pursuers too godless), he received sanctuary. At a later time, only priests could approach the altar.

THE CONCLUSION **28–9**

28. Thou art my God: the speaker is once again the King or the representative of the community (cf. Exod. 15:2). *RSV* repeats this phrase in verse 28*b* where M.T. has 'my God' which may well be a vocative (so Johnson, *PNT*, *NEB*).

29. The Psalm ends with the same words as it began (see verse 1). In 11QPs[a] (col. xvi) the Psalm is apparently concluded with the liturgical formula 'Praise the Lord' (see on 104:35, 106:1).

Psalm 119 A Eulogy of the Law of God

This is by far the longest Psalm in the Psalter; it consists of twenty-two strophes corresponding to the twenty-two letters of the Hebrew alphabet. Each strophe has eight verses, or *bicola* (two-line units), and each *bicolon* of a particular strophe begins with the same Hebrew letter. Conseqently the whole Psalm forms a very elaborate acrostic poem (see introduction to Ps. 9–10), since the strophes are arranged according to the alphabet sequence. The nearest *OT* parallel is the acrostic poem in Lam. 3, which also has twenty-two strophes; but each strophe contains only three *bicola* or verses beginning with the same letter of the alphabet.

The fact that there are eight *bicola* in each strophe can hardly be an accidental choice, although its real significance is not clear. It is possible that the number 'eight' was regarded as the completion of the number 'seven', thus expressing a wholeness or totality, which may also be the meaning of the acrostic scheme itself. This view finds some support in the fact that each strophe uses the same eight synonyms for 'law', each verse containing one equivalent (there are, however, two synonyms in verses 160, 168, 172). It does not follow that there were only eight different ways in which the Hebrews could describe 'law', but rather that the *same eight* were employed by our author (for some exceptions, see verses 3, 15, 37). (For a detailed discussion on the meaning of the number 'eight', see A. Deissler, *Psalm* 119 (118) *und seine Theologie* (1955), pp. 71–4.)

The impressive emphasis on the law, or its ultimate author, may provide some justification for defining the Psalm as a Hymn in praise of the law, or of God who was its giver. This Psalm incorporates many elements of different psalm-types, e.g. blessing (verses 1–3), lamentation (verses 153–60), thanksgiving (verse 7), and assertion of innocence (verses 97–106). Consequently Mowinckel (*PIW*, II, p. 139) thinks that the Psalm was a lamentation 'and prayer for help, using his (the author's) love of the law as a "motive for being heard".' Also v. Rad (*PHOE*, p. 248) has suggested that the author was 'making use of the form of the ancient cultic "lament" in compiling his prayer-like "confession".' He describes the Psalm as 'a highly composite mosaic of proverbial wisdom-material' and therefore he calls the Psalmist 'a wisdom-writer'. Similarly, Deissler (op. cit., pp. 270–81) characterizes the poem as an anthology, because it contains many allusions to other books of the *OT*, in particular to Deuteronomy, Proverbs, Isaiah, and Jeremiah. From this we may conclude that it is unwise to associate the Psalmist *exclusively* with the Wisdom circles (cf. K. Koch, *ThLZ*, III (1958), pp. 186f.) One could, however, think of the author as a teacher of a 'Wisdom school', whose main basis of learning was the canonical writings, which did not necessarily have their present form and extent. The fact that every verse of the Psalm either addresses, or refers to, God, and mentions at least one of the synonyms of law, may imply that the chief purpose of the Psalmist was to glorify the law and its author. The sheer length of the Psalm, as well as its structure and acrostic nature, have prevented any real development of thought in the poem; each strophe appears to be a variation of the main theme of the Psalm, and the effect is a monotonous repetition which is, nevertheless, impressive even in its repetitiveness.

It is quite possible that the intention of the author was to produce a Wisdom poem in the widest sense of the word, without imitating any particular psalm-type. If this is the case, it has a certain bearing also upon the setting of the Psalm. The lack of cultic allusions may indicate that the Psalm did not belong, at least originally, to a cultic setting, but that it may have been at home in what might be described as a 'house of instruction' (Sir. 51:23).

Little is known about the Psalmist himself. Delitzsch once described him as a young man (cf. verses 9ff., 100, 141), while Ewald regarded him as advanced in years, which may be more likely. In a similar fashion it had been argued that the writer was a prisoner who passed the time in creating this highly intricate composition (so Hitzig), or that the author was a king (so Widengren); but there is little concrete evidence to substantiate any of these views. If anything, he must have been a scribe or a teacher who experienced considerable difficulties with some of his contemporaries; in all these tribulations he recognized a divine discipline for his own good (verses 67, 71, 75, 107, 153). He suffered scorn and contempt (verses 22, 42, 51, 69, 78), and at times his very life was in grave danger (87, 95, 109). His enemies included also the princes or the representatives of the community (verses 23, 161), and it is possible that their hostility to the Psalmist was due to their lax attitude to the divine law.

Although the Psalm lays such a great stress upon the law, it is not immediately apparent what is meant by that term and its equivalents. Some such view as that of Kirkpatrick (*BPCB*, p. 700) may well be near the mark, in affirming that this law is not 'the Mosaic legislation or the Pentateuch' in the narrower sense, but rather 'all Divine revelation as the guide of life'. This law is neither an intolerable burden, nor a mere reference book, but a gracious gift of God, which is the faithful man's delight and joy, his comfort and the source of the fulness of life.

The date of the Psalm must be post-Deuteronomic, but not necessarily as late as the second century B.C. The third century may be an appropriate date (cf. Deissler, op. cit., p. 288).

More recently some scholars have suggested that Ps. 119 may originally have been the conclusion to the Psalter, thus balancing Ps. 1 which formed its introduction (cf. Guthrie, *ISS*, p. 191; C. Westermann, *Forschung am Alten Testament* (1964), pp. 338ff.).

The metre of the Psalm is chiefly 3 + 2, but there are a number of other variations, such as 2 + 3, 3 + 3, 2 + 2.

Strophe One **1–8**

1. Blessed are those . . .: or 'How rewarding is the life of those . . .'; see on 1:1.

whose way is blameless: i.e. whose way of life is irreproachable (cf. Prov. 11:20, 13:6). The same phrase is also used in the Dead Sea Scrolls, as an attribute of the sect (cf. 1QS iv:22; 1QSa i:28; 1QM xiv:7; 1QH i:36).

who walk in the law of the Lord: these are people whose lives are characterized by integrity (26:1,11) and obedience to the will of Yahweh (81:13 (M.T. 14); Jer. 26:4, 32:23, 44:10,23). It is tantamount to keeping God's Covenant (as it was defined at each particular time; cf. 78:10). The word *tôrāh* ('law') is usually derived from *hôrāh* ('to instruct, teach', 'to throw') (from the root *y-r-h*). For a detailed discussion of the etymology, see G. Östborn, *Tōrā in the Old Testament* (1945), pp. 4–22. In his view, one of the primary meanings of *tôrāh* was that of 'showing the way', while the others included 'direction, instruction'. At a later stage it became a comprehensive term for 'law'. For *tôrāh* in the sense of 'instruction, teaching', see Dt. 17:11; Ps. 78:1; Prov. 1:8, 3:1; Isa. 1:10, 8:16; Mal. 2:6. Vriezen (*OOTT*, p. 254) points out that *tôrāh* 'means in the first place "indication" ("hint"), namely as to what should be done in a particular case; and secondly "instruction".' It can be given by both the priest and the prophet (Isa. 1:10, 8:16,20), or even by a Wisdom teacher (Prov. 13:14). Ultimately the source of the *tôrāh* is Yahweh himself. The divine instruction can be codified for future use in the form of a law code (Dt. 4:44, 17:18f.; Jos. 8:31f.), and eventually the *tôrāh* denoted the whole Pentateuch as the *Tôrāh par excellence*. The 'law' which the poet describes in Ps. 119 is not a yoke which 'neither our fathers nor we have been able to bear' (Ac. 15:10). To the Psalmist the *tôrāh* is a gift of God, which was both preceded and followed by divine grace. Before the events of Sinai there was the Exodus, and after Sinai the Entry into the Promised land. Whatever may have been the historical details of these key events, the basic truths illustrate the pre-eminence of God's grace.

2. Blessed: see verse 1.

who keep his testimonies: i.e. who observe his laws (105:45). A good illustration is Dt. 33:9: 'they observed thy word, and kept thy covenant'.

ᶜĒḏôṯ ('testimonies') (LXX *ta marturia*) is derived from *ᶜ-w-d* ('to bear witness, testimony') (another, less likely, possibility is the derivation from *yāḏaᶜ*, 'to know'). In Exod. 31:18 the word 'testimony' is applied to the two tables of stone (i.e. to the Ten

Words written by the finger of God), and in Exod. 25:22 we have the expression 'the ark of the testimony' (cf. 'the ark of the covenant of the LORD' in Jer. 3:16). In 25:10, 132:12 'Covenant' and 'testimonies' are parallel terms, and similarly, perhaps, in 93:5. It is thus possible that the word was originally associated with the solemn charges of the Sinai Covenant (cf. J. Gray, *I & II Kings* (1964), p. 97). S. R. Driver (*Deuteronomy* (*ICC*, 1896), p. 81) suggests that under the influence of Deuteronomy the word came to be used as 'a general designation of moral and religious ordinances, conceived as a Divinely instituted standard of conduct' (cf. Dt. 4:45, 6:17,20; Ps. 99:7).

seek him: see on 24:6.

with their whole heart: this is a Deuteronomic expression (Dt. 4:29, 6:5, 10:12, 11:13, etc.). The reward of worshippers who seek God with absolute sincerity is that they will find him (Dt. 4:29; Jer. 29:13).

3. wrong: the Hebrew *ʿawlāh* often denotes injustice or wrong in general, as in 64:6: 'Who can search out crimes?' (cf. 92:15 (M.T. 16), 125:3). Sometimes the emphasis may be on legal injustice (cf. 2 Chr. 19:7; Mic. 3:10). The word occurs quite frequently in 1QS and 1QH, where it describes the evil principle in the universe (cf. 1QS iv:17,18), etc.

but walk in his ways: the adversative 'but' is rightly supplied from the context. The phrase itself is a synonym of verse 1*b*. Deissler (op. cit., p. 91) suggests that this expression has its home in the Deuteronomic circles, where it is usually coupled with loving Yahweh (Dt. 19:9, 30:16) and keeping his commandments (Dt. 8:6, 26:17, 28:9, 30:16). Sometimes it may express one of the essential aspects of Israelite religion, as in Jer. 7:23: 'Obey my voice . . . and walk in all the way that I command you . . .' (cf. 1 Kg. 2:3; 2 Chr. 6:31; Isa. 48:17).

4. precepts: the Hebrew *piḳḳûḏîm* is found only in the Psalter (but also in CD xx:2). In 103:18 it is parallel to 'Covenant' (or 'the Covenant law') and in 111:7 it goes with 'the works of his hands' (i.e. his self-revelation). In Ps. 119 the term is usually synonymous with 'law', but in verse 40 it may refer to God's saving judgments.

The use of the second person, when referring to God, can indicate that the author was primarily concerned with the Giver of the law rather than merely with law itself.

to be kept diligently: a similar construction is found in Dt.

24:8: 'to be very careful (to do) . . .'. We could also assume that the letter *m* had fallen out (by haplography) after *lišmōr* ('to keep') reading 'to keep *them* diligently' (similarly *NEB*).

5. . . . my ways: or, paraphrasing verse 5*a*: 'Oh that my obedience might be unwavering' (see verse 3).

statutes: the Hebrew *ḥuḳḳîm* has a wide application. In 2:7 *ḥōḳ* is used of a special decree of Yahweh, or of the so-called 'royal protocol', while in 148:6 it is practically identical with what we might call 'the natural law'. *Ḥōḳ* is frequently parallel to Covenant (50:16, 105:10), referring to the Covenant conditions and promises, or it is employed as a synonym of law, or of one of its many equivalents (18:22 (M.T. 23), 105:45, 147:19).

6. put to shame: apart from its psychological use, it may also have religious implications in suggesting that one is forsaken by God and punished by him (6:10 (M.T. 11), 25:2, 83:17 (M.T. 18), etc.). This usage is frequent in the Psalms of Lamentation.

commandments: the Hebrew *miṣwōṯ* (singular *miṣwāh*) denotes commands or decrees issued by a person in authority, as the order which Solomon gave to Shimei (1 Kg. 2:43); similarly all that God commands or forbids can be called *miṣwāh* (cf. L. Koehler, *Old Testament Theology* (1957), pp. 203, 206). In Deuteronomy the word *miṣwāh* is one of the main designations of 'law' (cf. N. Lohfink, *Das Hauptgebot* (1963), pp. 55f.).

7. I will praise thee: or 'I will keep on thanking you' (see on 18:49). This is a frequent expression in the Psalter, and the majority of *OT* occurrences of the verb *hôḏāh* ('to thank') are found in the Psalms.

with an upright heart: usually the Psalmists are said to praise God with their 'whole heart' (see 9:1 (M.T. 2), 111:1, 138:1), i.e. sincerely, and it is probable that both expressions are synonymous. See on 7:10.

when I learn: i.e. as I go on learning (cf. verse 62). In the Psalmist's view this was not a 'do-it-yourself' exercise, but rather a recognition that it was God who was doing the teaching (see verse 73).

thy righteous ordinances: perhaps, 'your judgments which bring liberation' (or 'deliverance'; similarly also in verses 39 and 43). Ordinances (*mišpāṭîm*) can be described as '*ad hoc* decisions which are accumulated as legal precedents' (J. Gray, p. 97) for future guidance. They may also be defined as judgments given by a judge (*šōp̄ēṭ*), and not infrequently the emphasis is upon the precedent. It may denote the casuistic law (see A. Alt, *Essays on Old Testament History and Religion* (1966), p. 123, n.106) as well as the customs of the community. Sometimes the term may even suggest 'salvation, deliverance' (or 'salvation-history' (?); cf. verse 52), as in Isa. 42:1,4, where the word 'justice' seems too narrow (cf. Dt. 33:21; Isa. 30:18). Mowinckel and W. D. Davies take Isa. 42:1,4 in the sense of 'the true religion'. (Cf. W. D. Davies, *The Setting of the Sermon on the Mount* (1964), p. 134.) See on 36:6, and the detailed discussion in *TDNT*, III, pp. 923–33.

8. For verse 8*a*, see verse 5, for they are practically identical. There is probably no need to emend *ḥuḳḳêḵā* ('your statutes') into *ʾimrāṯeḵā* ('your word') (so Duhm, Schmidt), because it is not impossible that the author repeated the same term in one verse.

forsake me not utterly: although I am in difficulties do not let me continue in this affliction permanently (cf. 27:9, 71:9,18). The word 'utterly' (*ʿaḏ meʾōḏ*) should not be taken with verse 8*a* (so Gunkel, Oesterley), for the Psalmist writes against the background of troubles, and therefore his plea is not to be left to his own devices *for ever*.

Strophe Two **9–16**

9. The second strophe opens with a question and answer—a style reminiscent of Wisdom writings (see Prov. 23:29f.; Sir. 1:6f., 10:19, 22:14; cf. Ps. 25:12f., 34:12f. (M.T. 13f.), 107:43). Also the 'young man' (verse 9*a*) reminds us of the 'my son' of the sapiential literature.

keep his way pure: *PNT* has 'remain sinless', which may be more than is intended by the Psalmist; see Prov. 20:9: 'Who can say "I have made my heart clean; I am pure from sin"?'. Righteousness need not be identical with sinlessness, although it is possible that various authors may have had slightly different views on this subject (cf. Job 15:14; Ps. 73:13; 1QS ix:9; v. Rad, '"Righteousness" and "Life" in the Cultic Language of the Psalms', *PHOE*, pp. 243–66).

By guarding it: *RSV* supplies the accusative **it** which refers to **his way** (verse 9*a*). The versions regard **thy word** as the object of 'to guard', omitting the preposition *ke* ('according to'; cf. Prov. 7:1f.), which may be regarded as an emphatic particle (cf. *JAOS*, LXIII, pp. 176–8). Hence we may render verse 9*b* as: 'By keeping your word'. 'Word' (*dāḇār*) usually refers to an utterance of men or

God, or to the matter spoken about. It can also denote things and events as such (Gen. 15:1, 22:1), legal cases (Exod. 18:16), manner (Est. 1:13), one's cause (56:5 (M.T. 6)), etc. Very often, when the speaker is God, it is the 'dynamic, creative or destructive element that comes to the foreground' (so Procksch, quoted from Vriezen's *OOTT*, p. 94). In 119:9 the *dāḇār* is the divine word which proceeds from the mouth (or lips) of God (17:4, 33:6). Consequently this word or words may also signify divine commands (50:17); so the 'ten words' (Exod. 34:28) is the Decalogue, and the 'words of this law' (Dt. 17:19) may refer to the Deuteronomic code. *Dāḇār* may indicate not only a particular message of Yahweh (Isa. 2:1; Jer. 7:2), but also the sum total of his revealed will, as perhaps in Dt. 4:2; Prov. 30:6.

10. With . . . whole heart: i.e. with utmost sincerity. For 'heart', see on 27:3.

I seek thee: cf. 24:6.

let me not wander: the verb *š-g-h* is a rather strong expression; cf. Dt. 27:18: 'Cursed be he who misleads a blind man on the road' and Isa. 63:17: 'why dost thou make us err from thy ways . . .' (cf. also Mt. 6:13). Verse 10*b* might be understood from Prov. 19:27, which states that when a man ceases to obey instructions he begins 'to stray from the words of knowledge'. So 119:10 is a recognition of man's dependence upon God. For 'commandments', see verse 6.

11. I have laid up: i.e. I have treasured your word in my heart (see on 27:3) in order that it might determine my actions (cf. Prov. 7:1: 'keep my words and treasure up my commandments'). This is paralleled by Dt. 6:6, 30:14; Jer. 31:33. The 'word' in this verse is the Hebrew *ʾimrāh*, which is a poetical synonym of *dāḇār* (see verse 9). In Ps. 119 it often means the law of God in general, or his promises in particular (verse 140). The 'word of Yahweh' may also be a circumlocution for 'Yahweh' (see on 105:19).

sin against thee: i.e. fail you by disobeying your commands. So in Jer. 3:25: 'we have sinned against the Lord . . . we have not obeyed the voice of the Lord our God' (cf. Jer. 14:7,20, 16:10).

12. Blessed be thou belongs to the language of praise and thankfulness. See on 28:6.

teach me is an imperative which is rather unusual after an initial 'Blessed be . . .' which is generally followed by an explanation as to why God should be praised (as in 28:6, 31:21 (M.T. 22), 66:20, 68:19 (M.T. 20), etc.); consequently some scholars read, '(for) you teach me . . .' (*tᵉlammᵉḏēnî*) (cf. verse 171). For **statutes,** see verse 5.

13. I declare: the verb *s-p-r* can mean both 'to count' (22:17 (M.T. 18)) and 'to recount, declare'. It has been suggested that the divine commands may have been memorized by being counted as they were recited. *NEB* has 'I say them over, one by one'.

the ordinances of thy mouth: some Hebrew and Greek MSS. and S read: '. . . of your righteousness' (*ṣiḏḳeḵā* for M.T. *pîḵā*), i.e. 'your righteous ordinances', as in verse 7.

14. In the way of thy testimonies: see verse 2. Perhaps its meaning is: 'In a life which is governed by your commands'; *PNT* has: 'I rejoiced to do your will'. The law, as yet, has not been overlaid by trifling casuistry, the result of which was that it became a heavy burden for many (Mt. 23:4).

as much as: perhaps we should read with S 'more than in (all riches)'. This is supported by similar thoughts in verses 72 and 127 (cf. Prov. 3:13f., 8:10f., 16:16). In fact it is only when the will of God becomes more important than material values that one begins to understand the meaning of God and his fellowship (see Prov. 2:4f.). So it is a 'variant' on Mt. 6:33: 'But seek first his kingdom and his righteousness . . .'.

15. I will meditate probably refers to the reading or reciting of the precepts (see verse 4) in a low tone, as in 1:2, although the verbs are different. The verb *ś-y-ḥ* is also found in 1QH in the sense of talking (i:35), speaking (ix:7), and meditating (xi:5; cf. 11QPsᵃ xviii:14).

thy ways are the paths which God has chosen and made known to his people (cf. verse 6*b*).

16. I will delight: cf. verses 24, 47, and 70. For 'statutes', see verse 5. There is not enough justification to alter 'thy statutes' into 'thy law' (*bᵉṯôrāṯᵉḵā*), although the former term occurs in this strophe also in verse 12.

I will not forget: this involves not only one's memory but also a deliberate act of the will (cf. 13:1 (M.T. 2), 44:24 (M.T. 25), 74:19, 77:9). In the *OT* to forget God means much more than an inability to remember; it can be described as a guilty forgetfulness (cf. 106:13,21), or as being false to his Covenant (44:17 (M.T. 18)), and as turning to other gods (44:20 (M.T. 21)). Cf. 4Q166 ii:3f.: 'they forgot God. . . his commandments they cast behind them . . .' (cf. 78:7).

thy word: see verse 9.

Strophe Three **17–24**

17. Deal bountifully: probably 'deliver (your servant from his trouble)'; a similar usage is found in 13:6, 116:7, 142:7. 'Thy servant' is more than a poetic variation on the first person pronoun 'I'; in Deissler's view (op. cit., p. 109) it emphasizes the God-man relationship, and alludes to the Covenant concept. For **servant**, see on 36:1.

that I may live: this does not refer to eternal life, but to a full life among the Covenant people in the Land of promise (cf. verses 77, 116, 144, 175).

thy word: most versions read the plural 'words' (*d^e^ḇārêḵā*); see verse 9.

18. Open my eyes: lit. 'uncover . . .'. The Psalmist is asking for divine help. See Num. 22:31, 24:4,16.

wondrous things: just as the created world and the great salvation events reflect the glory and majesty of God, so also does the divine law (see on 9:1).

19. a sojourner on earth: in a sense the Israelites were aliens (*gērîm*) in Yahweh's land (Lev. 25:23), but in this verse the expression emphasizes the fact that man is but a *passing* guest in God's world (cf. 39:12f. (M.T. 13f.); 1QH iii:25, v:5).

commandments: see verse 6. The Psalmists usually beseech God not to hide his face from them (27:9, 69:17 (M.T. 18), 102:2 (M.T. 3), 143:7), but here the object is his commandments. Since the world and all that is in it belong to God, it is only right that the sojourner should learn the laws of Yahweh's world; on this knowledge depends his whole existence (cf. 2 Kg. 17:26f.).

20. My soul: i.e. 'I myself'; see on 33:19.

is consumed: this verb is found only here and in Lam. 3:16 (a causative form). The versions understood it as 'to long' while in Syriac the verb *g-r-s* means 'to be broken to pieces, be shattered' (so also in Aramaic) which may also be the meaning of the Hebrew verb; hence, 'I am (practically) shattered by (the intensity of my) longing'. The object of 'longing' is God's ordinances (see verse 7) which can mean here either a knowledge of the divine will, or God's help in the form of a judgment (see verse 21ff.). The former alternative is more likely in view of 'at all times' (cf. Prov. 17:17).

21. rebuke is not merely a verbal reproof but an effective action of Yahweh in judgment (see on 9:5).

the insolent (*zēḏîm*) are well described in this Psalm. They

deride the Psalmist (verse 51*a*) and tell lies about him (verses 69*a*, 78*a*); they oppress him (verse 122*b*) and try to ensnare him (verse 85*a*); see verse 51.
accursed ones are taken by *RSV* (following M.T. and T) as in apposition to 'the insolent', while the other versions (so also *NEB*) take it with verse 21*b*: 'cursed are those who . . .' (so Gunkel, Nötscher, Kraus, *et al.*). The term 'cursed' (*ʾārûr*) is more at home in the formulae of curses (cf. Dt. 27:15–26) than in the Psalter (where it is found only once out of some 61 occurrences of the verb in the *OT*). G. von Rad (*Deuteronomy*, p. 167) has argued that the word for 'cursed' (*ʾārûr*) 'denotes a curse coming from God'. Many of the crimes which are condemned are those done in secret and therefore the punishment must be left in the hands of God who alone sees those things that are hidden from the eyes of mortals (cf. W. Zimmerli, *The Law and the Prophets*, Eng. tr. by R. E. Clements (1965), p. 40).
who wander: the verb *š-g-h* may occasionally describe a sin of inadvertence (cf. Lev. 4:13; Num. 15:22), but the present context suggests a deliberate action, as in verse 118 and 1 Sam. 26:21. For **commandments**, see verse 6.

22. take away: the Hebrew *gal* comes from *g-l-h* ('uncover, remove'), or it could be regarded as a by-form of *gōl* from *g-l-l* ('to roll away'). The latter alternative receives some support from the ancient versions.
their scorn: the possessive pronoun 'their' is supplied from the context. 'Scorn' (*ḥerpāh*) usually denotes the taunts and reproaches of the enemies (71:13, 79:12, 89:50), or the humiliating situation itself (69:19, 78:66, etc.) which is also the cause of the enemy's scorn. It can also describe the sufferer himself as the object of reproach (22:6 (M.T. 7), 31:11 (M.T. 12), 39:8 (M.T. 9), 79:4, 89:41 (M.T. 42), etc.).
and contempt is omitted by S, and perhaps rightly so. For *bûz* ('contempt'), see on 123:3.

23. princes: S reads *rešāʿîm* ('the wicked') but M.T. is more likely (cf. verse 161). The Hebrew *śārîm* (cf. the Akkadian *šarru*, 'king') is one of the most popular words for 'rulers' or 'leaders', but it ought not to be confused with the 'sons of the King' (cf. Zeph. 1:8) although the latter might occupy an office designated by *śar*. The *śārîm* may be chieftains (Jg. 5:15), heads of families (Ezr. 8:29), elders (Job 29:9), or it may denote military officers (1 Kg. 9:22; 2 Kg. 1:14, etc.) and civil officials of the

King (1 Kg. 4:2; Ps. 105:22; Jer. 26:10, etc.). It is also used of heads or chiefs of particular classes (Gen. 40:2; 1 Chr. 15:22) or, perhaps, as a term of dignity in general (cf. Isa. 23:8; Ps. 45:16 (M.T. 17), 82:7). In verse 23 the word *śārîm* refers to the officials of the community, or its powerful representatives; *NEB* 'the powers that be'.

sit plotting against me: cf. Jer. 36:12. It is not impossible that the Psalmist saw his life reflected in the experiences of Jeremiah. The latter, too, found delight in the words of Yahweh (Jer. 15:16), although he had to bear the scorn and enmity of his fellow men (Jer. 37:15; see Deissler, op. cit., p. 116). Yet while the Psalmist's enemies scheme against him, he finds comfort and help in God's statutes (see verse 5).

24. testimonies: see verse 2. In this strophe it is found in verse 22 also, where some emend it to *piḳḳûḏêḵā* ('thy precepts').

my delight: the Hebrew word is *šaᶜᵃšûᶜîm*, which is comparatively rare in the *OT*; Prov. 8:30,31 may have influenced the usage of this term in our verse. Irrespective of circumstances, the will of God is the object of the Psalmist's delight.

my counsellors: LXX reads: 'your judgments are my counsellors', but two synonyms of 'law' in one verse are rather unexpected. For the Hebrew phrase, see Isa. 40:13, 46:11. The purpose of their counsel may be to frustrate the plotting of the enemies.

Strophe Four **25–32**

25. This verse continues the description of the Psalmist's plight mentioned in verses 21–3.

My soul: Deissler (op. cit., p. 118) takes it in the sense of 'neck' (as perhaps in 44:25 (M.T. 26)), or it may simply mean 'my life' (see on 33:19) which 'cleaves' to the dust (*ᶜāp̄ār*). 'Dust' may be a symbolic term for the underworld. *ᶜĀp̄ār* can be used in several senses; it may denote the dry, loose earth (2 Sam. 16:13), the substance of which our bodies are made (i.e. in popular speech) (Gen. 2:7; Ps. 103:14), or the place to which they return (104:29; Ec. 3:20). It may connote the whole earth (Job 19:25), or ground (Isa. 25:12, 26:5), and occasionally it stands for the netherworld (22:15,29 (M.T. 16,30), 44:25 (M.T. 26); Isa. 26:19), or the grave (Job 7:21; Ps. 30:9 (M.T. 10)). Cf. also Tromp, *PCD*, pp. 85ff.

revive me: or, 'restore me to a full life', undisturbed by the threats of enemies or other afflictions (see verses 40, 107, 154,

156). Sometimes this restoration is seen as synonymous with deliverance from Sheol (30:3 (M.T. 4), 71:20), i.e. from a very grave situation. It can also mean 'to spare one's life' (1 Kg. 20:31). Of some relevance may be Dt. 8:3, where it is pointed out that a man does not live by bread alone but by 'everything that proceeds out of the mouth of the LORD'.

26. my ways: or 'my troubles' (cf. 37:5) or 'my fate' (49:13 (M.T. 14), 139:3). This may be a reference to the past experience of the author. When he was in distress, he appealed to God (by means of a Psalm of lamentation or prayer) and Yahweh answered him by granting him the help needed. For similar expressions see 3:4 (M.T. 5), 18:41 (M.T. 42), 34:4 (M.T. 5), 118:5. Sometimes God's answer involves the punishment of the wicked, as in 1QH iv:18: '. . . you will answer them in judging them by your might'. *NEB* has 'all I have done'.

teach me: see verse 12. For 'statutes', see verse 5.

27. Make me understand: or 'Instruct me' (cf. 1QS iii:13, vi:15). Yahweh is the real teacher of law and Wisdom, for he is the ultimate source of them both (Isa. 40:14). For **precepts**, see verse 4, and on verse 27*b*; cf. verse 15*a*.

28. soul: see on 33:19. Here it may be a circumlocution for the pronoun 'I'. The word-picture created by the *nepeš* ('soul') melting away is that of weeping. The verb *dālap̱* ('to drip') is associated by some scholars with the Akkadian *dalāpu*, and given a similar meaning, namely, 'was restless' (cf. *KBL*, p. 211a; *NEB* has 'I cannot rest for . . .'; see also F. Horst, *Hiob* (*BK* 16_4, 1963), pp. 254f.).

sorrow: the Hebrew *tûḡāh* is found only here and in Prov. 10:1, 14:13, 17:21.

strengthen me: or 'establish me' is synonymous with verse 25*b*. 'Thy word' (see verse 9) is the divine promise to those who keep the law.

29. Put . . . far from me: or 'Keep . . . far from me' (so *NEB*; cf. Deissler, op. cit., p. 123). Similarly in Exod. 23:25: 'I will take sickness away from . . .' may mean: 'I will keep sickness away from . . . ' (cf. Dt. 7:15).

false ways are the opposite of 'the way of thy precepts' (verse 27*a*) and of 'the way of faithfulness' (verse 30*a*). Therefore LXX may be right in rendering 'the way of iniquity' (*hodon adikias*), and similarly S and V. 'Falsehood' (*šeḳer*) is that which is without a real basis and therefore everything characterized by it must collapse sooner or later. J. J. Stamm and M. E. Andrews (*The*

Ten Commandments in Recent Research (*SBT*, 2nd Ser. 2, 1967), p. 107) suggests that *šeḳer* means primarily 'lie', 'deceit', and that from here it comes to suggest 'that which is delusive', 'pointless' (cf. Klopfenstein, *LAT*, pp. 2–173).

graciously teach me thy law: or 'favour me with your law' (for a similar construction, see Gen. 33:5). For 'law', see verse 1.

30. the way of faithfulness: cf. verse 29*a*. This is the way God has instructed him to choose (25:12); it is a path that is reliable (see on 36:5).

I set thy ordinances before me: *RSV* has supplied 'before me' (so also *NEB*), following 16:8, and this is a possible interpretation. The verb *š-w-h* could be linked with the other root, meaning 'to be like, agree with', rendering 'I consent to your ordinances'. Cf. CD xv:14: 'though he had consented (agreed) to it (i.e. the law)'. On 'ordinances', see verse 7.

31. I cleave to thy testimonies: see verse 2. This phrase is reminiscent of Deuteronomy, where cleaving to God is usually associated with obeying his voice (Dt. 30:20), serving him (Dt. 10:20, 13:4), and walking in his ways (Dt. 11:22). The verb *dāḇaḳ* ('to cleave') may also suggest oneness. Just as a man 'cleaves to his wife and they become one flesh' (Gen. 2:24) so the will of the Psalmist becomes one with that of God. This being the case, he can pray: 'let me not be put to shame', i.e. 'let me not be abandoned by you' (cf. 25:2).

32. I will run: some scholars (e.g. Wellhausen) have emended it to: 'I take pleasure in' (*ʾerṣeh*), or have assumed that there was a verb *rûṣ* II, a by-form of *rāṣāh* ('to be pleased with') (so A. Sperber). Yet *RSV* gives a satisfactory sense: the Psalmist will run, or follow (cf. Prov. 4:11f.), the way of God's commandments (see verse 6).

thou enlargest my understanding: lit. 'you have enlarged my heart'. 'Heart' is often used as a seat of intellect (see on 27:3), and therefore it can be rendered as 'understanding, mind'. In 1 Kg. 4:29 (M.T. 5:9) 'breadth of heart' means 'great understanding' (cf. M. Noth, *Könige* (*BK* 9_2, 1965), p. 81) and a similar meaning is found in 119:32. In Isa. 60:5 a 'wide heart' means freedom from trouble and therefore happiness.

Strophe Five **33–40**

33. Teach me: Yahweh is regarded as the teacher of his people, and therefore Elihu rightly exclaims: 'who is a teacher like him?' (Job 36:22); some other relevant passages are Ps. 25:4,9, 27:11, 86:11. Yahweh can delegate the teaching office to others; e.g. it is said that the Levitical priests 'shall direct you; as I commanded them, so you shall be careful to do' (Dt. 24:8). For **statutes,** see verse 5.

to the end: this is a difficult phrase in M.T. and the versions, as well as commentators, differ in their interpretation of it. So Weiser reads 'as a reward' (similarly Gunkel, Kraus; cf. *NEB*; for this usage of *ᶜēḳeḇ*, see 19:11 (M.T. 12); Prov. 22:4); Oesterley suggests: 'in gratitude' (i.e. what is given to God in return) and Cohen renders it 'at every step'. *RSV* rcceives some support from verse 112 and T (LXX reads *dia pantos*), but the idea of a reward seems more likely. This usage is attested in the Psalter (19:11 (M.T. 12), and probably also by 40:15 (M.T. 16) and 70:3 (M.T. 4), where the word is found in a prepositional expression). The keeping of the law is a reward in itself, although it obviously brings other rewards with it (cf. verse 1). This thought is inherent in the very understanding of the Covenant.

34. Give me understanding: or, 'Teach me'. This seems to be a variation of verse 33. For **law,** see verse 1.

with my whole heart: i.e. 'with my utmost ability' (cf. verse 2).

35. Lead me . . .: this calls to mind Prov. 4:11–19. The 'path of thy commandments' (see verse 6) is the conduct characterized by obedience to the revealed divine will.

I delight in it: cf. 112:1. This is an attitude which is the opposite to that of the people described by Jer. 6:10: '. . . the word of the Lord is to them an object of scorn, they take no pleasure in it' (cf. Prov. 18:2).

36. Incline my heart . . .: this is a confession of man's utter dependence upon God (cf. 1 Kg. 8:58; Ps. 141:4). 'Heart' in this verse denotes not only the volitional aspect but the whole man (see on 27:3).

not to gain: *AV* '. . . covetousness', better, '. . . unjust gain' (cf. Isa. 33:15); *NEB* '. . . ill-gotten gains'.

37. my eyes: i.e. 'me' (cf. 13:3 (M.T. 4)).

vanities: the Hebrew *šāwᵓ* has two main shades of meaning. It can denote either what is materially unsubstantial (i.e. unreal, empty), or what is morally unsound (i.e. false, frivolous, insincere). Thus it can also connote idols (24:4 (?), 31:6; Jer. 18:15), whose essence is both unreal and false. It is possible that originally the term 'may well have signified magic' (v. Rad, *OTT*, 1, p. 183).

thy ways: so many MSS., as well as S and V, while some Hebrew MSS. and LXX read the singular: 'thy way' (cf. verse 3). The reference is to the way (or ways) of obedience to God, which is, at the same time, the path in which God leads his people. Those who walk in God's ways receive life abundant (30:3 (M.T. 4), 119:25). Dahood reads 'by your power, quicken me' and for such a use of *derek̲* ('way'), see *PAB*, I, p. 2. *NEB* reads 'by thy word' (*bid̲ebārek̲ā*).

38. thy promise: lit. 'your word' (see verse 11). For 'servant' (*ᶜeb̲ed̲*) see on 36:1; here it is a humble self-designation.

for those who fear thee: lit. 'which (is) for your fear', meaning either the promise given to those who fear God, or the assurance which encourages the fear of God. Dahood (*PAB*, I, p. 33) takes the abstract 'your fear' in a concrete sense (by reason of the parallel expression 'your servant'), as 'those who fear you' (similarly *NEB*) which may well be right.

39. the reproach must refer to the troubles of the Psalmist which he is already experiencing (see on verse 22), and which are the cause of the ridicule of his enemies. Kirkpatrick (*BPCB*, p. 711) takes 'reproach' as the scorn which the Psalmist 'has to bear for his loyalty to God's law' (cf. Isa. 51:7).

thy ordinances are good is a possible rendering, but the context possibly suggests that the ordinances (*mišpāṭîm*, see verse 7) may mean judgment upon the enemies of the writer. 'Good' would have the sense of 'fitting' or 'right', as in Mic. 6:8: 'He has showed you, O man, what is good (i.e. what is right)'.

40. I long for thy precepts: this seems to be a parallel to verse 39*b*. In the situation envisaged by the Psalm, the poet is waiting for divine help, and therefore 'precepts' (*pik̲ḳūd̲îm*, cf. verse 4) may refer not so much to divine commands as to divine acts of judgment which bring help to the afflicted. This is supported by verse 40*b* where 'righteousness' (*ṣed̲āḳāh*) may mean 'deliverance' (see on 33:5). Deissler (p. 139) suggests that in the Psalter the emphasis is usually more upon the helping righteousness of God than upon its legal aspect (cf. 22:31 (M.T. 32), 36:6 (M.T. 7), 40:10 (M.T. 11), 51:14 (M.T. 16), etc.). In the context of a Covenant relationship 'righteousness' may manifest itself either as a gracious help, or as a strict justice, depending upon the particular circumstances (cf. 71:24).

give me life: or '(by your gracious help) restore me' (see verse 25).

Strophe Six **41–8**

41. come to me: the verb is written as a defective plural, as is **thy steadfast love** (see on 26:3), while LXX has the singular forms. The plural of *ḥesed* ('steadfast love') may be used either for the sake of emphasis, or it denotes the numerous gracious deeds of Yahweh whereby the Covenant relationship is maintained.

thy salvation: i.e. your vindication or your deliverance of me (see on 35:3). The Hebrew word for salvation is *tᵉšûᶜāh*, which is identical in meaning with *yᵉšûᶜāh* (in verses 123, 166, 174). In the Psalter it is made clear more than once that all deliverance comes from Yahweh alone (37:39), and that it is not attained by means of human might (33:16f., 60:12 (M.T. 14), 108:13 (M.T. 14)).

42. an answer: this is not necessarily a reply to a question, but rather a refutation of the affirmation of the enemies. Those who taunted him may well have said (as in 3:2 (M.T. 3)): 'there is no help for him in God'; but Yahweh's intervention will provide the substance to his answer. As long as the faithful man was in trouble, he had to remain silent in face of the enemies' scorn.

I trust in thy word: or, 'I am confident that you are both able and willing to fulfil your promises' (26:1). For 'word', see verse 9.

43. take not: the verb is derived from *n-ṣ-l*, which in the causative form denotes 'to snatch away, deliver', rather than from *ʾ-ṣ-l* ('to take away') (so Perles). The exact meaning of this phrase may be 'do not withhold', for the reference is either to the forthcoming aid of Yahweh, or to the opportunity to give an account of the true facts which would include also the help of God. The 'word of truth' may be the record of God's faithfulness which cannot be declared in Sheol because its inhabitants are outside the Covenant relationship with God (cf. 30:9 (M.T. 10), 88:11 (M.T. 12)). But the Psalmist is still in the land of the living, and so he pleads with God not to deprive him of the privilege to praise God's faithfulness (or 'truth'); in other words, he begs for divine help.

utterly: the Hebrew *ᶜaḏmᵉʾōḏ* overloads the line and should probably be omitted, following S.

my hope: lit. 'I have hoped' (or 'waited') (cf. Isa. 51:5; Mic. 7:7). The object is God's ordinances (*mišpāṭîm*, see verse 7) and, in this case, they may be the righteous judgments of Yahweh, which will bring relief to the Psalmist.

44. To keep the law of God means to obey it. The opposite is described by Jer. 16:11, where it is said concerning the fathers that they 'have forsaken me and have not kept my law'.
for ever and ever: or, 'as long as I live'.

45. at liberty: lit. 'in a broad place' (see on 18:19). 'To give room to one who is in trouble' means: 'to deliver one from affliction' (4:1 (M.T. 2), 31:8 (M.T. 9), 118:5). Therefore 'to walk in a broad, roomy place' is a metaphor of a happy life which is free from the 'restrictive hand' of misfortune. Deissler (op. cit., p. 145) sees here an allusion to the life of blessing in the Promised Land, which is occasionally described as a 'good and broad land' (Exod. 3:8), or a 'large and rich land' (Neh. 9:35).

I have sought: the Hebrew *dāraš* usually means to seek Yahweh in order to worship him, or to obtain an oracle (see on 24:6). In late Hebrew the verb could be used of exposition, and this usage is reflected by the term 'Midrash' which is the rabbinic exegesis of the *OT*. Here the verb portrays the Psalmist as preoccupied with God's precepts (see verse 4). This would involve both their study and their application to life.

46. thy testimonies: see verse 2. The Psalmist affirms that he would speak of God's law even before kings (and this may be based on the command found in Dt. 6:7). The term **kings** is probably a poetical exaggeration for the sake of emphasis, and there is no need to speculate whether the allusion is to the Persian or the Syrian kings (cf. Davies, *Cent. BP*, II, p. 263).
shall not be put to shame: (cf. Isa. 49:23, 50:7) or 'I shall not be ashamed' (of your testimonies) (cf. Mt. 10:18ff.; Ac. 26:1ff.).

47. While others find their delight in material things, the Psalmist derives his satisfaction from obedience to God's commandments (see verse 6).
which I love: LXX adds *sphodra* ('exceedingly'). The Hebrew *ʾāhēḇ* ('to love') may denote both human and divine love. When *ʾāhēḇ* is used of man loving God, it has not only an emotional content, but it also suggests a love which is manifested in the doing of God's will as expressed in his law. Cf. Dt. 5:10, 7:9, 10:12f., etc. For a detailed discussion, see *TDNT*, I, pp. 21–35.

48. I revere . . .: lit. 'I lift up my hands (unto your commandments)' (see verse 6), which is an unusual phrase. It is often suggested (as against the versions) that 'your commands which I love' is a dittograph from the previous verse, and that

we should read instead 'unto you' (*ʾēlêḵā*), thus restoring the 3 + 2 metre prevailing in Ps. 119. This would avoid the repetition of two synonyms for law in the same verse. 'To lift up one's hands' is a gesture common in prayer (see on 28:2), as in Neh. 8:6; Ps. 63:4 (M.T. 5), 141:2. *NEB* omits 'which I love'.
meditate: see verse 15.

Strophe Seven **49–56**

49. Remember thy word: (so LXX and S). This is an echo of 105:8: 'He is mindful of his covenant . . . of the word that he commanded' (cf. 105:42). 'The word' in verse 49 is most likely a reference to God's promise to his servant (see on 36:1). Childs (*MTI*, p. 34) states that the 'essence of God's remembering lies in his acting toward someone because of a previous commitment'.
in which: or 'because' (*RV*).
made me hope: the causative meaning of the intensive form of *y-ḥ-l* ('to wait for') is unusual and therefore some scholars (e.g. Gunkel, Oesterley) read *yiḥāltî* ('I wait for (it)').

50. my comfort: this is the divine promise, or the divine word whose power can bring healing (107:20), and did bring forth the whole creation (Gen. 1). It has also the power to raise one above affliction and misfortune. It is difficult to define the actual nature of the distress, yet the Psalmist was not only scorned and taunted by his enemies (verses 22, 39, 42, 51, etc.), but his very life was in danger (verses 87, 109). Nevertheless, he recognized his tribulations as part of the divine discipline intended for his own good (verses 67, 71, 75).

51. Godless men are the *zēḏîm* (see verse 21). A good definition of them is provided by Prov. 21:24: ' "Scoffer" is the name of the proud, haughty man (i.e. *zēḏ*) who acts with arrogant pride'.
deride me: LXX omits the pronoun 'me', but M.T. is preferable. The reason for the derision must have been the Psalmist's faithfulness to God (cf. 44:17f. (M.T. 18f.)), even in times of adversity. But in spite of all this, he has not turned away from God's law (see verse 1). The word 'law' (*tôrāh*) occurs three times in this strophe (in verses 51, 53, 55), and it is possible that in two of these instances synonyms of 'law' must have been replaced by the word *tôrāh*.

52. When I think: lit. 'I have remembered'. This verse may reflect the same thought as 105:5: 'Remember the wonderful works that he has done, his miracles, and the judgments he uttered' (cf. 77:5 (M.T. 6), 106:7, 143:5). Childs (op. cit., p. 65) suggests that, for the Israelite, to remember 'is to grasp after, to meditate upon, indeed, to pray to God' (cf. 78:35).

thy ordinances: *mišpāṭîm* in this context may have more than merely a legal connotation. It is not improbable that they allude to the salvation-history of Israel, or to the saving judgments of God in the past, whereby the righteous have been delivered (cf. Kraus, *PBK*, p. 826).

I take comfort: or, 'I am comforted'.

53. Hot indignation: the Hebrew *zalʿāp̄āh* is a rare word (elsewhere in 11:6; Lam. 5:10); LXX renders it by *athumia* ('despondency'), while T has *reṭîṭāʾ* ('trembling'; cf. 1QH v:30 'horrors' (?)). The thought of verse 53*a* may be that the Psalmist is horrified by the disregard of the law by his fellow men, and this emphasizes his own reverential attitude to it.

the wicked: *rešāʿîm* is a characteristic designation of the enemies of the Psalmists (see on 28:3). They are men who are guilty before God, because of their neglect of the divine law and revelation (verse 53*b*).

54. my songs: *zemîrôṯ* is not a frequent term; it can also mean songs of praise (95:2; Isa. 24:16), the object of the homage being the statutes of God (see verse 5). The word occurs in Job 35:10, where Pope (*JAB*, pp. 228f.) renders it by 'strength' associating it with the Arabic *ḏmr* ('violent, mighty'). The same connotation may fit our verse also, if the etymology is right; hence 'Your statutes have been a (great) strength to me'.

the house of my pilgrimage is this earth. In verse 19 the author described himself as 'a sojourner on earth' (cf. 1QS vi:2; 1QH v:8).

55. I remember: see verse 52. This is a recognition of, and a turning to, God. The phrase 'thy name, O LORD' may stand for 'you, O Yahweh'. For various reasons the night was regarded as a fitting occasion to seek Yahweh's presence. Not infrequently it was a time of dread and anxiety (Job 24:14–17, 36:20). In later Judaism night was thought of as a time of demonic activity (cf. E. Langton, *Essentials of Demonology* (1949), pp. 47, 49). See verse 62.

thy law: see verse 1.

56. This blessing: M.T. has only 'This' (*zōʾṯ*); *RSV* is an interpretative rendering, following T which adds *zeḵûṯāʾ* ('blessing, reward'). The demonstrative 'this' refers, most likely, to verse 56*b*. *NEB* has 'This (is true of me)'.

Strophe Eight **57–64**

57. The LORD is my portion: this formula is found several times in the Psalter (16:5, 73:26, 142:5 (M.T. 6)) but some MSS. of LXX, and V take 'the LORD' as a vocative, in which case we might paraphrase: 'I call it my privileged lot, O Yahweh, to keep your words' (see verse 9). This rendering would avoid the change from the third person (verse 57*a*) to the second (in verse 57*b*), although the expression in Hebrew becomes rather clumsy. For the thought that Yahweh is his people's portion, see on 16:5 and 73:26. The special feature is that in the Psalter Yahweh is not only Israel's portion (cf. Jer. 10:16), but also the individual's. On the other hand, the people of Israel can occasionally be described as the portion of Yahweh, or his own immediate possession (Dt. 32:9).

58. I entreat thy favour: Mal. 1:9 provides a commentary on this phrase: 'And now entreat the favour of God, that he may be gracious to us.' There was, however, a difference; the worship of the people in Malachi's time was characterized by a grudging spirit bordering on disrespect, while the Psalmist served God with all his heart, i.e. whole-heartedly (cf. 27:3).
thy promise: or 'your word' (*ʾimrāṯeḵā*); see verse 11.

59. When I think of thy ways: (following LXX), M.T. has 'my ways', which may be the right reading (so also T, S, and V). In Prov. 16:9 it is *man* who plans his way, but the last word belongs to Yahweh. Similarly also our Psalmist plans *his* life, but he maps out his path in constant reference to the law of God, or his testimonies (see verse 2).
I turn: this is taken by Cohen (*PSon*, p. 402) in the sense of 'repented and returned', suggesting that the previous conduct of the Psalmist had been defective. This, of course, was true (verse 67), but it may not be the correct interpretation of verse 59.

60. With the same eagerness with which others hasten to do evil (Prov. 6:18), the Psalmist is quick to keep the commandments (see verse 6), for he realizes that the observance of the divine law is not a matter of formality but a question involving his very existence.

61. the cords of the wicked is a figurative description of the means used by the enemies as they prepare the downfall of the Psalmist. These adversaries are portrayed as hunters setting their snares to entrap their victim (cf. Job 36:8; Ps. 140:6 (M.T. 7)). A similar word-picture can be used of death (18:4,5 (M.T. 5, 6), 116:3), or of sin (Prov. 5:22). Although the wicked (see on 28:3) scheme against him, and God, for the time being, seems inactive, he neither questions Yahweh, nor forgets his law (see verse 1).

62. midnight, as well as night in general, was often regarded as the time of divine judgment (Job 27:19f., 34:20; Lk. 10:20; 1 Th. 5:2), and the classic example was the night of Passover in Egypt (Exod. 12) when 'At midnight the LORD smote all the first-born in the land of Egypt . . .' (Exod. 12:29). It is not impossible that our verse offers a conscious contrast: just as the Pharaoh and his servants rose that night to make a lamentation (Exod. 12:30), so the servant of God rises at midnight to praise God (see on 18:49). On the other hand, it is probable that prayers at night were simply part of the tradition irrespective of the original significance. In the Qumran community the members of the sect spent a third of every night reading and studying the law (1QS vi:8; see Leaney *RQM*, p. 185).

righteous ordinances: see verse 7.

63. a companion: *ḥāḇēr* was at a later time used of the members of the Pharisaic communities or associations (cf. Ch. Rabin, *Qumran Studies* (*Scripta Judaica* 2, 1957), p. 32), but it is unlikely that the Psalmist was alluding to any well-defined party. He had in mind all those who feared Yahweh (see on 34:7, 9) and who kept his precepts (see verse 4). This was a spiritual union rather than an organizational unity.

64. The earth is not simply the Promised Land but the whole world (33:5; Isa. 6:3).

thy steadfast love is usually an expression belonging to the Covenant terminology (see on 26:3), but here it embraces the whole 'universe', although not in the same manner as it surrounds Israel. In its universal application the relationship is not based upon a Covenant, but upon creation (cf. 136:1–9; Eichrodt, *TOT*, I, p. 239).

teach me: see verse 33*a*.

Strophe Nine **65–72**

65. Thou hast dealt well: this is an acknowledgment of Yahweh's faithfulness. Loyalty on the part of the servant (see on 36:1) is answered by blessings on the part of Yahweh (cf. Dt. 30:15f.), according to his word or promise (see verse 9).

66. good judgment: the word 'good' (*ṭûḇ*) is probably a dittograph from verse 65, and is often deleted. 'Judgment' (*ṭaᶜam*) can mean 'taste' (Exod. 16:31; Jer. 48:11), or it can be used figuratively of 'judgment, discernment' (34:1 (M.T. 2); Prov. 11:22) and even of 'decree' (Jon. 3:7).

knowledge can be a familiarity with persons, things, and facts as well as an awareness of the special relationships involved. Here it is not merely information, but also, if not more so, responsibility and it carries a religious overtone (cf. Hos. 4:1,6, 6:6). Vriezen (*OOTT*, p. 128) defines 'knowledge of God' as 'essentially a communion with God', and N. W. Porteous (*OTMS*, p. 343) describes it as an 'intimate response of man's whole being to God'. *Daᶜaṯ* ('knowledge') is frequent in the Dead Sea Scrolls (cf. Leaney, *RQM*, pp. 121f.).

I believe: or 'I trust'. A similar phrase, but in a negative sense, is found in 1QpHab ii:14: 'they shall not believe in the laws (*ḥuḳḳê*) of God'. See on 78:22.

67. Before I was afflicted: this makes clear the Psalmist's present situation. It is not certain whether this distress consisted only of the hostility of the adversaries, or whether the particular misfortune was the *cause* of the ridicule and enmity.

I went astray: the Hebrew verb and noun from *š-g-g* usually refer to unintentional sins, but in this case they may include deliberate sins, as perhaps in Job 12:16 (cf. verse 21 where we find *šāḡāh*, a synonym of *šāḡaḡ*).

68. Thou art good: (cf. 25:8, 34:8 (M.T. 9), 73:1). This hymnic praise of God is an account of the Psalmist's own experience. Yahweh is not only good, but he also does good; his goodness is a dynamic quality.

69. the godless: (*zēḏîm*), see on verse 21.

besmear me with lies: i.e. they blacken him with falsehood (see verse 29) (cf. Job 13:14, 14:17). The same idea is also expressed by verses 78 and 86; cf. 27:12, 31:18 (M.T. 19), 120:2.

with my whole heart: see verse 2. Some scholars (e.g. Oesterley) omit the phrase as a gloss which overloads the line.

70. their heart is gross: the verb *ṭāp̄aš* is a *hapax legomenon* in the *OT* (except, perhaps, for Job 33:25 where it may be found meaning 'to be plump'). The Targum on Isa. 6:10 reads: 'Make the heart of this people fat (*ṭpyš*) . . . lest they . . . understand with their heart'. A similar meaning may suit verse 70*a*: 'their heart is truly fat' (or '. . . fat with fat') and therefore they are insensible to God's law (see on 17:10). The Psalmist, on the contrary, delights in the will of God.

71. good . . . that I was afflicted: this is a striking affirmation of faith in the providence of God, in which even affliction is seen as a mark of divine favour, and as a fatherly correction (see Eichrodt, *TOT*, II, p. 177). A similar expression occurs in 94:12: 'Blessed is the man whom thou dost chasten, O LORD . . .' (cf. Job 5:17; Prov. 3:11f.). The Psalmist accepts his suffering as a divine education which spurs him on to learn more of God's statutes (see verse 5).

72. The law of thy mouth: i.e. *your* law (see verse 1). To the Psalmist, God's law is more precious than any amount of silver and gold (cf. verses 103, 127; Prov. 3:13f.). M.T. omits the monetary unit after the numeral **thousands** and probably we should assume the word 'shekels', or simply 'pieces', since the expression was intended to suggest a very large but indefinite amount; cf. *NEB*: 'a fortune in gold and silver'.

Strophe Ten **73–80**

73. Thy hands: i.e. you by your own power.
have made: the verb *ʿāśāh* is often used in the Psalter of divine creation e.g. of heavens (96:5), moon (104:19), heaven and earth (146:6), sea (95:5), and all that is in it (146:6); also of the creation of man (95:6, 100:3, 138:8).
fashioned me: or, 'established me' (as in Dt. 32:6).
give me understanding . . .: Kirkpatrick (*BPCB*, p. 716) comments: 'Thou has made my bodily frame, perfect my spirit.' It is not enough for man to be created by God, he must also be instructed by him.

74. shall see me: i.e. those who fear Yahweh (see on 34:7, 9), or the faithful shall share in the deliverance of the Psalmist (as in 107:41f.). In the Hebrew there may be a word play on 'those who fear' and 'shall see' (i.e. *yᵉrēʾêḵā* and *yirʾunî*). The salvation of the afflicted was linked with his trust in the word of Yahweh. *Dāḇār* (see on verse 9) is either the divine promise, or the dynamic word judging and healing (107:20, 147:15).

75. thy judgments are right: see verse 7. God's help and retribution are dispensed not arbitrarily, but justly (cf. verse 40).

in faithfulness: (see on 36:5) i.e. in faithfulness to the Covenant, or to his word in general, God must chastise the disobedient or the negligent, and bless the loyal servants (cf. 89:28–37 (M.T. 29–38)). In 2 Sam. 7:14f. Yahweh speaks concerning the son of David: 'I will be his father, and he shall be my son. When he commits iniquity, I will chasten him . . . but I will not take my steadfast love from him, as I took it from Saul . . .'.

thou hast afflicted me: the Psalmist acknowledges that his punishment has been just and deserved (cf. verses 67 and 71), for God does not capriciously afflict his people (Lam. 3:33). Dt. 8:16 summarizes the general *OT* attitude on this point: trials come upon the people 'that he (i.e. God) might humble you and test you, to do you good in the end'.

76. In his troubles, the poet appeals to God's steadfast love or his Covenant faithfulness (see on 26:3) to comfort him. The basis of his plea was probably a previous experience of the goodness of God (cf. 94:17ff.).

77. mercy is the compassion which Yahweh shows to those in distress (69:16f. (M.T. 17f.), 79:8), and in particular to those who fear him and are in a Covenant relationship with him (103:13, 106:45f.; Isa. 14:1, 30:18). In 'mercy' we see God in action, forgiving (51:1 (M.T. 3), 79:8), and delivering the oppressed. If God's mercy and steadfast love were withdrawn from the people, their life would come to an end sooner or later (Jer. 16:5f.).

that I may live: i.e. that I may not die an untimely death, but that I may enjoy life in all its fullness (see verse 25).

78. The prayer for the godless (see verse 21) to be put to shame is a well-known theme in the Psalms of Lamentation (6:10 (M.T. 11), 31:17 (M.T. 18), 35:4,26, 83:17 (M.T. 18), etc.). This is part of the law of life, rather than essentially an expression of a spirit of bitterness and malice. When the oppressed man is delivered, the schemes of his oppressors are naturally frustrated and so they are put to shame.

they have subverted me: i.e. they have perverted my cause, as in Lam. 3:36: '. . . to subvert a man in his cause, the LORD does not approve' (cf. Job 19:6).

with guile: or 'falsely' (see verse 29). For verse 78*b*, see verse 15*a*.

79. turn to me: the verb *šûḇ* may mean 'to return', implying that even the pious had been aloof from the Psalmist in his trouble because they might not have been sure about his guilt or innocence.

that they may know: follows the *Kᵉṯîḇ* and T, while the *Ḳᵉrê* (LXX and S) reads: 'that is to say, those who know' (similarly Weiser, Kraus, *PNT*, *RP*, *NEB*, *et al.*). If the suggestion about the verb 'to return' is right, then the *RSV* rendering may be preferable, and verse 79*b* would express the reason for their sudden interest in the Psalmist. When God reverses the fortunes of the afflicted, the worshipping community shares in the experience of his saving power.

80. A man whose heart is blameless in God's statutes (see verse 5) is one who reflects in his actions something of the very life of God (cf. 78:72*a*), and who does the will of God (1 Kg. 9:4). Such a man will not be forsaken by God or put to shame by him (see verse 6).

Strophe Eleven **81–8**

81. My soul languishes: i.e., 'I (see on 33:19) waste away waiting for your salvation or help' (see on 35:3). This salvation is not found in earthly powers (33:16f., 60:11 (M.T. 13), 108:12 (M.T. 13), 146:3) but in God alone (37:39, 62:2 (M.T. 3), 144:10; Isa. 45:17; Jer. 3:23).

I hope in thy word: or, 'I wait for your word (of power)' (see on 31:24). For parallels, see 69:3 (M.T. 4), 130:5f.

82. My eyes fail: (see on 13:3) may be a picturesque way of saying: 'I am worn out' (cf. Isa. 38:14; 1QH ix:5).

thy promise: lit. 'your word' (*ʾimrāṯᵉḵā*). Perhaps we should paraphrase it as 'the fulfilment of your promise'.

I ask: lit. 'saying' (*lēʾmōr*). This is often deleted as a gloss, restoring the prevailing 3 + 2 metre.

When wilt thou comfort me?: Yahweh is the comforter of his people (cf. Isa. 12:1, 49:13, 51:3,12, 52:9; Jer. 31:13; Zech. 1:17) and the Psalmists see him also as the consoler of the individual (71:21, 86:17, 119:76).

83. like a wineskin in the smoke: this simile does not refer to the mellowing of wine by placing the wineskins in the smoke, for in that case the result would be desirable. The allusion seems to be to the wineskins, which shrivel up in the smoke of the primitive house, becoming black and unsightly (cf. Job 30:30; Lam. 4:8). The Psalmist feels that his trials have had a similar effect upon him (see Kirkpatrick, *BPCB*, p. 718).

forgotten: see on verse 16.

84. How long: lit. 'How many are the days of . . .' (i.e. they are comparatively few in number, and therefore God must hasten the vindication of his servant (see on 36:1) before the latter passes away (cf. 39:5 (M.T. 6), 89:47 (M.T. 48)).

When wilt thou judge: or, '. . . execute justice (*mišpāṭ*)' (see verse 7).

85. godless men: see on verses 21 and 51. These are the men who do not conform to the divine law (see verse 1).

have dug pitfalls: cf. Jer. 18:22. The enemies are represented as hunters (see on 35:7, 57:6) who seek to entrap their innocent victims.

86. God's **commandments** (see on verse 6) are characterized by truth and reliability: they are a true expression of his nature, and the blessing or curse implicit in the commandments will be manifested in due time.

they persecute me . . .: i.e. the enemies afflict him for no reason at all (cf. verse 161).

help me: see verses 173 and 175. Yahweh is the helper of the fatherless (10:14), or of the afflicted in general (30:10 (M.T. 11), 37:40, 54:4 (M.T. 6)).

87. on earth: probably we should translate: '(They almost exterminated me) from the earth (or 'land')' (similarly *NEB*), taking the preposition *b*[e] in the sense of 'from', as in Ugaritic. Cf. Exod. 32:12; Dt. 28:21; 11QPs[a].

I have not forsaken thy precepts: see verse 4. This expression presents a contrast to the accusation of the fathers in Jer. 16:10, where Yahweh complains that they 'have forsaken me and have not kept my law', which means that they have forsaken his Covenant (Dt. 29:25; 1 Kg. 19:10).

88. steadfast love: see on 26:3; cf. Exod. 20:6; Dt. 5:10.

spare my life: or 'quicken me' (so Weiser); see on verse 25.

the testimonies of thy mouth: lit. 'the testimony of . . .', meaning perhaps the sum total of the divine law (cf. 19:7 (M.T. 8)). 'Thy mouth' is a roundabout expression for 'you' (i.e. 'your testimony'; *NEB* 'all thy instruction').

Strophe Twelve **89–96**

89. thy word: (*d*[e]*ḇār*[e]*ḵā*) is probably the expression of God's all-embracing purpose and will (cf. Isa. 40:8). At a later time it could also denote the written word (Dt. 4:2; 2 Chr. 34:21, 35:6; cf. van Imschoot, *ThOT*, 1, pp. 188-95).

is firmly fixed: Deissler (pp. 188f.) argues that the verb *n-ṣ-b* does not suggest any idea of firmness and that we should render it by 'stands'; but see *NEB* 'planted firm'. S reads: 'You, O Lord, are for ever, your word abides in the heavens'.

90. Thy faithfulness: see on 36:5. As an example of the divine reliability and loyalty, the Psalmist adduces the creation of the earth (cf. 89:2 (M.T. 3); Jer. 33:25f.) and his care for it.

established the earth: i.e. upon the waters of the cosmic ocean (24:2). See Eichrodt, *TOT*, II, pp. 94f.

it stands fast: or 'it lasts, endures' (cf. Isa. 48:13, 66:22).

91. By thy appointment: or, 'According to your ordinances' (similarly *AV*, *RV*); see on verse 7.

they stand: the subject of the verb is not expressed, and some have suggested: 'The day and the night' (so Ewald, Davies) or, more likely: 'Heaven and earth' (so Ibn Ezra, Kirkpatrick), which are mentioned in verses 89f. (cf. Isa. 48:13). *RP* (similarly *NEB*) reads: 'Surely thine ordinances stand firm this day', while LXX could be rendered: 'By your arrangement the day continues'.

all things are thy servants: or, 'all things serve you' (*ᶜᵃḇāḏûḵā*) (so *PNT*, following Jerome); similarly *NEB*.

92. The law (see verse 1) was the Psalmist's delight (cf. verse 24), i.e. he found joy in *doing* it. Had it not been so, he would have died in his affliction, for 'those who are far from thee shall perish' (73:27). The affliction may have been due both to his sin and to his enemies (see verse 50).

93. The Psalmist affirms that he will not forget (cf. verse 16) God's precepts (see verse 4) for in the obeying of them he finds his true life. God gives him life as a reward for his obedience, or it could be regarded as the natural consequence of loyalty to God.

94. I am thine (cf. verse 125) emphasizes the author's certainty that he belongs to God, which, at the same time, forms the basis for his appeal for help (cf. 143:12; Isa. 43:1, 44:5).

save me is an expression frequently found in the Psalms of Lamentation (see on 54:1).

thy precepts: this term also occurs in verse 93, and therefore many scholars read for it: 'thy statutes' (*ḥuḵḵêḵā*).

95. The wicked: see on 28:3. For 'lie in wait', see the parallel in 56:6 (M.T. 7).

to destroy me: cf. Ezek. 22:27. Deissler (op. cit., p. 195) suggests that the Psalmist may have had in mind the passage from Ezekiel.

I consider: or, 'I observe (thy testimonies)' (cf. Dhorme, *CJ*, p. 567a).

96. a limit: the Hebrew *ḳēṣ* is often regarded as an ancient gloss on 'perfection' (*tiḵlāh*, a *hapax legomenon*), in which case we could translate verse 96*a*: 'To everything I have seen an end'. **perfection:** the Hebrew *tiḵlāh* may be identical in meaning with *taḵlîṯ*, which is usually rendered by 'boundary, limit'. Both nouns come from *k-l-h* ('to be complete, finished'). The author contrasts the limitations of all earthly things with the unlimited (or 'exceedingly broad') nature of the divine word (or 'commandment', *miṣwāh*).

Strophe Thirteen **97–104**

97. I love thy law: as in verses 113 and 163; see on verse 47.
my meditation: i.e. the law of God is the object of my study.

98. Thy commandment makes me wiser . . .: lit. 'Your commandments . . .' (*miṣwōṯeḵā*; see on verse 6); the verb is, however, singular (cf. *GK* 145k). LXX reads: 'You have made me wiser . . . (in) your commandment'. A reasonable parallel is found in 19:7: 'the testimony of the LORD is sure, making wise the simple' (cf. Dt. 4:6).
for it is ever with me: or 'for it belongs to me for ever' (cf. verse 111*a*).

99. The Psalmist may not boast of his personal intellectual attainments but he may contrast the two sources of practical wisdom: namely, the instruction derived from Wisdom teachers in general, and that gained from the law of God. Jeremiah (9:23f.) provides a good commentary on our passage: 'Thus says the LORD: "Let not the wise man glory in his wisdom . . . but let him who glories glory in this, that he understands and knows me . . ."'

100. According to the Psalmist, true wisdom does not necessarily depend upon a life-long experience but rather upon obedience to God's **precepts** (see verse 4). The background of this thought is the dictum: 'The fear of the LORD is the beginning of knowledge' (Prov. 1:7; cf. Job 28:28).

101. every evil way: Hebrew *ʾōraḥ* is a favourite term of the Wisdom writers. It can be used of 'the path of the righteous' (e.g. Prov. 4:18) as well as of 'the path of the wicked' (Prov. 4:14), or 'the path of life' (Prov. 5:6). 'The evil path' is the way of life of the godless who 'rejoice in doing evil and delight in the perverseness of evil' (Prov. 2:14).

to keep thy word: see on verse 9.

102. I do not turn aside . . .: this is regarded as a typical Deuteronomic expression (Dt. 9:16, 17:11,20, 28:14, etc.). To turn aside from God's ordinances means to neglect and to disobey them (Mal. 3:7).

thou hast taught me: Yahweh and no one else is the true teacher of his people (see verse 33), and therefore one cannot go astray as long as one is willing to be taught by him. Davies (*Cent. BP*, II, p. 273) remarks that the 'Divine word is its own interpreter'.

103. thy words: so LXX and some Hebrew MSS. *PNT* (similarly *NEB*), following M.T., reads: 'your promise' (Kissane 'thy word'). The Psalmist likens the divine instruction to the sweetest thing imaginable—namely, to honey; in other words, the law of God is more enjoyable than the most delicious food (cf. 19:10 (M.T. 11); Prov. 16:24; Ezek. 3:3).

honey (*d^e^ḇaš*) is usually the honey of wild or 'domesticated' bees (2 Chr. 31:5), but it may also denote grape syrup (cf. the Arabic *dibs*) which was used for sweetening purposes (so perhaps in Gen. 43:11; Ezek. 27:17).

104. The Psalmist's understanding comes from the divine precepts (see on verse 4), and he re-echoes 94:12: 'Blessed is the man . . . whom thou dost teach out of thy law' (cf. also verses 99f.).

I hate every false way: this is the result of his understanding of the divine purposes manifested in the law, for 'the fear of the LORD is hatred of evil' (Prov. 8:13). Every path that leads away from God is a 'false way' (see on verse 29), and therefore the Psalmist hates, or shrinks from, evil. For the concept of hatred in the Dead Sea Scrolls, see *Revue de Qumrân*, II (1959–60), pp. 345–56.

Strophe Fourteen **105–112**

105. Thy word: see on verse 9. The divine word or law is a lamp (cf. Prov. 6:23) to the Psalmist's feet (i.e. to the writer himself), shedding light (that is, blessing and happiness) into his life (cf. 18:28 (M.T. 29), 97:11, 112:4; Jn 8:12). *RSV*, in reading **my feet,** follows LXX and S, while M.T. has 'my foot'. For 'my path' (=M.T.) LXX and S have 'my paths' (*n^e^ṯîḇōṯāy*).

106. I have sworn an oath: some scholars have thought that the reference is to a cultic oath, on the occasion of the entry into the Temple (cf. J. Horst, 'Der Eid im Alten Testament', *Evangelische Theologie*, XVII (1957), p. 371).
and confirmed it: this and the preceding verb may be co-ordinated: 'I have undertaken a solemn oath' (cf. *GK* 120e). Perhaps the Hebrew *waʾaḳayyēmāh* could be rendered: 'and I have promised' (cf. 1QS v:8,10; Deissler, p. 205); *RP* has '. . . am steadfastly purposed'.
thy righteous ordinances: (see on verse 7; cf. 1QS iii:1, iv:4; 1QH i:23,26). These ordinances are not arbitrary, but they are an expression of what is right.

107. I am sorely afflicted: i.e. any distress brings a man near to Sheol, and his life is greatly weakened. Therefore the writer asks God to revive him, to give him life (see on verse 25*b*).

108. Accept: or, 'Be pleased' (cf. 19:14 (M.T. 15)). The verb *r-ṣ-h* can be used as a technical term for accepting one's sacrifice (Lev. 7:18, 19:7, 22:25, etc.).
my offerings of praise: lit. 'the freewill offerings of my mouth' which suggest prayers of praise and thanksgiving (cf. 50:14, 51:17 (M.T. 19); Heb. 13:15).

109. I hold my life in my hand: i.e. I risk my life (cf. Jg. 12:3; 1 Sam. 19:5, 28:21). LXX and S read: 'My life (i.e. 'soul') is in your hands', which is reminiscent of Job 12:10: 'In his hand is the life of every living thing . . .'. The context, however, supports the *RSV* rendering; although the Psalmist is in constant danger (cf. verse 61), he does not neglect God's law (see verse 1).

110. The wicked: see on 28:3. They are depicted as hunters laying snares for their victims. This and similar metaphors are quite frequent in the Psalms of Lamentation (cf. 9:15 (M.T. 16), 35:7, 38:12 (M.T. 13), etc.), as well as in the Prophetic literature (cf. Isa. 8:14, 24:17; Jer. 18:22; Hos. 9:8; Am. 3:5, etc.).
a snare: *paḥ* is primarily a bird-trap or a snare of the fowler, composed of a base and two nets which could spring up and trap the victim (cf. *ANEP*, pl. 189). Cf. Am. 3:5: 'Does a snare spring from the ground, when it has taken nothing (i.e. when it has not been triggered off)'.
I do not stray: cf. 58:3 (M.T. 4), 95:10. In Prov. 21:16 we find a warning that 'A man who wanders from the way of understanding will rest in the assembly of the dead' (i.e. he will die prematurely). For the verb *t-ʿ-h* ('to err'), see on 107:4.

111. my heritage for ever: lit. 'I have taken as my inheritance' (cf. Exod. 32:13). The verb *n-ḥ-l* ('to inherit') and the noun *naḥ^a^lāh* ('inheritance') belong to the Covenant phraseology, although not exclusively. In this verse, the heritage or special possession is not the Promised Land, but the testimonies of God (see verse 2).

the joy of my heart: cf. 15:16: 'thy words became to me a joy and the delight of my heart'. For 'heart', see on 27:3.

112. I incline my heart: i.e. I have determined to obey your statutes (see on verse 5). The heart (cf. 27:3), as the centre of the will, can determine one's actions: it can turn one away from the Lord (1 Kg. 11:9), or it can incline or be directed 'to the Lord' (Jos. 24:23).

to perform thy statutes: this and similar constructions reflect the parallel thought found in Deuteronomy (cf. Dt. 26:16, 30:14).

for ever, to the end: or 'lasting (is) the reward' (cf. *NEB*); for this use of *ᶜēḳeḇ* ('end, reward'), see on 19:11 (cf. 119:33). In Prov. 22:4 the reward (*ᶜēḳeḇ*) for humility and the fear of the Lord is riches and honour and life.

Strophe Fifteen **113–120**

113. double-minded men: the Hebrew *sēᶜ^a^pîm* is a *hapax legomenon* in the *OT*, and there are a number of possible interpretations, although the general idea is clear. LXX has *paranomoi* ('transgressors'), and similarly S and V. T reads: 'people who think vain thoughts'. Some more recent suggestions are: 'high-sounding ideas' (Leslie), 'half-hearted men' (*PNT*), 'the fickle' (Nötscher, Kraus).

I love thy law: see on verses 1 and 47.

114. my hiding place: the Hebrew *sēṯer* is the favourite term of the Psalmists (as in 27:5, 31:20 (M.T. 21), 32:7, 61:4 (M.T. 5), 91:1). The idea may have originated in the ancient belief and practice that the sanctuary offered a right of asylum (cf. de Vaux, *AI*, p. 276).

my shield: see on 3:3. Yahweh as the shield (*māḡēn*) of his people is a frequent metaphor in the Psalter (cf. 28:7, 33:20, 84:11 (M.T. 12), 115:9, etc.), and it may have been an ancient description of God (cf. Gen. 15:1; Dt. 33:29).

I hope: see on verse 81*b*.

115. Depart from me: cf. 6:8 (M.T. 9), 139:19.

the commandments of my God: see on verse 6. Of some

interest is the stylistic change from the second to the third person, when speaking of God.

116. Uphold me: the verb *s-m-k* is often used of divine help in general (3:5 (M.T. 6), 37:17, 54:4 (M.T. 6), 145:14, etc.) which brings deliverance and blessing.

according to thy promise: see verse 11.

that I may live: i.e. 'that my life may be renewed' (see on 40:2).

put to shame: see verse 6; or 'let me not be disappointed in my hope'. The Hebrew *śēḇer* ('hope') is found elsewhere only in 146:5; also the corresponding verb is rare in biblical Hebrew, but frequent in Aramaic.

117. Hold me up: the Hebrew *sāʿaḏ* is yet another verb which can describe the divine help (cf. 20:2 (M.T. 3), 41:3 (M.T. 4), 94:18).

be safe: or 'be saved' (Cohen); see verse 94.

have regard for: cf. Isa. 17:7: 'In that day men will regard their Maker', and not idols! Some of the ancient versions (LXX, S (?), T (?)) may have read the verb *š-ʿ-ʿ* ('to delight in'), but there is no need for emendation.

118. Thou dost spurn: or, 'You have rejected'. The verb *s-l-h* is probably an Aramaism.

go astray: deliberately (see verses 10 and 21).

their cunning: *RSV* follows the reading suggested by LXX, S, and Jerome: *tarʿîṯām* ('their planning, cunning'); this noun is often found in Aramaic. M.T. has 'their deceit' (*tarmîṯām*), so also 11QPs[a].

119. the wicked of the earth: Gunkel (*PGHAT*, p. 530) is of the opinion that the reference is to the Jews and not to foreigners. See on 28:3.

thou dost count: (*ḥiššaḇtā*) this follows some Hebrew MSS., Aquila, Sym, and Jerome; LXX has 'I reckon' which suggests the Hebrew *ḥiššaḇtī* (=11QPs[a]), while M.T. has *hišbattā* ('you cause to cease'). The *RSV* rendering seems to be more suitable in the present context.

dross: in its literal sense, the word is a technical metallurgical term (cf. H. Wildberger, *Jesaja* (*BK* 10_1, 1965), p. 60). 'Dross' refers to the refuse produced in the process of smelting, and consequently it could be used as a symbol of all that is worthless (cf. Isa. 1:22; Jer. 6:29f.; Ezek. 22:18,19); *NEB* has 'scum'.

120. My flesh: see on 38:3.

trembles: or 'shudders' (the reference may be to goose-flesh; cf. Dhorme, *CJ*, p. 51a). A similar expression is found in Job 4:15*b*.
for fear of thee: i.e., for fear of God's judgment (see verse 7). Although the Psalmist has been zealous to keep the law, he is also aware of his failures in God's sight (cf. verse 176).
I am afraid: the Hebrew *yārē'* denotes, in this verse, a psychological state. For other uses of this verb, see on 25:12.

Strophe Sixteen **121–8**

121. I have done: 6 MSS. read 'You have done'; but M.T. is supported by the ancient versions, and is possible in itself.
what is just and right: these are the qualities which God loves (see on 33:5), and they are the very foundation of God's throne or rule (see on 89:14).
my oppressors: cf. 72:4, 105:14; Jer. 21:12. In Prov. 14:31 it is said that the 'oppressor of the weak insults his Maker'.

122. Be surety: in legal terminology this would mean that a person is held legally responsible for the debt of another man (see Gen. 43:9, 44:9; Prov. 6:1, 11:15, 17:18, 20:16, etc.). In this verse the expression means: 'Be my protector and helper'.
the godless: see verses 21 and 51.

123. my eyes fail: similarly in verse 82.
thy salvation: or 'your help' (see on 35:3).
for the fulfilment of thy righteous promises: lit. 'for the word of your righteousness', of which *RSV* is probably a correct interpretation. The 'word' (*'imrāh*) is the dynamic word of God which accomplishes the righteous divine purpose underlying it (Isa. 55:11).

124. steadfast love: see on 26:3. God's Covenant loyalty will find expression in assisting the oppressed (cf. 109:21).
statutes: see verse 5. This phrase in verse 124*b* is also found in verses 12, 26, and 68.

125. I am thy servant: cf. 36:1 (M.T. 2). The term 'servant' (see on 36:1) may suggest, not only the writer's dependence upon God, but also the more personal relationship based on a Covenant.
that I may know: this may be an expression of one's willingness to accept the claims of God as they are made known in the law (cf. H. B. Huffmon, 'The Treaty Background of Hebrew *YADA'*', *BASOR*, 181 (1966), p. 37).

126. . . . time for the LORD to act: it is possible to take the preposition *l^e^* (*RSV* 'for') as a particle indicating the vocative

(see on 75:9), rendering: 'It is time, O LORD, to act'. The intervention of Yahweh would be manifested in administering justice by saving the oppressed and punishing the wicked (cf. Jer. 18:23). Such a prayer for divine help is a frequent motif in the Psalms of Lamentation (cf. 3:7 (M.T. 8), 7:6 (M.T. 7), 17:13, 35:1f.).
thy law has been broken: in the Prophetic literature the same thought could be expressed by the phrase: 'So-and-So has broken my Covenant' (cf. Isa. 24:5, 33:8; Jer. 11:10, 31:32, etc.).

127. Therefore . . .: this may imply that the more God's laws are broken, the more the Psalmist loves them (so Kirkpatrick), but many scholars suggest, following Duhm, a slight emendation: 'Above all' (*ᶜal kōl*) for 'Therefore' (*ᶜal kēn*); *NEB* has 'Truly'.
I love thy commandments: see verse 47 and Prov. 8:17.
above fine gold: the idea that wisdom is superior to gold and silver is quite a common concept in the Sapiential literature (cf. Job 22:25, 28:15f.; Prov. 3:14, 8:10,19, 16:16, etc.). Here the comparison is between the commandments of God and gold. 'Fine gold' (*paz*) is one of the several words used to denote gold in the *OT*, and the main difference between the various types of gold was probably in the degree of purity.

128. The first part of this verse may contain some textual corruption which is borne out by the different readings suggested by the ancient versions (see Deissler, p. 225f.). The word 'Therefore' at the beginning of the line may be a vertical dittograph from the previous verse, and the rest could be translated: 'All your precepts I indeed find agreeable' (*kol piḳḳûḏêḵā lᵉyāšartî*), taking the preposition *lᵉ* as an emphatic particle (see on 89:18).
I hate: see the parallel in verse 104*b*.

Strophe Seventeen **129–36**

129. God's **testimonies** (see verse 2) are works of wonder (cf. 77:14 (M.T. 15), 78:12, 88:10 (M.T. 11)), or they bring about wonderful results (see verse 18). 'Wonders' (*pᵉlāʾôṯ*) may refer to God's revelation both in word and deed; see on 77:11.
my soul: i.e. 'I' (see on 33:19).

130. The unfolding: probably 'revelation, manifestation' (so LXX; cf. *NEB*), while Sym and Jerome suggest 'gate' (*peṯaḥ* for M.T. *pēṯaḥ*); cf. 1QM xi:9.
gives light: see verse 105.
to the simple: perhaps '(even) to the simple' (see on 19:7). The term *peṯî* is often used to denote a person who is apt to believe

every word (Prov. 14:15), or who is a simpleton (Prov. 1:22, 14:18, etc.). In 116:6 it has a more positive connotation (cf. also 1QpHab xii:4: 'the simple ones of Judah who keep the law').

131. . . . I pant: see Job 29:23, where men wait for the counsel of Job, opening 'their mouths as for the spring rain'. With a similar eagerness the Psalmist pants for God's commandments (see verse 6).

I long: Hebrew *y-ʾ-b* is a *hapax legomenon* in the *OT*; it may be an Aramaism.

132. Turn to me: see on 25:16. The same phrase occurs in 86:16.

as is thy wont: lit. 'according to what is just' (cf. Exod. 21:31; Heb. 6:10).

those who love thy name: see on 5:11.

133. Keep steady my steps: i.e. direct me.

according to thy promise: (see on verse 11) *RSV* follows the reading of LXX, while M.T. has 'by your law' (cf. Job 31:7; Ps. 17:5; Prov. 1:15, 4:26). M.T. is more likely, and a similar thought is found in verse 35: 'Lead me in the path of thy commandments'.

iniquity: see on 36:4. Kirkpatrick (*BPCB*, p. 726) took it as 'a comprehensive term for sin as moral worthlessness or antagonism to God'.

get dominion over me: it is possible that the Psalmist was not thinking of his own possible disobedience, but rather of the mischief caused by his opponents. This may be supported by the following verse.

134. Redeem me: the Hebrew *p-d-h* can denote the redemption of a slave or captive (cf. Exod. 21:8), as well as the ransom of a person (or an animal) from death, either by a substitute or by the payment of money (cf. Exod. 13:13,15; Num. 18:15f.). It can also be used figuratively to describe deliverance from any sort of trouble or from death (cf. 26:11, 78:42; J. J. Stamm, *Erlösen und Vergeben im Alten Testament* (1940), pp. 7–33).

135. The first part of this verse is reminiscent of the Priestly blessing (Num. 6:25), and it has many parallels in the Psalter (see on 31:16; cf. Eichrodt, *TOT*, II, pp. 36f.).

teach me . . .: see on verse 33 (cf. verses 12, 26, 64, 68).

136. streams of tears: the Hebrew *peleḡ* means 'channel' or 'irrigation canal', but it can be used metaphorically of tears, as in this verse (cf. Lam. 3:48).

because: the preposition *ʿal* is apparently used for *ʿal ʾašer*, or it has the force of a conjunction (cf. *BDB*, p. 758a). The Psalmist is grieved at his contemporaries' disregard for God's law (see verse 1), because ultimately they are dishonouring God himself.

Strophe Eighteen **137–44**

137. Righteous art thou: see on 1:5. Righteousness is one of God's fundamental attributes, and it can express itself in the rewarding of the faithful and in the punishing of the wicked (cf. Neh. 9:33; Ps. 11:6f.). It can also be seen in the help given to the needy and oppressed (116:5f., 145:17f.). In a legal sense it means that God is beyond reproach, and that no accusation can be brought against him (Jer. 12:1; cf. also Job 34:10–30; 1QH xiv:15).

thy judgments: (see on verse 7) LXX and Jerome have the singular 'your judgment' (*mišpāṭeḵā*), which agrees with the singular 'right' (*yāšār*). The term probably refers to the divine law rather than to judgment as such.

138. The divine testimonies (see verse 2) are a summary of the will of Yahweh, and they are distinguished by righteousness and faithfulness. This contrasts with those authorities who issue iniquitous decrees (cf. Isa. 10:1; Jer. 8:8).

139. A similar idea is also found in verse 53 and 69:9 (M.T. 10). 'My zeal' (*ḳin'āṯî*) denotes an enthusiastic, exclusive devotion (1 Kg. 19:14) which at times may border on fanaticism, as in the case of Jehu (2 Kg. 10:16f.). The same noun (*ḳin'āh*) can also describe Yahweh's zeal, or his exclusive character (see van Imschoot, *ThOT*, 1, pp. 81f.). In some texts *ḳin'āh* has become a synonym of 'anger' (e.g. in 79:5; Isa. 42:13, 59:17; cf. Ps. 78:58). The Psalmist is consumed with the desire to maintain the honour of God and of his words (see verse 9).

my foes: the Hebrew *ṣar* is a frequent term in the Psalter, to denote the enemies of the Psalmists (see on 28:3, 107:2).

140. The promise of God (see verse 11), or his law, is well-tried and true; it is like a refined precious metal without any dross and impurity (cf. 12:6 (M.T. 7), 18:30 (M.T. 31) (=2 Sam. 22:31)).

thy servant: see on 36:1.

141. I am small: the Hebrew *ṣā'îr* ('small, insignificant') may be a sort of proverbial expression describing a person chosen in spite of his insignificance (cf. Jg. 6:15; 1 Sam. 9:21; Ps. 68:27 (M.T. 28); Isa. 60:22; Mic. 5:2).

despised: the Psalmist may have had in mind 22:7 (M.T. 8) and Isa. 53:3, which depict the sufferer as despised by others. In a small way he is a reflection of the suffering servant of the Lord.

142. Thy righteousness: see on 33:5. This is the saving and sustaining activity of God (cf. Isa. 51:6,8) within the Covenant context (see verse 40).

143. The author resumes the theme of verse 141, affirming that, although troubles have befallen him, God's commandments (see verse 6) still remain the source of his joy.

144. This verse is a partial repetition of verses 116, 138, and 142. The testimonies of God (see verse 2) are not only right, but they are also of a lasting significance (Mt. 5:17f.); and in them is found the life-giving wisdom, the author of which is God (cf. Prov. 4:4,13).

Strophe Nineteen **145–52**

145. With my whole heart: i.e. with all my being.
I cry: this is a common expression in the Lamentations of the Individual (cf. 17:6, 31:17 (M.T. 18), 88:9 (M.T. 10), etc.).
answer me: (see verse 26; cf. 1 Kg. 18:37) by helping me or by delivering me (cf. verse 146).

146. This verse is a repetition of the thought of verse 145. For **save me**, see verse 94, and for **observe**, see verse 44.

147. I rise before dawn: the early morning was a recognized time for prayer; so in Wis. 16:28: 'one must rise before the sun to give thee thanks and must pray to thee at the dawning of the light.'
cry for help: this expression is often found in the Psalter (cf. 22:24 (M.T. 25), 28:2).
I hope: see verse 81.

148. the watches of the night: the night was divided into several watches (Jg. 7:19; 1 Sam. 11:11; Ps. 90:4; Lam. 2:19); in the later Jewish system there were three such nightly divisions; it is possible that their origin goes back to much earlier times (cf. Jg. 7:19). The Psalmist's devotion to God's law (*RSV* **thy promise**) is so great that he uses even the hours (i.e. certain periods) of the night to meditate upon, or to study, the divine law or word (*ʾimrāh*; see verse 11). For similar ideas, see 63:6 (M.T. 7), 119:62.

149. in thy steadfast love: so some Hebrew MSS.; M.T. reads '*according to* your Covenant loyalty' (see on 26:3).

in thy justice: (similarly S); M.T. has 'according to thy judgments' (so *RV*), which may suggest the many precedents of God's gracious help; Cohen renders: 'as Thou art wont' (*PSon*, p. 413).

150. who persecute me . . .: so LXX, Sym, and S; M.T. could be rendered: '(my) mischievous persecutors', who may well have plotted for his life (cf. verses 87, 95, 109). The reason for their hostility is not to be found in the Psalmist himself, but primarily in the godlessness of the enemies who are far from God's law (see verse 1).

151. But thou art near: this contrasts with the drawing near of the enemies (verse 150), and it gives comfort to the afflicted man, for the nearness of *God* means deliverance and protection (cf. 69:18 (M.T. 19), 73:28; Isa. 50:8).

thy commandments: LXX suggests 'your ways'.

152. Long have I known: rather than 'Of old . . .' (*RV*). The poet affirms his conviction that the testimonies of God (see verse 2) are eternally valid, and that no vicissitudes of life can call in question the faithfulness of the divine lawgiver (cf. 111:7f.).

Strophe Twenty **153–60**

153. Look on my affliction: this is a well-known prayerful appeal to God in the Psalms of Lamentation (9:13 (M.T. 14), 25:18, 31:18 (M.T. 19), etc.). A similar expression also occurs in Exod. 3:7f., where Yahweh, before his intervention in Egypt, says: 'I have seen the affliction of my people . . . and I have come down to deliver them.'

154. Plead my cause: so also in 43:1. For the Hebrew verb *r-y-b* and its cognate accusative, see B. Gemser, 'The *Rîb*—or Controversy—Pattern in Hebrew Mentality', *Wisdom in Israel and in the Ancient Near East* (*SVT*, 3, 1955), pp. 120–37.

redeem me: the Hebrew *g-ʾ-l* usually refers to the redemption of what is one's own. According to A. R. Johnson ('The Primary Meaning of *GʾL*' (*SVT*, 1, 1953), pp. 67ff.) the original meaning of the verb is 'to protect'. In the *OT* usage of *g-ʾ-l*, the emphasis is generally upon the restoration of the original relationship, and so one who performs this function is the restorer, kinsman, or redeemer (*gōʾēl*). Vriezen (*OOTT*, p. 273, n.1) argues, however, that in the religious sense *gōʾēl* is a protector rather than a redeemer. In the Psalter the verb is usually used in a figurative sense, denoting deliverance from trouble and afflictions. The object of the verb may be both the nation and the individual.

give me life: see verse 25*b*.

155. The first part of the verse is a negative expression of the positive statement in 85:9: 'Surely his salvation is at hand for those who fear him'.

Salvation: see on 35:3.

they do not seek: i.e. they do not apply God's law to practical life.

156. Great is thy mercy: cf. 2 Sam. 24:14; Neh. 9:19, 27:31. God's mercy is not a sentiment, but a concrete manifestation of pity to the weak and afflicted (69:16 (M.T. 17), 103:13, 106:46; Isa. 14:1, 30:18, etc.).

give me life: see verse 25.

157. Although the Psalmist's enemies are countless, he has not swerved from God's will (verse 2).

158. the faithless: they are men who act treacherously (cf. 25:3; Isa. 48:8), especially within the Covenant relationship (Jer. 5:11; Mal. 2:10f.).

with disgust: or, 'I feel disgust'. See also 139:21: 'And do I not loathe them that rise up against thee?'

159. Consider: lit. 'See'. In the Lamentations it is customary for the nation or the individual to ask God to behold their distress (cf. 25:19; Lam. 1:11,20), but in the present verse the Psalmist pleads with God to consider his devotion to the divine precepts (see verse 4). On the second half of the verse, see verses 25 and 88.

160. The sum of thy word: (LXX and Jerome read '...words'; so also 11QPs[a]), or 'The essence (or 'substance') of your word (is truth)'. 'Truth' (*ʾemeṯ*) in this verse may mean 'dependability (itself)' (see on 25:5).

thy righteous ordinances: see verses 7, 62, 164.

Strophe Twenty-one **161–8**

161. Princes: see verse 23. Why these representatives of the community should persecute the Psalmist is not clear. Perhaps he had shown his disapproval of their deficient attitude to the divine law.

but my heart stands in awe: i.e., 'but I am afraid only of your words' (or 'word' as in T and S).

162. This and the preceding verse show the tension between awe (verse 161) and joy (verse 162), and it may be a reflection of the two opposites implicit in the Covenant law: blessing and curse (cf. Dt. 27:11–28:68).

spoil: the Hebrew *šālāl* is usually the booty of war. The division of the spoils of war was an occasion of great rejoicing, e.g., 'they rejoice before thee . . . as men rejoice when they divide the spoil' (Isa. 9:3; cf. Jg. 5:30).

163. The Psalmist hates and abhors falsehood, while the opposite attitude is well described by Amos (5:10): 'They hate him who reproves in the gate, and they abhor him who speaks the truth.' This disposition of the Israelite ruling classes may well have been mirrored by the 'princes' of the Psalmist's time (see verse 161).

164. Seven times: this is not to be taken literally (cf. Job 5:19; Prov. 24:16, 26:25), but it may suggest 'many times' or 'constantly'. The number 'seven' plays an important role in the *OT*, and in the Near East as a whole it was regarded as both sacred and effective. For a more detailed discussion, see M. H. Pope, *IDB*, IV, pp. 294f.
I praise thee: the Hebrew *h-l-l* ('to praise') is a word commonly used in the Psalter, and the verb usually praises 'God in the totality of his dealings with men . . . it looks at the "mighty God's great deeds" in all times and in all places and praises him for them all' (Westermann, *PGP*, p. 32). The same verb is also used in the cultic exclamation 'Hallelujah', or 'Praise Yahweh'.

165. peace: the Hebrew *šālôm* is a comprehensive term. Gray points out that its primary meaning is 'wholeness', of which 'well-being' is but one aspect; the meaning 'peace' is secondary (*I &II Kings*, p. 99). Von Rad (*OTT*, I, p. 372, n.6) defines *šālôm* as 'a state where things are balanced out, where the claims of a society are satisfied, a state . . . which can only be made effective when protected by a society governed by justice'. Thus *šālôm* is a term describing the relationships between man and man, or man and the community, or even between man and God. It may also extend to the realm of nature, in which case it would denote 'prosperity' (cf. 72:3). *Šālôm* is not so much an attitude of inward peace as an external well-being (cf. v. Rad, *TDNT*, II, p. 406); it is a dynamic entity rather than a static condition.
nothing can make them stumble: or 'and find therein no stumbling-block' (*RP*). Cf. Ezek. 3:20.

166. I hope for thy salvation: or, 'I await eagerly your help' (cf. Gen. 49:18; Ps. 145:15), and the reason for his confidence is, partly, his loyalty to the commandments (see verse 6).

167. My soul: i.e. I myself (see on 33:19).
I love them: see verses 47 and 119.

168. thy precepts and testimonies: these are two synonyms for 'law' in one verse; but the metre, as well as the ancient versions, support M.T.

all my ways: i.e. my daily conduct is known to God. Cf. Job 31:4: 'Does not he see my ways, and number all my steps?'

Strophe Twenty-two **169–76**

169. Let my cry come before thee: Hebrew *ḳ-r-b*, in its causative form, is practically a technical term for the presenting of an offering to God. It is possible that the Psalmist thought of his cry (i.e. prayer) as an offering to God, although not to the exclusion of material sacrifices.

give me understanding: some exegetes follow S in reading *ḥayyēnî* ('revive me'), but it lacks the support of other ancient versions.

170. my supplication: or 'my prayer for favour' (cf. 86:6).

come before thee: i.e. be acceptable to you (cf. 79:11, 102:2 (M.T. 3)).

deliver me: for this frequent call for help, see on 59:1.

171. . . . will pour forth praise: cf. 19:2 (M.T. 3), 145:7. The same verb *n-b-*[c] can also denote the uttering of proud and arrogant words (94:4). For 'praise', see on 65:1; it is man's fitting response to God. In a way, it is one's gratitude to God, and a public witness and testimony to his help, and to his goodness in general. Consequently the Psalmist can say: 'Praise befits the upright' (33:1).

172. My tongue: this is often a circumlocution for the pronoun 'I' (as is 'my lips' in verse 171); see 35:28, 51:14 (M.T. 16), 71:24; cf. Johnson, *VITAI*, pp. 45f.

of thy word: Gunkel, Kraus, *et al.* read *ᵓemûnāṯeḵā* ('of your faithfulness'), but there is no real reason for this emendation; 11QPsª = M.T.

173. thy hand: this suggests Yahweh in action, either helping the needy (80:17 (M.T. 18), 139:10) or punishing the wicked (32:4; Isa. 5:25). 'Hand' is sometimes merely a synonym of 'power', as in Dt. 32:36: 'when he sees that their power (i.e. hand) is gone', or in Isa. 28:2: 'he will cast down to the earth with violence' (i.e., with hand).

I have chosen thy precepts: cf. Dt. 30:19 where Moses sets before his people the two possibilities: blessing or curse, life or death. The Psalmist has chosen to obey God's commandments by loving him and by walking in his ways (see Dt. 30:15f.), and therefore he can claim the promises of God.

174. This verse is a variant of verses 77 and 81.

175. Let me live: lit. 'Let my soul live' or 'Let my life be spared' (cf. 1 Kg. 20:32). For 'soul', see on 33:19. The main reason for the wish to live is the Psalmist's desire to praise God, for the 'dead do not praise the LORD' (115:17; similarly in 88:10 (M.T. 11)).

176. I have gone astray: the author may have been thinking of unwitting sins or temporary deviations from the true path. This would not, however, alter his fundamental desire to serve God and to do his will. Therefore the confession of sin—if such it is—and the affirmation of loyalty are not necessarily inconsistent. The above phrase refers to human frailty and helplessness rather than faithlessness (see Nötscher, *PEB*, p. 271).

like a lost sheep: Duhm, Gunkel, *et al.* delete this phrase as a gloss which overloads the metre, but M.T. has the support of the ancient versions and 11QPs[a]. The metaphor is used in the *OT* more than once, to depict defencelessness (cf. Jer. 50:6; Ezek. 34:4ff.,16; see also Isa. 53:6).

Psalm 120 THE MAN OF PEACE AND HIS PROBLEMS

Ps. 120–34 all have the title: 'A Song of Ascents' (with a slight variation in Ps. 121); this may suggest that they formed a separate collection of songs. Occasionally Ps. 120–36 are called 'the Great Hallel' (see introduction to Ps. 113). The actual meaning of 'ascents' (*maᶜᵃlôṯ*) is far from clear, and there are a number of explanations of greater or lesser probability. Some exegetes have argued that 'ascents' refer to the 'step-like' repetition of certain words or phrases in successive verses (e.g. in 121:1 and 2, 3 and 4, 4 and 5), but this is not a peculiarity belonging exclusively to this group of Psalms. Another suggestion is to link the fifteen 'songs of ascents' with the fifteen steps leading from the court of the women to the court of Israel (cf. Mishnah, *Middoth* ii:5). Yet the Mishnaic reference only stresses the correspondence in number, and does not actually say that the Levites sang the 'songs of ascents' on these steps: for the opposite view, see Mowinckel, *PIW*, II, p. 82. An ancient interpretation is to associate the 'songs of ascents' with the 'ascending' of the exiles from the Babylonian captivity (cf. Ezr. 2:1, 7:9), but some of these Psalms speak of the Temple as already in use (cf. Ps. 122, 134) and therefore some, at least, of the songs must be later than the return from Babylon, or earlier than the Exile. A more recent view regards the 'songs of ascents' as a collection of Psalms chanted by pilgrims on their way to Jerusalem. This is possible, because the verb *ᶜ-l-h* is often used as a technical term for going on a pilgrimage (cf. 24:3, 124:2) or for the processional ascent to the sanctuary. Taylor (*PIB*, p. 639) describes the collection as a 'handbook of devotions for the use of pilgrims', while Mowinckel (*PIW*, II, p. 208) calls it 'The Songs of the festal processions' which may well be right. See also C. C. Keet, *A Study of the Psalms of Ascents: A Critical and Exegetical Commentary upon Psalms CXX to CXXXIV* (1969), pp. 1–17.

The *Gattung* of Ps. 120 is not certain; the *RSV* rendering of verse 1 would suggest that the Psalm is an Individual Lament (see Introduction, pp. 37ff.), while M.T. implies that the poem is a Thanksgiving of the Individual (so also Schmidt, Weiser, Kraus, *NEB*, *et al.*, see Introduction, pp. 35f.). If we adopt the latter alternative, then verse 1 points to the answered prayer, while the rest of the Psalm is a recapitulation of the situation before the petition was answered by Yahweh. Verses 2–4 are a brief prayer for help, uttered by the Psalmist in the time of his need, and verses 5–7 describe the actual plight of the author.

The Psalm contains no direct reference to pilgrimage, but a thanksgiving presupposes a journey to the Temple where all vows would be paid. The metre is irregular.

GOD HAS ANSWERED MY PRAYER **1**

1. In my distress: (similarly in 18:6 (M.T. 7), 66:14) for the general meaning of *ṣārāh*, 'distress', see on 107:2. It is impossible to determine the detailed circumstances which gave rise to this Psalm but most of the trouble seems to have been caused by treacherous and lying enemies (see verse 2).

I cry to the Lord: M.T. has: 'I cried . . .' which may be the more likely interpretation.

that he may answer me: (*wᵉyaᶜᵃnēnî*) M.T. has 'he answered me' (cf. 3:4 (M.T. 5), 22:21 (M.T. 22), 118:21). Yahweh's answer was to deliver the Psalmist out of his afflictions.

A PRAYER FOR HELP AND A CRY FOR RETRIBUTION **2–4**

In his thanksgiving the Psalmist incorporates a quotation or a summary of his prayer during the time of his distress; and so, once more, he relives and shares the past trials (false accusations?) with his fellow-worshippers.

2. Deliver me: lit. 'Deliver my soul' (for *nepeš*, 'soul', see on 33:19). The verb *n-ṣ-l* ('to deliver') is discussed on 59:1.
from lying lips: i.e. from liars; the 'lips' denote their owners as *pars pro toto*. For *šeḳer* ('lie, falsehood'), see on 119:29.
a deceitful tongue: or 'a tongue (which is) deceit', i.e. full of deception and duplicity; the expression is synonymous with 'lying lips'. Some scholars (e.g. Gunkel, Oesterley, G. R. Driver) prefer to delete this phrase although the M.T. may be right.

3. What shall be given to you: the Psalmist is not so much motivated by a wish for revenge as by the conviction that an agreement or Covenant with its oaths and conditions is binding to all parties involved. If the Psalmist actually lived as a *gēr*, or a protected alien (see on 39:12) among foreign people, then their relationships may well have been defined by a Covenant (cf. Gen. 26:26–33) safeguarded by oaths. This may be implied in verse 3*ab*, which brings to mind the customary formula used in solemn affirmations: 'God do so to me and more also . . .' (2 Sam. 3:35, 19:13 (M.T. 14); 2 Kg. 6:31; cf. also Weiser, *POTL*, p. 742).

4. This verse is the reply to the rhetorical question in verse 3; the culprits will be taken at their word.
A warrior's sharp arrows: it is usually thought that this military metaphor was suggested by the frequent descriptions of the tongue as a deadly weapon, e.g., 'their tongues (are) sharp swords' (57:4 (M.T. 5)), 'who whet their tongues like swords, who aim bitter words like arrows' (64:3 (M.T. 4)); cf. also Jer. 9:8 (M.T. 7). Since the liars had used their tongues like swords and arrows, their punishment will be by similar means; they broke the harmony (*šālôm*) by their hostilities (verse 7) and by hostilities they will be chastised (cf. Klopfenstein, *LAT*, p. 53). Delitzsch (*BCP*, III, p. 270) thinks that 'warrior' (*gibbôr*) refers to God himself (cf. Isa. 42:13); this is possible but unlikely.
the broom tree is probably the leguminous *Retama raetam*, or the white-flowered broom, which reaches the height of some twelve feet. It provided good fuel, and it could be used for making good quality charcoal. The words of the enemies may have been like a 'scorching fire' (cf. Prov. 16:27), and therefore their 'reward' will be a fiery retribution (cf. 11:6, 140:10 (M.T. 11)).

THE PREDICAMENT OF THE PSALMIST 5–7

5. Meshech denotes a people (or their country) in eastern Anatolia near the Black Sea (cf. also Gen. 10:2; 1 Chr. 1:5; Ezek. 38:2).

the tents: or, 'dwellings' (see on 118:15).

Kedar: according to Gen. 25:13, 'Kedar' was the second son of Ishmael, and the eponymous ancestor of an Arab tribe which inhabited the Syro-Arabian desert (cf. Isa. 21:13–17; 42:11). They were primarily herdsmen (cf. Isa. 60:7; Jer. 49:29).

A problem is created by the fact that Meshech and Kedar appear to be two localities separated by a considerable distance, while verse 5 implies that both locations are practically synonymous. Consequently some scholars (e.g. Gunkel, Leslie) have emended the distant 'Meshech' (*mešeḵ*) into 'Massa' (*maśśāʾ*) which was a north Arabian tribe. A better solution may be to take the two geographical terms in a figurative sense, equivalent to 'barbarians' or 'heathens', just as we might use the words 'Tartar' and 'Philistine'. Thus the Psalmist may have lived in the *Diaspora*, but the exact location was not specified: Meshech and Kedar would simply denote any hostile and unreasonable enemies.

6. who hate peace: the Hebrew equivalent is singular in form but it may have been used collectively; some MSS., LXX, and S have the plural *śôneʾê* ('who hate') for *śônēʾ* ('who hates').

7. I am for peace: for the construction, see on 109:4. For *šālôm*, 'peace', see on 119:165. Cf. Mt. 5:44.

but when I speak: perhaps it means '(As for me) I speak nothing but (peace)' or '. . . I speak (of it)'. Gunkel, Leslie, *et al.* follow the emendation *weḵēn* ('and truth') for *weḵî* ('but when'). If an alteration is necessary, we might take the Hebrew *ʾdbr* as a *puʿal* form, meaning: '(I am for peace even when) I am driven out'. For this meaning of *d-b-r*, and for further references, see Dahood, *PNWSP*, p. 45; he links *d-b-r* with the Amarna *duppura* ('to drive out, pursue').

they are for war: probably '. . . for hostilities'. However much the Psalmist worked for harmonious relationships with his neighbours, they could think of nothing but enmity.

Psalm 121 'My Help Comes from the Lord'

This is one of the most popular Psalms, and it belongs to the so-called Pilgrim Songs (see introduction to Ps. 120). It is essentially a dialogue, which is either a poetical device in which the Psalmist both asks the question and provides the answer, or an actual dialogue between two individuals such as a father and a son, or, more likely, a worshipper and a priest. It is possible that the 'worshipper' represents a whole group (cf. Mowinckel, *PIW*, II, p. 50; similarly Eaton).

It seems that the question, with all its implicit fears, is expressed in verse 1, while the answer is given in verses 2–8. A difficulty is created by verse 2, which refers either to the speaker's personal experience or to a general truth (in which case it requires a minor emendation; see *in loc.*). On the whole, the Psalm is a blessing and a promise of help, and in some ways it is reminiscent of the Psalms of Confidence. Its *Sitz im Leben* is problematic; Schmidt links it with the Entrance Liturgies (cf. Ps. 15 and 24), but it is more plausible that it should be associated with some ceremony in which the person departing (from the Temple for his own home?) is blessed by the one remaining behind. If so, the Psalm might be described as a farewell liturgy, and the main speaker must be a priest. For a summary of the various interpretations of Ps. 121, see O. Eissfeldt, *Kleine Schriften*, III (1966), pp. 494–500.

The date of the Psalm is hard to determine, but a number of commentators suggest a post-Deuteronomic origin (e.g. Taylor, Deissler). This is, however, far from certain.

The metre is uneven, and it varies from 3 + 3 (in verses 1 and 2) to 3 + 2 (verses 4, 5, and 8) and 2 + 2 + 2 (verses 3, 6, and 7).

A Song of Ascents: see introduction to Ps. 120.

THE ANXIOUS THOUGHT 1

The verse is obviously a question (see *NEB*) and not a statement of fact as it was understood by Luther; this may be primarily a stylistic device to pave the way for the priestly blessing, or it may suggest that the Psalm was sung antiphonally.

1. I lift up my eyes: i.e., 'I look anxiously'. A similar phrase is used in 123:1, where it suggests expectancy. *AVm* has: 'Shall I lift mine eyes to the hills?' (where the false gods are worshipped) (cf. Jer. 3:23; also 1 Kg. 20:23), but this is less likely (cf. however *NEB*).

to the hills: it is not clear what is actually meant by this simple term; it is often suggested that the allusion is to the hills of Jerusalem or to the mountains surrounding the Holy City, but more probably the Psalmist was thinking apprehensively of the hills which he will have to cross on his homeward journey. Travelling in antiquity was always linked with many possible hazards, and therefore the fear implied by the verse was a very natural feeling. Some exegetes explain the 'hills' as the sanctuaries or high places of other cults, or they see here a veiled question as to which is the true place of Yahweh's worship (cf. E. H. Blakeney, 'Psalm 121:1–2', *ET*, LVI (1944–5), p. 111), but such suggestions appear less convincing. Dahood (*PAB*, II, p. 85) thinks of the heavenly mountain, God's abode.

my help: i.e. my guidance and protection on the dangerous journey.

THE PRIESTLY BLESSING **2–8**

2. Most commentators are rightly of the opinion that this verse could hardly have been spoken by the same speaker as verse 1. A probable solution is to assume that due to an unintentional scribal error the pronominal suffix (i.e. the pronoun 'my') came to be attached also to the first word of verse 2, which originally was 'Help' (*ᶜēzer* and not *ᶜezrî*, 'my help'); thus all the help needed comes from Yahweh. Another possibility is to suppose that the priest or speaker of verse 2 is drawing upon his own experience, i.e. my God has helped me, and he is also able to help you. Gunkel (*PGHAT*, p. 541) *et al.* emend *ᶜezrî* ('my help') into *ᶜezrᵉḵā* ('your help').

who made heaven and earth: Kirkpatrick (*BCPB*, p. 737) has pointed out that this phrase is often used to describe Yahweh in the later Psalms (115:5, 124:8, 134:2, 146:6) but, on the other hand, this tradition may be far older than the Exilic period or Deutero-Isaiah; it may be part of Jerusalem's cultic heritage (see Gen. 14:19; Ps. 65:6). The doctrine of creation is not used as a convenient 'gap-filler' but as one of the basic facts of faith, vitally relevant to one's daily life (see Weiser, *POTL*, p. 747).

3. He will not let your foot be moved: see on 66:9; cf. 15:5. G. R. Driver has suggested: 'Will he let . . . will he slumber . . .', taking the negative *ʾal* (*RSV* 'not') as an interrogative particle = Akkadian *ali* ('where?') (cf. *JSS* XIII (1968), p. 37). This is a possible reading (cf. *NEB*), but in such a case the possessive pronouns in verse 3 are slightly problematic. Cf. also J. Gray, *The Legacy of Canaan* (*SVT*, 5, 1957), p. 203. Usually this verse is taken as the beginning of the priestly assurance and blessing.

he who keeps you: i.e. who watches over you (cf. 127:1) or guards you.

will not slumber: this may have a slightly polemic ring; Yahweh is not like the nature deities (such as Baal) who need to be awakened from their seasonal sleep (cf. 1 Kg. 18:27; J. Gray, *I & II Kings*, pp. 354f.), but he is the living, ever-present God.

4. This verse resumes the thought of the previous verse, and it contains a special allusion to the *Heilsgeschichte* of the people of God. This Drama of Salvation is not a means of entertainment, but a source of new courage and confidence: as Yahweh has watched over the nation of Israel, so shall he also preserve the individual member of his people.

5. The LORD is your keeper: or, '. . . guardian'. 11QPs[a] (col. 3) adds 'By night' (*blylh*) at the beginning of verse 5, but omits 'the Lord' (*yhwh*) from verse 5*b*; it yields a reasonable rendering: 'By night the Lord is your guardian, (by day he is) your shade at your right hand'. This may anticipate verse 6, but such a repetition of thought is a characteristic of this Psalm.

your shade: that is, your protection. This metaphor would be very meaningful to those who have known the full heat of the sub-tropical sun. For the use of this figure of speech, see Num. 14:9; Jer. 48:45; Lam. 4:20.

on your right hand: i.e. at your side as your helper; see on 109:31.

6. The sun shall not smite . . .: sunstroke was a real danger to travellers, and it was common in the ancient Near East (cf. 2 Kg. 4:19; Jon. 4:8; Jdt. 8:2f.). Equally frightening was the so-called 'moonstroke', and even our word 'lunatic' bears witness to this belief. Certain illnesses (such as epilepsy, fever) were frequently ascribed to the baneful influence of the moon. The parallelism between the sun and the moon is meant to be complementary (as in Jos. 10:12); Yahweh cares for his people *both* day *and* night.

7. . . . from all evil: Yahweh will protect his worshippers from every misfortune; the Hebrew *ra*[c] ('evil') is a comprehensive term.

your life: lit. 'your soul' (see on 33:19) which is a circumlocution for 'you'.

8. The LORD will keep . . .: 11QPs[a] omits 'the LORD' (*yhwh*), probably rightly.

your going out and your coming in: either 'your departure and your return home' (or 'your return to the sanctuary next time'), or 'all your undertakings and affairs' (cf. Dt. 28:6, 31:2; Jos. 14:11; 1 Kg. 3:7).

from this time forth . . .: (see on 113:2, 115:18) i.e. continuously.

Psalm 122 A PRAYER FOR THE PEACE OF JERUSALEM

This is the third of the Pilgrim Songs (see introduction to Ps. 120) and this description is substantiated by verses 1*b* and 4. Its *Gattung*, or psalm-type, can be defined as a Song of Zion (see Introduction, p. 35). Verses 1–2 depict the pilgrim's joy at being able to visit Jerusalem, and in verses 3–5 we find a praise of the Holy City, the cultic centre of the nation, the place where justice is (or should be) honoured and enforced. The Psalm ends with a prayer for the welfare of Jerusalem and the people of God (verses 6–9).

It was used at the annual pilgrimage festivals, perhaps at the Feast of Tabernacles in particular (so e.g. Mowinckel, G. W. Anderson). Nötscher (*PEB*, p. 274) is of the opinion that the Psalm was sung by the pilgrims as they entered Jerusalem, while Leslie (*PAP*, p. 44) suggests that the composition was 'a pilgrim's parting salutation to Jerusalem'. There is little evidence one way or the other, but the former alternative may be slightly more likely. The singer probably represents a whole group (cf. verse 1).

The date of the Psalm is uncertain; its language and some of its expressions may point to a post-Exilic origin (so also Davies, Gunkel, Taylor, *et al.*), but the reference to the Davidic house implies a pre-Exilic period unless the Psalmist speaks in retrospect. The significance of the Davidic dynasty, however, did not suddenly cease with the fall of Jerusalem (cf. Hag. 2:23; Zech. 6:12), and therefore the allusion to it may not be out of place even in a post-Exilic work.

The prevailing metre of the Psalm is 3 + 2.

A Song of Ascents: see introduction to Ps. 120.

Of David: see Introduction, pp. 43ff.

THE JOY OF PILGRIMAGE **1–2**

1. I was glad . . .: the Psalmist recalls the feeling of gladness when he and his companions began to make the preparations for the pilgrimage. Such a sentiment may sound strange to our ears but, on the other hand, visits to the Temple were not weekly events.

when they said presupposes *bᵉʾomrām* for M.T. *bᵉʾōmᵉrîm* which may be paraphrased: 'when folks said'.

Let us go: this may have been a common formula, or an expression of self-encouragement (cf. Isa. 2:3) to visit the sanctuary.

the house of the LORD is a fairly frequent designation for the Temple, as in 23:6, 27:4, 135:2 (cf. de Vaux, *AT*, p. 282; Patton, *CPBP*, p. 22). In the Ugaritic texts *bt* ('house') is often used as a 'house of god' or 'temple' (cf. Gordon, *UT*, p. 371).

2. Our feet have been standing: perhaps '(Then) our feet stood' or '(Now) our feet are standing'; *AV* has 'shall stand' which is unlikely. For the Hebrew construction, see S. R. Driver, *UTH*, pp. 169f. 11QPsª reads *rgly* ('my feet') for M.T. *raḡlênû* ('our feet'); 11QPs ª(=S) may well be right.

within your gates . . .: i.e. within Jerusalem. 'Gates' may denote the city itself (see on 87:2).

PRAISE OF JERUSALEM **3–5**

3. built as a city: not '. . . that art rebuilded (i.e. by the returned exiles)' (so Barnes, *PWC*, II, p. 597) although some commentators propose a similar interpretation (so e.g. Delitzsch, Briggs, Kissane). The intention of the Psalmist is to emphasize the strength and might of Jerusalem; she is a city indeed! For similar sentiments, see 48:12f. (M.T. 13f.).

which is bound firmly together: the reference is either to the compactly built city or to the worshippers in her, who are closely united in fellowship (so *NEB*). Although Oesterley (*TP*, p. 506) argues that the Hebrew *ḥ-b-r* is never used of a building being joined together, the former alternative seems more likely. Cf. Exod. 26:11: 'and couple the tent together that it may be one whole' (similarly Exod. 36:18); for the use of the verb *ḥ-b-r*, see *BDB*, p. 288. 11QPsª omits *yḥdw* ('together'), which is hardly required by the context because it is already implicit in the verb.

4. to which the tribes go up: this does not automatically presuppose the Deuteronomic law of a single sanctuary (cf. Dt. 12:5f.,

14, 16:6), because Jerusalem was the central shrine of *all* Israel from the time of David, and this unique position of Jerusalem was never entirely abandoned. On the other hand, it is not impossible that the Psalm is post-Deuteronomic, and that the Psalmist is thinking of the distant past.

the tribes of the LORD is a rare expression for the more common 'tribes of Israel'. This term may suggest a later date. For 'the LORD' (*yāh*), see on 68:4.

as was decreed for Israel: lit. 'a testimony for Israel' (*RV*); perhaps '(It is) an ordinance for Israel (11QPs[a] has 'an ordinance of') to praise . . .'. For the Hebrew *ᶜēḏûṯ* ('testimony'), see on 119:2. According to ancient sacral traditions (cf. Exod. 23:14–17; Dt. 16:16f., etc.) all Israelite males had to appear before the Lord (i.e. to visit the sanctuary) three times a year on the Feasts of Unleavened Bread, Weeks, and Tabernacles. The solemn enactment (*ᶜēḏûṯ*) probably included also a reminder of the special privileges granted to Jerusalem.

to give thanks: see on 18:49, 30:12.

the name of the LORD: see on 20:1, 124:8. This concept is characteristic of the Book of Deuteronomy, but is not confined to it; yet verse 4 may be more at home in the post-Deuteronomic period than in the preceding era (cf. also E. W. Nicholson, *Deuteronomy and Tradition* (1967), pp. 55ff.).

5. There thrones . . .: or 'For there are set the thrones . . .' (*RV*). The Davidic king was the highest legal authority in the realm (cf. 2 Sam. 8:15, 15:2,6; 1 Kg. 3:28; Isa. 16:5; Jer. 21:12), and it is possible that this royal function was a continuation of the office of 'judge of Israel' (cf. Dt. 17:8f.) in the pre-monarchic period (cf. Noth, *LPOE*, p. 245; Kraus, *PBK*, pp. 840f.). The function of the King as a judge is not an exclusive characteristic of the Israelite kingship (cf. Johnson, *SKAI*, pp. 3ff.).

the thrones of the house of . . .: the plural 'thrones' (*kisᵉʾôṯ*) may be used for the sake of emphasis, and it does not follow that other members of the royal family also exercised a judicial role. 11QPs[a] has *ksʾ* ('throne'); see on 9:4.

PRAYER FOR JERUSALEM **6–9**

6. the peace of Jerusalem: the word *šālôm*, 'peace', (see on 119:165) occurs three times in verses 6–8; it may also be a word play on 'Jerusalem' (*yᵉrûšālā(y)im*) (see on 102:21). Verse 6 provides an example of some sort of alliteration (accidental?)

with the recurrence of the *š*-sounds, e.g. *šaʾalû šelôm yerûšālā(y)im.* The phrase: 'Pray for the peace . . .' (lit. 'Ask for . . .') (cf. Jer. 15:5) may mean 'Wish for the prosperity of . . .', or simply 'Greet . . .' (cf. Exod. 18:7; Jg. 18:15; 1 Sam. 10:4; etc.). Kirkpatrick (*BPCB*, p. 741) remarks that 'the Psalmist prays that the *nomen* may become an *omen*' (i.e. 'may the "city of peace" (?) know peace'). Cf. Lk. 19:42. Mowinckel (*PStud*, v, pp. 39f.) understands verse 6 as a call to the priests to offer a prayer for the Holy City; this, however, seems unlikely.

May they prosper . . .: the verb *š-l-h* usually means 'to be quiet, secure'.

who love you: one MS. reads 'your tents' (*ʾōhālāyiḵ*), i.e. all the homes of Jerusalem (cf. Job 12:6); the ancient versions and 11QPs[a] support M.T.

7. within your walls: or, '. . . ramparts'. The collocation of **walls** ('ramparts') and **towers** is also found in 48:13 (M.T. 14).

8. my brethren: together with 'companions' denote the Psalmist's fellow-Israelites.

9. I will seek your good: i.e. 'I will intercede for your good' (for the verb *b-ḳ-š* ('to seek'), see on 40:16), or I will strive for your well-being (cf. Dt. 23:6 (M.T. 7)). In Jer. 29:7 we have a similar thought: 'But seek (the verb is *d-r-š*) the welfare of the city . . . and pray to the LORD on its behalf' (cf. also Neh. 2:10).

Psalm 123 'Have Mercy Upon Us, O Lord'

This Psalm begins like an Individual Lamentation (verse 1) which changes into a Congregational Lament in verses 2–4. This transition may be due to the antiphonal singing of the Psalm, and the individual speaking in verse 1 may be a representative of the congregation.

The community has endured the contempt and scorn of its proud and arrogant foes, but we can only guess whether those adversaries were foreign overlords or oppressors from among its own people; the group involved in this description need not be identical with the whole nation.

The Psalm dates, perhaps, from post-Exilic times, but it is hardly as late as the Greek period; the time of Nehemiah is a plausible guess (so, e.g., Kirkpatrick and Deissler).

The metre of the lament is mainly 3+2.

A Song of Ascents: see introduction to Ps. 120.

THE HOPE OF THE WEAK **1–2**

1. To thee I lift up my eyes: for this gesture of hopeful expectancy, cf. 121:1.

who art enthroned in the heavens: lit. 'who sits (enthroned) ...' (cf. 2:4, 11:4, 115:3; see also Brockelmann, *HS*, 73b). The throne of God was set in the heavens (for *šāmayim*, see on 19:1), and it was established 'from of old' (93:2). This does not contradict the belief that the Ark or Jerusalem itself might be called the throne of Yahweh (cf. Jer. 3:16f.) because they represent, and therefore are linked with, his heavenly throne.

2. The **hand** of the **master** or the **mistress** may deal out blows or provide the necessities of life; it could also be used to express a command, etc. The simile in the verse seems to point to the humble but trustful dependence of the servant (see on 36:1) upon his master, and it is this same attitude of mind that characterizes the servants of God when they wait for his intervention. This is not so much a 'slave mentality' as a right sense of proportion.

their master: the Hebrew *ʾaḏônêhem* is a plural of excellence (cf. *GK* 124g,h).

the Lord our God: i.e. our Covenant God; see on 113:5.

till he have mercy upon us: see on 6:2, 57:1.

PLEA FOR GOD'S GRACE **3–4**

3. Have mercy upon us: or 'Be gracious to us'; the repetition of this phrase stresses the extent and gravity of the affliction. See on verse 2.

we have had more than enough: lit. 'we are completely sated with contempt'. *Bûz* ('contempt') may spring from a false pride and wickedness (cf. Job 31:34), but it may also be a justifiable reaction (see 107:40). In our Psalm we may assume that this scorn was undeserved (cf. 119:22).

4. Too long our soul has been sated: or 'Our soul (i.e. we; see on 33:19) has been fully sated'; this resumes the second half of verse 3. For the structure, see Brockelmann, *HS*, 101.

the scorn: the Hebrew word is *laʿaḡ*, which usually means 'mocking, derision' (cf. 44:13 (M.T. 14)).

who are at ease: *NEB* 'the wealthy'. The substantive *šaʾanan* ('one at ease') often implies a person who is arrogant and who adopts an 'I couldn't care less' attitude. Cf. Isa. 32:9,11; Am. 6:1.

the contempt of the proud: this may be a variant on verse 4*b* (so Gunkel, Taylor). 'The proud', *gaʾᵃyônîm* (so *Keṯîḇ*) are probably those who do not recognize the rights of the weaker members of the society, and who therefore reject the authority of God. *Ḳerê* reads *geʾê yônîm* ('proud oppressors'). Delitzsch (*BCP*, III, p. 281) thinks that *yônîm* may be an allusion to *yewānîm* ('the Greeks'); if this is so, then verse 4*c* is a late addition, adapting the Psalm to the contemporary situation.

Psalm 124 A Grateful Song of Deliverance

This is a National Thanksgiving (see Introduction, pp. 35f.) which begins with a reflective survey of the past dangers (verses 1–5) emphasizing the disasters that might have come upon the nation had not Yahweh intervened. Verses 6–7 represent the main section in which Yahweh is briefly but thankfully praised for the deliverance. The Psalm concludes with an expression of confidence (verse 8).

The description of the peril shows in a picturesque way the magnitude and intensity of the threatening dangers; yet it is too general to enable us to define the actual distress. It may have been a particular threat (as e.g. the hostilities recounted in Neh. 4), or it may refer to the past deliverances wrought by God on behalf of the people, and re-presented in the cult. On reflection the only reasonable reaction is a grateful praise and an immense relief.

The language of the Psalm points to the post-Exilic period as the time of the origin of the composition. Cf. F. Crüsemann, *Studien zur Form geschichte von Hymnus und Danklied in Israel* (*WMANT*, 36, 1969, pp. 161ff.).

The metre is irregular.

A Song of Ascents: see introduction to Ps. 120.

Of David: see Introduction, pp. 43ff.

What might have happened 1–5

1. If it had not been the Lord . . .: the repetition of this phrase in verse 2 is not a dittograph, but a literary or/and cultic device employed for the sake of emphasis (see 129:1f.). It may also be an echo of the words of Jacob, in Gen. 31:42; since the very beginning of the nation, Yahweh had watched over them (cf. 94:17, 119:92).

who was on our side: lit. 'who was for us' (see on 118:6).

let Israel now say is a liturgical formula inviting the people to take part in the thanksgiving (cf. also 118:2, 129:1).

2. when men rose up against us: to fight against us (cf. 3:1 (M.T. 2), 54:3 (M.T. 5)). The word used for 'men' is the collective noun *ʾāḏām* (see on 84:5), which may be intended to offer 'the sharpest possible contrast with God' (Cohen, *PSon*, p. 425); cf. Jacob, *TOTe*, pp. 156f., and for a corrective, see Barr, *SBL*, pp. 144ff. *ʾĀḏām* does not mean, in this context, 'all mankind'.

3. swallowed us up alive: it is clear that the enemies threatened the people of God with a sudden destruction (Num. 16:30), but some of the details of this word-picture are not obvious. The metaphor is probably derived from the language of myth (in its technical sense) and the foes are depicted as some terrible primeval monsters (for a parallel, see Jer. 51:34) or as Sheol (i.e. the netherworld) which, in its insatiable greed, is always hungry for new victims (cf. Prov. 1:12; also Ps. 55:15 (M.T. 16)). It is less likely that in this verse the adversaries are described as wild beasts of prey, although such figures of speech are frequent in the Psalter (cf. 22:12f. (M.T. 13f.)).
when their anger was kindled: either at some success of their prospective victims (cf. e.g. Neh. 4:1,7 (M.T. 3:33, 4:1)) or at their resistance.

4–5. In these verses the metaphor changes, and the opponents are represented as a destructive flood and a raging torrent. This word-picture is probably influenced both by the observation of the sudden rush of flood-waters in a wadi after heavy rains (cf. Jg. 5:21; Mt. 7:27), and by the mythological language of stories which describe Yahweh's combat against the primeval waters (see on 89:10, 93:3; cf. also N. C. Habel, *Yahweh versus Baal* (1964), p. 66).
the raging waters: lit. 'the proud waters' (for similar expressions, see Job 38:11; Ps. 89:9 (M.T. 10)). The word *zēḏôn* ('proud') is a *hapax legomenon* in the *OT*, but other words of the same root tend to suggest insolence, presumptuousness; see on Ps. 119:21.

GOD PRESERVES HIS PEOPLE 6–7

6. Blessed be the LORD: Yahweh is worthy of the highest praise; see on 28:6. This may be called a laconic expression of the most heartfelt thanks; in fact the whole Psalm conveys a spirit of gratitude and a sense of amazement at the great salvation.

as prey to their teeth: see the parallel in 7:2 (M.T. 3). Here the enemies are thought of as wild beasts.

7. We have escaped as a bird: lit. 'Our soul escaped . . .'; *nepeš* ('soul') is used as a substitute for the personal pronoun (see on 33:19). The bird-simile rather appropriately denotes a defenceless people (cf. 11:1; Lam. 3:52) whose only hope was the help of God. For *ṣippôr* ('bird'), see on 84:3.

the snare: see on 119:110. The description envisages the bird as already in the nets of the snare. It is, however, immaterial whether the trap was thought to have been broken by the bird or by some-one else; the basis of faith lies in the belief that had Yahweh not helped his people, they would have perished. G. R. Driver suggests: 'surely the snare is broken' (adding the infinitive absolute *nišbōr* before the verb *nišbār* ('is broken')); this would be in line with the 3+2 metre in verse 7*a* (*JTS*, XLIV (1943), p. 21).

we have escaped: *RP* renders: 'we are delivered', which may be closer to the original thought.

AFFIRMATION OF TRUST IN YAHWEH **8**

8. Our help: 11QPs[a] (col. iv) reads *ʿwzrnw* for M.T. *ʿezrēnû* ('our help'), but the significance of the additional *wāw* is not clear. The word *ʿwzrnw* may mean 'our helper', but it does not give a satisfactory sense.

the name of the LORD: (see on 122:4; cf. 135:1) or, to para-phrase: 'the effective reality of the saving God'. Eichrodt (*TOT*, II, p. 43) is of the opinion that the name Yahweh is regarded as 'the medium of his operation', and that in such instances we find 'a transition from the Name as an interchangeable term for the divine person to its use as a designation for the divine power . . .'.

who made heaven and earth: see on 121:2. Of special interest is the association of the concept of God as saviour with that of creator.

Psalm 125 THE PROTECTION OF YAHWEH IS ROUND ABOUT HIS PEOPLE

The *Gattung* of this Psalm is not very clear, but most scholars define the poem as a National Psalm of Trust. Mowinckel (*PIW*, I, p. 207) describes it as 'a national psalm of lamentation' while Leslie (*PAP*, p. 125) calls it 'a prayer liturgy' associated with the New Year Festival. Verses 1–3 express a confidence in Yahweh, whose protection is both reliable and permanent, and whose nature is such as to inspire reliance. Verse 4 voices a brief intercession for the righteous, and the Psalm concludes with a mild imprecation against the evildoers (verse 5*ab*). The phrase 'Peace be in Israel' (verse 5*c*) may be a later addition (so Kraus).

The date of the Psalm seems to be post-Exilic, and its language points in the same direction (cf. Gunkel, *PGHAT*, p. 549).

The metre is irregular.

A Song of Ascents: see introduction to Ps. 120.

THE PEOPLE'S TRUST IN YAHWEH **1–3**

1. who trust in the LORD: see on 37:5, 78:22. These are the righteous who are like the immovable Mount Zion (cf. 46:5 (M.T. 6), 78:68f.). The faith of the upright is not shaken by unfavourable circumstances; any apparent inconsistencies in the divine government of the world will soon be rectified.

Mount Zion: see on 65:1.

but abides for ever: according to *RSV*, this is a further description of the durability of Zion (so also *AV*, *RV*); LXX reads: 'he who dwells in Jerusalem (shall never be shaken)'—the term 'Jerusalem' is transferred here from verse 2.

2. As Jerusalem (see on 102:21) is (practically) encircled by higher mountains like a fortress by indestructible walls, so, in a similar way, Yahweh protects his faithful people; (for an analogous idea, see Zech. 2:5 (M.T. 9); cf. Ps. 34:7 (M.T. 8)).

from this time . . . for evermore: see on 113:2, 115:18. Many scholars (e.g. Gunkel, Taylor, Kraus) regard this phrase as a gloss.

3. For the sceptre of wickedness: LXX and S suggest 'of the wicked' (so *AV*; reading *hārāšā*ᶜ). This verse introduces one of the reasons for the confidence expressed in verses 1f. 'The sceptre of wickedness' is usually taken as a symbol of foreign domination (for a parallel, see Isa. 14:5), or of the domination of evil, the source of which is the ungodly in Israel. The reference may well be to the foreign overlordship which extends over the land of Israel (i.e. the land allotted to the righteous), and which brings with it the influences of foreign cults; the latter often had to be adopted by the vassal states as a complement to their national religion. The Hebrew *šēḇeṭ* (*RSV* 'sceptre') may have several connotations (see on 23:4, 45:6), but here it is a metaphor of rule or domination (as in Gen. 49:10).

shall not rest: i.e. it will not *always* rest; this presupposes that the powers of wickedness are already at work.
the land allotted: lit. 'the lot' (*gôrāl*) which may denote the share of land given by lot to a tribe or family (cf. v. Rad, *PHOE*, p. 82; de Vaux, *AI*, p. 166).
the righteous: see on 1:5. These are not a special party within Israel or Judaism, such as existed at a later time, but simply the faithful in Israel. The Psalmist himself belongs to this 'true Israel', and his primary concern is not any material loss, but the fear that the people of God might be tempted to lose their faith.

INTERCESSION AND PETITION **4–5**

4. Do good: i.e. manifest your righteousness and fulfil your promises (cf. Jos. 24:20; Jg. 17:13; Isa. 57:13, 60:21, 65:9).
those who are good: that is those who are loyal to Yahweh, and who are upright in their hearts (see on 7:10, 119:7). They will inherit Yahweh's land, and they will be his people (cf. Prov. 2:21f.). 11QPs[a] (col. 4) reads *blb* ('in heart') for M.T. *b^elibbôṯām* ('in their hearts') but the essential meaning remains unchanged.

5. those who turn aside . . .: these are the apostates and renegades, the unfaithful among the people of Israel; their share will be with the evildoers (for *pōᶜalê hāʾāwen*, see on 28:3), who in this Psalm seem to be the Gentiles, or the heathen nations.
the Lord will lead away: i.e. to punishment.
upon their crooked ways: 11QPs[a] has *ᶜḳlḳwlwt* ('crookedness') for M.T. *ᶜaḳal^eḳallôṯām* ('their crooked ways' (or 'crookednesses')).
Peace be in Israel: as in 128:6. This may be either a later addition or the culmination of the whole poem. Cf. 122:6ff.; Gal. 6:16.

Psalm 126 Restore our Fortunes, O Lord

This Psalm is usually classed as a National Lament (see Introduction, pp. 37ff.); it begins with a retrospective description of Yahweh's saving help (verses 1–3). Luther, Gunkel, Oesterley, *RP*, *et al.* have taken this section as a prophetic pronouncement of future salvation but this interpretation is unlikely. Verse 4 is a prayer for the restoration of the fortunes of the community, while verses 5–6 contain words of promise which may have been uttered by a cultic prophet or a priest. *RSV* makes verses 5–6 part of the prayer in verse 4.

The setting of the Psalm may be the Autumnal Festival or the Feast of Tabernacles. This is implied by the reference to Yahweh's mighty works (verses 1–3), and by the metaphors associated with rain (verse 4*b*) and with sowing and reaping (verses 5–6). In this case the Psalm could be a sort of festal liturgy voicing a prayer for blessings upon the nation during the coming year. Leslie (*PAP*, p. 126) describes Ps. 126 as 'a fervent New Year prayer'. On the other hand, the Psalm may allude to a concrete situation; Kraus (*PBK*, p. 855) has argued that it must have originated some time after 538 B.C. (i.e. after the return from the Babylonian exile, which was the first restoration of the nation's fortunes) in circumstances such as those depicted in Isa. 59:9–11. Yahweh had indeed wrought a great deliverance, but many prophetic promises were still to be fulfilled. Therefore Ps. 126 could be an appropriate prayer in a similar historical setting; cf. Hag. 1:6. Kirkpatrick (*BCPB*, p. 748) connects the Psalm with the time of Ezra-Nehemiah. In some ways Ps. 85 is reminiscent of Ps. 126.

The metre is mainly 2+2+2 and 3+2.

A Song of Ascents: see introduction to Ps. 120.

THE RESTORATION OF FORTUNES **1–3**

1. the fortunes of Zion: (similarly *NEB*) *AV*, *RV* render 'the captivity of Zion'. The M.T. *šîḇaṯ* is usually regarded as a scribal error for *š^{e}ḇûṯ* (*K^{e}ṯîḇ*) or *š^{e}ḇîṯ* (*Ḳ^{e}rê*) (so verse 4), and the derivation is generally traced either to *š-b-h* ('to take captive') or to *š-w-b* ('to turn back'). The latter alternative seems more likely, and the phrase *šûḇ š^{e}ḇûṯ* may literally mean 'to turn a turning', i.e. to restore one's fortunes or prosperity. Johnson (*CPAI*, p. 67, n. 4) derives *š^{e}ḇûṯ* from *š-b-t** ('to be firm'), rendering 'to restore well-being'. The expression 'to restore the fortunes of. . .' occurs a number of times in the *OT* (Dt. 30:3; Ps. 14:7, 53:6 (M.T. 7), 85:1 (M.T. 2); Jer. 29:14, 30:3, etc.); Weiser (*POTL*, p. 760) suggests that it 'is used as a formula for the cultic-eschatological realization of salvation'. The term 'Zion' (see on 65:1) probably denotes Israel as a people whose spiritual home is Jerusalem.

who dream: *RP* (cf. *TRP*, p. 51) has '. . . that renew their strength' (similarly *NEB*), and it links the Hebrew *ḥōl^{e}mîm* (*RSV* 'who dream'), not with *ḥ-l-m* II ('to dream'), but with *ḥ-l-m* I ('to be healthy, strong'). 11QPs^a (col. 4) reads *kḥlwmym* (for M.T. *k^{e}ḥōl^{e}mîm*), which may be a passive participle meaning: 'like those who are healed' (cf. J. Strugnell, 'A Note on Ps.

126:1', *JTS*, n.s., VII (1956), pp. 239–43); a similar reading may be implied by LXX, T, and V. According to the *RSV* rendering, the people were so amazed at the wonderful help of Yahweh that it all seemed unbelievable, like a wild dream. The alternative translation points to the magnitude of the transition, from weakness and distress (cf. 137:1) to joyful deliverance (cf. Isa. 51:11).

2. our mouth was filled with laughter: this is a picturesque way of saying that we were overjoyed (similarly Job 8:21).
the nations: (for *gôyīm*, see on 59:5, 106:5); they are usually depicted as enemies or as being sceptical of Israel's God (cf. 79:10, 115:2), but on this occasion they, too, are impressed by the restoration of Israel (cf. 98:2; Isa. 52:10; Ezek. 36:36).

3. The Psalmist resumes the latter part of the preceding verse, but this time it is the Zion community that re-echoes the words of the Gentiles.

THE PRAYER OF THE NATION **4**

4. Restore our fortunes: see the discussion on verse 1. The people pray for a new deliverance which would alter the situation; just as the dry river-beds become streams of water, so may God's help transform the lot of the nation.
the watercourses in the Negeb: this may have been a proverbial picture for a sudden and complete change; in a short space of time the dry wadis could turn into whirling torrents (see Y. Aharoni, *The Land of the Bible* (1966), p. 24). 'Negeb' is the name of an ill-defined region in Judah, S. of Hebron; it is also used as an equivalent of 'the south' and as designation of a steppe or semi-arid country (cf. Gray, *JJR*, p. 115). During the biblical period the Negeb may have been less arid than during more recent years.

THE WORDS OF ASSURANCE **5–6**

The translation of *RSV* makes verses 5–6 into a continuation of the prayer in verse 4, but it is more likely that this section is an expression of promise which sounds like a prophetic or priestly oracle (so Taylor, Leslie); it is not certain, however, that it required a priest or a cultic prophet to utter these verses. It is possible that the thought of this passage is taken from an ancient proverbial saying, the origin of which may be found in the Canaanite cult, particularly in the myth of the death and rising of the fertility god. Sowing was associated, in the thought of many ancient peoples, with the dying and burial of the nature deity, and therefore lamentations and weeping were appropriate to the scattering of the seed, and as a result they would help to secure a plentiful harvest. Thus he who sows with weeping, reaps with rejoicing. This does not mean that the Hebrews subscribed to those beliefs, but they definitely used many metaphors derived from the language of Canaanite mythology. For some relevant Canaanite material, see *ANET*, pp. 138b–141a; Jirku, *MK*, pp. 89f.; F. Hvidberg, *ZAW*, LVII (1939), pp. 150–2.

6. bearing the seed for sowing: some commentators delete *nōśē*ʾ ('bearing'), as a dittograph from verse 6*d*, but it is probably repeated for stylistic reasons (cf. verses 2*b* and 3*a*). The Hebrew *mešeḵ* may be a leather bag for carrying the seed (see *KBL*, p. 575a; so also *NEB*), and verse 6*b* could be rendered 'bearing the bag of seed'; there is less support for the *RSV* rendering.
shall come home: he shall most certainly come home rejoicing when, at the harvest time, he has gathered his abundant crops. Cf. also Jn 16:20.

Psalm 127 'Unless the Lord, It is in Vain'

This Psalm consists of two parts: verses 1–2 depict the ultimate futility of all human enterprise if God is not taken into account, while verses 3–5 show that many sons, or a large family, are a blessing of God (and not the result of human error). The poem is often described as a Wisdom Psalm (see Introduction, p. 40), and a number of exegetes (e.g. Briggs, Weiser, Taylor) have argued that it is composed of two independent fragments. G. W. Anderson (*PCB*, 385e) has aptly remarked that 'the desire to separate the two parts is simply a manifestation of the occupational disease of commentators', and this may well be right. Kraus (*PBK*, p. 861) quotes a Sumerian song dedicated to the goddess Nisaba, in which she is praised as the one without whom no house, city, or palace, is built, and as the one who grants children to the family. This collocation of themes similar to Ps. 127, shows that there is no real reason to doubt the unity of our Psalm.

The *Sitz im Leben* of the Psalm is uncertain, but it could be associated with the Feast of Tabernacles during which blessings would be implored and advice sought. Mowinckel (*PIW*, II,

p. 103) links it with the consecration of the Temple, although he thinks that the poem (like Ps. 1) may not have been used ritually at all (op cit., p. 114). Schmidt (*PHAT*, p. 228) regards the composition as a song of greeting on the birth of a son (cf. Ru. 4:14f.; Isa. 9:6f. (M.T. 5f.)); this is a plausible suggestion but, if it is correct, at some later time it may have been re-interpreted. In its present form the poem is ascribed to Solomon, but it is unlikely that he is its author. The reasons for this ascription may be found in the tradition about Solomon's proverbial wisdom, the view that the 'house' in verse 1 refers to the Solomonic Temple, and in the reference to the 'beloved' (Solomon was also called 'Jedidiah', 'beloved of Yah(weh)', in 2 Sam. 12:25).

The Psalm is probably post-Exilic; its metre is irregular.

A Song of Ascents: see introduction to Ps. 120.

MAN'S UTTER DEPENDENCE UPON GOD **1–2**

1. Unless the LORD builds the house: it is unlikely that the Psalmist is speaking of the building of the Temple, although it may be described as a house. Possibly the expression 'to build a house' has a double meaning—that is, to found a family and to build a dwelling for it. Both Sarah (or Sarai) (Gen. 16:2) and Rachel (Gen. 30:3) speak of being 'built up' in the sense of obtaining children through their maids, and in Dt. 25:9 the raising up of a family is described as the building of a house (see Exod. 1:21; Ru. 4:11; 1 Sam. 2:35; 2 Sam. 7:27).

those who build it labour in vain: if the world is indeed God's creation, then man's life and work cannot prosper without God. From the Psalmist's point of view, 'in vain' is a fitting motto of a godless existence.

over the city: this need not be Jerusalem, but simply any city. A family or a community that is not bound together by a common allegiance to God is like a doomed city in the path of a conquering army. Pathetic is the effort to guard it, if there is not the slightest chance of holding it.

2. The Psalmist does not depreciate diligence or honest work, but he sees that even our best efforts are ultimately futile (from a theological point of view) if God has no share in them.

for he gives to his beloved sleep: this is, exegetically, a difficult phrase. *AV*, *PBV* render: 'for so he giveth his beloved sleep' (similarly *RV*). The *PLE* paraphrase: 'is it not in the hours of sleep that he blesses the men he loves?' represents another possible rendering. Dahood (*PNWSP*, p. 22) takes the Hebrew *kēn* (*RSV* 'for') in the sense of 'reward' (parallel to *naḥalāh* ('heritage') and *śāḵār* ('reward') in verse 3), and reads: 'He gives his beloved a reward in sleep' (cf. also Kraus, *PBK*, p. 858). Some commentators think that 'sleep' may be a euphemistic allusion to marital intercourse, but this is not a convincing explanation; it is more likely that the reference is to the growth of crops and flocks. See also Keet, op. cit., pp. 56–60.

CHILDREN ARE THE BLESSING OF GOD **3–5**

3. . . . a heritage from the LORD: 'heritage' or 'inheritance' (*naḥalāh*) is often used to denote the land of Israel as the gift of Yahweh (see on 105:11; cf. 2 Sam. 20:19, 21:3). Similarly children, and particularly sons, are a gift from God, and the strength of the family. Cohen (*PSon*, p. 429) points out that the rabbis taught 'that a child had three parents: God, in addition to father and mother.' In other words, there can be no true family without God; such a household lives, metaphorically speaking, in the shadow of bereavement, whether they know it or not.

fruit of the womb: i.e. children, as in Gen. 30:2; cf. Dt. 7:13; Ps. 132:11.

4. Sons are likened to arrows in a warrior's hand; they are the first line of God-ordained human defence of the family in times of need. The simile may have been suggested by the description of arrows as 'the sons of the quiver' (cf. Lam. 3:13, rendered by *RSV*: 'the arrows of his quiver'). In more modern terms, one could venture to say that the alternative to a geriatric ward is a God-centred family.

the sons of one's youth: i.e. the sons born during the early part of one's marriage, as opposed to the sons of old age (cf. Gen. 37:3). When the father gets old, his sons are about to reach their prime. This lends some support to Schmidt's view that the Psalm was a song of congratulation at the birth of a son to a young couple.

5. Happy is: see on 1:1.

who has his quiver full of them: this is a continuation of the simile in verse 4. The archer who has a quiver full of arrows will not be defenceless, and similarly the father of many sons will have no cause to be ashamed.

He shall not be put to shame: (*yēḇōš*) so *RSV*, following some Greek MSS.; M.T. has 'they shall not be put to shame' (*yēḇōšû*), but it seems slightly inferior to the *RSV* rendition.
when he speaks with his enemies in the gate: the *RSV* is an emendation of *yᵉḏabbᵉrû* ('they shall speak') into *yᵉḏabbēr*. For the significance of the term 'gate', see on 69:12. A man who has many sons will not be wrongly deprived of his rights or justice due to him in judicial proceedings; the contrary was often the case with widows, orphans, and aliens who had no families to protect their interests. Dahood retains M.T. but he takes the verb *d-b-r* to mean 'to pursue, drive away', rendering: 'but they will drive their foes from the gate' (for details, see *PAB*, I, p. 9). If this suggestion is accepted (it offers no great advantage), the word-picture may still refer to a legal dispute rather than to warfare.

Psalm 128 The Blessings of a God-fearing Man

Luther once described this Psalm as a 'Marriage song', and its contents seem to justify this description. Strictly speaking, however, the poem is a Wisdom Psalm (see Introduction, p. 40). The composition begins with a beatitude (verse 1), which is followed by an address to the righteous man in the second person (verses 2–6). This latter section promises happiness to the upright even in the common things of life: in work, in family circle, and in the membership of one's people. Verses 2–6 are reminiscent of a priestly blessing, and the setting of the Psalm appears to be the Jerusalem Temple, perhaps at the time of the Feast of Tabernacles. It could be a blessing pronounced upon the pilgrims as they set out on their homeward journey. Other scholars (e.g. Nötscher) see little connection with the Temple liturgy.

The date of the Psalm must be post-Exilic, and the metre of the poem is 3+2, except for verse 5, which is in 3+3+2 rhythm.
A Song of Ascents: see introduction to Ps. 120.

BENEDICTION **I**

1. Blessed is . . .: see on 1:1.
who fears the Lord: see on 34:7,9, 85:9, 102:15.
who walks in his ways: this is the man who in grateful reverence does the will of Yahweh (see on 119:3). Verse 1 describes in brief the main traits of a righteous man.

THE HAPPINESS OF THE GODLY **2–6**

2. You shall eat: i.e. you shall most certainly enjoy . . . The Hebrew *kî* (not translated by *RSV*) is probably an emphatic particle, 'surely' (cf. G. R. Driver, *CML*, p. 144, n. 17).

. . . the fruit of the labour of your hands: (cf. Isa. 3:10) man's toil is not automatically rewarded by an abundant harvest, etc. It was believed that if a man did not keep God's commandments, he would sow in vain, or his enemies would eat his crop (Lev. 26:15f.; cf. Dt. 28:30ff.; Am. 5:11), or drought, blight, and other disasters would ruin his work (cf. Hag. 1:11, 2:17). The righteous, however, would know divine blessing. The author has avoided the problem caused by the not infrequent delays in the smooth working of the doctrine of rewards and punishments. Perhaps he felt that if his positive assertion was true, then, God being God, he could be sure of justice at all times whether he could understand its workings or not.

you shall be happy: or, 'how rewarding will be your life for it will be well with you'. The Targum explains the double blessing in verse 2*b* as referring to the blessedness both in this world and in the life to come, but it is unlikely that this was the Psalmist's meaning.

3. Your wife will be like a fruitful vine: 'vine' is often a symbol of Israel (see on 80:8), but in this verse it is a fitting metaphor of the fruitfulness of the wife (not of her gracefulness or dependence; so Kirkpatrick). Monogamy is, perhaps, taken for granted, or is the general rule.

within your house: better 'in the innermost parts of your house', referring, most likely, to a room or a corner of a room, set apart for the wife's use.

olive shoots: in this verse they are not so much 'emblems of freshness and vigour' (Davies, *Cent. BP*, II, p. 301) as a parallel to the metaphor of the fruitful vine. The numerous shoots may also point to the vigour of the olive tree (cf. 52:8 (M.T. 10); Hos. 14:6); even when it is cut down, new shoots spring up from the old roots. The word-picture may presuppose a prolonged time of peace (see on 52:8).

table: see on 23:5, 69:22.

4. Lo, thus: M.T. has *hinnēh kî kēn* ('Behold, for thus'). The particle *kî* ('for') is often regarded as a partial dittograph of *kēn*, and therefore it is deleted (following some MSS., LXX, and S).

be blessed: the verb is *b-r-k* (see on 67:1) while verse 1 has *ʾašᵉrê*. In a way, verse 4 re-echoes verse 1.

5. the LORD bless you from Zion: i.e. from his earthly dwelling-place, from Zion (see on 65:1) where he is present (cf. 134:3).

the prosperity of Jerusalem: this suggests that the fortunes of the individual are bound together with the prosperity of the whole community. The opposite is equally true: the welfare of the nation rests upon the 'health' of the family.

6. May you see your children's children: that is, 'may you have a long life (cf. Gen. 50:22), and may "all the days of your life" (verse 5*c*) be characterized by unbroken success and happiness.' Descendants are not only the strength of the family, but also its future life.

Peace be upon Israel: see on 125:5. This is probably an integral part of the Psalm: the future of one lies in the future of all. A man whose prosperity is not a sign of the welfare of the whole people may be the latter's curse; and a community which does not share its wealth with its weaker members is already accursed. The Psalmist envisages a society in which one can not only enjoy one's blessings but also rejoice in the happiness of all. This may be a Utopian dream, but it offers an inspiring vision and a lofty goal.

Psalm 129 Sorely Tried but Not Destroyed

It seems reasonably clear that this Psalm was some sort of liturgical formulary (cf. verse 1; Weiser, *POTL*, p. 770), but its *Gattung* is uncertain. The Psalm consists of two main parts: verses 1–4 and 5–8. The first part is not infrequently regarded as an element of collective thanksgiving (so Gunkel, G. W. Anderson), but it could well be an expression of trust. The Psalmist surveys, in a few sentences, the whole history of Israel, and concludes that, in spite of all the hardships and afflictions, Yahweh has set his people free. The second part of the poem is described as a 'Psalm of Revenge' (so R. Kittel), since it appears to be an imprecation on the foes (so Davies) or a prayer for judgment. It is possible that the Psalmist has taken up and adapted a prophetic oracle, thus expressing his certainty in the divine justice. In view of all this, the psalm-type can be defined only tentatively. The two main possibilities are either a 'Communal Song of Thanksgiving' (G.W. Anderson, *PCB*, 385g), or a National Psalm of Confidence (so

Kraus, Deissler); the latter suggestion may well be right. Cf. F. Crüsemann, *Studien zur Formgeschichte von Hymnus und Danklied in Israel* (*WMANT*, 32, 1969), pp. 168f.

Most scholars assign the Psalm to the post-Exilic period, and it is impossible to be more specific.

The metre is mainly 3+2.

A Song of Ascents: see introduction to Ps. 120.

A HISTORICAL RETROSPECT **1–4**

1. Sorely have they afflicted me: 11QPs[a] (col. 5) seems to suggest: 'Many times' (reading *rbwt* (cf. Neh. 9:28) for M.T. *rabbaṯ*, 'sorely' (or 'greatly') which is used adverbially); this is also supported by LXX *pleonakis*, 'several times'. The speaker in the Psalm is Israel personified, or a cultic representative of the people, who 'represents the "corporate, greater I" of the congregation' (Mowinckel, *PIW*, 1, p. 45).

from my youth: the nation's youth was usually regarded as the time of the Exodus and the Wilderness wanderings; see Hos. 2:15: 'as in the days of her youth; as at the time when she came out of the land of Egypt'; similarly Hos. 11:1: 'When Israel was a child. . . out of Egypt I called my son' (cf. Jer. 2:2; Ezek. 23:3).

let Israel now say: this liturgical call is found also in 118:2, 124:1.

2. Sorely . . .: see verse 1*a*. The repetition seems to be a forceful poetic device.

they have not prevailed against me: although the assaults of the enemy have been many, Israel has not been annihilated; the people of God have outlived all their oppressors—the successive dynasties of the Egyptians, the Philistines and the Arameans, the Assyrians and the Babylonians. So the 'anvil of God' has worn out many a sledge-hammer. For a *NT* parallel, see 2 C. 4:8–10.

3. The ploughers . . .: 11QPs[a] (col. 5) reads *rš*ʿ*ym* ('the wicked') for M.T. *ḥōrešîm*, which may have been derived from the following verse. 'The ploughers' is a metaphorical picture of the cruel oppressors; the allusion is probably to the use of the taskmasters' whips, which would leave welts or weals resembling furrows. Micah (3:12) applies a similar metaphor to Zion. Cf. also the picture of the brutality of the enemies in Isa. 51:23, and the expression of sorrow in *Baal* 1, vi:20–2 (*CML*, p. 109a).

they made long their furrows: the treatment was excessively harsh. The exact significance of this phrase is not certain, and this ambiguity is also reflected in the renderings of the ancient versions (cf. Gunkel, *PGHAT*, p. 560). The 'furrows' may denote, perhaps, the ploughed-up area (cf. 1 Sam. 14:14).

4. The Lord is righteous: the construction of this phrase is difficult; Gunkel thinks that the term *ṣaddîḳ* ('righteous') (see on 119:137), is in apposition to 'The Lord' (i.e. 'Yahweh, the righteous one'), while Kraus regards the phrase as emphatic, rendering 'The righteous Yahweh' (cf. 7:9 (M.T. 10)). Whatever alternative is accepted, the meaning is clear: Yahweh is loyal to his Covenant, and therefore he saves his people and punishes their oppressors.

the cords of the wicked: the Hebrew *ᶜaḇôṯ* ('cord(s)') may be used figuratively of the yoke or the domination of the wicked (for *rᵉšāᶜîm* ('wicked'), see on 1:1, 28:3, 92:7) as in 2:3 (cf. also Lev. 26:13; Isa. 9:4 (M.T. 3); Ezek. 34:27). It is probable that in this word-picture Israel is depicted as a yoke-animal harnessed to the plough (cf. Job 39:10).

AN IMPRECATION ON THE ENEMIES OF ZION **5–8**

5. who hate Zion: this expression is a *hapax legomenon* in the *OT*, and most scholars apply it to the foreign enemies. The theme of the onslaught of the nations is quite frequent in the Psalter and in the *OT* (cf. G. Wanke, *Die Zionstheologie der Korachiten* (*BZAW*, 97, 1966), pp. 70–99), but it is possible that the 'haters of Zion' refers to certain influential Israelites who, for some reason or other, have rejected the claims of Zion (see on 65:1), as is suggested by Weiser (*POTL*, p. 771). The Psalmist may be pointing out that, just as the hostilities of the foreign oppressors in the past came to nothing, so also the internal opponents would be put to shame (see on 25:2, 119:2).

turned backward: cf. 9:3 (M.T. 4), 35:4, 40:14 (M.T. 15).

6. The Psalmist expresses his wish (or certainty?) that the enemies of Jerusalem might become like the weeds that sprout on the flat roof-tops but are blasted by the sun and winds before they are grown (cf. Isa. 37:27). The roofs of the houses were usually constructed of beams and rafters, covered with reeds and branches; on top of this was a layer of earth (or clay) plastered with a clay and lime mixture.

before it grows up: or, 'before it produces a stalk' (cf. G. R. Driver, 'Studies in the Vocabulary of the Old Testament', *JTS*, XXXI (1930), p. 270).

7. fill his hand: the reaper usually grasped a handful of stalks and cut them with a flint or metal sickle, a foot or so below the ears of corn (cf. Job 24:24). The stalks were left standing, and were eventually burnt; the ears were gathered into sheaves, and taken to the threshing floor (cf. Corswant, *DLBT*, p. 25). It is very likely that from time to time there may have been some slight variations in this process of harvesting. Thus 'to fill one's hand' refers, in this context, to the reaper grasping fistfuls of stalks for the purpose of cutting off the ears. At the same time he would also separate the weeds from the corn (cf. Mt. 13:30,40); the former might have been left on the field with the stalks, to be burnt. Verse 7 seems to depict the uselessness of the grass on the housetops, and thus represents one of the essential characteristics of the life of the wicked.

his bosom: the fold of his garment or his lap; the verb is to be supplied from the preceding line. The allusion is to the gathering of the handfuls of corn to bind them into sheaves and bundles (cf. Gen. 37:7).

8. The blessing of the Lord . . .: 11QPs^a^ seems to have read (ʾ)*lwhykm*, 'your God', for *yhwh* (RSV 'the Lord'). This verse may well continue the word-picture in verses 6–7; since there is no harvest, there is no harvest blessing (cf. Ru. 2:4; Gray, *JJR*, p. 413). Similarly, there will be no blessing upon the wicked. If, on the other hand, the metaphor is changed, and the harvesters are the opponents, then the implication may be that they are no longer regarded as members of the cultic community, but are treated as foreigners. Some scholars (e.g. Briggs) think that verse 8*c* is a gloss and a variant on verse 8*b* but it is more likely that it is an integral part of the Psalm, perhaps a priestly blessing upon the worshipping community, or a reply of the reapers (cf. Ru. 2:4).

We bless you . . .: see on 66:20.

the name of the Lord: see on 124:8; cf. v. Rad, *OTT*, I, p. 182.

Psalm 130 'In His Word I Hope'

This is one of the Penitential Psalms of the ancient Church (see introduction to Ps. 6), which also belongs to the Songs of Ascents. It was one of the favourites of Martin Luther who described it as one of the 'Pauline' psalms (the others were Ps. 32, 51, and 143). According to its *Gattung* it belongs to the Lamentations of the

Individual (see Introduction, pp. 37ff.), but it is by no means a classic example of this psalm-type.

Verses 1–2 are a cry for help which is a characteristic of the Laments, but the place of the description of the plight is taken by an indirect confession of sins (verses 3–4). This is followed by an expression of hope (verses 5–6), based upon the knowledge of the goodness of Yahweh to his Covenant people.

The date of the Psalm is post-Exilic; the metre of the composition is irregular.

A Song of Ascents: see introduction to Ps. 120.

1. the depths: the Hebrew *maᶜamakkîm* refers to the depths of the seas (see on 69:2; cf. Isa. 51:10; Ezek. 27:34), but here it is used figuratively of troubles and misfortunes. This symbolism is very apposite, because the deep or the seas can often represent Sheol or its sphere of influence (cf. Jon. 2:2f. (M.T. 3f.)). It is less likely, however, that 'Out of the depths' means 'steeped in sin', as suggested by Oesterley (*TP*, p. 526). The metaphor in verse 1 does not say anything concrete about the situation envisaged, except that it is characterized by a distance from God, and by its similarity to the Sheol-existence. It is pointless to speculate about the many possible troubles because the writer is thinking, primarily, of typical, recurring situations, and not of one definite individual experience (cf. W. H. Schmidt, 'Gott und Mensch in Ps. 130', *ThZ*, XXII (1966), p. 243).

2. Lord, hear my voice: i.e. my cry for help (see on 28:2, 54:2). This phrase probably belongs to the preceding verse.

Let thy ears be attentive: similarly in 2 Chr. 6:40, 7:15. 11QPsᵃ (col. 5) has: 'Let your ear . . .' (i.e. it uses singulars in this phrase for the plurals in M.T.).

the voice of my supplications: that is, my loud entreaties for favour (see on 68:6).

3. O LORD: for *yāh*, the shorter form of *yhwh*, 'Yahweh', see on 68:4.

mark iniquities: Moffatt: '. . . didst keep a strict tally of sins'. The verb *š-m-r* means 'to keep, guard', and has many other similar shades of connotation. Here it probably suggests 'to keep in mind' (cf. Gen. 37:11) in order to act upon it in due course.

who could stand?: the answer expected is 'None', and the suggestion is that no man is without sin; see also the similar view in 1 Kg. 8:46; Ps. 143:2; Prov. 20:9; 1QH iv:30f. 'To stand' may suggest the privilege of living in the presence of God. This verse brings to mind the so-called Entrance Liturgies with their questions: 'who shall stand in his holy place?' (24:3), and 'who shall sojourn in thy tent?' (15:1); there must have been many who claimed to have walked blamelessly and to have done what is right. There is no reason to doubt that in most cases the claim was justified, because the requirements were within the realm of the possible. On the other hand, such liturgical questions and implicit or explicit answers could easily become merely formal exercises (see Jer. 7). It seems that our Psalm represents a deeper appreciation of the demands of God and a better understanding of human nature, although the contradiction between the Entrance Liturgies and Ps. 130 is not as great as it may appear to us (see v. Rad, ' "Righteousness" and "Life" in the Cultic Language of the Psalms', *PHOE*, pp. 243–66).

4. But there is forgiveness with thee: (see on 103:3). This verse is probably an indirect prayer for God's forgiveness. Because Yahweh is ready to forgive (Neh. 9:17), he enables man to 'stand' or 'to live' in this world; otherwise man would descend into the depths of the underworld.

that thou mayest be feared: the *nipᶜal* imperfect (*tiwwārēᵓ*; for *yārēᵓ* ('to fear'), see on 102:15) is unusual, because otherwise only the participle of this reflexive form is in use. This may account for the different readings found in the versions. LXX has: 'for your name's sake (O Lord, I have waited for you)'; V could be rendered 'because of your law'. M.T. may, however, be right, meaning 'that you might be revered (and trusted) the more'. The 'fear of God' is a response to him which manifests itself in awe and reverence, and leads to obedience (cf. Ringgren, *IR*, p. 127). Although the forgiveness of God is a free gift, there are obviously certain prerequisites, e.g. in order to be forgiven, one must see the need for forgiveness, and without the reverence for God, sin and forgiveness have little, if any, significance. The fear of Yahweh is sometimes equivalent to having faith in him because he is the one who inspires faith and trust (cf. S. Plath, *Furcht Gottes* (1963), pp. 94f.).

5. I wait for the Lord: for the verb *ḳ-w-h*, see on 25:3, 40:1. This is a spiritual reaching-out of one's whole being toward God; the totality of the effort is indicated by the repetition of the same thought in the phrase 'my soul waits'. For *nepeš* ('soul'), see on 33:19.

in his word I hope: or 'for his word I wait'. It is possible that the hoped-for word is an oracle of salvation (cf. 1 Sam. 12:13; Ps. 107:20; Lam. 3:55ff.; Kraus, *PBK*, p. 872; v. Rad, *OTT*, 1, p. 401). Another possibility is that the awaited answer is provided by the Psalmist himself in verses 7–8, and that behind it lies the unforgettable knowledge of the nation's *Heilsgeschichte* in which the character of Yahweh has been clearly manifested.

6. my soul waits for the LORD: M.T. has 'my soul for the LORD'. The missing verb is supplied by 11QPs[a] (col. 5) which adds *hwḥlty* ('I wait'), at the beginning of the verse; it is probable that if 11QPs[a] is right, the verb may have fallen out through haplography because the same verbal form occurs also at the end of verse 5.

watchmen: this denotes persons who are posted on various watch duties usually at night. Targum thinks of these guards as Levites keeping watch in the Temple and waiting for the signs of the dawn that the daily morning sacrifice might be duly offered. Whether these watchmen are military sentries or Levites is, however, comparatively unimportant; the point is their waiting for the morning, and the certainty that it will come. The repetition of verse 6*b* in 6*c* is not a dittograph, but serves the purpose of emphasis.

7. . . . hope in the LORD: cf. 131:3; for the verb see 71:14. This call to Israel (verses 7–8) is occasionally regarded as a gloss to adapt the Lament of the Individual for congregational worship, but this seems unlikely because of the close theological and other similarities between verses 1–6 and 7–8.

steadfast love: Yahweh is distinguished by his unstinted devotion (cf. J. M. Myers, *Ezra-Nehemiah* (*AB* 14, 1965), p. 160) to the Covenant with his people. On *ḥesed̲* ('steadfast love, Covenant loyalty'), see on 26:3.

plenteous redemption: Moffatt 'a wealth of saving power'. For *p[e]d̲ûṯ* ('redemption'), see on 111:9.

8. he will redeem: see on 119:134; cf. 25:22.

iniquities: this term may denote either 'iniquity itself' or 'punishment for it'; in this verse the reference may be to both, or only to the latter. The redemption from sins is rather a unique expression in the *OT*, at least in this explicit form, and it is tantamount to forgiveness which involves deliverance from the afflictions caused by the sins (cf. W. H. Schmidt, pp. 252f.; Mt. 9:1–8; Mk 2:1–12; Lk. 5:17–26).

Psalm 131 THE SECRET OF INWARD PEACE

This beautiful little poem is a Psalm of Confidence or Trust (see Introduction, p. 39), and it reflects something of the spirit of the Psalms of Lamentation. The speaker in the Psalm seems to be an individual rather than the personified Israel, because of the intensely personal language of the composition. It is possible that verse 3 is a later liturgical addition to adapt the Psalm to communal worship. On the other hand, the poem could be regarded as a declaration of loyalty to Yahweh (cf. Kraus, *PBK*, p. 874); it presents, at the same time, an example of a righteous man, and sets it before the community to inspire a new hope. As the *Heilsgeschichte* of the nation can be a source of courage for the individual, so also one individual's experience can benefit the many.

The date of the Psalm may well be post-Exilic. The metre is 3+2, except for verse 2 where it is 4+3+3.

A Song of Ascents: see introduction to Ps. 120.

Of David: see Introduction, pp. 43ff.

1. my heart is not lifted up: i.e. 'my heart is not haughty', or, simply, 'I am not proud' (for similar expressions, see 2 Chr. 26:16, 32:25; Prov. 18:12; Ezek. 28:2). Cf. Eichrodt, *TOT*, II, p. 143.

my eyes are not raised too high: that is, 'I have not been arrogant' (see on 18:27, 101:5).

I do not occupy myself with . . .: lit. 'I do not walk in . . .', i.e. my life does not revolve round ambitions and schemes which are impossible (because they are not right?).

marvellous: for *niplāʾôṯ*, see on 9:1, 78:11. Here it probably means 'too difficult' (cf. Dt. 17:8, 30:11).

2. But I have calmed: for *ʾim lōʾ* ('but') see *GK* 149b.

my soul: the Psalmist speaks of his soul as if it were a distinct entity (cf. Eaton, *PTBC*, p. 291), but this differentiation is based on poetical expediency rather than on anthropological considerations.

like a child quieted: lit. 'like a weaned child at his mother's side'. If 2 Mac. 7:27 is a representative example, then children were weaned at approximately the age of three. This may imply that the older infants (before they were weaned) may have received an insufficient amount of milk, and therefore their restlessness and crying may have been proverbial. On the other hand, a weaned child could have been symbolic of contentment.

is my soul: this . . . is occasionally deleted (so Oesterley), but such a repetition is quite frequent in the Songs of Ascents. Some scholars (Gunkel, Weiser, Kraus, *et al.*) alter *kaggāmūl* ('like a child') into *tiggāmēl* (or *tiḡmōl*), '(so my soul) is quieted (within me)'; a verb is also suggested by LXX.

3. hope in the LORD: see 130:7.

from this time forth: that is, continually. See on 113:2, 115:18.

Psalm 132 THE ELECTION OF ZION AND OF DAVID

This Psalm is a liturgical composition which may have been used at a festal procession. Ps. 132:8ff. occurs in 2 Chr. 6:41f. as the concluding part of the prayer offered by Solomon at the dedication of the Jerusalem Temple. This section of Ps. 132 is not, however, found in 1 Kg. 8, the parallel to 2 Chr. 6, and therefore it might be argued that the addition was made for a specific reason which may have been the contemporary liturgical usage. The dedication of the Temple took place in the seventh month (1 Kg. 8:2; 2 Chr. 5:3) at the Feast of Tabernacles (see Introduction, p. 51), and it is reasonable to conclude that Ps. 132 was part of the festal liturgy at a similar celebration. There is no reason to doubt that originally the Psalm may have been connected with the Autumnal Festival. Recent scholarly studies have shown that the Feast of Tabernacles had more than one aspect, although certain exegetes have tended, to a greater or lesser extent, to separate and to emphasize one particular facet of the complex celebrations. Mowinckel (*PIW*, I, p. 175) assigns the Psalm to 'the new year festival, the enthronement of Yahweh', while Kraus (*WI*, pp. 183–8) speaks of 'the royal festival on Zion'; Weiser (*POTL*, p. 779) prefers to call it 'the Covenant Festival of Yahweh'. The solution to this problem may well be found in some form of synthesis (see J. R. Porter, '2 Samuel VI and Psalm CXXXII', *JTS*, n.s., V (1954), pp. 161–73).

The main themes of the Psalm are the Ark, the election of Zion, and the choice of the Davidic house. Since the Ark (see on 68:1) is closely associated with the presence of Yahweh, the divine king, it may follow that Ps. 132 was used on an occasion which celebrated not only the accession of the Davidic king but also the kingship of Yahweh. During this cultic event the life and faith of the community was renewed by the reliving of the basic events of the *Heilsgeschichte* and by fresh declarations of allegiance to Yahweh and his vicegerent.

The date of the Psalm must be pre-Exilic, but hardly as early as the time of Solomon (as implied by 2 Chr. 6). Some exegetes (e.g. Deissler) have contended for a post-Exilic date, round about the time of the Chronicler, but this view seems less likely than the former suggestion.

The metre of the Psalm is mainly 3 + 3.

A Song of Ascents: see introduction to Ps. 120.

AN APPEAL TO YAHWEH **1–10**

1. Remember, O Lord: act for the sake of David. The speaker may be the King (so Mowinckel, Taylor) or a priest (so Kraus). The verb *z-k-r* ('to remember') is dealt with on 8:4, 74:2.

all the hardships he endured: perhaps 'all his self-affliction' (cf. Lev. 23:29). It is unlikely that the allusion is to all the hardships endured by David during his lifetime or before he became King: the Psalmist is probably thinking of the preparations to recover the Ark which was, apparently, in the territory occupied by the Philistines, and to bring it to Jerusalem. LXX and S suggest 'his humility' (*ᶜanwāṯô*) (cf. Johnson, *SKAI*, p. 18).

2. how he swore to the Lord: in the account in 2 Sam. 6, there is no mention of such an oath, but this information may have been either derived from some more detailed tradition or part of the cultic elaboration. An oath was essentially a conditional curse (see 58:6–9 (M.T. 7–10), 69:22–8 (M.T. 23–9)), and it was usually accompanied by a symbolic action. The verb used in this verse is *š-b-ᶜ*, which is thought to be related to the word 'seven' (*šeḇaᶜ*), but the significance of this association is uncertain although it may have had certain magical implications (cf. *IDB*, III, p. 576b). It is unlikely, however, that the verb had retained its original meaning in the *OT* usage (cf. Vriezen, *RAI*, pp. 95f.).

vowed: i.e. promised (see on 61:5).

the Mighty One of Jacob: this is the name of the God of Jacob. It is an ancient divine title (cf. Gen. 49:24), but it has survived in poetry (see A. Alt, *Essays on Old Testament History and Religion* (1966), pp. 25f.). For the meaning of *ᵓaḇîr* ('Mighty One'), see on 78:25; for the name 'Jacob', see on 20:1, 85:1. Davies (*Cent. BP*, II, p. 310) renders the above phrase by 'Steer of Jacob'; Alt (p. 26) would describe this suggestion as an expression of 'bull-mania'.

3. my house: lit. 'the tent of my house', i.e. my dwelling place (for the construction, see *GK* 128m). The rendering: 'tent, which is my house' (Briggs, *CECBP*, II, p. 469) is misleading, for David dwelt 'in a house of cedar' (2 Sam. 7:2). Barnes (*PWC*, II, p. 613) understands the expression as a reference to abstinence from marital intercourse; this view seems a reasonable possibility (cf. 1 Sam. 21:5 (M.T. 6); 2 Sam. 11:11). The 'tent of my house' may mean 'the inner chamber of my house', i.e. what might be called a bedroom (cf. G. W. Ahlström, *Aspects of Syncretism in Israelite Religion*, Eng. tr. by E. J. Sharpe (1963), p. 29).

my bed: lit. 'the couch of my bed', perhaps 'the couch which is my bed' (see on 6:6).

4. This verse seems to be a proverbial expression, and it is quoted as a proverb in Prov. 6:4. The saying is a hyperbolic statement meaning, perhaps, no more than: 'I shall not rest till I have accomplished my promise' (similarly Kissane, *BP*, p. 592).

5. until I find a place for the Lord: Briggs (*CECBP*, II, p. 469) reads '. . . the place of Yahweh', i.e. the location where Yahweh (his Ark?) was to be found at that time; although this gives a satisfactory sense, the usual rendering seems slightly more likely. The Psalmist may have had in mind the preparation of the tent to house the Ark, which was the symbol of Yahweh's presence (cf. 1 Chr. 15:1). It is of some interest that the Psalm, apparently, makes David into the real founder of the Temple so that Solomon was only instrumental in bringing to completion what David had begun (cf. Kraus, *PBK*, p. 884).

a dwelling place: lit. '. . . places' (probably a plural for the sake of emphasis); see on 74:7, 84:1.

6. we heard of it in Ephrathah: this expression lends some support to the suggestion of Briggs in verse 5. The reference is to the bringing of the Ark from Kiriath-jearim (1 Sam. 7:1; cf. 2 Sam. 6:2; 1 Chr. 13:5). 'Ephrathah' was probably the native place of David (cf. Ru. 4:11; Mic. 5:2 (M.T. 1)) or the clan of Boaz, David's ancestor (cf. Gray, *JJR*, p. 422). This presupposes that David and his men were in Ephrathah when they received the news of the whereabouts of the Ark. Delitzsch (*BCP*, III, p. 313) suggests that 'Ephrathah' was the name of the district in which Kiriath-jearim was situated; less likely is the view that the Psalmist is speaking of Ephraim (i.e. the territory to which Shiloh, with its amphictyonic sanctuary, once belonged). Cf. also C. C. Keet, pp. 89ff.

the fields of Jaar: this is, most likely, a poetical designation of Kiriath-jearim. Johnson (*SKAI*, p. 19) takes it as 'woodland', and not as a proper name.

7. Let us go to his dwelling place: the people addressed are not David and his men, but the worshippers taking part in the festal procession. So the 'dwelling place' (see verse 5*b*) is the Temple in Jerusalem.

let us worship: (for the verb *š-ḥ-h* (or *ḥ-w-h*?), see on 29:9) or 'let us prostrate ourselves at . . .' (cf. A. S. Herbert, *Worship in Ancient Israel* (1959), p. 10).

his footstool: (see on 99:5, 110:1). The author probably means the Ark; Yahweh was enthroned above the cherubim (cf. 99:1), while the Ark itself could be regarded as the footstool of Yahweh's throne (cf. 1 Chr. 28:2). The verse refers to the homage before the divine king, which in turn indicates that this particular festival dealt not only with the election of Zion and the Davidic dynasty but also with the kingship of Yahweh.

8. Arise, O Lord: see on 3:7, 68:1. This cultic call was, apparently, derived from the ancient battle-cry (cf. Num. 10:35), and may have been uttered by the priest as the Ark was lifted up. Weiser (*POTL*, p. 781) is of the opinion that there is no allusion to the carrying of the Ark in a procession, because it was already in the Temple. This interpretation of verse 7 is, however, doubtful.

go to thy resting place: that is, the Temple on Mount Zion (cf. 1 Chr. 28:2). 'Resting place' (*m^enûḥāh*) may have a twofold significance: (i) it may point to the fact that at one time the Ark was a portable symbol of Yahweh that moved from place to place (for other views, see *IDB*, I, p. 222f.); (ii) it may also suggest that the present home of the Ark is its *permanent* dwelling place, and that its location in Zion marks the place as the city of God (see also verses 13f.).

the ark of thy might: Davies (*Cent. BP*, II, p. 311) renders 'Thy strong ark', while LXX has 'the ark of your holiness' (similarly V). Kraus (*PBK*, p. 885) points out that 'the ark of thy might' may be a reminiscence of the time when the Ark was the palladium of the Holy War, or the symbol of the safety of Israel (cf. 1 Sam. 4:3; Ps. 24:8). Although the Ark was closely associated with the self-revelation of Yahweh in power, this manifestation was not subject to human manipulation (cf. 1 Sam. 4).

9. clothed with righteousness: this expression may denote the priests as men characterized by righteousness (cf. Isa. 11:5;

61:10) and as channels of divine blessing. 'Righteousness' (*ṣeḏeḳ*) (see on 33:5) is here a synonym of 'salvation' (see verse 16; 2 Chr. 6:41) or of divine help and blessing. The allusion may be to their function as the givers of oracles of salvation (cf. Kraus, *PBK*, p. 886). Oesterley (*TP*, p. 532) suggests that verse 9*a* means that the priests must be clothed in 'fitting—i.e., festal—garments'; this may be true of the cultic dress as such but it is hardly the right interpretation of this verse.

thy saints: for *ḥªsîḏîm*, see on 30:4, 86:2. The author is referring to the cultic community, the 'votaries' of God (so Johnson).

10. thy servant: for *ᶜeḇeḏ*, see on 27:9, 36:1; here it is a title of David. The community prays for God's blessings on the reigning King on account of David's loyalty; for this view, see Exod. 20:5f.; Dt. 5:9f.

do not turn away the face of . . .: i.e. do not reject (but accept) your chosen servant (cf. 1 Kg. 2:16; 2 Kg. 18:24).

thy anointed one: (see on 2:2, 89:20) that is, the ruling Davidic king.

THE DIVINE ANSWER **11–18**

This section of the Psalm may have been uttered by a cultic prophet, just as similar promises were given to David through the instrumentality of Nathan.

11. The LORD swore to David . . .: the Psalmist alludes to Yahweh's promise to David mentioned in 2 Sam. 7:12–16. The divine oath is, probably, a poetical exaggeration to emphasize the unchangeability of the divine word. For the verb *š-b-ᶜ* ('to swear'), see verse 2.

a sure oath is a rendering of the Hebrew *ᵓemeṯ* (see on 25:5), and metrically it belongs to verse 11*b*: 'Yahweh has sworn to David, (he has given) a firm pledge (from which) he will not turn back'. In other words, Yahweh will not go back on his promise which is described in verses 11*cd* and 12. *AV*, *RV* take *ᵓemeṯ* as an adverbial accusative: 'in truth', but this rendering seems less likely.

One of the sons of your body: or, one of your descendants will always be on your throne; no dynastic change will take place. Although the promise of God is utterly reliable, it is a conditional oath which is further defined in verse 12. The term 'One' is not in the Hebrew text where a word is probably missing; Kraus (*PBK*, p. 877) reads 'kings (*mᵉlāḵîm*) from the fruit of your body'. 11QPsª (col. 6) adds *ky*, 'for (from the fruit . . .)'.

12. my covenant (for *b^e^rîṯ*, see on 55:20) and **my testimonies** (for *ᶜēḏôṯ*, see on 119:2) are synonymous (cf. v. Rad, *PHOE*, pp. 225–8), and the reference may be either to the Sinaitic covenant and its divine law, or the Davidic covenant and the royal duties and responsibilities which it outlined. The latter alternative may be more likely, but the former is not impossible, since the King is also a member of the Covenant community.

their sons also . . .: see 89:4,29 (M.T. 5,30); Jer. 33:20ff.

shall sit upon . . .: 11QPs^a^ (col. 6) 'shall ascend . . .' (reading *yᶜlw* for M.T. *yēš^e^ḇû*).

13–14. the Lord has chosen Zion: Zion (see on 65:1) has become 'the city of the great king' (48:2 (M.T. 3)), and the primary emphasis seems to be on the presence of the divine king rather than on the cultic site. For the verb *b-ḥ-r* ('to choose'), see on 65:4. In a way the stability and the permanence of the Davidic dynasty is based upon Yahweh's choice of Zion as his dwelling place. The presence of Yahweh is the guarantee of his conditional promise (cf. Zech. 2:12 (M.T. 16)). The election of Zion may also have other implications; e.g. it suggests that Jerusalem is entitled to the privilege of retaining the Ark, that Canaan is the land of Yahweh *par excellence*, and that Israel is the chosen nation (cf. Clements, *GT*, p. 50).

he has desired it . . .: this is parallel to '. . . has chosen', but it places more emphasis upon the subjective element.

habitation may suggest not only Yahweh's earthly abode, but also the place where he is enthroned as king (cf. Ezek. 28:2). The same double meaning may also be expressed by verse 14, in which 'here I dwell' could be paraphrased as 'here I will reign enthroned as king' (similarly W. H. Schmidt, *Königtum Gottes in Ugarit und Israel* (*BZAW*, 80, 1966), p. 70).

my resting place: see verse 8. This is both Yahweh's habitation and his throne (cf. Isa. 66:1).

I have desired: see verse 13*b*.

15. One consequence of Yahweh's presence with his people is abundant blessing (cf. Dt. 15:4).

her provisions: LXX has *thēran*, 'the pursued (?)'; this may be an error for *chēran*, 'widow', which would give a good parallel to 'her poor' (verse 15*b*); see also G. R. Driver, *JTS*, XLIV (1943), p. 21. *NEB* has 'her destitute'.

poor: for *ʾeḇyônîm*, see on 35:10, 86:1.

16. See the parallel verse 9.

17. a horn: (see note on 75:4). Here it is symbolic of the King (less likely, a messianic king; but cf. Lk. 1:68) or simply of the strength of the Davidic dynasty (so Oesterley *et al.*); cf. Ezek. 29:21.
a lamp: the metaphor may be derived from the lamp which was kept burning in the Temple, either perpetually or regularly (during the night). Noth (*LPOE*, pp. 137f.) suggests '(the possibility of) a "new break" (new beginning)', but this seems unlikely. In 2 Sam. 21:17 David is called 'the lamp of Israel', and in our psalm 'lamp' may be a metaphoric expression for the Davidic heir (or 'the Davidic line', so Leslie, *PAP*, p. 108).

18. clothe with shame: this is the opposite of verses 9 and 16. For a similar thought, see Job 8:22; Ps. 35:26, 109:29.
upon himself: i.e. upon David's head.
his crown: (see on 89:39). This is a symbol of the royal office. LXX has 'my holiness' (or 'consecration'), but it must have read the same Hebrew noun *nēzer* as in M.T.

Psalm 133 The Blessings of the Covenant Fellowship

Verse 1 is reminiscent of the proverbial sayings which praise the good fortune of those who know true wisdom, i.e. the law of God. Also, the comparisons in verses 2 and 3 show that the poem should be classed as a Wisdom Psalm (see Introduction, p. 40). Its interpretation is, however, difficult, and there are three main views as to what the original intention of the author was. Many commentators suggest that the Psalmist is praising the ancient Israelite practice of brothers (even when they are married) living together on their patrimony (cf. Dt. 25:5). Kirkpatrick, Cohen, *et al.* have argued that the Psalm arose out of a particular historical episode, such as Nehemiah's attempt to re-populate Jerusalem, and that it presented a lofty ideal to be aimed at by the new community. The most likely explanation seems to be the view that the Psalmist is thinking of the fellowship of the Covenant community in Jerusalem, during the pilgrimage festivals (cf. verse 1 (*NEBm*)). This would also explain why the Psalm was included among the Pilgrim Songs.

Its *Sitz im Leben* is uncertain. Schmidt (*PHAT*, p. 237) regarded the Psalm as belonging to secular poetry, and thought that it was a poem of greeting uttered by a guest entering the dwelling of a harmonious family. It is far more likely that the composition had a cultic use although we can only guess the actual setting.

The date of the Psalm is most likely the post-Exilic period; Deissler *et al.* assign it to the fourth century B.C.

The metre is irregular.

A Song of Ascents: see introduction to Ps. 120.

1. Behold is an introduction to the Wisdom saying (cf. 127:3; Gunkel, *EP*, p. 391).

when brothers dwell in unity: lit. 'the dwelling of brethren (or 'brothers') together'; this phrase may be an allusion to Dt. 25:5 but it is unlikely that the author was trying to revive some ancient custom (see above). The word 'unity' is not in M.T., but it is a reasonable interpretative addition.

2. To modern readers the comparison used in this verse may appear grotesque, if not absurd; it can only be appreciated by trying to look at it from the Israelite point of view.

like the precious oil: for *šemen* ('oil'), see on 104:15. Oil had many useful applications in the ancient Near East, but here the reference is to the anointing oil which was poured upon the head of the high priest (cf. Exod. 29:7; Lev. 8:12; see also K. Elliger, *Leviticus* (*HAT*, 1966), pp. 117f.). Kraus (*PBK*, p. 890) thinks that the reference is to the use of oil in daily life (cf. Mic. 6:15), but 'precious oil', lit. 'good oil', probably means scented or fragrant oil (see Gray, *I & II Kings*, p. 638) and therefore it may denote the sacred oil (cf. Delitzsch, *BCP*, III, p. 317).

running down: the verb *y-r-d* occurs three times in verses 2 and 3, but it is difficult to say whether this repetition had any special significance, as is often suggested.

Aaron denotes not only the ancestor of the priestly family, but also any High Priest.

the collar of his robes: lit. 'the mouth (or 'opening') of his robes' (11QPs[a] reads *mdyw* for M.T. *middôṯāyw*, but both mean 'his robes'). What is 'running down' the priest's collar may be either the anointing oil or his long, uncut beard—perhaps the latter.

3. like the dew of Hermon: Mount Hermon (see on 42:6) was situated in Syria, and therefore it is rather odd to speak of the dew of Hermon falling on the mountains of Zion. In view of this, it is likely that 'the dew of Hermon' was a proverbial expression for 'heavy dew'.

the mountains of Zion: 11QPs[a] (col. 23) reads 'the mountain (*hr* for M.T. *harᵉ rê*) of Zion'. There is no necessity to emend 'Zion' into anything else (as is suggested by Gunkel, Oesterley, Leslie, *et al.*).

For there: Kraus (*PBK*, p. 891) is of the opinion that 'there' refers back to verse 1, i.e. to the families where brothers live together on their undivided family heritage. On the other hand, 'there' may point to 'Jerusalem' (so Kirkpatrick, Davies, *et al.*) which is the immediate source of God's blessing.
has commanded: (cf. 42:8 (M.T. 9)) i.e. has bestowed.
the blessing: see on 24:5.
life for evermore: few exegetes would argue that the Psalmist is thinking of individual immortality; Oesterley (*TP*, p. 536) thinks of 'the perpetuation of the family'. 11QPs[a] (col. 23) reads: '. . . the blessing for evermore; prosperity upon Israel!' (i.e. it omits *ḥayyîm*, 'life', but adds *šlwm ˁl yśrʾl*, 'prosperity (or 'peace') upon Israel', which may be derived from 128:6, although such cultic formulae may have been used by more than one author (cf. also 11QPs[a] col. 4, l 8).

Psalm 134 The Blessing of the Blessed One

This Psalm is the last of the Songs of Ascents, and it consists of two parts: verses 1–2 are a hymnic exhortation to the priests or, more likely, to the worshippers to bless or to praise God, while verse 3 is a priestly blessing. Thus the poem is a liturgy in miniature, which probably belonged to the Feast of Tabernacles.

Its date may well be post-Exilic. The metre is varied.

A Song of Ascents: see introduction to Ps. 120.

INVITATION TO PRAISE YAHWEH 1–2

1. Come: lit. 'Behold'; the Hebrew *hinnēh* is unusual in such a hymnic introduction. Gunkel (*PGHAT*, p. 573) thinks that it is mistakenly inserted from 133:1. It is not clear who the speaker in verses 1–2 is; there are two main possibilities: either the priests are addressing the worshippers, or the congregation is speaking to the priests. The former alternative may be slightly more likely, although some of the expressions would suit the priests better than the laymen.
bless the Lord: see on 104:1. It is possible that this invitation to bless Yahweh refers to some specific prayer or formula used on such occasions. The task 'to bless God' is often described as one of the priestly functions (cf. Dt. 10:8, 21:5), but it is not confined to them.
servants of the Lord: this phrase may denote either the priests

or the whole congregation, as in 135:1 (see on 113:1). For 'servant' (*ᶜebed*), see on 36:1.

who stand by night: lit. '. . . by nights' (*NEB* 'night after night'). It does not necessarily suggest that there were regular nightly services year in year out (but cf. 1 Chr. 9:33); the reference may be to the special nocturnal worship at some of the pilgrimage festivals, especially at the Feast of Tabernacles (cf. *Sukkah* v:4). The verb *ᶜ-m-d* ('to stand') may connote 'to wait upon, serve, minister', and the object can be either certain men of importance, such as the King (1 Kg. 10:8; Jer. 52:12), or, more often, God (cf. Dt. 17:12, 18:7, etc.). This verb is frequently used to describe the ministry of priests and Levites.

the house of the LORD: i.e. the Temple. LXX and V add '(even) in the courts of the house of our Lord', but this phrase may well be borrowed from 135:2 although it is an accurate description of the actual place of congregational worship.

2. Lift up your hands: for this common gesture in prayers, see on 28:2 (cf. 1 Tim. 2:8).

to the holy place: or '(in) holiness' (*AVm*, *RVm*). It is more likely that the Hebrew *ḳōdeš* ('holiness, holy place') (see on 68:17), is used as an accusative of direction: 'towards the Temple' or 'in the direction of the Holy of Holies' (Cohen, *PSon*, p. 440); *NEB* has 'in the sanctuary'.

and bless the LORD: 11QPs[a] (col. 28) reads '. . . the name of the LORD' (adding *šm*, 'the name of'; cf. 135:1).

THE PRIESTLY BLESSING **3**

This verse is probably a priestly blessing upon the worshippers who seem to be addressed collectively; 'you' is singular in M.T.

3. May the LORD bless you . . .: see on 128:5. Cf. Num. 6:24; Ps. 135:21.

who made heaven and earth: for this not uncommon expression, see on 121:2.

Psalm 135 IN PRAISE OF THE COVENANT GOD

This Psalm can be described as a liturgical Hymn intended for one of the great pilgrimage festivals, perhaps for the Feast of Passover rather than for that of Tabernacles, because there is no explicit mention of the events at Sinai.

The poem follows the usual structure of the Hymns (see Introd., pp. 32f.): there is an introductory call to worship (verses 1–4), which is followed by the main section (verses 5–18). The corpus of the hymn reviews briefly the salvation-history of the nation (verses 5–12), and Yahweh is depicted as the creator of all, and as the helper of Israel, who gives to his people both triumph over the nations and a goodly land as an inheritance. Verses 15–18 are an indirect praise of Yahweh, by stressing the obvious uselessness of the idols. The Psalm ends with a renewed call to praise Yahweh (verses 19–21), and repeats the same phrase ('Praise the LORD') with which it began.

From the exegesis of the Psalm, it is reasonably clear that the poem is not an original composition, but more like a mosaic from fragments of other Psalms, especially Ps. 115, 136. The dependence need not be a literary one but it may be explained as due to a familiarity with the liturgical language which must have left its mark on many *OT* writers. Yet, regardless of everything, the author has created a coherent and impressive composition.

This Psalm is generally assigned to the late post-Exilic period. The metre is mainly 3 + 3.

A CALL TO PRAISE YAHWEH **1–4**

1. This verse is a variant on 113:1. 11QPs[a] (col. 14) inverts the order of M.T., and reads 1*cba*.

Praise the LORD: for this ancient formula, see on 104:35, 106:1.

the name of the LORD: see on 124:8. Weiser (*POTL*, p. 789) defines 'name' as: 'the compressed manifestation of the divine nature and will'.

servants of the LORD: see on 113:1. This expression comprises all Israel as described in verses 19f.

2. you that stand: 11QPs[a] (col. 14) adds *wrwmmw yh* ('and exalt Yah (i.e. Yahweh)') (cf. 99:5,9) but this seems to be a deliberate expansion. For the verb ᶜ*-m-d* ('to stand'), see on 134:1. Oesterley (*TP*, p. 540) sees here a reference to the ministering priests (so also Nötscher *et al.*) but a more comprehensive meaning is preferable (see verses 19f.).

the house of the LORD: cf. 134:1. This is a frequent designation of the Temple; see on 122:1.

in the courts . . .: i.e. in the Temple courts; see on 96:8.

our God: this may be an echo of the Covenantal formula; see on 113:5. 11QPs[a] (col. 14) enlarges the verse by adding *wbtwkk* *yrwšlym* ('and in your midst, O Jerusalem'); this phrase seems to be borrowed from 116:19, and is not required metrically.

3. Praise the LORD: 11QPsa (col. 14) has: 'Praise Yahweh (i.e. *yhwh*, not *yāh* as in M.T.) for (he is) good' (so also S); this reading gives a better parallel to the thought and structure of verse 3*b*.

sing to his name: this is parallel to 54:6 (M.T. 8). For the verb *z-m-r* ('to sing, play'), see on 66:4. 'Name' may be used as a circumlocution for Yahweh (see on 20:1).

for he is gracious: rather, 'for it (i.e. the name) is . . .'. The adjective *nāʿîm* usually means 'delightful, pleasant', and it seems as if 'good' and 'beautiful, pleasant' have become synonyms (cf. Prov. 23:8).

4. For the LORD has chosen: for *b-ḥ-r* ('to choose'), see on 65:4. 11QPsa (col. 14) omits 'the LORD', *yāh* (see on 68:4), perhaps rightly so.

Jacob: see on 20:1, 85:1. The term is used as a synonym of 'Israel'; this usage is frequent in the Psalter (cf. G. Wanke, *Die Zionstheologie der Korachiten* (*BZAW*, 97, 1966), p. 57).

as his own possession: Yahweh has chosen Israel as his own special treasure (cf. Exod. 19:5; Dt. 7:6; Mal. 3:17). The value of Israel is not to be found in the numbers, or in the quality, of the nation, but it depends upon Yahweh who gives worth to the object of his choice (cf. S. R. Driver, *Deuteronomy* (*ICC*, 1896), p. 100; M. Greenberg, *JAOS*, LXXI (1951), pp. 172ff.). 11QPsa (col. 14) adds at the end of the verse *lw* ('for himself'), which emphasizes the fact that Israel belongs to Yahweh alone.

YAHWEH'S MIGHTY DEEDS 5–12

In this passage Yahweh is portrayed as the Creator of all and the Deliverer of his people. Both these themes became central in the *Heilsgeschichte*, probably because each was associated with Yahweh's victory over hostile forces (cf. Ringgren, *FI*, p. 103).

5. I know: this may suggest that the speaker of the main section of the Psalm was an individual, perhaps a priest (cf. 119:75, 152).

the LORD is great: this is reminiscent of the words of Jethro: 'Now I know that the LORD is greater than all gods . . .' (Exod. 18:11).

and . . . our Lord: 11QPsa (col. 14) reads *wʾlwhynw*, 'and our God', for M.T. *waʾᵃḏōnênû*, 'and our Lord'.

is above all gods: Yahweh's mighty works make him incomparable in greatness (see Labuschagne, *IYOT*, p. 99). Whatever existence the other gods may have, they are of no significance in comparison with the God of Israel (see verses 15–18).

6. This verse is much longer in 11QPs^a, but M.T. has preserved the more original reading, because this Psalm in the Qumran MS. is often elaborated by various additions.

whatever the LORD pleases . . .: here we have a variant on 115:3*b*, which see.

all deeps: for the Hebrew *t*^{e}*hômôṯ*, 'deeps', see on 104:6. Pope (*EUT*, p. 63) suggests that *t*^{e}*hôm* or *t*^{e}*hômôṯ* 'generally refer to the subterranean supply of sweet-water, the source of fountains, springs, and rivers . . . as contrasted with the celestial reservoir whence comes the rain . . .'. Kraus (*PBK*, p. 897) is of the opinion that *t*^{e}*hômôṯ* alludes to the story of the defeat of the sea and its deeps. Cf. also 1QH i:14, xiii:9.

7. This verse re-echoes Jer. 10:13, 51:16. Yahweh is the giver of rain, the one who sends out lightnings and who creates storms. These were also the functions of the Canaanite Baal (cf. J. Gray, *The Legacy of Canaan* (*SVT*, 5, 1957), p. 208).

the end of the earth: i.e. from the most distant part of the world.

lightnings for the rain: this is rather an odd expression, but it is usually suggested that in Canaan there was seldom rain without lightnings; as a generalization this may be acceptable.

his storehouses contained winds, rain, snow, and hail, and they were brought forth when required (cf. Dt. 28:12; Job 38:22f.; Jer. 10:13, 51:16; Enoch 18:1, 41:4, 60:12; 1QM x:12).

8. Verses 8–12 only mention explicitly three mighty acts of Yahweh: the plagues in Egypt, the defeat of the nations, and the gift of the land to Israel. It would be wrong, however, to assume that the Psalm is based upon a tradition which did not *know* of the crossing of the sea and of the events at Sinai (see also E. W. Nicholson, *Deuteronomy and Tradition* (1967), pp. 41ff.).

the first-born of Egypt: see on 78:51; cf. Exod. 12:29.

9. signs and wonders: see on 65:8 and 71:7 respectively.

Pharaoh, or the Hebrew form *par*^{c}*ōh*, is derived from the Egyptian *pr-*^{c}^{ɔ}, 'the great house'. Originally this term was one of the designations of the royal palace but later it became a royal title (cf. *IDB*, pp. 773f.; *HDB*, p. 759).

10. many nations: or 'great . . .' (*AV*, *RP*). For 'nations' (*gôyīm*), see on 59:5, 106:5.

11. Sihon (see Num. 21:21–4; Dt. 2:30–33) and **Og** (see Num.

21:33f.; Dt. 3:1–6) were the first kings defeated by Israel, and therefore this conquest of Transjordan had a very important place in the traditions of the people of God (Y. Aharoni, *The Land of the Bible* (1966), pp. 187ff.).

12. as a heritage: for *naḥᵃlāh*, see on 105:11. The repetition of 'heritage' in verse 12*b* is a poetical device and it stresses the new significance of the one-time 'kingdoms of Canaan'.

A HYMN OF PRAISE TO YAHWEH **13–14**

13. Thy name: or, in this context, 'your fame (as manifested in the great triumphs over the nations)'. For *šēm*, 'name', see on 20:1, 124:8.

for ever: see on 117:2.

thy renown: the Hebrew *zēḵer* is parallel to *šēm* ('name, fame'), and in this verse there is probably no difference between the two. Sometimes *šēm* denotes the name of the deity which is cultically pronounced, while *zēḵer* may refer to the *act* of utterance (see Childs, *MTI*, pp. 70–3). Cf. Exod. 3:15: 'this is my name for ever, and thus I am to be remembered throughout all generations'.

throughout all ages: lit. 'for a generation and a generation' (cf. 72:5), so also in 102:12 (M.T. 13).

14. Here we have a verbatim quotation from Dt. 32:36; in Dt. 32:37ff. there is a reference to the failure of the idols, and a similar thought is expressed in 135:15–18.

will vindicate: the verb used is *d-y-n* ('to judge, vindicate'); see on 72:2. The special allusion may be to the difficulties of the post-Exilic period; the *Heilsgeschichte* would be a guarantee that Yahweh is able and willing to help.

... have compassion: (so also *NEB*) this is better than 'repent himself' (*AV*, *RV*); see on 71:21.

THE INEFFECTIVENESS OF IDOLS **15–18**

For the exegesis of this section, see 115:4–8, which is a very close parallel to 135:15–18. It is sometimes pointed out that such an ironic account of idols or the gods of other nations and an implicit emphasis on the exclusiveness of one's own God have no real parallels in non-biblical literature (cf. Ringgren, *FP*, p. 121).

17. nor is there any: 11QPsᵃ (col. 15) reads *wʾyn* ('and there is no . . .') for M.T. *ʾap̱ ʾên* ('nor is there any . . .').

THE CONCLUDING CALL TO PRAISE **19–21**

19–20. For a similar call, see 115:9ff., 118:2ff., but in our Psalm the author refers to the worshipping community by using *four* terms, adding 'the house of Levi'. In the post-Exilic cultus the Levites formed a subordinate order of Temple officials in charge of various minor tasks, while the priests (or the Aaronites) performed all the important duties (see Rowley, *WAI*, pp. 100f., 171ff.; de Vaux, *AI*, pp. 388–94).

bless the LORD: see on 104:1.

21. Blessed be the LORD: 11QPs[a] (col. 15) has *ybrkkh*, '(The LORD) bless you . . .' for M.T. *bārûḵ*, 'Blessed be . . .'; 11QPs[a] may be an adaptation of 134:3.

Praise the LORD: see verse 1. This formula is transferred by LXX and V to the beginning of Ps. 136.

Psalm 136 THANKS TO THE GOD OF UNCHANGING LOYALTY

This liturgy of thanksgiving was traditionally known as the 'Great Hallel' (for further details, see introduction to Ps. 113) and it was associated with the Feast of Passover (see Introduction, pp. 51f.). It is probable that this comparatively late Jewish tradition has preserved the original cultic setting of the Psalm. In more recent years some exegetes have been inclined to associate it with the New Year Festival, or Tabernacles (see Introduction, pp. 52f.); so e.g. Oesterley, Weiser, Leslie.

The structure of the poem is reasonably plain: verses 1–3 form the introit with its invitation to thank Yahweh; this is followed by the main section (verses 4–9), the deliverance from Egypt (verses 10–16), the entry into the Promised Land (verses 17–24), and God's care in general. Verse 26 resumes the theme of the introduction, and concludes the Psalm.

Psalm 136 in its present form consists of 26 verses each of which is made up of two lines. The first lines of the successive verses develop the main themes (i.e. the creation and the *Heilsgeschichte*), while the second lines form a monotonous but forceful refrain which may well have been sung by the congregation (or a choir?) as a response to the priestly choir (or a single priest?). Sometimes it has been argued that our poem was an expansion of a shorter original version made up of verses 1–9, 25–26. At some later point this nucleus was enlarged by the insertion of verses 10–24 and the refrain (cf. Taylor, *PIB*, p. 699). A variation of this view is the proposal that only the refrain is a later liturgical addition (cf. Oesterley, *TP*, p. 542). These suggestions are possible, but they are not entirely convincing.

The date of the composition is to be found in the late post-Exilic period.

The metre is, with a few exceptions, 3 + 3 (Oesterley suggests 3 + 2) assuming that the Hebrew *kî* ('for') represents one stressed syllable.

CALL TO WORSHIP 1–3

1. O give thanks: for this common liturgical formula, see on 106:1.

for his steadfast love: or 'for his Covenant loyalty is endless'. This phrase is a refrain which recurs in each verse, and is discussed on 107:1. It is also found in a cultic setting in 2 Chr. 7:3,6.

2. the God of gods: this is reminiscent of Dt. 10:17: 'For the LORD your God is God of gods and Lord of lords'. The expression must have had its origin in a polytheistic background (so Kraus, *PBK*, p. 901), but in its present context it simply has a superlative force, meaning 'God who is God indeed' (cf. G. Henton Davies, *PCB* 236f; Labuschagne, *IYOT*, p. 145).

3. the Lord of lords: i.e. Yahweh is the undisputed Lord. For this way of expressing a superlative, see Brockelmann, *HS*, 79b. For *ʾăḏôn*, 'lord', see on 8:1.

YAHWEH AS THE CREATOR GOD 4–9

For the relationship between Yahweh's creative activity and his saving work, see Labuschagne, *IYOT*, pp. 89–112; v. Rad, *PHOE*, pp. 131–43.

4. great wonders: 11QPs^a (col. 15) rightly omits *g^{e}ḏōlōṯ* ('great'), thus restoring the prevailing 3 + 3 metre. For *nip̱lāʾōṯ* ('wonders'), see on 9:1, 78:11. The thought is similar to that expressed in 72:18, 86:10; Yahweh is not only the God who has done the creative work alone, but he is also the only one who could do it. This is yet another proof of his incomparability.

5. who by understanding made the heavens: this is a reflection of Prov. 3:19*b* (cf. Jer. 10:12). *T^{e}ḇûnāh* ('understanding') is one of the divine attributes manifested especially in Yahweh's works of creation (cf. Job 9:10; Ps. 104:24). For the 'heavens' (*šāmayim*), see on 19:1.

6. who spread out: the verb *r-ḳ-*ᶜ means 'to beat out' and probably also 'to spread out (by beating)'; so the earth is picturesquely described as if it were a thin sheet of metal spread over the waters (cf. Isa. 42:5, 44:24). For the general thought, see on 24:2.

7. the great lights: i.e. the sun and the moon (cf. Gen. 1:16). The plural *ʾôrîm* ('lights') is found only here in the *OT*; 11QPsᵃ (col. 15) has *mʾwrwt* ('lights' or 'luminaries'), as in Gen. 1:14, 15,16.

8. the sun to rule over the day: cf. Gen. 1:16; for *šemeš* ('sun'), see on 19:5. 11QPsᵃ (col. 15) inserts between verses 7 and 8 another verse: 'the sun and the moon, for his steadfast love. . .'; but this addition is not attested by the versions, and it seems to be an exegetical gloss.

9. the moon and the stars: the word *wᵉḵôḵāḇîm* ('and the stars') is often deleted by exegetes for metrical reasons. Furthermore, according to Gen. 1:16 only the moon was given that task.

ISRAEL'S DELIVERANCE IN EGYPT **10–15**

10. See on 78:51, 135:8.

11. and brought Israel out: i.e. from Egyptian slavery (cf. Exod. 18:1, 20:2; Dt. 1:27, 4:20, 5:15, etc.).

12. with a strong hand: this expression is often found in Deuteronomy (cf. Dt. 4:34, 5:15, 7:19, 11:2, 26:8). It probably means: 'with an irresistible power, effective in delivering the oppressed and in punishing the oppressors'.

13. who divided the Red Sea: lit. 'who cut the Sea of Reeds in pieces' (for the verb *g-z-r*, 'to cut', cf. 1 Kg. 3:25; for a possible (?) Ugaritic parallel, see Kraus, *PBK*, p. 902). Deissler *et al.* think that the underlying metaphor is based on the mythological conflict with Chaos (see on 93:3). *Yam sûp̱* ('Red Sea' (so *RSV*)) is discussed on 106:7.

14. Cf. Exod. 14:22.

15. overthrew: lit. 'shook off'; i.e. Yahweh effortlessly shook off into the sea both Pharaoh (see on 135:9) and his army, as if they were a locust (cf. 109:23). See Exod. 14:27.

ISRAEL IN THE DESERT AND IN THE PROMISED LAND **16–25**

16. See on 78:52. This theme of the divine guidance during the wilderness period is frequent in the *OT*; cf. Dt. 8:15; Jer. 2:6; Am. 2:10.

17. who smote great kings: this appears to be a parallel of verse 18*a* 'and slew famous kings'; the allusion may be to the events recorded in Jos. 12.

19–20. See on 135:11.

21–22. See on 135:12.

Israel his servant: cf. Isa. 41:8, 44:1,2; C. R. North, *The Second Isaiah*, p. 97. For *ʿeḇeḏ* ('servant, slave'), see on 36:1.

23. who remembered us: i.e. who acted on our behalf; for the verb *z-k-r*, see on 74:2, 79:8. The reference may be either to the period of the Judges, or to the history of Israel from the time of the Settlement to the Exile. Some scholars (e.g. Ibn Ezra, Kirkpatrick, Deissler) think that 'in our low estate' (cf. Isa. 32:19) recalls the particular humiliation suffered at the time of the fall of Jerusalem and during the Babylonian exile.

24. rescued us . . .: this may be a general allusion to the many acts of deliverance, while Deissler *et al.* are more specific, and suggest the return from the Babylonian captivity (cf. Lam. 5:8).

25. who gives food . . .: cf. 104:27f.

all flesh: see on 38:3, 56:4; the writer probably means all mankind rather than the Jewish people in particular. Cf. Eichrodt, *TOT*, II, p. 146f.

FINAL CALL TO GIVE THANKS **26**

This verse is a repetition of the theme in verses 1–3.

26. the God of heaven: this phrase occurs only here in the Psalter. A variation of it (which has the synonymous *ʾᵉlōhê* for *ʾēl*, 'God') is frequent in the later writings of the Persian period (cf. Ezr. 1:2, 5:12, 6:9; Neh. 1:4, 2:4; Jon. 1:9; etc.).

In some Greek MSS. we find an additional verse: 'Give thanks to the Lord of lords . . .'; but this is obviously borrowed from verse 3.

Psalm 137 'By the Waters of Babylon'

The brief but difficult Psalm does not fit easily into any of the common psalm-types. The poem could be analysed as follows: verses 1–4 are reminiscent of a Congregational Lament, while verses 5–6 affirm the Psalmist's loyalty to Zion, in the form of a self-cursing; the Psalm concludes with words of hatred and imprecation (verses 7-9). If the emphasis is placed upon the opening verses, then the Psalm could be described as a Communal

Lament (see Introduction, pp. 37ff.); if, on the other hand, we stress the last three verses, then the poem could be defined as a Psalm of Cursing (so e.g. Gunkel, Mowinckel, Taylor, *et al.*). Another possibility is to regard verses 5–6 as forming the main theme, in which case the composition resembles the Songs of Zion (see Introduction, p. 35). Perhaps the best solution is to class Ps. 137 as a Communal Lament culminating in an imprecation upon the enemies. In verse 1 the author describes how he and his fellow exiles *remembered* Jerusalem; how he was ready to be cursed if he were to *forget* Jerusalem (verse 5) and if he did not *remember* her (verse 6); therefore, God simply must *remember* the 'day of Jerusalem' (verse 7) against the foes. The most likely date for this Psalm is during the early years of the return, perhaps between 537 and 515 B.C. During this period much of the city, including the Temple, was in ruins, while Babylon, even after her empire had come to an end, was still one of the chief cities of the new Persian empire. The Psalm may have been intended for one of the Days of Lamentation (cf. Zech. 7:1–5) on which prayers would be offered for the full restoration of Jerusalem and its people. So far they had been 'a byword of cursing among the nations' (Zech. 8:13), but the Psalmist pleads with God to reverse the situation.

The author of this Psalm must have been exiled after the fall of Jerusalem in 587 B.C., and he may have been one of the Temple musicians taken to Babylon as an entertainer. So, e.g., Sennacherib in his account of the siege of Jerusalem states that Hezekiah sent to him 'male and female musicians' as part of his tribute (cf. *DOTT*, p. 67). It is plausible that the Psalmist and his colleagues shared a similar fate (see *ANEP*, pl. 205). When the Psalm was written its author was no longer in Babylon (see verses 1 and 3), but he must have belonged to the generation which had seen the destruction of the Holy City (see verses 7f.); therefore the date could hardly be later than the rebuilding of the Temple in 515 B.C., and not earlier than 537 B.C.

The Psalm has no title in M.T. but LXX reads: 'For David. (A Psalm of) Jeremiah'; this probably means: 'An imitation of a Davidic psalm by Jeremiah'. Jeremiah did not, however, share the *Babylonian* exile, and in any case the above title is hardly authentic.

The metre of the Psalm is irregular.

THE LAMENTATION **1–4**

1. By the waters of Babylon: lit. 'By the rivers (*nah^arôṯ*) of . . .'. The reference seems to be to the many irrigation channels which intersected Babylonia. Ezekiel (1:1, 3:15) mentions a Jewish settlement at Tel-abib by the river (*nāhār*) Chebar, but this 'river' may have been one of the canals (cf. *NBD*, p. 206b). 'Babylon' is the rendering of the Hebrew *bāḇel* which is based on the Babylonian *bab-ili* ('gate of god') (for further details, see *IDB*, I, pp. 334ff.; *NBD*, pp. 116ff.).

there we sat down: or 'there we settled down'. Ewald, Kraus, *et al.* think that this suggests a gathering of the exiles for prayer and lamentation (cf. Lam. 2:10f., 18f., 3:48ff.), but it does not imply that synagogues were already in existence (cf. Rowley, *WAI*, p. 230). It is not imperative, however, to assume that the author was speaking of religious gatherings of the captives and that 'weeping' and the 'remembering of Zion' must refer to cultic activities (cf. also W. Schottroff, *'Gedenken' im Alten Orient und im Alten Testament* (*WMANT*, 15, 1964), pp. 144f.).

2. willows: or 'poplars' (*PNT*).

we hung up our lyres: for *kinnôr*, 'lyre', see on 98:5. This may imply that inanimate objects could express sorrow and mourning, as in Lam. 1:4: 'The roads of Zion mourn . . .'. Another possibility is to take the phrase as a metaphor for deep sorrow unrelieved by any joys.

3. required of us songs: this may be a variant of the mocking question 'Where is their God?', found elsewhere (79:10, 115:2). The request may be tinged with sarcasm: 'Sing about that indestructible Jerusalem and its so-called almighty God'.

our tormentors: the M.T. *tôlālênû* is a *hapax legomenon* in the *OT*, and its originality is dubious. Kraus (*PBK*, p. 904) derives it from *y-l-l* which, in the causative form, means 'to howl' or 'to make someone else to howl'. One could also follow T, reading *šôl^elênû* ('our plunderers'). *NEB* has 'our captors'.

the songs of Zion: this may denote the Psalms which are often called the Hymns of Zion (see Introduction, p. 35), such as Ps. 76, 84, 87, 122. Nötscher (*PEB*, p. 291), on the other hand, argues that the allusion may be to religious songs in general.

4. the Lord's song: this is simply a synonym of a 'song of Zion'.

a foreign land is essentially an unclean land (Am. 7:17), and even its food is unclean (Ezek. 4:13; Hos. 9:3f., but cf. Jer. 29:5ff.). Perhaps the meaning of verse 4 is 'How can we who are unclean (in that we are punished) sing Yahweh's praises to an unclean people in an unclean land?, (cf. Isa. 6:5).

LOYALTY TO ZION **5–6**

This is not an expression of chauvinism, but a description of a courageous faith in the promises of God. The real significance of Jerusalem is the fact that it was, and will be, the earthly dwelling place of God, while its ruins are a testimony to the reality of God's uncompromising righteousness (cf. N. W. Porteous, 'Jerusalem-Zion: The Growth of a Symbol', *Living the Mystery* (1967), pp. 103ff.). *

5. If I forget . . .: i.e. if I no longer remember where my loyalty lies.

let my right hand wither: *AV* 'let my right hand forget (her cunning)' but the words bracketed are not in M.T. It is possible that there is a deliberate word-play on the verb *š-k-ḥ*, which in verse 5*a* means 'to forget' while in verse 5*b* it may have the meaning 'to wither away', similar to the Ugaritic *ṯkḥ* ('wilted') (see Driver, *CML*, p. 151; Winton Thomas, *TRP*, p. 52; Dahood, *PNWSP*, pp. 11f.). Some other exegetes (e.g. Gunkel, Oesterley, Kraus) have resorted to emendations such as *teḵaḥēš* ('may it fail (me)') for M.T. *tiškaḥ*, 'let (my right hand) forget' or 'wither'.

6. Let my tongue . . .: i.e. let me be struck dumb. For the expression, see Lam. 4:4; Ezek. 3:26; 1QH v:31. The Psalmist's self-cursing is not a mere figure of speech, but it underlines his determined devotion to all that Jerusalem represents. In a way this is a challenging example to those who may have been more concerned with their own houses than with the restoration of the Temple (cf. Hag. 1:9).

HATRED OF EDOM AND OF BABYLON **7–9**

7. Remember, O Lord: i.e. punish (the Edomites) (cf. Neh. 6:14, 13:29). For *z-k-r* ('to remember'), see on 79:8.

the Edomites: Esau and Jacob, the traditional ancestors of Edom and Israel respectively, were brothers (cf. Gen. 25:25f.; Mal. 1:2f.) and consequently the two peoples were closely related. The territory of Edom stretched, at times, from the southern end of the Dead Sea as far as the Red Sea.

the day of Jerusalem: i.e. the day of punishment, the time of the destruction of the Holy City. There was a long standing hostility between Edom and Israel or Judah, but the culmination of this enmity was reached during the fateful days of Jerusalem when the Edomites not only looted the defenceless city, but also killed the fugitives (cf. Ob. 11–14; also Ezek. 25:12ff., 35:5f.). Later they occupied the territory of southern Judah which in *NT* times was known as Idumaea and which was the native country of Herod the Great.

Raze it, raze it: this repetition is for the sake of emphasis, and may stress the Edomite thirst for vengeance; in the past centuries Edom had been subject to Israel on more than one occasion. The verb *ᶜ-r-h* means 'to be bare, naked', and in the intensive form it may suggest the laying bare of the foundations, i.e. the tearing down of walls.

8. O daughter of Babylon: Barnes (*PWC*, II, p. 630) thinks that 'Babylon is a *mother*', while 'the "daughter of Babylon" is her people' (cf. 45:12 (M.T. 13)).

devastator: *RSV* reads (with T and S) *haššāḏôḏāh* for M.T. *haššᵉḏûḏāh* ('you who are devastated' (*RSVm*), or 'who art to be destroyed' (*AV*)). The reading of M.T. is less likely because, when Babylon fell to the Persians in 537 B.C., the city was not even partly destroyed (see 'Cyrus Cylinder', *DOTT*, pp. 92ff.).

Happy shall he be: see on 1.1.

9. dashes them against the rock: Kraus (*PBK*, p. 907) has well said that this verse is not so much an expression of hatred as of the barbarity of ancient warfare, and the *OT* accounts of various wars provide many instances of the same kind of cruelty (cf. 2 Kg. 8:12; Isa. 13:16; Hos. 10:14, 13:16 (M.T. 14:1); Nah. 3:10). The author of Ps. 137 longs essentially for the application of the *lex talionis*, or the legal principle of 'eye for eye, tooth for tooth' (cf. Exod. 21:24). The whole verse (9) may be taken figuratively; the dashing of the babes upon the rocks (scarce in Babylonia!) was an experience well known to the Israelites; that was the meaning of war for those who were defeated. So the Psalmist prays that the ruthless conqueror might himself taste the bitterness of defeat and helplessness.

The Psalmist is often accused of giving way to unpardonable human passion (so Oesterley, *TP*, p. 548), but it is only fair to say that anyone who depends upon military force for the protection of country and family is a modern replica of the ancient poet; both are in the same predicament of how to serve God in a sinful world. J. Bright (*The Authority of the Old Testament* (1967), p. 238) has remarked that the Psalmist is 'typical of that man in every age who is godly and devoted to things of God, yet who—theologically speaking—lives in B.C. His name is Legion'.

Psalm 138 Even Kings shall Praise Yahweh

The Psalm consists of three main sections: verses 1–3 praise and thank Yahweh for his help, verses 4–6 depict the majesty and grace of God, and their effect upon the rulers of the earth, while the concluding verses (7–8) express the author's trust in Yahweh.

Most scholars regard the Psalm as an Individual Thanksgiving (see Introduction, pp. 35f.), while some (e.g. Mowinckel, Eaton) treat the composition as a Royal Psalm; perhaps we should define it as a Thanksgiving of the Community (see Introduction, p. 36), which is offering thanks for its deliverance from the Babylonian exile. The reason for favouring the last view is the many points of contact with Isa. 40–66; this may also point to the post-Exilic period as the more likely date for the composition of the Psalm. Verses 4–6 would be more appropriate to a communal Psalm than to an individual thanksgiving, although the Psalmist could have borrowed certain themes from the Royal or National Psalms (cf. Gunkel, *EP*, 147).

The metre is varied, but is mainly 3 + 3.

THE THANKSGIVING FOR AN ANSWERED PRAYER **1–3**

1. I give thee thanks, O Lord: the vocative 'O Lord' is not in M.T. but it is found in most ancient versions and in 11QPs[a] (col. 21). For the verb 'to give thanks', see on 18:49, 30:12; cf. Isa. 12:1, 25:1.

with my whole heart: see on 119:2. Some Greek MSS. and V insert after this phrase: 'For you have heard the words of my mouth'; but this seems to be an addition derived from verse 4*b*.

before the gods: the interpretation of this expression is rather difficult. LXX has *enantion angelōn* ('before the angels') (so also V); S reads *ḳ*[e]*ḏām malkēʾ* ('before kings'), while T has *dayyāynayyāʾ* ('judges'). These are all more or less plausible interpretations to which we may add a few others. The Hebrew *ʾ*[e]*lōhîm* (**gods** (*RSV*)) may mean 'heavenly beings', who are occasionally portrayed as surrounding the throne of God and serving him (see on 29:1, 58:1). If this is right, then these 'gods' are the witnesses to the testimony of Yahweh's majesty and power. Thanksgiving is never a purely private affair (see 22:25 (M.T. 26), 52:9 (M.T. 11)). Another possible suggestion is to assume that *ʾelōhîm* refers to the gods of the foreign peoples, who powerlessly watch the praise of the Most High God (cf. Kraus, *PBK*, p. 911). Perhaps 'before the gods' means 'in the country where these (so-called) deities are worshipped', but hardly 'in one of their temples' (for this view, see Oesterley, *TP*, p. 551). Weiser's rendering of the above phrase is 'before God' but *RSV* is preferable. *NEB* has 'boldly, O God . . .'.

I sing thy praise: for the verb *z-m-r* ('to sing'), see on 66:4.

2. I bow down: or 'I worship'; see on 29:2. Verse 2*a* is similar to 5:7*b* (M.T. 8*b*).

toward thy holy temple: see 5:7; cf. 28:2, 134:2. This need not imply that the speaker in the Psalm is far from the sanctuary (cf. 1 Kg. 8:48; Dan. 6:10); he may well be prostrating himself in the Temple courts towards the main building or the Holy of Holies.

to thy name: this probably means 'to you'; for *šēm* ('name'), see on 20:1. Where Yahweh's name is, there also is Yahweh himself.

thy steadfast love and thy faithfulness: for this not uncommon pair of divine attributes, see on 57:3; cf. Exod. 34:6; Ps. 25:10, 61:7 (M.T. 8), 89:1f. (M.T. 2f.).

thou hast exalted . . .: lit. 'you have magnified your word above your name' which sounds slightly odd; it may suggest, however, that Yahweh's gracious deeds have far exceeded even his known fame or his past prowess. Cf. Eph. 3:20: 'who . . . is able to do far more abundantly than all that we ask or think'. *RSV* adds 'and' (*wᵉ*) before 'thy word' (*ʾimrāṯeḵāh*) (so also Schmidt, Kraus, *et al.*), while some other scholars (e.g. Oesterley) delete *ʾimrāṯeḵāh*, reading: '. . . magnified thy name over all'. Deissler (*PWdB*, III, p. 186) renders '. . . magnified your word on account of all your name'. 'Your word' may refer to the promises of God to his people.

3. On the day I called: this was the turning point of the trouble but we need not take 'the day' in its literal sense. When the afflicted man (or community) calls for help, God answers (cf. 17:6; Isa. 40:29).

thou didst increase: so *RSV*, following most of the ancient versions, and reading *tarbēnî* (or *tarbeh*) for M.T. *tarhīḇēnî* ('you have made me proud') (cf. 18:35 (M.T. 36)). *NEB* renders 'and make me bold and valiant-hearted'.

UNIVERSAL HOMAGE TO YAHWEH **4–6**

4. All the kings . . .: i.e. the kings and the nations which they rule; therefore the Psalmist means that the whole world will praise Yahweh (cf. 68:32 (M.T. 33), 96:1,3,7f., 97:1, 98:4, 100:1, 102:15 (M.T. 16).

the words of thy mouth: this seems to suggest the promises of Yahweh to the people rather than to a single worshipper, even though what God promises to one, may have a great significance for many. Deissler (*PWdB*, III, pp. 187f.) sees here an allusion to Yahweh's promise to deliver his people from Exile (cf. Isa. 40:5), and the many similarities between Ps. 138 and Deutero-Isaiah lend some support to Deissler's view. Oesterley (*TP*, p. 551) thinks that the 'words' refer to the decree of Cyrus (cf. Ezra 1:2ff.), but this seems unlikely.

5. of the ways of the LORD: M.T. 'in the ways . . .' (so also LXX, *AV*). 'The ways' may be Yahweh's gracious dealings with Israel (see on 103:7).

the glory of the LORD: see on 26:8, 57:5. The kings (and the nations) will magnify Yahweh when they see his power at work (cf. Isa. 40:5, 60:1).

6. the LORD is high: although Yahweh is exalted above everything, he is not too proud to help the least of his creatures (cf. 113:4–8; see also Isa. 57:15, 66:2).

he regards the lowly: the verb *r-ʾ-h* ('to see') may also mean 'to look after (or 'to look with favour')'. Cf. 106:44; Lk. 1:48,52.

the haughty: Dahood (*PAB*, I, p. 62) regards the adjective *gāḇōah* (*RSV* 'haughty') as a divine title 'the Lofty One'; this is a possible interpretation, but not necessarily superior to the *RSV* rendering.

he knows from afar: the Hebrew *y-d-ʿ* in this verse may not be the common verb 'to know', but a cognate of the Arabic *waduʿa*, meaning 'to humble'. Winton Thomas (*TRP*, p. 53; cf. also *JTS*, n.s., XII (1961), p. 50) suggests *yᵉyaddāʿ* ('he humbles (the haughty)') (similarly *NEB*) for M.T. *yᵉyēḏāʿ* ('he knows'). 'From afar' may be another way of saying 'from the heavens', as suggested by the interpretation of T ('from the distant heavens').

CONFIDENCE IN YAHWEH'S COVENANT LOYALTY **7–8**

7. in the midst of trouble: the author does not specify of what sort of troubles he is thinking. It may refer to the hardships

of the early years of the post-Exilic period. *NEB* improves the parallelism by rendering: 'among foes'.
thou dost preserve my life: see on 30:3, 119:25; cf. 71:20, 143:11.
thou dost stretch out thy hand: this is figurative speech describing Yahweh's intervention to help or to punish (cf. 144:7). The word *yāḏ* ('hand') may be rendered, perhaps, as 'left hand' (see on 74:11), balancing 'thy right hand' in verse 7*d*.
thy right hand delivers me: cf. 60:5 (M.T. 7), 139:10.

8. The LORD will fulfil his purpose: for a similar expression see 57:2 (M.T. 3). T paraphrases 'Yahweh shall reward them with evil, on account of me' (similarly LXX and V).
for me: Dahood (*PAB*, I, p. 19) suggests '(Yahweh will deal bountifully) as long as I live', reading *beᶜōḏî* for M.T. *baᶜaḏî* ('for me').
thy steadfast love: for this expression, see on 107:1.
the work of thy hands: lit. 'the works of . . .', referring either to the course of action which God has undertaken, or to the people of God, as in Isa. 60:21, 64:8 (M.T. 7).

Psalm 139 The Thanksgiving of an Acquitted Man

The Psalm is made up of two parts: verses 1–18 and 19–24. The first part deals with three main themes: Yahweh's unlimited knowledge of the Psalmist (verses 1–6), his omnipresence (verses 7–12), and his awe-inspiring wonders of creation (verses 13–18). The second part of the Psalm consists of a malediction on the enemies of God (verses 19–22) and a prayer to Yahweh (verses 23–4).

Since verses 1–18 are reminiscent of a Hymn and verses 19–24 of an Individual Lamentation, some scholars (e.g. Schmidt) have regarded them as two independent poems or fragments. There is little doubt, however, that the Psalm is a literary unity (cf. verses 1 and 23).

The definition of the *Gattung* of the Psalm must be tentative, but whereas verses 23f. are a petition to God to search the accused man's heart, verse 1 states that Yahweh has *already* scrutinized the motives and deeds of the suppliant. The best explanation of this is the assumption that the Psalm is an Individual Thanksgiving offered after the accused had been acquitted by God. This would also account for the unusual structure of the composition because the Thanksgiving Psalms not infrequently recount the past troubles and quote parts of the previous prayers. It seems that the person concerned was accused of idolatry (see verse 24), and the imperatives in verse 23 suggest the tension of the suspected man. In verses 21f. he dissociates himself from all the godless and stresses that he has nothing in common with them; we could regard verses 19–24 as an affirmation of innocence. So it seems that much of Ps. 139 is based upon the lamentation offered while the accused man was awaiting the divine decision or as a preparation for it. This hypothetical lament may have been a formulary used on such occasions of ordeal (cf. Dt. 13:13–16, 17:2–7).

Since the *Gattung* of the Psalm and its *Sitz im Leben* are far from certain, it is worth mentioning some other views. A. Bentzen thought that the Psalm was a prayer of an accused man (similarly Weiser, Deissler), while Eaton (*PTBC*, p. 301) has suggested that the poem may have been 'composed for a ruler beset with fierce enemies'. G. W. Anderson (*PCB* 387c) views the poem as a 'highly individual meditative psalm', but Mowinckel (*PIW*, II, p. 74) takes it as a lament in which the introduction is elaborated into a complete hymn.

The date of the Psalm is uncertain, but it may be a post-Exilic composition; Deissler suggests a late post-Exilic date.

The metre of the Psalm is mainly 3 + 3.

To the choirmaster: see Introduction, p. 48.

A Psalm of David: see Introduction, pp. 43ff. and 46.

THE AMAZING KNOWLEDGE OF YAHWEH **1–6**

1. thou hast searched me: i.e. Yahweh has examined the heart and mind of the accused (cf. 7:9 (M.T. 10), 17:3, 26:2; Jer. 17:10; Sir. 42:18–21), and it seems that he has passed a favourable decision on the man who had been charged with a serious offence (see verse 24).

and known me: so *RSV*, after LXX, V, reading *wattēḏāᶜēnî* for M.T. *wattēḏaᶜ* ('you know'). The pronoun 'me' (or the verbal suffix) in verse 1*a* probably has a double function, i.e. its force extends also to verse 1*b* (see on 3:3). The meaning of verse 1*b* is: 'you know that I am not guilty' (cf. Job 10:7; Jer. 12:3). The affirmation or praise of God's omniscience serves a twofold purpose: it glorifies him, and shows that his judgment cannot possibly be wrong.

2. Thou: the Hebrew *ᵓattāh* seems to be used for the purpose of emphasis: 'You alone'.

when I sit down . . . rise up: this comprises one's whole life. For a similar expression, see Dt. 6:7; Ps. 127:2.

my thoughts: or 'my intentions'. The Hebrew *rēa*ᶜ ('thought, purpose') occurs only here and in verse 17, and may be an Aramaism. The preposition *l*ᵉ before *rēa*ᶜ may be used as a sign of the accusative (so in Aramaic).

from afar: for this phrase, see on 138:6*b*.

3. Thou searchest out: the verb *z-r-h* usually means 'to scatter' or, in a derived sense, 'to sift, winnow'. Some associate *zērîṯā* (**thou searchest out** (*RSV*)) with *zereṯ* ('span') (cf. *KBL*, p. 266a), which would give some such meaning as 'you measure', but the former alternative is more likely. Cf. also *JBL*, LXXXV (1966), p. 456.

my path and my lying down are parallel with 'all my ways', and together they picturesquely depict a man's entire life. The Hebrew *ʾorḥî* ('my path') can be regarded as an infinitive construct with a suffix (analogous to the infinitives in verse 2*a*), denoting 'my journeying' or 'my going'.

art acquainted: G. A. Danell ('Psalm 139', *Uppsala Universitets Årsskrift* (1951) I, p. 11) views verse 3*b* as a circumstantial clause: 'being acquainted . . .'.

4. Yahweh knows not only the uttered words but also the thoughts of man. The description of God's omniscience is practical in nature rather than theoretical.

5. Thou dost beset me: the Hebrew *ṣ-w-r* could mean either 'to besiege, confine' (so *RSV*), or 'to create, fashion' (so LXX, S, and V), but this latter alternative would anticipate verses 13–16. The former rendering need not suggest any hostility; Yahweh may surround the suppliant for the purpose of protecting him. This seems to be suggested by verse 6, which would sound rather strange if God were to be regarded as an adversary.

layest thy hand upon me: this expression can be a gesture of blessing, as in Gen. 48:14,17. For a similar thought, see Exod. 33:22 where the hand of Yahweh protectively covers Moses. Cf. Psalms of Solomon 13:1: 'The right hand of the Lord hath covered me; the right hand of the Lord hath spared us.'

6. The Psalmist exclaims that such awareness of Yahweh's gracious omniscience is too wonderful for him; it is far beyond his understanding.

Such knowledge: LXX reads *hē gnōsis sou* ('the knowledge of you'), which may be a correct interpretation of the M.T.; Mowinckel (*PIW*, I, p. 92) has '(Thy) insight'.

YAHWEH'S OMNIPRESENCE **7–12**

7. thy Spirit is parallel to 'thy presence' (lit. 'your face', see on 66:8), and both refer to Yahweh as present in his power and might. 'Spirit', *rûaḥ*, may be a circumlocution for Yahweh himself (see on 76:12). T understood *rûaḥ* as 'wind, wrath' (an allusion to the story of Jonah?). The verse as a whole is a rhetorical question, expecting a negative answer. It does not imply that the Psalmist wanted to escape from God (as Jonah tried to do; cf. Jon. 1:3,10); on the contrary, he seems to be glad that there is no place in this world where he might find himself beyond God's care (see verse 10). In a way this is also an implicit protestation of innocence; believing what he does, he would have been absolutely foolish to rebel against God, or to try to hide his guilt, had he committed some offence. Therefore he feels safe with God, and is not afraid to ask God to search his thoughts and motives.

8. Danell (op. cit., p. 28) cites a parallel from the Amarna Letters (no. 264, lines 15–19) in which the sender affirms that whether he goes up to heaven or goes down to the earth (the underworld (?)), his life is in the hands of the Pharaoh. It is possible that both the writer of the above letter and the Psalmist are using a well-known figure of speech which describes the unlimited might of some king or deity (cf. also Am. 9:2), and consequently verse 8 does not necessarily contradict the views of other Psalmists who affirm that God's Covenant love is not manifested in Sheol (see on 6:5, 30:9), and that those who are in the underworld are cut off from God's help (cf. 88:5 (M.T. 6)). It is doubtful if we are justified in arguing that in the view of the Psalmist God was actually present in Sheol (cf. Oesterley, *TP*, p. 556), although his authority did not end at the gates of Sheol (cf. v. Rad, *OTT*, I, p. 389).

If I ascend: this does not refer to the miraculous ascent of Enoch and Elijah (see on 73:24), as suggested by Davies (*Cent. BP*, II, p. 329), but it is merely a hypothetical supposition.

9. If I take the wings of the morning: this metaphor may be derived from some mythological story, although the myth itself may not have had any significance to the Psalmist. The Hebrew *šaḥar* (**morning** (*RSV*)) is etymologically linked with the Ugaritic

šḥr, which may denote the god of dawn (?) (cf. Driver, *CML*, p. 123b; Jirku, *MK*, pp. 58f.). A dependence upon Greek mythology (so Oesterley, *TP*, p. 556) is unlikely. The above expression is reminiscent of 55:6 (M.T. 7): 'O that I had wings like a dove'. Another possibility is that verse 9*a* is a word-picture for being in the extreme east; this would offer a good contrast to verse 9*b*, which speaks of the extreme west (cf. heaven—Sheol (verse 8) and darkness—light (verse 11)). Dahood ('Congruity of Metaphors', *SVT*, 16 (1967), p. 44) renders verse 9*a*: 'Should I lift my wings (*kenāpay* for M.T. *kanepê*, 'wings of . . .') in the east', but the improvement, if any, does not justify the re-vocalization.
the uttermost parts of the sea: the extreme west or the end of the earth. Danell (op. cit., p. 15) thinks that this is a 'designation of the abode of the dead'; this would be a unique expression in the *OT*, but it is not impossible, since similar ideas existed among Israel's neighbours (cf. H. Frankfort, *Ancient Egyptian Religion* (1961), p. 106). Yet verse 9 is connected more with verse 10 than with 8*b*, and therefore 'uttermost parts of the sea' refers rather to the most distant parts of the world or to the farthest west.

10. If the Psalmist went to the ends of the earth, even there he would experience Yahweh's guidance. (Cf. Clements, *GT*, p. 132.)
thy hand: probably 'your left hand' being a complementary parallel to 'thy right hand' (verse 10*b*); see on 74:11.
. . . shall lead me: some scholars read *tiḳḳāḥēnî* ('. . . shall seize me' (in a hostile sense ?)) for M.T. *tanḥēnî* ('. . . shall lead me'), but it is doubtful whether the emendation is justified. The following line (verse 10*b*) can quite well mean that God has taken hold of the Psalmist not in anger but in gracious care (as in 73:23).

11. If I say: rather 'When I said' which may allude to the past troubles.
Let only darkness cover me: or 'Surely darkness will spread over ('envelop') me'. The Hebrew *š-w-p* means 'to bruise, crush' (cf. Gen. 3:15; Job 9:18), and in a derived sense it may mean 'to overwhelm'. Some commentators (cf. Thomas, *TRP*, p. 53) change *yešûpēnî* ('it will overwhelm me') into *yeśûkkēnî* ('it shall cover me'). 'Darkness' may be a metaphor for the distress experienced by the suppliant, and need not allude to any magic art (cf. Eaton, *PTBC*, p. 302).
and the light about me be night: 11QPsa (col. 20) has: 'and night has (already) encompassed me', reading *ʾzr* ('has encompassed') for M.T. *ʾôr* ('light'). The Psalmist apparently states

that when troubles were about to overwhelm him (from the human point of view), they could not force God's hand (verse 11), or they could never be too much for him.

12. even the darkness is not dark: or, 'yet even (the very) darkness is not too dark for you' (similarly Kissane), i.e. no trouble is too great for you (unless verses 11f. are to be taken literally).

the night is bright as the day: or, 'and (to you even) the night will be as light as the day', which may imply that God can transform the worst adversity into an occasion of blessing.

for darkness is as light with thee: i.e. darkness and light are both alike to you (similarly *AV*, *RV*). Some scholars (e.g. Kraus) delete this phrase as a gloss. The words 'with thee' are not in M.T.

YAHWEH AS THE MAKER OF MAN **13–18**

Yahweh's omniscience is based upon the fact that he is the creator of all (cf. 94:9).

13. For thou didst form: or, 'You have indeed formed me'. The verb used is *ḳ-n-h*, which is often used of divine creative activity, but it is less frequent than its synonym *b-r-ʾ* ('to create'). Von Rad (*OTT*, I, p. 142) regards *ḳ-n-h* as of Canaanite origin (cf. also P. Katz, *JJS*, v (1954), pp. 126ff.). LXX, V, *AV*, *RV* take *ḳ-n-h* in the other sense, 'to possess', which is less likely in the present context. Cf. J. Gray, *The Legacy of Canaan* (*SVT*, 5, 1957), p. 194.

my inward parts: lit. 'my kidneys' (*AV*, *RV* 'my reins'). The Hebrew *k^elāyôṯ* ('kidneys' or 'reins') is often employed in a figurative sense as the seat of emotion (cf. *DB*, p. 550a; Pedersen, *ILC*, I–II, pp. 173f.); see on 7:9.

thou didst knit me together . . .: rather than '. . . hast covered me . . .' (*AV*, *RV*). Cf. Job 10:8–11; Jer. 1:5. See also M. Dahood, *Biblica*, XLIV (1963), p. 301.

14. I praise thee: lit. 'I thank you' (see on 18:49). In M.T. this is followed by *ʿal kî*, 'for' (so *RSV*), but Dahood (*PAB*, I, p. 195) suggests that *ʿl* is to be regarded as a divine appellative: 'Most High'. This is possible, but not necessary.

for thou art fearful and wonderful: following LXX, T, S, and V. This rendering is partly supported by 11QPs[a] (col. 20), which reads *nwrʾ ʾth* ('you are awesome') for M.T. *nôrāʾôṯ* ('fearful'). For M.T. *niplêṯî* ('I am wonderfully made') 11QPs[a] has *nplʾwt* ('(your works are) exceedingly (wonderful)'). M.T. could

be translated literally: 'for I am fearfully and wonderfully made' (so *AV*, *RV*).
Thou knowest me right well: this involves a change from M.T. *yōḏaʿaṯ* ('(my soul) knows') (so also LXX, T, S, V) into *yāḏaʿtā* ('you know'), and verse 14*c* forms the parallel to verse 15*a*.

15. my frame: lit. 'my bones' (a collective noun). 11QPs^a (col. 20) reads *ʿṣby*, 'my body (?)' (the verb *ʿ-ṣ-b* means 'to fashion, shape') for M.T. *ʿoṣmî* ('my frame').
when I was being made in secret: the reference may be to the formation of the embryo in the womb, or it is possible that the author is making use of certain mythological word-pictures which portrayed man as being created in the depths of the earth, i.e. the Mother Earth (cf. Job 1:21; 2 Esd. 5:48; Sir. 40:1; see also Tromp, *PCD*, pp. 122ff.). The metaphor may refer to the creation of the first man rather than of each successive generation as such, and therefore there is no inconsistency with verse 13*b*.
intricately wrought: the verb *r-ḳ-m* primarily means 'to embroider, weave', hence, perhaps, 'to fashion with care'. It is unlikely that the Psalmist is describing the veins and arteries of the human body (so Cohen, *PSon*, p. 453).
in the depths of the earth: this is parallel to 'in secret' (verse 15*a*) and it supports the Mother Earth theory (cf. Kraus, *PBK*, 920). A similar idea is also found in Job 1:21: 'Naked I came from my mother's womb, and naked shall I return' (lit. '. . . return *there*' which may allude to the above myth). Cf. also Pope, *Job* (*AB* 15, 1965), p. 16; Danell, op. cit., p. 30; Eichrodt, *TOT*, II, p. 141.

16. my unformed substance: probably 'my embryo'. Some exegetes (e.g. Gunkel, Oesterley, Kraus) suggest *g*^{e}*mūlay* ('my deeds') for M.T. *golmî* ('my embryo'). The emendation is more in line with what follows in the text.
thy book: 11QPs^a (col. 20) reads *sprykh* ('your books'). For this concept of the divine books, see on 51:1, 69:28.
every one of them: referring either to 'my deeds' (if we adopt the emendation), or to 'the days' mentioned in the following line. Some of the older commentators (e.g. Ibn Ezra, Ḳimḥi, *AV*, *RV*) thought that the reference is to all the members of the embryo, but this is hardly likely.
when as yet there was none of them: probably the days. M.T. is, however, obscure.

17. How precious: or 'How incomprehensible (to the finite man)'.
thy thoughts may be a synonym of 'your works' (as in 92:5 (M.T. 6); cf. Job 42:3; Ps. 40:5 (M.T. 6)). The word *rēᶜîm* could mean 'friends' (LXX *hoi philoi*, similarly V), but this is less likely than the *RSV* rendering.
the sum of them: i.e. their immeasurable totality.

18. If I would count them: i.e. the works of God.
more than the sand: this is a well-known figure of speech describing what is innumerable (cf. Gen. 22:17, 32:12 (M.T. 13), 41:49; Jos. 11:4, etc.).
when I awake: T and Sym understood the phrase as an allusion to resurrection, but this is not very likely. On the other hand, the more recent interpretations are equally unsatisfactory, and it seems that a line or lines may have been accidentally omitted between verse 18*a* and *b*. *RSVm* (following Halévy, Gunkel, *et al.*) renders: 'were I to come to the end', *hᵃḳiṣṣôṯî* (for M.T. *hᵉḳîṣōṯî*), but this offers no real improvement. *NEB* suggests 'to finish the count, my years must equal thine'.
I am still with thee: cf. 73:23: 'I am continually with thee'.

AN IMPRECATION ON THE ENEMIES **19–22**

The sentiments expressed in this section are far from those reflected in the Sermon on the Mount, but, on the other hand, it must be remembered that for the Psalmist and his contemporaries evil was no abstract idea but was embodied in evil men (so Kirkpatrick, *BPCB*, p. 790). This also explains, at least partly, the hate which the poet feels against the enemies.

19. the wicked: the Hebrew *rāšāᶜ* (see on 1:1, 28:3, 92:7) is used collectively. The prayer that God might slay the wicked would amount to a self-cursing if the accused man were to be proved to be in the wrong (cf. Würthwein, op. cit., p. 173).
men of blood: see on 5:6; cf. Prov. 29:10.
. . . would depart from me: i.e. from persecuting me (see on 6:8). *RSV* presupposes *yāsûrû* for M.T. *sûrû* (11QPsᵃ *swr*), 'depart' (imperative, second person plural).

20. who maliciously defy thee: or 'they speak (against) thee wickedly' (so *AV*, *RV*). Some exegetes emend M.T. *yōʾmᵉrūḵā* into *yamrûḵā* (from *m-r-h*): 'they are rebellious against you'.
who lift themselves up . . .: similarly 11QPsᵃ (col. 20) which

reads *nś*ʾ*w* ('they lift up . . .') for M.T. *nāśû*ʾ, which seems to be a passive participle of *n-ś-*ʾ ('to lift up').

against thee: M.T. has ᶜ*ārêḵā* which means 'your cities' (so LXX, S, V) but *AV*, *RV* renders it as 'thine enemies'; in Aramaic ᶜ*ār* can mean a 'hater', or 'enemy' (cf. *DTTM*, p. 1109b). *RSV* accepts the emendation ᶜ*ālêḵā* ('against you') for M.T. ᶜ*ārêḵā*.

21. Do I not hate them: this rhetorical question is probably an emphatic way of saying: 'I indeed hate . . .' (see verse 22); *NEB* 'How I hate them'. The enemies of the Psalmist are also God's enemies, or they are the opponents of the poet because they are rebels against God (cf. 26:5, 119:113). For the verb *ś-n-*ʾ ('to hate'), see on 68:1; cf. 1QS i:10.

do I not loathe them: cf. 119:158.

22. I count them my enemies: the Psalmist's hatred is not really an expression of personal feelings; he is primarily concerned with the honour of God and with the upholding of the Covenant.

A PRAYER TO GOD **23–4**

23. Search me . . .: this is a petition to the righteous judge for a decision in a capital case (cf. verse 19), and it may be a quotation from the lamentation uttered during the distress (cf. the introduction to this Psalm); see verse 1.

know my heart: for *lēḇāḇ* ('heart'), see on 27:3. Note also the urgency of the appeal, which manifests itself in the repetition of the synonymous requests: 'search me', 'try me', and 'know my thoughts'.

24. any wicked way: the Hebrew ᶜ*ōṣeḇ* can be associated either with ᶜ*-ṣ-b* I ('to pain, hurt') or with ᶜ*-ṣ-b* II ('to shape, fashion'). Consequently the noun may denote either 'hurt' or 'idol'; the latter seems more likely. If so, the allusion is to 'the way of idolatry' (similarly T) (i.e. the Psalmist may have been accused of worshipping idols), or of apostasy. The punishment for this would be death (cf. Dt. 13:13–16, 17:2–7).

the way everlasting: or 'the ancient way' (*dereḵ* ᶜ*ôlām*). This expression is a *hapax legomenon* in the *OT*, but it is found in 1QH iv:4 where it is parallel with the paths which God has chosen. Kraus (*PBK*, p. 921) thinks it possible that the concept of 'two ways' may have arisen out of certain cultic practices involved in the ordeal (cf. J. Morgenstern, 'Trial by Ordeal', *HUCA*, II (1925), pp. 113ff.; R. Press, 'Ordal im alten Israel', *ZAW*, LI (1933), pp. 121–40, 227–55). Dahood (*PAB*, I, p. 33) translates: 'the eternal assembly', i.e. the heavenly council, but this is doubtful. Würthwein suggests, more plausibly, that *dereḵ ʿôlām* denotes 'the way to the Temple' (op. cit., p. 174); cf. 24:7,9, where the Temple gates are called 'the ancient doors'. Another possibility is that the Psalmist is thinking of the paths (i.e. way of life) followed by the forefathers (cf. Jer. 6:16, 18:15); *NEB* 'the ancient ways'.

Psalm 140 Yahweh is the Refuge of the Afflicted

This Psalm belongs to the Individual Laments (see Introduction, pp. 37ff.) and it may, perhaps, be further defined as a Prayer of an accused man (so Schmidt, Deissler). The poet portrays himself as beset by ruthless slanderers, who were, most likely, false accusers. He does not describe the trumped-up charges, but they must have been serious. If this suggestion is right, then the lament was a petition and preparation for Yahweh's judgment.

Some scholars (e.g. Eaton) regard the composition as a Royal Psalm, and certain features (see verses 2 and 7) indeed support this view. On the whole, however, the former interpretation seems more applicable to the Psalm, and it can account for the similarities to the Royal Psalms.

The poem begins with a call for help and a lamentation in fairly general terms (verses 1–5). This is followed by an appeal to the righteous judge (verses 6–11), and the Psalm ends on a note of confidence that God will establish justice (verses 12–13.)

The date of the Psalm is uncertain; Oesterley (*TP*, p. 558) places it in the fourth or third century B.C., but an earlier date is not improbable. The *language* of the Psalm favours the post-Exilic period.

The metre of the Psalm is irregular.

To the choirmaster: see Introduction, p. 48.

A Psalm of David: see Introduction, pp. 43ff. and 46.

PRAYER AND LAMENTATION **1–5**

1. Deliver me: such cries for help are frequently used to introduce Laments (cf. 41:3, 51:1 (M.T. 3), 54:1 (M.T. 3), 56:1 (M.T. 2), 57:1 (M.T. 2), etc.). For the use of the verb *ḥ-l-ṣ*, cf. 119:153; 1QS xi:13.

evil men: the Hebrew *ʾāḏām* ('man') is to be taken collectively (so *RSV*, *PNT*, *NEB*; *AV*, *RV*, *RP* have 'man') as suggested by verses 2f.

preserve me: i.e. guard me from violent men (lit. 'man of violences' or 'man of exceptional violence'). It is not very likely that in our context 'evil men' refers to persons of low social standing, and 'violent men' (*ʾîš ḥamāsîm*) to persons of importance (as suggested by Barnes, *PWC*, II, p. 641); see on 18:48, 49:2.

2. who plan . . . in their heart: i.e. secretly but with great determination (cf. 21:11 (M.T. 12), 35:4; Zech. 7:10, 8:17).

stir up wars continually: the Hebrew *yāḡûrû* (from *g-w-r* II, 'to stir up strife (?); the more common *g-w-r* I means 'to sojourn') is thought to be dubious, and many exegetes propose *yeḡārû*, 'they provoke, stir up' (from *g-r-h*); this reading may be implied by 11QPsa (col. 27) which was *ygrw*. 'Wars' and the reference to 'the day of battle' (verse 7) may suggest that the Psalm was intended for the King or some military leader (so Eaton) but it is equally possible, if not more likely, that expressions proper to the Royal Psalms could have been borrowed and applied to this and other Laments of the Individual (cf. Kraus, *PBK*, p. 925). The speaker in Ps. 140 appears to be an ordinary person of no special office, and his opponents are his own countrymen.

3. They make their tongue sharp: lit. 'They have sharpened' (cf. 64:3 (M.T. 4)); i.e. their tongue is as sharp as that of a serpent (see on 58:4). The allusion is to the forked tongue of the snake, which may have been popularly (although mistakenly) regarded as a sting.

under their lips is the poison of vipers: the Hebrew word *ʿaḵšûḇ*, 'viper', is a *hapax legomenon* in the *OT* (*NEB* has '. . . spiders' poison'); LXX renders it by *aspis* ('asp' or 'Egyptian cobra') (similarly S, V) but T has *ʿakkôbîṯāʾ* ('spider'), and similarly 11QPsa (col. 27), which reads *ʿkbyš* ('spider'). Verse 3*b* is quoted in Rom. 3:13.

Selah: see Introduction, pp. 48f.

4. Guard me: so also in 16:1, 17:8, 141:9.

from the hands of the wicked: i.e. from the clutches (or 'power') of the godless. The Hebrew *rāšāʿ* ('wicked') (see on 1:1, 28:3, 92:7) is a person for whom the divine law 'has no existential significance, so that his sin is not simply his *actus peccandi*, but embraces his life as such' (K. H. Rengstorf, *TDNT*, I, p. 322).

preserve me . . .: see verse 1*b*.

. . . to trip up my feet: or 'to overthrow my steps' (cf. 118:13).

5. Arrogant men: see on 94:2. These are men who reject the brotherhood of *all* Israelites, and thereby they disinherit *themselves* (cf. verse 11). These supercilious men are portrayed as hunters hiding their traps (for *paḥ*, 'snare, trap', see on 119:110) and nets (see on 9:15, 31:4) in order to ensnare (metaphorically) their human prey. Such a description of the enemies of the individual is quite frequent in the Psalter (cf. 9:15 (M.T. 16), 31:4 (M.T. 5), 35:7, 64:5 (M.T. 6), 141:9, 142:3 (M.T. 4)).

with cords . . .: some scholars (e.g. Oesterley, Kraus) read *m^eḥabb^elîm* ('those who work for (another's) ruin') for M.T. *ḥ^ab̲ālîm* ('cords'). A simpler change would be read *ḥōb̲^elîm*, 'corrupters' (so Gunkel) or *ḥabbālîm* ('knaves') (so G. R. Driver; *NEB* 'rogues'), which is found in Syriac but not in the *OT*.

snares: for *môḳēš*, see on 64:5.

Selah: see Introduction, pp. 48f.

A PRAYER FOR JUDGMENT ON THE WICKED **6–11**

6. I say: or 'I said' (*AV*, *RV*, *RP*); cf. 16:2. Perhaps the Psalmist's loyalty to Yahweh is implicitly contrasted with the arrogant godlessness of the wicked.

to the LORD: Dahood (*PAB*, I, p. 87) renders this phrase by 'O Yahweh', and he regards the preposition *l^e* ('to') as a *lāmed̲ vocativum.*

Thou art my God: a similar expression occurs in 16:2, 31:14 (M.T. 15). For 'my God', see on 52:5, 113:5. Since Yahweh is the Covenant God (cf. Exod. 20:2) of the righteous, the upright man can turn to him for protection and vindication.

give ear . . .: i.e. attend to my prayer and answer me with your help (see on 141:1).

the voice of my supplications: see on 28:2, 86:6.

7. O LORD, my Lord: lit. 'O Yahweh, my Lord'. The *RSV* rendering is due to the traditional practice of replacing the tetragrammaton, or the divine name Yahweh, by a less sacred substitute, such as 'the Lord', 'the Name', etc. (cf. *DB*, pp. 334f.; for a brief bibliography on the subject, see *IDB*, II, p. 417).

my strong deliverer: lit. 'the strength of my salvation' (*AV*, *RV*, *RP*); this phrase is found only here in the *OT*. Yahweh is the saving strength of the afflicted man.

thou hast covered my head: commentators usually suggest that God is portrayed as covering with a shield or helmet the defenceless head of the harassed man (cf. 3:3 (M.T. 4); Isa. 59:17; Eph. 6:17; 1 Th. 5:8).

the day of battle: lit. 'the day of weapons (?)'; the phrase is a *hapax legomenon*. Kraus (*PBK*, p. 925) is of the opinion that this particular day refers to the giving of the divine judgment rather than to a time of battle. For *nešeḳ* ('battle, armour'), see N. H. Tur-Sinai, *The Book of Job* (1957), p. 550.

8. the desires of the wicked: i.e. may Yahweh frustrate the pernicious schemes of the men who are in the wrong and are proud of it. *Rāšā*ᶜ ('wicked') (see verse 4) is probably a collective term (so *NEB*) as against the rendering of *AV*, *RV*, *RSV*, etc.

do not further his evil plot: for the verb *p-w-ḳ* ('to further, promote') cf. the Ugaritic *pḳ* (see Driver, *CML*, p. 162b), which may have a similar meaning. The noun *zāmām* ('plan, device') is found only here in the *OT*, but its meaning must be synonymous with that of *zimmāh* (see on 26:10) and *mᵉzimmāh* (cf. 37:7), both of which suggest 'purpose, wicked device, etc.'. *AV*, *RV*, following M.T., have after verse 8*b*: '*lest* they exalt themselves. Selah' (similarly LXX), while *RSV* transfers the verb *yārûmû* ('they are high') to verse 9, changing it into *yārîmû* ('they lift up'; so also two Hebrew MSS.).

9. their head: M.T. of verse 9*a* could be rendered: 'the head of those who surround me', but a verb seems to be missing. Therefore some such change as that adopted by *RSV* and *NEB* is preferable. Jerome (also Sym) understood the Hebrew *rōʾš* (*RSV* 'head') as 'poison', i.e. poisonous words (cf. Boylan, *PSVP*, II, p. 359); this gives a reasonable rendering: '. . . lift up (their) venomous speech' (for the construction cf. Gen. 39:15).

the mischief of their lips: for *ᶜāmāl* ('toil, mischief'), see on 55:10. The allusion may be to the slanders and false accusations which, if proved wrong, would bring punishment upon the liars (see on 27:12); cf. 7:16 (M.T. 17), 64:8 (M.T. 9).

10. burning coals: (*gaḥᵃlêʾ ēš*). This reading is also suggested by some Greek MSS. and Jerome; M.T. has *geḥālîm bāʾēš* ('coals with fire'). Verse 10*a* may be a figurative description of divine punishment, derived from the story of Sodom and Gomorrah (Gen. 19); less likely is the suggestion that the Psalmist had in mind some sort of ordeal by fire (so Schmidt, *PHAT*, p. 246).

Let them be cast into pits: the noun *mahᵃmōrôṯ* (*RSV* 'pits') is a *hapax legomenon* in the *OT*, and its meaning is dubious. *BDB* (p. 243a) proposes 'flood' which is also supported by Sym (*bothunos*), T, and Jerome. Cf. also the Ugaritic *mhmrt* ('gullet (?)') and *hmry* ('miry' (?)) which is the name of Mot's town in the underworld (see Gordon, *UT*, p. 391, no. 779; Driver,

CML, p. 137b). Dahood (*PAB*, I, p. 224) suggests 'the miry depths' as a translation of *mahamōrôṯ*. The Psalmist may have thought of a divine judgment similar to that inflicted on Korah and his company (Num. 16:32f.), or of the fate of some of the followers of the kings of Sodom and Gomorrah (Gen. 14:10). See also Tromp, *PCD*, p. 54.

no more to rise: their fall will be final (cf. 36:12 (M.T. 13); Isa. 26:14).

11. slanderer: lit. 'a man of tongue'; this phrase occurs only here in the *OT*, but it is a very effective word-picture of a calumniator (see also verse 3).

established in the land: Weiser (*POTL*, p. 810) is of the opinion that the Psalmist may be referring to the exclusion of the wicked from the cultic community, which brings with it the loss of the privilege of owning property in Yahweh's land. Cf. Lev. 25:23: 'the land is mine; for you are strangers and sojourners with me'; consequently those who have rejected Yahweh's authority have no claim to this privilege to dwell in his land. The practical implications of this are not clear, however (cf. 101:5). See v. Rad, 'Promised Land and Yahweh's Land', *PHOE*, pp. 79–93.

let evil hunt down . . . speedily: just as the violent man (see verse 1*b*) hounded his innocent prey, so he himself shall be afflicted without having the comfort of a clear conscience. T paraphrases 11*b*: 'evil shall hunt down (the violent man), the angel of death shall push him down into Gehenna'.

THE CONFIDENCE IN YAHWEH **12–13**

12. I know . . .: (so *Ḳerê*; *Keṯîḇ* suggests *yāḏaʿtā* ('you know'), which is unlikely). This is an utterance of confidence and certainty, but it does not necessarily imply that the divine decision (or an oracular sign) has been given. The assurance may be based on the knowledge of Yahweh's previous interventions on behalf of his people. Cf. 20:6 (M.T. 7), 56:9 (M.T. 10).

the afflicted: for *ʿānî*, see on 34:2. Yahweh will do justice to the cause of his servant (cf. 9:4 (M.T. 5)).

13. righteous: see on 1:5; cf. Rom. 8:33.

give thanks: or, 'praise' (see on 18:49).

to thy name: or, 'to you'. For *šēm* ('name'), see on 20:1.

the upright: the term *yāšār* is discussed on 92:15; it is a synonym of 'the righteous'.

shall dwell in thy presence: i.e. they shall have the right to worship Yahweh and to dwell in his land, in contrast to the wicked (see verse 11). See on 25:13, 37:9. The phrase may also mean 'to live under Yahweh's protection' (cf. 11:7, 31:20 (M.T. 21)), thus enjoying his favour and blessings.

Psalm 141 THE DANGER OF BAD COMPANY

This Psalm is an Individual Lament (see Introduction, pp. 37ff.) in which the Psalmist pleads for divine protection against his enemies, and for deliverance from evil and temptation.

The poem opens with the customary cry for help (verses 1–2), and is followed by a prayer that he might be preserved from sinning in word and deed (verses 3–5). Verses 6–7 are beset by textual uncertainties or corruptions, but the theme appears to be the punishment of the wicked. The Psalm ends with a petition that the pernicious plans of the enemies may come to nothing (verses 8–10).

It is probable that the Lament was used by the appropriate people at the time of the evening sacrifice (see verse 2). Taylor (*PIB*, p. 722) describes the poem as 'substantially Ps. 1 put into the form of a prayer', i.e. it is a didactic prayer.

The Psalm is to be placed in the post-Exilic period, and its metre is 4+4 for the most part.

A Psalm of David: see Introduction, pp. 43ff. and 46.

THE INTRODUCTORY CALL FOR HELP **1–2**

1. I call upon thee: lit. 'I called . . .'. This is a frequent expression in *OT* prayers (cf. 17:6, 31:17 (M.T. 18), 88:9 (M.T. 10), 119:146, 130:1.

make haste to me: as in 70:5 (M.T. 6). It stresses the urgency of the situation rather than his impatience with God. Far more common is the synonymous phrase 'hasten to my aid' (22:19 (M.T. 20), 38:22 (M.T. 23), 40:13 (M.T. 14), 70:1 (M.T. 2), 71:12).

Give ear: i.e., 'Be willing to hear my prayer'. 'Ear' as the organ of hearing is often employed to denote 'hearing' or 'attention'; hence 'to give ear' means 'to give attention'.

2. prayer: for *teᵉpillāh*, see on 65:2.

incense: the Hebrew *ḳeṭōreṯ* may signify the smoke of a sacrifice (66:15) or incense (Exod. 25:5, 30:7, etc.). Here it probably refers to the incense burnt with the burnt offerings (cf. H. Wildberger, *Jesaja* (*BK* 10_1, 1965), p. 42; M. Haran, 'The Uses of Incense in the Ancient Israelite Ritual', *VT*, x (1960), pp. 113–29). Cohen (*PSon*, p. 458) has argued that the Psalmist was precluded from bringing an offering, and that he hoped that his prayers would prove an efficacious substitute. Weiser (and some others) has stated that 'prayer is counted before God as incense and as an evening sacrifice and, consequently, is meant to take the place of the sacrifice' (*POTL*, p. 811). It is true that in the post-Exilic period there was a process of spiritualizing much of the sacrificial system, but it is very doubtful if the Psalmists ever intended to replace sacrifices by prayers and praises (cf. v. Rad, *OTT*, I, pp. 368f.). It is obvious that in certain circumstances (e.g. in the Babylonian exile and in the Dispersion) the sacrificial cult was impossible, but such situations were regarded either as anomalies or temporary deprivations. Cf. 11QPs[a], 45:10f.

the lifting up of my hands: for this prayerful attitude, see on 28:2.

evening sacrifice: for *minḥāh* ('sacrifice'), see on 40:6; cf. Lev. 2:1. In post-Exilic times prayers were often said thrice a day (cf. 55:17 (M.T. 18); 2 Enoch 51:4), and the time of the evening sacrifice was a well-known occasion for supplications (cf. Ezr. 9:5; Dan. 9:21; Jdt. 9:1). It is possible that the Psalm was uttered at some point during the evening offering, but not as its substitute. Verse 2 is essentially a plea to God to accept the prayers of the afflicted man even as he accepts the sacrifices which he himself had ordained.

A PRAYER AGAINST TEMPTATION 3–5

3. Set a guard . . .: i.e. preserve me from falling into sins of speech. The Psalmists and the Wisdom writers were well aware of the dangers of the misuse of the tongue. So Prov. 13:3: 'He who guards his mouth preserves his life; he who opens wide his lips comes to ruin' (cf. Ps. 34:13 (M.T. 14), 39:1 (M.T. 2); Prov. 21:23; Sir. 22:27, 28:25f.).

. . . the door of my lips: i.e. control my thinking and speaking. A similar expression is found in Mic. 7:5. The Hebrew *dal* ('door') occurs only here in the *OT*, but it is attested in Phoenician (cf. Kraus, *PBK*, p. 929). The usual word for 'door' is *deleṯ*.

4. Incline not my heart to any evil: it is possible that the author and his contemporaries believed that *all* human actions can ultimately be traced back to Yahweh; e.g. Yahweh was thought to have enticed David to commit a sin by numbering the people of Israel (2 Sam. 24:1). At a later time, such an explicit statement seemed unacceptable, and the Chronicler attributed this enticement to Satan (1 Chr. 21:1; for another example, see 1 Kg. 22:20–3). Probably the Psalmist's plea: 'Incline not my heart . . .', is an expression of his dependence upon, rather than an attribution of his sin to, Yahweh (cf. 119:36). For *lēḇ* ('heart'), see on 27:3. It often denotes 'reason' and 'will' in Hebrew idiom.

to busy myself: or 'to practise (deeds of wickedness)'.

wicked deeds: lit. 'deeds in wickedness'. Oesterley (*TP*, p. 561) renders: 'the doings of the wicked', reading *rāšāᶜ* ('wicked man') for *rešaᶜ* ('wickedness') (so also Gunkel).

who work iniquity: for *pōᶜᵃlê ᵓāwen* ('evildoers, doers of iniquity'), see on 28:3. Verse 4*cd* is a description of the fellowship of the godless who are bound together by their common devotion to wickedness (*ᵓāwen*, see on 36:4). By means of his prayer the Psalmist wishes to dissociate himself from the wicked, who are well typified in Prov. 4:16 as men who 'cannot sleep unless they have done wrong'.

their dainties are probably their hospitality (not necessarily prompted by altruistic motives); it need not suggest a 'participation in idolatrous sacrifices' (cf. Kirkpatrick, *BPCB*, p. 798); for the opposite view, see Barnes, *PWC*, II, p. 645; cf. 106:28; Isa. 65:4,11. The company of the wicked is always a potential danger, and therefore the Wisdom writers often warn the naïve optimists to avoid such companionship. In the Story of Aḥiḳar there is the advice: 'My son, pour out thy wine on the graves of the righteous, rather than drink with evil men' (cf. *APOT*, II, p. 730, no. 10). It is not impossible that verse 4*d* should be taken metaphorically, and that 'dainties' refers to the flattering words of the godless. Cf. Prov. 5:3: 'the lips of a loose woman drip honey'.

5. Let a good man strike . . .: this is reminiscent of Prov. 9:8: 'reprove a wise man, and he will love you', because this correction is for his own good. Similarly in the Story of Aḥiḳar (*APOT*, II, p. 738, no. 73) we read: 'let the wise man strike thee with many blows, and let not the fool salve thee with sweet salve'. Cf. also D. J. Wiseman, 'Alalakh', *AOTS*, p. 128.

oil of the wicked: so *RSV* and *NEB*, reading *rāšāᶜ* ('the wicked') for M.T. *rōᵓš* ('head'), following LXX, S and V. The anointing of the head of important and welcome guests was a common oriental custom. For 'oil' (*šemen*), see on 104:15.

for my prayer . . .: lit. 'for continually and my prayer is . . .' (*RSVm*). Perhaps we should render 'while I live (let) my prayer (be) against their wicked deeds', reading *ᶜôḏî* ('while I live') for M.T. *ᶜôḏ* ('yet'; *RSV* 'continually'), following the proposal by Winton Thomas (*TRP*, p. 54).

THE FATE OF THE WICKED **6–7**

6. When they are given over . . .: *RV* 'Their judges are thrown down by the sides of the rock'; or, 'Their rulers (see on 72:2) shall be thrown down (a prophetic perfect ?) from the sides of the rock' (for this use of the preposition *bᵉ*, see on 18:8); if the latter suggestion is adopted, then the allusion may be to a form of punishment mentioned in 2 Chr. 25:12; Lk. 4:29.

then they shall learn . . .: lit. 'and (then) they shall hear my words, for they (i.e. the words) are pleasant (kind?)'. For this verse, see H. Junker, 'Einige Rätsel im Urtext der Psalmen', *Biblica*, XXIV (1943), pp. 197–212; cf. R. Tournay, 'Le Psaume 141', *VT*, IX (1959), pp. 58–64.

7. As a rock which one cleaves . . .: perhaps 'as a ploughman (cf. *DTTM*, II, p. 1178) cleaves the earth (scattering the clods)', reading *yᵉḇaḳḳaᶜ* ('cleaves') for M.T. *ûḇōḳēaᶜ* ('and he who cleaves'); similarly *RP* (cf. LXX, S, V).

their bones: lit. 'our bones' (11QPsᵃ has 'my bones'), but *RSV* (following some Greek MSS. and S) seems right in reading *ᶜaṣᵉmêhem* for M.T. *ᶜaṣāmênû*.

at the mouth of Sheol: (for 'Sheol', see on 6:5) i.e. at the entrance of the underworld or, perhaps, at the opening of the family grave (cf. Pedersen, *ILC*, I–II, pp. 460ff.) as in Jer. 8:1f. (cf. Ezek. 6:5); this would undo the value of the previous burial rites, and it would be tantamount to a great dishonour and disaster. Cf. also Tromp, *PCD*, pp. 39f.

THE CONCLUDING PETITION **8–10**

8. my eyes are towards thee: for the phrase, see on 25:15.

in thee I seek refuge: see on 7:1, 16:1.

leave me not . . .: lit. 'pour not out my soul' (or 'life'); LXX renders 'take not away my life' which is a reasonable interpretation of M.T. The idiom may be derived from the belief that life can be poured out with the blood of a man or an animal, which is the seat of life (see Dt. 12:23f.); cf. Isa. 53:12. For *nep̱eš* ('soul'), see on 33:19.

9. Keep me . . .: see on 140:4. The enemies are frequently depicted as hunters (see on 7:15).
from the trap: (see on 119:110) lit. 'from the hands (or 'clutches') of the trap'. Cf. L. Wächter, *Der Tod im Alten Testament* (1967), pp. 35–8.
the snares: for *môḳēš*, see on 64:5.

10. the wicked: the Psalmist prays that the schemes of the wicked (for *rᵉšāᶜîm*, see on 1:1, 28:3, 92:7) might back-fire. For a similar thought, see on 7:16, 9:16, 140:9.
nets: the Hebrew *maḵmōr* is a *hapax legomenon* in the *OT*; its cognate in Isa. 51:20 denotes a net for catching animals, while another noun of the same root (Hab. 1:15) is used of a fishing-net.
while I escape: the Hebrew phrase is difficult—perhaps: 'while I escape all in one piece.' *NEB* 'whilst I pass in safety, all alone'.

Psalm 142 No Hope but Yahweh

This is a Lament of the Individual (see Introduction, pp. 37ff.), but its more detailed interpretation is difficult. Much depends upon the meaning of 'prison' in verse 7. If it is to be taken literally, :hen the Psalm may be a prayer of a falsely accused man; if, on the other hand, 'prison' is a metaphor for distress, then the composition is a lamentation of a persecuted man (verse 6) in desperate trouble, with none but God to help. Some of the earlier exegetes (e.g. Baethgen, Briggs) thought that the Psalm described the experiences of Israel in the Babylonian exile. In view of the personal nature of the Psalm, this collective interpretation is unlikely.

There is no indication as to the date of the Psalm, but Oesterley assigns it to the late post-Exilic period (*TP*, p. 564), probably rightly so.

The metre varies between 3+3 and 3+2.
A Maskil: see Introduction, p. 47.
of David: see Introduction, pp. 43ff.
when he was in the cave: the intended allusion may be either to the cave (or stronghold) of Adullam (1 Sam. 22:1; cf. H. W. Hertzberg, *I & II Samuel* (*OTL*, 1964), p. 184) or, less likely, to the cave (?) of Engedi (cf. 1 Sam. 24; so Davies). This historical note is generally regarded as a later attempt to provide an appropriate setting for the Psalm.
A Prayer: see on 65:2.

THE INVOCATION OF YAHWEH **1–3ab**

This prayer to God is expressed in an indirect form, and it is actually a description of the invocation (cf. 30:8 (M.T. 9), 77:1 (M.T. 2)).

1. I cry with my voice: i.e., 'I cry aloud'. Similarly in 3:4 (M.T. 5), 77:1 (M.T. 2). Prayer was not merely a personal matter in *OT* times, but also a corporate concern, if not more so. Therefore most prayers would be said aloud (see 1 Sam. 1:13). Cf. Rowley, *FI*, pp. 144f.; C. W. F. Smith, 'Prayer', *IDB*, III, pp. 857–67.

I make supplication: the verb *ḥ-n-n* in the *ḳal* means: 'to be gracious' but in the *hiṯpaᶜēl* form it signifies: 'to seek or implore favour (of man or of God)' (cf. 1 Kg. 8:59; Job 8:5; Ps. 30:8 (M.T. 9)). Dhorme (*CJ*, p. 114) suggests that etymologically the verb means to 'endeavour to conciliate some one'.

2. I pour out my complaint . . .: (cf. 42:4 (M.T. 3), 62:8 (M.T. 9)). The noun *śîaḥ* often expresses plaintive musing or complaint.

I tell my trouble . . .: see on 107:2.

3ab. When my spirit is faint: (for *rûaḥ*, 'spirit', see on 76:12). A similar expression is found in 77:3 (M.T. 4), 143:4. The same thought could be denoted by the phrase 'my soul fainted within me' (Jon. 2:7 (M.T. 8)).

thou knowest my way: the pronoun 'thou' (*ʾattāh*) is emphatic; for the idea, see on 1:6: 'the LORD knows the way of the righteous'. The Hebrew *n*ᵉ*ṯîḇāh* ('way') usually means 'path'; it can also be used metaphorically of one's course of life or moral direction.

THE LONELY MAN'S LAMENT **3c,d–4**

3c,d. the path (*ʾōraḥ*) is a synonym of *n*ᵉ*ṯîḇāh* ('path, way') and *dereḵ* ('way'), and can be employed figuratively of one's way of life or fortunes (see on 119:101).

a trap: Hebrew *paḥ*; see on 119:110. The exact nature of the enemies' activities is uncertain, but their schemes were designed to destroy the afflicted man.

4. I look to the right and watch: so *RSV*, following LXX, T, S, V; 11QPsª (col. 25) has *ʾbyṭh* ('I look') and *wʾrʾh* ('and I watch' (or 'see')) for the imperatives in M.T. ('Look . . . and see'), which would be addressed either to Yahweh (cf. Lam. 1:11, 2:20, 5:1) or, less likely, to fellow-worshippers. The phrase 'to the right' alludes to the place usually taken by the helper (see on 109:31; cf. 16:8, 110:5, 121:5). Some scholars (e.g. Wellhausen, Gunkel) add after 'watch' the term 'to the left' (*ś^e^mōˀl*), but this expansion is unnecessary.

who takes notice of me: i.e., 'who still recognizes me as a friend' (cf. Ru. 2:10).

no refuge remains to me: lit. 'refuge is perished from me', and there is no escape. For a similar expression, see Job 11:20; Jer. 25:35; Am. 2:14.

no man cares for me: lit. 'there is no one who cares for my soul'. For *nepeš* ('soul'), see on 33:19. The verb *d-r-š* usually means 'to seek, inquire of', hence: 'to seek with care' (cf. Dt. 11:12; Job 3:4), 'to regard, care for' (Jer. 30:14,17). This feeling of being forsaken may be due to the imprisonment of the unfortunate man (see verse 7).

A FURTHER APPEAL FOR HELP **5–7**

5. I cry to thee: this is a resumption of the thought of verse 1. **Thou art my refuge:** for *maḥ^a^seh* ('refuge'), see on 61:3; cf. 71:7; Jer. 17:17. The phrase may be associated with the idea that the sanctuary offered an asylum to the persecuted man, but it does not follow that the Psalmist envisaged himself as a fugitive seeking refuge in the Temple.

my portion: the Hebrew *ḥēleḳ* ('portion') is discussed on 73:26. Weiser (*POTL*, p. 816) sees here an allusion to the redistribution of the land in the festival cult. The particular reference may be to the tribe of Levi whose inheritance was not a portion of the Promised Land but Yahweh himself (Dt. 10:9). Thus they did not depend for their livelihood upon the cultivation of the soil but upon God (Num. 18:20). It seems that this Levitical privilege has been spiritualized (cf. Kraus, *PBK*, p. 933) and applied to the afflicted man who was forsaken by all but by his enemies.

in the land of the living: i.e. in this life, as against the existence in the underworld. See on 27:13.

6. Give heed to my cry: see on 17:1.

I am brought very low: for this phrase, see on 116:6; cf. 79:8. The verb *d-l-l* ('to be low') is used metaphorically of distress.

Deliver me: for *n-ṣ-l* ('to deliver, snatch away'), see on 59:1.

they are too strong for me: cf. 18:17 (M.T. 18).

7. prison: some scholars (e.g. Kirkpatrick, Davies, Cohen) take it as a metaphor for wretchedness or distress, as perhaps in

107:10; Isa. 42:7. On the other hand, it may denote actual imprisonment or custody, as in Lev. 24:12; Num. 15:34; there the accused person was confined till the divine judgment was made known. The ancient law did not usually provide for imprisonment as a legal punishment, although temporary confinement was well attested (cf. M. Greenberg, 'Prison', *IDB*, III, pp. 891f.).

that I may give thanks: for *hôḏāh* ('to give thanks'), see on 18:49.

to thy name: or, 'to you' (see on 20:1).

The righteous: see on 1:5. They 'will surround' the acquitted man (similarly *AV*, *RV*, *RP*), or 'because of me shall the righteous crown (Thee)' (Cohen, *PSon*, p. 461); LXX has 'the righteous shall wait for me' (so also S). The Psalmist probably had in mind the thanksgiving in the midst of the worshipping community (see on 22:26), after his deliverance. There is no indication that the righteous were at fault for waiting till *after* the vindication of the accused man; if the allusion is to the 'great congregation' (cf. 22:25 (M.T. 26)), then they would be together only at the great pilgrimage festivals.

thou wilt deal bountifully with me: see on 13:6, 116:7; cf. 1QH ix:30.

Psalm 143 'Hide Not Thy Face from Me'

This Psalm belongs to the Laments of the Individual (see Introduction, pp. 37ff.), and it is the last of the so-called Penitential Psalms (see introduction to Ps. 6). Although it does not contain any explicit statement about repentance, it voices a penitential note; thus the discernment of the Early Church was not wrong. The Psalmist is aware that no man is righteous before God (verse 2), and that every one needs divine guidance (verse 8); this amounts to an implicit confession. Consequently it is understandable that he does not appeal to any merits or achievements of his own, but he bases his prayer on Yahweh's faithfulness and righteousness (verse 1). His only hope is the precedent of Yahweh's gracious intervention in the past (see verse 5).

The Psalm consists of three sections: verses 1–2 form the introductory prayer, verses 3–6 contain the actual lamentation, while verses 7–12 are made up of a series of petitions.

The poet is pursued by his enemies (verses 3 and 9); and Schmidt, Leslie, *et al.* are of the opinion that he is falsely accused and in danger of losing his life. This is plausible, but the account of the distress is too general to enable us to reconstruct the details of the situation.

The Psalm was probably recited in the Temple (cf. verse 9) the evening before the expected divine decision (cf. verse 8), but it need not necessarily imply a rite of incubation (Leslie, *PAP*, p. 359); see on 3:5.

The date of the Psalm is late post-Exilic; this is suggested by the numerous allusions to other Psalms and certain theological points, e.g., the awareness of a universal sinfulness.

The metre is irregular.

A Psalm of David: see Introduction, pp. 43ff. and 46. LXX adds a historical note to the title: 'when his son pursued him', and the reference is obviously to Absalom (so some Greek MSS.; cf. 2 Sam. 15–18). This interpretation is, however, very unlikely.

THE INTRODUCTORY PRAYER **1–2**

1. Hear my prayer: this and similar expressions are frequently used in the introductory petitions of the Laments (see on 54:2; cf. 5:1 (M.T. 2), 17:1, 28:2, 39:13 (M.T. 14), 64:1 (M.T. 2), etc.). For *t*^{e}*p̱illāh* ('prayer'), see on 65:2; here it is a synonym of *taḥ*^{a}*nûnîm* ('supplications') (see on 86:6), and serves as a designation for a lament.

give ear . . .: see on 141:1.

In thy faithfulness: S reads 'with your word', which suggests the Hebrew *b*^{e}*ᵓimrāṯ*^{e}*ḵā* for M.T. *be*^{ᵓe}*mûnāṯ*^{e}*ḵā* (see on 36:5); if the variant found in S is correct, then the allusion may be to the awaited oracle of deliverance.

in thy righteousness: this is not simply an uncompromising legal justice but a determination, on the part of God, to mend rather than to rend. It may denote deliverance, which would be an expression of Yahweh's Covenant faithfulness, and a response to his servant's desperate plight. For *ṣ*^{e}*ḏāḳāh* ('righteousness'), see on 33:5.

2. The thought expressed in this verse is rather unique in a lament: instead of hinting at his own righteousness and protesting innocence (see on 7:3ff.), the Psalmist recognizes that *all* men are sinful in the sight of God.

Enter not into judgment . . .: i.e. do not subject me to a strict examination in which my human insignificance and sinfulness would become painfully obvious; rather judge between your servant and his persecutors (see verse 12). If the standard were certain absolute principles, then no one would be righteous before God (cf. Job 4:17, 9:2f., 15:14, 25:4ff.; Ps. 14:2f., 130:3; Rom. 3:20); on the other hand, if the criterion is the Covenant of Yahweh, then the difference between the servants of God and their adversaries would become clear.

thy servant: see on 27:9, 36:1.

no man living is righteous: this being so, the Psalmist dares to beg for God's mercy. It does not necessarily follow that no Israelite is (or ever has been) righteous in the sense of being loyal to God's Covenant (cf. Ps. 15 and 24), although *no* man's devotion to God is perfect; such righteousness does not, however, constitute a claim upon God (cf. v. Rad, *OTT*, I, p. 383).

THE LAMENT OF THE PERSECUTED MAN **3–6**

3. the enemy has pursued me: for *nep̱eš* ('soul'), see on 33:19. The Psalmist does not state the reasons for, and the actual manner of, his persecution, but the motives of his enemies are far from pure (see verse 12) and their methods are characterized by ruthlessness. The term used for the enemy (*ʾôyēḇ*) is singular (and so are the verbs in verse 3), but it may be employed collectively (cf. verse 9 where the same noun occurs in the plural form). It is less likely that the Psalmist in verse 3 has singled out one particular adversary. Verse 2 need not imply that the author is suffering for his own sins.

he has crushed my life . . .: see on 94:5; cf. Isa. 53:10. The word used for 'life' is *ḥayyāh*; the usual term is *ḥayyîm* which is a masculine plural in form, and may convey a suggestion of intensity (so Johnson, *VITAI*, p. 103); see also on 21:4; v. Rad, '*Zaō*', *TDNT*, II, pp. 843–6.

in darkness: this refers either to an actual imprisonment (cf. 142:7) or to calamity in general; both alternatives are linked with the sphere of Sheol, or the underworld, which is often described as a place of gloom and darkness (cf. 88:6 (M.T. 7)). For a similar idea, see Mic. 7:8.

like those long dead: lit. 'like the dead ones of eternity'; for *ʿôlām* ('eternity, long duration'), see on 117:2. Gunkel, Kraus, *et al.* regard this phrase as a later addition from Lam. 3:6. It has been suggested that there is a gradual ebbing away of life (such as it is) even in Sheol, and that 'those long dead' are those most remote from life (so Eaton, *PTBC*, p. 307). Whether or not this was the popular belief is hard to say. The above-mentioned phrase probably denotes the dead whose names and memory have long ceased to exist. The Psalmist feels that he has become like a nameless shade (see on 88:10) whose existence is no longer of any significance to his fellow men. To all intents and purposes the Psalmist finds himself in the shadow of the netherworld.

4. my spirit faints . . .: as in 142:3 (M.T. 4); similarly in 61:2 (M.T. 3), 77:3 (M.T. 4). The Psalmist has become entirely dispirited; for *rûaḥ* ('spirit'), see on 76:12.

my heart . . . is appalled: the expression is a *hapax legomenon* in the *OT* but a similar idiom occurs in 1QH vii:3, xviii:20. LXX has 'my heart was troubled . . .', which is a reasonable interpretation of M.T.

5. the days of old: as in 77:5 (M.T. 6). The allusion is to the salvation-history of the nation although it may also include God's providential care for the individual. Yahweh's saving acts on behalf of Israel were the one firm factor in the poet's spiritual turmoil; in them he found a new assurance that Yahweh was, and still is, the God of might and faithfulness. 'Personal experience gives vitality to faith, but its solid ground is the divine action in history' (Rodd, *PEPC*, II, p. 121).

I meditate . . .: this verb (*h-g-h*, see on 1:2) is parallel to 'I remember' (for *z-k-r*, see on 119:52) in verse *5a*, and to 'I muse' (for *ś-y-ḥ*, see on 77:3; Ringgren, *FP*, p. 57). The object of these actions is the wonderful works of Yahweh. Cf. 11QPs[a] Plea, verses 12f.: 'When I remember thy might, my heart is brave, and upon thy mercies do I lean'.

what thy hands have wrought: lit. 'the work of your hands' (see on 8:3, 102:25), i.e. your own work. LXX, T, 11QPs[a] have: 'the works of (*maᶜaśê*) . . .'.

6. I stretch out my hands to thee: the extended hands in prayer symbolize the suppliant's dependence on God (see on 28:2, 44:20; cf. Lam. 1:17).

my soul thirsts for thee . . .: for the thought cf. 42:1f. (M.T. 2f.), 63:1 (M.T. 2). There is no verb in M.T., which can literally be rendered: 'my soul (or 'I', see on 33:19) as a dry land to you'. 11QPs[a] (col. 25) has: 'in a dry land my soul (looks) for you', reading *bʾrṣ* ('in a land') for M.T. *keʾereṣ* ('like a land'); for the construction, see Jer. 5:3.

Selah: see Introduction, pp. 48f.

THE PSALMIST'S PETITION **7–12**

7. Make haste: see on 69:17 (cf. 40:13 (M.T. 14), 102:2 (M.T. 3)).

My spirit fails: this phrase occurs only here in the *OT* but it is similar to 'my soul fails' (see on 84:2), and means: 'my energy is fully spent'.

Hide not thy face . . .: this expression is also found in 27:9, 102:2 (M.T. 3), and there is a similar instance in 69:17 (M.T. 18). The author pleads with God not to withdraw his favour permanently (see on 27:9).

like those who go down to the Pit: see on 28:1, 88:4. For a Ugaritic parallel, cf. *Baal* II, viii: 7–9: 'and go down to the lowest depths of the earth, be counted with them that go down into the earth' (Driver, *CML*, p. 103a).

8. in the morning: it is possible that salvation (i.e. oracles of deliverance) was usually made known in the Temple liturgy at the break of day (for a hypothetical life-setting, cf. Ringgren, *IR*, p. 236). For this expectation of divine help in the early morning, see on 46:5.

steadfast love: that is devotion and loyalty to the Covenant relationship (see on 26:3).

I put my trust: for the verb *b-ṭ-ḥ*, see on 78:22. LXX has 'for I have hoped in you' (cf. R. Bultmann, '*Elpis*', *TDNT*, II, pp. 521ff.).

Teach me the way . . .: similarly in 86:11 (which see); cf. 5:9 (M.T. 10), 25:4, 32:8, 142:3 (M.T. 4). For *dereḵ* ('way'), see on 103:7.

I lift up my soul: see on 25:1, 86:4.

9. Deliver me . . .: for this brief petition, see 59:1 (M.T. 2).

fled to thee for refuge: so *RSV*, after LXX, V, reading *nastî* ('I have fled') for M.T. *kissīṯî* ('I have hidden') (the object is lacking); Delitzsch (*BCP*, III, p. 372) renders: 'I have hidden myself'. Perhaps we should read *kᵉsūṯî* (for *kissīṯî*): '(with you is) my covering (i.e. my protection)'; similarly Kraus (*PBK*, pp. 935, 936).

10. Teach me to do thy will: for a synonymous expression, see on 25:4f. The Hebrew *rāṣôn* can denote 'favour' (5:12 (M.T. 13), 106:4), 'acceptance' (19:14 (M.T. 15)), and 'will' (40:8 (M.T. 9), 103:21). Only in 16 cases is the word *rāṣôn* associated with human emotions and attitudes; in some forty instances it signifies the divine will, favour, or acceptance (see G. Schrenk, '*Eudokia*', *TDNT*, II, p. 743).

for thou art my God: this is the essence of Yahweh's Covenant promise (cf. 31:14 (M.T. 15), 40:5 (M.T. 6), 86:3, 118:28, 140:6 (M.T. 7)). See on 91:2.

Let thy good spirit lead me: for an analogous use of *rûaḥ*, 'spirit', cf. Neh. 9:20; see on Ps. 76:12. Kraus (*PBK*, p. 938) describes the 'good spirit' as a manifestation of the guiding presence of Yahweh, while Ringgren (*IR*, p. 93) thinks that 'the spirit almost appears in the guise of a guardian angel' (cf. his *Word and Wisdom* (1948), p. 166). The term 'holy spirit' is mentioned in 51:11 (M.T. 13).

on a level path: so *RSV* (similarly *NEB*), following some Hebrew MSS., reading *beʾôraḥ* ('in the path') (27:11) for M.T. *beʾereṣ* ('in the land (of uprightness)'), which is a *hapax legomenon* in the *OT*. Eaton (*PTBC*, p. 307) interprets the phrase in M.T. as 'a fertile plain'; in Dt. 4:43 *ʾereṣ mîšôr* (lit. 'a land of uprightness') is used as a term for 'table-land' (cf. Jer. 48:21). Its usage in Ps. 143 may be figurative (cf. Isa. 26:7, 42:16).

11. For thy name's sake: for the expression, see on 106:8 (cf. 31:3 (M.T. 4)).

preserve my life: see on 30:3, 119:25.

in thy righteousness: i.e. being true to your Covenant promises. For *ṣedāḳāh*, 'righteousness', see on 33:5. Dahood (*PAB*, I, p. 34) takes *ṣedāḳāh* as 'a poetic term for Paradise'; but this suggestion seems unlikely.

12. steadfast love: i.e. by your unfailing devotion and loyalty (see verse 8).

cut off my enemies: i.e. annihilate them; cf. 54:5 (M.T. 7), 73:27, 94:23.

destroy all my adversaries: the prayer for the extermination of the adversaries is in line with the *OT* Covenant tradition according to which blessings and curses for the obedient and disobedient, respectively, were equally real.

I am thy servant: as in 116:16. For *ʿeḇeḏ* ('servant'), see on 36:1.

Psalm 144 ALL VICTORIES ARE GIVEN, NOT GAINED

Many commentators have argued that this Psalm is composed of two originally independent units (verses 1–11 and 12–15) which have been accidentally or deliberately combined into one poem (so e.g. Gunkel, Leslie, Taylor). Verses 1–11 resemble a Royal Lament, while verses 12–15 are reminiscent of a prayer or a Psalm of Blessing (cf. Ps. 127 and 128). The first part is largely a mosaic of various fragments of other Psalms, especially Ps. 18; the second part may be original unless it is dependent upon some lost poem (so Davies, *Cent. BP*, II, p. 349).

The simplest, if not the best, solution is to assume that the present Psalm is a literary unity, although the writer has leaned heavily upon older traditions. The resultant composition could be described as a National Lamentation (see Introduction, pp. 37ff.). The speaker in verses 1–11 seems to be a King or military leader, but since the language, style, and character of the Psalm are more at home in the post-Exilic period the poem may have been spoken by a representative of the Judaean community of the Persian period. The cultic setting could have been the Feast of Tabernacles (see Introduction, pp. 52f.), and the historical background the hostilities of the treacherous neighbours.

Many exegetes (e.g. Gunkel, Schmidt, Weiser, Kraus) assign the Psalm to the late pre-Exilic period, and regard it as a Royal Psalm, uttered by the King before going to war (so Gunkel, *PGHAT*, p. 605), or during the ritual of the Autumn Festival (cf. Eaton, *PTBC*, p. 308; similarly Schmidt, Weiser, *et al.*).

The metre is varied but mainly 3 + 3, especially in verses 1–11.

A Psalm of David: see Introduction, pp. 43ff. LXX adds to the title *pros ton Goliad*, 'against Goliath' (a similar idea is found in T, on verse 10); but this is obviously a late interpretation of the Psalm.

A HYMNIC INVOCATION OF YAHWEH **1–2**

1. Blessed be the LORD, my rock: in 18:46 (M.T. 47) we have 'blessed be my rock'. For *bārûḵ* ('blessed be'), see on 16:7, 28:6. The divine title 'rock' (*ṣûr*) is discussed on 28:1, 42:9; it depicts God as a place of security and refuge.

who trains my hands for war: this phrase is practically the same as 18:34*a* (M.T. 35*a*), which uses the word *milḥāmāh* ('war') for *ḳ*^e^*rāḇ* ('war') in 144:1. The former noun occurs some 319 times in the *OT*, while the latter is used only nine times (cf. *BDB*, pp. 536, 898) but is frequent in Aramaic.

my fingers for battle: this is probably a variant of the previous expression. The author praises God for instructing him in warlike skills. Dahood (*UHP*, p. 31) proposes that 'my fingers' is a poetic description of 'my arms', parallel to 'my hands' in verse 1*b*.

2. my rock: following 18:2 (M.T. 3) and 2 Sam. 22:2. M.T.

has 'my loyal friend' (?), *ḥasdî* (*RSVm* 'my steadfast love'), which is rather a unique divine appellation or descriptive title. Delitzsch (*BCP*, III, p. 380) regards *ḥasdî* as an abbreviation of *ᵓelōhê ḥasdî* ('God of my Covenant loyalty'), i.e. the God who is gracious and loyal to his Covenant 'partner' (as in 59:17 (M.T. 18)). Some exegetes resort to emendations (so Cheyne, Gunkel, Kraus, *et al.*), but no changes are required; *ḥasdî* seems to be a synonym of 'my deliverer', just as 'my fortress' (see on 18:2) is parallel to 'my stronghold' (see on 18:2). *NEB* paraphrases it as 'my help that never fails'.

my shield: see on 3:3, 18:2. A metaphor of Yahweh's protecting care.

I take refuge: this is similar to 18:2 (M.T. 3). For the verb *ḥ-s-h* ('to seek refuge'), see on 7:1, 16:1.

who subdues the peoples under him: so *RSV*, following 18:47*b* (M.T. 48*b*), reading *ᶜammîm taḥtāyw* for M.T. *ᶜammî taḥtāy* (*Ḳᵉrê* suggests *taḥtāyw*) ('my people under me' (*Ḳᵉrê* '. . . under him')). 11QPsᵃ (col. 23) and most ancient versions suggest *ᶜammîm* (i.e. foreign enemies; see verse 11). If we follow M.T. (so *AV*, *RV*), then the allusion is to a local rebellion among the King's own subjects; the *RSV* rendering, however, seems to be superior. *RP*, *PNT*, *NEB* indicate that God subdues the nations under the rule of the Davidic king.

A CONFESSION OF MAN'S INSIGNIFICANCE **3–4**

3. what is man: this is an echo of 8:4 (M.T. 5) and Job 7:17. For 'man', *ᵓāḏām*, see on 84:5. This rhetorical question emphasizes the humble status of the suppliant, in comparison with the greatness and majesty of God.

that thou dost regard him: or, 'that you care for him'. For this use of the verb *y-d-ᶜ* ('to know'), see on 1:6, 37:18; cf. Winton Thomas, *TRP*, p. 1.

the son of man: see on 8:4.

4. Man is like a breath: i.e. he is a transitory being. The expression may be a variation of 39:5 (M.T. 6): 'Surely every man stands as a mere breath' (cf. 39:11 (M.T. 12), 62:9 (M.T. 10)).

his days are like a passing shadow: the thought of the ephemeral nature of man's life is a common theme in Wisdom literature (cf. Job 8:9, 14:2; Ps. 102:11 (M.T. 12), 109:23; Ec. 6:12, 8:13; Wis. 2:5; etc.).

A PRAYER FOR DIVINE INTERVENTION **5–8**

5. Bow thy heavens: the Psalmist prays for the manifestation of Yahweh's presence, as he once made himself known at Sinai.
and come down: Kraus (*PBK*, p. 943) describes the verb *y-r-d* as a technical term of the condescension of God (cf. Gen. 11:5, 18:21; Exod. 3:8, 19:11, 18, 34:5; Isa. 64:1 (M.T. 63:19)). *NEB* regards 'the heavens' as the subject of the verb.
Touch the mountains . . .: for this phrase, see on 104:32*b*.

6. Flash forth the lightning . . .: this verse is an adaptation of 18:14 (M.T. 15). It is possible that the imagery was derived from the past experiences of the winter storms; similar descriptions are also used of Baal (cf. *Baal* II, v:6–9; Driver, *CML*, p. 97b).
scatter them: the allusion is probably to the enemies (so Kirkpatrick, Davies, Cohen, *et al.*) rather than to the lightnings (so *NEB*).
thy arrows: i.e. your lightnings (see on 18:14).
and rout them: or 'throw them into a panic' (as in Jos. 10:10). Confusion and panic were often regarded as the instruments of Yahweh in the Holy War (see L. E. Toombs, 'Ideas of War', *IDB*, iv, pp. 796–801).

7. Stretch forth thy hand: this is a variation of 18:16 (M.T. 17) and a vivid way of saying 'help me!' *RSV* follows all the ancient versions in reading the singular *yāḏeḵā* for M.T. *yāḏêḵā*, 'your hands' (similarly *NEB*).
from on high: i.e. from the heavens. For *mārôm* ('on high'), see on 68:18.
rescue me: this usage of the verb *p-ṣ-h* is frequent in Aramaic, but in the *OT* it is attested only here and in verses 10 and 11. It is possible that 'deliver me' (see on 59:1) is a gloss on the rare *peṣēnî* ('rescue me'), or perhaps the right reading is preserved in verse 11*ab*.
from the many waters: see on 18:16, 69:1; H. G. May, 'Some Cosmic Connotations of *Mayim Rabbîm*, "Many Waters",' *JBL*, LXXIV (1955), pp. 9–21. The 'many waters' symbolize the hostile forces—in this case the might of the aliens which is, at the same time, also an expression of the power of Sheol (cf. 18:4f. (M.T. 5f.)).
the hand of aliens: or, 'the clutches of the foreigners'. For 'aliens' (*benê nēḵār*), cf. Isa. 56:6, 60:10, 61:5, 62:8. The Hebrew *nēḵār* denotes that which is foreign or strange, and consequently

it can also suggest what is hostile or unclean (ritually); cf. Neh. 9:2; Ezek. 44:9. *NEB* regards verses 7*c*, 8 as a later addition.

8. lies: for *šāwᵓ*, see on 119:37.

a right hand of falsehood: see 106:26; for *šeḳer*, 'falsehood', see on 119:29. The aliens either swear falsely or break their oath. The raising of the right hand towards heaven was the usual gesture of a person taking an oath; it was, apparently, a symbolic appeal to God as witness (cf. Dt. 32:40).

THE VOW **9–11**

9. I will sing: i.e., 'I will praise'. Verse 9 may be an imitation of 33:2f.

a new song: for *šîr ḥādāš*, see on 33:3, 96:1. This is a thanksgiving for the hoped-for deliverance. It is not certain that this song of praise was originally understood eschatologically.

O God: the Hebrew *ᵓelōhîm* occurs very seldom in Ps. 90–150; apart from this Psalm it is found only in Ps. 108, which is composed of parts of two Elohistic Psalms (57 and 60).

a ten-stringed harp: see on 33:2. *NEB* '. . . lute'.

10. who givest victory to kings: for 'victory' (or 'salvation'), see on 35:3; cf. 33:16. This may be a statement of general truth or it may allude to the salvation-history of the nation exemplified in the reigns of the Davidic kings (cf. 18:50 (M.T. 51)).

who rescuest David thy servant: when a Davidic king is made triumphant over his foes, it is also David who is 'delivered' in his successor (cf. Kraus, *PBK*, p. 944). On the other hand, 'David' may simply denote the reigning King of the house of David (as in Ezek. 34:23; Hos. 3:5; cf. W. Zimmerli, *Ezechiel* (*BK*, 13_{II}, 1963), pp. 842f.). Deissler (*PWdB*, III, p. 207) thinks that the reference is to the coming David, i.e. the Messiah (cf. Ezek. 34:20–31). For 'servant' (*ᶜeḇeḏ*), see on 27:9, 36:1; cf. *DOTT*, p. 123, n.26.

11. from the cruel sword: in M.T. (and in the ancient versions) this phrase belongs to verse 10, but *RSV* (also *PNT*, *RP*) provides a better parallelism. Verse 11 is a slightly varied repetition of verses 7–8; it is unlikely that they form a refrain in the Psalm; rather verse 11 is a resumption of the previous prayer. T renders the expression: 'from the evil sword of Goliath', but this is a late interpretation.

A PRAYER FOR THE PROSPERITY OF THE NATION **12–15**

12. May our sons . . .: M.T. begins with the relative particle *ᵓašer* which is usually regarded as a gloss from verse 11*c*, or as a connecting particle; Eaton (*PTBC*, p. 309) renders it: 'so that (our sons may be . . .)'. Some scholars (e.g. Graetz, Kissane, Weiser) change *ᵓᵃšer* into *ᵓašᵉrê* ('Oh (our) happiness!') (cf. Leslie, *PAP*, p. 431; similarly *NEB*). Another possibility is to interpret verses 12–15 as an expression of future blessings by taking *ᵓᵃšer* as *ᵓāšūr* ('surely'), which is attested in post-Biblical literature (see G. R. Driver, 'Hebrew Homonyms', *Hebräische Wortforschung* (*SVT*, 16, 1967), pp. 52f.).

in their youth . . .: i.e. while they are still young, they will be cared for like saplings or plants in a plantation; they will not become fatherless (cf. Isa. 1:2).

like corner pillars . . .: the exact translation is uncertain, but the daughters seem to be likened to the carved pillars of the palace (or Temple). The point of comparison may be their beauty and strength rather than their height and stateliness (cf. Sir. 26:18; *VT*, IV (1954), p. 175).

13. all manner of store: lit. 'from kind to kind'. The Hebrew *zan* ('kind') occurs elsewhere only in 2 Chr. 16:14, and it is thought to be a Persian loan-word (cf. J. M. Myers, *II Chronicles* (*AB* 13, 1965), p. 93).

14. may . . . heavy with young: this phrase is textually suspect; for various possible readings, see Barnes, *PWC*, II, p. 658. Perhaps we should transfer 'in our fields' from verse 13 to verse 14, reading: 'in our fields may our cattle be . . .', thus providing a parallel to 'may our sheep bring forth . . .' (verse 13*c*). This would allow us to translate verse 14*bc*: 'may there be no breach (in our walls), and may there be no going forth (into captivity; cf. Ezek. 12:4, 20:38), may there be no cry . . .' (similarly *PNT*); such a rendering would be preferable metrically. For the thought, see 72:3f. The 'going forth' may suggest a surrender of a besieged city, as in 2 Kg. 24:12; Am. 4:3.

15. Happy . . .: see on 1:1.

to whom such blessings fall: lit. 'to whom (it happens) like this.'

Psalm 145 YAHWEH'S DOMINION ENDURES FOR EVER

This is an acrostic poem, its verses beginning with the successive letters of the Hebrew alphabet (see introduction to Ps. 9–10). In M.T. the verse beginning with the letter *nûn* has been accidentally omitted; it is preserved in 11QPs[a] and in the ancient versions.

This Psalm is a Hymn (see Introduction, pp. 32f.) which Westermann (*PGP*, pp. 130ff.) further classifies as an Imperative Psalm; its main characteristic is the imperative calls to praise God, alternating with descriptions of his majesty and goodness. In Ps. 145 these summonses are, however, indirect; here we have a threefold invocation (verses 1–2, 4–7, and 10–12), and each call is followed by a description of the character of Yahweh and his works (verses 3, 8–9, and 13–20 respectively).

Weiser (*POTL*, p. 827) is of the opinion that the hymn was probably 'recited at the feast of the covenant', or we could simply say that the cultic setting of the Psalm was the great Autumn Festival or the Feast of Tabernacles.

The Psalm is usually regarded as belonging to the post-Exilic period; Oesterley (*TP*, p. 572) calls it 'one of the latest in the Psalter'. This view is also suggested by the language of the Psalm, which has more in common with later Hebrew than with the language of the early period, as well as by the acrostic structure, dependence upon other Psalms, and certain comparatively late concepts, such as *maᵉḵûṯ* ('kingship (of Yahweh)').

The metre is irregular.

A Song of Praise: see Introduction, p. 47.

Of David: see Introduction, pp. 43ff.

THE PRAISE OF YAHWEH'S GREATNESS **1–3**

1. I will extol thee: for this hymnic introduction, see on 30:1.
my God: perhaps 'my (Covenant) God'; the speaker seems to be a representative of the whole community. See on 91:2, 113:5.
King: for *meleḵ* as a divine title, see on 68:24. The Psalmists usually employ the epithet 'my King' (cf. 5:2 (M.T. 3), 68:24 (M.T. 25), 84:3 (M.T. 4)), but it is not clear whether there was any real difference in their respective meanings.
bless thy name: i.e. I will praise Yahweh for his manifold and awe-inspiring self-manifestation. For *b-r-k* ('to bless'), see on 104:1; *šēm* ('name') is discussed on 20:1.
for ever and ever: see on 9:5. The Psalmist is suggesting that his praise of God will never end, as long as he lives on this earth. It is doubtful whether there is an allusion to a fully developed after-life here (cf. 2 Enoch 42:3).

In 11QPsa145 we find after each verse a refrain or a congregational response: 'Blessed is Yahweh, and blessed is his name, for ever and ever' (*brwk yhwh wbrwk šmw lᶜwlm wᶜd*). It is unlikely, however, that this refrain is original, although it may reflect a later cultic usage. See Ps. 136 for a similar congregational participation.

2. Every day . . .: my praise of God will be continual (cf. 34:1 (M.T. 2)). It is said that this Psalm was recited 'thrice daily in the synagogue by many pious Jews' (Oesterley, *TP*, p. 574).
praise thy name: this expression is similar to the cultic call 'Praise the LORD' (*halᵉlû yāh*); for the verb *h-l-l* ('to praise'), see on 119:164. The object of the praise is the name of Yahweh, which may be a circumlocution for Yahweh himself (see on 20:1; cf. 1QM xiv:12).

3. Great is the LORD . . .: for the same phrase, see on 48:1, 96:4; cf. 147:5.
his greatness is unsearchable: i.e. the full extent of his greatness and power is beyond human comprehension. For the thought, cf. Job 5:9, 9:10; Isa. 40:28.

YAHWEH'S WONDROUS WORKS AND GRACIOUSNESS **4–9**

4. One generation . . . to another: this expression occurs only here in the *OT*, but, for a similar idea, cf. 19:2 (M.T. 3), 22:30f. (M.T. 31f.).
shall laud: the verb used is *š-b-ḥ*, for which see on 63:3.

5. 11QPs[a] (col. 16) seems to have preserved the more likely reading of this verse: 'They shall speak of the glorious splendour of your majesty, and I will meditate on your wondrous works'; this involves the change of M.T. *wᵉḏiḇᵉrê* ('and the words of . . .') into *ydbrw* ('they shall speak'), and the addition of the conjunction *wᵉ* ('and') before M.T. *nip̄lᵉʾôṯêḵā* ('wondrous works'); see on 9:1; cf. 1QH ix:7.

6. the might of thy terrible acts: or '. . . awe-inspiring deeds' (see on 65:5). In verses 4–7 the Psalmist uses a number of synonyms to describe Yahweh's works in creation and in salvation-history, and it is unlikely that in this context there was any differentiation in their meaning. Also the verbs are more or less synonymous.

7. They shall pour forth . . .: (see on 19:2), i.e. they shall declare ceaselessly (cf. 119:171).
the fame of . . .: for *zēḵer* ('fame, praise'), see on 135:13. 'Thy . . . goodness' is parallel to 'thy righteousness' (see on 33:5), and both may refer to the faithfulness and graciousness of Yahweh, expressed in all his saving acts (cf. 1QH x:16).

shall sing aloud: see on 33:1.

8. This verse, with slight alterations, is found in 103:8; cf. Exod. 34:6; Ps. 86:15; Jl 2:13; Jon. 4:2. It seems to be a liturgical formula.

9. The LORD is good to all: a number of Greek MSS. render: '. . . to those who wait for (him)' (*tois hupomenousin*), but the parallel line (verse 9*b*) supports M.T. 'All' refers to the entire creation or to 'all that he has made' (cf. 103:19); they, too, experience Yahweh's faithfulness and mercy manifested in the regular and unfailing maintenance of the world (cf. Eichrodt, *TOT*, I, p. 239).

his compassion: see on 51:1.

THE PRAISE OF YAHWEH'S ROYAL RULE **10–20**

10. shall give thanks . . .: see on 18:49.

all thy saints: the Hebrew *ḥ^a^sîḏîm* are those who practise *ḥeseḏ* or Covenant loyalty (see on 30:4, 86:2); the emphasis may be, however, on the fact that they are the recipients of God's grace and care. This usage largely corresponds to that of 'saints' in NT (cf. Rom. 1:7; 1 C. 1:2; etc.).

shall bless thee: see verse 1.

11. the glory of thy kingdom: for 'glory', see on 19:1, 57:5. The Hebrew *mal^e^ḵûṯ* ('kingdom') is often used in the *OT* of a political kingdom (1 Sam. 20:31; 1 Kg. 2:12; 2 Chr. 36:22; etc.), but here it denotes Yahweh's kingdom or kingship, kingly rule. This usage was, perhaps, a half-way stage to the thought of the 'kingdom of God' in the *NT*. See further, v. Rad, '*Basileus*', *TDNT*, I, pp. 570f.; O. E. Evans, 'Kingdom of God', *IDB*, III, pp. 17–26.

12. the sons of men: (*b^e^nê ʾāḏām*), see on 49:2, 84:2.

thy mighty deeds: so *RSV* following LXX and S. M.T. has 'his . . .'.

thy kingdom: (so also LXX and S). M.T. has 'his . . .' (see verse 11).

13. This verse occurs also in Dan. 4:3 (M.T. 3:33), 4:34 (M.T. 4:31). For a Ugaritic parallel, see *Baal* III*, A:10: 'Thou shalt take thy everlasting kingdom, thy dominion for ever and ever' (Driver, *CML*, p. 81).

an everlasting kingdom: lit. 'a kingdom of all ages' (for *ʿôlām* ('age'), see on 9:5, 117:2). Yahweh's dynamic rule extends from the remotest past to the present, as well as to the most distant future. This dominion is unlimited either in space or in time, and it is characterized by a just and merciful rule (see verses 13*cd*–20). Only in the case of Yahweh is there no danger that power might corrupt its wielder.

The Lord is faithful . . .: this line or verse has been accidentally omitted from M.T., but it is found in 11QPs[a] (col. 17) and most ancient versions. 11QPs[a] reads *nʾmn ʾlwhym bdbryw wḥsyd bkwl mʿśyw* ('God is faithful in his words (i.e. deeds), and loyal in all his works'). This line supplies the missing verse beginning with the letter *nûn*.

14. upholds: or 'supports' (see on 119:116).

all who are falling: cf. 1QM xiv:11.

and raises up: the Hebrew *z-ḳ-p* ('to raise up') is found only here and in 146:8 (and Ezr. 6:11, which is in Aramaic), but is frequent in Aramaic.

who are bowed down: similarly in 146:8 (cf. Isa. 58:5).

15–16. These two verses are an adaptation of 104:27f. The whole creation is dependent upon Yahweh.

Thou openest thy hand: this corresponds to 11QPs[a], which reads *ʾth ʾt* for M.T. *ʾeṯ* (=the accusative sign); the pronoun *ʾth* (i.e. *ʾattāh*, 'thou') must have dropped out due to haplography. 11QPs[a] is supported by LXX, S, V.

thou satisfiest . . .: or, 'you satisfy with (your) favour every living thing' (cf. Dt. 33:23).

17. is just: for *ṣaddîḳ* ('just'), see on 119:137.

in all his ways: i.e. in all his dealings (cf. 103:7).

kind: for *ḥāsîḏ*, see on 30:4, 86:2; cf. 18:25 (M.T. 26).

18. The Lord is near . . .: i.e. he answers and helps (cf. Dt. 4:7; Ps. 34:18 (M.T. 19)).

who call upon him: (cf. 75:1 (M.T. 2), 116:13), i.e. who call on his name, which is the pledge of his presence (cf. Kraus, *PBK*, p. 949).

in truth: that is, earnestly and faithfully; see on 25:5. Verse 18*b* reminds us of Jn 4:24; cf. Isa. 10:20.

19. He fulfils the desire . . .: for *rāṣôn* ('desire, favour'), see on 106:4; cf. Prov. 10:24.

who fear him: or 'who worship him' (see on 34:7, 85:9, 102:15).

hears their cry: i.e. he responds to their prayer and saves them (see on 54:1).

20. The Lord preserves: i.e. he protects (cf. 121:4).

who love him: 11QPs[a] (col. 17) reads *yrʾyw* ('who fear him';

see verse 19*a*); this also has the support of LXX, S, and T. For ʾ-*h-b* ('to love'), see on 26:8; cf. Eichrodt, *TOT*, II, pp. 311f.
the wicked: the term *rᵉšāʿîm* is dealt with on 1:1, 28:3, 92:7.
he will destroy: cf. 104:35, 143:12. The ultimate triumph of truth and goodness will mean the end of falsehood and evil.

THE CONCLUSION **21**

The finale of this Psalm takes up the opening theme of praise (verses 1–2).

21. My mouth: i.e. I myself; cf. Johnson, *VITAI*, p. 45.
praise: (*tᵉhillāh*), see on 65:1, 119:171.
all flesh: or 'all mankind'. For *bāśār* ('flesh'), see on 38:3, 56:4.
his holy name: see on 106:47.
for ever and ever: for this formula of life-long commitment, see on 9:5.

Psalm 146 HAPPY ARE THOSE WHO FIND THEIR HELP IN YAHWEH

Although the speaker in the Psalm is an individual (see verses 1f.), it is a Congregational Hymn (see Introduction, pp. 32f.). It is unlikely that it should be regarded as 'a song of personal thanksgiving' (so Leslie, *PAP*, p. 313). In the later Jewish usage Ps. 145–50 were described as the Hallel Hymns, and they formed part of the daily morning prayer in the synagogue.

The structure of this poem is unusual: like all hymns it opens with a call to praise Yahweh (in the form of a self-exhortation; verses 1–2). This is followed by a warning not to place trust in human beings (verses 3–4) if it interfered with one's faith in God (verse 5), whose praise is described in verses 6–9. This description of Yahweh's works and attributes forms the main section of this hymn. Rather impressive is the fivefold repetition of the name 'Yahweh' (*RSV* 'the LORD'). The Psalm ends with a final shout of praise and a call for a congregational participation (verse 10).

LXX and V ascribe this Psalm (as well as Ps. 147–8 which in LXX are Ps. 146–8, i.e. Ps. 147 is divided into two Psalms) to Haggai and Zechariah. There is, however, no evidence for this view, although the Psalm may be of post-Exilic origin; it depends upon earlier Psalms or traditions, and some aspects of its language appear to be comparatively late.

The metre is mainly 3 + 3.

A CALL TO PRAISE GOD **1–2**

1. Praise the LORD: for this doxology in miniature, see on 104:35, 106:1; cf. H. H. Rowley, 'Hallelujah', *DB*, p. 360.
Praise . . . O my soul: see on 103:1, 104:1. The expression probably means: 'I shall personally take part in praising Yahweh'.

2. I will praise . . . as long as I live: i.e. the main purpose of my life is to praise God, and my praise shall be life-long. For a similar phrase, see on 104:33 (cf. 34:1 (M.T. 2), 63:4 (M.T. 5)).
I will sing praises . . .: for *z-m-r* ('to sing'), see on 66:4. Verse 2*b* is identical with 104:33*b*.

AN EXHORTATION TO TRUST YAHWEH **3–4**

3. Put not your trust in princes: i.e. do not place unreserved confidence in men; this expression is nearly the same as 118:9*b*. For the verb *b-ṭ-ḥ* ('to trust'), see on 78:22. 'Princes' (*nᵉḏîḇîm*) probably denotes 'men of excellence', whose superiority is not always manifested in moral values (cf. de Vaux, *AI*, p. 69).
in a son of man: *AV*, wrongly, '*nor* in the son of man' (so also *RV*, *RP*) because verse 3*b* is not a real alternative to verse 3*a*, but rather defines it. Hence we can paraphrase: 'Your problems will not be solved even by the rich and powerful, for each one of them is no more than a mortal man.' At best this would be an instance of the blind leading the blind. The Psalmist does not depreciate human help as such, but rather he shows the folly of a misplaced trust.
help: or 'salvation', see on 35:3; cf. 33:16, 60:11 (M.T. 13).

4. This verse is quoted in 1 Mac. 2:63.
his breath: lit. 'his spirit' (for *rûaḥ*, see on 76:12). The reference is to the spirit of life; when God takes it away, the living creature dies (104:29), or 'the dust returns to the earth as it was, and the spirit returns to God who gave it' (Ec. 12:7).
he returns to his earth: this may be a deliberate play on *ʾāḏām* ('man') and *ʾᵃḏāmāh* ('earth') (see on 84:5). For the thought of death as man's return to the earth, cf. Gen. 3:19; Ps. 104:29; Ec. 3:20; 1QH x:4, xii:26; Tromp, *PCD*, p. 88.
his plans: the word used is *ʿeštōnāh* (cf. Sir. 3:24) which may be an Aramaism, derived from *ʿ-š-t* ('to think') (cf. Dhorme, *CJ*, p. 170), which is found elsewhere only in Jon. 1:6. *NEB* has 'his thinking'.

A DIDACTIC GLORIFICATION OF YAHWEH **5–9**

5. Happy is he . . .: see on 1:1.
whose help is . . .: for the construction, see *GK* 119i; Brockelmann, *HS*, 106g; cf. 35:2.
the God of Jacob: this is one of the ancient Israelite divine names (cf. A. Alt, 'The God of the Fathers', *Essays on Old Testament History and Religion* (1966), pp. 3–77). The Psalmist may have had in mind the idea expressed in 46:7,11 (M.T. 8,12): 'the God of Jacob is our refuge'.
hope: *śēḇer* occurs elsewhere only in 119:116. It is common in Aramaic.

6. who made heaven and earth: as in 115:15, 121:2, 124:8, 134:3. This verse has *ᶜōśeh* ('who made') for the more common *ᶜōśēh* ('the maker of . . .').
the sea was usually regarded as a dangerous element, and among the neighbouring peoples it often had a mythological significance, traces of which still survive in the *OT*, mainly as metaphors (see on 74:13).
and all that is in them: i.e. in the entire created world.
who keeps faith for ever: for *ᵓemeṯ* ('faith, truth'), see on 25:5. Perhaps we should render 'he upholds his Covenant faithfulness . . .'. 'For ever' (*leᶜôlām*) describes the commitment of Yahweh as unchangeable (see on 9:5).

7. who executes justice . . .: this is a shorter version of 103:6.
he gives food . . .: see on 107:9*b*.
. . . sets the prisoners free: this phrase may be taken either figuratively of deliverance from trouble in general, or literally of the release of actual prisoners (exiles, captives, those unjustly accused, etc.). Cf. 68:6 (M.T. 7), 107:10–16; Isa. 42:7, 61:1.

8. the LORD opens the eyes of the blind: the word 'eyes' is rightly supplied from the context; it is not in M.T. LXX suggests 'the Lord (gives) wisdom to the blind' but this seems to be an interpretative translation. The description is probably to be taken figuratively: Yahweh is able to help even the most helpless. Blindness was not only a very common affliction in Palestine, but it was also a most distressing condition in which the unfortunate man was entirely at the mercy of his fellow-men. Although it was often regarded as a divine punishment (cf. Exod. 4:11; Jn 9:2), it also created a serious social problem which was, to some extent, dealt with in the Israelite laws (cf. Lev. 19:14; Dt. 27:18).

The LORD lifts up: see on 145:14*b*.

loves the righteous: Gunkel (*PGHAT*, p. 613) and *NEB* link this phrase with verse 9*c*, perhaps rightly so. For 'righteous', see on 1:5, and for the verb 'to love', see on 26:8.

9. sojourners: for *gērîm*, see on 39:12. It is quite possible that the 'salvation-history' of the individual was meant to bring to mind the saving works of God in the life of the nation.

he upholds: perhaps 'he restores (their rights)'.

widow: O. J. Baab ('Widow', *IDB*, IV, p. 842) remarks that 'in every code except the Hebrew, the widow has rights of inheritance . . .', and he goes on to say that one of the reasons for such an attitude may have been the belief that untimely death was a divine punishment for sin, which included also the widow. This and other possible factors often made the position of a widow very difficult, and her ill-treatment was not uncommon in ancient Israel. Therefore the widow, as well as the orphan (and the sojourner) were objects of God's special concern (cf. de Vaux, *AI*, p. 40).

the fatherless: see on 82:3.

the way of the wicked: both their life and their work (cf. 1:6). See also A. Kuschke, 'Die Menschenwege und der Weg Gottes im AT', *Studia Theologica*, V (1951), pp. 106–18.

he brings to ruin: the verb *ʿ-w-t* means 'to be bent, crooked'; hence Yahweh bends the path of the wicked, i.e. he frustrates their crookedness so that they miss their goal.

11QPs[a] (col. 2) seems to have had an additional verse(s) after verse 9, but the fragmentary state of the text makes it impossible to reconstruct it.

THE CONCLUDING PRAISE **10**

10. The LORD will reign: similarly in Exod. 15:18; Ps. 29:10. It is also reminiscent of the phrase 'the LORD reigns' (see on 93:1). One of the main functions of the King was the maintaining of justice and welfare; Yahweh, the Great king, is incomparable as the upholder of justice and the giver of blessings. Since his dominion is unlimited (**for ever**; see on 9:5), it provides a striking contrast to the inadequacy of all human help which does not operate within the framework of the divine will.

Zion: see on 65:1. Here it is a synonym for the people of God (cf. Isa. 52:7).
Praise the LORD: see verse 1.

Psalm 147 It is Good to Praise God

This Psalm consists of three main parts (verses 1–6, 7–11, 12–20) each of which forms a more or less self-contained hymn. LXX and V divide this Psalm into two independent Psalms (i.e. verses 1–11 = Ps. 146 in LXX, while verses 12–20 = Ps. 147 in LXX). Nevertheless, this Psalm may well be a literary unity.

The setting of this composition may be the Feast of Tabernacles (see Introduction, pp. 52f.), for it would be at this time in particular that men would think of God's providence.

The Psalm is of post-Exilic origin, and this is implied by verses 2 and 13, which suggest a date after the restoration of Jerusalem. There are also similarities of phrase and thought between Ps. 147 and Ps. 33, 104, and Isa. 40–55. LXX ascribes the Psalm to Haggai and Zechariah, although this is unlikely.

The metre is, with a few exceptions, 3 + 3.

THE LORD OF THE UNIVERSE AND THE HELPER OF THE WEAK 1–6

1. Praise the LORD: see on 104:35, 106:1, 146:1. The Psalm begins and ends with the same liturgical formula.
For it is good . . .: better 'Surely, it is good . . .', taking the Hebrew *kî* (*RSV* 'for') as an emphatic particle (see on 118:10). It could not very well be the usual hymnic *kî* ('for'), because the phrase 'Praise the LORD' is outside the metrical arrangement, and it may not be an integral part of the Psalm.
for he is gracious . . .: or 'surely, it is pleasant . . .'; see above.
and a song of praise is seemly: rather 'to make a fitting praise'. The Hebrew *nā'wāh* (*RSV* 'seemly') is clearly parallel to the *pi'ēl* infinitive *zammerāh* (*RSV* **to sing praises**; for the form, see *GK* 52p) in verse 1*a*, and therefore it too may be an infinitive (see J. Blau, *VT*, IV (1954), pp. 410f.).

2. The LORD builds up Jerusalem: (cf. 51:18 (M.T. 20), 102:16 (M.T. 17)). It is not certain that the Psalm must have been written *shortly* after the rebuilding of the walls of the city in Nehemiah's time (cf. Neh. 6–7) *c.* 445 B.C. The hymnic participle *bōnēh* (*RSV* 'builds') may allude to the *continual* building up of the city rather than to one particular incident. For a similar usage of *b-n-h* ('to build' or 'to make to flourish'), see 28:5; Prov. 14:1; Jer. 24:6, 42:10.

he gathers the outcasts of Israel: similarly in Isa. 11:12, 56:8 where two different but synonymous verbs are used. The reference may be to the return of the exiles (cf. Kraus, *PBK*, p. 956), or to the great ingathering of the dispersed people of God, of which the restoration from the Babylonian exile was only a prelude.

3. He heals the brokenhearted: lit. '. . . the broken in heart' (*šᵉḇûrê lēḇ*, only here in the *OT*); for similar expressions, see 34:18 (M.T. 19), 51:17 (M.T. 19); Isa 61:1; 11QPs[a] 155:17. For Yahweh as the true healer, see on 30:2; cf. Dt. 32:39; Isa. 19:22, 57:18f.; Jer. 30:17.

binds up their wounds: for the idea, see Isa. 61:1; Hos. 6:1. The description is figurative, and it depicts the divine succour in times of trouble.

4. He determines the number . . .: the verb *m-n-h* may mean 'to count' or 'to number', but here it probably suggests that Yahweh *knows* the number of all the stars (cf. Isa. 40:26). In other words, what is impossible for men (cf. Gen. 15:5) is possible for God.

he gives . . . them their names: this may imply both Yahweh's creative ability and his lordship over the stars, which may represent the *whole* world. The mention of the stars in particular may have a special significance: in the ancient Near East they were regarded as deities, and it was believed that they determined the destinies of mortals. Thus the Psalmist disposes of all these ideas in a single verse by affirming that *all* the stars are but servants of Yahweh (cf. Jg. 5:20; Isa. 40:26; *ANET*, p. 429).

5. Great is our LORD: similarly in 48:1 (M.T. 2), 96:4, 145:3. For *ʾāḏôn* ('Lord'), see on 8:1, 77:2. *RSV* erroneously has 'LORD' for 'Lord' in some editions; the former rendering would suggest the tetragrammaton, but M.T. has *ʾaḏônênû*.

abundant in power: cf. Isa. 40:26.

his understanding is beyond measure: lit. '. . . has no number' or '. . . is infinite' (cf. Isa. 40:28).

6. the downtrodden: in 146:9 we find some concrete examples of this class of persons. Yahweh lifts up (or restores the rights of) the oppressed (for *ʿanāwîm*, see on 34:2); for the thought cf. 113:7f., 145:14: Lk. 1:52.

he casts the wicked to the ground: this is a poetic description of the outworking of the divine justice.

YAHWEH'S PROVIDENTIAL CARE **7–11**

7. Sing: the verb *ᶜ-n-h* is a synonym of the far more common *z-m-r* and *š-y-r*. The verb *ᶜ-n-h* is found elsewhere in the Psalter in 119:172 and in the title of Ps. 88.
thanksgiving: for *tôḏāh*, see on 69:30.
lyre: see on 98:5; cf. 33:2.

8. This verse consists of three lines, and it is possible that one line had been omitted owing to a scribal error. LXX adds the line from 104:14*b*: 'and green herb for the service (or 'use') of man'; this would give a reasonable parallel to verse 8*c*.
he prepares rain for the earth: i.e. Yahweh is the giver of rain and fertility, not Baal or some other deity (cf. Job 5:10, 36:27ff.; Vriezen, *RAI*, pp. 40ff.).

9. the beasts: *bᵉhēmāh* is employed collectively, and it may denote animals as distinct from man, or simply domestic animals; it is seldom used of *wild* beasts.
young ravens: are probably mentioned because, according to unjustified popular beliefs, ravens neglected their young (cf. G. E. Post, 'Raven', *HDB*, IV, pp. 201f.; N. H. Tur-Sinai, *The Book of Job* (1957), pp. 537f.). The croaking of the young ravens is regarded as their 'prayer' to God (LXX has 'that call upon him (i.e. God)'). Cf. Job 38:41; Lk. 12:24.

10. The theme of this verse may have been associated with the concepts of the Holy War (for a brief discussion and bibliography, see de Vaux, *AI*, pp. 258–67, 537).
the strength of the horse: the reference is to the war-horse or, perhaps, to 'the well-mounted warrior' (*PLE*). Yahweh is not favourably disposed towards those who put their trust in men and horses, instead of turning to him for help (cf. 20:7 (M.T. 8), 33:17; Am. 2:15).
. . . legs of a man: i.e. Yahweh does not derive any pleasure from men who stake *their* future upon the swiftness of their warriors. The right attitude is expressed by: 'Not by might, nor by power, but by my Spirit' (Zech. 4:6).

11. In contrast to those who have a distorted sense of values, this verse portrays men who fear God (see on 19:9, 25:12, 85:9) and who hope (see on 71:14) or believe in Yahweh's Covenant loyalty. *These* are the people who experience God's favour and blessing (cf. 149:4), because they know that they need his help and they are willing to accept it on *his* terms (cf. Exod. 14:13f.).

YAHWEH CARES FOR HIS PEOPLE **12–20**

12. Praise the LORD: for the verb *š-b-ḥ*, see on 63:3.

O Jerusalem: (see on 102:21). The Psalmist is addressing the worshipping community. 'Zion' (see on 65:1) is parallel to 'Jerusalem'.

Praise your God: the verb used is *h-l-l*; see on 119:164. 'Your God' may be an allusion to the Covenant formula; cf. 113:5.

13. the bars of your gates: this may refer to the restoration of the walls of Jerusalem by Nehemiah (cf. Bright, *HI*, pp. 365ff.), but not necessarily so.

he blesses your sons: for *b-r-k* ('to bless'), see on 67:1. The object of Yahweh's blessing is the post-Exilic community, the children of Zion.

14. He makes peace . . .: lit. 'He makes your border peaceful'. *Šālôm* ('peace') is not simply the cessation of war, but also positive well-being and prosperity. Cf. Isa. 60:17–22; v. Rad, '*Eirēne*', *TDNT*, II, pp. 402–6.

the finest of the wheat: lit. 'the fat of the wheat' (*RVm*); see on 81:16.

15. He sends forth his command . . .: i.e. the created world is not left to run its course on its own, but Yahweh controls it through his word. Even the firmly established patterns, such as seed-time and harvest, summer and winter, night and day, life and death, do not function independently (cf. H. W. Robinson, *Inspiration and Revelation in the Old Testament* (1956), p. 24). The 'word' of Yahweh is his revealed will which can manifest itself, either in the form of a creative word, or as 'promise and hope, demand and power' (O. Procksch, '*Legō*', *TDNT*, IV, p. 100; see also pp. 91–100; Eichrodt, *TOT*, II, pp. 71–92).

his word runs swiftly: it is effective and attains its goal (cf. Isa. 45:23, 55:11; Heb. 4:12).

16. He gives snow like wool: (cf. Isa. 1:18; Dan. 7:9). Severe winters are comparatively rare in Palestine, but the rarity of the phenomenon makes it the more impressive as an illustration of Yahweh's power.

like ashes: this simile may have been chosen on account of the word-play on *k^{e}pôr* ('hoar frost') and *kāʾēp̱er* ('like ashes'); the similarity to *kōp̱er* ('ransom') seems purely accidental.

17. ice like morsels: i.e. the hailstones were as large as pieces of bread (cf. Prov. 17:1, 28:21).

who can stand before his cold: many recent commentators adopt the old emendation *mayim yaᶜᵃmōḏû* ('the waters stand still'), i.e. covered with ice they seem to have ceased to flow. This would give a better parallel with verse 17*a*, and would prepare the way for verse 18*b*.

18. He sends forth his word: see verse 15; cf. 107:20*a*; Isa. 9:8 (M.T. 7); Zech. 7:12. The word of Yahweh is described as if it were a divine messenger (cf. H. Ringgren, *Word and Wisdom* (1947), p. 158).

he makes his wind blow: the Hebrew *n-š-b* ('to blow') is found only here and in Gen. 15:11 ('to drive away') and Isa. 40:7. 'Wind' is a translation of *rûaḥ* (see on 76:12), alluding probably to the breath of Yahweh's mouth (see on 33:6), i.e. his word.

the waters flow: i.e. they had been frozen (see verse 17*b*); but now the ice has melted (verse 18*a*), and the movement of water is seen once more.

19. He declares his word . . .: (cf. 78:5), that is, Yahweh reveals his will to his people, Israel. For the use of **Jacob**, see on 20:1, 85:1. This revealed word is defined as **statutes** (see on 119:5) and **ordinances** (see on 36:6, 119:7).

20. This verse refers to the election of Israel. Their privilege is that they are called to render obedience to Yahweh by keeping his law. Cf. Dt. 4:8; Bar. 4:4.

they do not know his ordinances: *RSV* follows LXX, S, and V. M.T. omits the pronoun 'his'. The nations indeed have their own ordinances some of which may be identical with those found in Israel, yet whatever useful purpose these laws may serve, they are not used as means to express devotion to *Yahweh*.

Praise the LORD: see verse 1.

Psalm 148 LET THE WHOLE WORLD PRAISE YAHWEH

This Psalm is a development of the usual type of Hymn (see Introduction, pp. 32f.), in which the hymnic introduction forms practically the entire Psalm. Only verses 5*b*–6 and 13*b*–14*a* could be described as the 'equivalents' of the main section of the Hymns. On the other hand, this extended call to praise Yahweh is in itself an implicit glorification of him, for the very enumeration of creatures and created things displays the unsurpassable majesty of the creator.

This systematic listing of the creatures and natural phenomena follows a certain pattern which is also found in Job 38 and in the apocryphal Song of the Three Young Men, and it shows similarities with the ancient Egyptian compendium, the *Onomasticon* of Amenope, which lists all that Ptah (the god of Memphis) has created (for details see v. Rad, 'Job XXXVIII and Ancient Egyptian Wisdom', *PHOE*, pp. 281–91).

Verses 1–6 are addressed to the heavenly world, while verses 7–14*a* call upon the earthly creatures, created things, and meteorological phenomena to magnify their creator. Verses 14*bc* may be an editorial note indicating the nature of the Psalm, i.e. it is a praise for the use of the people of God. The cultic setting of the Psalm is not clear, but it must have been used in communal worship.

The date is post-Exilic. The metre of the composition is 3 + 3, except for verse 8 (4 + 4).

LET ALL THE HEAVENLY BEINGS PRAISE YAHWEH **1–6**

1. Praise the LORD: see on 104:35, 106:1, 146:1. This cultic call both begins and ends the Psalm.

from the heavens: this is set in contrast to 'from the earth' in verse 7*a*. These two phrases describe the two spheres where praise is possible; Sheol is not included (cf. 6:5 (M.T. 6), 30:9 (M.T. 10)).

in the heights: for *mārôm*, see on 68:18.

2. Here the Psalmist addresses the angels of Yahweh (see on 91:11) and all his host (see on 24:10, 59:5), i.e. the heavenly beings which surround his throne and do his will (cf. 103:20f.).

all his host: so *Keṯîḇ*; *Ḳerê* and the versions have the masculine plural 'his hosts' (*ṣeḇāʾāyw*).

3. The sun, moon, and stars also are summoned to offer their praise to Yahweh; they may be regarded as part of his heavenly host (cf. Job 38:7; Isa. 40:26).

shining stars: lit. 'stars of light'; LXX, S, and V read 'stars and light'.

4. highest heavens: lit. 'heavens of heavens' (cf. Dt. 10:14; 1 Kg. 8:27; 2 Chr. 2:6 (M.T. 5); Sir. 16:18). It is not certain that the Psalmist thought of a plurality of heavens (cf. 2 C. 12:2; F. C. Grant, 'Heaven', *DB*, pp. 369f.), or successive strata such as are depicted in later Jewish literature (cf. the Testament of

Levi 3:1–8). The expression 'heaven(s) of heavens' may simply be a superlative (as in *RSV*), or an idiomatic way of saying 'heaven itself' (cf. J. Gray, *I & II Kings*, p. 205).
waters above the heavens: i.e. the celestial ocean above the firmament (Gen. 1:7), which was regarded as the source of rain (cf. Gen. 7:11, 8:2).

5. the name of the LORD: see on 124:8.
for he commanded: (cf. 33:9, 147:15), i.e. God spoke his creative word (as in Gen. 1), and the world was brought into being.
were created: for the verb *b-r-*ᵓ ('to create'), see on 51:10.

6. he established them: cf. 93:1, 96:10.
for ever: i.e. permanently (cf. 9:5 (M.T. 6)).
he fixed their bounds . . .: the Hebrew *ḥōḳ* can sometimes mean 'boundary' (as in Job 23:10, 38:10), but usually it denotes 'statute, ordinance'. It is possible that the Psalmist had in mind an unalterable law or ordinance which cannot be broken by the created world.

LET THE EARTH AND ALL THAT IS IN IT PRAISE YAHWEH **7–14**

7. sea monsters: for *tannînîm*, see on 74:13. Weiser (*POTL*, p. 838) thinks that the mention of the dragons is an indication 'that the creation story with its tradition of the combat of the gods against the powers of chaos forms the background of the psalm'. It is possible, however, that the list of created things, etc., which was used (?) by the Psalmist, pre-dated his time; if this is so, then the battle motif may have played little or no part in the author's thinking (cf. v. Rad, pp. 282f.). In this Psalm the 'sea monsters' are not Yahweh's enemies but his creatures and servants; perhaps it simply suggests the marine animals (see J. Skinner, *Genesis* (*ICC*, 1912), p. 28). *NEB* has 'water-spouts'.
all deeps: for *tᵉhōmôṯ* ('deeps'), see on 104:6.

8. fire: i.e. lightning (cf. 18:12 (M.T. 13)), which often accompanied hailstorms. It may be slightly odd to think of the varied meteorological phenomena as praising God, yet it may not be too much of a rationalization to say that the creature or created phenomenon renders the highest praise to its creator by fulfilling the task for which it was created (as is implied in verse 8*b*).
frost: the Hebrew *ḳîṭôr* and its cognates usually mean 'smoke' (so also in Ugaritic, Arabic, etc.); perhaps in this context it means 'mist'. LXX reads *krustallos* ('ice'); *NEB* has 'ice'.
stormy wind: see on 107:25.

9. Mountains and all hills represent the whole earth, while 'fruit trees and all cedars' (cf. 104:16) stand for the entire vegetation.

10. Beasts and all cattle: i.e. the wild and domesticated animals respectively (see on 147:9).

creeping things: (cf. Gen. 1:24), i.e. reptiles, worms, and insects. See J. A. Kelso, 'Creeping Things', *DB*, p. 188.

flying birds: lit. 'bird(s) of wing'; for a similar expression, see Gen. 1:21; Prov. 1:17.

11–12. The list of the created things and beings reaches its climax with the mention of mankind, the crown of all creation (cf. 8:5 (M.T. 6)). All people, irrespective of their status, age, or sex, are called upon to render praise.

13. Let them praise: as in verse 5. In both instances (i.e. in verses 5 and 13) this phrase introduces the hymnic main section.

his name alone is exalted: i.e. Yahweh and his deeds are beyond comparison, for only he can utter the creative word (cf. Isa. 44:24), and he alone sustains the universe.

his glory: the Hebrew *hôḏ* usually means 'majesty' (so *NEB*), 'splendour'.

above earth and heaven: i.e. Yahweh is exalted above everything mentioned in the previous verses, and that indeed represents *all*. The phrase 'earth and heaven' is found elsewhere in Gen. 2:4*b*, but it is unlikely that a special significance should be attached to this unusual word order.

14. . . . a horn for his people: 'horn' (*ḳeren*) is often used as a symbol of strength and power (see on 75:4). The Psalmist probably means that Yahweh has given fresh strength and courage to his people (cf. 112:9). LXX suggests that this reversal of fortunes is a future occasion (i.e. 'he *shall* exalt . . .').

praise: see on 65:1, 119:171. If verse 14*bc* is an integral part of the Psalm, we could render: '(He) is the praise of all his saints . . .'; cf. Dt. 10:21: 'He is your praise . . .'. For 'saints', see on 30:4, 86:2.

who are near to him: cf. Lev.10:3.

Psalm 149 A Hymn of Triumph

This Psalm is clearly a Hymn (see Introduction, pp. 32f.) which praises Yahweh as the giver of victory to his people (verse 4). Some exegetes have assigned this poem to a particular historical situation: to the Maccabean wars (so Briggs) or to Nehemiah's triumph over the hostile neighbours (so Cohen). Gunkel, Kittel, *et al.* assume that the Psalm looks forward to the final judgment of God, but a cultic interpretation seems more likely. The shouting of the warriors (verse 6) and the praises of the people may well belong to the ritual of the cultic drama which portrayed, from the point of view of faith, the salvation-history of the nation. The conventionalized re-presentation of the past events also had a present and future significance: as Yahweh has acted in the past, so he is also involved in the present situation, and he will bring to a glorious completion *all* his purposes. The reference to the kingship of Yahweh (verse 2) may indicate that the cultic event alluded to in the Psalm may have belonged to the Feast of Tabernacles; see Introduction, pp. 52f.

The date of the Psalm is hardly pre-Exilic; the language of the poem and its apocalyptic tone (verses 7–9) favour a later origin.

The metre is 3 + 3 except for verses 1 and 9 which are in 4 + 3 metre.

THE INTROIT TO THE HYMN **1–3**

1. Praise the Lord: see on 104:35, 106:1, 146:1. The same phrase also forms the conclusion of the Psalm.

a new song: see on 33:3, 96:1. This might be paraphrased as: 'the song of the re-created people of God'. Cf. Rev. 14:3; Jdt. 16:2,13.

praise: see on 65:1, 119:171.

in the assembly of the faithful: it is unlikely that the 'faithful' (*ḥᵃsîḏîm*; see on 30:4, 86:2) are to be identified with the Hasidaeans who appear in history during the Maccabean period (cf. 1 Mac. 2:42). The *ḥᵃsîḏîm* in this Psalm may refer to the worshipping community, synonymous with 'Israel' and 'the sons of Zion' in verse 2. For *ḳāhāl*, 'assembly', see on 89:5.

2. Israel: this name may designate the patriarch Jacob, but far more frequently it is used as the name of the sacral league of the twelve tribes. The earliest mention of this name in non-biblical sources is found in the Stele of Merenptah (see *DOTT*, pp. 137ff.), but it is not clear what tribe or tribes were designated by this thirteenth-century B.C. inscription. During the period of the Divided Monarchy, 'Israel' came to be used as a political name for the northern tribes, but after the end of the northern kingdom in 722 B.C., it was employed again as the name for the people of God, although the allusion was usually to Judah as the existing nucleus. For a more detailed account, see G. A. Danell, *Studies in the Name of Israel in the Old Testament* (1964).

his Maker: cf. 95:6, 100:3; Isa. 44:2, 51:13. It was Yahweh who had transformed a group of slaves and semi-nomads into a nation, and who had preserved them throughout the vicissitudes of their history. The Hebrew *ᶜōśāyw* is plural in form, probably a plural of majesty (cf. *GK* 124k).

the sons of Zion: i.e. the worshippers of Yahweh. This same phrase is also found in Lam. 4:2; Jl 2:23. For 'Zion', see on 65:1.

their King: for Yahweh as 'king', see on 68:24.

3. his name: see on 20:1, 124:8.

dancing: this was not an uncommon cultic activity, see on 30:11.

timbrel (*tōp̄*) and **lyre** (*kinnôr*) are discussed on 81:2 and 98:5 respectively. See *ANEP*, pll. 206–11.

THE REASON FOR PRAISING YAHWEH **4**

4. the LORD takes pleasure: cf. 147:11.

he adorns: i.e. he grants victory (*yᵉšûᶜāh*, 'salvation', see on 35:3) to his people (see Isa. 44:23, 55:5, 61:3).

the humble: see on 34:2. The parallelism with verse 4*a* shows that the Psalmist is thinking of all the people of God rather than of a *party* of pious men within the nation.

THE DESTRUCTION OF THE ENEMIES **5–9**

5. The **faithful** (see on verse 1) are exhorted to exult (see on 94:3) in glory, i.e. in their God-given triumph (cf. 112:9).

let them sing: for *r-n-n*, see on 33:1.

on their couches: Gunkel, Kraus, *et al.* read *ᶜal mišpᵉḥôṯām* ('according to their families'; cf. Num. 1:18) for M.T. *ᶜal miškᵉḇôṯām* ('on their couches'), which gives a better sense. Perhaps M.T. means 'upon their places of prostration' ('prayer mats' (?); cf. Hos. 7:14), i.e. the place where each worshipper does homage to God. Eaton (*PTBC*, p. 315) *et al.* think that the 'couches' may be the seating used at the sacrificial meal (cf. Isa. 57:8; Am; 2:8).

6. high praises: the Hebrew *rômām* is found elsewhere in 66:7 (cf. Yadin, *SWSLSD*, p. 275).

two-edged swords: lit. 'a sword of mouths'; *AV*, *RV*, *RSV* follow LXX which has *rhomphaiai distomoi*. Kraus calls it a 'double axe', but the expression may simply mean a 'sharp sword' or a 'devouring sword' (cf. the phrase 'to smite with the edge (or 'mouth') of the sword'; cf. Jos. 6:21, 11:12; Jg. 1:8; etc.).

A parallel to our passage is found in Jdt. 15:13, where Judith went before the people dancing, 'while all the men of Israel followed, bearing their arms and wearing garlands and with songs on their lips'.

7. to wreak vengeance: cf. Isa. 62:1, 63:4; Ezek. 25:14. The War Scroll (1QM) would have provided a 'practical' manual of how to apply verses 7–9 (in their literal sense) to a future situation.
chastisement on the peoples: lit. 'corrections of . . .'. Many modern readers are, no doubt, appalled at the martial language of this Psalm, yet essentially the Psalmist is saying no more than: 'Thy will be done . . .' (Mt. 6:10), although the actual words are clearly those of a man of his own time. He is not dreaming of a national war of conquest but of a Holy War, to execute the divine judgment, not of a universal pogrom, but of the establishment of divine justice.

8. to bind their kings . . .: this is what defeat meant in the Psalmist's time; for similar ideas cf. Isa. 45:14, 49:7, 23. For a pictorial testimony, see *ANEP*, pll. 325, 332, 358, 447, 524.
their nobles: i.e. their honoured ones (cf. Isa. 23:8,9; Nah. 3:10; 1QM xiv:11; 4Q169 3–4,iv:4).

9. . . . the judgment written: Bentzen, Mowinckel, *et al.* think of a rite corresponding to that connected with the Egyptian execration texts (cf. *ANET*, p. 328f.). In Egypt pottery bowls were occasionally inscribed with the names of various enemies, and then smashed; it was believed that, as the pottery was smashed, so also the power of the foes would be broken. It is more likely, however, that the allusion is to the heavenly books in which all the deeds of men were recorded (see on 51:1). An alternative suggestion is that the 'judgment' refers to the prophecies of the earlier prophets (cf. Kissane, *BP*, p. 655).
This is glory . . .: for *hāḏār* ('glory'), see on 90:16, 96:6. A less likely rendering is: 'He is the glory of His saints' (cf. Cohen, *PSon*, p. 478).
Praise the LORD: see verse 1. It is lacking in LXX and S.

Psalm 150 PRAISE THE LORD

It is fitting that the Songs of Israel should end with an emphatic call to universal praise. This Psalm is a Hymn (see Introduction, pp. 32f.), although it consists only of an expanded introit without the characteristic hymnic main section; thus it is similar to Ps.

148. The praise of Yahweh is, however, implicit in the repeated summons to glorify him. The tenfold repetition of the imperative call: 'Praise him', or 'Praise God' (once in verse 1) may sound rather monotonous, but it is, no doubt, used for the sake of special emphasis. Deissler (*PWdB*, III, p. 225) sees here an allusion to the ten words of creation in Gen. 1 (cf. *Aboth* v:1: 'By ten Sayings was the world created') and to the Ten Commandments (cf. Exod. 20). This may be so, although the number 'ten' may be purely accidental.

This hymn is often regarded as the concluding doxology to the entire Psalter, just as each of the first four books is concluded with an appropriate blessing (see Introduction, p. 27). It is not certain, however, that this Psalm was composed with this purpose in mind. Actually Ps. 146–50 all begin and end with the phrase 'Praise the LORD,' and they may have formed a small collection (or part of one) on their own. Ps. 150 is an impressive hymn, but it would be an exaggeration to call it 'the grandest symphony of praise to God ever composed on earth' (Oesterley, *TP*, p. 593).

The date of the psalm is post-Exilic. Its metre is 3 + 3.

1. Praise the LORD: see on 104:35, 106:1, 146:1. It is lacking in some Hebrew MSS. and in S.

Praise God: S and Jerome read: 'Praise the Lord'. The other imperative calls to magnify Yahweh begin with 'Praise him'; this may imply that 'Praise the LORD' at the beginning and at the end of the Psalm, is a later liturgical addition.

in his sanctuary: (for *ḳōḏeš*, see on 68:17). The reference may be either to the Jerusalem Temple (so Gunkel, Barnes, Deissler, *et al.*), or to Yahweh's dwelling place in heaven (Kirkpatrick, Cohen, etc.). If the parallelism in verse 1 is synonymous (see Introduction, p. 41), then the latter alternative is the right interpretation; it seems that verse 1 describes not the place where God is to be praised but rather the 'place' where he dwells. On the other hand, the Temple is a symbol of the heavenly dwelling of God, and therefore both are closely associated (cf. 11:4). Verses 3–5 suggest that it is the human worshippers (at least primarily) who are addressed.

his mighty firmament: this phrase is found only here in the *OT*. The Hebrew *rāḳîa*ᶜ ('firmament') (from Latin *firmamentum*; LXX has *stereōma*) was thought to be a solid vault which arched over the earth, and separated the waters above the firmament from those below it (cf. Gen. 1:6f.). If it were to fail, the primeval conditions of Chaos would return (see Eichrodt, *TOT*, II, pp. 93ff.). In this verse 'firmament' is simply a synonym for 'heavens' (cf. 8:2 (M.T. 3)). See also Stadelmann, *HCW*, pp. 56ff.

2. his mighty deeds: cf. 106:2, 145:4,11,12; these are his acts of creation, deliverance, and preservation.

according to his exceeding greatness: some Hebrew MSS. and S read *b^e^rōḇ* ('for (his) exceeding (greatness)') for M.T. *k^e^rōḇ* ('according to . . .'); this emendation, if such it is, would restore the same structure in verse 2*b* as that found in the other phrases in verses 2*a*, 3–5.

3. with trumpet sound: 11QPs^a^ (col. 26) suggests 'with the blowing of trumpet', reading *btḳwᶜ* ('with the blowing of') for M.T. *b^e^ṯēḳaᶜ* ('with the sound of'). The trumpet (*šôp̄ār*) was primarily an instrument for giving signals, and this may be its use here. See on 47:5, 98:6.

lute: see on 33:2.

harp is discussed on 98:5.

4. timbrel: cf. 149:3; see on 81:2.

strings: the Hebrew *minnîm* is found only here and, possibly in 45:8 (M.T. 9). It may be a term for stringed instruments in general.

pipe: *ᶜûgāḇ* ('flute'). This was probably an instrument used in secular activities; only here is it mentioned in a religious setting (cf. Gen. 4:21; Job 21:12, 30:31).

5. sounding cymbals and **clashing cymbals** refer to two different kinds of percussion instrument, and the difference may have been in the sound produced. For more details on musical instruments, see Curt Sachs, *The History of Musical Instruments* (1940); P. Grandenwitz, *The Music of Israel* (1949). Cf. *ANEP*, pl. 202.

6. everything that breathes: lit. 'every breath' or 'all life'. The same phrase occurs in Dt. 20:16; Jos. 10:40, 11:11,14, etc. It usually refers to human beings; only in Gen. 7:22 does it include animals.

Praise the Lord: see verse 1.

INDEX

INDEX OF HEBREW WORDS